S0-BFE-119

N

BOLLINGEN SERIES LXXXVIII

THOMAS TAYLOR THE PLATONIST

SELECTED WRITINGS

EDITED, WITH INTRODUCTIONS, BY

KATHLEEN RAINE

AND

GEORGE MILLS HARPER

BOLLINGEN SERIES LXXXVIII

PRINCETON UNIVERSITY PRESS

TO

THE SACRED

MAJESTY

OF

TRUTH.

PREFACE

This book is an offspring of the Yeats International Summer School. When the editors met for the first time at Sligo, Ireland, in the summer of 1965, they discovered that both had intended to edit a selection of the writings of Thomas Taylor the Platonist (1758–1835). Bollingen Foundation had agreed to publish such a work, and Kathleen Raine's essay and a proposed list of contents were already in their hands. As a result of an extended discussion leading to some modifications, the editors decided to collaborate. In the selections included here, Taylor's spelling has in the main been preserved. Some minor changes have been made: misprints have been corrected, the typography has been modernized, several footnotes have been omitted, and here and there punctuation has been altered when that seemed to lend clarity. Other editorial devices—introductory headnotes for each selection; supplementary footnotes and translations of Latin poems, in brackets—have been clearly differentiated from Taylor's own work.

For permission to reproduce illustrations used in this edition, we are indebted to The British Museum; The Royal Society of Arts; Josiah Wedgwood, Ltd.; Arlington Court, North Devon; The National Gallery of Ottawa; The Historical Society of Pennsylvania; Dr. Frances Yates; Mr. Geoffrey Watkins. We are indebted also to many people who have helped with information about Taylor and with editorial assistance, especially to Professor Franklin P. Johnson, of Osceola, Missouri; the staff at the Library of the Missouri Historical Society, in St. Louis; the Concord Public Library, in Massachusetts; the University of Florida Library, in Gainesville; Professor Louise S. Boas; Mr. Geoffrey Watkins. Finally, we would like to express our appreciation of the invaluable editorial assistance of Mrs. Janet Morrell Glover and Mrs. George Mills Harper.

London and Gainesville　　　　　　　　KATHLEEN RAINE
January, 1968　　　　　　　　　　　　GEORGE MILLS HARPER

CONTENTS

Contents

The Platonic Philosopher's Creed

An Apology for the Fables of Homer

Bibliography

LIST OF ILLUSTRATIONS

The dedication on p. v is from Taylor's translation of *The Commentaries of Proclus* (London, 1788–1789); see p. 17. A profile engraving of Taylor on p. 103 is explained there. All the other illustrations are in a section following p. 48.

List of Illustrations

THOMAS TAYLOR THE PLATONIST

SELECTED WRITINGS

The wish to see some of the writings and translations of Thomas Taylor reprinted came to me while I was reading the source books from which William Blake learned traditional wisdom. Foster Damon in 1924[1] first surmised Blake's indebtedness to Taylor, and no serious Blake scholar has since denied it. But with few exceptions[2] the importance of that debt has been minimized; and as with Blake, so with the other Romantic poets.

John Livingston Lowes, in his delightful book *The Road to Xanadu*, could not altogether ignore Coleridge's debt to Taylor, whose name appears in the poet's often quoted self-portrait: "Metaphysics, & Poetry, & 'Facts of mind'—(i.e. Accounts of all the strange phantasms that ever possessed your philosophy-dreamers from Tauth [Thoth], the Egyptian to Taylor, the English Pagan,) are my darling Studies."[3] Yet to Lowes this Neoplatonism, admittedly "one of Coleridge's inveterate preoccupations," was "one of the strangest tendencies which marked the tumultuous exit of the century";[4] one of the many curious beads upon Coleridge's string, and not—as is nearer the truth—the thread upon which the beads are strung.

As with Coleridge so with Shelley, whose Platonism has always been known, yet disregarded in the reading of his poems.[5] The nineteenth century has praised, and the twentieth condemned as impressionistic description, the subtle and exact symbolism of the imagery in Shelley's best poems, clear to those (among them

[1] *William Blake, His Philosophy and Symbols* (London, 1924).

[2] See especially Milton O. Percival, *William Blake's Circle of Destiny* (New York, 1938) and George Mills Harper, *The Neoplatonism of William Blake* (Chapel Hill and Oxford, 1961).

[3] Letter to Thelwall, Nov. 19, 1796, in *Collected Letters of Samuel Taylor Coleridge*, ed. E. L. Griggs (Oxford and New York, 1956), p. 260. Lowes cited this, with slight modifications, in his *Road to Xanadu* (Boston, 1927), p. 231.

[4] Ibid., p. 232.

[5] See, however, as a reversal of this tendency, Neville Rogers, *Shelley at Work: a Critical Inquiry* (Oxford, 1956).

Yeats) qualified to understand its language.[6] As for Yeats himself, since it has not been possible to deny, it has been tacitly agreed to forgive in so great a poet whatever can loosely be called his "occultism," a word made to embrace all esoteric doctrine from Plotinus to MacGregor Mathers.[7] But the truth cannot be hidden: the "darling studies" of the poets are just those their academic commentators would like to disregard. Dante studied, besides the scholastic theologians, Dionysius the Areopagite; Spenser venerated Plato's intellectual beauty; Milton learned from that same Thoth the Egyptian[8] and read Plato not for his dialectical method but to unfold

> *What Worlds, or what vast Regions hold*
> *The immortal mind that hath forsook*
> *Her mansion in this fleshly nook. . . .*

The divergence between those "two cultures" whose frontiers may be variously drawn goes back to Greece; and the ultimate distinction lies in what is thought to be the nature of the primary reality. All normal traditional cultures (Hindu, Buddhist, Judaeo-Christian, or Islamic, besides the Orphic and Pythagorean tradition which lies behind Platonism) assume the primacy of mind, and see nature as a system of appearances, or images, in which a metaphysical order is reflected. The first beginnings of the opposite view (which at the present time dominates the world) are to be found in certain pre-Socratic Greek philosophers; this view has since been associated with Aristotle, in whom the naturalistic bias is strong; while the traditional metaphysics has continued under the name of Platonism. The Platonic mainstream descends through Plotinus, and after him through the Neoplatonists of the early Christian centuries; there is a strong Platonic element in St. Augustine, and the Pseudo-Dionysius is a Plato-

---

[6] The late C. S. Lewis was another.

[7] F.A.C. Wilson's two books, *W. B. Yeats and Tradition* (London, 1958) and *Yeats's Iconography* (London, 1960) have done much to remedy this neglect.

[8] The "thrice great Hermes" of *Il Penseroso*. Both Coleridge and Milton are referring to the *Hermetica*.

nist whose celestial hierarchies are the old gods and daemons thinly Christianized. The Hermetic tradition, which survived within Christendom as prophetic of Christ until the seventeenth century, when Isaac Casaubon established the date of the *Hermetica* as A.D. and not B.C., must also be considered as Platonic; and so, in a lesser degree, with alchemy and even with the Jewish Cabala, which embodies strong Platonic elements. These are the most important branches of a current of thought which has flowed unbroken through European civilization, sometimes within Christendom, at other times outside it.

At the time of the Renaissance, Humanism and the mentality which has since developed quantitative science entered, by a reversal in the premises of civilization itself, upon the phase of dominance which has continued to the present time. Spokesmen of the now dominant culture speak of an "advance" from "ignorance" and magic, to "knowledge" and material science; yet in terms of philosophy, religion, and the arts the same event can only be seen in opposite terms, as a decline from knowledge to ignorance. Since each gnosis has its own terms of reference, each to the other must to a certain degree appear "meaningless"— a word whose application, by materialists, in the fields of philosophy, religion, and the arts grows ever more confident as the positivist mentality extends its power. Philosophy has, in post-Renaissance England, been dominated by the Humanist and positivist mentality which stems from Bacon; its premises, in the century of Newton and Locke, seemed self-evident. Religious thought was affected by this climate of opinion, and iconoclastic Protestantism was itself one of the expressions of the reversal of values which took place between the fifteenth and seventeenth centuries.

Dr. Frances Yates in her book on Giordano Bruno[9] has studied the causes and crosscurrents of this reversal, and reminds us that what mankind chooses to study and to regard as important is a matter of the will; premises which to one age seem self-evident

---

[9] *Giordano Bruno and the Hermetic Tradition* (London, 1964).

to another become incomprehensible. Whatever the advantages of the new direction in the field of mechanical sciences, its accompanying repudiation of images, both visual and mental ("idolatry" to the new mentality, or merely meaningless), deprived religion and the arts of their normal language and cut away the foundations of their thought. Poetry Shelley defines as the language of the imagination; a language not of definitions which measure, but of images which evoke, knowledge; meaningless to the positivist, this language is, in relation to "facts of mind," exact.

The passage in the *Republic* in which Plato banishes the poets is often invoked (disregarding the reasons he gives, which relate to the excessive naturalism of certain artists and poets of the time) to show Plato as the enemy of the poets. But in fact Plato is the philosopher of the arts, the Platonic philosophy is the necessary basis of all imaginative art. Therefore it is that the Platonic tradition has lived on as the learning of the poets, like a secret language. Together with the philosophy are associated those gods, myths, symbolic figures, and stories which not only Plato himself but Plotinus and all the later Platonic philosophers employ. The Platonic artist and poet philosophize; the Platonic philosopher mythologizes.

The Platonic tradition may be likened to an underground river that from time to time sends up a spring; wherever its waters flow, the soul is reborn, and with it the conception of intellectual form, the beautiful, and true art. Yeats wrote: "The mystical life is the centre of all that I do and all that I think and all that I write. . . . I have always considered myself a voice of what I believe to be a greater renaissance—the revolt of the soul against the intellect—now beginning in the world."[10]

[10] Letter to John O'Leary, July 1892, in *The Letters of W. B. Yeats*, ed. Allan Wade (London, 1954). Yeats uses the word "intellect" to mean the dianoetic power, as in the modern phrase "an intellectual" in the sense of a discursive reasoner or a scientist. The word "reason" was used by Milton and revived by Coleridge (who quarrels with Taylor's preference for the word "intellect") to mean νοῦς: but in English, whatever the word used to describe this faculty, so little understood except by the poets, it

6

The Irish Renaissance, like every renaissance in Europe, was accompanied by a revival of Platonism and the Hermetic tradition, the European branch of the learning of the soul or *mens*. What Yeats here calls mysticism is not piety but a great body of knowledge with its own terms of discourse, including those magical images by which he sought to discover and express a kind of knowledge which only the symbol can mediate, since it is of a mental kind and is immeasurable. Our own time has been enriched by tributaries from Indian metaphysics, from the philosophy and art of China and Japan; all the mythologies of the world lie open to us; yet there can never be anything essentially new, or essentially other than is contained in our native tradition of Platonism as it has lived on both apart from, and within, Christianity. Plotinus and Porphyry, Proclus and Pythagoras, with Plato himself, have at all times been the "singing masters of the soul." In England it is to the poets rather than to the philosophers (Berkeley is the notable exception) that we must look for the continuity of this tradition. Milton, Spenser, Shelley, Yeats, Blake, and Coleridge are poets of (in the Platonic sense of the word) intellect: they are more, not less, "intellectual" in content than such a poet as Donne, whose intricate thought is at the level of dianoetic reason, and whose ingenious imagery is almost without intellectuality or metaphysical content. The understanding of these poets requires (as with Raphael, Botticelli, and Michelangelo) not only a higher intelligence, but also a much greater learning than that of the superficially more complex "metaphysical" poets. Beauty as such has, within this philosophy, an intellectual content; experience of the beautiful is a mode of knowledge, of *gnosis*; is indeed the supreme intellectual experience, though "meaningless" within the context of quantitative thought. The concept of the beautiful invariably accompanies the

---

soon becomes degraded into the lower sense; even Blake's words "vision" and "imagination" a Nation of Shopkeepers will sooner or later use in the sense of business acumen. Yeats, however, uses the word "intellect" in Taylor's sense in many contexts, as in the line "Monuments of unageing intellect."

traditional metaphysics of which Platonism is the European expression.

It was Thomas Taylor who took upon himself, at the close of the eighteenth century, the task of placing before his contemporaries the canonical Platonic writings, in which are embodied the essential learning of the imaginative tradition. The texts Taylor placed in the hands of the Romantic poets were the same that Ficino[11] had made accessible to Botticelli, Raphael, and Michelangelo;[12] Coleridge and Shelley alone among the Romantic poets habitually read their Greek authors in the original; Taylor's translations were the texts, his interpretations the guide. Flaxman and probably Blake were close friends of Taylor during the formative years of all three; Shelley's friend Thomas Love Peacock knew him later in life. Keats, though not a scholar, may at a remove have caught the enthusiasm of his Greek polytheism from Taylor;[13] and the gleam from Plotinus that illuminates Wordsworth's most famous Ode (and other of his poems) certainly comes through Taylor. Samuel Palmer, F. O. Finch, George Richmond, and Edward Calvert affirmed, in the name by which they called themselves, "the Shoreham Ancients,"[14] an intention to revive, in their art, a traditional vision, restored to their generation by the rediscovery not only of the arts, but of the philosophy of ancient Greece.

Samuel Palmer, in a letter written to his sister-in-law Elizabeth Linnell from Pompeii, July 8, 1838, recalls evenings spent in reading what can only have been Thomas Taylor's translation of the works of Plato; declaring himself a Platonist in no uncertain terms: ". . . Blessed also will be the mind that is imbued with Plato—would that mine were so!—the very antithesis of the literary impudence, dandyism and materialism with which most of our modern periodicals tend imperceptibly to imbue

[11] See Plates 4 and 5.
[12] See Edgar Wind, *Pagan Mysteries in the Renaissance* (London, 1958).
[13] See Bernard Blackstone, *The Consecrated Urn* (London, 1959), *passim*.
[14] Shoreham in Kent; the home of Samuel Palmer for seven years during the 1820's and 1830's.

8

the mind. If I am ever to open a book again & not to 'live a fool & die a brute,' may I open once more the divine leaves of Plato in some happy Grove St. evening with you and dear Anny by my fireside—but it is too good to be hoped for in this world except with Euripides in his cave; too deep to hear the rumbling of her rubbish carts. . . ."[15]

The Platonic mainstream has gathered tributaries in every age. Volumes of Taylor crossed the Atlantic, there to fertilize a flowering of American culture.[16] Emerson, Bronson Alcott, and their friends dreaming of an America that should approach to Plato's never-to-be-realized Republic, read the same books that a generation earlier had inspired Blake's prophecies of an England whose national life should reflect, like Plato's city, the order of eternal perfection. And in this century, when "the sceptre of intelligence had passed to Dublin"[17] we find that the same works were fertilizing the thought of AE and the poetry of Yeats.

In the eighteen-eighties the Theosophical Society became interested in Taylor; G.R.S. Mead and other members and associates of the Society edited and reissued a number of his works. During the period between Taylor's death and this rediscovery there was nothing in England comparable with the cult of Taylor in America which stemmed from the Transcendentalists and Thomas M. Johnson's *The Platonist*; but there is one curious link between Taylor's own revival of the ancient gods and the theosophical and magical societies of the end of the nineteenth century: Mrs. Mary Anne Atwood's *A Suggestive Inquiry into the Hermetic Mystery*, "with a dissertation on the more celebrated of the Alchemical Philosophers, being an attempt toward the recovery of the ancient experiment of nature." This rare book (reprinted in 1920 by the theosophical publisher J. M. Watkins) is

[15] See *Samuel Palmer's Italian Honeymoon*, by Edward Malin (Oxford, 1968); Grove St., Paddington Green, was Palmer's home.

[16] See below, George Mills Harper's introductory essay.

[17] A telegram sent to George Moore by Yeats on the occasion of the first performance of the latter's *The Countess Cathleen*; quoted in Moore's *Ave* (London, 1911), p. 72.

9

a work of quixotic learning compiled from long extracts from the Hermetica, Dionysius, Aquinas, Boehme, Saint-Martin, Henry More, Paracelsus, the Alchemists, and Thomas Taylor. Mary Anne Atwood was the daughter of Thomas South, a Hampshire country gentleman with a fine library of classical, philosophical, and metaphysical works, and a taste for all the new sciences of magnetism, hypnotism, mesmerism, spiritism, and the like. His daughter wrote and published her *Suggestive Enquiry* at the age of twenty-three, and then was persuaded by her father to withdraw a book which he regarded as a betrayal of a secret tradition. Mrs. Atwood, born in 1817, lived on to 1910; in the 1880's she presented the fine library which had been her father's to the Theosophical Society, whose President at that time was A. P. Sinnett. She seems to have hoped that the Society would develop into a school upon Pythagorean lines in which students would pass through an ordered course of spiritual instruction. Later she lost interest in the Society and her library passed into other hands.

The interest of the Theosophical Society, and even more so the Hermetic Society of the Golden Dawn, in traditional *gnosis* was less learned and more practical than Taylor's own, though Taylor himself had started a fire in the Freemason's Hall while attempting to demonstrate a perpetual flame. It was in the context of the theosophical movement that Yeats and AE came to know Taylor, and they no doubt read his work in the reprints and new editions promoted by the Society. If Taylor's polytheism was philosophic, Yeats's was above all magical.

Yet the Platonic ground was never abandoned; AE in a letter compares the Irish revival to that of the New England Transcendentalists; nor is it only in poetry and the arts that the resemblance holds, but, in the original sense of the word, in politics also, again and again fertilized by Platonic thought. Wordsworth's remark to Emerson, quoted in George Mills Harper's essay (below, p. 54), illustrates the deep-rooted unwillingness of the English to attempt to relate, like the Transcendentalists or the makers of Eire (to use the words of AE) "the politics of time" to "the politics of eternity"; yet never to do so may in the long run destroy a nation.

Stephen MacKenna gave to the Irish literary movement his fine translation of Plotinus, but Taylor's works also were in Yeats's library, as they had been on the shelves of Coleridge and Shelley. There were reprints of a few of these, both in England and in America, at the turn of the nineteenth century, following the revival of theosophical studies.[18] Taylor did not write for the many, but the few who have valued him have been the intellectual aristocracy of their time; AE called him "The Uncrowned King."[19]

Taylor was more than a man of learning. G.R.S. Mead (whose own interpretation of Orphism[20] is but an expansion of Taylor's preface to the Hymns) called him "more than a scholar, he was a philosopher in the Platonic sense of the word."[21] His object was "to diffuse the salutary light of genuine philosophy." For Taylor, erudition was not an end but a means. His learning was inspired by a zealous wish to combat the mentality of his age—the same mechanistic materialism denounced by Blake, Coleridge, and Shelley—and to bring about, by making known the literature of the Platonic tradition, long neglected (and to the increasing number of otherwise literate persons unable to read Greek, inaccessible), a return to traditional wisdom. Taylor neither wished nor attempted to isolate the teachings of Plato from the continuous tradition of "Platonism," which can no more be arrested at any historical moment than can Christianity or Buddhism[22] be abstracted from the continuous vitality of their

[18] The Theosophist G.R.S. Mead, closely associated with Helena Blavatsky, and the publisher J. M. Watkins were the moving spirits and agents of this work. No doubt AE (George Russell) and Yeats first heard of Taylor through their association with the Theosophical Society. See *Letters from AE to Yeats* (Dublin, 1936).

[19] This I was told by Mrs. Constance Sitwell, friend of AE, Yeats, and others of their circle.

[20] *Orpheus* (London, 1896).

[21] *Select Works of Plotinus* (London, 1895), p. ix.

[22] "The Buddha Himself was always at pains to repudiate, as a monstrous heresy, any suggestion that he had come to teach anything new in the matter of doctrine." Marco Pallis, *The Way and the Mountain* (London, 1960), p. 180.

history. Platonism, as Taylor saw it, is an informing principle rather than a formulation, transmitted through a "golden chain of philosophers": a doctrine received by Socrates and Plato from the Orphic and Pythagorean past, and transmitted to the future, to reemerge, enriched, in the school of Alexandria. We find it again in the Florentine "School of Athens," fertilizing in the Renaissance an art as authentically Platonic as any in Greece, and so in the works of Spenser, Shelley, Yeats, and whatever works of poetry, music or architecture have received and transmitted its current.

"And as to the philosophy, by whose assistance these mysteries are developed, it is coeval with the universe itself; and however its continuity may be broken by opposing systems, it will make its appearance at different periods of time, as long as the sun himself shall continue to illuminate the world. It has, indeed, and may hereafter, be violently assaulted by delusive opinions; but the opposition will be just as imbecil as that of the waves of the sea against a temple built on a rock, which majestically pours them back, 'Broken and vanquish'd foaming to the main.' "[23]

Already during Taylor's boyhood the Greek Revival was transforming taste in the visual arts. Perhaps the most important single work in inspiring the passion for things Greek which was to possess a generation was Stuart and Revett's *Antiquities of Athens*,[1] published in four volumes between 1762 and 1816; Taylor's *Pausanias* (1794) is illustrated by several of Stuart's engravings that were taken from that work (see Plate 6). Already the collectors were at work, bringing into the country gems and intaglios, vases, sculptures, sarcophagi. Yet one has the impression that Taylor was not himself much interested in the visual arts; he makes no mention of them, and this omission is striking when

[23] *A Dissertation on the Eleusinian and Bacchic Mysteries* (London, 1790), below, p. 345.

---

[1] *The Antiquities of Athens*, "measured and delineated by James Stuart F.R.S. and F.S.A. and Nicholas Revett, Painters and Architects" (London, 1762–1816).

we consider the immense excitement such things were causing at the time. He never cites any work of visual art as a source of iconographic evidence or confirmation of myth or symbol. When he came to have his portrait painted, although he had known Romney, it was by the fashionable Sir Thomas Lawrence[2] (see Plate 1), and of the maker of the bust of Taylor in later life (Plate 2) nothing is known except the self-evident fact that it is not by "Flaxman the statuary," in whose house Taylor had, at some time in the 1780's, given his twelve lectures on Platonic philosophy. Yet Flaxman had been one of the moving spirits at the very heart of the Greek revival in the visual arts, and it was to Flaxman and his circle that Taylor's message was first delivered.

In an autobiographical sketch (see below, p. 105) Taylor tells that as a schoolboy at St. Paul's School (famed for its excellence in the classics and in Hebrew) he was already noted for his interest in the philosophic aspect of the classics. In the same work he says that he was led to his Platonic studies through his interest in mathematics. But Taylor moved in that small circle which was, then as now, the "world" of the artists and men of letters of his time, and it was among these that the Greek revival was a living reality.

His lectures at Flaxman's house were, he said, attended by "Sir William Fordyce, the Hon. Mrs. Damer, Mrs. Cosway, Mr. Romney and others"; among those "others" William Blake must have been one; for he was at that time an intimate friend of Flaxman. In that world the same names constantly reappear in different contexts, as lives cross and recross. So we find that William Pars (1742–1782), whose brother Henry Pars's drawing-school Blake attended as a boy, went to Greece with Nicholas Revett to work on *Ionian Antiquities*.[3] James Basire (Plate 7), to whom Blake was later apprenticed, was one of the engravers of Stuart's drawings and Blake himself another (Plate 8). At the time Blake was with

[2] Son-in-law of Taylor's patron William Meredith.

[3] "Published by the Society of Dilettanti," R. Chandler, N. Revett, and W. Pars (2 vols.; London, 1769, 1794).

Basire, the work in hand included Bryant's *Mythology*,[4] which played so great a part in turning the thoughts of a generation toward myth and symbol (Plate 12). Flaxman was already working for Wedgwood and Bentley by the time he was twenty (Plate 11), and it was he who interested Josiah Wedgwood in the Barberini (afterward the Portland) Vase (Plate 9), when in 1784 he wrote a letter in which he urged his employer to come to London to "see Sir Wm. Hamilton's Vase; it is the finest production of Art brought to England."[5] Blake (who also worked for the Wedgwoods from time to time as an engraver) made the engravings of the Portland Vase (Plate 10) for Erasmus Darwin's *The Botanic Garden* (1789–1791). Darwin, an intimate friend of the Wedgwoods, believed the emblems on the vase to be representations of the Eleusinian Mysteries; and Taylor's *Dissertation* on those Mysteries appeared within the same year. In which of those fertile young minds did this idea (never before suggested in accounts of the vase) originate? In that *Island in the Moon* (1784–1785) in which Blake has represented Taylor (Sipsop the Pythagorean?) and Flaxman (Etruscan Column?) was the vase one of the topics of those wild, irrational discussions? And the Eleusinian Mysteries? Was Fuseli (Blake's friend) ever among those present, and did he propound the views of the ancient Greeks given by the Abbé Winckelmann, whose work on ancient Greek painting and sculpture[6] he had translated into English as early as 1765? In that work is pictured a race of ancient Greeks whose physical beauty and intellectual and moral qualities were as far from the moderns as perfection is from imperfection. Had Taylor read this work? His friend and patron George Cumberland certainly had, and his own *Thoughts on Outline* (1796), illustrated by drawings some of which were engraved by another friend, William Blake (see Plate 13), is the product of a similar enthusiasm for the ancient world.

[4] Jacob Bryant, *A New System of Ancient Mythology* (3 vols.; London, 1774).

[5] Feb. 5, 1784. Quoted in Wolf Mankowitz, *The Portland Vase and the Wedgwood Copies* (London, 1952).

[6] Johann Joachim Winckelmann, *Reflections on the Painting and Sculpture of the Greeks*, tr. Henry Fuseli (London, 1765).

So ideas are, within a generation, exchanged and transmitted; the written records of such interchanges are but the unconsumed residue of a once-living organism. Thus when a generation later Palmer, Calvert, and their friends called themselves "the Shoreham Ancients" they were perpetuating an idea long current among those in revolt against "progressive" science, of an ancient tradition, lost and recovered, from which true art is at all times drawn; a veneration for some symbolic antiquity is (as in Plato himself) the constant accompaniment of such thought; as against science, whose truths are experimental, and whose future is a perpetual invalidation of its past. Yeats and the Irish Renaissance were again to turn (as all poets must) to the riches of the past; for renewals in the arts are never iconoclastic, they come about through reorientation and return to the source.

Taylor was therefore in the heart of the excitement of his generation. The revolutionary Mary Wollstonecraft was Taylor's lodger, Blake's friend Johnson the bookseller's translator and reader, and mother of Shelley's wife. If later in life Taylor worked himself into scholarly seclusion, this was by no means his character as a young man. One has the impression that Taylor as he grew older moved less among such wild friends; and the books of his later years are correspondingly less enthusiastic and imaginative. His immense scholarly labors have since been superseded, and the works for which he will most certainly be remembered are his early expositions of myth and symbol, undertaken not only for the love of learning but above all in order to change the world and to help to create that New Age of which Blake too was a prophet, in those days before the French Revolution when everything seemed possible.

But if we catch only glimpses of Taylor's relations with the artists and firebrands of his own generation we have from his own account a clear picture of his relations with Floyer Sydenham (1710–1787), who between 1759 and 1780 had translated nine of Plato's fifty-five dialogues.[7] Of these the *Io*, the *Greater*

---

[7] Taylor gets fifty-five by counting the *Republic* as ten and *Laws* as twelve.

Hippias, the *Lesser Hippias,* and the *Banquet* were published in 1767, when Taylor was ten years old; the First and Second *Alcibiades* in 1773; and in 1779 the *Philebus.* The *Meno* and the *Rivals* were published after Sydenham's death, in 1804; all these (revised and edited) are included in Taylor's own *Works of Plato,* and there can be no doubt that the idea of translating the whole of Plato grew out of his acquaintance with Sydenham (in whose translations he may first have read Plato), whose self-appointed task he completed. In the Introduction to his *Plato*[8] Taylor gives an account of his acquaintance with the old and ailing Floyer Sydenham in which we see the young Taylor, warm in his sympathy for Sydenham's private troubles, but already assured of his own superiority as scholar and philosopher (he was twenty-nine when Sydenham died) and prepared rather to teach and to proselytize than to learn. Already, as in his earliest written works, we see Taylor fired with enthusiasm for the Neoplatonists:

". . . this excellent though unfortunate scholar died before he had made that proficiency in the philosophy of Plato which might have been reasonably expected from so fair a beginning. I personally knew him only in the decline of life, when his mental powers were not only considerably impaired by age, but greatly injured by calamity. His life had been very stormy: his circumstances, for many years preceding his death, were indigent; his patrons were by no means liberal; and his real friends were neither numerous nor affluent. He began the study of Plato, as he himself informed me, when he had considerably passed the meridian of life, and with most unfortunate prejudices against his best disciples, which I attempted to remove during my acquaintance with him, and partly succeeded in the attempt; but infirmity and death prevented its completion. Under such circumstances it was not to be expected that he would fathom the profundity of Plato's conceptions, and arrive at the summit of philosophic attainments. I saw, however, that his talents and his natural dispositions were such as might have ranked him among the best of Plato's interpreters, if he had not yielded to the pressure of

[8] I, cvi–cvii.

calamity, if he had not nourished such baneful prejudices, and if he had not neglected philosophy in the early part of his life."

Taylor when he was young no doubt hoped, naïvely we may say (as did Blake, that other prophet of a New Age), for an easy victory. Those who have seen some truth can never imagine others cannot see what to them is plain: "Truth can never be told so as to be understood, and not be believ'd,"[9] Blake wrote; and Taylor dedicated his Proclus's *Commentaries* "To the Sacred Majesty of Truth" (see p. v). In 1787, in a style reminiscent of Blake's, and perhaps caught from him in the enthusiastic days of their early acquaintance, while Blake was proclaiming Swedenborg's "A new heaven is begun,"[10] Taylor was summoning the men of the New Age to the standard of Plotinus:

"Impetuous ignorance is thundering at the bulwarks of philosophy, and her sacred retreats are in danger of being demolished, through our feeble resistance. . . . The foe is indeed numerous, but, at the same time, feeble: and the weapons of truth, in the hands of vigorous union, descend with irresistible force, and are fatal wherever they fall."[11]

What young man would ever set out upon such a task without the belief that truth is great and will prevail? But experience taught Taylor, as it taught Blake, that the victories of truth are not so easily or obviously won; for in 1805 he wrote more soberly of "that sublime theology which was first obscurely promulgated by Orpheus, Pythagoras and Plato, and was afterwards perspicuously unfolded by their legitimate disciples; a theology which, however it may be involved in oblivion in *barbarous,* and derided in *impious* ages, will again flourish for very extended periods, through all the infinite revolutions of time."[12]

[9] *The Marriage of Heaven and Hell,* in *Poetry and Prose of William Blake,* ed. Geoffrey Keynes (London, 1932), p. 152.

[10] *The Marriage of Heaven and Hell,* Keynes, Plate 3, p. 149.

[11] Plotinus, *Concerning the Beautiful* (London, 1787), below, p. 160 n.

[12] *Miscellanies in Prose and Verse* (London, 1805), p. viii. This statement is based upon the tradition of the Great Year, as described in Plato's *Laws.* The same doctrine is taught in India. The revolution of the Great Year is an ever-recurring theme in European poetry—Virgil, Shelley, and Yeats come to mind.

Why, then, is the name of Thomas Taylor so seldom found in works of literary history and criticism? Let it be said at once that if Taylor had written better English his translations might have been more widely read. Yeats called his style atrocious, and Coleridge wrote that Taylor translated Proclus from "difficult Greek into incomprehensible English." MacKenna, who praised him as a pioneer, objected to his translations for reasons "mainly literary."[13] Taylor was first a mathematician, then a metaphysician; he used words for the communication of precise but abstruse meanings, often lying outside the genius of the English language, the English being, in Yeats's words, "babes in philosophy" and possessing the poorest philosophical literature in Europe. He does not, like MacKenna, make Plotinus a delight to read; he even—which might seem no less difficult—makes Apuleius unreadable; but he does compel attention to the subtleties of ideas and in this he is often superior to MacKenna. "The gold that was in them the Platonist thought deserved the trouble of toilsome digging."[14] If he never makes the way smooth, he does not approximate or blur, or in any other way allow us to evade the exacting demands of philosophy: "in perusing the works of these great men, the reader must not expect to find the sublimest truths explained in a familiar manner, and adapted, like many modern publications, *to the meanest of capacities.*"[15]

Yet he writes with intellectual passion, and passion is infectious. Of the theology of the ancients he reminds us that "its intrinsic excellence and truth will extend its existence beyond the wreck of modern systems, and the desolation of ages."[16] Taylor understood that the most excellent cannot be obtained without effort, and wisdom is not to be had at the cheap rate our age demands. The best that can be said of Taylor's style is that it does not allow us to think that we have understood the philosophy because we have admired a work as literature.

[13] *Plotinus: The Enneads*, tr. Stephen MacKenna (London, 1917–1930), Introduction.

[14] W.E.A. Axon, *Thomas Taylor the Platonist*, below, p. 132.

[15] *Commentaries of Proclus* (1792), I, xxiv.

[16] Ibid., II, i.

Thomas Taylor in England

There is good reason for not reading Plato and Plotinus in Taylor's translations now that better versions exist, but why in his own day was he not thanked for his labors? "His efforts were unfavourably—almost contemptuously—received," according to the *Encyclopaedia Britannica* (11th edition). In the answer to this question lies the secret of the quality of greatness that sets Taylor above men of mere learning.

Men who, like Taylor, become learned not for the sake of erudition but of truth must always be an embarrassment and a reproach to the merely erudite. Taylor was calling in question received values of his time; his Platonism was too obviously subversive. History was repeating itself: as scholastic theologians and humanists alike would have none of Ficino, Pico, and Bruno, so did the pedants of Oxford and Edinburgh unite against the English Pagan. He was not, like Bruno, burned, nor like Shelley driven into exile; but he suffered continual attack and ridicule for his defense of that philosophy which has again and again been the inspiration of sublime art and anathema to dull minds. He was, besides, disturbing the sleep of the Universities. As the son of a nonconformist father, Oxford and Cambridge had been barred to him, and because of a rash, romantic (but apparently very happy) early marriage he did not go up, as his father had intended, to Aberdeen. It is true that in 1802 he was invited to Oxford, was entertained at New College, and worked at the Bodleian; but the clerical hosts of the first translator of Plato into English, whose books "were produced without regard to, and hopeless of, profit,"[1] cannot have forgotten that they themselves, with every advantage of security and leisure, had not done what he had done. Taylor, in poverty and obscurity, carried to completion the translation of Plato begun by Floyer Sydenham, who died at seventy-seven years of age, in a debtor's prison. B. G. Niebuhr, the German classical scholar, thanked God, a propos Taylor, that he was not born a poor scholar in England. In our own century the premature death of MacKenna was, also, hastened by the hardship of poverty. Oxford, for whatever reasons,

[1] Axon, below, p. 132.

assaulted Taylor with "black melancholy," and he made his escape as soon as he possibly could.[2]

Nor was the hostility to Taylor merely that of all entrenched authorities toward those who invade "their" field of study; what was worse, he presented "the classics" in an entirely new, and revolutionary, light. Whatever Taylor's faults may have been it was not for these but for his excellencies that he was castigated. Possessed of a genius for metaphysical thought in an uncomprehending age, the nearer he approached those premises which are, in terms of the philosophy he expounded, most fundamental (and therefore most subversive) the more angrily he was derided.

The *Edinburgh Review*[3] devoted twenty-four angry pages to

[2] A letter from Taylor, published in an article by Edward Peacock in *The Antiquary* (July 1888), pp. 1–5, describes this visit. The letter (see Plate 21) is dated June 20, 1802, and tells that the Dean of Christ Church, "as he received me in a very flattering manner, said he was well acquainted with my works, and professed himself a great admirer of Plato and Aristotle; and he told me yesterday that he would subscribe to my Plato. I have also received great civilities from Dr. Smith, the head of Trinity College, Dr. Winstanley, Professor of History in Corpus [Christi] College; and particularly from the Professors in New College, where I reside. I have, likewise, found the manuscripts which I expected to find in the Bodleian Library, to which I have the liberty of access after the usual hours. . . .

"I shall perhaps surprise you by saying that Oxford, independent of the Bodleian Library, has no charms for me. For though I have received the greatest civilities from the black-coated gentlemen, yet they appear to me to be in general haughty and superficial, and they flaunt through the streets with that self-importance, as if wisdom and wit were inseparable from the robe. And as to the numerous Colleges and Halls in Oxford, these, though they may be considered as so many palaces, are to me so gloomy from their Gothic structure, that they give a melancholy aspect to the town and its vicinity. Even the trees, in which these proud edifices at a distance seem to be embosomed, appear to me to lose all their verdure as the barbaric towers and spires tower above them. In short everything is infected with monkish gloom; and I am not yet reconciled to my apartments, which are very much in the style of some of the rooms in Mrs. Radcliffe's castles. If it were not, therefore, that I consider my residence here for a short time as necessary to the accomplishment of an object to which I shall always consider everything else as secondary, whatever and wherever be my situation in life, I should leave Oxford immediately, so black is the melancholy with which it assaults me."

[3] Vol. 14 (April 1809), pp. 187–211.

an attack on Taylor's *Plato*, but the reviewer turns aside for a moment to describe the state of classical learning in England. In spite of the immense amount of education devoted to "the classics," England had contributed very little of value to classical learning: "the preposterous share of time, labour and esteem . . . bestowed upon the comparatively unimportant business of prosody" (regarded as a cardinal point in English education) was the cause of the rarity, even among the most celebrated scholars in England, of "anything like a familiar acquaintance with the orators, the philosophers, and the historians of Greece."

It must also be remembered that the academic world at that time consisted of Protestant clergymen, to whom the Platonic theology must have been extremely distasteful. Taylor's defense of the polytheism of the philosophers whose mythological discourse suggested "idolatry," so detestable to the Protestant mentality, must have seemed as outrageous as Shelley's "atheism" did a generation later to the Master and Fellows of University College. Edward Peacock[4] wrote that Taylor, "though saturated with Greek learning was a self-taught man, and therefore never acquired the kind of scholarship which is useful for schoolmasters and has a commercial value at British universities. . . . It has therefore been the fashion during the last half-century for prigs, who find it by no means easy to stumble through a chapter in the 'Acts,' to jeer at him as a man who translated Aristotle and Plato without knowing Greek grammar. . . . The same young men will assure us with edifying calmness that the Pauline epistles present no difficulties to them. . . ." Peacock also says that Taylor was "a mortal foe to Greek accents, treating them with a righteous scorn. . . . This opinion laid him open to the charge of avoiding accents from ignorance. This was certainly not the true reason why he hated them. It was, however, too telling a point for popular writers to neglect."

A display of critical apparatus is no proof of intelligence; and Taylor had no illusions about the "verbal critics" who "look with great disgust on a translation at the bottom of which no variety

[4] *The Antiquary*, XVIII (July 1888), 1–3.

of different readings, no critical acumen of verbal emendation presents itself to view." Such notes are of no use to an English reader who does not know Greek; the pedants who set so much store by this "egregious trifling" have, as he truly says, "become so mentally imbecile, as to mistake *words* for *things*."[5] It is very much easier, besides, to count commas and breathings than to experience a poem, or to understand an idea. Taken all in all, Taylor was not a man likely to be loved by the academic profession.

René Guénon, who as a metaphysician of the perennial philosophy has in this century occupied a position not unlike that of Taylor, writes of a danger always present in academic studies: "As soon as erudition becomes a 'speciality' it tends to be regarded as an end in itself, instead of a means to an end, as it normally should be. It is this invasion of the intellectual field by erudition with its special methods which constitutes a genuine danger . . . because the habits which grow with the use of such methods narrow the intellectual horizon and cause irremediable harm to those who submit to them."[6]

Taylor criticized Fabricius in similar terms. Fabricius had blamed Proclus for "uniting to the doctrine of Plato a thousand dogmata, foreign to his philosophy"; and Taylor comments: "When men mistake their abilities, they always act absurdly, and often dangerously. As a laborious and accurate critic on philological matters, Fabricius merits the highest commendation such attainments can deserve; but when he leaves the beaten road in which nature designed him to walk, and attempts the trackless paths of philosophy, he perpetually stumbles, and often falls on the ground. The wings of philology, like those of the swallow, were never destined for a lofty flight;—it must be the eagle wing of genius, which can alone soar to the sun of philosophy."[7]

G.R.S. Mead, in his foreword to the 1895 edition of Taylor's

[5] *The Phaedrus of Plato* (London, 1792), Introduction.
[6] *Introduction to the Study of Hindu Doctrine*, tr. Marco Pallis (London, 1945), p. 19.
[7] *Commentaries of Proclus* (London, 1792), I, 38.

Select Works of Plotinus, wrote: "It is true that the perfected scholarship of our own times demands a higher standard of translation than Taylor presents; but what was true of his critics then is true of his critics today: though they may know more Greek, he knew more Plato. . . . Taylor was more than a scholar, he was a philosopher in the Platonic sense of the word." Taylor's knowledge was, besides, of a kind that his world (and still, to a great extent, our own) did not want. It is not merely that the mechanistic scientific phase of Western culture is not interested in traditional metaphysics; there is a positive wish to not know, to shut out a body of knowledge incompatible with existing values, and with the ends to which our civilization as a whole is directed. There is at all times a kind of criticism that takes up trifling points for attack to disguise the real motives of hostility. It is always possible to pick upon some minor fault and to use this as a pretext for avoiding the only important question, which is: does a work succeed in fulfilling its real purpose, and is that purpose a worthy one?

The violence with which Taylor has been over and over again consigned to oblivion is reminiscent of the positive force which, according to modern psychologists, is necessary in order to forget what we do not want to remember. De Quincey[8] wrote in 1846 that Taylor was "far more distinguished [than Taylor of Norwich] for absurdity and is now equally illustrious for obscurity." An examination of the *Edinburgh Review*[9] article that states that "the hand of oblivion has passed over him" reveals the attack on Taylor as, in reality, a violent rejection of the Neoplatonists, and of all those aspects of Plato himself which are at variance with the Scottish school of philosophy. Taylor incurs the indignation of the Lowland Scots "by exhibiting Plato as the mortal foe both of reason, and of taste" (those enthroned values of the Enlightenment): "He has not translated Plato; he has travestied him, in the most cruel and abominable manner. He has not elucidated, but covered him over with impenetrable

[8] *Works* (Edinburgh, 1860), Vol. 13, p. 60.
[9] Vol. 14 (April 1809), pp. 187ff.

darkness." How so? By adding, by way of notes, Proclus's commentaries: "In the character of commentator, Mr. Taylor has scarcely done anything, or indeed professed to do anything, but to fasten upon Plato the reveries of Proclus, and of the other philosophers of the Alexandrian school." How can any reader follow Plotinus without "disgust"? Here the ghost of Knox rises to denounce witchcraft and superstition: Plotinus and his school "were, almost without exception, impostors and mountebanks, THAUMATURGI *par métier.*"

The names of the current pillars of reason and taste—Jacob Bryant, Cicero, Horace, Brucker, and Gibbon—are invoked as witnesses against the "wild, and mystical, and obscure" writings of Proclus and Plotinus, their extravagant fancies, absurd reveries, strange allusions, forced etymologies; "the solemn trifling and impenetrable obscurity of those sages, who professed to reveal the system of the universe." Did not Plato himself, in the *Timaeus*, speak the same language? Not at all—the *Timaeus* and the *Parmenides*, far from expressing Plato's thought, were written with the intention of exposing the follies of those "ridiculous quibblers" whose names they bear! Another Edinburgh publication—*Blackwood's Magazine*[10]—abused Taylor as unscholarly: he is "an ass, in the first place; secondly he knows nothing of the religion of which he is so great a fool as to profess himself a votary. And thirdly he knows less than nothing of the language about which he is continually writing. . . ."

But the *Monthly Magazine*[11] used another stick to beat him— he was too accurate: "The philosophy of Aristotle, wrapped in the deepest mysteries by the Platonicians, has been relieved from its long night of darkness by the luminous interpretation of Dr. Gillies," it begins; "Mr. Thomas Taylor, however, indignant that the philosophy of Aristotle should be made intelligible to common understandings, and convinced, with Mr. Burke, that obscurity is a principal source of the sublime, has written a virulent *'Answer'* to Dr. Gillies, in which the unfaithfulness of that excel-

[10] Vol. 17 (June 1825), p. 737.
[11] Vol. 18, No. 124 (January 1805), p. 579.

lent Grecian's translation of the Ethics is inferred from the want of that creeping verbal accuracy which distinguishes his own."

Let us give Dr. Gillies a hearing: "The nature and scope of my literary labours are so totally different from those of Mr. Taylor, that it is not easy to understand how our roads could cross. . . . Utility, common and vulgar utility, above which that sublime author proudly soars was my great, or rather sole aim."[12] Such complacency is only to be found in a man who knows that public opinion is with him; what Englishman at the turn of the nineteenth century could resist that blessed word "utility"?

Taylor's views, not his Greek, are the real motives of attack; he held the opinion—a usual one now—that "Aristotle did not essentially differ from Plato on the doctrine of ideas."[13] Blakey, in his *History of the Philosophy of Mind*, fairly describes his position: "Mr. Taylor strenuously contends that Aristotle was not only the pupil, but in the strictest sense a holder of the Platonic dogmas, contrary to what he considered the ignorant and rash deductions of some modern writers, who, never having fully comprehended either master or scholar, have fancied the Stagyrite the founder of an opposing sect. . . ."[14]

Taylor's denial of an *essential* antagonism between the Platonic and Aristotelian schools turns, again, upon what we consider "essential" in the two philosophies. "My object in translating the whole of Aristotle's works," wrote Taylor, "was not to comment copiously on all that he has written, but to bring to light all the sublime and most important dogmas of his philosophy . . . and, also, to prove that these dogmas are perfectly conformable to those of Plato. . . . For if it shall appear that I have faithfully unfolded these dogmas from genuine sources, I shall neither envy those who have illustrated Aristotle better in less particulars, nor regard the criticism of those who may censure me in failing where it would have been easy to excel."[15] Great as are the dif-

[12] John Gillies, *Aristotle's Ethics and Politics . . . and a new analysis of his speculative works* (London, 1797), Supplement, p. xlvii.

[13] *An Answer to Dr. Gillies's Supplement* (London, 1804), p. 6.

[14] (London, 1848), IV, 67.

[15] *The History of Animals . . .* (London, 1809), p. xviii.

ferences between Plato and Aristotle in method and in formulation, it may be said that there is no essential difference in their metaphysical doctrine; or, to put it more carefully, it is possible for the metaphysician to find as many essential points of resemblance as it is for the logician or the moralist to find points of difference. Taylor found in Aristotle (as did Aquinas) an exponent of traditional metaphysics; and Aristotle himself would scarcely have shared the anti-metaphysical thought of those who claim him as the father of modern empiricism. But Aristotle's name had become associated with a whole structure of rationalist thought, from which had stemmed the philosophy of Bacon, Newton, Locke, and the experimentalists. The last thing such Aristotelians wanted was to have Aristotle made, after all, into a Platonist.

In reply to those who would object that Taylor fails to appreciate precisely what was original and new in "the Greek miracle," we may quote from Guénon once more, who saw in those originalities the germ of the development which all but divorced dialectic method from spirituality in the West. "Any new tendencies in the Graeco-Roman world are really almost entirely of a restricting and limiting nature," he writes. Their originality was of a purely dialectical order; indeed their dialectical subtlety amounts to no more than (as in many of Plato's dialogues) "an apparent desire to examine each question interminably, under all its aspects and in minutest detail, in order to arrive finally at a rather insignificant conclusion."[16] If Taylor found a residue of Platonic truth in Aristotle, Guénon discerned the seeds of Aristotelian pedantry in Plato. Wherever we may choose to discover its origin, the divergence itself is a real one, between an ancient metaphysical view of reality, and a new naturalist bias which now has, for the time being, prevailed. Guénon has described the present phase of civilization as "The Reign of Quantity"—a reversal of the due order of things, an abnormal exaltation of quantitative above qualitative value. Taylor, like Guénon, saw this reversal in terms of those gyres that Plato describes in *The Laws*:

[16] Guénon, *Hindu Doctrine*, p. 40.

". . . the circle of time, as it produces continual variations, at length reverses the objects of pursuit; and hence, that which was once deservedly first, becomes at length, by a degraded revolution, the last in the general esteem."[17] It is not abnormal that Proclus and Plato should be, to the average reader, obscure; nor that a minority only should understand the Mysteries; but it is abnormal that those who have knowledge should be objects of the contempt of the ignorant, that ignorance should with unchallenged assurance pass judgment upon knowledge.

The *Edinburgh Review* and the rest knew that they could flatter the vanity of "the modern reader" by making their appeal to his own prejudices (the same thing is done in the critical journals of every generation), and we may quote that glass of fashion Horace Walpole,[18] who, with less caution than the men of Edinburgh, says what he (and they) really think of Plato: "Taylor's book was shown to me this summer by one of those wiseacres that call themselves learned men, and who told me it was tremendous. I was neither alarmed nor curious: yet, on your Ladyship's notice, I borrowed the 'Monthly Review,' and find that the world's future religion is to be founded on a blundered translation of an almost unintelligible commentator on Plato." (So much for Proclus.) "I guess, however, that the religion this new apostle recommends is, not belief in the pantheon of Pagan divinities, but the creed of the philosophers, who really did not believe in their idols, but whose metaphysics were frequently as absurd; and yet this half-witted Taylor prefers them to Bacon and Locke, who were almost the first philosophers who introduced common sense into their writings, and were as clear as Plato was unintelligible—because he did not understand himself."

After this complacent revelation of the mentality of an unphilosophic age, Walpole (whose worldly wisdom was unquestionable) foretold that "Taylor will have no success; not because

---

[17] *Commentaries of Proclus*, I, cvi.

[18] Letter to the Countess of Ossory, November 26, 1789, in *Letters of Horace Walpole* (Oxford, 1903–1905), XIV, 238.

nonsense is not suited to making Proselytes—witness the Methodists, Moravians, Baron Swedenborg, and Loutherburg[19] the painter; but it should not be learned nonsense, which only the *literati* think they understand after long study."

These adverse judgments reveal just as well as praise wherein the originality of Taylor's classicism lies, and its revolutionary and subversive character, as it seemed to the Enlightenment; and as it seemed no less to the Romantic poets who read Taylor with a delight equal to the indignation of his (and their) opponents. One may recall the divisions over Chatterton and *Ossian*: were the real motives in these cases also different from those alleged? Would poor Chatterton have been accused of "fraud" if he had written smooth couplets instead of rough ballads, on Roman themes instead of "Gothic"? And was Dr. Johnson's moral indignation really aroused against Macpherson for taking too great license with his folklore sources (the "improvement" of Shakespeare, Chaucer, and the classics was freely interpreted by the Augustans), or was it because in the free rhythmic prose-poetry of *Ossian* and its romantic and novel themes he saw a threat to established literary values? It was from *Ossian* that Blake developed his highly original long free lines; and no "exposure" by

[19] Philip de Loutherburg, an Alsatian by birth, painter and scene designer at Drury Lane, where he worked for Garrick. He was the inventor of the "transformation scene," first used in 1781-82. He also invented the "eidophusicon," a model theater in Pall Mall, where by means of lighting effects and moving scenery spectators were entertained by "Fallen angels raising the Palace of Pandemonium," "Eruption of Vesuvius," the Armada, the Fire of London, etc.

Walpole, however, is referring to another of his activities, the faith-healing practiced by de Loutherburg and his wife at their house in Hammersmith Terrace. On "healing days" as many as three thousand people sometimes assembled, selling tickets of admission for as much as five guineas. The crowds caused annoyance to neighbors, who at last put a stop to the practice. In 1789 Cagliostro made friends with de Loutherburg and defrauded him of a large sum of money. Rumor reported an almost successful projection of the Philosophers' Stone, "only spoiled by the crucible breaking"—an episode reminiscent of Taylor's experiments on a Perpetual Flame. (See pp. 114, 129.)

Johnson could stem the tide of the "Gothic" taste, or save his world.

The Greek revival was as hateful to the Augustans as the Gothic. Walpole (agreeing in this with the Transcendentalists) couples Taylor with Swedenborg; and the *Edinburgh Review* writes that "the ravings of Jacob Behmen are not a more abominable misinterpretation of the New Testament than the commentaries of Proclus and Company are of the writings of Plato."[20] Coleridge and Blake turned to precisely these as the prophets of the New Age. Not all classicism is Augustan, as Edgar Wind said in lecturing on Classicism at Cambridge, and Taylor's was an integral part of the rise of the soul against mechanism, empiricism, and rationalism, the dynamic impulse of the Romantic movement.

Let us now turn to the Romantics in whom the Neoplatonists inspired an enthusiasm equal to the chagrin they aroused in the Augustans. Coleridge, by way of contrast with the *Edinburgh Review*, Walpole, and the rest, wrote that "the most beautiful and orderly development of this philosophy, which endeavors to explain all things by an analysis of Consciousness, and builds up a world in the mind out of materials furnished by the mind itself is to be found in the Platonic Theology of Proclus."[1]

He even went so far as to make Proclus the touchstone of a capacity for metaphysics. "Let a prepared Scholar" (so he wrote in the margin of his copy of Taylor's *Proclus*) "attentively peruse Chapter VI, Book I (concerning the essence of Mathematical Genera and Species) . . . if possible in the original Greek: and the result in his mind will inform him, whether Nature has intended him for metaphysical Research.—If I have any conception

---

[20] April 1809, p. 193.

[1] Letter to Lady Beaumont, January 21, 1810, in *Collected Letters of Samuel Taylor Coleridge*, ed. Griggs, III, 279. Coleridge is speaking specifically of the philosophy of Jacob Boehme.

of Sublimity as arising from a majestic vision of tranquil Truth, it will be found in this Chapter."[2] Those who wish to know what Coleridge considered the necessary qualifications of a "prepared Scholar" will find them set forth in the same place. Those qualifications are possessed by very few. What to Coleridge was "beautiful and orderly" was to Walpole "nonsense" and to the *Edinburgh Review* "impenetrable darkness." When we read that philosophers are unintelligible, may we not ask, "to whom?"

Taylor raises the question in relation to one of those "Cambridge Platonists" as overrated in the academic world as Taylor has been underrated. "I find my indignation roused by the following words of Dr. Cudworth, in his Intellectual System, p. 306. 'Proclus (says he) had some peculiar fancies and whims of his own, and was indeed a confounder of the Platonic theology, and a mingler of much unintelligible stuff with it.' I must confess, (and I am neither afraid, nor ashamed of the declaration,) that I never found any thing in Proclus, but what by patient thought, accompanied by a sincere and vehement thirst after truth, I have been able to fathom. Had Dr. Cudworth been endued with these requisites, he would doubtless have had equal success; but without them, the sublimest truths will certainly appear to be *unintelligible stuff.*"[3]

One of the subterfuges used in the name of scholarship for dismissing the Alexandrian school is to appeal to a kind of archaeological snobbery by which the responsibility of making a judgment is evaded by making "early" a synonym for "good" and "authentic" and "late" for "bad" or "spurious": because Plotinus is "late" and Proclus even later, they must be inferior, as philosophers, to Plato and Aristotle. But fidelity to tradition is not to be equated with a reverence for antiquity, as such; human thought has at different periods approached, or receded from, authentic knowledge. Neither antiquity nor novelty can increase or diminish inherent truth, or inherent beauty. If our approach is genu-

[2] Appendix B in *The Notebooks of Samuel Taylor Coleridge*, ed. Kathleen Coburn, Vol. 1 (New York and London, 1957), Notes, p. 455.
[3] *Commentaries of Proclus*, I, 36.

inely metaphysical, it will be obvious that the period from the second to the fourth centuries A.D. was a golden age in philosophy, including the last fine flower of the pre-Christian, and the first of the Christian era. In St. Augustine, as in Plotinus, many currents united to reemerge with gathered power. Taylor thought that no one for a thousand years had understood the Neoplatonists; and in a "Gothic" flight of fancy he likens their neglected philosophy to "a lamp shining on some venerable statue amidst dark and solitary ruins. And yet," he goes on "though these philosophers have been treated with such undeserved contempt by a pigmy race of critics and sophists, will any man undertake to prove, that since the age of Plato there has lived a philosopher of so much profundity as Plotinus, so learned as Porphyry, so skilled in the deepest mysteries of theology as Jamblichus, so acute as Syrianus, or who has unfolded such treasures of wisdom as Proclus?"[4] But the ignorance of the Lowland Scots and the complacency of the English are not easily charmed away by divine philosophy.

Taylor's road was a hard and solitary one; he attacked on two fronts at once, religion on the one hand, mechanistic science on the other. To the empiricist, men like Taylor must appear as intransigent; but the certainty of those who hold, with Plotinus, that "there is nothing higher than the truth," is different in kind from the fanaticism of opinion. Opinion may be changed, hypothesis discarded, but we cannot un-know. There is unanimity among those who have traveled farthest. This claim would be understood even at the present time if it were made, for example, by a physicist; but that "facts of mind" may also transcend personal opinion has been forgotten. Taylor's impatience with his critics, and, in general, with the religious and philosophic thought of his day, was that of a metaphysician of genius in an environment entirely unable to perceive "facts of mind" which to him were clear. The frequent unashamed allusions to the "murkiness" of the Platonists illustrates the point.

Whatever may be said against Taylor, or against the philoso-

---

[4] *An Answer to Dr. Gillies's Supplement*, pp. 87-88.

phers whose doctrines he attempted to restore, they cannot be called vague; Yeats wrote to his father[5] of "a religious system more or less logically worked out" that was to give him a new form of poetry. "One goes on year after year gradually getting the disorder of one's mind in order, and this is the real impulse to create." Taylor's friend Edward Peacock understood that "Taylor was a metaphysician, not a poet . . . he was an ardent enthusiast for that form of thought which we will call Neoplatonism, but which was in fact much more nearly like the beliefs of the men of the Italian Renaissance than any form of Platonic thought."[6] But this historical distinction is one that to a metaphysician does not exist; since the final appeal is to ideas whose truth is intrinsic and unaffected by history.

Robert Blakey, in his *History of the Philosophy of Mind,*[7] gives a generous account of Taylor, who was, as he realized ". . . justly entitled to honourable mention in any history of mental speculation. He spent above forty years in an exclusive devotion to what he considered the first and most august philosophy; and is the only modern, since the days of the Emperor Julian, or the age immediately succeeding, who has penetrated to its remotest sources, and effected its perfect mastership." It is not possible that Blakey had forgotten the Florentine school, and his praise of Taylor is high indeed.

"Mr. Taylor conceives that all which the moderns possess of moral science consists of nothing else than small and broken, though splendid, fragments of the great Platonic union of the universe. He employed himself not in studying the truth by their inspection, but in elaborate re-constructions of the whole as a concatenated and perfect system, according to its pristine form and splendour. He therefore, with a contempt which appears narrow and somewhat arrogant, rejects acceptance of, and declines all attention to, the dark and partial systems of modern writers;

[5] Letter to J. B. Yeats, June 14, 1917, in *Letters,* ed. Allan Wade, p. 627.
[6] *The Antiquary,* XVIII (July 1888), 2.
[7] IV, 66–68.

not, however, out of deficiency of powers for judging of them, but from a conceived previous fulness and redundancy of loftier and better knowledge."

But although Blakey understood the grounds of Taylor's rejection of humanist and experimentalist notions, he adds a very fair criticism: "Amongst other peculiarities of this extraordinary man, there is one which is deeply to be lamented. The Platonic Philosophy being strictly and essentially theological—in which, accordingly, all other principles and knowledge become themselves religionised, so to speak—Mr. Taylor adopts it in its fullest extent, with all the old profoundly significant and representative mythology attached to it. . . . This has led him to throw a gorgeous halo around the Grecian system; and to look at pure and undefiled truth through a dim and hazy atmosphere."

To give the title of "pure and undefiled truth" to Christianity in the debased forms in which it existed in England at the turn of the eighteenth century would be absurd. Taylor was the son of a nonconformist family of mean culture, and his early struggles to free himself from this background no doubt helped to embitter his contempt for Methodists and Presbyterians. He knew Christianity in a form devoid of intellectuality; but his conviction that "genuine philosophy and genuine religion . . . always amicably and inseparably accompany each other" was equally evident to Augustine and Aquinas, Eckhart and Scotus. Taylor valued Dionysius the Areopagite, and his rare Florentine copy of the *Celestial Hierarchies* is now in the possession of Mr. Geoffrey Watkins, son of the theosophical publisher who reissued several of Taylor's works. Nevertheless the same incompatibility between Christianity and the Hermetic tradition had been brought to light at the time of the Italian Renaissance, whose best minds had found Christianity, as Taylor did, intellectually stifling.

Like Blake and Shelley, Taylor was bound to reject Christianity as he found it; but, unlike these, his anti-Christianity took its tone of intellectual contempt, though not its philosophical substance, from Gibbon (whose influence on Taylor's sentence structure was even more regrettable): "For in our times, the voice of wisdom is no longer heard in the silence of sacred solitude; but *folly*, usurping her place, has filled every quarter with the deafening clamours of despicable sectaries, while the brutal hand of commerce has blinded the liberal eye of divine contemplation."[8] Like Gibbon, Taylor admired the Aristotelian virtues of high-mindedness and magnanimity, seeing in Christian "meekness" the mentality of the populace—the rising lower-middle classes: "meekness suppresses the effervescence of desire, restrains the restless spirit of enquiry, and calms the impetuosity of genius. Hence though we are no longer surprised with the daring exploits, and prodigious talents which distinguished the ancient world, yet we can boast a greater uniformity of character, a more general equality in moderate attainments, and a more interested spirit. In consequence of this universal mediocrity, our capacity for commerce is increased, and our abilities enlarged, for accumulating wealth by groveling pursuits."[9]

Taylor was as far from sharing Gibbon's skeptical Humanism as he was "the delirious visions of Swedenborg" or "the unconnected and impious effusions of Methodistical rant." Southey's jibe at Taylor as "a pagan Methodist" was certainly unjust; his anti-Christianity may be emotionally colored, but his Platonism is that of a true philosopher.

If Taylor scorned Christianity as a vulgarization of the Perennial Philosophy, still more absolute was his rejection of the scientific philosophy of Bacon, Newton, and Locke. There can be little doubt that the first to define the grounds of Blake's well-known rejection of these philosophers was Taylor:

"As little as the eye of a fly at the bottom of the largest of the Egyptian pyramids sees of the whole of that pyramid, compared

[8] *Commentaries of Proclus*, II, 317. The Platonic Philosopher of Isaac Disraeli's novel *Vaurien* (1797) expresses his contempt for the religious beliefs of "the moderns" in a manner whose style and substance are as close to the original as satire can well be. See Axon's account below, p. 130.

[9] *Commentaries of Proclus*, II, 317–18.

with what is seen of it by the eye of a man, so little does the greatest experimentalist see of the whole of things, compared with what Plato and Aristotle saw of it, through scientific reasoning founded on self-evident principles."[1]

The *Edinburgh Review* felt itself on safe ground when it accused Taylor of having "not so much as a tincture of modern science," and Coleridge himself called him a "blind bigot" for his objections to Bacon, adding, "the modern chemists talk of Bacon," as if the approval of a Humphry Davy could decide a point that is essentially metaphysical. Taylor is not concerned to discuss the utility of modern science, but purely and simply its metaphysical grounds. "The doctrine of causes was the object of ancient investigation: the enumeration of effects is the busy employment of the moderns."[2] By a strange irony of fate, Taylor earned his living for many years as Secretary to the Society for the Encouragement of Arts, Manufactures and Commerce (Plates 23, 24), at the very center of the promotion of agriculture, industrial, engineering, and scientific projects. There are letters from Taylor about the planting of larches near Kendal; the building of locks by the Stratford-upon-Avon Navigation Company, by Arkwright; on the cultivation of turnips; he is said to have been an excellent Secretary. If he rejected modern science it was not in ignorance of its uses. Blake understood what Coleridge apparently did not (and he must surely have talked the matter out with Taylor during the years of their acquaintance), that "Bacon's philosophy has ruined England."

"The mischief began at the end of the seventeenth century when men became passive before a mechanized nature," wrote Yeats, "that lasted to our own day with the exception of a brief period between Smart's *Song of David* and the death of Byron, wherein imprisoned man beat upon the door."[3] It was Blake above all who "beat upon the wall," as Yeats elsewhere writes; but fine as Blake's reasoning powers certainly were, it is likely that it was

[1] *The Creed of the Platonic Philosopher* (London, 1805), below, p. 441 n.

[2] *Commentaries of Proclus*, II, 318.

[3] *Oxford Book of Modern Verse*, p. xxvii. Cf. Blake, *Jerusalem*, ed. Keynes, Plate 91, p. 739: ". . . all his pyramids were grains / Of sand, & his pillars dust on the fly's wing. . . ."

Taylor whose metaphysical exactness of thought prepared Blake's position for him. Blake uses the curious but expressive term "labyrinths" (those spectral mazes into which his Tharmas pursues ever-vanishing Enion, and the male and mental principle of *A Mental Traveller* pursues the feminine material principle) in a sense comprehensible only in the sense the word is given by Taylor in such passages as the following comment on Bacon:

"The conceptions of the experimental philosopher who expects to find truth in the labyrinths of matter, are not much more elevated than those of the vulgar; for he is ignorant that truth is the most spendid of all things; that she is the constant companion of Divinity, and proceeds together with him through the universe, that the shining traces of her feet are conspicuous only in form; and that in the dark windings of matter she left nothing but a most obscure and fleeting resemblance of herself. This delusive phantom, however, the man of modern science ardently explores, unconscious that he is running in fog and darkness and infinite perplexity, and that he is hastening after an object which eludes all detection and mocks all pursuit."[4]

Taylor was engaged on his *Commentaries of Proclus* during the days of his presumed acquaintance with Blake. From *An Island in the Moon* we must conclude that Blake knew Taylor well before 1787; in (probably) 1788 Taylor delivered his twelve lectures on Platonism at the house of Flaxman. The substance of those lectures may very well have been the substance of the several Dissertations (on the Platonic Doctrine of Ideas, on the Demonstrative Syllogism, on the Nature of the Soul, and on the End of Geometry) included in the first volume of the *Commentaries*. Taylor's *History of the Restoration of the Platonic Philosophy*, in which his attacks on Locke and Bacon, Johnson and "the moderns" were first launched (included in the second volume of the *Commentaries*), must have appeared at least one year earlier, that is to say in or before 1788, the date of Blake's *Tractates* against "Natural Religion," and it may have been the substance of this Dissertation rather than the four listed above which

[4] *Theoretic Arithmetic* (London, 1816), p. xxxiv.

formed the substance of those famous lectures; it is at all events highly probable that the lecturer would have worked up his material for subsequent publication, and that it lies somewhere embedded in the two volumes of Proclus. There are therefore strong grounds for concluding that Blake learned his arguments against Bacon, Newton, and Locke from Taylor; whose objections, as a mathematician and metaphysician, are precise. Blake, who must have learned these Platonic objections from Taylor, merely gave his characteristically vigorous expression to objections which, from their Platonic character, we may reasonably conclude were first formulated by the "feeder of poets" and not by the poet himself.

To his contemporaries, it must have seemed mere arrogance in Taylor to declare with so much assurance that the thought of Locke and Bacon would sooner or later perish with ". . . the variety of other self-taught systems which, like nocturnal meteors, blaze for a while, and then vanish in obscurity. . . ."[5] Yet in the light of metaphysics he could not have thought otherwise: "self-taught" is an accurate description of knowledge reached by the experimental method.

For the natural scientists, the laws of mathematics are the laws of nature; whereas for Proclus, Euclid, and the Pythagorean tradition, number expresses the order of the soul, "facts of mind." The modern physicist, no less than the modern mathematician, is once again compelled to ask whether mind may not be the limiting factor to all measurement of the universe of nature; and Proclus's teaching that quantity originates in mind has meaning once more: "The essential number they [the Platonic philosophers] considered as first subsisting in the intelligible world, together with being."[6] "And if it be enquired how number subsists in the human soul, we must say, that the soul, by her self-moving energies, procreates number, while she numerates, and by this energy, causes the existence of quantity."[7] Bacon, accord-

[5] Ibid.
[6] *Commentaries of Proclus*, I, xiv.
[7] Ibid., p. xv.

ing to Taylor, in treating mathematics as a natural science, lost sight of its real nature.

The force of these philosophic objections must seem clearer at the present time; and a point of view practically identical with Taylor's was formulated not long ago by Guénon in *Les Principes du Calcul Infinitesimal*.[8] Both Taylor and Guénon were mathematicians before they were metaphysicians; and Guénon's objection, like Taylor's, to the natural scientists since Descartes and Bacon also rests upon the nature of number.

Pythagoras and Plato made mathematics the foundation of philosophic studies. There is a persistent modern misconception that the mental world is "personal," "subjective," and necessarily vague, whereas whatever order there may be is to be found in matter. Yet "the numerative art is essentially inherent in the soul, and is therefore present with all men,"[9] Taylor wrote; and the purpose of mathematical study is "no other than the enjoyment of that felicity congenial to the soul previous to her immersion in body."[10]

"But if it should be asked in what these energies of intellect consist, to which all science ultimately refers? I answer, in the contemplation of true being, or those ideal and divine forms, with which the intelligible world is replete."[11]

Thus the Greek "know thyself" may be better achieved by the study of mathematics than by introspection. Formlessness in the arts, far from being a mark of their "subjective" truth, betrays an ignorance of the order of the soul, and reveals the bankruptcy of a culture that, when it abandons the imitation of natural appearance, is left with no ordering principle whatsoever.

The arts are, according to the Platonic tradition, embodiments of mental forms. Iamblichus tells that whereas Pythagoras taught his disciples by means of music he himself listened to the inaudible "music of the spheres": "Pythagoras . . . seems to have said that he heard the celestial harmony, as understanding the har-

[8] Paris, 1946.
[9] *Commentaries of Proclus*, I, xvii.
[10] Ibid., p. cxvi.
[11] Ibid., p. cxv.

monic proportion in numbers, of the heavenly bodies, and that which is audible in them."[12] As Taylor says, "according to the Orphic and Pythagoric doctrine, the lyre of Apollo is an image of the celestial harmony . . . caused by the orderly revolutions of the celestial spheres." "The Comparison and conjunction of the musical and astronomical elements are most ancient."[13] Music has, until recently, retained its Pythagorean foundation in the diatonic scale. Architecture like music is an art based upon number and proportion; and the widespread abandonment of the art of architecture for the science of engineering reflects the modern purely quantitative understanding of mathematics for which Taylor held Bacon responsible.[14]

Taylor admired Kepler, and wrote in praise of his *De Harmonia Mundi*: "Kepler was skilled in the platonic philosophy, and appears to have been no less acquainted with the great depth of our author's [Proclus's] mind than with the magnificence and sublimity of his language. Perhaps Kepler is the only instance among the moderns, of the philosophical and mathematical genius being united in the same person."[15] Although Taylor considered Newton to be no philosopher, he fully recognized his genius as a mathematician.

Taylor printed on the first page of his *Commentaries* a sentence adapted from Isaac Disraeli's *Curiosities of Literature*, a true word, as he must have thought, spoken in jest, and in full calculation of

---

[12] *Life of Pythagoras* (London, 1818).

[13] *Mystical Hymns of Orpheus* (London, 1792), note on the Hymn to Apollo. See below, p. 247 n.

[14] Blake, who truly perceived (or learned through Taylor) that Greek art is an expression of "mathematical form," was not aware (and neither, it seems, was Taylor) that the "living form" of the Gothic was itself the flowering of a revival of the Pythagorean mathematics, studied by the monks of Cluny. Enthusiasm for geometric form led the Carthusians to banish the imitative naturalistic arts of sculpture and painting from their churches. See Otto von Simson, *The Gothic Cathedral* (London and New York, 1958). Le Corbusier and his school have more recently attempted to reintroduce a Greek system of proportion into architecture.

[15] *Commentaries of Proclus*, I, 114 n.

the irreverent spirit in which it would be taken: "Mr. T. Taylor, the Platonic Philosopher and *the modern Plethon,* consonant to that philosophy, professes polytheism." Taylor, who, like Pletho, rejected Christianity, was a polytheist only in the sense in which the Florentine painters of so many mythological scenes may be so called; he was always willing to shock the prejudices of the orthodox, whose ignorance in philosophy he held in the greatest contempt. Taylor's polytheism, so challengingly professed on the title page of Proclus's *Commentaries,* could not fail to give rise to countless rumors and anecdotes—that he was turned out of his lodgings for wishing to sacrifice a lamb (in other versions a bull) to Jupiter; that he believed his cats and dogs (he was an animal lover and a vegetarian) to be inhabited by transmigrant human souls, and so forth. Blake, in his *An Island in the Moon,* introduces Taylor as "Sipsop the Pythagorean," who is seen "stroking the cat," and dismissing Giotto as of no importance because he is not in Plutarch's *Lives.* Isaac Disraeli, in his *Curiosities of Literature,* fanned the flame: "The divinities of Plato are the divinities to be adored, and we are to be taught to call God, Jupiter; the Virgin, Venus; and Christ, Cupid! The Iliad of Homer allegorized, is converted into a Greek bible of the arcana of nature!"[1] Disraeli and Taylor seem to have been good friends, and Disraeli is said to have attended Taylor's funeral. He is also the "Mr. Mystic" of Thomas Love Peacock's *Melincourt.*

Nothing could be more untrue than to suppose that polytheism is unphilosophic; it is, on the contrary, a feature of those metaphysical systems which most clearly realize that "the deep truth is imageless"—a thought Shelley himself may quite possibly have first seen stated in Taylor's arguments against the Christian Trinity in his essay *On the Restoration of the Platonic Philosophy.* Polytheism is a most subtle symbolic mode of apprehension of "facts of mind," incomprehensible only to those who, like Locke,

[1] *Curiosities of Literature* (London, 1830), p. 370. This is journalism—the falsification of fact by style. *De Antro Nympharum* is certainly "the Iliad of Homer allegorised"; and if for "cupid" we read "love" the statement ceases to be blasphemous. Disraeli's satire is indeed finely two-edged.

regard mental processes as mere elaborations of sense impressions. "If by polytheists we mean," Taylor wrote, "men who believed in a multitude of self-existent beings independent of each other, and of one first cause, there were no such men among the Greeks and Romans, as must be obvious to everyone who is conversant with the writings of the heathens, and as is fully evinced by Dr. Cudworth in his *Intellectual System*; nor am I acquainted with any nation who entertained an opinion so monstrous and dire. But if by polytheists he intends to signify men who believed in the existence of divine natures, the immediate progeny of one first cause with which they are profoundly united, Aristotle is so far from opposing this doctrine in his Metaphysics, that in the eighth chapter of the twelfth book he demonstrates their existence."[2]

All poets are natural polytheists; a wave of polytheism characterized the Romantic movement, and Taylor's expositions of the Greek mythology became sacred books of the poets. It is chiefly the early essays of Taylor which retain their interest, both in themselves and because the poets learned from them. Coleridge's *Ancient Mariner*[3] with its spirits and daemons; Keats's reanimation of the Greek myths with imaginative meaning;[4] the Platonic polytheism of Shelley, all in various ways and degrees reflect Taylor's "restoration of the Platonic philosophy." But the strangest of the Romantic polytheists, and the one most demonstrably influenced by Taylor, is Blake. Blake must have loved Taylor's translation of Porphyry's *De Antro Nympharum* in his youth—for it inspired his art in his old age (Plate 14). Of the part played by Taylor in forming Blake's elaborate pantheon of "gods" that "emanate" from "the Human Imagination" I have written elsewhere.[5] Blake adopted (with tributaries from Christian Caba-

---

[2] *An Answer to Dr. Gillies's Supplement*, p. 18.

[3] See John Beer, *Coleridge the Visionary* (London, 1959).

[4] See Bernard Blackstone, *The Consecrated Urn*.

[5] *Blake and Tradition* (A. W. Mellon Lectures in the Fine Arts; Princeton and London, 1968). C. G. Jung's archetypes may also be described as composing a "pantheon" of the "divine natures" as these are manifested and diversified in the psyche.

lism, alchemy, Boehme, Swedenborg, and related systems) the Orphic and Neoplatonic theology, and many of its myths. A beautiful page of *The Marriage of Heaven and Hell* illustrates a text that tells how "The ancient Poets animated all sensible objects with Gods or Geniuses. . . ." It seems that there was a break between Blake and Taylor, and that when *Milton* was written (1802) Blake wished to dissociate himself from some former assent to Taylor's pagan manifesto: "We do not want either Greek or Roman Models if we are but just & true to our own Imaginations, those Worlds of Eternity in which we shall live for ever in Jesus our Lord."[6] But Blake retained the elements of Neoplatonic polytheism within his Christian framework; and in his later years his love of Plato increased. His Christianity, informed as it was by the study of Platonic metaphysics and Orphic mythology, was no more acceptable or comprehensible than Taylor's paganism; the two rebels had more in common than had either with their amazed contemporaries.

The modern Western mentality has little sense of the relative. Taylor in a late essay[7] shows up Bacon's naturalistic interpretation of myths for the shallow thing it is, in terms whose dispassion contrasts with the fiery indignation of his youth:

"As the mythology of the Greeks is intimately connected with their philosophy and theology, it is not at all wonderful, since the moderns are ignorant of the latter, that they have not genuinely developed the former. Lord Bacon, indeed, has done all, in attempting to unfold this mythology,[8] that great genius, without the assistance of *genuine philosophy*, is able to effect. But the most piercing sagacity, the most brilliant wit, and the most exquisite subtilty of thought, without this assistance, are here of no avail. It is indeed easy for ingenious men to explain an ancient fable, in a way which to the superficial observer shall appear to be the precise meaning which its inventors designed to convey, though

[6] Preface to *Milton*, Book I, p. 460.

[7] "On the Mythology of the Greeks," *Classical Journal*, XXIII (March and June 1821), 33–41.

[8] Taylor is presumably referring to Bacon's *The Wisdom of the Ancients*.

it be in reality very far from the truth. This may be easily accounted for, by considering that all fables are images of truths; but those of the Greeks, of truths with which but few are acquainted."

Taylor's importance as a teacher of mythological thought to the Romantic poets cannot be exaggerated. In his Introductions to the first and second editions of the *Hymns of Orpheus* and in his *Dissertation on the Mysteries*, in particular, he presents, with the mastery of a true metaphysician, those first principles of symbolic thought which had long been lost. He translated Sallust's *On the Gods and the World*, and included a passage from that work in his *Dissertation* that may, for those "mythological poets," Keats, Shelley, Blake, and Coleridge, have been a key placed in their hands to the whole body of European mythological poetry; nor was it only classical literature upon which this illumination must have fallen, but also upon Spenser and Milton, the two poets to whom the Romantics chiefly turned. Sallust's distinction of the four kinds of myth, the theological, the animastic (which would now be called the psychological, applying to the soul or *anima*) the natural, and the "mixed," is the key to the correct reading not only of Greek mythology but of all mythological poets since. To a modern reader, indebted as we are to Jungian and other reexaminations of the language of mythology, these distinctions may not seem strange. But how far the mentality of the eighteenth century had strayed from any possibility of understanding the symbolic thought embodied in myths can scarcely be credited unless we read such writers as Bryant and Warburton. It is true that mythology was beginning to capture the imagination even of such authors as these—they would scarcely have devoted their lives to erecting their monuments of unenlightened erudition had this not been so; nor must we forget the growing interest in Norse mythology, embodied in such works as Mallet's *Northern Antiquities*, translated by Bishop Percy (himself the collector of ancient ballads), the *Celtic Researches* of Edward Davies, and the work of other investigators of British antiquities, and the oriental studies of Sir William Jones and his circle. The myths spoke to the imagination of such authors, the inadequacy of their rationalizations notwithstanding.

Jacob Bryant's *New System of Ancient Mythology* is a work of extensive learning used in the service of an idea of such naïveté as to excuse Taylor's most contemptuous diatribes against the folly of "the moderns."[9] Bryant, observing that the Flood myth occurs in many versions besides that in the Bible, drew the conclusion—applauded by the learned of his day (the clergy of that time and place were of course committed to a purely "historical" reading of even those parts of the Bible that are quite evidently symbolic stories), commentated, substantiated, and discussed at length in the pages of learned journals—that all pantheons are based upon the eight persons saved from the Flood in Noah's Ark. Scarcely an adverse voice was raised; Sir William Jones[10] went so far as to say that he was not convinced—no doubt a polite understatement by that man of sophisticated intelligence and vast learning; and only Taylor, unheeded, said that the theory was nonsensical. Reason and taste, outraged by Proclus and Plotinus, were satisfied with a theory that could not better illustrate the inability of the English of that time to comprehend symbolic thought. To such lengths could a naïvely "historical" reading of the Bible lead learned clerics. Bryant's *Mythology*, once so widely read, is remembered today chiefly because William Blake as an apprentice assisted Basire in the engraving of some of the plates.

Taylor's warnings against the interpretation of mythology with-

[9] Bryant, however, seems an original thinker when compared with Warburton, whose *Divine Legation of Moses* was no less highly esteemed in its day. Taylor's *Dissertation* refers to Warburton's explanations of the Mysteries of Eleusis. The truth "pure and undefiled" taught by Protestant Christian divines of the eighteenth century, on anything of a symbolic character, is too fantastic to be satirized.

[10] Jones was himself the author of several remarkable essays on the Mythology of the Hindus, and of comparative studies of these myths with Italian and Classical mythology. He was remarkable at that time for his understanding of the subtler meanings of such myths: and also pointed out the similarities of the Indian metaphysics to Berkeley's Immaterialist philosophy.

out full knowledge of the body of thought of which the symbolic stories from an integral part has as much force, however, now as then; as may be seen from the many "psychological" interpretations that find too ready credence among the followers of one or another school. Such works may have a value of their own; but like the elaborate symbolic commentaries made upon Biblical stories by medieval theologians—or later by Swedenborg—their value has little or nothing to do with the real or "orthodox" meaning of the myths upon which they are fastened. Freud's Oedipus, Neumann's Psyche, or Jung's Job[11] are no less period pieces than is Pater's Dionysus; and perhaps less memorable. But Taylor's essay *On the Eleusinian and Bacchic Mysteries* is written in strict accordance with the continuous and living philosophic tradition of the civilization to which those myths belong, and in full understanding of the metaphysical system of which they form a part.

The *Dictionary of National Biography* says, "Critical faculty he had none. No doubt of the historic personality of Orpheus or the authenticity of the hymns ascribed to him ever crossed his mind...."[12] Of the "critical faculty" Taylor is said not to possess, enough has been said on the relative value of erudition to place his work in a perspective that makes such a judgment of little weight: Taylor possessed a power of discrimination of a much higher order. All the other objections arise, likewise, from a misconception of the relative importance of the matters under discussion. It will be obvious that the historicity or otherwise of Orpheus would not, from the standpoint of metaphysics, either establish or diminish the "authenticity" of the Hymns that bear his name. In this charge against Taylor's unhistorical point of view we hear an echo of Isaac Casaubon's "discrediting" of the *Hermetica* a century and a half earlier, by his establishing of the date of the principal *Tractates* as A.D. and not, as had been supposed, B.C. But as with the *Hermetica*, so with the Orphic Hymns which Ficino

[11] Cf. Erich Neumann, *Amor and Psyche: The Psychic Development of the Feminine* (New York and London, 1956); C. G. Jung, *Answer to Job* in *Collected Works*, vol. 11 (New York and London, 1958).
[12] J. M. Rigg (1898), XIX, 468ff.

had sung to the lute—they embody a tradition, and it is not upon their date but upon their content that their authenticity rests. "Of what consequence is it whether Moses wrote the Pentateuch or no?" Blake asked, answering in advance the "higher critics" who were presently to turn the same arguments against the Hebrew scriptures.

As it happens, Taylor did discuss, in his Introduction to the Hymns, the historicity of Orpheus and the various figures, real or imaginary, who bore the name, and concludes, reasonably enough, that while nothing certain is known of the first bearer of the name later attached to several figures associated with the cult, ". . . this alone may be depended on, from general assent, that there formerly lived a person named Orpheus, who was the founder of theology among the Greeks."[13] Jane Harrison, W.K.C. Guthrie, and later scholars, have reached much the same conclusion.[14] In the historical field modern scholarship has of course superseded his work; but his exposition of the theology of Orphism as a metaphysical system is never likely to be bettered.

Taylor mentions in his autobiographical memoir that the Platonic Marquis de Valady had been his guest during his stay in England in 1788, before his return to France where, his liberal principles

[13] Third edn., Introduction, p. xliv.

[14] Taylor says that the Hymns were written by Orpheus, and used in the Eleusinian Mysteries. He qualifies the first statement, not only by listing the several bearers of the name, but also by allowing that they are late translations in the Doric dialect; their authenticity lies, therefore, in their content alone: it is a doctrinal and symbolic, not a literary authenticity. As to their use as a hymn-book in the cult-centers of the Mysteries, modern scholarship has made this view seem probable. Kern first put forward the view, supported by Guthrie and Linforth, that the Hymns were used at the temple of Demeter at Pergamon. Guthrie thinks that they belonged to a Dionysiac cult; but Linforth believes they were all along associated with the cult of the Two Goddesses: "The author of the *Rhesus* credited Orpheus with the foundation of certain honored mysteries of Persephone at Athens. It may be noted that one of the *Orphic Hymns* (xl) is addressed to Demeter Eleusinia, and that another (xxix) is addressed to Persephone" (Ivan M. Linforth, *The Arts of Orpheus*, Berkeley, 1941, pp. 189–90).

notwithstanding, he was guillotined in 1793. Mrs. Louise Schutz Boas has published her reasons for believing Taylor to be the author of the article on the Marquis de Valady in *Biographical Anecdotes of Founders of the French Revolution* (1797). Taylor never shared the liberal views of so many of his friends, who may have imagined that, being himself anticlerical, he would have done so. He was at no time either a revolutionary or an egalitarian.[1]

To complete his rejection of current values, Taylor, as a Platonist, ventured to attack the democratic ideal itself. Society, so Plato argued, depends upon the maintaining of due order and upon the rule of wisdom. Since wisdom must always belong to a few, in proportion to "a number of the middle sort and a countless multitude of the ignorant," the most excellent, in politics, like the beautiful in aesthetics, cannot be decided by the voice of the majority. Taylor went so far as to point out that "the present efforts to enlighten by education the lowest class of mankind is an attempt to break the golden chain of beings, to disorganise society. . . ."[2] This defense of a caste system finds its echoes, equally unheeded, in the writings of Coomaraswamy and Guénon, who, as exponents of tradition in this century, have many points of resemblance to Taylor. Those who lament the submergence of the highest by the lowest in obedience to the voice of the majority are in danger of being regarded as enemies of society and of mankind.[3] Yet Taylor's view—which is that of tradition— cannot be dismissed by anyone who has seriously considered the present state of the arts and of public morals: ". . . there cannot I think be a more egregious instance of the barren state of philosophy at present, than the prevailing opinion that the most valuable knowledge is derived from common life and the general

---

[1] See below, p. 127, n. 7.

[2] *Select Works of Plotinus*, Introduction, p. lxix, n.

[3] For holding a similar view both Yeats and T. S. Eliot have been called "Fascist," most unjustly, since Plato's conception of aristocracy, like the Indian caste system, is based not upon power but upon knowledge and a system of spiritual values from which the idea of caste is inseparable, as both these poets understood, Yeats as a student of the Upanishads, and Eliot having in mind rather the hierarchic structure of mediaeval Christendom.

conduct of mankind. The manners of the multitude, so far from affording any really valuable information, exhibit nothing but specimens of folly and vice, astonishingly various, and differently combined."[4] *A Vindication of the Rights of Brutes* is a light-hearted *reductio ad absurdum* of the theories of his former lodger Mary Wollstonecraft and of Thomas Paine.

Perhaps there is a note of bitterness and arrogance in Taylor—as indeed there is in Guénon—when he turns from pure meta-physics to consider the imperfections of the temporal world. Blake (as also AE) was in some ways a better Platonist than Taylor, for like Plato he labored in the hope and belief that the invisible City might, at least in some measure, be realized at all times, though never completely or permanently at any time. Blake could see, where Taylor could not, the "golden builders" at work in London streets. But Taylor remained steadfast and dignified, serene in those consolations wisdom brings those who choose its service in preference to the rewards of the world. He undertook, in full knowledge of what this would entail, a life work in the service of the minority who value the highest achievements of human thought. His *Commentaries of Proclus* are dedicated to that principle than which Plotinus says there is none higher, which Loyola declares is great and will prevail, "To the Sacred Majesty of Truth." Truth, like virtue, is its own, and frequently its only, reward. "He was an enthusiast, and only an enthusiast could have done his work. His translations represent a side of Greek thought that but for him would be unrepresented in English literature."[5]

KATHLEEN RAINE

[4] *Commentaries of Proclus*, II, 318.
[5] Axon, below, pp. 131–32.

Thomas Taylor the Platonist, painted by Sir Thomas Lawrence for
William Meredith, Taylor's patron, about 1812

Anonymous bust of Taylor, from a photo-
graph found in Mr. Geoffrey Watkins' copy
of Taylor's *Arguments of Celsus, Porphyry,
and the Emperor Julian, against the Christians.* The bust itself is now lost

For according to Empedocles, it is necessary that

From the blest wandering thrice ten thousand times*
Thro' various mortal forms the soul should pass

—— This being the case, it is requisite to believe that men are committed to the care of certain inspective guardians of this prison the body.

"That the least of things, however, are allotted guardian powers, may be learnt from the Egyptians, who say that the human body is divided into thirty-six parts, & that dæmons, or certain ethereal Gods, who are distributed into the same number of parts, are the guardians of these divisions of the body. Some also assert, that there is a much greater number of these presiding powers, different corporeal parts being under the inspection of different powers. The names of these also in the vernacular tongue of the Egyptians are, Chnoumen, Chnachoumen, Knat, Sicat, Biou, Erou, Erebiou, Ramanor, Reianoor, & such others as they denominate in their language. Those when invoked heal the parts of the body over which they preside. What therefore should prevent him from making use of these & other powers,

* This 30,000 times must not be considered mathematically; since it symbolically indicates a certain appropriate measure of perfection. For in unity there is a perfect number as having a beginning, middle & end. And again, 10 is perfect, because it comprehends all numbers in itself.

Working page from Taylor's *Arguments of Celsus, Porphyry, and the Emperor Julian, against the Christians* (1830)

DIVINI
PLATONIS
OPERA OMNIA
MARSILIO FICINO
INTERPRETE.

Recens editio, summo studio, & diligentia à vitiis ema-
culata, & ad exemplar Græcum fideliter collata.

His accesserunt sex Platonis dialogi, nuper à Sebastiano
Conrado tralati, neque vnquam adhuc
in hoc volumen recepti.

LVGDVNI,
APVD ANTONIVM VINCENTIVM.
M. D. LXVII.

Cum priuilegio.

Title page of Taylor's copy of Marsilio Ficino's edition of *Divini Platonis Opera Omnia* (Lyons, 1567). This book afterwards belonged to Derwent Coleridge. A manuscript note in the handwriting of E. H. Coleridge, to whom the book afterwards passed, records that the book had been bequeathed by Mrs. Joseph Henry Green to Derwent Coleridge; he thinks it unlikely that the book ever belonged to Samuel Taylor Coleridge (who died in 1834, a year before Thomas Taylor) and that Mrs. Green must have acquired it after Taylor's death. If there was any link between the Taylor and Coleridge families, it remains obscure (see Plate 5)

Specimen of Taylor's handwriting, from the flyleaf of his copy of the Ficino *Plato*. "This book upwards of fifty years ago belonged to a Mr. Ballow, who was a lawyer, & a very eccentric character. After he had made as complete a collection of books relative to the philosophy of Plato & Aristotle, as could be obtained, he sold his collection, & began to collect the same works again. I bought this, & several others of his books, after his death, of a Mr. Thornton, at that time a bookseller in Southampton Street in the Strand. He has made many remarks in the margin of this copy, & in a similar manner in all his other books. But though he appears to have diligently read the works of Plato & Aristotle, yet he had by no means fathomed the depths of their meaning. His annotations therefore, are merely philological. In his will, he left ten pounds to a surgeon to dissect his body in order to ascertain the cause of his death, but by committing suicide through blowing out his brains deprived the surgeon of his legacy. Peace however be to his manes, for he deserves great praise for having made such a valuable collection of philosophical works.

T.T."

{5}

Doric Portico at Athens. Engraving after a drawing by James Stuart. From
Stuart and Revett's *Antiquities of Athens*, Vol. I (1762), Chap. I, Plate I. Taylor
used the same engraving as an illustration to his *Pausanias*, Vol. I (1794)

Sculpture from the Tower of the Winds, Athens. Engraving by James Basire after a drawing by James Stuart. From Stuart and Revett's *Antiquities of Athens*, Vol. I (1762), Chap. III, Plate XII

Centaurs and Lapithae, from the Parthenon Frieze. Engraving by William Blake after drawings by William Pars. From Stuart and Revett's *Antiquities of Athens*, Vol. III (1794), Chap. I, Plates XXI–XXIII

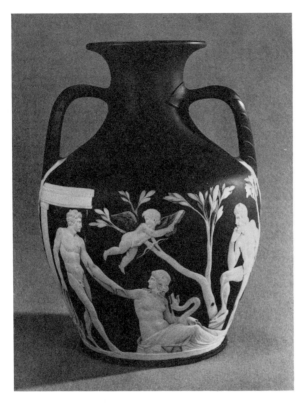

Josiah Wedgwood's copy of the Portland Vase. Several replicas of the Portland Vase were exhibited at the Wedgwood showrooms in Greek Street in 1790, and Wedgwood lectured on the vase and the reproduction. Wedgwood's friend Erasmus Darwin, in Part I of *The Botanic Garden* (1789–1791), put forward the theory that the figures are emblems of the Eleusinian Mysteries (see Plate 10)

The first Compartment.

The first compartment of the Portland Vase. Engraving by Blake for Erasmus Darwin's *Botanic Garden.* It was Flaxman who first interested Josiah Wedgwood in the vase, at the time when Sir William Hamilton had bought it from the Barberini family and brought it to England. A letter of Flaxman's, dated February 5, 1785, urges Josiah Wedgwood to come to London to "see Sir Wm. Hamilton's Vase . . . the finest production of Art brought to England" (see Plate 9)

John Flaxman's medallions (c. 1775), made for Wedgwood jasper ware. Flaxman was at this time twenty years old

(a) The Marriage of Cupid and Psyche. Copied from an antique medallion,
    which was also copied by Bartolozzi (see Plate 12)

(b) Sacrifice to Hymen. Flaxman's own invention, made in the style of the
    antique

The Marriage of Cupid and Psyche. Engraving by Bartolozzi for Bryant's *Mythology*, Vol. II (1774). Copied from an antique medallion (see Plate 11a)

Psyche Disobeys. Engraving by William Blake (1794) after an original invention by George Cumberland. From Cumberland's *Thoughts on Outline, Sculpture, and the System that Guided the Ancient Artists in Composing their Figures and Groups* ... (1796)

Thetis ordering the Nereids to descend into the sea
Ye sister Nereids, to your deeps descend
Engraving by Thomas Piroli after the composition of John Flaxman (1793). From Alexander Pope's translation of *The Iliad*

Briareus

Then call'd by thee, the Monster Titan came,
Whom gods Briareus, men Aegaean name

Engraving by Thomas Piroli after the composition of John Flaxman (1793). From Pope's *Iliad*

Leucothea and Odysseus
All radiant on the raft the goddess stood
Engraving by Thomas Piroli after the composition of John
Flaxman (1793). From Pope's *Odyssey*

Scylla
When Lo fierce Scylla stoop'd to seize her prey
Stretch'd her dire jaws, & swept six men away
Engraving by Thomas Piroli after the composition of John Flaxman (1793). From Pope's *Odyssey*

William Blake's tempera painting discovered in 1948 at Arlington Court (North Devon). An illustration of Porphyry's *De Antro Nympharum* (1822), which Blake knew in Taylor's translation

Adelphi, Society of Arts Oct.r 7.th 1798

Dear Sir

A Volume will be published next month entitled "Public Characters of the Year 98". In this Volume I am to make my appearance: and as the Editor requested me for this purpose to give him some memoirs of my stormy life, I have drawn up as accurate an Account of myself as memory would permit; thinking it was better to be my own executioner, than to be murdered by any editor, or hireling Author in Great Britain. In the course of these memoirs, I have taken care to inform the world, that it was principally owing to you, that I was enabled to emerge from the obscurity & servility of a Bankers Clerk; & have mentioned you as well known; by the publication of several ingenious works. This I thought no more than justice, & hope you will consider what I have done in that light. Wishing you health, peace & temperance,

I remain Yours Sincerely
Thomas Taylor.

Taylor's letter of October 7, 1798, to George Cumberland concerning his appearance in *Public Characters of 1798*

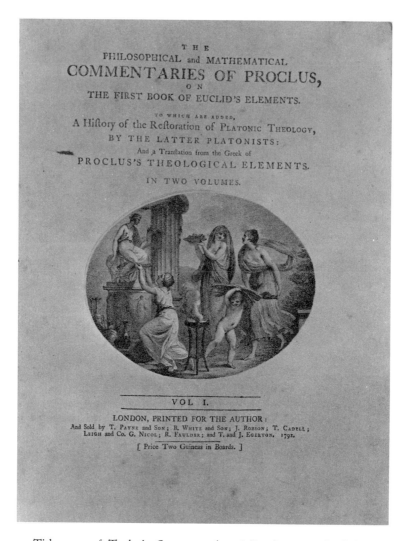

THE
PHILOSOPHICAL and MATHEMATICAL
COMMENTARIES OF PROCLUS,
ON
THE FIRST BOOK OF EUCLID'S ELEMENTS.
TO WHICH ARE ADDED,
A History of the Restoration of PLATONIC THEOLOGY,
BY THE LATTER PLATONISTS:
And a Translation from the Greek of
PROCLUS'S THEOLOGICAL ELEMENTS.

IN TWO VOLUMES.

VOL I.

LONDON, PRINTED FOR THE AUTHOR:
And Sold by T. PAYNE and SON; B. WHITE and SON; J. ROBSON; T. CADELL;
LEIGH and Co. G. NICOL; R. FAULDER; and T. and J. EGERTON. 1792.
[Price Two Guineas in Boards.]

Title page of Taylor's *Commentaries of Proclus*, second edition, Vol. I (1792). The two volumes of the first edition carried separate publication dates (1788 and 1789) and title-page illustrations. Lacking only two lines of Greek from Homer, the wording of the page reproduced here is that of Vol. II in the first edition

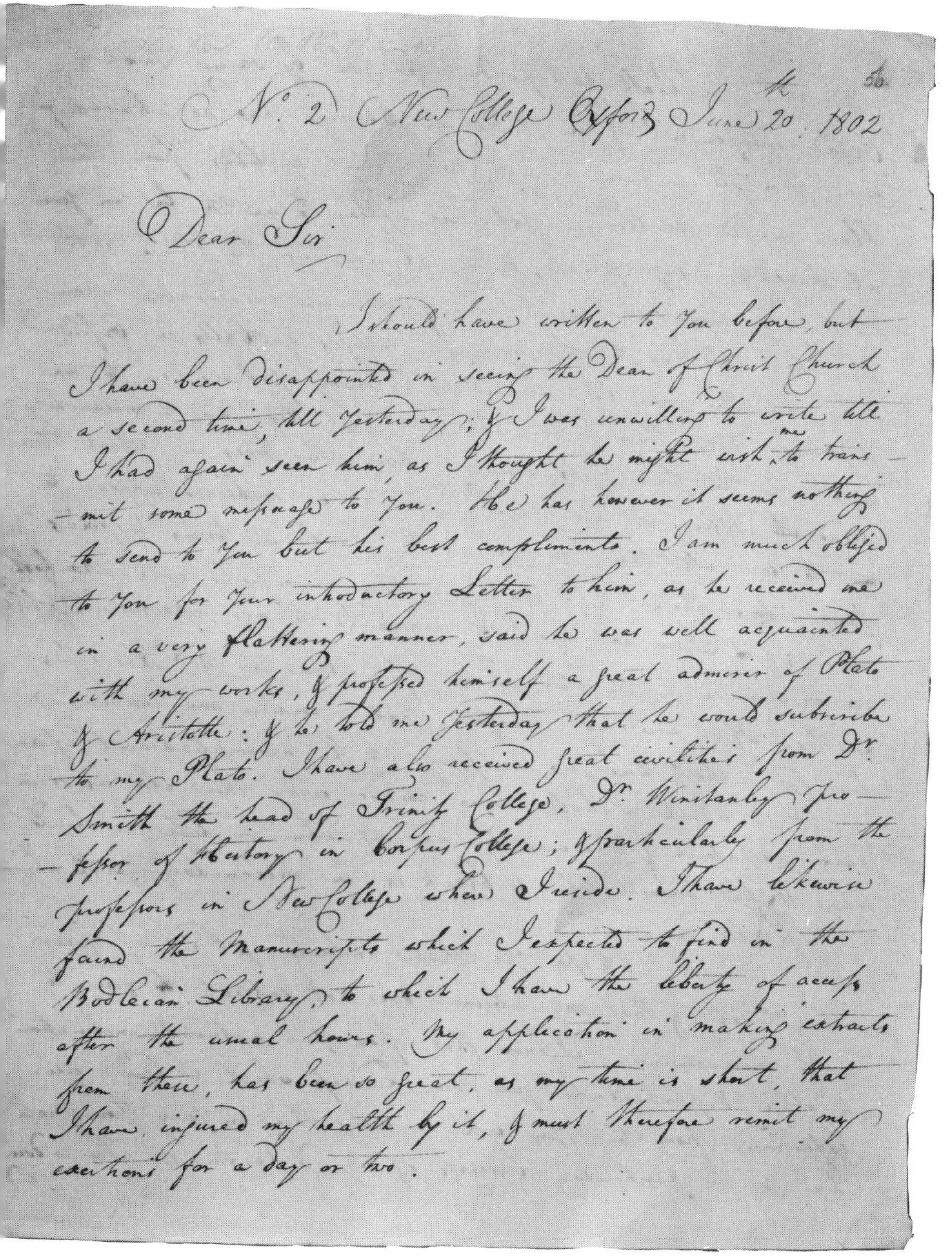

No. 2 New College Oxford June 20th. 1802

Dear Sir

I should have written to you before, but I have been disappointed in seeing the Dean of Christ Church a second time, till yesterday; & I was unwilling to write till I had again seen him, as I thought he might wish me to transmit some message to you. He has however it seems nothing to send to you but his best compliments. I am much obliged to you for your introductory Letter to him, as he received me in a very flattering manner, said he was well acquainted with my works, & professed himself a great admirer of Plato & Aristotle: & he told me yesterday that he would subscribe to my Plato. I have also received great civilities from Dr. Smith the head of Trinity College, Dr. Winstanley professor of History in Corpus College; & particularly from the professors in New College where I reside. I have likewise found the Manuscripts which I expected to find in the Bodleian Library, to which I have the liberty of access after the usual hours. My application in making extracts from these, has been so great, as my time is short, that I have injured my health by it, & must therefore remit my exertions for a day or two.

Page of a letter from Taylor to Charles Taylor (no kin) concerning a visit to the Bodleian Library (see transcript, p. 20, n. 2)

THE

HYMNS OF ORPHEUS,

Tranſlated from the original Greek :

With a Preliminary Diſſertation on

THE LIFE AND THEOLOGY OF ORPHEUS.

London, printed for the Author,

And ſold by T. Payne, at the Mews-gate ; B. White and Son,
Fleet-ſtreet ; G. Nicol, Pall-Mall ; R. Faulder, New
Bond-ſtreet. 1792.

[Price Five Shillings, Boards.]

Title page of Taylor's *Hymns of Orpheus* (1792), first issued in 1787

Gentlemen

I beg leave to offer myself as a Candidate for the vacant Office of Assistant Secretary to this Society; presuming that my knowledge of ancient literature, and the theoretical part of Mathematics, will be considered by you as a recommendation of some weight on the present occasion. If an acquaintance with the best Greek & Roman writers was productive of no other benefit, yet it is universally acknowledged to be the best means of acquiring an elegant & accurate style; & you cannot be insensible that the Mathematical Science is the origin of almost all Arts, & an abundant source of advantage to human affairs. I omit to mention, that long habits of study, necessarily produce habits of attention, together with a vigilance which is seldom surprized into negligence, I

Taylor's letter of application for the position of Assistant Secretary of the Royal Society of Arts (see Plate 24)

{ 23 }

a perseverance which obstacles cannot easily retard.

If upon examination I shall appear to you to be sufficiently qualified for the present vacant office, & shall have the honour to be elected, I shall endeavour by every possible exertion to prove myself worthy the choice you have made.

I remain,

Gentlemen,

with the greatest respect,

Your most Obedient, & most humble serv.t

Thomas Taylor.

Verso of Taylor's letter of application (see Plate 23)

In the introductory chapter of *Studies in New England Transcendentalism*, Harold Clarke Goddard insists, after quoting from Emerson, Parker, and others, that "there is little dispute as to what the New England transcendental philosophy was; but as to just whence it came, just what its various sources truly were, no answer really definite has been given."[1] Although Goddard underestimated how "little dispute" there is over the ingredients of the transcendental philosophy, he was no doubt right that the question of sources was more important. Despite the fact that much sound investigation has been conducted since Goddard was writing in 1908, the issue of sources has not yet been resolved to the satisfaction of many students, and the definitive study remains to be done.

It is the purpose of this essay to introduce briefly one of the largely overlooked sources of the transcendental stream in America—Thomas Taylor the Platonist, to point out his importance to several of the chief figures in the movement, and to suggest the significance of several now almost forgotten transmitters of the Platonic philosophy. I make no pretense to comprehensiveness, which indeed can be achieved only after the study of many largely unexamined materials such as Bronson Alcott's voluminous journals; the files of the Plato Club and the American Akademe of Jacksonville, Illinois; and the papers of Thomas M. Johnson, the editor of *The Platonist*—to cite only the more obvious.

Although transcendentalism certainly was "that complex product of most varied forces,"[2] and many of those forces were indigenous, it is clear, I think, that the movement would have been greatly different without the revival of the Platonic philosophy imported first and chiefly through the translations and commentaries of Thomas Taylor. It must be remembered that Emerson and Alcott, the two great figures in the transcendental movement,

---

[1] (New York, 1908), p. 9.
[2] Ibid., p. 32.

were early and faithful readers of Taylor, and found in him the primary elements of their philosophical system. In spite of John S. Harrison's convincing if overemphasized and somewhat disorganized pioneer work on Emerson and Taylor,[3] students of transcendentalism have not properly recognized how early the young Emerson was reading eagerly and steadily in Taylor's translations. Harrison, for example, though rather indifferent to chronology, presumes that Ralph Cudworth's *The True Intellectual System of the Universe* "was perhaps the first book to draw Emerson's attention to Platonism."[4] Thanks to the zealous efforts of Kenneth W. Cameron, we now know that Emerson had discovered Thomas Taylor's *Works of Plato* as early as 1826, and that he continued to read it over and over again during the late 1820's and early 1830's while he was absorbing the material and organizing the thought that was to culminate in his *Nature* (1836), the bible of transcendentalism. In 1836 also was founded the famous "Transcendental Club" for the promulgation of the "new views."[5] Out of this desire grew *The Dial* (1840–1844). Although it contains Alcott's often-parodied "Orphic Sayings," obviously indebted to Thomas Taylor, and many of Emerson's poems and essays, *The Dial* was, by this time, too conservative for these arch-Neoplatonists.[6]

Years earlier, in March 1835, Emerson had projected an "organ of a Spiritual Philosophy" which would no doubt have conformed more nearly to the new philosophy as he and Alcott conceived it.[7] Perhaps no important stream of philosophy ever had for its basis a more widely eclectic body of reading, but it should not be forgotten, as Goddard long ago pointed out, that "all these transcendentalists whom we have been considering knew and took delight in Plato."[8] Moreover, the most readily available edition was

[3] *The Teachers of Emerson* (New York, 1910).
[4] Ibid., p. 15. See also Goddard, p. 70.
[5] See Goddard, pp. 35ff.
[6] See F. B. Sanborn and William T. Harris, *A. Bronson Alcott: His Life and Philosophy* (Boston, 1893), II, 359–60. Hereafter cited as Sanborn and Harris.
[7] Ibid., p. 364.
[8] Goddard, p. 112.

Taylor's monumental five-volume *Works of Plato* published in 1804. In any discussion of the influence of Plato on English and American literature for the next half century or so, we should be mindful of two facts about Taylor's *Plato*: it was the only complete English translation, and it was a book with a mission. In the long Introduction, in extensive footnotes and appendices, and in the phraseology of the translation, Taylor sought to convey the idealistic convictions about the nature of man and the universe which he had acquired from a lifetime of reading in the Neoplatonists. As a result, of course, almost all readers of Taylor's works were either greatly fascinated by his allegorical and symbolic interpretations as a glimpse of arcane truth or repulsed by them as the reveries of a madman. It was difficult to be neutral.

American readers of the early nineteenth century who wanted to know Plato well were almost forced to read Taylor's translation, and Ralph Waldo Emerson did. Early in his college career at Harvard, he decided that *Plato* was among the important "Books to Read."[9] In 1826, according to Cameron, Emerson "seems to have begun the systematic study which he continued throughout his life."[10] And he pursued his study in Taylor's *Plato*, which had been left to the Harvard Library in 1820.[11] Beginning in November 1826 with Volume IV, which contains the dialogues concerned with the trial and death of Socrates, Emerson embarked upon a lifelong study of Plato and the Neoplatonists through Taylor's translations, as the journals, the letters, the poetry, and the essays as well as the records of two libraries testify. After borrowing various volumes of the *Works* first from Harvard, then from the Boston Athenaeum, Emerson purchased, in 1845, the copy which Charles Lane and Bronson Alcott had brought to America for the library at Fruitlands. He

[9] *Journals of Ralph Waldo Emerson*, ed. E. W. Emerson and W. E. Forbes (Boston and New York, 1909–1914), II, 68. Hereafter cited as *Journals*.
[10] Kenneth Walter Cameron, *Emerson the Essayist* (Raleigh, N.C., 1945), I, 38.
[11] Ibid.

also owned Taylor's translation in one volume of *The Cratylus, Phaedo, Parmenides and Timaeus of Plato*.[12] I cite these details to emphasize that Emerson was reading Taylor's translations steadily during the greatly impressionable years when he broke away from the Church and led in the formulation of the philosophic pattern—it should not be called a system—that was to be known as transcendentalism, reaching an early climax perhaps in the most important single work of the movement, Emerson's *Nature*. A strange, often bewildering mélange of Platonic and Neoplatonic impressions and borrowings, *Nature* is deeply indebted to Taylor's *Plato*, and the proper study of Emerson's pioneer work, which has yet to be made, must begin with this book.

But it is not easy to follow the various strands of Emerson's thought to their source, and he always transmutes his borrowings. Moreover, he read Taylor, as he read others, for stimulation rather than system: "There are also prose poets. Thomas Taylor, the Platonist, for instance, is really a better man of imagination, a better poet, or perhaps I should say a better feeder to a poet, than any man between Milton and Wordsworth."[13]

In the years when Emerson was reconciling himself emotionally and intellectually to the break with the Church, Taylor's translations must have been especially appealing. An entry in the Journal for 1867 suggests the part Taylor played in Emerson's "reconciliation of paganism and Christianity" (to borrow a phrase from William Butler Yeats, who was to wrestle with a similar dilemma): "Thomas Taylor and Winckelmann would have preferred, to all meeting-houses and churches, to have restored the old native service of the temples on whose ruins these had been constructed, and to have worshipped, with Horace for the psalmbook, chanting, '*Mercuri facunde nepos Atlantis*,' or '*Sic te diva potens Cypri*,' with tibia and theorbus and lyre, to all the psalters and all the organs of the Romish or the English congregations."[14]

[12] Ibid., p. 39.

[13] *The Complete Works of Ralph Waldo Emerson*, centenary edition (Boston and New York, 1903–1904), VIII, 50. Hereafter cited as *Complete Works*.

[14] *Journals*, X, 185.

In one sense, no doubt, Emerson felt that he was building temples on the ruins of the meeting-houses. From Plato, he could "get ethics without cant."[15] "I delight in the votaries of the genius of Plato," he wrote in 1859, then added, two sentences later: "Culture is a pagan."[16] Although Emerson was no doubt emotionally ready to be convinced, it is clear, I think, that much of the evidence upon which he based his reconciliation came from Plato and his followers.

After Plato the most important of these was Plotinus. He was, of course, accessible in tantalizing, incomplete fragments throughout the *Works of Plato*, but Emerson was not long satisfied with such tidbits. Although we cannot be certain when he acquired Taylor's *Select Works of Plotinus*, we do know that it became a cherished volume "which for many years he kept within easy reach of his writing table and which he marked and indexed as a favorite possession."[17] Since the *Select Works* was one of the books in the library at Fruitlands, Emerson may have acquired it when he purchased the *Plato* from Charles Lane in 1845. But he had read Plotinus with care long before as he sought to prove to himself what many of the English Romantics had already decided: that "All religions are one." In the Journal for January 20, 1841, Plotinus was already among the select few: "Of these unquiet daemons that fly or gleam across the brain what trait can I hope to draw in my sketch-book? Wonderful seemed to me as I read in Plotinus the calm and grand air of these few cherubim—great spiritual lords who have walked in the world—they of the old religion—dwelling in a worship that makes the sanctities of Christianity *parvenues* and merely popular. . . ."[18] By this time certainly the reconciliation had been accomplished.

When this passage became a part of the concluding paragraph of "Intellect," it was introduced by a quite revealing sentence: "But I cannot recite, even thus rudely, laws of the intellect, without remembering that lofty and sequestered class who have been its prophets and oracles, the high-priesthood of the pure reason,

---

[15] Ibid., IV, 266. [16] Ibid., IX, 187.
[17] Cameron, I, 46. [18] *Journals*, V, 510–11.

the *Trismegisti*, the expounders of the principles of thought from age to age."[19] By now, it is not Plotinus but "these few" whose "abstruse pages" reveal the secrets of the "old religion," the fundamental laws of all truth. Emerson continues with a catalogue of the *Trismegisti*, most of whom were readily accessible only in the translations and commentaries of Taylor: "This band of grandees, Hermes, Heraclitus, Empedocles, Plato, Plotinus, Olympiodorus, Proclus, Synesius and the rest, have somewhat so vast in their logic, so primary in their thinking, that it seems antecedent to all the ordinary distinctions of rhetoric and literature, and to be at once poetry and music and dancing and astronomy and mathematics. I am present at the sowing of the seed of the world. With a geometry of sunbeams the soul lays the foundations of nature. The truth and grandeur of their thought is proved by its scope and applicability, for it commands the entire schedule and inventory of things for its illustration."[20] From the oracular tone of this passage one might surmise that Emerson, like Taylor, considered himself a link in the golden chain of Platonic successors destined to reveal the truth to a lapsed and fallen world. At any rate, many of Emerson's contemporaries were ready to invest him with the mantle.

Although Emerson never ceased to be amazed at the "wealth of perception in Plotinus, Proclus, Jamblichus, Porphyry, Synesius," and the rest of Plato's marvelous "school,"[21] most of his reading in them was confined to Plotinus and Proclus for the very simple reason that these two had received the greatest attention from Taylor. Emerson may have exaggerated a bit to impress Wordsworth when he visited at Rydal Mount in 1848, but there is no reason to believe that his remark about the circulation of Taylor in America was not essentially true—of the libraries he knew at any rate: "I told him it was not creditable that no one in all the country knew anything of Thomas Taylor, the Platonist, whilst in every American library his translations are

[19] *Complete Works*, II, 345.   [20] Ibid., p. 346.
[21] *Journals*, VIII, 474.

found."[22] In May of the same year Emerson had visited with Patmore, Tennyson, Hallam, and others, and had been more than a little disillusioned that Hallam "knew nothing of Thomas Taylor, nor did Milman, nor any Englishman."[23] But Emerson was not easily discouraged. As Thomas M. Johnson recorded more than thirty years later, "Emerson, when in England, made diligent enquiry about Thomas Taylor, but declared that he could only ascertain one fact about him, viz.: that he had a son and named him Proklos."[24]

Emerson shared Taylor's respect for Proclus: "What literature should be, he is."[25] There is evidence in the Journals that he read with care two of Taylor's translations from Proclus: *Six Books on Plato's Theology* and *The Commentaries on the Timaeus of Plato*.[26] A journal entry for June 16, 1842, suggests that Emerson was reading the *Commentaries on the Timaeus*: "I read the *Timaeus* in these days, but am never sufficiently in a sacred and holiday health for the task. The man must be equal to the book. A man does not know how fine a morning he wants until he goes to read Plato and Proclus."[27] Three years later he copied several choice sentences from Proclus's *Timaeus* into the Journal, and commented on philosophy with great enthusiasm: "*Proclus.* I not only do not think he has his equal among contemporary writers, but I do not know men sufficiently athletic to read him.

[22] Ibid., V, 295. The continuation of this conversation, as Emerson records it, is interesting: "I said, if Plato's Republic were published in England as a new book to-day, do you think it would find any readers?—he confessed it would not: 'And yet,' he added after a pause, with that complacency which never deserts a true-born Englishman, 'and yet we have embodied it all.'"

[23] Ibid., VII, 450. It is unfortunate that Emerson did not direct his question to Patmore, who was much better informed. A copy of Taylor's *Five Books of Plotinus*, now in my possession, was once in Patmore's library. A penciled note inside the front cover points out that Patmore had praised Taylor "in his article on Keats."

[24] "Tayloriana," *The Platonist*, II (1884–1885), 69.

[25] Quoted by Harrison, p. 220.

[26] See *Journals*, VII, 7–8, 516–17. Both of these books were in the library at Fruitlands along with three others of Taylor's translations of Proclus.

[27] Ibid., VI, 213.

There is the same difference between the writings of these Platonists and Scotch metaphysics as between the sculptures of Phidias
and the statues of Tam o' Shanter and my Uncle Toby. They
abound in personification. Every abstract idea, every element, every
agent in nature or in thought, is strongly presented as a god, in this
most poetic philosophy, so that the universe is filled with august
and exciting images. It is imaginative and not anatomical. It is
stimulating."[28] Proclus ranked high among the *Trismegisti* of
the old religion.

So too did Jamblichus. "What a vitality has the Platonic philosophy!" Emerson once exclaimed. "I remember I expected a revival in the churches to be caused by a reading of Iamblichus.
And Plutarch: if the world's library were burning, I should fly
to save that, with our Bible and Shakespeare and Plato. Our debt
to Thomas Taylor, the translator of the Platonists. A Greek
born out of his time, and dropped on the ridicule of a blind and
frivolous age."[29] We should not be surprised, I am sure, to find
that Jamblichus's *On the Mysteries of the Egyptians, Chaldeans,
and Assyrians* was in the library at Concord, along with Proclus's
Theology of Plato and *Commentaries on the Timaeus*, the *Works
of Plato,* and Plotinus's *Select Works.*[30] The last contains an extract from Synesius's *On Providence*, for which Emerson had the
highest praise in the essay on "Books" as the work of one of "the
Platonists, who also cannot be skipped": "If any one who had read
with interest the Isis and Osiris of Plutarch should then read a
chapter called Providence, by Synesius, translated into English by

[28] Ibid., VII, 7–8. It is rather surprising that Emerson did not know the
most fascinating of Taylor's translations from Proclus, *The Philosophical
and Mathematical Commentaries . . . on the First Book of Euclid's Elements,* which appeared in two editions (1788–1789, 1792) and was also at
Fruitlands. It is perhaps futile to speculate on the probable reaction, but
I am certain that he would have been excited by Taylor's long explication of
the symbolic meaning in Ulysses' wandering and his translation of Porphyry's *Cave of the Nymphs* as well as the extended essay on "The Restoration of the Platonic Theology, by the Latter Platonists."

[29] Quoted by Thomas M. Johnson, in *The Platonist*, III (1887), 559.
Johnson is quoting from Cabot's *Emerson*.

[30] Harrison, p. 5.

Thomas Taylor, he will find it one of the majestic remains of literature, and like one walking in the noblest of temples, will conceive new gratitude to his fellow men, and a new estimate of their nobility."[31] Having "come down by natural steps from the master to the disciples," "the imaginative scholar will find few stimulants to his brain like these writers. He has entered the Elysian Fields." As a reader of these books, Emerson felt that he had made "new acquaintance with his own mind; new regions of thought are opened."[32] They had, in fact, been the vehicle for his reconciliation of the old religion with the new: "The acolyte has mounted the tripod over the cave at Delphi; his heart dances, his sight is quickened. These guides speak of the gods with such depth and with such pictorial details, as if they had been bodily present at the Olympian feasts."[33]

To the whole transcendental group, then, and especially to Emerson, the high priest of the movement, the gates to the "Elysian Fields" were opened by these latter Platonists, whose works, Emerson declared, "I do not hesitate to read . . . in translations"; and he meant Thomas Taylor's.[34] As Emerson pointed out in 1842, at the height of his exhilaration over the Neoplatonists, "The first thing we have to say respecting what are called *new views* here in New England, at the present time, is, that they are not new, but the very oldest of thoughts cast into the mould of these new times."[35] "What is popularly called Transcendentalism among us," he explained, "is Idealism; Idealism as it appears in 1842."[36] At this stage certainly, and in fact for most of his creative life, Emerson's conception of idealism was essentially Neoplatonic.

A more thoroughly Neoplatonic idealist in many respects was

[31] *Complete Works*, VIII, 202–03. The rather long paragraph from which this passage comes is a panegyric to Taylor's translations: in addition to Synesius, Emerson names Plotinus, Porphyry, Proclus, and the Emperor Julian.

[32] Ibid.   [33] Ibid.   [34] Ibid.

[35] Ibid., I, 329. This is the opening sentence of his essay on "The Transcendentalist."

[36] Ibid.

Emerson's friend Amos Bronson Alcott. His first contact with Emerson, in September 1828, is revealing; after hearing the brilliant young preacher on "The Universality of the Notion of Deity," Alcott commented wryly in his Journal: "A very respectable effort."[37] It may well be, indeed, that he had already reached a stage in the journey to idealism which the more conservative Emerson had not yet attained. When he was once offered a position as a young man to teach "only that which could be 'demonstrated to the senses and perceptions of the children,'" Alcott realized how distasteful Lockean psychology had become to him, and he refused a salary of more than twice what he was making at the time. The comment upon his prospective employers, the Free Enquirers, was, as usual, both forthright and instructive: "[They] are a low party in religion. . . . I shall have nothing to do with them."[38] Alcott was, in fact, groping for the metaphysical framework he needed for the idealism he had been working out by a process of elimination.

Then came the light, the discovery of Plato. During the early summer of 1833, Alcott left his family in Germantown, Pennsylvania, where he had been teaching, and went to live in an attic room on Library Street in Philadelphia in order to be near two good libraries. Among the many books which stirred him in those exciting months, the most important was Thomas Taylor's translation of Plato's *Cratylus, Phaedo, Parmenides and Timaeus.* "Plato I had long wished to read," as he phrased it, "but could never before find a translation."[39] And when he recalled this memorable event many years later, he recorded it in the red ink usually reserved for life's climactic experiences: "his marriage, the births of his daughters, the opening of the Civil War, and the assassination of Lincoln."[40] During this period also, according to Odell Shepard, Alcott discovered Taylor's Proclus and Plotinus. The young idealist had certainly come to the right fountain, and one cannot help wishing that he could have met the aged Taylor.

[37] Odell Shepard, *Pedlar's Progress: The Life of Bronson Alcott* (Boston, 1937), p. 126.
[38] Ibid., p. 133.   [39] Ibid., p. 151.   [40] Ibid., p. 160.

When he did at last get to England in 1842, Taylor was seven years in his grave, but Alcott paid him the fine compliment of collecting, with Charles Lane, a library which perhaps included as many of Taylor's books as they could find. Of the 214 titles which were brought to America for the library of their "new Eden" at Fruitlands, 16 bore the name of Thomas Taylor as translator, editor, or author. Not even in his most popular days, I suppose, was Taylor to receive such homage; and not again perhaps until a Missouri lawyer named Thomas M. Johnson, who became a friend of Alcott in his old age, put together the finest collection of Taylor's books in America. With Alcott as with Emerson, it was Plato who fired the imagination but his followers who kept the flame burning. Emerson may have been right when he said that Alcott "could go into any strange library and lay his hand at once upon the one book that he most needed to read, even if he did not know the language."[41]

At any rate, he found the right book in a Philadelphia library. From 1833, certainly, Taylor's translations were indispensable to Alcott, whose "natural attitude explains Plato."[42] Alcott was, Emerson wrote in a famous passage, one of those "few persons who give flesh to what were, else, mere thought, and which now I am not at liberty to slight, or in any manner treat as fictions. It were too much to say that the Platonic world I might have learned to treat as cloud-land, had I not known Alcott, who is a native of that country, yet I will say that he makes it as solid as Massachusetts to me."[43] Although Emerson was aware that Alcott "has not wrought his fine clay into vases, nor his gold dust into ingots," he considered Alcott "an inestimable companion, because he has no obligations to old or new; but is free as if new born."[44] For this reason perhaps, because he could live the life of the spirit as well as preach its doctrines, Alcott was better able to effect a personal reconciliation of paganism and Christianity than Emerson. But the two of them together, strangely different as they were, had a powerful impact on the "new views here in

[41] Ibid., p. 161. The phraseology is Shepard's.
[42] *Journals*, IX, 119.   [43] Ibid., VIII, 303.   [44] Ibid., p. 396.

New England" as well as in that great cultural desert, the Middle West, which for a time responded even more excitedly to the new views than New England. (There is a rather interesting analogy in the fact that the New England had reacted more strongly to transcendental idealism than the old had.) But the flowering of Platonism in the Middle West would hardly have been possible without Alcott and Emerson, their friends and followers.

Bronson Alcott, and perhaps even the direction of American transcendentalism, were so greatly changed by his experience in the Library Street attic, that it may be well to repeat the explanation he recorded in his diary:

"Plato I had long wished to read, but could never before find a translation. It had long been my impression that there were in his writings great and profound ideas which the light of existing thought and science had not been bright enough to attain. This impression I find confirmed on perusal of the few fragments of his writings translated by Taylor.

"Modern philosophy has widely departed from the genius of the ancient school. The living spirit has departed from it, and left it but a dead and corrupt mass of material elements. *That* had intercommunion with the invisible and infinite; *this* is limited to the consideration of the finite and the visible, and is incompetent to investigation of primary causes and ultimate laws. It stops at secondary causes and can penetrate no deeper. It limits and circumscribes the infinite by the frail and powerless energies of the finite. It shuts God from the universe, and, carried to its legitimate issues, results in Pantheism—building up on an inconceivable basis the whole fabrick of religion, which it must assume as independent of man and nature. It makes of exterior nature a self-existent substance, and sees not in the laws and vicissitudes of things the movement of Spirit.

"These illusions, which never had much influence over my own mind, have all been swept away by the Platonic theory, and I see clearly what before was obscured by the gloss of exterior matter: Spirit all in all—matter its form and shadow."[45]

[45] *The Journals of Bronson Alcott*, ed. Odell Shepard (Boston, 1938), p. 36. Hereafter cited as Shepard, *Journals*.

The concept of nature here suggested in its extreme f⟨
Alcott is very different from the commonly accepted vie⟨
philosophy espoused by the English Romantics, Wordsw⟨
particular. Blake alone would have subscribed wholeheartedly to
Alcott's Neoplatonic assumptions. This passage from the Journal
makes clear that Alcott could not long be satisfied with a "few
fragments" of Taylor's *Plato*. Unfortunately, as he discovered,
there was not a complete edition in Philadelphia, but he soon
moved back to Boston, where he no doubt found in the Athenaeum the very copy Emerson had read steadily throughout the
thirties. Indeed, there is good reason to believe that the availabil-
ity of the books he wanted may have prompted his return to
Boston: "I doubt," he confided to his Journal, in 1835, "if there
be a complete edition of the works of Plato in three-fourths of our
college libraries. There is none in Philadelphia. The Boston Athenaeum contains Taylor's translation, which I own."[46] In the two
years since his great awakening in Philadelphia he had acquired
a copy of what was even then a rare and expensive item. Three
years later, after the nightmarish experience with the Temple
School,[47] the unfortunate Alcott was forced to sell his beloved
books, Taylor's *Plato* among them. A passage in the Journal
records his feeling for these lost friends and at least partially reveals the basis for Alcott's veneration of Emerson: "Valued authors, whose works served to cheer my solitude and quicken my
faculties, I was compelled to dispose of last spring to meet demands of creditors. Then did I lose society of Plato, ever in company with Socrates and the wise Stagyrite; then did Taylor
(Jeremy) turn his face from me, and other souls familiar with
beings of faery, Spenser among the rest.—And living friends?
Alas, of these how few? Emerson, single contemporary with me
who seeth the same visions, haunteth the same tracts of faery,
goeth and returneth, knoweth the passway to the Island of
Beauty!"[48]

[46] Ibid., p. 66.

[47] See Shepard, *Pedlar's Progress*, pp. 164ff., for a very good account of
the controversy which led to the disaster.

[48] Shepard, *Journals*, pp. 98–99. The entry is for January, Week II, 1838.

The following year, 1839, the two friends planned their "Bible of the Nations," which was to make readily available many of the favorite books Alcott had given up: "I proposed," he wrote, "that some measures should be taken to put English readers in possession of the works of these great minds. Confucius, Zoroaster, Paracelsus, Galen, Plato, Bruno, Behmen, Plotinus, More, Swendenbourg [sic], etc., should be in the hands of every earnest student of the Soul."[49] From the titles in this list as well as the proposed name for the project, it is evident that an unusual religious amalgamation was being planned. Although Emerson was the more influential of the two, Alcott was better fitted temperamentally to be the prophet of the new order because, as Thoreau was quick to recognize, he was freer from commitments to tradition than almost any man of his time: "Of yore we had sauntered and talked and effectually put the world behind us; for he was pledged to no institution in it—free-born, *ingenuus*."[50] On the other hand, Alcott had stronger emotional attachments than Emerson to both pagan and Christian elements of their universal religion, perhaps because Alcott was less original, less capable of subtle distinctions, and more dependent on the thoughts of others. Or it may be that there were fewer strands in the religious skein Alcott was weaving for himself. Whatever the cause, he tended after 1833 to think of Plato and Christ together: "My debt to Plato is greater, perhaps, than to any mind— greater than to Christ, I sometimes think, whose spirit is an element of humanity but whose genius I did not entertain and comprehend till Plato unsealed my eyes and led me to the study of his fair performance. . . . Plato and Christ interpreted each other and the mind of mankind."[51] That, I suggest, would serve as a kind of simplified statement of the religious ideal of the whole transcendental movement, until at the end, at least, when it lost much of its Christian urgency and became more formally phil-

[49] Ibid., pp. 136–37.
[50] Quoted from the original manuscript of *Walden* by Shepard, *Pedlar's Progress*, p. 403.
[51] Shepard, *Journals*, p. 23. Entry for March 28, 1850.

osophical. Numerous entries in the Journal reveal both Alcott's delight in Platonic doctrines and his own attempts to fuse Greek and Christian thought. In 1835, as he surveyed the route of his spiritual development to 1833, he recalled:

"I was then a disciple of Experience, trying to bring my theories within the Baconian method of induction, and took the philosophy of Aristotle as the exponent of humanity while my heart was even then lingering around the theories of Plato without being conscious of it. A follower of Aristotle was I in theory, yet a true Platonist in practice. Christianity had not found its philosophical interpretation at that time in my heart. . . . I was looking outward for the origin of the human powers, making more of phenomena than I ought, studying the concrete without a sense of the grounds to which this was dependent for its forms and continuance."[52]

Here Alcott stood, then, until the great illumination in Philadelphia. Although, in his words, "It was Coleridge who lifted me out of this difficulty," it was surely Plato who at last furnished the "philosophical interpretation" he needed to explain "the elements of human consciousness not in the impressions of external nature but in the spontaneous life of Spirit itself, independent of experience in space and time."[53]

Three of Coleridge's works were influential in the early stages of the transcendental movement: *The Friend, Biographia Literaria,* and *Aids of Reflection.* Alcott owned a copy of the *Aids* in the important James T. Marsh edition (Burlington, Vermont, 1829) as early as 1830 and wrote excitedly about it in 1832, but Plato not Coleridge led him to record the red-letter date "in 1833" after which he was no longer a "disciple of Experience": "Thus was I released from the Philosophy of Sense. Since that time I have been steadily pursuing the light then let in upon me,

[52] Ibid., pp. 66–67.

[53] Ibid. I do not intend to belittle the influence of Coleridge on Alcott but rather to suggest the striking impression and continuing significance of Plato and the Neoplatonists. See Shepard, *Pedlar's Progress,* p. 159, and Goddard, p. 59, for brief discussions of Coleridge's influence at this time.

and striving to apprehend, represent, and embody it, not only in theory but in practice."[54] It is, of course, precisely this issue of theory versus practice which distinguishes so clearly the personal philosophy of Emerson from that of Alcott. As a rule Emerson was the sage and seer who watched and commented, whereas Alcott followed his impulses and practiced his convictions, at least through the time of the experiment at Fruitlands in 1843. After that disastrous experience, Alcott himself was more the sage, though he always insisted upon the importance of both thought and action, for which his idols, Plato and Christ, seemed perfect complements:

> *'Tis much to have the company of Plato*
> *in these pinched times of ours.*
> *Plato for thought,*
> *Christ for action.*[55]

If this is a fair distinction, Emerson was perhaps the better Platonist of the two, and he greatly admired the strength of Alcott's commitment, though he deplored the many unfortunate results of his friend's impulse to act.

But fate's stern blows had not yet fallen in 1835 as Alcott was still radiating the excitement of the Philadelphia discovery: "My own conceptions of life are confirmed in the happiest manner in the Platonic theory. In Plato, as in Jesus, do I find the Light of the World, even the *supersensual* light, that lighteth every man who cometh into the world of sense, and essayeth to regain that spirit it seemeth to have lost by the incarnation of itself." "When this is felt as it ought to be," Alcott continued, "natural science will receive an impulse that we cannot at present conceive of," and we will see "all Nature, in its manifold relation," by "the method of philosophy." "Such," Alcott concluded his entry, "are my topics of speculation and inquiry."[56] To him, as to friends and associates of 1835, this method, "the only true way of apprehend-

[54] Shepard, *Journals*, p. 67.
[55] Ibid., p. 394. Entry for March 23, 1869.
[56] Quoted by Goddard, p. 58.

ing" the phenomenal world, was Platonic, no matter what the immediate source of their information. As Emerson said in 1842, "What is popularly called Transcendentalism . . . , is Idealism"; "the Transcendentalist adopts the whole connection of spiritual doctrine."[57]

More thoroughly than any of the other transcendentalists Alcott adopted the "spiritual doctrine," and he never wavered. He was quite as certain as William Blake that "There exist in that Eternal World the Permanent Realities of Every Thing which we see reflected in this Vegetable Glass of Nature."[58] "The comfort of Alcott's mind is," in Emerson's words, "the connexion in which he sees whatever he sees. He is never dazzled by a spot of colour, or a gleam of light, to value that thing by itself, but forever and ever is prepossessed by the undivided one behind it and all. I do not know where to find in men or books a mind so valuable to faith. His own invariable faith inspires faith, in others. . . . He is as good as a lens or mirror. . . ."[59] Over and over again— in the Journal, in the controversial "Orphic Sayings" of *The Dial*, in the educational and social experiments—Alcott insisted to his countrymen that "Matter is ever pervaded and agitated by the omnipresent soul," that "All things are instinct with spirit,"[60] and that we must

> *Recall the memories of man's ancient state,*
> *Ere to this low orb had his form dropt down.*[61]

[57] *Complete Works*, I, 329–35.

[58] *The Complete Writings of William Blake*, ed. Geoffrey Keynes (London and New York, 1957), p. 605.

[59] *Journals*, IX, 35–36.

[60] *The Dial*, I (1841), 94.

[61] "Ion: A Monody," in Alcott's *Emerson* (Boston, 1882), p. 64. In the preceding two stanzas of this elegy for Emerson, Alcott had named Plato, Charmides, and Orpheus, revealing perhaps his continuing preoccupation with Taylor's books and the Neoplatonic theory of the Fall as a lapse or descent in terms of Plotinus's theory of Emanation:

> *Oblivious here of heavenly glories flown,*
> *Lapsed from the high, the fair, the blest estate,*
> *Unknowing these, and by himself unknown.*

Alcott's early knowledge of Taylor was apparently confined to the translations of Plato, which, of course, contain many references to and passages from the Neoplatonists. From the Journals, I would assume that his knowledge of the Neoplatonists was not extensive before the 1840's. But the trip to England, in 1842, broadened his base considerably. Here he came in daily contact with the followers of James Pierrepont Greaves, a vegetarian reformer and admirer of Thomas Taylor who had accumulated a considerable library of esoteric books. After a series of discussions at the English school which had been named in his honor—Alcott House, near Richmond—Alcott, Henry Wright, and Charles Lane decided to establish a "second Eden" somewhere in New England. "Britain," Alcott had concluded, "with all her resources and talent, is not the scene for the education of humanity. Her spirit is hostile to human welfare, and her institutions averse to the largest liberty of soul."[62] The new friends proposed, as a part of the plan, to collect a philosophical library for the "new Eden," and Alcott was elected to choose the volumes which were to supplement the library of Greaves. We are fortunate that Alcott made a "List of Books Bought by Me in London, 1842"[63] because it tells us something of his own interests and tastes at the time; and we are even more fortunate to have also a list of the library that was to become the center of the experiment at Fruitlands for the "education of humanity." The editors of the *The Dial* considered the establishment of this library in America such an important event that they published the entire list, introduced by the following notice:

"Mr. Alcott and Mr. Lane have recently brought from England a small but valuable library, amounting to about a thousand volumes, containing undoubtedly a richer collection of mystical writers than any other library in this country. To the select Library of the late J. P. Greaves, 'held by Mr. Lane in trust for universal ends,' they have added many works of a like character by purchase, or received as gifts. In their Catalogue, from which the

---

[62] Quoted in Shepard, *Pedlar's Progress*, p. 338.
[63] Ibid., pp. 340–41.

following list is extracted, they say, 'the titles of these books are now submitted, in the expectation that the Library is the commencement of an institution for the nurture of men in universal freedom of action, thought, and being.' We print this list, not only because our respect is engaged to views so liberal, but because the arrival of this cabinet of mystic and theosophic lore is a remarkable fact in our literary history."[64]

That library is indeed "a remarkable fact in our literary history," for it includes a large number of the titles which became standard fare for the transcendentalists and were to be greatly influential until the end of the century. Hitherto almost unavailable translations of Plotinus, Porphyry, Proclus, Jamblichus, and other Neoplatonists now apparently became daily fare. We would, of course, like to know what Alcott wrote in his Journal as he discovered these exciting new books, but there is little hope that we ever will. It is one of the great tragedies of our social and intellectual history that the six lost volumes of the Journal Alcott kept from 1826 to 1882 should encompass the years 1840 to 1845. The intimate details we would so like to have about the experience in England and the establishment and dissolution of Fruitlands as well as Alcott's spiritual evolution at a critical time in the development of American transcendental thought can never be recovered. Alcott himself set a high store by the accounts of these years, and never ceased to mourn his tragic loss.

From the published parts of the Journal after 1845 and from Emerson's Journal, however, we can get a good impression of how important the Neoplatonists became to the movement and to Alcott in particular. At this distance the record can never be as full as we would wish, but it seems fairly clear that the transcendentalists acquired an intimate knowledge of the Neoplatonists only after their writings in Taylor's translations had been assembled in one collection—the library which Alcott had brought home in September 1842. Before that time even Emerson's knowl-

[64] *The Dial*, III (1843), 545. The list may be found also in Clara Endicott Sears, *Bronson Alcott's Fruitlands* (Boston and New York, 1915), pp. 177–85.

edge must have come chiefly from secondary sources such as Cudworth's *True Intellectual System of the Universe* and Taylor's *Works of Plato*. At any rate, this assumption is suggested if not adequately supported by the record of Emerson's reading in his Journal. Not only Taylor, it should be said, but many another of Emerson's favorite authors and books was represented in the Greaves library—notably, Boehme, Hermes, Agrippa, Plutarch, Dacier, Coleridge, Henry More, and William Law, to cite the most obvious.[65] And the record of withdrawals from the Boston Athenaeum includes none of the Neoplatonists who were to be primary texts for the remainder of his life.

If only we could have Alcott's lost Journal, perhaps we could know what other enthusiasts came to consult Taylor's transcendental translations and to talk the hours away about the revival of the old religion in the new world. But we do know that both Emerson and Alcott, who were "carved out of the same cloud," read Plato and the Neoplatonists for the remainder of their lives. Alcott inserted twelve "Pythagorean Sayings" from Jamblichus's *Life of Pythagoras* at the end of his "Days from a Diary," which appeared in *The Dial*.[66] In 1853, according to one of Shepard's notes, "he read Thomas Taylor's *Hymns of Orpheus*, Aristotle's *Ethics* and *Politics* for the fourth or fifth time, Lyell's *Principles of Geology*, Swedenborg's *Heaven and Hell*, Bishop Berkeley's *Siris*, and the *Confessions of St. Augustine*—all in his own library."[67] Although I can only conjecture, the Aristotle he read was probably in Taylor's translations. The library at Fruitlands included his *Metaphysics* and the *Dissertation on the Philosophy of Aristotle* but not the monumental *Works of Aristotle*,

[65] Some weeks after Alcott's return from England in the fall of 1842, Emerson made an entry in his Journal of books "thou shalt read": he included "Plato, Proclus, Plotinus, Jamblichus, Porphyry, Aristotle, Virgil, Plutarch, Apuleius," in that order (VI, 282). Taylor had translated all but Virgil and Plutarch. Again in the Journal, some months later, Emerson observed: "I think one would grow handsome who read Proclus much and well" (VI, 376), as apparently Emerson had not until about this time.

[66] *The Dial*, II (1842), 436–37.

[67] Shepard, *Journals*, p. 264.

which was perhaps—even in 1842—too rare and too expensive. By 1853, apparently, Alcott had reassembled his personal library of favorite books, the sale of which had pained him so much. One can only hope that he had recovered his beloved *Works of Plato*. And perhaps he had, for he was rereading the Bible, Swedenborg, Plato, and Aristotle in March 1859.[68] It would be difficult to find a better illustration than this of Alcott's catholic tastes and his desire, possibly unconscious, to fuse the Pagan and the Christian. After 1833, he was firm in his conviction that the ideal religion must combine the teachings of Christ and Plato, one for the heart and one for the head, as Alcott phrased it:

"Nothing like Comparative Divinity for forcing the mind from traditional teaching. Like travel, it opens out new and distant aspects of the globe on which men live, and shows their relationships in thought and purpose. Christianity cannot suffer by comparison with the faiths of the races. Its advocates need to learn its affinities with all religions and to discriminate its special merits, claiming no more than belongs to it.

"As a religion for the heart it stands preeminent and alone, a revelation of the common brotherhood of the races. We must look elsewhere for a religion for the head. And where but to Plato's philosophy? The culture of the world today were as incomplete without the infusion of the Attic mind as it would be without Christianity: nor has this been virtually denied in all the colleges of Christendom since the advent of Christ. Indeed Christianity, as such, has done little directly for pure intellectual culture. The influences have been indirect, not organized and brought to bear systematically upon the mind. The Classics still maintain their high place."[69]

Although the reverence of Alcott and Emerson for Plato's philosophy is surely sincere, we need to keep reminding ourselves that the Plato they knew was Taylor's Plato and that the "infusion of the Attic mind" which the transcendentalists continually extolled was essentially Alexandrian rather than Athenian.

How many times Alcott reread his favorite Neoplatonists and

[68] Ibid., p. 312.   [69] Ibid., p. 394.

just which of their books he owned himself in the years after 1842 will have to wait for a careful study of the unpublished letters and Journals, but we do know that he was still excited in March 1878 when he wrote: "Return Thomas Taylor's translation of Jamblichus' book on the Mysteries to Emerson, and dine with him." In the same entry he records the basis for the chief distinction between his idealism and Emerson's:

"His faith is purely ethical, and demands the certainty of facts experienced individually. His idealism hesitates and pauses, appalled at the dread facts of the Personality. True to his convictions, he modestly rests in his Individualism, and is silent concerning what lies beyond. Perhaps he may be classed as an ideal theist, with that film of pantheistic haze that hovers always about that school of thinkers. This latent pantheism has from the first characterized the New England school of Transcendentalists, and has not yet cleared itself from the clouds, most of its disciples being still touched with its indefiniteness, unable to find the certainty they seek. While it has modified favorably the materialistic tendencies of New England thinking, it has failed of planting itself upon the intuition of the Personal and Immortal. . . ."[70]

Looking at the movement from the vantage point of the twentieth century, we feel, I think, that Emerson and Alcott are able "to find the certainty they seek," and we can agree that they and their followers have "modified favorably the materialistic tendencies of New England thinking." That story has frequently been told, but the pattern of the movement as it is modified has not received the same attention. For that we must turn our attention to the West, as all good transcendentalists were inclined to. In the words of Thoreau, "My needle is slow to settle—varies a few degrees, and does not always point due southwest, it is true, and it had good authority for this variation, but it always settles between west and south-southwest." Less addicted to "Walking" than his friend Thoreau, Alcott was quite as convinced that "there is a subtle magnetism in Nature" and that "we would fain take that walk, never yet taken by us through this actual world, which

[70] Ibid., pp. 484–85.

is perfectly symbolical of the path which we love to travel in the interior and ideal world." In his lifelong "saunter toward the Holy Land," Alcott was always "in the best of spirits," as he wrote to Thomas M. Johnson (on September 21, 1880), "with my face turned West and South."

It is sadly prophetic that Alcott should have opened the entry in his Journal for April 28, 1878, with Milton's famous consolatory line: "They also serve who only stand and wait." Like William Blake, Alcott had found appreciative disciples only in old age. Admitting to "not a little of restlessness, and a sense of justice withal," he writes that the "passage of years brought reconcilement, and ... acceptance, ... without which I might have proved a waste power in my time." After all, "waiting may be the noblest serving," he philosophized, for "the idealist may be said to stand in relation of parent to his time, and needs must wait for his young generation to come to maturity in order to appreciate his claims to authority and apply his genius to practical uses."[71]

He was indeed standing on the threshold of the last noble edifice of transcendentalism, his Concord School of Philosophy; and although the plan may have been his and Emerson's, perhaps directly traceable to their dream of the Bible of the Nations, the organization and much of its execution would not have been possible without their disciples, the informal offspring of the Transcendental Club which had grown up in the Middle West. Their beginning may be pinpointed fairly exactly.

In the winter of 1856–1857, the young William T. Harris, "in a state of protest against many of the habits and practices that existed around"[72] him at Yale, was invited to hear Alcott's series of conversations at the College. "As I listened to him," Harris recalled, "I began to form some notion of higher native powers in the soul, by which the limits of mere sensuous experience could be passed over or transcended. This glimpse of Transcendentalism was like glad tidings to me. . . . Idealism was not a mere fanciful theory to him, but the sober truth."[73] As a result of this

[71] Ibid., pp. 486–87.   [72] Sanborn and Harris, II, 544.
[73] Ibid., pp. 549–50.

experience, Harris concluded that it was worth his time "to understand this strange doctrine" of "Berkeley's idealism" and "the philosophy of the Neo-Platonists," and Alcott recommended for his reading Thoreau's "Walden," Jamblichus's "Life of Pythagoras," and the writings of Emerson. The following spring Harris read Alcott's "Orphic Sayings" in *The Dial,* and "came to see that the world of matter, instead of being the ultimate reality, is only the initial reality."[74]

The significance of Harris's conversion to idealism is hard to underestimate. In the winter of 1858–1859, he invited Alcott to St. Louis, where he held a series of conversations which were attended by many of the people who are usually identified as the St. Louis Hegelians. "Mr. Alcott found us interested," Harris records, "especially in his idealism, and to a less degree in his social views and reforms."[75] This difference, which became even stronger as time went on, was therefore clear from the beginning: the Westerners were more interested in metaphysics than ethics, in philosophy than religion. And as Henry Pochmann has shown,[76] not all Alcott's auditors were pleased with his brand of idealism. The members of the Philosophical Society who were most strongly committed to Hegelianism, especially Henry C. Brokmeyer, the translator of Hegel's *Logic,* were, in fact, openly antagonistic when Alcott returned to St. Louis in 1866. Although aware of Brokmeyer's scorn for Alcott, Harris insisted that "his presence was a powerful influence to stir into activity whatever philosophical thought there might be in a place. All people entering upon the stage of the 'clearing up,' or the intellectual declaration of independence, felt something congenial in the atmosphere of such a conversation as he conducted."[77] And Harris is certainly right. Unfortunately, because Pochmann has told so

[74] Ibid., pp. 550–52. Further reading led Harris to see a relationship between the Orphic Sayings and the doctrines of the German idealists, toward whom he ultimately veered.

[75] Ibid., p. 553.

[76] *New England Transcendentalism and St. Louis Hegelianism* (Philadelphia, 1948), p. 35. Hereafter cited as *New England Transcendentalism.*

[77] Sanborn and Harris, II, 593.

well the story of the negative reaction, the positive response to the gospel of Platonism has never been adequately narrated. I can only suggest briefly the materials and the directions of the yet unwritten history of transcendental idealism in the West.

An ironic notice in the Detroit *Free Press* will suggest the widespread attention the movement was to receive: "The strong cards of the party are Alcott, Harris, and Jones. . . . If you have never heard of Jones you had better say you never heard of Plato and confess yourself an ignoramus at once."[78] If to these three men the *Press* had added Thomas M. Johnson, it would indeed have named the seminal figures, but many another almost forgotten name was important in the dissemination of ideas which was to stamp an indelible pattern upon the cloth of American thought.

And indeed Johnson, the one significant member of this group who has received little serious attention, might well have been forgotten if he had not chosen to spend so many years in editing *The Platonist*, a periodical "Devoted Chiefly to the Dissemination of the Platonic Philosophy in all its Phases." Since in some respects Johnson is a rather typical figure in the Western development of American transcendentalism, it is perhaps worthwhile to examine his career briefly before the establishment of *The Platonist*.

Born in Osceola, Missouri, the son of a United States and Confederate States senator, Johnson graduated from Notre Dame in 1871 and was admitted to the bar in Missouri.[79] Although he was an excellent lawyer and practiced sporadically for the remainder of his life, his heart was in idealistic philosophy. Before graduation, he had acquired Plotinus and Damascius in the Greek, and many of his office hours, as they are recorded in his unpublished

[78] Quoted by Paul R. Anderson, "Hiram K. Jones and Philosophy in Jacksonville," *Journal of the Illinois State Historical Society*, XXXIII (1940), 500. Hereafter cited as "Hiram K. Jones." See also Anderson's *Platonism in the Midwest* (New York, 1963).

[79] For biographical facts I am indebted to the brief account by Johnson's son Franklin, which appears in a brochure on *The Thomas Moore Johnson Collection* published by the University of Missouri in 1949. The degree was not actually conferred until 1876.

diary, were spent reading Plato and the Neoplatonists, chiefly
in the translations of Emerson's "divine Thomas Taylor." Less
than two years after graduation, while yet in his twenty-second
year, Johnson was deeply engrossed in Taylor's volumes and
planning a book which, presumably, would outline the transcendental philosophy to which he was already deeply committed.
The stature of Alcott is suggested in the fact that the young aspirant should almost automatically turn to him for advice. On
March 8, 1874, Johnson opened a correspondence with the master
that was to last for many years:

"Mr. A. Bronson Alcott,
"Dear Sir,

"I have in course of preparation a work which I have entitled
the 'Autobiography of a Modern Platonist.' In this work I propose to give a systematic account of the Philosophy of Plato as
expounded by the Neo-Plato-icians—so called. After a diligent
study of Plotinus, Proclus, Julian, Taylor, etc., etc., I consider
myself qualified to explain the dogmas of Plato and his disciples.
Will you please favor me with your opinion as to the probable
success of such a work, etc.?

Yours respectfully."[80]

Alcott responded on March 21 that he was "curious to learn
more fully of yourself and your studies than your note informs
me. And I shall gladly learn any thing further which you may
choose to communicate." Then, in the oracular tone he had assumed by this time, Alcott offered the encouraging but guarded
advice of an old man to a young enthusiast:

"Your proposed 'Autobiography of a Platonist' interests me, as
it should all students of *Ideas*. Whether there is a public for a
literary venture of the kind I am unable to predict. Students of
Plato and of the Alexandrians are rare. A reaction, however, ap-

[80] This letter is in the Free Public Library, Concord, Massachusetts. The
transcription was made for me by the Librarian, Miss Dorothy E. Nyren,
who obtained permission from Alcott's descendants for its use here.

74

pears to be setting in against the materialism of the scientists, and idealism may have its day presently.

"At any rate I shall be glad to see your purpose carried out fully. The design appears to be excellent, and deserving of prosecution for the editor's benefit, at least."[81]

Coming from Alcott, such half-bitter irony must have been unexpected. The prospect of another move, to be made the first of April, may have disturbed his usual cheerful optimism.

But the young Johnson was not deterred. By this time he was a dedicated disciple of Thomas Taylor, and he apparently asked Alcott for information in a letter I do not have. Alcott replied to Johnson's inquiry on July 26, 1874: "I have been hoping to find something of importance to communicate concerning Taylor, the Platonist. But have little to give you in answer to your inquiries." In the meantime, however, Alcott had carried his young friend's problem to Emerson, who had already inquired at length about Taylor in England. Alcott's letter continues: "Mr. Emerson tells me that the most he learned when last in England, after many inquiries was 'that Taylor named his son Proclus.'— Wordsworth nor the Professors at Oxford and Cambridge, knew little or nothing of him, nor were his translations at the University libraries." In a typical burst of indignation Alcott added: "to such depths of ignorance had the scholars of England attained!" It needs to be recalled, of course, that Alcott had insisted, after a visit in 1842, that "Britain . . . is not the scene for the education of humanity. Her spirit is hostile to human welfare, and her institutions averse to the largest liberty of the soul."[82] His "second Eden" must be planted in America, and Thomas Taylor was to

[81] From an unpublished letter in the possession of Franklin P. Johnson, through whose kind permission it appears here. Other Alcott letters quoted will be from the same collection.

[82] Shepard, *Pedlar's Progress*, p. 338. Even Carlyle, who shared some of his transcendental views, was disappointing to Alcott: "I have seen Carlyle once more, but we quarreled outright, and I shall not see him again. Greatness abides not here; her home is in the clouds, save when she descends on the meadows or treads the groves of Concord" (pp. 316–17).

play a large part in restoring "Man to his rightful communion with God in the Paradise of Good."[83] (The library at Fruitlands contained 16 titles from Taylor.) Johnson was surely delighted to find Alcott's judgments so completely in accord with his own: "I owe to Taylor's translations my first reading in Greek philosophy, and my love for Taylor's learned text," Alcott wrote, "and much [?] prefer it still before the later versions."

In the remainder of the letter for July 26 Alcott paraded his erudition for the benefit of his young follower, pointing out that "Taylor and 'Thomas Stanley's History of Philosophy' appear to be the best authorities on matters relating to Greek thought," and that "Coleridge is the only Englishman since Berkeley, who seem [sic] fitted to do the Greek idealists full justice." Finally, Alcott enclosed an article about Taylor which he had copied for Johnson from Volume XII of the *Encyclopedia Americana*, adding: "It is the most that I can now do for your literary venture."

This venture was no doubt the projected life and works of Thomas Taylor which Johnson was to discuss for many years to come. But, as the response to Alcott reveals, the disciple was already better informed than the master. "Your kind and encouraging letters have been received," Johnson answered on August 18; "Many thanks for the 'Biographical Sketch,' etc. I send you a copy of Taylor's Miscellanies in Prose and Verse. Possibly you may not have the work. Please accept it as a very slight expression of my esteem and admiration for you and your works. The work is interesting—especially the Platonic Creed." And then, with a touch of his own scholarly pride, he informed the informer: "The greater portion of it, as you will perceive, is taken from the writings of Proclus, and the work of Sallustius 'On the Gods and the World.' The latter work is an admirable compendium of Platonic sentiments. The account you send, extracted from the 'Encyclopedia Americana,' will be of value; for though I had read it before, I have no access to the work at present." Whether or not he was being ironic, the young Johnson, barely twenty-three, was already well versed in Platonic philosophy and

[83] Ibid., p. 338.

especially in the works of Taylor. One wonders, of course, where he had found the books he was already accumulating and how much of the discussion of Neoplatonism in the remainder of this letter he was merely remembering from his college days, if indeed the esoteric writers he mentions were in the library at Notre Dame. After offering his "thanks to Mr. Emerson for the references which he so generously furnished," Johnson expresses his own dissatisfaction that "the English Universities have done but little for Plato and his disciples. About the best thing Oxford University [has] ever done in this respect, was the publication of an edition of Plotinus which came forth in 1835. It was edited, however, by Creuzer, and not by an *English* scholar." In the rather long discussion which followed, Johnson referred to Taylor, Stanley, Gemistus Pletho, Marsilius Ficino, Jamblichus, Porphyry, Eunapius, Diogenes Laertius, Marinus, Proclus, Damascius, and Isidorus—books by and about whom are "all replete with entertaining information." That surely was enough to impress the great man, as the conclusion was no doubt intended to. Thinking of himself surely, Johnson suggested that "the biography of a philosopher should be written by a philosopher," and concluded: "I trust to be able, in the course of time, to do *something* for the cause of Ideas. As at present situated, I am unable to labor continuously on my contemplated works, but think that ere the end of next winter, I will have accomplished something."[84]

Three days later, on August 21, 1874, probably before he received this letter, Alcott wrote about his continuing effort to help with the biography of Taylor:

"R. W. Emerson has kindly handed me the enclosed note of reference which may chance aid you in your quest of information covering Thomas Taylor. Probably no American has preached more fully and faithfully for what is preserved of this Platonic Briton than Mr. Emerson.

"I sincerely hope your purpose of giving us some account of him may be carried out by you and we may read here in New England

[84] From Miss Nyren's transcript and with the permission of the Alcott family.

with new admiration and hope, the fruits of your Western Studies."

There is, I think, something almost symbolic in the changed tone of Alcott's letters in such a brief time. The baton has been passed; the hope lies with the West.

But Johnson's dream was never to be realized. More than twenty years later, with both Emerson and Alcott dead, he was still searching for information about Taylor. On November 6, 1896, obviously in answer to an appeal, Emerson's son Edward wrote to Johnson: "I have looked in my Father's note books in England and find no mention of any visit to Walworth [Taylor's home], or indeed of Thomas Taylor at all, except this sentence: 'Hallam knew nothing of Taylor, nor did Milman, nor any Englishman.' "[85] The letter then points out three references to Taylor in Emerson's books, alludes to the "familiar anecdote" of Taylor's desire "to sacrifice a bull to Jupiter in his lodgings," and ends with a regret that "I cannot find more to your purpose." By this time surely Johnson had little hope of finding the information he needed: he had corresponded with various people in England, and had advertised repeatedly in *The Platonist* for news of Taylor, his books and manuscripts, and his family.

He continued also to correspond with friends of Platonic idealism, and he made a trip to the East in 1876. Some time in the fall of 1874 Alcott invited Johnson to meet him in St. Louis. Unfortunately, we have neither the letter of invitation nor the reply, but Johnson must have been disappointed, as was Alcott. On October 14, 1874, he wrote to his young friend: "I regret that I am not to form your personal acquaintance while I am at the West and must look forward in the future for this pleasure. I am the guest of W. T. Harris while in St. Louis, and so at the fountainhead of philosophic thought in these parts." As might be expected, Johnson did know of Harris, having written to him on November 12, 1871, when Johnson was twenty years old: "While in St. Louis, a few months ago, I procured the Volume of the Journ. of Spec. Phil. for 1870. I wish to inquire whether

[85] Unpublished letter in Franklin P. Johnson's possession and quoted with his permission.

78

any other Greek fragments, except those of Parmenides, have been presented in your Journal?' 'The Journal of Speculative Philosophy' is very valuable, and I wish it every success."[86] This was, I believe, the first note of a correspondence that was to last more than thirty years. By the time of Alcott's letter in October 1874, Johnson had written several letters (eight are extant) to Harris and had informed Alcott of his correspondence. As a result Alcott's regret is twofold: "I wish heartily that you might form his acquaintance personally, as well as read his Journal. Perhaps no high influence, within our time, has done so much to kindle and diffuse the spark of thought in America as this torch of his. Presently the thinkers of New England will feel and acknowledge his mind and the countries' [sic] debt to his labors. I must apologize for my negligence in not acknowledging the gift of Taylor's translation of the Orphic Hymns—a most valued addition to my library."

It is clearly apparent from Alcott's high praise of Harris that the time was fast coming for New England to recognize that the Middle West had reached maturity. A few days after the return from the long tour of 1874–1875, Alcott wrote in the Journal: "I question whether many of my acquaintance will take without large allowance my estimates of the intelligence and gentility of western people. Need I remind them that not a few of the intelligent and cultivated settlers are from New England, and carry their attainments with them to plant cities and institutions wherever they settled? I regard the more thriving and cultivated portions as new New England; and, in many respects, an improvement on our population."[87]

---

[86] I quote from a letter in the W. T. Harris papers, with the permission of the Missouri Historical Society, St. Louis. All letters to Harris hereafter cited are in this collection.

The Journal of Speculative Philosophy, perhaps the most famous journal of its kind in America, grew out of discussions in the Philosophical Society, as *The Dial* had from the Transcendental Club. Harris was its editor from its beginning in 1867 to its demise in 1893.

[87] Shepard, *Journals*, p. 455. Contrast the entry for December 28, 1858, which has little good to say for the "Journey Westward."

But the inhabitants of the "new New England" still looked upon the East as the center of American culture. Harris made an annual trip to Concord, as though it were a shrine,[88] and here too came the young Johnson at the first opportunity. Because Johnson was disappointed at not having met Emerson on his pilgrimage to Concord, the ever-gracious Alcott invited him to return. Addressing him at the Parker House, Boston, on July 13, 1876, Alcott wrote: "I have a conversation at Emerson's next Sunday evening, and shall gladly introduce you should you think it worth your pains to visit Concord again; meanwhile, Mr. Sanborn will probably attend, and wish to speak with you, and you would meet with some of our people to advantage." Johnson had, I imagine, visited Concord during the week of June 28, when Emerson was gone for a lecture at the University of Virginia. Since we have no record that Johnson ever met Emerson, I suppose he was unable to accept Alcott's invitation to return in July. He did meet Sanborn, who was to become the Secretary of the Concord Summer School and deliver a Special Lecture at its first session on "Philanthropy and Social Science." A firm friend of the Westerners—Johnson, in particular—Sanborn was denounced as "a Yankee renegade for his part in foisting the Western set of philosophers upon Emerson's Concord." Almost forty years after that first meeting, Johnson was writing to him for scholarly advice about four Latin lines. Sanborn's response suggests an intimate friendship:

"Dear Friend,

"Here is my classmate, B. S. Lyman's version of your four lines. He is a good Latin scholar and may have got nearer the meaning than I."[89]

Sanborn's concluding remarks about Bliss Perry, Bergson, and "my Engineer philosopher, Palmer" remind us how close he and Johnson are to our own time.

Johnson's visit to Boston also has an interesting history. His

[88] Ibid., p. 463.
[89] Unpublished letter of January 2, 1913, in Franklin P. Johnson's possession and quoted with his permission.

first letter to Harris was prompted by the discovery of Thomas Davidson's article on Plato's *Parmenides* in Harris's *Journal*, which no doubt prompted a letter to Davidson. And another of his philosophical friendships developed. A member of the St. Louis group but more interested in the Greeks than in Hegel, Davidson had left St. Louis in 1875 to settle temporarily in the East. Professing himself a "classic heathen," and known among his friends as the last of the wandering scholars, the "militant, mercurial" Davidson must have reminded Johnson of Thomas Taylor. When he left Concord in July 1876 Johnson visited Davidson in Magnolia, Massachusetts, where, as he wrote to Harris on July 9, 1876, "Prof. Davidson gave me a cordial reception & I have had several interesting conversations with him. He appears to be very much opposed to Hegel's Philosophy—says that he cannot see any sense in it." Davidson warned the young aspirant that "it will be very difficult to translate Plotinus" and apparently offered advice about books to read in the Boston Public Library, where Johnson was going "about Wednesday next" for a week of study on the way to other libraries with Neoplatonic resources in New York and Philadelphia.

The next extant letter from Alcott to Johnson suggests that the two-year hiatus in their correspondence had been broken by a letter from Johnson, who had as usual been less concerned with lawyers than Neoplatonists, especially Plotinus. On August 17, 1878, Alcott wrote:

"I am much gratified to learn by your letter, which reached Concord during a visit of mine to Connecticut, that you are still pursuing your philosophic studies, and promise a translation of Plotinus before long. If I remember rightly, we agreed when you did us the honor of visiting Concord, that, of the works of the new Platonists, those of Plotinus were most likely to interest thinking minds of our time. Taylor's translation of his Select Works is now difficult to obtain anywhere. My copy is lent most of the time and kept long.

"I hope your 'Biography of Taylor' will not long be delayed from us. I have known of but one importation of his translations lately, and that was incomplete. It was purchased, I believe, by some College at the West."

Alcott's letter continued with a reference to a Concord visit by another Westerner who was to become a significant figure in the development of American Platonism:

"Lately we have had with us for a fortnight, Dr. Jones and his friends from Jacksonville and Quincy, Ill. Theirs was quite an invasion of Platonism from the prairies and surprised our Concord circle wonderfully. If you see the St. Louis Globe of August 10th you may find an account of their visit by Sanborn of the Springfield Republican.

"I think we may promise ourselves the uprise of the *Old Idealism* to submerge the many shallow swimmers who are venturing beyond their depth both here and in foreign seas of thought."[90]

The visit of Dr. Hiram K. Jones and his friends had the effect of spurring Alcott's plans for the School of Philosophy, which had been discussed at length during a western tour in 1871, the Jacksonville Plato Club having promised $5,000 for the support of the School.[91] That "world at the West," as Alcott was to write

[90] The extended article in the St. Louis *Globe Democrat* calls Dr. Jones "the most accomplished Platonist in America" and suggests that Platonism is the basis of transcendentalism: "So completely was the Platonic Idealism reproduced in New England Transcendentalism, and so thoroughly did the latter become identified with Concord, that this country-village has been regarded for more than forty years as the Home of a New Platonism, of which Alcott and Emerson were the leaders." Among the topics taken up during the fortnight of the invasion from the prairies "were Faith and Reverence Clubs, Plato's Timaeus, Goethe, Evolution, Shakespeare, Faust, Primeval Man, and the Oracles of Mankind. In the last-named were included, besides the Hebrew and Christian Scriptures, the books of Homer, Plato, Dante, Shakespeare, Goethe, and other great men, whom Dr. Jones styles 'Angels.'" Among those present at Dr. Jones's "series of remarkable conversations" were Emerson, Alcott, Elizabeth Peabody, and F. B. Sanborn, who commented that "Miss Peabody had watched by the cradle of New England Transcendentalism, in Dr. Channing's Boston study, more than half a century ago, and had since witnessed the rising and setting of many of its stars; and she took a peculiar pleasure in observing this new mysticism which has established itself among the prairies, and now turns back toward the East from whence its light first came."

[91] Shepard, *Journals*, p. 417.

in the Journal on his return, represents "a culture and society to pique the curiosity and invite inquiries," "and we here in New England begin to feel its thought and enterprize reacting on ours." "*Westernize*," he concluded, "is a verb meaning progress."[92] How little times change!

It was to be eight years, however, before the Westerners finally effected the opening of the School in the summer of 1879. Sometime that spring Alcott had received the prospectus of a journal which fulfilled his fondest expectations. Just how much he had to do with its intent we can only conjecture from his reply, on April 24, 1879, to Johnson's proposal:

"I have distributed most of the prospectus [sic] which you sent me, and have been looking for the appearance of No. 1 of '*The Philosopher.*' I trust no impediment has arrested your purpose of publication. The Philosopher will fill a place in American Journalism becoming more and more obvious to observers of the undercurrent of Philosophic thought both here and abroad. 'The Journal of Speculative Philosophy' begins to touch upon Pure Mysticism in April No. giving us a translation of Hegel's estimate of Boehme's Theosophy and promises more. I have wished more than has been given in its former issues. There is hope for us when Boehme is studied in good earnest."

Although we cannot know how long Johnson had been planning his journal, which was to be called *The Platonist* when it appeared in 1881, he had apparently written about it to Harris in a letter I do not have, possibly as early as 1878. He wrote to Harris again on January 20, 1879, that he was "highly gratified and much encouraged by your kind wishes concerning *The Philosopher*," which he hoped "to make worthy of the attention of thinkers of this age." It is likely, I believe, that Johnson's reading of *The Journal of Speculative Philosophy* prompted him to plan a Platonic periodical to fill the void left by Harris's Hegelian journal. Like Alcott, Johnson had "wished for more than has been given in its former issues," and we can well imagine that the inception of *The Platonist* may be traced to some evening of

[92] Ibid., pp. 418, 423.

fine talk with "the American Plato" during Johnson's visit to Concord in 1876. Alcott's conversation mesmerized his listeners, as Emerson and many another testified.

Also, since the Concord School of Philosophy had been planned in the West as a platform for the dissemination of Platonism, Alcott had probably encouraged his enthusiastic disciple to start a literary organ that would carry the Platonic message to the whole world. At any rate, the timing suggests the likelihood. Although the first issue of *The Platonist* did not appear until February 1881, it was planned for 1879, the year of the School's beginning: Harris had mailed a check for his subscription in January 1879, and Alcott urged Johnson on April 24 to have the first issue ready for the opening of the School that summer: "Mr. Harris writes that he will stop most of the month of July with us in Concord. Inquiries come almost daily to hand from all parts, particularly from the West about our Summer School of Philosophy. Shall we not have No. 1 of '*The Philosopher*,' if not its Editor, with us by that time?"

The School opened as planned, on July 15, 1879, without either Johnson or his journal. In search of health and relief from the law, he had gone to Denison, Texas, in early summer to consider a teaching position in the public schools, but he found the Texas people indifferent to education and the Texas climate "debilitating and enervating." "It is almost unnecessary to say," he added in a letter (of June 22) to Harris, "that *Philosophy* is virtually unknown in Texas. The very air is unfavorable to it." Fortunately, however, the young Platonist had gone forearmed if not forewarned: "I brought with me your Journal, Plotinus, a vol. or two of Plato and Proclus, and a few other works. These tomes furnish me with subjects for thought and contemplation, when I am wearied of the sight of the cow-boy, and the yell of the cattle-auctioneer." So it was that Thomas Taylor reached Texas. But he was not to stay long, for the disillusioned Johnson no doubt took his precious books with him when he returned to Missouri later in the summer. Although he had "definitely abandoned the practice of law" and was seeking, in his words, "any vacant professorship that you consider me competent to fill," he was back in the law office by September and inquiring of Harris for a translation of Hegel's *Phenomenology* which the Philosophical Club in St. Louis had proposed. For the remainder of his life the ambitious young philosopher was to struggle with an uncongenial profession and the unscholarly atmosphere of a rural town. In May 1880 he was writing wistfully to Harris, who had lectured at the first session of Alcott's School: "I have seen the Circular of the Summer School of Philosophy. The Lectures are on attractive subjects, and ought to induce a large number to attend. The School has been a surprising success from the beginning, and you and your associates have good reason to be proud of it."

In the meantime, however, Johnson was not idle. Determined, as he wrote to Harris in 1875, "to contribute *Something* towards the diffusion and propagation of the Platonic Philosophy," he planned several translations in obvious emulation of Thomas Taylor. On September 21, 1880, Alcott wrote to thank Johnson for his "translation of Plotinus" which had made favorable mention of Alcott: "I was pleased to have it, and gratified, I must confess, at finding my name associated with his. Having now made a beginning, I trust you will complete your translation of his works. It is an auspicious moment, since philosophical studies are beginning to interest our most thoughtful minds, and our Summer School finding favor with the public, or that better portion of it which values transcendant thought. My thanks for this hopeful beginning." With such stimulation from Alcott, Harris, and probably his friend Hiram K. Jones, it is not surprising that Johnson should have organized in 1880 "a club for the systematic study of the History of Philosophy,"[93] which was certain to emphasize Taylor rather than Plato, as indeed most of the Western Plato clubs did.

In the first issue of *The Platonist*, Johnson announced that "The republication of the writings of Thomas Taylor, that noble and

[93] *The Platonist*, I (1881), 114.

most genuine Platonist of modern times, will be made a specialty,"[94] and he was soon appealing for Taylor manuscripts: "We have reason to believe that there are still in existence, both in England and this country, many manuscript works of Thomas Taylor, the Platonist. Do any of our readers know where these precious manuscripts are?"[95] And the most extensive project of Volume I was Johnson's "Life and Works of Thomas Taylor the Platonist," which remains an important accumulation of source materials.[96] The conclusion to Johnson's extended sketch will illustrate the tone and character of this strangely exciting journal which has not yet received the attention it deserves:

"Take him all in all Thomas Taylor the Platonist was certainly the most extraordinary and admirable philosophic character of Modern times. In his own age he was not appreciated—save by a few discerning spirits—and his labors were received by the rabble with unmeaning ridicule, and by the superficially learned with senseless derision. Neither dismayed nor discouraged, however, he pursued his useful, philosophic course of life, trusting to Divinity for reward, and to posterity for appreciation. His trust in neither Divinity nor Posterity was misplaced. Today, amid the business, turmoil, and strife of this commercial age, Taylor's memory and character are reverenced, and his immortal works studied and appreciated by hundreds of cultured philosophic minds living within themselves, apart from the mass of mankind."[97]

Like Alcott, obviously, Johnson saw an analogy between his position and Taylor's. Scholarly pariahs all, they enjoyed a perverse pleasure in the fact that "the *profanum vulgus* are still barking and snarling at you," as Johnson wrote to Harris. The stated "mission" of *The Platonist* would have expressed the convictions of Alcott and Taylor quite as well as Johnson: "to release the soul from the bonds of matter, to lead it to the vision of true

[94] Ibid., p. 1.
[95] Ibid., p. 49.
[96] Ibid., pp. 61–64, 102–09, 147–54, 179–87.
[97] Ibid., p. 187.

being—from images to reality,—and, in short, to elevate it from a sensible to an intellectual life."[98]

Although Johnson, Alcott, Emerson, Harris, Jones, and their transcendental associates knew other translations, their primary source for the study of Plato as well as the Neoplatonists was the work of Taylor. Both Alcott and Johnson were, of course, avowed disciples of Taylor, insisting that "he possessed an insight into the esoteric meaning of the Greek philosophic text which has never been equalled or even approached by any 'scholar' of Modern times." In answer to the most frequent objection to Taylor's scholarship, Johnson insisted that "he knew more Platon if others knew more Greek."[99] "It may be truly said," he wrote, "that, in all human probability, no one will ever present the works of Platon to the public 'on a more extensive plan' than that of Mr. Taylor. His edition leaves but little to be desired."[100] Although none of the other Western Platonists was quite this enthusiastic, all of them seemed to prefer Taylor. Even Dr. Jones, who "eschews commentaries and elucidations," made "an exception to this rule . . . in favor of the translation and notes of Thos. Taylor."[101] And the leaders of other Plato Clubs at Quincy, Decatur, Chicago, St. Louis, and Osceola, apparently, chose Taylor consistently. Johnson's advice, in an early number of *The Platonist*, perhaps expressed an almost if not wholly unanimous sentiment: "In conclusion, we say to the student of Platon: Get Taylor's translation, if possible. Otherwise, get Bohn's, Whewell's, or Jowett's."[102] It would be hard, I think, to imagine a greater tribute to Taylor than the enthusiastic study he received up and down the Mississippi Valley in the latter half of the nineteenth century.

The Platonist continued sporadically for most of eight years, being discontinued with the June issue of 1888, only a few weeks after the death of Alcott and less than a year after the final session of the Concord School of Philosophy. For a few months

[98] Ibid., p. 1.
[99] Ibid., p. 187. *Platon* is Johnson's usual spelling.
[100] Ibid., p. 108.
[101] Ibid., p. 84 [Lewis J. Block].
[102] Ibid., p. 50.

more in 1889–1890 Johnson was to edit the *Bibliotheca Platonica,* but a period was coming to an end.

Although this is not the time to trace the history of Johnson's thankless editorial labors, it is appropriate to emphasize the place his periodicals had in reflecting American idealism and popularizing Neoplatonic doctrines. Always in financial straits, *The Platonist* was nevertheless widely distributed, going "to nearly all sections of the globe": according to an editorial note in the first volume, it had "subscribers in America, Great Britain, France, Germany, India, Greece, etc."[103] Johnson corresponded with the thinkers of two continents, and continued to disseminate the doctrines of Platonic idealism, though he fought a losing battle against an adverse philosophic climate. In part at least he was stimulated by the impulse which led Emerson and Alcott to attempt the fusion of Paganism and Christianity, as the epigraph or motto to Volume II indicates: "Christianity is esoterically identical with Philosophy." But there is a great difference, suggested clearly in the word *esoteric.* With both Emerson and Alcott, Christianity was a powerful ingredient. Not so with Johnson and his fellow worshipers at the shrine of Plato and his "golden chain" of followers. Their interest, in varying degrees to be sure, lay in philosophy rather than organized religion, to which they were in fact antagonistic. In the last year of *The Platonist* (1888) Johnson adopted for his title page a motto from Proclus which illustrates ironically the strength of his commitment to a losing cause: "I should say that the Platonic Philosophy came to mankind for the benefit of terrestrial souls, in place of statues, temples and the whole of sacred institutions, and that it is the leader of salvation alike to the men that now are and to those who shall come hereafter."

Even a fairly casual examination of the Tables of Contents in *The Platonist* will reveal that the steady fare of the early numbers consisted chiefly of reprints from Taylor and translations and commentaries which were heavily indebted to him, but gradually moved toward theosophy and spiritualism. Neoplatonic idealism

[103] Ibid., p. 48.

interpreted by an Emerson is one thing, by a Madame Blavatsky quite another. One sentence from an article on "The Way and the Wisdom-Teachers" will suggest the gradual transmutation: "The present revival of mysticism, more especially the return of many modern Christians to the beliefs of the Neoplatonician 'heretics,' is largely a mere reaction from the cold, barren dogmas of modern science."[104] Alcott might not have known quite what he disagreed with in such a passage, but he would have been uneasy at the tone. Like Thomas Taylor and Emerson, he did not denigrate the sciences, insisting rather that they should function ideally as symbolic projectors of a higher truth. Although Johnson was inclined toward the more formally philosophic side of Neoplatonism, he extended the scope of his journal "to include not only the Wisdom-Religions of the archaic period, Oriental as well as Occidental philosophy, and expositions of the intrinsic and esoteric nature of the various beliefs of the world. . . ."[105] The late issues of *The Platonist* are loaded with such articles as "The Theosophical Leaders," "The Kabbalah," "The Philosophers' Stone," "The Tarot," etc. But this trend is clearly contrary to the editor's original intention and may have been largely responsible for the discontinuance of *The Platonist* and the founding of its short-lived successor *Bibliotheca Platonica*, which reaffirmed Johnson's desire "to make the writings of Plato and his chief disciples generally accessible to the thinkers of this country."[106]

Lonely, I fear, frequently misunderstood, rarely appreciated, Thomas M. Johnson was in many respects a remarkable man. Like Thomas Taylor, he was something of an anachronism almost from the beginning. But he fought the good fight, and when the history of transcendentalism in the West is written, he will be recognized for what he was: the staunch defender of the ancient faith. Although he faced the incredible odds of materialism's resistless tide, he never doubted that he would at last be justified;

[104] Ibid., III (1887), 362.
[105] Ibid., II (1884–1885), 1–2.
[106] Ibid., IV (1888). The notice of the new journal, including this quotation, appeared on the back cover of the last six issues of *The Platonist*.

and America would surely be the less without men like him and his master Alcott.

A far better-known man, whose impact on American thought will ultimately be less enduring, was Hiram K. Jones, the philosopher-physician of Jacksonville, Illinois, who founded an important "Plato Club" in 1865 and became one of the chief lecturers in Alcott's Concord School. Like Johnson and Harris, Jones became a convert to transcendental idealism while still in college. His recollection of the experience will help to remind us of Emerson's seminal position in the Platonic revival as well as the strength of the movement: "When I was a student in Illinois College there were two other students and myself who got hold of Emerson's writings. Of course we were ridiculed for dabbling in such nonsense. These writings were then denounced on all sides. Now within one short lifetime that thought has conquered and subdued all minds."[107] Even with a reasonable discount for enthusiasm, this statement is surely impressive, as indeed was Jones himself. "He was led," as Henry Pochmann puts it, "by natural stages from Emerson to Plato."[108] Although his Plato Club was less historical in its orientation than the Philosophical Society in St. Louis, Jones himself was a good scholar, and the Club attracted remarkable attention. In the words of its Secretary, Lewis J. Block, it "has been honored by the presence of many distinguished visitors. Among these may be mentioned A. Bronson Alcott, Dr. Wm. T. Harris, Ralph Waldo Emerson, D. J. Snider, Thos. M. Johnson, H. H. Morgan, and Thos. Davidson. These visitations have given rise to animated discussions, and clear enunciations of opinions. Clubs in the neighboring city, Quincy, have shown their interest in the interpretations of Dr. Jones, and considerable correspondence has ensued with various individuals and associations."[109]

From time to time throughout its erratic history *The Platonist* carried notices about Dr. Jones's Club and its international brother,

---

[107] Anderson, "Hiram K. Jones," p. 487.
[108] *German Culture in America* (Madison, Wisconsin, 1957), p. 290.
[109] *The Platonist*, I (1881), 84.

The American Akademe; and Johnson was clearly in sympathy with its aims and its approach to idealistic philosophy. Though never such an avowed disciple of Thomas Taylor as Johnson was, "Jones possessed and consulted Taylor's books," and "they were . . . the scriptures from which [he] drew his Platonic texts, as appears from the resume of the club creed." These are the conclusions of Ronald Levinson, who had the good fortune to consult Lewis Block about the Jacksonville Club. According to Block, "the mythologic atmosphere in which Taylor lived and his doctrine of the interwoven spheres, appealed profoundly to Jones, and deeply influenced his lectures. If ever Thomas Taylor possessed an American follower and close parallel that man was Dr. Jones." Jones, like Emerson and Johnson, sought information about Taylor's family and burial place, and was like them disappointed that people in his native country should have taken so little notice of Taylor. Levinson's observation about the importance of Taylor to the Jacksonville group is equally true of other Plato clubs, most of which were modeled on the parent club. It was, Levinson writes, "a western wing of the great movement of New England transcendentalism on its Neo-Platonic side. The important fact for our purpose is that for the Neo-Platonism of the entire movement Taylor is practically the sole source. As in Concord, so here in the middlewest, no admirer of Plato could make his way without Taylor's translations and comments, while the student of Plotinus, of Iamblichus, and of Proclus was obliged to build wholly upon Taylor's foundations."[110]

The best-known child of the parent club was the one organized at Quincy, Illinois, by Samuel H. Emery. Although its motives were similar to those of the Jacksonville Club, it was apparently much less formal in its recording and hence of much less value to the student of the movement. The interests of the Quincy group were about equally divided between Hegelianism and Platonism, but their Platonism did not have the strong Neoplatonic bias of the other groups, and the Quincy Club is not therefore impor-

[110] Ronald B. Levinson, "Thomas Taylor, the Platonist" (unpublished dissertation, University of Chicago, 1924), pp. 170–71.

tant to this study, though Emery was to become the permanent director of the Concord School.[111]

The most famous development of all this ferment was, of course, the Concord School of Philosophy. Although it was long a dream of Emerson and Alcott, it would never have been more than that without the active endorsement of the Westerners, especially Jones and Harris. During Alcott's visit to Jacksonville in 1871, Jones and his friends had urged him to establish the School, but nothing happened until Jones visited Concord in the summer of 1878 and prompted Alcott to action. As a result, the School opened in 1879. A glance at the prospectus for the first two terms reveals how important the Westerners were. Among the five "regular professors" for 1879 were W. T. Harris and H. K. Jones. They were joined in 1880 by Denton J. Snider (of St. Louis), and S. H. Emery, Jr., was listed as Director.[112]

"It is significant," as Pochmann points out, "that Dr. Jones the Platonist and not Dr. Harris the Hegelian was the co-founder of the School. Jones and Alcott originally conceived a Platonic institution; but once Harris was invited to participate, the die was cast."[113] In one sense, of course, the inception of the School may be traced to the Bible of the Nations for the fusion of Paganism and Christianity which Alcott and Emerson had dreamed of, and in fact the two dreamers had even conceived a plan for an organization not unlike that of the Concord School. In August 1840 Emerson went so far as to ask Margaret Fuller, the first editor of *The Dial*, if she did "not wish to come here and join in such a work," which he then described: "Alcott and I projected the other day a whole university out of our straws. George Ripley, Henry Hedge, Theodore Parker, Mr. Alcott, and I shall in some country town—say Concord or Hyannis—announce that we shall hold a semester for the instruction of young men, say, from Octo-

---

[111] See Paul R. Anderson, "Quincy, an Outpost of Philosophy," *Journal of the Illinois State Historical Society*, XXXIV (1941), 50–83, and Pochmann, *German Culture in America*, pp. 290–94.

[112] From my copy of the original notice.

[113] *German Culture in America*, p. 294.

ber to April."[114] Since these names are all prominent in the history of transcendental thought, the direction the School would have taken is perhaps obvious, and several of the subjects Emerson proposed are suggestive of their desire to preach the union of all religions; among the several topics he listed: History of Opinion, Theology, Metaphysics, Philosophy of History, the Catholic Church, History of Paganism, the Modern Crisis, and the Ideal Life.[115]

Nevertheless, there would have been no School without the enthusiasm of the Western Platonists. That it should have been from the very beginning a great debate between the forces of Platonism and the forces of Hegelianism and that the latter were to prevail—if a winner need be declared—are perhaps sure indications of the changing times. Alcott's Journal reveals that he was disturbed at the trend of the lectures and in his own ineffectual way sought to promote a less speculative and logical method than the Hegelians were following: "I confess full faith in Mr. Harris' logic," he wrote wistfully on July 16, "but am incapable of following the steps leading to his conclusion." Again that evening after "discussing the Hegelian Idea and methods": "I find my thinking is ideal, my method analogical rather than logical, and thus reaching the conclusion by concrete symbols. . . . For theological ends this method is the more significant and effective, reaching the many while the other affects but the few."[116]

Although Alcott was to insist that "we have allowed Plato's text to sleep too long" and that "it should be read along with St. John and St. Paul," he noted before the session was over that "Harris has won general acceptance from all who have heard him speak." Even more significant perhaps, as an ironic foreshadowing of things to come, is an entry in the Journal for August 1: "Dr. Jones' Conversation on Plato's Dialectic, preparatory to his doctrine of Reminiscence, is listened to with much interest. He treats of the natural and supernatural states of the

[114] Sanborn and Harris, II, 507–08.
[115] Ibid.
[116] Shepard, *Journals*, p. 497.

soul and illustrates his subject in modern experience. Darwinism is noticed and partially discussed."[117] The time had come, of course, when Darwin could no longer be dismissed by partial discussion. Alcott was whistling in the dark.

Among the early lecturers of the School were two people who have some place in the history of Taylor's rise and fall in America. The first of these is Thomas Wentworth Higginson. As a friend of Alcott and Emerson and a participant in many reform movements of the century, he perhaps deserves more credit than he has thus far received in the study of American transcendentalism. Although Pochmann is doubtless right that he "followed more the literary tradition of Margaret Fuller than Emerson and Parker's concern with philosophy and theology,"[118] Higginson was an admirer of Thomas Taylor and a collector of his books and manuscripts. On July 16, 1881, responding to an appeal from Thomas M. Johnson, Higginson wrote:

"In answer to the inquiry made in *The Platonist* after original manuscripts of Thomas Taylor, I am glad to contribute a few facts respecting autograph notes made by him in two volumes in my possession. It may be well to begin by saying that I have long been in the habit of picking up such of his translations as came in my way, and have now some twenty-five volumes. In addition to these, I possess the two following Greek texts, both of which belonged to his library and bear his autograph.... I must say that the whole effect of these volumes has been to enhance my respect for the scholarship and literary method of Thomas Taylor. He is certainly one of the most unique and interesting figures in English literary history, and deserves at least—what he never has had—a full and accurate bibliography of his works. I do not know that even their exact number has ever been ascertained."

The extent of Higginson's commitment to Taylor is suggested by the amount of information about Taylor's works he possessed. Although he does not presume himself capable of giving the full

[117] Ibid., pp. 507, 505, 504.
[118] *German Culture in America*, p. 637.

and accurate bibliography needed, he had made a fairly accurate count and, in concluding his article, observed: "This makes fifty-nine volumes known to exist, representing forty-three distinct works, and there are doubtless others. I wish some American admirer of Thomas Taylor would undertake a careful bibliography of his publications."[119] Since Higginson was for many years the mentor and friend of Emily Dickinson, whose favorite philosopher was Plato, she undoubtedly came to know his works through Taylor's translations. How many others may have been converted by Higginson's enthusiasm we can only conjecture. It is clear, however, that Taylor's books were basic texts in transcendental circles.

Higginson's plea for "a careful bibliography" was answered. Johnson pointed out in *The Platonist* that "Mr. Orlin Mead Sanford of New York City has probably the most notable set (sixty-two volumes) of the writings of Thomas Taylor, in this country. He has printed an annotated catalogue of his collection, which is very interesting to the numerous admirers of the great Platonist." Being a bibliographical authority himself by this time, Johnson observed that Sanford "lacks three volumes, two of which I have," and concluded with the hope that "Mr. Sanford's unique collection will remain intact, and ultimately find a permanent abiding place in some public library, where it may delight and benefit the scholars of future ages."[120]

One other name needs mention: Dr. Alexander Wilder. In the session of 1882 at the Concord School he spoke on Alexandrian Platonism, a subject on which he was well informed. Although Wilder is now almost forgotten, he was apparently a well-known author, editor, and lecturer in his day; and he was an early devotee of Thomas Taylor. In 1875 he had published an edition of Taylor's *Dissertation on the Eleusinian and Bacchic Mysteries*, with introduction, notes, emendations, and glossary; and almost

[119] *The Platonist*, I (1881), 68–69. I have learned through Mrs. Louise S. Boas that Higginson's collection is now in the Huntington Library.

[120] *The Platonist*, II (1884–1885), 168. Sanford's *Annotated Catalogue . . . of the Works of Thomas Taylor* was published in New York in 1885.

from the beginning he was the most prolific contributor to *The Platonist*. His translation of *Jamblichus: A Treatise on the Mysteries*, beginning in 1881 and ending in 1887, was heavily indebted to Taylor's translation, and so too was the "Platonic Technology: A Glossary of Distinctive Terms used by Platon and other Philosophers in an Arcane and Peculiar Sense," which appeared in four issues of Volume I. But he also contributed many articles and may have assisted in editing and publishing *The Platonist* from August to December 1885, when it was issued from Orange, New Jersey, near his home. Johnson praised Wilder as "a critical scholar and profound thinker," and pointed out proudly that Wilder was Professor of "Psychological Science, in the United States Medical College, in New York City," where he "is now delivering a course (the second) of valuable lectures."[121] But he was already well known to many readers of *The Platonist* through his contributions to *The Theosophist*, whose editor wrote to Johnson:

"So far we are sincerely charmed with *The Platonist*. It comes in good time, and will fill one of the greatest needs of our age. Its value is the more enhanced in our sight by the promise we find in it from our respected friend and brother, Professor Alexander Wilder, to become one of its chief contributors. The news is gratifying, indeed. We trust his too sensitive modesty may forgive the enthusiastic, though never too exaggerated, opinion of his sincere admirers and far-away friends—if we repeat again that which we all honestly believe, namely: that there is not in the United States a scholar more competent than himself to elucidate to the reader the hidden beauties, as well as the esoteric meaning underlying Platonic philosophy."[122]

With such a background and interests Wilder was obviously much more sympathetic with the Western Platonists than the Easterners, and when the Westerners broke off from the Concord School in 1882 as a result of a decision against holding the sessions in the West on alternate years, Wilder joined with Jones

---

[121] Ibid., I (1881), 114.
[122] Ibid.

to organize The American Akademe "as a winter school . . . to be an antidote and in some sense a rival of the Hegelian school at Concord, which continued as a summer school."[123] Whether or not they felt this rivalry, the founders of the Akademe no longer participated in Alcott's School. At the organizational meeting on July 2, 1883, Jones presided and Wilder acted as secretary. Among the thirty-three people present, according to Paul R. Anderson, were Johnson, Harris, and Block.[124] Although Harris moved to the East and became United States Commissioner of Education, he remained a link between East and West, writing to thank the second editor of the *Journal of the American Akademe* for a copy of the *Journal* with her "report of the Plato Banquet at Jacksonville," which he described as "a sort of university city for Philosophy in this country." "I have hoped before this time," he added, "to see a volume from Dr. Jones giving his Platonic studies."[125]

Elected Corresponding Secretary at the organizational meeting, Thomas M. Johnson was closely associated with the Akademe throughout its existence, and it was the intention apparently that he should publish notices of meetings and worthy papers. In fact, the formation of the Akademe in 1883 may have furnished the impetus for the revival of *The Platonist*, which had lapsed in January 1882. At any rate, the first issue of Volume II (January 1884) carried a notice of the new society, outlining the organization, membership, purpose, etc.; and a subsequent issue quoted a resolution of the Akademe that "the several contributions were ordered to be transmitted to *The Platonist* for publication."[126] Still another issue in 1884 emphasized the President's remark that "this association is not *local* but CONTINENTAL," alluding

---

[123] Pochmann, *New England Transcendentalism*, p. 103.

[124] "Hiram K. Jones," pp. 503–04.

[125] Quoted in *Journal of the American Akademe*, V (1890), 18. In this Harris was to be disappointed. Many of Jones's lectures, perhaps all he thought worthy of publication, were copied out in a fair hand, passed at his death into the possession of his friend Johnson, and are now in the library of Franklin P. Johnson.

[126] *The Platonist*, II (1884–1885), 48.

ironically, I think, to the closed corporation represented by the Concord School.[127] And indeed the Akademe did grow astonishingly. By May 1884 there were 180 members. "Fourteen new members were elected" at the eighth monthly meeting, and "the attendance was large."[128] On June 21, 1892, when the Akademe held its last meeting, having existed just nine years, "the cumulative roll of members contained 433 names."[129] They came, as its President pointed out in 1884, "from Maine to California and from Canada to the Dutch West Indies." Obviously proud of their international flavor, Jones insisted that "we shall continue to maintain this character. We do not claim to be an Akademe of Philosophers, but desire to be regarded simply as students of Philosophy, united as disciples for mutual help."[130]

The aim of "this association," Jones observed on the same occasion, "is to find out persons of kindred thought and appreciations." They also sought, of course, to study writers with interests kindred to their own. The full record of their nine years' deliberations would, I think, reveal an exciting chapter in American intellectual history which is too often unnoticed or denigrated. As it is now, we are confined, for the early meetings, to such fascinating fragments as Johnson could find space for. His account of the eighth meeting is particularly suggestive in recording an early reference to William Blake, who shared their desire for "communion with the diviner ideas and natures" through the occult lore of Jacob Boehme and Plato's followers. In the discussion following a paper on "Natural Law in the Spiritual World," Elizur Wolcott is said to have commented: "William Blake claimed open vision of the supernatural. 'I do not see the external world,' said he; 'it is only a hindrance.' Like Blake, there is more reality to me in the glorious company of the angelic hosts; but like Paul, I am conscious of the two natures

[127] Ibid., p. 64.
[128] Ibid.
[129] Pochmann, *New England Transcendentalism*, p. 135.
[130] *The Platonist*, II (1884–1885), 64.

within me."[131] And not surprisingly, Thomas Johnson himself had found and appreciated the poet who conceived the material world as "the delusion of Ulro." On a scrap of note paper which I found in his library, Johnson had registered his pleasant surprise at Blake's cosmological idealism.

With the July number in 1884, Johnson was once more unable to continue *The Platonist*, and the Akademe felt it necessary to found a journal to record its transactions for nonresident members. Alexander Wilder became its first editor. Five years later, in a strange reversal, the *Journal of the American Akademe* carried a flattering notice of one more of Johnson's valiant efforts to carry the message to the world, the *Bibliotheca Platonica*, which lasted for only four issues from July 1889 to December 1890. Quoted in translation from the *Journal of the Savantes*, Paris, the article observes: "We believe America occupies an unique place in useful inventions and industries, but it appears that in that country there are many persons who cultivate philosophy, history, and also Greek and Latin literature. It is evidently the country of the future; and if unfortunately the study of antiquity becomes an extinguished light in Europe, we may hope the torch will be relighted in America." So it was that a surprised but pleased Paris writer named H. Weil introduced his review of the first volume of Johnson's last journalistic venture. Much of Weil's space was reserved for a paper by Alexander Wilder entitled "Platonic Reflections on the Nature of the Soul" which, before publication here, had been "the leading discourse in a symposium given Nov. 7, 1888, in celebration of the

---

[131] Ibid. It was, ironically, Wolcott who read a paper on Evolution to the Akademe about which Johnson recorded in the monthly notices of meetings: "The decision of the majority was that the doctrine of Evolution can in no wise be accepted, till certain gaps which are still yawning widely are successfully bridged over" (II, 80). He had already published Lewis J. Block's comment about Darwin in the "Doctrines" of the Plato Club: "Man has always been man. Darwinism is an inversion of the truth. Nature had descended from man, not man sprung from it. All religions are the same in content, however different as to form" (I, 85). Block's language sounds much like Alcott's.

terrestrial descent of Plato, at the home of the editor of the Bibliotheca Platonica, Osceola, Mo." After pointing out that a similar
symposium is planned for the home of Mrs. Julia P. Stevens in
Bloomington, Illinois, for the following November, the reviewer
observes that "these things seem the beginnings and promise of
a new Platonic Academy." Although he finds it "very natural
that the New Platonism of the 19th century should feel itself in
harmony with the beliefs of the ages of antiquity," Weil registers
considerable amazement at this Platonic movement in "the far
West" for which "love of erudition, interest in the history of
philosophy are not a sufficient explanation": "The founding of
a periodical devoted to the study of Platonism in the valley of
the Mississippi is certainly very extraordinary."[132]

And indeed it was extraordinary. The great surprise, I suppose,
is that the movement endured for so long and with such strength.
I find it hard to believe, as I look back over this summary study,
that literary historians should have paid so little attention to one
of the great movements in our intellectual history. The entire
transcendental movement needs reexamination as the heroic attempt it was to revive Platonic idealism and reconcile the Mystery
religions and Christianity; in particular, the Western extension of
New England idealism deserves the thorough study which only
one part, its Germanic features, has received in the work of Henry
Pochmann. In this brief space I have done little more than suggest
several important names and groups, and have in fact omitted
many who were once significant in the propagation of an idealistic
philosophy which never dies.

It does, of course, wane as the cycle changes. And a great change
occurred about 1890, when the idealistic movement seemed to
falter. Although Johnson, Wilder, Jones, and others of the Westerners lived on past the turn of the century, the movement may
be said to have come to a close with the last meeting of The
American Akademe in "the Athens of the West," on June 21,
1892. The virtually stillborn *Bibliotheca Platonica* had expired in

[132] *Journal of the American Akademe*, V (1890), 28–29.

1890, *The Journal of Speculative Philosophy* in 1888.[133] Emerson had died in 1882 and Alcott in 1888; his Concord School had closed the year before. Finally, as though to climax the end of an era's quest for proof that "all religions are one," in 1891 Alexander Wilder reissued Taylor's *Dissertation on the Eleusinian and Bacchic Mysteries* in a very attractive edition with eighty-five illustrations by A. L. Rawson. "There are many," Wilder wrote, "who still cherish a regard, almost amounting to veneration for the author; and we hope that this reproduction of his admirable explanation of the nature and object of the Mysteries will prove to them a welcome undertaking." By this time the number of those "who still cherish a regard" for Taylor was obviously diminishing, and Wilder was surely wrong in bravely insisting that "there is an increasing interest in philosophical, mystical, and other antique literature."[134] In reproducing Taylor's defiant "Advertisement" to the first edition, Wilder is perhaps recognizing ironically that the philosophic climate is against him and his Neoplatonic friends: "And as to the philosophy, by whose assistance these Mysteries are developed, it is coeval with the universe itself; and however its continuity may be broken by opposing systems, it will make its appearance at different periods of time, as long as the sun himself shall continue to illuminate the world."[135]

With the optimistic faith that Platonic idealism was certain to reassert itself as well as with the pessimistic implication that the tide has ebbed, Bronson Alcott himself would have agreed, I think. "Opposing systems" had indeed "broken the continuity." Although he could insist almost to the end that "I see not why my morrow should differ from my yesterday,"[136] the last entry in his Journal is a sadly wistful recognition of at least a temporary defeat for Western idealism: "Evening," he began propheti-

---

[133] Two more numbers did appear, one in 1892 and one in 1893. See Pochmann, *German Culture*, pp. 277–81 and 651 (n. 118).

[134] Alexander Wilder, ed., *The Eleusinian and Bacchic Mysteries: A Dissertation*, by Thomas Taylor, fourth edition (New York, 1891), pp. 27–28.

[135] Ibid., pp. 29–30.

[136] Shepard, *Journals*, p. 536.

cally; "Harris comes and takes me to tea at the 'Orchard House.' Ames is now there. We have much discussion of the Lapse. I do not succeed in showing them the place of this in my theory of the Genesis, or of the Renovation of man from the ruins of sin."[137] The end of an age had come: the moon was behind the clouds; and the once familiar landscape was "grown up in sweet-fern, barren, unfenced, and all gone to ruin."[138]

GEORGE MILLS HARPER

[137] Ibid., p. 537.
[138] Ibid., p. 536.

BIOGRAPHICAL ACCOUNTS OF
THOMAS TAYLOR

Engraving of Taylor,
from *Public Characters of 1798*

I

*"MR. TAYLOR, THE PLATONIST"**

The subject of this article, from his enthusiastick and undiverted attachment to the religion and philosophy of Plato, has been called by different writers, "the modern Pletho,"[1] "the apostle of Paganism,"[2] and "the gentile priest of England."[3]

This very singular man was born in London, in the year 1758, of obscure but worthy parents; and though in his literary career he has accomplished Herculean labours, yet we are informed that his body has been from his childhood weak and diseased; for at the early period of six years of age, alarming symptoms of a consumption induced his family to remove him for three years to Staffordshire. On returning thence, in his ninth year, he was sent to St. Paul's School, to be educated for a dissenting minister. Here, it seems, he soon gave indications of that contemplative turn of mind, and that aversion to merely verbal disquisitions, which have since become such predominant features in his character. In proof of this, Mr. Ryder, one of the masters of the school, whenever a sentence occurred remarkably moral or grave, in any classick which young Taylor was translating to him, would always preface it by saying to the youthful Platonist: "Come, here is something worthy the attention of a philosopher."[4] The boy, indeed, was so disgusted with the arbitrary manner in which the dead languages are taught in that, as well as in all other publick schools, that he entreated, and at length prevailed on his father

* [From *Public Characters of 1798* (Dublin, 1798–1799), pp. 100–124. (". . . this is, if not autobiographical, evidently based on information supplied by the subject"—W. E. A. Axon, *Thomas Taylor the Platonist*.) See manuscript letter, Plate 19, for proof that it is autobiographical. Also, p. 105.]

[1] In the second edition of the Curiosities of Literature.

[2] See Analytical Review of his Sallust.

[3] See Pursuits of Literature.

[4] Thus too, at an early period, one of the first scholars of the age, discovered the critical turn of his mind: for when, on reading the Latin Testament, *at Jesus* was printed instead of *ait Jesus*, he shrewdly conjectured that *at* must be a verb, and be derived from *ao*.

to take him home, and abandon his design of educating him for the ministry. The parent complied indeed, but with great reluctance, as he considered the office of a dissenting minister the most desirable and the most enviable employment upon earth!

About this time Mr. T. happened to become acquainted with a Miss Morton, the eldest daughter of a respectable coal merchant in Doctor's Commons, for whom, although he was but twelve years of age, he conceived such an attachment, as neither time nor distance could dissolve or impair. This young lady (his present wife) had received an elegant education, and united with an agreeable person, uncommon modesty, liberality, and artless manners. Mr. T. has often declared that he was then as deeply in love as the most famous hero of romance, and that to see and converse with his adored fair one formed the very summit of his wishes.

During Mr. T's residence at home, while his father was yet undetermined as to his future situation in life, he happened to meet with Ward's Young Mathematician's Guide, and was so struck, in looking over the book, with the singularity of *negative quantities*, when multiplied together producing *positive* ones, that he immediately conceived a strong desire to become acquainted with mathematicks. His father, however, who was deeply skilled in modern theology, but utterly unacquainted with this sublime and most useful species of learning, was, it seems, averse to his son's engaging in such a course of study; but Mr. T's ardour soon enabled him to triumph over all opposition, by devoting the hours of rest to mathematical lucubrations, though to accomplish this he was obliged to conceal a *tinder-box* under his pillow.

To this early acquaintance with those leading branches of mathematical sciences, arithmetick, algebra, and geometry, Mr. T. ascribes his present unrivalled attachment to the philosophy of Plato, and all the substantial felicity of his life.

About this time, viz. at the age of fifteen, Mr. T. was placed under an uncle-in-law at Sheerness, who happened to be one of the officers of that dock yard. Here at his leisure hours, which were but few, he still pursued the study of the speculative part of mathematicks; for he was of opinion that those sciences were degraded when applied to practical affairs, without then knowing that the same sentiment had been adopted by Pythagoras, Plato, and Archimedes. Here, likewise, he read Bolingbroke and Hume, and by studying their works became a convert to the *sceptical philosophy.*

The behaviour, however, of his uncle-in-law was so very tyrannical, and his opportunities for the acquisition were so very inadequate to his thirst for knowledge, that after having been in what he considered a state of slavery during three years, he determined to break his fetters, and, as he could find no other refuge from oppression, cast himself once more into the arms of the church.

For this purpose he left Sheerness, and became, during the space of two years, a pupil of one of the most celebrated dissenting preachers. Under this gentleman he recovered his knowledge of the rudiments of the Latin and Greek tongues, but made no great advances in the attainment of those languages, as his mind, naturally propense to the study of things, required an uncommon stimulus to make it stoop to an attention to words. This stimulus, the philosophy of Plato and Aristotle could alone inspire.

Mr. T. it seems, during this course of ministerial study renewed with redoubled ardour his acquaintance with Miss M. and, what indeed is singular in the extreme, was able to unite in amicable league, courtship and study. Hence he applied himself to Greek and Latin in the day, paid his addresses to his fair one in the evening, and had the courage to begin and read through the Latin quarto of Simson's Conic Sections at night.

About this time Mr. T. entered on the study of the modern philosophy, and thinking himself qualified by his knowledge of the more abstruse parts of mathematicks, to understand the system of the universe as delivered in the *Principia* of Newton, he began to read that difficult work. We are informed, however, that he soon closed the book with disgust, exclaiming, "Newton is indeed a great mathematician, but no philosopher!" He was principally induced it seems to form this conclusion by Sir Isaac's assertion[5] that "every the least possible particle of matter or body, attracts all bodies at all distances; that the being, whatever it is, that attracts or impels bodies towards each other, proceeds from those bodies to which it belongs, and penetrates the whole substance of the bodies on which it acts." It appeared to him, that from this assertion it must inevitably follow, that bodies act immediately or by themselves, without the intervention of any other being, in a place where they are not, since attraction is the *immediate* action of attracting bodies; that they thus act in many places at the same time; that they penetrate each other; and that the least particle of matter is extended as far as the limits of the universe: all which consequences he considered as glaringly absurd.

Thus far the stream of Mr. T.'s life may be said to have run with an equal tenour, limpid, and unruffled, compared with its course in the succeeding period, in which it resembled some dark river rolling with impetuous rage to the main.

The time now drew nigh in which Mr. T. was to leave his fair one for the university. But as her father, in his absence, intended to marry her to a man of large fortune, who had made her the offer of his hand, Miss M. to secure herself from the *tyrannical* exertion of parental authority, generously consented to unite herself to our philosopher, on condition that nothing further than the marriage ceremony took place till he had finished his studies at Aberdeen. This he immediately assented to, and the indissoluble knot was tied.

But when the fates are adverse, how vain are the most prudent projects! how unfortunate the most generous intentions! The low cunning of Mr. T.'s mother-in-law discovered the secret, soon after the union of the platonick pair; who, from a combination of ecclesiastical indignation with parental rage, were for a time exposed to the insult of undeserved reproach, and bitterness of real distress.

We are happy to find, however, that Mr. and Mrs. T. exculpate their parents on this occasion: Mr. T. entirely ascribing his father's

[5] Prop. 6. 7. & 8. L. 3.

conduct to the malicious misrepresentation of his mother-in-law, and the anger of the church, and Mrs. T. to the unnatural and selfish conduct of some of her very near relations.

Whether Mr. T.'s great aversion to presbeterians and presbeterian ministers originated in this or some other circumstance, we are unable to determine. Certain, however, it is, that he has ever since considered the clergy of this description as men implacable in their resentments, whom neither pity can soften, nor penitence appease; and has often been heard to say, that of all the christian sects, the members of the church of England are the best, and the presbeterians the worst.

Such indeed was the distressed situation of this young couple at this period, that we are informed they had no more than seven shillings a week to subsist on, for nearly a twelvemonth! This was owing to the base artifice of one of Mrs. T.'s relatives, who was left executor, and who prevailed on her father, at this time in a dying state, to let him pay her what he had left her as he pleased. Mr. T. endeavoured indeed to obtain employment as an usher to a boarding-school; but it was some time before he was able to effect this, as he was abandoned both by friends and relatives, and could not even borrow ten shillings and sixpence, which it seems is the usual fee of those who procure such situations.

At length he was separated from his partner in affliction, and settled as usher to a boarding-school at Paddington. As his embarrassments were such, that he was unable to remove Mrs. T. from Camberwell, where she then resided, and the only time he was permitted to see her was on Saturday afternoon, he could enjoy but little of her company. This little, however, was doubtless dear in proportion to its brevity, and the remembrance of past pain would, it may be presumed, be lost in the overflowings of reciprocal love.

Mrs. T.'s affection was, indeed, as we are informed, so great for her unfortunate husband, that though then in a state of pregnancy, she almost deprived herself of the necessaries of life, that she might purchase out of her weekly pittance of seven shillings a comfortable dinner for Mr. T. on Saturday; and letters, it seems, during this painful separation passed between them, replete with sentiments which express the most tender and disinterested regard.

Mr. T. however, finding the situation of an usher in itself extremely disagreeable, and when attended with such a separation from his partner in calamity, intolerable, determined if possible to obtain a less irksome employment; and at length, by the exertions of his few friends, he obtained a clerk's place in a respectable banking-house in the city. In this situation, however, he at first suffered greatly; for as his income was but fifty pounds a year, and this paid quarterly, and as he had not any money to spare for himself, and could not from his embarrassments quit his lodging at Camberwell, he was unable to procure nutriment in the course of the day, adequate to the great labours he endured. Hence, he was so exhausted by the time he had reached home in the evening, that he frequently fell senseless on the floor.

We are informed that Mr. T. soon after he was settled in this new employment, took a house at Walworth, by the assistance of a friend, who had been his schoolfellow; finding a residence at some small distance from town, necessary for his own health and that of Mrs. T. and much more favourable to the cultivation of his mind, of which he never seems to have lost sight, even amidst the lassitude of bodily weakness, the pain incident to uncommon fatigue, and the immediate pressure of want.

About this time Mr. T.'s studies, it seems, were chiefly confined to chemistry. Of all the authors in this branch of natural philosophy, he was most attached to Becher, whose *Physica Subterranea* he read with great avidity, and became a complete convert to the doctrines of that illustrious chemist. He did not, however, neglect mathematicks; but, in consequence of having thought much on the quadrature of the circle, and believing he had discovered a method by which the rectification of it might be geometrically, though not arithmetically, obtained, he found means to publish a quarto pamphlet on that subject, which he entitled "A new Method of reasoning in Geometry." The substance of this pamphlet, as it did not attract the attention of the publick, he has since given to the world in a note, in the first volume of his translation of Proclus on Euclid.

Hitherto Mr. Taylor's studies may be considered as merely preparatory to those speculations which were to distinguish him in the literary world; at least, they are considered in this light by the followers of Plato. It appears too, that, without knowing it, he was led to the mystick discipline of that sublime philosopher, in the exact order prescribed by his disciples; for he began with studying the works of Aristotle. He was induced, it seems, to engage in this course of study, by a passage in Sir Kenelm Digby's treatise "on Bodies and Man's Soul," in which he says that "the name of Aristotle ought never to be mentioned by scholars but with reverence, on account of his incomparable worth." This eulogium from a man who was very far from being a Peripatetick, determined Mr. T. to enter on the study of Aristotle, as soon as he could procure any of his works, and had sufficiently recovered his knowledge of Greek.

By a fortunate circumstance, he soon met with a copy of that philosopher's Physicks, and before he had read a page, was so enamoured with his pregnant brevity, accuracy, and depth, that he resolved to make the study of Aristotle's philosophy the great business of his life. Such, indeed, was his avidity to accomplish this design, that he was soon able to read that great master in the original; and has often been heard to say, that he learned Greek rather through the Greek philosophy, than the Greek philosophy through Greek.

However, as he was engaged every day in the banking-house till at least seven in the evening, and sometimes till nine or ten, he was obliged to devote part of the night to study. Hence we are informed, that for several years, while he was at the banker's, he seldom went to bed before two or three o'clock in the morning; and having, by contemplative habits, learned to divest himself during the time which he set apart for study of all concern about the common affairs of life, his attention was not diverted from Aristotle, either by the inconveniencies arising from his slender income, or solicitude about the business of the day.

By the assistance of Aristotle's Greek Interpreters, therefore, Mr. T. read the Physicks, books *de Anima, de Caelo*, Logick, Morals, and Metaphysicks, of that philosopher: for, in the opinion of Mr. T. a man might as reasonably expect to understand Archimedes, who had never read Euclid, as to comprehend either Aristotle or Plato, *who wrote obscurely from design*, without the assistance of their Greek commentators. Hence he has often been heard to say, that the folly of neglecting the invaluable commentaries of the ancients, on those philosophers, is only to be equalled by the arrogance of such as affect to despise them; since these interpreters possessed a traditional knowledge of the Greek philosophy, had books to consult on that subject which are now lost, spent their whole lives in the study of it, were men of the deepest erudition, and must be infinitely better qualified to explain the meaning of the text of Plato and Aristotle than any modern can pretend to be, because the Greek was their native tongue. Mr. T. even carries his attachment to these interpreters so far as to assert, that from the oblivion in which they have been so long concealed, the philosophy of Plato and Aristotle has not been accurately understood for upwards of a thousand years.

Mr. T. therefore, who, by divesting himself at night of those habits of business which he had been contracting in the day, may be said in this respect to have resembled Penelope, made it a constant rule to digest what he had learned from Aristotle, while he was walking about with bills. This, when he was once master of his employment, he accomplished with great facility, without either committing mistakes, or retarding his business. We are, indeed, informed from good authority, that while in that department, he was always distinguished for accuracy and dispatch.

Mr. T. having in this manner applied himself to the study of Aristotle, and presuming that he was sufficiently instructed in his philosophy, betook himself to the more sublime speculations of Plato; considering the Peripatetick discipline, when compared with that of Plato, as bearing the relation of the less to the greater mysteries: and in this light it seems, the two philosophies were always considered by the best of the Platonists.

Mr. T. had not long entered on the study of Plato before he met with the works of Plotinus, which he read, we are told, with an insatiable avidity and the most rapturous delight, notwithstanding the obscurity of his diction, and the profundity of his conceptions. After having been well imbued in the doctrines of Plotinus, he betook himself to the six books of Proclus on the Theology of Plato, a work which he found to be so uncommonly abstruse, that he has been heard to say he did not thoroughly understand it till he had read it thrice over.

While he was engaged in the study of Proclus, who appears upon the whole to be of all the Platonists, Mr. T.'s greatest favourite, the celebrated Mrs. Wollstonecraft, and her friend Miss Blood, resided with our Philosopher for nearly three months. Mr. T. has been known to observe of Mrs. W. that during her stay with him, he thought her a very modest, sensible, and agreeable young lady; that she often heard him explain the doctrines of Plato, and was always pleased with his conversation on that subject; but confessed herself more inclined to an active than a contemplative life. She often too complimented him on the tranquillity of his manners, and used to call the little room which he made his study, "the abode of peace."

Mr. T. observed, that he afterwards called on her when she lived in George-street, and that he has there drunk wine with her out of a *tea cup*; Mrs. W. remarking at the time, that she did not give herself the trouble to think whether a wine-glass was not a necessary utensil in a house. He added, he has heard her say, that one of the conditions she should make previous to marriage, with the man she intended for her husband, would be this—that he should never presume to enter the room in which she was sitting, till he had first knocked at the door.

But to return from these eccentricities, which would not have been worthy of remark in a woman of less merit, to our Platonist. When Mr. T. had been nearly six years at the banking-house, he became so disgusted with the servility of the employment, and found his health so much impaired from the combination of severe bodily and mental efforts, added to an incurable disorder in the bladder, which he had laboured under for a long time, that he determined to emancipate himself, if possible, from slavery, and live by the exertion of his talents.

In order to effect this, he turned his attention to a subject which he had often thought on in the days of his youth, viz. the possibility of making a *perpetual lamp*; as he was convinced from Licetus[6] and Bishop Wilkins,[7] that such lamps had been constructed by the ancients. He began, therefore, to make some experiments with phosphorus, determining for a while to descend from mind to matter, and stoop in order to conquer. In the course of these experiments, he found that oil and salt boiled together, in a certain proportion, formed a fluid which, when phosphorus was immersed in it, both preserved and increased its splendor.

In consequence of this discovery, he exhibited at the Free Masons' tavern a specimen of phosphoric light, sufficient to read by at the distance of a yard; but the room in which this was shewn being small, and very warm from the weather and the number of persons that came to see it, the phosphorus caught fire, and thus raised a prejudice against the invention, which could never afterwards be removed. This exhibition, however, procured Mr. T. such friends[8] as at length enabled him to emancipate himself from the banker's, and procure subsistence for himself and his family by literary toil.

His first effort after this, to emerge from obscurity, was by composing twelve Lectures on the Platonic philosophy, at the request of Mr. Flaxman, the statuary, who had been one of the auditors of Mr. T.'s Lecture on Light, and who very benevolently

---

[6] [Fortunius Licetus (1577–1657), Italian physician and philosopher. In his *De motu sanguinis, origineque nervorum* . . . (Udine, 1647), he countered Harvey's theory of blood circulation with a bizarre theory of his own. Of his numerous writings, now of only historical interest, the best known is *De monstris* (3d edn., Amsterdam, 1665).]

[7] [John Wilkins, Bishop of Chester. One of the first members of the Royal Society and author of several books, including *Mathematical Magic*, which Taylor apparently knew well.]

[8] This, we are informed, was principally through the means of Mr. Geo. Cumberland, the author of several ingenious works. [See Plate 13.]

permitted him to read his Lectures in the largest room of his house. He likewise procured for him some very respectable auditors, such as Sir William Fordyce, the Hon. Mrs. Damer, Mrs. Cosway, Mr. Romney, &c. &c.[9] and was the means of his becoming acquainted with Mr. Bennet Langton,[10] well known for his great intimacy with the late Dr. Johnson.

To this gentleman he read his Platonic Lectures, with which Mr. L. was so much pleased, as likewise with the conversation and uncommon application which our Platonist had given to study, that he at length mentioned him to the king, under the appellation of *a gigantic reader*, in hopes that the rays of royal attention might be so strongly collected upon him as to dissipate the obscurity in which he was then involved, and give additional vigour and ardour to his pursuits. Mr. L., it seems, mentioned him thrice to his majesty, who was pleased to enquire after his family, and to express his admiration of Mr. T's. ardour and perseverance in the pursuit of knowledge, in a situation so unfavourable to its acquisition as that of a banker's clerk; but we do not find that this well-meant effort on the part of Mr. L. procured our Platonist any patronage from the throne.

About this time, Mr. T. became acquainted with Mr. William Meredith[11] of Harley-place, a circumstance which he justly considers as forming, by far, one of the most important and fortunate events of his life. This gentleman, as we are informed, in addition to an ample fortune, possesses a most elegant and liberal mind; and though concerned in a very extensive trade, has found

[9] [Sir William Fordyce, a distinguished and learned physician who wrote widely for medical journals and received a gold medal from the Society of Arts for a work on rhubarb; knighted in 1782. Mrs. John Damer (Anne Seymour), a well-known sculptor and an intimate of Horace Walpole, who left her his home at Strawberry Hill. Mrs. Maria Cosway, the wife of Richard Cosway, and like him a popular miniature painter. George Romney, the portrait painter; like Taylor, a warm friend of Flaxman.]

[10] [Bennet Langton, a great friend of Dr. Johnson, whom he succeeded as Professor of Ancient Literature at the Royal Academy in 1787.]

[11] [William Meredith, a wealthy business man and patron of the arts. His subsidies freed Taylor from uncongenial labor and made possible many of his publications.]

leisure for the study of the best English writers, and the best English translations of the works of the ancients. He became deeply enamoured with the doctrines of Plato, from reading Mr. Sydenham's translation of some of that philosopher's dialogues; and this fondness for Plato at length occasioned his attachment to Mr. Taylor.

We are happy in being able to assure the public on good authority, that under the very noble and singular patronage of this gentleman, and his brother Mr. George Meredith, Mr. T. was enabled to give the world his translation of "The Hymns of Orpheus," "The Commentaries of Proclus on Euclid," and "The Fable of Cupid and Psyche." The abilities of the latter of these gentlemen in the art he professes,[12] and his knowledge of the Gothic architecture, which he has displayed in many beautiful drawings, have seldom been equalled, and will rarely be excelled. We likewise do not in the least doubt but that Mr. T. in the course of his stormy life has experienced the liberality of these gentlemen upon occasions with which we are entirely unacquainted.

While Mr. T. was engaged, under the patronage of Messrs. W. and G. M. in translating and illustrating at his leisure hours the Commentaries of Proclus (for the principal part of his time was employed in teaching the Classics), the Marquis de Valady[13] took up his residence for three or four months at Mr. T.'s house. As the public have already been much gratified with anecdotes[14] of this singular character, and particularly with his adventures with Mr. T. we shall insert in addition to those, the following particulars, which our Platonist has been heard to mention respecting him.

The Marquis, who professed himself a rigid Pythagorean, under the notion that a community of possessions in *every thing*

[12] Architecture.
[13] [See W.E.A. Axon, below, p. 127n.]
[14] See "Biographical Anecdotes of the Founders of the French Republick," vol. I. [See p. 127n.]

was perfectly Pythagoric, often conversed with Mr. T. on this subject, and once asked him if he did not think it consistent with Pythagorean friendship for the wife of the married to be shared by the unmarried friend? The *hint was broad*, but Mr. T. thought proper not to take it; on the contrary, he severely reprobated the idea, as entirely foreign from that purity of conduct which forms the basis of the Pythagoric and Platonic philosophy.

He likewise once told Mr. T. that if he had a son, he should make him, as soon as he had the proper use of his limbs, climb a high tree every morning for his breakfast, and afterwards fling him into a river in order to learn him to swim.

Dining once at Mr. Bennet Langton's with Mr. T., Mr. (now Dr.) Burney,[15] and many other eminent scholars, he exclaimed to his friend, as soon as he left the house, "God keep me from Critics!" This was occasioned by a dispute which arose at that time respecting the propriety of the epithet *ocean stream*, which Mr. T. had made use of in his translation of one of the Orphic hymns. Mr. T. urged in his defence, that this epithet was employed by Homer, Hesiod and Plato. To this Dr. B. replied, that Homer indeed had the expression ωκεανον ποταμον, *the ocean-river*, but that a *river* was not a *stream*. Mr. T. then observed, that these words were considered as synonymous by no less poets than Milton and Sir John Denham. By Milton, when speaking of the leviathan (Paradise Lost, Book I), he says,

> *. . . or that sea beast*
> *Leviathan, whom God of all his works*
> *Created hugest, that swim th' ocean stream.*

And by Denham, in the first of those famous lines on the Thames:

> *O could I flow like thee, and make thy stream*
> *My great exemplar, as it is my theme.*

The genius of the Marquis seemed naturally inclined to war.

---

[15] [Charles Burney, a distinguished organist and musicologist, the father of Fanny Burney, whose *Evelina* and *Cecilia* were popular novels.]

Whenever he went to bed, he was heard to repeat as he was going upstairs, those animated lines of Neptune to the Greeks, from the Iliad by Pope:

> . . . *On dastards, dead to fame,*
> *I waste no anger, for they feel no shame!*

And if ever any one attempted to prove that modern warriors were equally heroic with the ancient ones, he would indignantly exclaim, in the words of Minerva to Tydides:

> *Such Tydeus was, and such his martial fire;*
> *Gods! how the son degenerates from the sire.*

We find that Mr. T. soon after the Marquis left him came into the possession of six or seven hundred pounds, in consequence of the death of a relation of his wife. A considerable part of this, it seems, Mr. T. spent in relieving the necessities of his own relations; but was not sufficiently a man of the world to know how to dispose of the remaining part of it to his own advantage. About five or six years after this, he again seems to have laboured under the pressure of want; to relieve which, with incredible diligence, he translated, and illustrated with copious introductions and some notes, five of the most abstruse of Plato's Dialogues, in the short space of about seven months; the copy of which he sold for no more than forty pounds!

After this, he wrote his "Dissertation on the Eleusinian and Bacchic Mysteries," in consequence of some considerable information on that subject which he had obtained from the perusal of three Greek manuscripts in the British Museum. One of these, it seems, is the Commentary of Proclus on the Parmenides of Plato, and is a folio volume consisting of upwards of five hundred pages. This with the other two, which are likewise folio volumes of no inconsiderable size, Mr. T. had the courage to copy for his own private use.

Shortly after this, he translated the Platonic Sallust "On the Gods and the World"; the "Pythagoric Sentences of Demophilus"; and Five Hymns of Proclus; likewise Two Orations of the Emperor Julian; and Five Books of Plotinus: all which, we are informed, he sold for no more than twenty pounds!

But the most labourious of all his undertakings, and for which he seems to have received less in proportion than for any of his other publications, was his translation of Pausanias. When this task was first proposed to Mr. T. by the bookseller, Mr. Samuel Patterson, well known to the literary world by several very ingenious publications, happening to be present, observed that "it was enough to break a man's heart." "O (replied the bookseller) nothing will break the heart of Mr. T.!" This Herculean labour our Platonist accomplished in the space of ten months, though the notes are of such an extent, and so full of uncommonly abstruse learning, that the composition of them might be supposed to have taken up a much longer time. For that arduous work, we almost blush to say, Mr. T. received no more than sixty pounds; and we are grieved to add, that his health was greatly injured by his excessive application on that occasion. We are indeed informed, that the debility of his body became so extreme after this, that at times he was incapable of any exertion; and what is singular, he has ever since been deprived of the use of his forefinger in writing.

Our Platonist, however, in a short time exhibited an indubitable proof that he possesses an ardour which neither toil can abate, embarrassments impede, nor even debility extinguish; and which, like gunpowder set on fire, seems to rise with renewed vigour, in proportion as it has been compressed. Notwithstanding the extreme lassitude of his whole bodily frame, and the difficulty with which he was able to write, he engaged, under the patronage of an anonymous gentleman of fortune,[16] to translate all those dialogues of Plato which have not been clothed in our native dress by Mr. Sydenham and others, together with his epistles, in order that by revising what has been already done, he might

[16] [Charles Howard, 11th Duke of Norfolk, 1746–1815, succeeded 1786, to whom Taylor's *Works of Plato* is dedicated; a Whig who lapsed from his Catholic faith in order to enter Parliament; F.R.S., 1767, F.S.A., 1779; patron of the arts and literature; President of the Society of Arts, 1794.]

give the whole of Plato to the world in an English garb. This great undertaking we understand he accomplished in the space of about two years; and the work now only waits for a liberal patronage to be made public.

Under the patronage too of the same gentleman, he has translated the greater part of Aristotle's Nichomachean Ethics, and at present we hear Messrs. W. and G. Meredith have engaged him to translate Aristotle's Metaphysics, of which he has already nearly accomplished the three first books.

We are likewise happy to inform the public, from good authority, that Thomas Brand Hollis, esq. has been for many years very much attached to our Platonist; that he frequently invites him to his table; and that he has always shewn himself active in promoting his welfare, though we are uncertain as to the time when Mr. T.'s intimacy with Mr. Hollis commenced.

We shall only add, that Mr. T. is at present assistant secretary to the Society for the Encouragement of Arts, Manufactures, and Commerce;[17] a situation which he obtained by a very considerable majority of votes, through the uncommon exertions of his friends; and that prior to this, some of them had procured him a situation in one of the public offices, to the fatigues of which finding his strength by no means adequate, and the employment appearing to him extremely servile, he relinquished it almost immediately after his nomination, and composed the following lines on the occasion:

> *To ev'ry power that reigns on high,*
> *Swifter than light my thanks shall fly,*
> *That, from the B——'s dark dungeons free,*
> *I once more hail sweet liberty.*
> *For sure, I ween, fate ne'er me doom'd*
> *To be 'midst sordid cares entomb'd,*
> *And vilely waste in groveling toil*
> *The mid-day blaze and midnight oil,*
> *To some poor darkling desk confin'd;*

[17] [See Plates 23, 24.]

Biographical Accounts

While the wing'd energies of mind
Oppress'd and crush'd, and vanquish'd lie,
And lose at length the power to fly.
*   A doom like this be his alone,*
To whom truth's charms were never known;
Who many sleepless nights has spent,
In schemes full fraught with cent. per cent.
The slave of av'rice, child of care,
And lost to all that's good and fair.

II

*THOMAS TAYLOR THE PLATONIST**

Thomas Taylor the Platonist has been variously judged.[1] "To strain human curiosity to the utmost limits of human credibility," says Isaac Disraeli, "a modern Plato has arisen in Mr. Thomas Taylor, who consonant to the Platonic Philosophy, religiously professes polytheism! At the close of the eighteenth century, be it recorded, were published many volumes in which the author affects to avow himself a zealous Platonist, and asserts that he can prove that the Christian religion is 'a bastardized and barbarous Platonism.' The divinities of Plato are the deities to be adored, and we are to be taught to call God, Jupiter; the Virgin, Venus; and Christ, Cupid! The Iliad of Homer, allegorized, is converted into a Greek Bible of the Arcana of Nature!"[2]

T. J. Mathias styles Taylor "the would-be restorer of unintelli-

---

* [The following account of Taylor's life is given in "Thomas Taylor the Platonist: a Biographical and Bibliographical Sketch," by W.E.A. Axon, published in *The Library* (July and August 1890), and reprinted for private circulation (London, 1890), very largely based on the article in *Public Characters*. See ms. letter reproduced in Plate 19. Axon's account continues the record of Taylor's life and death. The account has been slightly abridged.]

[1] The materials for the following sketch are in Allibone's *Dictionary of English Literature; An Annotated Catalogue of an Unique and Exceptionally Complete Set of the Works of Thomas Taylor, the Platonist*, by Orlin Mead Sandford, New York, 1885, also in *Book-Lore*, vols. 2 and 3; *The Antiquary*, August 1888 (by Edward Peacock); *The Survival of Paganism* (*Fraser's Magazine*, November 1875); Lowndes' *Bibliographer's Manual*, British Museum General Catalogue; Barker's *Literary Anecdotes; Public Characters*, 1798 (this is, if not autobiographical, evidently based on information supplied by the subject; there is a portrait of him, representing a rather ascetic but kindly face); Disraeli's *Curiosities of Literature*; Mathias' *Pursuits of Literature; Nouvelle Biographie Générale*, par Hoefer; *A Brief Notice of the Life of Mr. Thomas Taylor, the Celebrated Platonist, with a Catalogue of his Works*, London, 1831, signed J.J.W. [i.e., James Jacob Welsh].

[2] "Modern Platonism," *Curiosities of Literature* (New York and Boston, 1863), I, 295.

gible mysticism and superstitious pagan nonsense," and speaks of—

> *The hymns that Taylor, England's Gentile priest,*
> *Sung spousal at fair Psychè's marriage feast.*

Another critic, writing in *Blackwood's Magazine* in 1825, said, "The man is an ass, in the first place; secondly, he knows nothing of the religion of which he is so great a fool as to profess himself a votary; and thirdly, he knows less than nothing of the language about which he is continually writing."[3] De Quincey also had a poor opinion of him, yet read what Ralph Waldo Emerson, in his conversation with Wordsworth, has said:—"I told him it was not creditable that no one in all the country knew anything of Thomas Taylor, the Platonist, whilst in every American library his translations were found. I said, 'If Plato's Republic were published in England, as a new book, to-day, do you think it would find any readers?' He confessed it would not; 'and yet,' he added, after a pause, with that complacency which never deserts a true-born Englishman, 'and yet we have embodied it all.'"[4]

The singular and interesting man who is known to us as Taylor the Platonist was born in London in the year 1758, and his parents, we are told, were "obscure but worthy." His father was Joseph Taylor, staymaker, of Round Court, St. Martins-le-Grand, where the future Platonist was probably born.[5] He was a weakly child, and signs of consumption induced his family to send him into Staffordshire. He returned to the metropolis in his ninth year, and was admitted at St. Paul's School, April 10, 1767. His parents designed him for the Nonconformist ministry. His affection for philosophy, as distinguished from the mere verbal acquaintance with classics, was so marked that when an ethical or specially grand sentence occurred in an author he was construing, the surmaster, Mr. William Rider, would say, "Come,

---

[3] Quoted by Dr. Allibone.

[4] *Representative Men* (London, 1850), p. 39. See also pp. 18, 38, 40–44.

[5] Mr. Edward Peacock says that he was born May 15, 1758, in a street at or near Bunhill Fields, London (*Antiquary*, XVIII [1888], 1).

here is something worthy the attention of a philosopher." He early discovered critical powers which enabled him to notice and correct a blunder in the printing of a Latin Testament. He had now to disappoint his father, whose reverence for the ministerial office led him to regard it as "the most desirable and most enviable employment upon earth," and who was correspondingly troubled when he found that his talented son had no desire to occupy that office, and had so great a dislike to the public school teaching and languages—as it then was—that he begged to be taken home again. He had also been for a time a pupil of Mr. Worthington, the dissenting minister of Salter's Hall. Taylor was precocious in another direction, for his passion for the lady who was afterwards his wife began when he was only twelve years old.

At home young Taylor picked up a copy of Ward's *Young Mathematician's Guide*, and this gave him a turn for mathematics, in which he afterwards excelled, and to which he himself ascribed no small share of his success afterwards as a translator of Greek philosophy. Owing to his father's opposition his early studies in mathematics were pursued in hours stolen from rest, and he slept with a tinder-box under his pillow. He was sent at fifteen to work under an uncle-in-law at Sheerness Dockyard, but rather than endure this unpleasant situation he attempted to fall in with his father's views and became pupil to a dissenting minister. He studied Greek and Latin in the day, courted Miss Morton in the evening, and at night read Simson's *Conic Sections* in the Latin edition. His judgment on Newton, after reading the *Principia*, was that he was a great mathematician but no philosopher! Miss Morton's father intended his daughter for a richer man, but the young couple decided upon the immediate performance of the marriage ceremony, whilst postponing married life until the return of the bridegroom from Aberdeen University, where he was to finish his education. The stepmother[6] of Taylor found out the secret, and the young couple had a bad time of it. The bride's father was induced when dying to leave

[6] It is said to be the mother-in-law in the sketch in *Public Characters*, but the context seems to indicate that it was his father's wife.

any payments to her to the discretion of a relative whose fault was not that of open-handed liberality. For about a year the philosopher and his wife had only about seven shillings a week on which to live. Taylor obtained a situation as usher, and was only able to see his wife upon the Saturday afternoon. He next obtained a position in Lubbock's Bank at a salary of fifty pounds, paid quarterly, and endured great privations from want of money, so that frequently from want of food he would be in a fainting condition on reaching home. Even under these discouraging circumstances Taylor did not neglect study, and turned his mind to the unprofitable consideration of Becher's *Physica Subterranea* and quadrature of the circle. His first essay, a quarto pamphlet, entitled *A New Method of Reasoning in Geometry*, bears upon the last-named subject, and its substance is reproduced in a note to his translation of Proclus *On Euclid*. A passage in Sir Kenelm Digby sent him to the writings of Aristotle, and he was soon able to read him in the original. He used to say himself that he learned Greek rather through the Greek philosophy than the Greek philosophy through Greek. The earnest student was always engaged at the bank until seven and often until ten, and in order to continue his abstract researches seldom went to bed until two or three o'clock in the morning. He had that power of abstraction from the common cares of life that is indispensable for successful thinking. The fact that he was accurate and "business-like" in his employment did not in the least prevent him from digesting, whilst walking about delivering the bills of the bank, that which he had read in Aristotle and his interpreters. He paid great attention to the commentaries upon Aristotle. He next proceeded to study Plato with equal or greater avidity. In this new path he soon came upon Plotinus and Proclus, whose dissertation on the theology of Plato he found so profound that it was not until he had thrice read it over that he thoroughly comprehended its abstruse matter.

Whilst engaged with Proclus he had residing in his house Mary Wollstonecraft and her friend Miss Blood. Their three months' company was mutually agreeable. The lady listened attentively to his explanations of Plato, called his study the "Abode of Peace," but avowed her preference for an active, rather than a contemplative, life. He called upon her when she lived in George Street, and there drank wine with her out of a *tea-cup*; Mrs. Wollstonecraft observed at the time, that she did not give herself the trouble to think whether a glass was a necessary utensil in a house. He has also heard her say that one of the conditions she should make previous to marriage, with the man she intended for her husband, would be this—that he should never presume to enter the room in which she was sitting, till he had first knocked at the door.

After six years at the bank, the drudgery proved too much, even for the philosophic spirit of Taylor. Nights of arduous study following days of uncongenial employment had injured his health. He had a notion that a perpetual lamp might be made, and he gave an exhibition of his invention at the "Freemasons' Tavern." He found that oil and salt boiled formed a fluid vehicle, which when phosphorus was immersed in it, both preserved and increased the splendour of light. Unfortunately, at the exhibition the phosphorus took fire, "and thus raised a prejudice against the invention which could never afterwards be removed." The failure was not, however, without result, for it attracted the attention of Mr. George Cumberland, who, with other friends, enabled Taylor to leave the bank "and procure subsistence for himself and his family by literary toil"—but of what nature is not stated. Flaxman, the sculptor, induced him to write twelve lectures on the "Platonic Philosophy," which were read at the artist's house, where he had amongst his auditors Sir William Fordyce, the Hon. Mrs. Damer, Mrs. Cosway, Mr. Romney and others. Flaxman also introduced him to Bennet Langton, who thrice mentioned him to the king as "a gigantic reader." George III expressed his admiration of Taylor's ability and industry, but did not take any further notice of his Platonic subject. But if royalty was not liberal another patron arose. A wealthy man, Mr. William Meredith, of Harley Place, who had become acquainted with Plato in the fine translation of Sydenham, took him by the hand, and enabled him to print his translations of the *Hymns of*

Orpheus, the *Commentaries of Proclus on Euclid,* and the *Fable of Cupid and Psyche.* In William Meredith and his brother George, who was one of the architects who early studied Gothic, Taylor had liberal and sympathetic friends.

It was at this period that the Marquis de Valady lodged with Taylor. The extraordinary letter in which the marquis introduced himself is dated "12 Xbre 1788, vulg. aera," was printed by Taylor, and is quoted in *Fraser's Magazine* (Nov. 1875). The Frenchman professed to be a Pythagorean, and thought that the philosophic doctrine of community should be extended to the conjugal relations. He asked the English Pythagorean's opinion; but Taylor severely condemned the loose morality of the suggestion.[7]

Taylor had the true literary dislike of critics. Dining once at

[7] There is a biographical sketch of J.G.C.S.X.J.J. Izarn de Valady in the *Lives of the Remarkable Characters of the French Revolution,* and it is limned in very dark colours. "The persons to whom he was known assert with him madness was the result of immorality, not immorality the result of madness." He acted with the Girondins, and was arrested at Périgueux, and condemned to death, December 5, 1794.

[Mrs. Louise Schutz Boas in *Notes and Queries* (forthcoming) gives her reasons for supposing Taylor himself to be the author of this article, which contains letters from the Marquis de Valady to Taylor, to which only their recipient could have had access. She has identified the anonymous editor of this work as Richard (afterward Sir Richard) Phillips, through the preface to the first edition dated from Phillips's Bookshop, 71 St. Paul's Churchyard. Phillips was a friend of Taylor, and, like him, a vegetarian. Taylor did many pieces of hackwork of this kind, and according to Mrs. Boas is also the author of an unsigned article on the Eleventh Duke of Norfolk (in *Public Characters of 1798*), which concludes with a reference to the Duke's patronage of a scholar, clearly Taylor himself, and of one on Porson (in a later volume) which is written in a distinctly ironic tone. Mrs. Boas believes on good internal evidence that Mary Wollstonecraft wrote the article on Madame Roland.

Taylor himself was, like Plato, a supporter of an aristocratic government and the caste system as interpreted by Plato in his *Republic*; but as an anticlerical he found himself necessarily among many of the liberals and revolutionaries of the time. In France esotericism and social subversion went together, as is well known; and it was natural for the Marquis de Valady, a compatriot of Saint-Martin, to address himself to the English Pythagorean in terms of admiration, as the English counterpart of a French group whose political sympathies were the very reverse of those of Taylor.]

Mr. Bennet Langton's, with Dr. Burney and other eminent scholars, he exclaimed to his friend, as soon as he left the house, "God keep me from critics!" . . .

Under the encouragement of an anonymous patron[8] Taylor undertook to translate all the Platonic dialogues that had not been turned into English by Mr. Sydenham. For this purpose he visited the Bodleian at Oxford in 1797, and was "handsomely treated" by the University. The Merediths engaged him to translate Aristotle's *Metaphysics*.[9] Mr. Thomas Brand Hollis was another of his friends.

The elder Disraeli wrote a now-forgotten novel entitled *Vaurien* which appeared anonymously in 1797. In this there is a satirical sketch of the Platonist. It is not easy to select passages from it sufficiently brief and unobjectionable. Vaurien waits in conversation with the wife of the Platonist until he has completed his morning worship: "By this time the Platonist had concluded his long hymn to Apollo. Vaurien now ascended with difficulty. At the bottom of the stairs was a large kennel of dogs of various nations, who lived in a good understanding with each other, excepting when a bone was thrown among them, for then the dogs behaved like men, that is, they mangled and tore each other to pieces with sagacity and without remorse. Monkeys and apes were chained on the banisters. A little republic of cats was peaceably established on the first landing place. He passed through one room which was an aviary and another which was an apiary. From the ceiling of the study of the Platonist, depended a polished globe of silvered glass, which strongly reflected the beams of the sun. Amidst this aching splendour sat the Platonist, changing his seat with the motions of his god, so that in the course of the day he and the sun went regularly round the apartment. He was occupied in constructing a magic lanthorn, which puerile amusement excited the surprise of Vaurien."

[8] [The 11th Duke of Norfolk; see above, pp. 119n and 127n.]

[9] Mr. Peacock states that the translations of Aristotle were published at the expense of the Duke of Norfolk. ["This is incorrect."—written in an old-fashioned hand in K. Raine's copy.]

The Platonist accounted for it. "My dissertation on the Eleusinian mysteries is not all understood. The whole machinery, reflected on a white sheet, will be more intelligible than any I could give on a sheet of paper. In the presence of the gods, in the most holy of the mysteries, daemons appeared with the heads of dogs; Pletho says this, who lived a thousand years after the mysteries. Then I have 'omniform and terrific monsters'; then the demiurgus, the progress of purgation, inspection, crowning, torch-bearing, and, finally, friendship with the gods. But here is the great difficulty. How shall I represent 'the intolerable effulgence of the divine light'? Much it grieves me, that for this sublime purpose a candle and a piece of coloured tin are all I can get into the lanthorn. The gods are not always favourable to my attempts. After long experiments, I conceived I had discovered the perpetual sepulchral lamp of the ancients. Last week I invited my friends to a philosophical lecture on my perpetual lamp; I triumphed in my discovery; but ere my lecture closed my lamp was suddenly extinguished. Good Gods!"[10]

After more, which is best left untouched, we read:

"Vaurien having felicitated the Platonist on the new world he had opened to himself, said, 'You propose to overturn Christianity by the publications of the Platonists, and to erect a Pantheon, that the gods may be honourably reverenced.'

" 'That is my important pursuit; I have already prepared the soaring and ecstatic Olympiodorus, the noble and obscure Heraclitus; I join the Asiatic luxuriancy of Proclus, divinely explained by Jamblichus, and profoundly delivered by Plotinus. Plotinus, who was surnamed "Intellect" by his contemporaries, such was the fervour of his mind, that he was accustomed to write without attending to the orthography or the revision of his works, which perhaps occasions their divine unintelligibility; for the celestial vigour rendered him incapable of trifling concerns, and he therefore committed them, as fast as he wrote, to Porphyry, who, perhaps labouring under the same divine influence, was equally incapable of orthography or sense.' " The Platonist con-

[10] Vol. II, p. 192.

cluded this conversation with an invective, of which the style appears to us so curious that we shall give the exact expressions, as a specimen of the Platonic effervescence in a Ciceronian period:

" 'I have long perceived the ignorance and malevolence of Christian priests, from the most early fathers to the most modern retailers of hypocrisy and cant; every intelligent reader must be alternately excited to grief and indignation, to pity and contempt, at the barbarous mythological systems of the moderns; for in these we meet with nothing but folly and delusion, opinions founded either on fanaticism or atheism, inconceivably absurd, and inextricably obscure, ridiculously vain, and monstrously deformed, stupidly dull, and contemptibly zealous, apostolically delirious, or historically dry, and, in one word, such only as arrogance and ignorance could conceive, impiety propagate, and the vapid spirit of the moderns be induced to admit.'

" 'My dear Platonist,' exclaimed Vaurien, 'if you can roll periods like these, your genius will be rewarded by yourself being chosen by the nation to lay the first stone of a Pantheon in London, for "the ascent of excellent daemons".' "[11]

There is nothing to show that Disraeli was personally acquainted with Taylor the Platonist, and the sketch in *Vaurien* is too obviously caricatured to be worthy of much attention.

Taylor, after leaving the bank, "had a place in one of the public offices, to the fatigues of which, finding his strength by no means adequate, and the employment appearing to him at the same time extremely servile, he relinquished it almost immediately after his nomination," and composed the following lines on the occasion. . . .[12]

Mr. Taylor finally, by the influence of his friends, was appointed assistant secretary of the Society of Arts.

Amongst Taylor's friends was Thomas Love Peacock, whose granddaughter says:—"My grandfather's friends were especially Mr. Macgregor Laird and Mr. Coulson, also the two Smiths of the 'Rejected Addresses'; Barry Cornwall (Mr. Procter), and a re-

[11] Vol. II, p. 213.
[12] [For the verses, see above, pp. 120–21.]

markable man, Mr. Thomas Taylor, of Norwich, commonly
called 'Pagan Taylor,' who always addressed grandpapa as
'Greeky Peeky'; he sacrificed lambs in his lodgings to the 'immortal gods,' and 'poured out libations to Jupiter,' until his
landlord threatened to turn him out; hence his nickname of
'Pagan.' "[13]

It is rather amusing here to see Thomas Taylor confounded
with Taylor of Norwich, as on other occasions he has been confounded with Robert Taylor, the Devil's Chaplain, and even with
Isaac Taylor! The origin of the story about the sacrifice, which
has more than once been taken seriously, was probably no more
than a good-natured jest.[14]

Thomas Taylor died at his residence at Walworth, November
1, 1835. The cause of death was a disease of the bladder, borne
with stoical resignation. Some days before his death he asked if
a comet had appeared, and being answered in the affirmative,
said, "Then I shall die; I was born with it and shall die with it."

He was buried in Walworth churchyard, but no stone marks
the spot, and the resting place of the Platonist is unknown.[15] He
was an enthusiast, and only an enthusiast could have done his
work. His translations represent a side of Greek thought that

[13] [Macgregor Laird (1808–1861), a London merchant, African explorer,
and prolific writer who sought to extinguish slavery in Africa; Walter
Coulson (1794–1860), a lawyer, newspaper editor, and "prodigy of knowledge" who lived on intimate terms with the chief men of letters in London;
the two Smiths (Horatio, 1779–1849, and James, 1775–1839), wits and
young men about town who reached the pinnacle of success with a series of
"Rejected Addresses" (1812), actually parodies of popular poets conceived
as imaginary addresses to be submitted in competition for a prize at opening of the Drury Lane Theatre; Bryan Cornwall Proctor (1787–1874), a
minor poet and playwright (under pseudonym of Barry Cornwall) who was
intimate with London's literati and established (in 1820) the *London
Magazine*; William (not Thomas) Taylor of Norwich (1765–1836), an
enthusiastic student of German literature who was well known for his
translations of Lessing's *Nathan*, Goethe's *Iphigenia*, and especially Bürger's
Lenore.]

[14] [A chronological list of Taylor's publications has been omitted. Its substance is included in the Bibliography at the end of this volume.]

[15] *Notes and Queries*, 7th S., IX, 194.

but for him would be unrepresented in English literature. The sneers at his command of Greek are evidently absurd, for surely no man's mind was ever more thoroughly suffused with the very essence of Neoplatonism. Whatever failure he may have made in unessential details would be more than compensated by the fidelity with which his sympathetic mind reproduced the spirit of the Pythagorean philosophers with whom he dwelt—apart from the noise and turmoil of the age in which he had been cast. His books remain a mighty monument of disinterested devotion to philosophic study. They were produced without regard to, and hopeless of, profit. They are not addressed to popular instincts, and there is no attempt made to give them clearness of style or to present their thoughts in an attractive fashion. The gold that was in them the Platonist thought deserved the trouble of toilsome digging.

The life of Thomas Taylor the Platonist is one which will receive a tribute of admiration from the thoughtful. However much of an anachronism a Pagan philosopher may seem in the London of the nineteenth century of Christianity, it must be acknowledged that a man who devotes himself to poverty and study in an age and country famous for the pursuit of wealth; who has the courage to adopt and the sincerity to avow opinions that are contrary to every prejudice of the time; who runs the risk of persecution and imprisonment; a man who "scorns delights and lives laborious days," is entitled to our admiration and respect. And such was Thomas Taylor the Platonist, whose name should be remembered by all friends of learning and freedom of thought.

III

A BRIEF NOTICE OF MR. THOMAS TAYLOR
*THE CELEBRATED PLATONIST**

Mr. Taylor has nothing remarkable in his exterior; he is of the middle size, well-proportioned, and firmly put together; his countenance is regular, open, and benevolent. There is a dignified simplicity and unaffected frankness of manner about him which are sure to win the affections of all who have the pleasure of seeing him. In his dress he is simple and unpretending; in his conduct irreproachable. Among friends, he is unreserved and sincere; a determined foe to falsehood; and always ready to make sacrifices, when the end to be obtained is worthy of a noble mind. I verily believe, that no man had ever a more passionate love of virtue, a loftier aspiration after truth, or a more vehement zeal for its diffusion. His manners, as already hinted, are peculiarly soft and graceful, alike destitute of pride, haughtiness, or vanity, which, together with his venerable appearance, never fail to inspire both love and reverence. Being gifted with a very extraordinary memory, he is not only enabled to retain the immense stores of knowledge, which, in the course of a long life, assiduously devoted to study, he has amassed, but to bring them into complete action at his will. Such is the comprehension and vigor of his mind, that it can embrace the most extensive and difficult subjects—such the clearness of his conception, that it enables him to contemplate a long and intricate series of argument with distinctness, and to express it with precision. An acute observer of men and manners, he possesses an inexhaustible fund of anecdote, so that the flow of his familiar chat, the cheerfulness of his disposition, and his easy communicativeness, are as attractive as his mental faculties are commanding. Very rarely has an understand-

---

* [A contemporary account of Taylor in his later life given by "J.J.W." (James Jacob Welsh) in *A Brief Notice of Mr Thomas Taylor the Celebrated Platonist with a Complete List of His Published Works* (London, 1831), reprinted in the *Philobiblion*, II (1863), 151–58.]

ing of such strength and comprehension been found united with a heart so pure and ingenuous. "Nihil unquam produxit rerum natura, aut pudentius, aut prudentius, aut candidius, aut benignius."[1] I have the honor to know him most intimately, and can truly say, that his whole conduct is in perfect harmony with the principles of his sublime philosophy, that his every thought is in accordance with the whole tenor of his blameless life; and that his intentions are wholly unsullied by views of personal interest. I could adduce many splendid instances of his great disinterestedness and singularly amiable disposition; but "on ne cherche point à prouver la lumière."

[1] Erasmus, Epist. 14. lib. 4. p. 286.

CONCERNING THE BEAUTIFUL

or, A Paraphrase Translation from the Greek of Plotinus,
Ennead I, Book VI

Slight as it is, *Concerning the Beautiful* (London, 1787) is an important volume in Taylor's battle against "barbarous ignorance." In the Introduction he states a position from which he never swerved: "modern pursuits" have little concern with wisdom. Like William Blake, Taylor insists that the "search . . . to detect the atoms of Democritus" is "ridiculous in the extreme." Although Taylor had published nothing significant before 1787, he was already well known among the intelligentsia of London, having conducted an experiment with a perpetual lamp and given "twelve lectures on the Platonic philosophy" at the home of John Flaxman. *Concerning the Beautiful* received substantial notices in the *Critical Review*, LXIV (1787), 286–88, and the *Monthly Review*, LXXIX (1788), 142–44, and it was reissued in 1792 as *An Essay on the Beautiful*.

INTRODUCTION

IT MAY SEEM WONDERFUL that language, which is the only method of conveying our conceptions, should, at the same time, be a hindrance to our advancement in philosophy: but the wonder ceases when we consider, that it is seldom studied as the vehicle of truth, but is too frequently esteemed for its own sake, independent of its connection with things. This observation is remarkably verified in the Greek Language; which as it is the only repository of ancient wisdom, has, unfortunately for us, been the means of concealing, in shameful obscurity, the most profound researches and the sublimest truths. That words, indeed, are no otherwise valuable than as subservient to things, must surely be acknowledged by every liberal mind, and will alone be disputed by him who has spent the prime of his life, and consumed the vigour of his understanding, in verbal criticisms and grammatical trifles. And, if this is the case, every lover of truth will only study a language for the purpose of procuring the wisdom it contains; and will doubtless wish to make his native language the vehicle of it to others. For, since all truth is eternal, its nature can never be altered by transposition, though, by this means, its dress may be varied, and become less elegant and refined. Perhaps, even this inconvenience may be remedied by sedulous cultivation; at least, the particular inability of some ought not to discourage the well-meant endeavours of others. Whoever reads the lives of the ancient Heroes of Philosophy must be convinced that they studied things more than words, and that Truth alone was the ultimate object of their search: and, he who wishes to emulate their glory, and participate their wisdom, will study their doctrines more than their language, and value the depth of their understandings far beyond the elegance of their composition. The native charms of Truth will ever be sufficient to allure the truly philosophic mind; and he who has once discovered her retreats will surely endeavour to fix a mark by which they may be detected by others.

But, though the mischief arising from the study of words is prodigious, we must not consider it as the only cause of darkening the splendors of truth, and obstructing the free diffusion of her light. Different manners and philosophies have equally contributed to banish the goddess from our realms, and to render our eyes offended with her celestial light. Hence we must not wonder, that, being indignant at the change, and perceiving the empire of ignorance rising to unbounded dominion, she has retired from the spreading darkness, and concealed herself in the tranquil and divinely lucid regions of mind. For, we need but barely survey modern pursuits to be convinced how little they are connected with wisdom. Since, to describe the nature of some particular place, the form, situation, and magnitude of a certain city; to trace the windings of a river to its source, or delineate the aspect of a pleasant mountain; to calculate the fineness of the silk-worm's threads, and arrange the gaudy colours of butterflies; in short, to pursue matter through its infinite divisions and wander in its dark labyrinths is the employment of the philosophy in vogue. But surely the energies of intellect are more worthy our concern than the operations of sense; and the science of universals, permanent and fixt, must be superior to the knowledge of particulars, fleeting and frail. Where is a sensible object to be found, which abides for a moment the same; which is not either rising to perfection, or verging to decay; which is not mixed and confused with its contrary; whose flowing nature no resistance can stop, nor any art confine? Where is the Chemist, who, by the most accurate analysation, can arrive at the principles of bodies; or who, though he might be so lucky in his search as to detect the atoms of Democritus, could by this means give respite to mental investigation? For every atom, since endued with figure, must consist of parts, though indissolubly cemented together; and the immediate cause of this cement must be something incorporeal, or knowledge can have no stability, and enquiry no end. Where, says Mr. Harris,[1] is the microscope which can discern

[1] [James Harris, a wealthy country gentleman and member of Parliament, was well known for a "singular and learned work" entitled *Hermes, or a Philosophical Inquiry Concerning Universal Grammar*.]

what is smallest in nature? Where the telescope, which can see at what point in the universe wisdom first began? Since then there is no portion of matter which may not be the subject of experiments without end, let us betake ourselves to the regions of mind, where all things are bounded in intellectual measure; where every thing is permanent and beautiful, eternal and divine. Let us quit the study of particulars, for that which is general and comprehensive, and, through this, learn to see and recognize whatever exists.

With a view to this desirable end, I have presented the reader with a specimen of that sublime wisdom which first arose in the colleges of the Egyptian priests, and flourished afterwards in Greece. Which was there cultivated by Pythagoras, under the mysterious veil of numbers; by Plato, in the graceful dress of poetry; and was systematized by Aristotle, as far as it could be reduced into scientific order. Which, after becoming in a manner extinct, shone again with its pristine splendor, among the philosophers of the Alexandrian school; was learnedly illustrated, with Asiatic luxuriancy of style by Proclus; was divinely explained by Iamblichus; and profoundly delivered in the writings of Plotinus. Indeed, the works of this last philosopher are particularly valuable to all who desire to penetrate into the depths of this divine wisdom. From the exalted nature of his genius, he was called Intellect by his contemporaries; and is said to have composed his books under the influence of divine illumination. Porphyry relates, in his Life, that he was four times united, by an ineffable energy, with the divinity; which, however such an account may be ridiculed in the present age, will be credited by every one who has properly explored the profundity of his mind. The facility and vehemence of his composition was such, that when he had once conceived a subject, he wrote as from an internal pattern, without paying much attention to the orthography, or reviewing what he had written: for, the celestial vigour of his intellect rendered him incapable of trifling concerns; and, in this respect, inferior to common understandings; as the eagle, which, in its bold flight, pierces the clouds, skims the surface of the earth with less rapidity than the swallow. Indeed, a minute attention to trifles is inconsistent with great genius of every kind; and it is on this account, that retirement is so absolutely necessary to the discovery of truths of the first dignity and importance; for how is it possible to mix much with the world, without imbibing the false and puerile conceptions of the multitude; and, without losing that true elevation of soul, which comparatively despises every mortal concern. Plotinus, therefore, conscious of the incorrectness of his writings, arising from the rapidity, exuberance, and daring sublimity of his thoughts, committed their revision to his disciple Porphyry; who, though inferior in depth of thought to his master, was, on account of his extraordinary abilities, called by way of eminence, the Philosopher.

The design of the following discourse is to bring us to the perception of the beautiful itself, even while connected with a corporeal nature, which must be the great end of all true philosophy, and which Plotinus happily obtained. To a genius, indeed, truly modern, with whom the crucible and the air-pump are alone the standards of truth, such an attempt must appear ridiculous in the extreme. With these, nothing is real but what the hand can grasp, or the corporeal eye perceive: and nothing useful but what pampers the appetite, or fills the purse: but, unfortunately their perceptions, like Homer's frail dreams, pass through the ivory gate; and are, consequently, empty and fallacious, and contain nothing belonging to the vigilant soul. To such as these, a treatise on the Beautiful cannot be addressed: since its object is too exalted to be approached by those engaged in the impurities of sense, and too bright to be seen by the eye accustomed to the obscurity of corporeal vision. But it is alone proper to him, who is sensible that his soul is strongly marked with ruin by its union with body; who considers himself in the language of Empedocles, as

Heaven's exile, straying from the orb of light;

and who so ardently longs for a return to his true country, that to him, as to Ulysses, when fighting for Ithaca,

Concerning the Beautiful

Slow seems the sun to move, the hours to roll;
His native home deep-imag'd in his soul.[2]

But here it is requisite to observe, that our ascent to this region of Beauty must be made by gradual advances: for, from our association with matter, it is impossible to pass directly, and without a medium, to such transcendent perfection; but we must proceed in a manner similar to those who pass from darkness to the brightest light, by advancing from places moderately enlightened to such as are the most luminous of all. It is necessary, therefore, that we should become very familiar with the most abstract contemplations; and that our intellectual eye should be strongly irradiated with the light of ideas which precedes the splendors of the beautiful itself, like the brightness which is seen on the summit of mountains, previous to the rising of the sun. Nor ought it to seem strange, if it should be some time before even the liberal soul can recognize the beautiful progeny of intellect as its kindred and allies: for, from its union with body, it has drank deep of the cup of oblivion, and all its energetic powers are stupefied by the intoxicating draught. So that the intelligible world, on its first appearance, is utterly unknown by us, and our recollection of its inhabitants, entirely lost: and we become similar to Ulysses on his first entrance into Ithaca, of whom Homer says,

> *Yet had his mind, thro' tedious absence, lost*
> *The dear remembrance of his native coast.*[3]

For,

> *Now all the land another prospect bore,*
> *Another port appear'd, another shore,*
> *And long continued ways, and winding floods,*
> *And unknown mountains crown'd with unknown*
> *woods:*

[2] Pope's Homer's Odyssey, book xiii. ver. 37.
[3] Odyssey, book xiii. ver. 223.

until the goddess of wisdom purges our eyes from the mists of sense, and says to each of us, as she did to Ulysses,

> *Now lift thy longing eyes, while I restore,*
> *The pleasing prospect of thy native shore.*[3a]

For then will

> *. . . the prospect clear,*
> *The mists disperse, and all the coast appear.*

Let us then humbly supplicate the irradiations of wisdom, and follow Plotinus as our divine guide to the beatific vision of the Beautiful itself: for, in this alone can we find perfect repose, and repair those destructive clefts and chinks of the soul which its departure from the light of good and its lapse into a corporeal nature have introduced.

But, before I conclude, I think it necessary to caution the reader not to mix any modern enthusiastic opinions with the doctrines contained in the following discourse: for there is not a greater difference between substance and shade than between ancient and modern enthusiasm. The object of the former was the highest good and the supreme beauty; but that of the latter is nothing more than a phantom raised by bewildered imaginations, floating on the unstable ocean of opinion, the sport of the waves of prejudice, and blown about by the breath of factious party. Like substance and shade, indeed, they possess a similitude in outward appearance, but in reality they are perfect contraries; for the one fills the mind with solid and durable good; but the other with empty delusions; which, like the ever running waters of the Danaides, glide away as fast as they enter, and leave nothing behind but the ruinous passages through which they flowed.

I only add, that the ensuing treatise is designed as a specimen (if it should meet with encouragement) of my intended mode of publishing all the works of Plotinus. The undertaking is, I am sensible, arduous in the extreme, and the disciples of wisdom are unfortunately few: but, as I desire no other reward of my

[3a] [See Plate 18 and p. 297.]

labour than to have the expence of printing defrayed, and to see Truth propagated in my native tongue; I hope those few will enable me to obtain the completion of my desires.

For then, to adopt the words of Ulysses,

> *That view vouchsaf'd, let instant death surprise,*
> *With ever-during shade these happy eyes!*[4]

[4] Odyssey, book vii. ver. 303.

CONCERNING THE BEAUTIFUL

BEAUTY,[1] for the most part, consists in objects of sight: but it is also received through the ears, by the skilful composition of words, and the consonant proportions of sounds; for in every species of harmony, beauty is to be found. And if we rise from sense into the regions of soul, we shall there perceive studies and offices, actions and habits, sciences and virtues, invested with a much larger portion of beauty. But whether there is, above these, a still higher beauty, will appear as we advance in its investigation. What is it then, which causes bodies to appear fair to the sight, sounds beautiful to the ear, and science and virtue lovely to the mind? May we not enquire after what manner they all partake of beauty? Whether beauty is one and the same in all? Or, whether the beauty of bodies is of one kind, and the beauty of souls of another? And again, what these are, if they are two? Or, what beauty is, if perfectly simple, and one? For some things, as bodies, are doubtless beautiful, not from the nature of the subjects in which they reside, but rather by some kind of participation: but others again appear to be essentially beautiful, or beauties themselves; and such is the nature of virtue. For, with respect to the same bodies, they appear beautiful to one person, and the reverse of beauty to another; as if the essence of body were a thing different from the essence of beauty. In the first place, then, what is that which, by its presence, causes the beauty of bodies? Let us

[1] It is necessary to inform the Platonical reader, that the Beautiful, in the present discourse, is considered according to its most general acceptation, as the same with the Good: though, according to a more accurate distinction, as Plotinus himself informs us, the Good is considered as the fountain and principle of the Beautiful. I think it likewise proper to observe, that as I have endeavoured, by my paraphrase, to render as much as possible the obscure parts evident, and to expand those sentences which are so very much contracted in the original, I shall be sparing of notes; for my design is not to accommodate the sublimest truths to the meanest understandings (as this would be a contemptible and useless prostitution), but to render them perspicuous to truly liberal and philosophic minds. My reasons for adopting this mode of paraphrase may be seen in the preface to my translation of Orpheus's Hymns.

reflect, what most powerfully attracts the eyes of beholders, and seizes the spectator with rapturous delight: for if we can find what this is, we may perhaps use it as a ladder, enabling us to ascend into the region of beauty, and survey its immeasurable extent.

It is the general opinion, that a certain commensuration of parts to each other, and to the whole, with the addition of colour, generates that beauty which is the object of sight: and that in the commensurate and the moderate alone, the beauty of every thing consists. But from such an opinion, the compound only, and not the simple, can be beautiful; the single parts will have no peculiar beauty; and will only merit that appellation by conferring to the beauty of the whole. But it is surely necessary, that a lovely whole should consist of beautiful parts; for the fair can never rise out of the deformed. But from such a definition, it follows, that beautiful colours, and the light of the sun, since they are simple, and do not receive their beauty from commensuration, must be excluded the regions of beauty. Besides, how, from such an hypothesis, can gold be beautiful? Or the glittering of night, and the glorious spectacle of the stars? In like manner the most simple musical sounds will be foreign from beauty; though, in a song wholly beautiful, every note must be beautiful, as necessary to the being of the whole. Again, since the same proportion remaining, the same face is to one person beautiful, and to another the reverse, is it not necessary to call the beauty of the commensurate one kind of beauty, and the commensuration another kind; and that the commensurate is fair, by means of something else? But, if transferring themselves to beautiful studies, and fair discourses, they shall assign as the cause of beauty in these, the proportion of measure; what is that which, in beautiful sciences, laws, or disciplines, is called commensurate proportion? Or, in which manner can speculations themselves be called mutually commensurate? If it be said, because of the inherent concord; we reply, that there is a certain concord and consent in evil souls, a conformity of sentiment, in believing (as it is said) that temperance is folly, and justice generous ignorance. It appears, therefore, that the beauty of the soul is every virtue; and this species of the beautiful possesses far greater reality than any of the superior we have mentioned. But, after what manner in this is commensuration to be found? For it is neither like the symmetry in magnitude, or in numbers. And since the parts of the soul are many, in what proportion and synthesis, in what temperament of parts, or concord of speculations, does beauty consist? Lastly, of what kind is the beauty of intellect itself, abstracted from every corporeal concern, and intimately conversing with itself alone?

We still, therefore, repeat the question, what is the beauty of bodies? It is something which, at first view, presents itself to sense; and which the soul familiarly apprehends, and eagerly embraces, as if it were allied to itself. But when it meets with the deformed, it hastily starts from the view, and retires abhorrent from its discordant nature. For since the soul in its proper state ranks according to the most excellent essence in the order of things, when it perceives any object related to itself, or the mere vestige of a relation, it congratulates itself on the pleasing event, and astonished with the striking resemblance, enters deep into its essence,[2] and, by rousing its dormant powers, at length perfectly

[2] The Platonic philosophy insists much on the necessity of retiring into ourselves in order to the discovery of truth: and on this account, Socrates, in the first Alcibiades, says, that the soul entering into herself will contemplate whatever exists, and the divinity himself. Upon which Proclus thus comments, with his usual elegance and depth, (in Theol. Plat. p. 7.) "For the soul (says he) contracting herself wholly into a union with herself, and into the centre of universal life, and removing the multitude and variety of all-various powers, ascends into the highest ($\pi\epsilon\rho\iota\omega\pi\dot{\eta}$) place of speculation, from whence she will survey the nature of beings. For if she looks back upon things posterior to her essence, she will perceive nothing but the shadows and resemblances of beings: but if she returns into herself, she will evolve her own essence, and the reasons she contains. And at first indeed she will as it were only behold herself; but when by her knowledge she penetrates more profoundly in her investigations, she will find intellect seated in her essence, and the universal orders of beings: but when she advances into the more interior recesses of herself, and as it were into the sanctuary of the soul, she will be enabled to contemplate, with her eyes closed to corporeal vision, the genus of the gods, and the unities of beings. For all things reside in us, ($\psi\upsilon\chi\iota\kappa\hat{\omega}\varsigma$) after a manner

recollects its kindred and allies. What is the similitude then between the beauties of sense, and that beauty which is divine? For if there be any similitude, the respective objects must be similar. But after what manner are the two beautiful? For it is by participation of species that we call every sensible object beautiful. Thus, since every thing void of form is by nature fitted for its reception, as far as it is destitute of reason and form, it is base, and separate from the divine reason, the great fountain of forms; and whatever is entirely remote from this immortal source is perfectly safe, and deformed. And such is matter,[3] which by

---

correspondent to the nature of the soul: and on this account we are naturally enabled to know all things, by exciting our inherent powers, and images of whatever exists."

[3] There is nothing affords more wonderful speculation than matter, which ranks as the last among the universality of things, and has the same relation to being, as shade to substance. For, as in an ascending series of causes, it is necessary to arrive at something, which is the first cause of all, and to which no perfection is wanting: so in a descending series of subjects, it is equally necessary we should stop at some general subject, the lowest in the order of things, and to which every perfection of being is denied. But let us hear the profound and admirable description, which Plotinus gives us of matter (lib. vi. Ennead. 3) and of which the following is a paraphrase. "Since matter," says he, "is neither soul nor intellect, nor life, nor form, nor reason, nor bound, but a certain indefiniteness; nor yet capacity, for what can it produce? Since it is foreign from all these, it cannot merit the appellation of being, but is deservedly called non-entity. Nor yet is it non-entity in the manner as motion, or station: but it is true non-entity, the mere shadow and imagination of bulk, and the desire of subsistence: abiding without station, of itself invisible, and avoiding the desire of him who wishes to perceive its nature. Hence, when no one perceives it, it is then in a manner present: but cannot be viewed by him who strives intently to behold it. Again, in itself contraries always appear, the small and the great, the less and the more, deficiencies and excess. So that it is a phantom, neither abiding, nor yet able to fly away: capable of no one denomination, and possessing no power from intellect; but constituted in the defect and shade as it were of all real being. Hence, too, in each of its vanishing appellations, it eludes our search: for if we think of it as something great, it is in the meantime small; if as something more, it becomes less; and the apparent being which we meet with in its image is non-being, and as it were a flying mockery. So that the forms which appear in matter, are merely ludicrous; shadows falling upon shadow, as in a mirror, where the position of a thing is

its nature is ever averse from the supervening irradiations of form. Whenever, therefore, form accedes, it conciliates in amicable unity, the parts which are about to compose a whole: for being itself one, it is not wonderful that the subject of its power should tend to unity, as far as the nature of a compound will admit. Hence beauty is established in multitude, when the many is reduced into one; and in this case it communicates itself both to the parts, and to the whole. But when a particular one, composed from similar parts, is received, it gives itself to the whole, without departing from the sameness and integrity of its nature. Thus at one and the same time, it communicates itself to the whole building, and its several parts; and at another time confines itself to a single stone: and then the first participation arises from the operations of art, but the second from the formation of nature. And hence body becomes beautiful, through the communion supernally proceeding from divinity.

But the soul, by her innate power, than which nothing is more powerful, in judging its proper concerns, when another soul concurs in the decision, acknowledges the beauty of forms. And, perhaps, its knowledge in this case arises from its accommodating its internal ray of beauty to form, and trusting to this in its judgment; in the same manner as a rule is employed, in the decision of what is strait. But how can that which is inherent in body accord with that which is above body? Let us reply by asking how the architect pronounces the building beautiful, by accommodating the external structure to the fabric in his soul? Perhaps, because the outward building, when entirely deprived of the stones, is no other than the intrinsic form, divided by the ex-

different from its real situation; and which, though apparently full of forms, possesses nothing real and true. But the things which enter and depart from matter are nothing but imitations of being and semblances flowing about a formless semblance. They appear, indeed, to affect something in the subject-matter, but in reality produce nothing: from their debile and flowing nature, being endued with no solidity, and no rebounding power. And since matter, likewise, has no solidity, they penetrate it without division, like images in water, or as if any one should fill a vacuum with forms."

ternal mass of matter, but indivisibly existing, though appearing in the many. When, therefore, sense beholds the form in bodies, at strife with matter, binding and vanquishing its contrary nature, and sees form gracefully shining forth in other forms, it collects together the scattered whole, and introduces it to itself, and to the indivisible form within; and renders it consonant, congruous and friendly to its own intimate form. Thus, to the good man, virtue shining forth in youth is lovely, because consonant to the true virtue, which lies deep in the soul. But the simple beauty of colour arises when light, which is something incorporeal, and reason and form, entering the obscure involutions of matter, irradiates and forms its dark and formless nature. It is on this account that fire surpasses other bodies in beauty, because, compared with the other elements, it obtains the order of form: for it is more eminent than the rest, and is the most subtle of all, bordering as it were on an incorporeal nature. Add too, that though impervious itself, it is intimately received by others; for it imparts heat, but admits no cold. Hence it is the first nature which is ornamented with colour, and is the source of it to others: and on this account it beams forth exalted like some immaterial form. But when it cannot vanquish its subject, as participating but a slender light, it is no longer beautiful: because it does not receive the whole form of colour. Again, the music of the voice rouses the harmony latent in the soul, and opens her eye to the perception of beauty, existing in many the same. But it is the property of the harmony perceived by sense, to be measured by numbers, yet not in every proportion of number or voice, but in that alone which is obedient to the production and conquest of its species. And thus much for the beauties of sense, which, like images and shadows flowing into matter, adorn with spectacles of beauty its formless being, and strike the respective senses with wonder and delight.

But it is now time, leaving every object of sense far behind, to contemplate, by a certain ascent, a beauty of a much higher order: a beauty not visible to the corporeal eye, but alone manifest to the brighter eye of the soul, independent of all corporeal aid. However, since, without some previous perception of beauty, it is impossible to express by words the beauties of sense, but we must remain in the state of the blind; so neither can we ever speak of the beauty of offices and sciences, and whatever is allied to these, if deprived of their intimate possession. Thus we shall never be able to tell of virtue's brightness, unless by looking inward we perceive the fair countenance of justice and temperance, and are convinced that neither the evening nor morning-star are half so beautiful and bright. But it is requisite to perceive objects of this kind with that eye by which the soul beholds such real beauties. Besides, it is necessary that whoever perceives this species of beauty, should be seized with much greater delight, and more vehement admiration, than any corporeal beauty can excite; as now embracing beauty real and substantial. Such affections, I say, ought to be excited about true beauty,[4] as admiration and sweet astonishment; desire also and love, and a pleasant trepidation. For all souls, as I may say, are affected in this manner about invisible objects, but those the most who have the strongest propensity to their love; as it likewise happens about corporeal beauty: for all equally perceive beautiful corporeal forms, yet all are not equally excited, but lovers in the greatest degree.

But it may be allowable to interrogate those who rise above sense, concerning the effects of love in this manner: of such we enquire, what do you suffer respecting fair studies, and beautiful manners, virtuous works, affections, and habits, and the beauty of souls? What do you experience on perceiving yourselves lovely within? After what manner are you roused as it were to a Bacchanalian fury; striving to converse with yourselves, and collecting yourselves separate from the impediments of body? For thus are true lovers enraptured. But what is the cause of these wonderful effects? It is neither figure, nor colour, nor magnitude; but soul herself, fair through temperance, and not with the false gloss of colour, and bright with the splendours of virtue herself. And

---

[4] Instead of περὶ τὸ ὅ τι ἄν ᾖ καλὸν, it should doubtless read περὶ τὸν αληθινον καλὸν, which sense is adopted in the paraphrase; and which I wonder Ficinus did not observe.

this you experience as often as you turn your eye inwards; or contemplate the amplitude of another soul: the just manners, the pure temperance; fortitude venerable by her noble countenance; and modesty and honesty walking with an intrepid step, and a tranquil and steady aspect; and, what crowns the beauty of them all, constantly receiving the irradiations of a divine intellect.

In what respect then, shall we call these beautiful? For they are such as they appear, nor did ever any one behold them, and not pronounce them realities. But as yet reason desires to know how they cause the loveliness of the soul; and what that grace is in every virtue which beams forth to view like light? Are you then willing we should assume the contrary part, and consider what in the soul appears deformed? for, perhaps it will facilitate our search, if we can thus find what is base in the soul, and from whence it derives its original.

Let us suppose a soul deformed, to be one intemperate and unjust, filled with a multitude of desires, a prey to foolish hopes, and vexed with idle fears; through its diminutive and avaricious nature the subject of envy; employed solely in thought of what is mortal and low; bound in the fetters of impure delights; living the life, whatever it may be, peculiar to the passion of body; and so totally merged in sensuality as to esteem the base pleasant, and the deformed beautiful and fair. But may we not say, that this baseness approaches the soul as an adventitious evil, under the pretext of adventitious beauty; which, with great detriment, renders it impure, and pollutes it with much depravity; so that it neither possesses true life, nor true sense, but is endued with a slender life through its mixture of evil, and this worn out by the continual depredations of death: no longer perceiving the objects of mental vision, nor permitted any more to dwell with itself, because ever hurried away to things obscure, external, and low? Hence, becoming impure, and being on all sides snatched in the unceasing whirl of sensible forms, it is covered with corporeal stains, and wholly given to matter, contracts deeply its nature, loses all its original splendor, and almost changes its own species into that of another: just as the pristine beauty of the most lovely form would be destroyed by its total immersion in mire and clay. But the deformity of the first arises from inward filth, of its own contracting; of the second, from the accession of some foreign nature. If such a one then desires to recover his former beauty, it is necessary to cleanse the infected parts, and thus by a thorough purgation to resume his original form. Hence, then, if we assert that the soul, by her mixture, confusion and commerce with body and matter, becomes thus base, our assertion will, I think, be right. For the baseness of the soul consists in not being pure and sincere. And as the gold is deformed by the adherence of earthly clods, which are no sooner removed than on a sudden the gold shines forth with its native purity; and then becomes beautiful when separated from natures foreign from its own, and when it is content with its own purity for the possession of beauty: so the soul, when separated from the sordid desires engendered by its too great immersion in body, and liberated from the dominion of every perturbation, can thus, and thus only, blot out the base stains imbibed from its union with body; and thus becoming alone, will doubtless expel all the turpitude contracted from a nature so opposite to its own.

Indeed, as the ancient oracle declares, temperance and fortitude, prudence and every virtue are certain purgatives of the soul; and hence the sacred mysteries prophesy obscurely, yet with truth, that the soul not purified lies in Tartarus, immersed in filth. Since the impure is, from his depravity, the friend of filth; as swine, from their sordid body, delight in mire alone. For what else is true temperance than not to indulge in corporeal delights,[5] but to fly from their connection, as things which are neither pure, nor the offspring of purity? And true fortitude is not to fear death: for death is nothing more than a certain separation of soul from body; and this he will not fear, who desires to be alone. Again, magnanimity is the contempt of every mortal concern; it is the wing by which we fly into the regions of intellect. And lastly, prudence is no other than intelligence, declining subordinate objects; and

[5] For a full account of the division and nature of the virtues, see Porphyry's Ἀφορμαὶ πρὸς τὰ Νοητά, p. 235.

directing the eye of the soul to that which is immortal and divine. The soul, thus refined, becomes form and reason, is altogether incorporeal and intellectual; and wholly participates of that divine nature which is the fountain of loveliness, and of whatever is allied to the beautiful and fair. Hence, the soul, reduced to intellect, becomes astonishingly beautiful; for as the lambent flame which appears detached from the burning wood, enlightens its dark and smoky parts, so intellect irradiates and adorns the inferior powers of the soul, which, without its aid, would be buried in the gloom of formless matter. But intellect, and whatever emanates from intellect, is not the foreign, but the proper, ornament of the soul: for the being of the soul, when absorbed in intellect, is then alone real and true. It is, therefore, rightly said, that the beauty and good of the soul consists in her similitude to the Deity; for from hence flows all her beauty, and her allotment of a better being. But the beautiful itself is that which is called beings; and turpitude is of a different nature, and participates more of non-entity than being.

But, perhaps, the good and the beautiful are the same, and must be investigated by one and the same process; and in like manner the base and the evil. And in the first rank we must place the beautiful, and consider it as the same with the good; from which immediately emanates intellect as beautiful. Next to this, we must consider the soul receiving its beauty from intellect; and every inferior beauty deriving its origin from the forming power of the soul, whether conversant in fair actions and offices, or sciences and arts. Lastly, bodies themselves participate of beauty from the soul, which, as something divine, and a portion of the beautiful itself, renders whatever it supervenes and subdues, beautiful, as far as its natural capacity will admit.

Let us, therefore, reascend to the good itself, which every soul desires; and in which it can alone find perfect repose. For, if any one shall become acquainted with this source of beauty, he will then know what I say, and after what manner he is beautiful. Indeed, whatever is desirable is a kind of good, since to this desire tends. But they alone pursue true good, who rise to intelligible beauty; and so far only tend to good itself, as far as they lay aside the deformed vestments of matter, with which they became connected in their descent. Just as those who penetrate into the holy retreats of sacred mysteries are first purified, and then divest themselves of their garments, until some one, by such a process, having dismissed every thing foreign from the God, by himself alone, beholds the solitary principle of the universe, sincere, simple, and pure, from which all things depend, and to whose transcendent perfections the eyes of all intelligent natures are directed, as the proper cause of being, life, and intelligence. With what ardent love, with what strong desire will he who enjoys this transporting vision be inflamed, while vehemently affecting to become one with this supreme beauty? For thus it is ordained, that he who does not yet perceive him, yet desires him as good: but he who enjoys the vision, is enraptured with his beauty; and is equally filled with admiration and delight. Hence, such a one is agitated with a salutary astonishment; is affected with the highest and truest love; derides vehement affections, and inferior loves, and despises the beauty which he once approved. Such, too, is the condition of those, who, on perceiving the forms of gods or daemons, no longer esteem the fairest of corporeal forms. What then must be the condition of that being, who beholds the beautiful itself? In itself perfectly pure,[6] not confined by any corporeal bond, neither existing in the heavens, nor in the earth, nor to be imaged by the most lovely form imagination can conceive; since these are all adventitious and mixt, and mere secondary beauties, proceeding from the beautiful itself. If, then, any one should ever behold that which is the source of munificence to others, remaining in itself, while it communi-

[6] This is analogous to the description of the beautiful in the latter part of Diotima's Speech in the Banquet; a speech which is surely unequalled, both for elegance of composition and sublimity of sentiment. Indeed, all the disciples of Plato are remarkable for nothing so much as their profound and exalted conceptions of the Deity; and he who can read the works of Plotinus and Proclus in particular, and afterwards pity the weakness and erroneousness of their opinions on this subject, may be fairly presumed to be himself equally an object of pity and contempt.

cates to all, and receiving nothing, because possessing an inexhaustible fulness; and should so abide in the intuition, as to become similar to his nature, what more of beauty can such a one desire? For such beauty, since it is supreme in dignity and excellence, cannot fail of rendering its votaries lovely and fair. Add too, that since the object of contest to souls is the highest beauty, we should strive for its acquisition with unabated ardor, lest we should be deserted of that blissful contemplation which, whoever pursues in the right way, becomes blessed from the happy vision; and which he who does not obtain is unavoidably unhappy. For the miserable man is not he who neglects to pursue fair colours, and beautiful corporeal forms; who is deprived of power, and falls from dominion and empire; but he alone who is destitute of this divine possession, for which the ample dominion of the earth and sea, and the still more extended empire of the heavens, must be relinquished and forgot, if, despising and leaving these far behind, we ever intend to arrive at substantial felicity, by beholding the beautiful itself.

What measures, then, shall we adopt? What machine employ, or what reason consult, by means of which we may contemplate this ineffable beauty: a beauty abiding in the most divine sanctuary, without ever proceeding from its sacred retreats, lest it should be beheld by the profane and vulgar eye? We must enter deep into ourselves, and, leaving behind the objects of corporeal sight, no longer look back after any of the accustomed spectacles of sense. For, it is necessary that whoever beholds this beauty, should withdraw his view from the fairest corporeal forms; and, convinced that these are nothing more than images, vestiges, and shadows of beauty, should eagerly soar to the fair original from which they are derived. For he who rushes to these lower beauties, as if grasping realities, when they are only like beautiful images appearing in water, will, doubtless, like him in the fable, by stretching after the shadow, sink into the lake, and disappear. For, by thus embracing and adhering to corporeal forms, he is precipitated, not so much in his body, as in his soul, into profound and horrid darkness; and thus blind, like those in the infernal regions, converses only with phantoms, deprived of the perception of what is real and true. It is here, then, we may more truly exclaim, "Let us depart[7] from hence, and fly to our father's delightful land." But, by what leading stars shall we direct our flight, and what means avoid the magic power of Circe, and the detaining charms of Calypso? For thus the fable of Ulysses[8] obscurely signifies, which feigns him abiding an unwilling exile, though pleasant spectacles were continually presented to his sight; and every thing was promised to invite his stay which can delight the senses, and captivate the heart. But our true country, like that of Ulysses, is from whence we came, and where our father lives. But where is the ship to be found, by which we can accomplish our flight? For our feet are unequal to the task, since

[7] Vide Hom. Iliad. lib. ii. 140 et lib. ix. 27.

Φεύγωμεν σὺν νηυσί φίλην ἐς πατρίδα γαῖαν.

[8] Porphyry informs us, in his excellent treatise, De Antro Nymph., "that it was the opinion of Numenius, the Pythagorean, (to which he also assents) that the person of Ulysses, in the Odyssey, represents to us a man, who passes in a regular manner, over the dark and stormy sea of generation; and thus, at length, arrives at that region where tempests and seas are unknown, and finds a nation, who

Ne'er knew salt, or heard the billows roar."

Indeed, he who is conscious of the delusions of the present life, and the enchantments of this material house, in which his soul is detained, like Ulysses in the irriguous cavern of Calypso, will, like him, continually bewail his captivity, and inly pine for a return to his native country. Of such a one it may be said as of Ulysses (in the excellent and pathetic translation of Mr. Pope),

But sad Ulysses by himself apart,
Pour'd the big sorrows of his swelling heart;
All on the lonely shore he sate to weep,
And roll'd his eyes around the restless deep;
Tow'rd the lov'd coast, he roll'd his eyes in vain,
Till, dimm'd with rising grief, they stream'd
again. (Odyssey, book v. 103)

Such a one, too, like Ulysses, will not always wish in vain for a passage over the dark ocean of a corporeal life, but by the assistance of Mercury, who may be considered as the emblem of reason, he will at length be enabled to quit the magic embraces of Calypso, the goddess of Sense, and to return again into the arms of Penelope, or Philosophy, the long lost and proper object of his love.

they only take us from one part of the earth to another. May we not each of us say,

> *What ships have I, what sailors to convey,*
> *What oars to cut the long laborious way?*[9]

But it is in vain that we prepare horses to draw, or ships to transport us to our native land. On the contrary, neglecting all these, as unequal to the task, and excluding them entirely from our view, having now closed the corporeal eye, we must stir up, and assume a purer eye within,[10] which all men possess, but which is alone used by a few. What is it then this inward eye beholds? Indeed, suddenly raised to intellectual vision, it cannot perceive an object exceeding bright. The soul must therefore be first accustomed to contemplate fair studies, and then beautiful works; not such as arise from the operations of art, but such as are the offspring of worthy men: and next to this, it is necessary to view the soul which is the parent of this lovely race. But you will ask, after what manner is this beauty of a worthy soul to be perceived? It is thus. Recall your thoughts inward, and if, while contemplating yourself, you do not perceive yourself beautiful, imitate

[9] See Pope's Homer's Odyssey, Book v. 181.

[10] This inward eye is no other than intellect, which contains in its most inward recesses, a certain ray of light, participated from the sun of Beauty and Good, by which the soul is enabled to behold and become united with her divinely solitary original. This divine ray, or, as Proclus calls it συνθημά, a mark or impression, is thus beautifully described by that philosopher, (Theol. Plat. p. 105). "The Author of the universe, (says he) has planted in all beings impressions of his own perfect excellence, and through these, he has placed all beings about himself, and is present with them in an ineffable manner, exempt from the universality of things. Hence, every being entering into the ineffable sanctuary of its own nature, finds there a symbol of the Father of all. And by this mystical impression, which corresponds to his nature, they become united with their original, divesting themselves of their own essence, and hastening to become his impression alone; and, through a desire of his unknown nature, and of the fountain of good, to participate him alone. And when they have ascended as far as to this cause, they enjoy perfect tranquility, and are conversant in the perception of his divine progeny, and of the love which all things naturally possess of goodness, unknown, ineffable, without participation, and transcendently full."

the statuary, who, when he desires a beautiful statue, cuts away what is superfluous, smooths and polishes what is rough, and never desists until he has given it all the beauty his art is able to effect. In this manner must you proceed, by lopping what is luxuriant, directing what is oblique, and, by purgation, illustrating what is obscure; and thus continue to polish and beautify your statue, until the divine splendor of Virtue shines upon you, and Temperance, seated in pure and holy majesty, rises to your view. If you become thus purified, residing in yourself, and having nothing any longer to impede this unity of mind, and no farther mixture to be found within, but perceiving your whole self to be a true light, and light alone; a light which, though immense, is not measured by any magnitude, nor limited by any circumscribing figure, but is every where immeasurable, as being greater than every measure, and more excellent than every quantity: if, perceiving yourself thus improved, and trusting solely to yourself, as no longer requiring a guide, fix now stedfastly your mental view, for with the intellectual eye alone can such immense beauty be perceived. But, if your eye is yet infected with any sordid concern, and not thoroughly refined, while it is on the stretch to behold this most shining spectacle, it will be immediately darkened and incapable of intuition, though some one should declare the spectacle present, which it might be otherwise able to discern. For, it is here necessary, that the perceiver and the thing perceived should be similar to each other, before true vision can exist. Thus the sensitive eye can never be able to survey the orb of the sun, unless strongly endued with solar fire, and participating largely of the vivid ray. Every one, therefore, must become divine, and of godlike beauty, before he can gaze upon a god, and the beautiful itself. Thus proceeding in the right way of beauty, he will first ascend into the region of intellect, contemplating every fair species, the beauty of which he will perceive to be no other than ideas themselves; for all things are beautiful by the supervening irradiations of these, because they are the offspring and essence of intellect. But that which is superior to these, is no other than the fountain of good, every where widely diffusing around the streams of beauty, and hence, in discourse, called the beautiful itself; because, beauty is its immediate offspring. But, if you accurately distinguish the intelligible objects, you will call the beautiful the receptacle of ideas; but the good itself, which is superior, the fountain and principle of the beautiful; or, you may place the first beautiful and the good in the same principle, independent of the beauty which there subsists.[11]

[11] But before I take my leave of Plotinus, I cannot refrain from addressing a few words to the Platonical part of my readers. If such, then, is the wisdom contained in the works of this philosopher, as we may conclude from the present specimen, is it fit so divine a treasure should be concealed in shameful oblivion? With respect to true philosophy, you must be sensible that all modern sects are in a state of barbarous ignorance: for Materialism, and its attendant Sensuality, have darkened the eyes of the *many*, with the mists of error; and are continually strengthening their corporeal tie. And can any thing more effectually dissipate this increasing gloom than discourses composed by so sublime a genius, pregnant with the most profound conceptions, and every where full of intellectual light? Can any thing so thoroughly destroy the phantom of false enthusiasm, as establishing the real object of the true? Let us then boldly enlist ourselves under the banners of Plotinus, and, by his assistance, vigorously repel the encroachments of error, plunge her dominions into the abyss of forgetfulness, and disperse the darkness of her baneful night. For, indeed, there never was a period which required so much philosophic exertion; or such vehement contention from the lovers of Truth. On all sides, nothing of philosophy remains but the name, and this is become the subject of the vilest prostitution: since it is not only engrossed by the Naturalist, Chemist, and Anatomist, but is usurped by the Mechanic, in every trifling invention, and made subservient to the lucre of traffic and merchandize. There cannot surely be a greater proof of the degeneracy of the times than so unparalleled a degradation, and so barbarous a perversion of terms. For, the word philosophy, which implies the love of wisdom, is now become the ornament of folly. In the times of its inventor and for many succeeding ages, it was expressive of modesty and worth: in our days, it is the badge of impudence and vain pretensions. It was formerly the symbol of the profound and contemplative genius; it is now the mark of the superficial and unthinking practitioner. It was once reverenced by kings, and clothed in the robes of nobility; it is now (according to its true acceptation) abandoned and despised, and ridiculed by the vilest Plebeian. Permit me, then, my friends, to address you in the words of Achilles to Hector:

Thomas Taylor the Platonist

> *Rouse, then, your forces, this important hour,*
> *Collect your strength, and call forth all your pow'r.*

Since, to adopt the animated language of Neptune to the Greeks,

> *. . . on dastards, dead to fame,*
> *I waste no anger, for they feel no shame;*
> *But you, the pride, the flower of all our host,*
> *My heart weeps blood, to see your glory lost.*

Nor deem the exhortation impertinent, and the danger groundless:

> *For lo! the fated time, th' appointed shore;*
> *Hark! the gates burst, the brazen barriers roar.*

Impetuous ignorance is thundering at the bulwarks of philosophy, and her sacred retreats are in danger of being demolished, through out feeble resistance. Rise, then, my friends, and the victory will be ours. The foe is indeed numerous, but, at the same time, feeble: and the weapons of truth, in the hands of vigorous union, descend with irresistible force, and are fatal wherever they fall.

THE HYMNS OF ORPHEUS
Translated from the Original Greek
With a Preliminary Dissertation on the
Life and Theology of Orpheus

Originally published in 1787 as *The Mystical Initia-tions; or, Hymns of Orpheus*, this is Taylor's first important book. A "Second Edition, with Consider-able Emendations, Alterations, and Additions" was published in 1824 as *The Mystical Hymns of Orpheus* (reissued by Bertram Dobell in 1896). Well known to Yeats and his contemporaries, this edition was probably the one read by Emerson, Alcott, and their fellow Transcendentalists; the English Romantics were best acquainted with the first edition and its reissue. By 1787, as Taylor points out, "the ancient philos-ophy" had already been "for many years, the only study of his retired leisure." The *Hymns* was dealt with at length in the *Critical Review*, LXIII (1787), 401–06) and the *Monthly Review*, LXXIX (1788), 133–42.

In the *Dissertation* several of Taylor's notes supply-ing Greek phrases have been deleted.

PREFACE

THERE IS DOUBTLESS a revolution in the literary, correspondent to that of the natural world. The face of things is continually changing; and the perfect and perpetual harmony of the universe subsists by the mutability of its parts. In consequence of this fluctuation, different arts and sciences have flourished at different periods of the world: but the complete circle of human knowledge has, I believe, never subsisted at once, in any nation or age. Where accurate and profound researches into the principles of things have advanced to perfection, there, by a natural consequence, men have neglected the disquisition of particulars: and where sensible particulars have been the general object of pursuit, the science of universals has languished, or sunk into oblivion and contempt.

Thus wisdom, the object of all true philosophy, considered as exploring the causes and principles of things, flourished in high perfection among the Egyptians first, and afterwards in Greece. Polite literature was the pursuit of the Romans; and experimental enquiries, increased without end, and accumulated without order, are the employment of modern philosophy. Hence we may justly conclude, that the age of true philosophy is no more. In consequence of very extended natural discoveries, trade and commerce have increased, while abstract investigations have necessarily declined: so that modern enquiries never rise above sense; and every thing is despised which does not in some respect or other contribute to the accumulation of wealth, the gratification of childish admiration, or the refinements of corporeal delight. The author of the following translation, therefore, cannot reasonably expect, that his labours will meet with the approbation of the many: since these Hymns are too ancient, and too full of the Greek philosophy, to please the ignorant and the sordid. However, he hopes they will be acceptable to the few, who have drawn wisdom from its source and who consider the science of universals as first in the nature of things, though last in the progressions of human understanding.

The translator has adopted rhyme, not because most agreeable to general taste, but because he believes it necessary to the poetry of the English language, which requires something as a substitute for the energetic cadence of the Greek and Latin Hexameters. Could this be obtained by any other means, he would immediately relinquish his partiality for rhyme, which is certainly when well executed, far more difficult than blank verse, as the following Hymns must evince, in an eminent degree.

And, here it is necessary to observe, with respect to translation, that nothing is more generally mistaken in its nature, or more faulty in its execution. The author of the Letters on Mythology gives it as his opinion, that it is impossible to translate an ancient author so as to do justice to his meaning. If he had confined this sentiment to the beauties of the composition, it would doubtless have been just; but to extend it to the meaning of an author is to make truth and opinion partial and incommunicable. Every person, indeed, acquainted with the learned languages, must be conscious how much the beauty of an ancient author generally suffers by translation, though undertaken by men who have devoted the greatest part of their lives to the study of words alone. This failure, which has more than any thing contributed to bring the ancients into contempt with the unlearned, can only be ascribed to the want of genius in the translators: for the sentiment of Pythagoras is peculiarly applicable to such as these, that many carry the Thyrsus, but few are inspired with the spirit of the God. But this observation is remarkably verified in the translators of the ancient philosophy, whose performances are for the most part without animation; and consequently retain nothing of the fire and spirit of the original. Perhaps, there is but one exception to this remark, and that is Mr. Sydenham: whose success in such an arduous undertaking can only be ascribed to his possessing the philosophical genius, and to his occasionally paraphrasing passages, which would otherwise be senseless and inanimate.

Indeed, where languages differ so much as the ancient and modern, the most perfect method, perhaps, of transferring the philosophy from the one language to the other is by a faithful and animated paraphrase: faithful, with regard to retaining the sense of the author, and animated, with respect to preserving the fire of the original; calling it forth when latent, and expanding it when condensed. Such a one will every where endeavour to improve the light, and fathom the depth of his author; to elucidate what is obscure, and to amplify what in modern language would be unintelligibly concise.

Thus most of the compound epithets of which the following Hymns chiefly consist, though very beautiful in the Greek language, yet, when literally translated into ours, lose all their propriety and force. In their native tongue, as in a prolific soil, they diffuse their sweets with full-blown elegance, but shrink like the sensitive plant at the touch of the verbal critic, or the close translator. He who would preserve their philosophical beauties, and exhibit them to others in a different language, must expand their elegance, by the supervening and enlivening rays of the philosophic fire; and, by the powerful breath of genius, scatter abroad their latent but copious sweets.

If some sparks of this celestial fire shall appear to have animated the bosom of the translator, he will consider himself as well rewarded, for his laborious undertaking. The ancient philosophy has been for many years the only study of his retired leisure; in which he has found an inexhaustible treasure of intellectual wealth, and a perpetual fountain of wisdom and delight. Presuming that such a pursuit must greatly advantage the present undertaking, and feeling the most sovereign contempt for the sordid drudgery of hired composition, he desires no other reward, if he has succeeded, than the praise of the liberal; and no other defence if he has failed, than the decision of the candid, and discerning few.

A DISSERTATION ON THE
LIFE AND THEOLOGY OF ORPHEUS

THE great obscurity and uncertainty in which the history of Orpheus is involved affords very little matter for our information; and even renders that little, inaccurate and precarious. Upon surveying the annals of past ages, it seems that the greatest geniuses have been subject to this historical darkness; as is evident in those great lights of antiquity, Homer and Euclid, whose writings indeed enrich mankind with perpetual stores of knowledge and delight; but whose lives are for the most part concealed in impenetrable oblivion. But this historical uncertainty is no where so apparent as in the person of Orpheus, whose name is indeed acknowledged and celebrated by all antiquity (except perhaps Aristotle alone); while scarcely a vestige of his life is to be found amongst the immense ruins of time. For who has ever been able to affirm any thing with certainty, concerning his origin, his age, his parents, his country, and condition? This alone may be depended on, from general assent, that there formerly lived a person named Orpheus, whose father was Oeagrus, who lived in Thrace, and who was the son of a king, who was the founder of theology among the Greeks, the institutor of their life and morals, the first of prophets, and the prince of poets; himself the offspring of a Muse; who taught the Greeks their sacred rites and mysteries, and from whose wisdom, as from a perpetual and abundant fountain, the divine muse of Homer, and the philosophy of Pythagoras and Plato, flowed; and, lastly, who by the melody of his lyre, drew rocks, woods, and wild beasts, stopt rivers in their course, and even moved the inexorable king of hell; as every page, and all the writings of antiquity sufficiently evince. Since thus much then may be collected from universal testimony, let us pursue the matter a little farther, by investigating more accurately the history of the original Orpheus with that of the great men who have, at different periods, flourished under this venerable name.

The Hymns of Orpheus

The first and genuine Orpheus was a poet of Thrace, and, according to the opinion of many, the disciple of Linus; who flourished, says Suidas, at the time when the kingdom of the Athenians was dissolved. Some assert that he was prior to the Trojan wars, and that he lived eleven, or according to others nine generations. But the Greek word γενεα, or generation, according to Gyraldus,[1] signifies the space of seven years; for unless this is supposed, how is it possible that the period of his life can have any foundation in the nature of things? Plutarch indeed, Heraclitus, Suidas, and some grammarians, assert that this word signifies a space of thirty years: but omitting the discussion of this latter opinion, from its impossibility, we shall embrace the former, agreeable to which Orpheus lived sixty-three years; a period, if we may believe the astrologers, fatal to all, and especially to great men, as was the case with Cicero and Aristotle.

Our poet, according to fabulous tradition, was torn in pieces by Ciconian women: on which account, Plutarch affirms the Thracians were accustomed to beat their wives, that they might revenge the death of Orpheus. Hence, in the vision of Herus Pamphilius, in Plato, the soul of Orpheus, being destined to descend into another body, is reported to have chosen rather that of a swan than to be born again of a woman; having conceived such hatred against the sex, on account of his violent death. The cause of his destruction is variously related by authors. Some report that it arose from his being engaged in puerile loves, after the death of Eurydice. Others, that he was destroyed by women intoxicated with wine, because he was the means of men relinquishing their connexion. Others affirm, according to the tradition of Pausanias, that upon the death of Eurydice, wandering to Aornus, a place in Threspotia, where it was customary to evocate the souls of the dead, having recalled Eurydice to life, and not being able to detain her, he destroyed himself; nightingales building their nests, and bringing forth their young upon his tomb; whose melody, according to report, exceeded every other of this species. Others again ascribe his laceration to his having

[1] Syntag. Poet. p. 54.

167

celebrated every divinity except Bacchus, which is very improbable, as among the following hymns there are nine to that Deity, under different appellations. Others report that he was delivered by Venus herself into the hands of the Ciconian women, because his mother Calliope had not determined justly between Venus and Proserpine, concerning the young Adonis. Many affirm that he was struck by lightning, according to Pausanias; and Diogenes confirms this by the following verses composed, as he asserts, by the Muses upon his death:

> *Here, by the Muses plac'd, with golden lyre,*
> *Great Orpheus rests; destroy'd by heav'nly fire.*

Again, the sacred mysteries called Threscian derived their appellation from our Thracian bard, because he first introduced sacred rites and religion into Greece; and hence the authors of initiation in these mysteries were called Orpheotelestae. Besides, according to Lucian, our Orpheus brought astrology and the magical arts into Greece; and with respect to his drawing trees and wild beasts by the melody of his lyre, Palaephatus accounts for it as follows.[2] The mad Bacchanalian nymphs, says he, having violently taken away cattle and other necessaries of life, retired for some days into the mountains. When the citizens, having expected their return for a long time, and fearing the worst for their wives and daughters, called Orpheus, and entreated him to invent some method of drawing them from the mountains. But he tuning his lyre, agreeable to the orgies of Bacchus, drew the mad nymphs from their retreats; who descended from the mountains bearing at first ferulae and branches of every kind of trees. But to the men who were eye-witnesses of these wonders, they appeared at first to bring down the very woods; and from hence gave rise to the fable.

But so great was the reputation of Orpheus, that he was deified by the Greeks; and Philostratus relates, that his head gave oracles in Lesbos, which, when separated from his body by the Thracian women, was, together with his lyre, carried down the river

[2] Opusc. Mythol. p. 45.

Hebrus into the Sea. In this manner, says Lucian,[3] singing as it were his funeral oration, to which the chords of his lyre, impelled by the winds, gave a responsive harmony, it was brought to Lesbos and buried. But his lyre was suspended in the Temple of Apollo; where it remained for a considerable space of time. Afterwards, when Neanthus, the son of Pittacus the tyrant, found that the lyre drew trees and wild beasts with its harmony, he earnestly desired its possession; and having corrupted the priest privately with money, he took the Orphean lyre, and fixed another similar to it, in the temple. But Neanthus considering that he was not safe in the city in the day time, departed from it by night; having concealed the lyre in his bosom, on which he began to play. But as he was a rude and unlearned youth, he confounded the chords; yet pleasing himself with the sound, and fancying he produced a divine harmony, he considered himself as the blessed successor of Orpheus. However, in the midst of his transports, the neighbouring dogs, roused by the sound, fell upon the unhappy harper and tore him to pieces. The former part of this fable is thus excellently explained by Proclus in his commentaries (or rather fragments of commentaries) on Plato's Republic; a work I would earnestly recommend to the liberal, for the great light it affords to the recondite theology of the Greeks. Orpheus, says he, on account of his perfect erudition, is reported to have been destroyed in various ways; because, in my opinion, men of that age, participated partially of the Orphic harmony; for they could not receive a universal and perfect science. But the principal part of his melody was received by the Lesbians; and on this account, perhaps, the head of Orpheus, when separated from his body, is said to have been carried to Lesbos. Fables of this kind, therefore, are related of Orpheus, no otherwise than of Bacchus, of whose mysteries he was the priest. Thus far Proclus, and thus much concerning the first, or Thracian Orpheus. The second Orpheus was an Arcadian, or, according to others, a Ciconian, from Bisaltia of Thrace, and is reported to be more ancient than Homer, and the Trojan war. He composed figments

[3] In Oratione ad Indoctum.

of fables called (μυθοποιια) and epigrams; and is, according to Gyraldus, the author of the following hymns; though I rather chuse to refer them, with the Fathers Vossius and Eschenbach, to Onomacritus, or the fourth Orpheus, of Crotonia. The third Orpheus was of Odrysius, a city of Thrace, near the river Hebrus; but Dionysius, in Suidas, denies his existence. The fourth Orpheus was of Crotonia, who flourished in the time of Pisistratus, about the fiftieth Olympiad; and is doubtless the same Onomacritus the author of these hymns. He writ Decennalia, δεκαετηρια, and, in the opinion of Gyraldus, the Argonautics, which are now extant under the name of Orpheus, with other writings called Orphical, but which, according to Cicero,[4] some ascribe to Cecrops the Pythagorean. The last Orpheus was Camarinaeus, a most excellent versifier; and the same according to Gyraldus whose descent into hell is so universally known. And thus much for the life of Orpheus.

SECTION II

Let us now proceed to his theology; exchanging the obscurity of conjecture for the light of clear evidence; and the intricate labyrinths of fable for the delightful though solitary paths of truth. And here I must acquaint the reader, that I shall every where deduce my information from the writings of the latter Platonists, as the only sources of genuine knowledge, on this sublime and obsolete enquiry.[5] The vulgar systems of mythology are here entirely useless; and he who should attempt to elucidate the theology, or hymns of Orpheus, by any modern hypothesis, would be as ridiculously employed, as he who should expect to find the origin of a copious stream, by pursuing it to its last and most intricate involutions. In conformity with modern prejudices, the author of the Letters on Mythology endeavours to prove, that the Orphic hymns deify the various parts of nature, not considered as animated by different intelligences but as various

[4] In 1. De Nat. Deor.
[5] In the latter part of this Dissertation, we shall discourse on the agreement between the doctrine of Orpheus and the Platonists.

modifications of inert and lifeless matter. This hypothesis is no doubt readily embraced by the present philosophers, a great part of whom deny the existence of any thing incorporeal; and the better sort, who acknowledge one supreme immaterial Being, exclude the agency of subordinate intelligences in the government of the world; though this doctrine is perfectly philosophical, and at the same time consistent with revelation. The belief indeed of the man who looks no higher than sense must be necessarily terminated by appearances. Such a one introduces a dreadful chasm in the universe; and diffuses the deity through the world like an extended substance; divided with every particle of matter, and changed into the infinite varieties of sensible forms. But with the ancient philosopher, the deity is an immense and perpetually exuberant fountain whose streams originally filled and continually replenish the world with life. Hence the universe contains in its ample bosom all general natures, divinities visible and invisible, the illustrious race of daemons, the noble army of exalted souls, and men rendered happy by wisdom and virtue. According to this theology, the power of universal soul does not alone diffuse itself to the sea, and become bounded by its circumfluent waters, while the wide expanse of air and aether is destitute of life and soul; but the celestial spaces are filled with souls, supplying life to the stars, and directing their revolutions in everlasting order. So that the celestial orbs in imitation of intellect, which seeks after nothing external, are wisely agitated in perpetual circuit round the central sun. While some things participate of being alone, others of life, and others are endued with sentient powers; some possess the still higher faculty of reason; and, lastly, others are all life and intelligence.

But let us rise a little higher, and contemplate the arguments by which the Platonists establish the Orphic doctrine of the existence and agency of subordinate intelligences. Thus then they reason.[6] Of all beings it is necessary that some should move only, that others should be entirely moved; and that the beings situated between these two should participate of the extremes, and

[6] Procl. lib. i. Theol. Plat.

both move and be moved. Among the first in dignity and order are those natures which move only; the second, those which move themselves; the third, those which move and are moved; and the fourth, those which are moved only. Now the second class of these, or the self-motive natures, since their perfection consists in transition and mutation of life, must depend upon a more ancient cause, which subsists perpetually the same; and whose life is not conversant with the circulations of time, but is constituted in the stable essence of eternity. But it is necessary that the third class, which both move and are moved, should depend on a self-motive nature. For a self-motive being is the cause of motion to those which are moved by another, in the same manner as that which is immovable inserts in all beings the power of moving. And again, that which is moved only must depend on those natures which are indeed moved by another, but which are themselves endued with a motive-power. For it is necessary that the chain of beings should be complete; every where connected by proper mediums, and deduced in an orderly and perpetual series, from the principle to the extremes. All bodies therefore belong to those natures which are moved only, and are naturally passive; since they are destitute of all inherent energy, on account of their sluggish nature, which participates of division, magnitude, and weight.

But of incorporeals some are divisible about bodies; while others are entirely free from such an affection about the lowest order of beings. Hence such things as are divided about the dead weight of bodies, whether they are material qualities or forms, belong to the orders of nature's moving, and at the same time moved. For such as these because incorporeal, participate of a motive faculty; but because they are also divided about bodies, they are on this account exempt from incorporeal perfection, are filled with material inactivity, and require the energy of a self-motive nature. Where then shall we find this self-motive essence? For such things as are extended with magnitude, oppressed by material weight, and inseparably reside in bodies must necessarily either move only, or be moved by others. But it is requisite, as we have before observed, that prior to this order, the self-motive essence should subsist. And hence we conclude that there is another certain nature exempt from the passivity and imperfection of bodies, existing not only in the heavens, but in the ever-changing elements, from which the motion of bodies is primarily derived. And this nature is no other than soul, from which animals derive their life and motive power; and which even affords an image of self-motion to the unstable order of bodies.

If then the self-motive essence is more ancient than that which is moved by another, but soul is primarily self-motive, hence soul must be more ancient than body; and all corporeal motion must be the progeny of soul, and of her inherent energy. It is necessary, therefore, that the heavens, with all their boundless contents, and their various natural motions (for a circular motion is natural to such bodies) should be endued with governing souls, essentially more ancient than their revolving bodies. According to the Platonic philosophers, therefore, these souls which orderly distinguish the universe and its contained parts, from their inherent cause of motion, give life and motion to every inanimate body. But it is necessary that every motive essence, should either move all things rationally, or irrationally; that is, either according to the uniform and unerring laws of reason, or according to the brutal impulse of an irrational nature. But the constant order observed in the periods of the celestial bodies, the convenience of their positions, and the admirable laws by which their revolutions are directed plainly evince that their motions are governed by a rational nature. If therefore, an intellectual and rational soul governs the universe, and if every thing eternally moved is under the directing influence of such a soul, may we not enquire whether it possesses this intellectual, perfect, and beneficent power, by participation, or essentially? for if essentially, it is necessary that every soul should be intellectual, since every soul is naturally self-motive. But if by participation, there must be another nature more ancient than soul, which operates entirely from energy; and whose essence is intelligence, on account of that uniform conception of universals, which it essentially contains. Because it is also necessary that the soul, essentially rational, should receive intellect by participation, and that intellectual energy should be of two kinds; one primarily subsisting in the divine intellect; but the other subsisting secondarily in its offspring soul. You may add too, the presence of intellectual illumination in body, which is received in as great perfection as its unstable and obscure nature will admit. For how is it possible that the celestial orbs should be for ever circularly moved in one definite order, preserving the same form, and the same immutable power, unless they participated of an intellectual nature. For soul is indeed the constant supplier of motion; but the cause of perpetual station, of identity and uniform life, reducing unstable motion to a circular revolution, and to a condition eternally the same, must be more ancient than soul.

Body, indeed, and whatever is the object of sense, belongs to the order of things moved by another. But soul is self-motive, embracing in itself, in a connected manner, all corporeal motions. And prior to this is immovable intellect. And here it is requisite to observe, that this immaterial nature must not be conceived as similar to any thing inert, destitute of life, and endued with no spirit, but as the principal cause of all motion, and the fountain of all life; as well of that whose streams perpetually return into itself, as of that which subsists in others, and has, on this account only, a secondary and imperfect existence.

All things, therefore, depend upon unity, through the medium of intellect and soul. And intellect is of an uniform essence; but soul of a mental form νοειδής, and the body of the world vivific, or vital ζωτικὸς. The first cause of all is indeed prior to intellect, but intellect is the first recipient of a divine nature; and soul is divine, so far as it requires an intellectual medium. But the body which participates a soul of this kind is divine, in as great a degree as the nature of body will admit. For the illustration of intellectual light pervades from the principle of things, to the extremes; and is not totally obscured, even when it enters the involutions of matter, and is profoundly merged in its dark and flowing receptacle.

The Hymns of Orpheus

Hence we may with reason conclude, that not only the universe, but each of its eternal parts is animated, and endued with intellect, and is in its capacity similar to the universe. For each of these parts is a universe if compared with the multitude it contains, and to which it is allied. There is, therefore, according to the Orphic and Platonic theology, one soul of the universe; and after this others, which from participating this general soul, dispose the entire parts of the universe into order; and one intellect which is participated by souls, and one supreme God, who comprehends the world in his infinite nature, and a multitude of other divinities, who distribute intellectual essences, together with their dependent souls, and all the parts of the world, and who are the perpetual sources of its order, union, and consent. For it is not reasonable to suppose that every production of nature should have the power of generating its similar, but that the universe and primary essences should not more abundantly possess an ability of such like procreation; since sterility can only belong to the most abject, and not to the most excellent, natures.

In consequence of this reasoning, Orpheus filled all things with Gods, subordinate to the demiurgus of the whole Δημιουργῷ, every one of which performs the office destined to his divinity, by his superiour leader. Hence according to his theology there are two worlds, the intelligible and the sensible. Hence too his three demiurgic principles: Jovial, Dionysiacal, and Adonical, Δίιος, Διονσιακὴ, Ἀδωνϊακὴ, from whence many orders and differences of Gods proceed, intelligible, intellectual, supermundane, mundane, celestial, authors of generation. And among these some in the order of guardian, demiurgic, elevating and comprehending Gods; perfecters of works, vivific, immutable, absolute, judicial, purgative, &c.; and besides these to each particular divinity, he added a particular multitude of angels, daemons, and heroes; for according to Proclus, relating the opinion of Orpheus, and the theologists:[7] "About every God there is a kindred multitude of angels, heroes, and daemons. For every God presides over the form of that multitude which receives the

[7] In Timaeum. p. 67.

divinity." He likewise considered a difference of sex in these deities, calling some male, and others female; the reason of which distinction[8] Proclus, with his usual elegance and subtilty, thus explains.

"The division of male and female comprehends in itself, all the plenitude of divine orders. Since the cause of stable power and identity, and the leader χόρηγος of being, and that which invests all things with the first principle of conversion, is comprehended in the masculine order. But that which generates from itself all various progressions and partitions, measures of life and prolific powers, is contained in the female division. And on this account Timaeus also, converting himself to all the Gods, by this division of generated natures, embraces their universal orders. But a division of this kind is particularly accommodated and proper to the present Theory, because the universe is full of this two-fold kind of Gods. For that we may begin with the extremes, heaven corresponds with earth, in the order and proportion of male to female. Since the motion of the heavens imparts particular properties and powers to particular things. But on the other hand earth receiving the celestial defluxions, becomes pregnant, and produces plants and animals of every kind. And of the Gods existing in the heavens, some are distinguished by the male division, and others by the female: and the authors of generation, since they are themselves destitute of birth, are some of this order and others of that, for the demiurgic choir is abundant in the universe. There are also many canals as it were of life, some of which exhibit the male and others the female form. But why should I insist on this particular? since from the absolute unities, whether endued with a masculine or a feminine form, various orders of beings flow into the universe." Thus far Proclus.

But that Orpheus was a monarchist, as well as a polytheist, is not only evident from the preceding arguments, originally derived from his Theology, but from the following verses quoted by Proclus.[9]

[8] In Tim. p. 290.   [9] In Tim. p. 95.

Hence with the universe great Jove contains
The aether bright, and heav'ns exalted plains;
Th' extended restless sea, and earth renown'd
Ocean immense, and Tartarus profound;
Fountains and rivers, and the boundless main,
With all that nature's ample realms contain,
And Gods and Goddesses of each degree;
All that is past and all that e'er shall be,
Occultly, and in fair connection,[10] *lies*
In Jove's wide womb, the ruler of the skies.

And in the same place, Proclus has preserved to us another copy of Orphic verses, which are also found in the writer (de Mundo); previous to which he observes, that the demiurgus, or artificer of the world, being full of ideas, comprehended by these all things within himself, as that theologer (Orpheus) declares. With these verses we have connected others, agreeable to the order of Stephens, Eschenbach, and Gesner, as follows:

Jove is the first and last, high thund'ring king,
Middle and head, from Jove all beings spring;
In Jove the male and female forms combine,
For Jove's a man, and yet a maid divine;
Jove the strong basis of the earth contains,
And the deep splendour of the starry plains;
Jove is the breath of all; Jove's wondrous frame
Lives in the rage of ever restless flame;
Jove is the sea's strong root, the solar light,
And Jove's the moon, fair regent of the night;
Jove is a king by no restraint confin'd,
And all things flow from Jove's prolific mind;
One is the pow'r divine in all things known,
And one the ruler absolute alone.
For in Jove's royal body all things lie,
Fire, night and day, earth, water and the sky;

[10] I have here followed the correction of Eschenbach, who reads σειρά instead of συῤῥά, which is I think more expressive and philosophical.

The first begetters pleasing love and mind;
These in his mighty body, Jove confin'd:
See, how his beauteous head and aspect bright
Illumine heav'n, and scatter boundless light!
Round which his pendant golden tresses shine
Form'd from the starry beams, with light divine;
On either side two radiant horns behold,
Shap'd like a bull's and bright with glittering gold;
And East and West in opposition lie,
The lucid paths of all the Gods on high;
His eyes, the sun, and moon with borrow'd ray;
His mind is truth, unconscious of decay,
Royal, aetherial; and his ear refin'd
Hears ev'ry voice, and sounds of ev'ry kind.
Thus are his head and mind immortal, bright,
His body's boundless, stable, full of light;
Strong are his members, with a force endu'd
Pow'rful to tame, but ne'er to be subdu'd;
Th' extended region of surrounding air
Forms his broad shoulders, back, and bosom fair;
And thro' the world the ruler of the skies
Upborne on natal, rapid pinions flies;
His sacred belly earth with fertile plains,
And mountains swelling to the clouds, contains;
His middle zone's the spreading sea profound,
Whose roaring waves the solid globe surround;
The distant realms of Tartarus obscure
Within earth's roots, his holy feet secure;
For these earth's utmost bounds to Jove belong,
And form his basis permanent and strong.
Thus all things Jove within his breast conceal'd,
And into beauteous light from thence reveal'd.

These verses contain what Dr. Cudworth calls the grand arcanum of the Orphic theology, that God is all things; which is likewise an Egyptian doctrine, from whence it was derived through Orpheus into Greece: and this sublime truth Plotinus[11] himself proves with his usual sagacity and depth. But here it is necessary to observe, that Orpheus and the Platonists do not conceive the Deity to be all things, as if he were a divisible, corporeal nature; but that he is all things, because present every where, and to every being totally, though more or less intimately present, according to the various gradations and approximations of being. So that he is to be considered as containing all things, and yet as separate and apart from all; as the source of all multitude, yet himself perfect unity; and as immensely prolific, yet divinely solitary and ineffably good. Thus, according to Porphyry, explaining the properties of incorporeal natures, "God, intellect, and soul are each of them every where, because no where. But God is every where, and at the same time, in no place of any being posterior to his nature; but he is only such as he is, and such as he willed himself to be. But intellect is indeed in the Deity, yet every where and in no place of its subordinate essences. And soul is in intellect, and in the Deity, every where and no where with respect to body; but body exists in soul, and in intellect, and in God. And though all beings, and non-entities, proceed from, and subsist in the Deity, yet he is neither entities, or non-entities, nor has any subsistence in them. For if he was alone every where, he would indeed be all things, and in all: but because he is likewise no where, all things are produced by him; so that they subsist in him because he is every where, but are different from him because he is no where. Thus also intellect being every where and no where, is the cause of souls, and of natures subordinate to soul: at the same time it is neither soul, nor such things as are posterior to the soul, nor has it any subsistence in them; and this because it is not only every where in its subordinate natures, but at the same time no where. Thus too, soul is neither body, nor in body, but is the cause of body; because while it is every where diffused through body, it is no

[11] Enn. 5. lib. vi.

179

where. And this procession of the universe extends as far as to that nature,[12] which is incapable of being at the same time every where and no where, but which partially participates of each. And in another place of the same excellent fragment, he tells us that the ancients explaining the property of an incorporeal nature, as far as this can be effected by discourse, when they affirmed it to be one, at the same time add, that it is likewise all things; that it is every where, and no where, and that it is totally present in every whole. He adds, they express its nature entirely by contrary properties, that they may remove from it the fictitious and delusive conceptions of bodies which obscure those properties by which true being is known.[13]

We have before observed, that the Platonic philosophers, agreeable to the doctrine of Orpheus, considered fecundity as, in an eminent degree, the property of a divine nature; and from this principle filled the universe with Gods.[14] This opinion a modern philosopher, or a modern writer on mythology, will doubtless consider as too ridiculous to need a serious refutation: the one, because he believes the phenomena may be solved by mechanical causes; and the other, in consequence of a system originating from prejudice, and supported without proof. However, prejudice apart, let us hear what the philosophers can urge in defence of this doctrine, in addition to what we have already advanced. To begin then with Onatus[15] the Pythagorean: "Those," says he, "who assert that there is but one God, and not many Gods, are deceived, as not considering that the supreme dignity of the divine transcendency consists in governing beings similar to itself, and in surpassing others. But the other Gods have the same

[12] Meaning material forms and qualities.

[13] It is remarkable that in the Hymn to Nature, among the following, the Deity is celebrated as all things, yet the poet adds that he is alone incommunicable; which perfectly agrees with the preceding account of his subsisting in all things, and at the same time being separate and apart from all.

[14] If the word Gods offends the ear of the reader, he may substitute in its stead, thrones, dominions, &c. for I do not discourse concerning words.

[15] Stob. Ecl. Phyf. p. 5.

relation to this first and intelligible God, as the dancers to the Coryphaeus, and as soldiers to their general, whose duty is to follow their leader. And although the same employment is common both to the ruler, and those who are ruled; yet the latter, if destitute of a leader, could no longer conspire together in one occupation; as the concord of the singers and dancers, and the expedition of the army, must fail, if the one is deprived of the Coryphaeus and the other of the captain or commander." To the same purpose Plotinus[16] shews that it is perfectly philosophical to suppose a multitude of Gods subordinate to the One supreme. "It is necessary," says he, "that every man should endeavour to be as good as possible, but at the same time, he should not consider himself as the only thing that is good; but should be convinced that there are other good men, and good daemons in the universe, but much more Gods: who though inhabiting this inferior region, yet look up to that higher world; and especially that most blessed Soul, the ruling Divinity of this universe. From whence a man ought to ascend still higher, and to celebrate the intelligible Gods, but above all their great King; declaring his majesty in a particular manner, by the multitude of Gods subordinate to his divinity. For it is not the province of those who know the power of God to contract all into one, but rather to exhibit all that divinity which he has displayed, who himself, remaining one, produces many, which proceed from him and by him. For the universe subsists by him, and perpetually speculates his divinity, together with each of the Gods it contains." Should it be objected, that if such Gods (or exalted beings) really existed, we should be able to demonstrate the reality of their existence, in the same manner as that of one supreme God; we cannot frame a better reply than in the words of Proclus.[17] "And perhaps," says he, "you may affirm that souls more swiftly forget things nearer to them; but have a stronger remembrance of superior principles. For these last operate on them more vigorously, through the sublimity of their power, and appear to be

[16] En. 2. lib. ix. cap. 9.
[17] In Tim. p. 286.

present with them by their energy. And this happens with respect to our corporeal sight; which does not perceive many things situated on the earth, yet observes the inerratic sphere, and the stars it contains; because these strongly irradiate our eyes with their light. So the eye of our soul is more forgetful, and sooner loses the sight of principles proximate to its nature, than of such as are more elevated and divine. In like manner all religions and sects confess that there is one highest principle, and men every where invoke God as their helper; but that there are Gods in subordination to this first cause, and that there is a providence proceeding from these to the universe, all men do not believe; and this because the one appears to them more perspicuously than the many."

Indeed in consequence of the Platonic doctrine of the pre-existence of the soul, it is not strange that we should know so little of those divine and exalted beings above us; since from our union with generation and material concerns, we are imbued with oblivion, ignorance, and error. "We are similar," as Porphyry[18] well observes, "to those who enter or depart from a foreign region, not only in casting aside our native manners and customs; but from the long use of a strange country we are imbued with affections, manners, and laws foreign from our natural and true religion, and with a strong propensity to these unnatural habits." As, therefore, it is not wonderful that the greatest part of those who inhabit a pestiferous region, should languish and decline, but that a very few should preserve their natural strength; so we ought not to wonder, that thus placed in generation, the multitude of mankind are obnoxious to passions and depraved habits; but we ought rather to be astonished if any souls, thus involved in the dark folds of the body, and surrounded with such great and unceasing mutations, are found sober, pure, and free from destructive perturbations. For it is surely astonishing that the soul should live immaterially, in material concerns; and preserve itself uncontaminated amidst such base defilements; that it should drink of the cup of oblivion, and not be laid asleep by the intox-

[18] De Abstinentia, lib. i.

icating draught; that it should elevate its eye above the sordid darkness with which it is surrounded; and be able to open the gates of truth, which, though contained in its essence, are guarded and shut by terrene and material species. But that it is possible to know more of such exalted natures than is generally believed, by the assistance of the ancient philosophy, accompanied with a suitable life, is, I am persuaded, true; and I would recommend the arduous and glorious investigation to every liberal mind.

Let us now consider the nature of sacrifice according to Orpheus and the Platonists; previous to which, I must beg leave to inform the reader, that the Greek theologists and philosophers were not (as they are represented by modern writers on mythology) so stupid as to worship the creature instead of the Creator; and to neglect or confound that homage and veneration, which is due to the first cause of all. On the contrary, they considered the supreme Being as honoured by the reverence paid to his most illustrious offspring; and carefully distinguished between the worship proper to the Deity, and to the subordinate Gods, as the following discourse will abundantly evince. How far, indeed, such opinions may be consistent with revelation, it is not my business to determine. It is sufficient for me, to give the most faithful account I am able of their sentiments on this subject; to free their opinions from misrepresentation; and to shew that God has not left himself without a witness among the wise and learned of the heathens. But as I cannot give a better account of the nature and antiquity of sacrifice than from the writings of Porphyry, I shall present the reader with the following paraphrase, on part of the second book of his excellent work on abstinence.

"The period of time appears to have been immensely distant, from which, as Theophrastus says, a nation the most learned of all others, and inhabiting the sacred region formed by the Nile, began first of all, from the domestic fire, to sacrifice to the celestial divinities; not with myrrh or cassia, nor with the first fruits of frankincense mingled with saffron, (for these were applied many ages afterwards, from error increasing in certain degrees: I mean at the period when men having surmounted the difficulties of a life formerly oppressed with the cares of procuring necessaries, and from the beginning to the end attended with many labours and tears, sacrificed perhaps a few drops to the Gods). For at first they performed sacrifices, not with aromatics, but with the first fruits of the green herb; plucking it with their hands, as a certain soft down or moss of prolific nature. Indeed the earth produced trees before animals; but prior to trees, the annually rising grass, the leaves, and roots, and entire produce of which having collected, they sacrificed with fire: by this sacrifice, saluting the visible celestial Gods, and rendering them through the ministry of fire immortal honours. For we preserve as sacred to those divinities, a perpetual fire in our temples; since this element is most similar to their lucid frames. But with respect to fumigations from herbs produced by the earth, they called the censer or pan, in which the herbs were burnt, θυμιατήριος, and to perform sacrifice θύειν, and the sacrifices themselves θυσίαι; all which we have erroneously interpreted, as if these words were signatures of that error, which afterwards crept in among us; and hence it is that we call the worship consisting from the slaughter of animals θυσίαι.

"Indeed so great was the care of the ancients in retaining their primaeval customs, that they uttered imprecations against those who deserted the old manner, and introduced a new one: and therefore they called those herbs with which we now fumigate ἀρώματα, aromatics. But the antiquity of the above mentioned fumigations will be perceived by him who considers that even now many odorous kinds of wood, cut into fragments, are employed in sacrifice. From whence it happened that the earth now bearing trees together with grass, its earliest production, men at first eating the fruits of oaks, burned only a few of these in sacrifices to the Gods, on account of the rarity of such sustenance; but sacrificed a multitude of the leaves. Afterwards human life passed to a gentle diet, and sacrifices were performed with nuts; from whence the proverb originated, ἅλις δρυὸς, enough of the oak.

"But among the fruits of Ceres, after the first appearance of leguminous barley, mankind were accustomed to sprinkle it, made into an entire mass, in their first sacrifices. Afterwards breaking the barley, and diminishing the nutriment into meal, having concealed the instruments of so great a work, which afford divine assistance to human life, they approached these as certain sacred concerns. But they cast the first fruits of the barley (when bruised into meal) and which was more esteemed than when whole, into the fire, in sacrifice to the Gods: from whence even now, at the conclusion of the sacrifice, we make use of meal mixed with wine and oil. By this custom indeed we indicate from whence, and from what beginnings sacrifices have increased to the present state: but, at the same time, we do not consider why such things are performed. Mankind proceeding from these small beginnings, and the earth yielding an abundant supply of corn and various fruits, they judged that the first produce of all the rest should be offered in sacrifices, with a view of pleasing the various orders of the Gods: selecting many things for this purpose, and mingling not a few others with these, if they possessed any thing beautiful, and on account of its odoriferous nature accommodated to divine sensation. With some of these, formed into garlands, they encircled the statues of the Gods; and others they sacrificed with fire. Likewise to the Gods as the proper causes, they poured forth the divine drops of wine, and honey, and oil, when their uses were first discovered.

"The truth of the preceding account appears to be confirmed by the procession celebrated even now at Athens, in honour of the sun and the hours. For in this solemnity grass is carried about, enwrapping the kernels of olives, attended with figs, all kinds of pulse, oaken boughs or acorns, the fruit of the strawberry, wheat, and barley, a mass of dried figs, cakes composed from the meal of wheat and barley, heaped in a pyramidal form, and last of all olives." Theophrastus then proceeds to shew the impropriety of animal sacrifices, after which he adds: "But the utility of fruits is the first and greatest of every production; the first fruits of which are to be sacrificed to the Gods alone, and to the Earth,

the prolific parent of every herb. For Earth is the common Vesta
of Gods and men, on whose fertile surface reclining, as on the soft
bosom of a mother or a nurse, we ought to celebrate her divinity
with hymns, and incline to her with filial affection, as to the
source of our existence. For thus, when we approach to the conclusion of our mortal life, we shall be thought worthy of a reception into the celestial regions, and of an association with the
race of immortal Gods, who now behold us venerating their
divinities with those fruits, of which they are the authors, and
sacrificing in their honour every herb of the all-bearing earth; at
the same time not esteeming every thing worthy or proper to be
offered as a testimony of our homage.

"For as every thing indiscriminately is not to be sacrificed to
the Gods, so perhaps we cannot find any thing sufficiently worthy,
with which we may worship them as they deserve." Thus far
Theophrastus. Porphyry then proceeds to shew after what manner those ought to sacrifice who propose an intellectual life, as
the ultimate object of their pursuit.

"Let us also," says he, "sacrifice, but in a manner becoming
the offspring of intellect, bringing with us the most exalted offerings, with our most exalted powers. To the Divinity indeed, who
is above all things, as a wise man said, neither sacrificing nor
dedicating any thing sensible or material; for there is nothing
subsisting by material concretion, which must not be deemed impure by a nature entirely free from the contagion of body. Hence
even the discourse, which is proffered by the voice is not proper
to be addressed to a cause so sublime and ineffable; nor the internal speech of the soul, if contaminated with any perturbation,
or mixed with any of the sensible phantasms of imagination. But
we ought to worship the supreme God, in the most profound
and pure silence; and with the purest thoughts concerning his
exalted nature. It is requisite, therefore, that having conjoined and
assimilated ourselves to him, we should approach this sublime
principle with a pious sacrifice, which may redound to his praise,
and to our safety. But such a sacrifice can only be performed by
contemplating his divinity with a soul free from material affec-

tions, and with the rational eye filled with intellectual light. But to the offspring of this first God (I mean the intelligible divinities) we should present the sacrifice of hymns, composed by the rational principle. For it is customary to offer the first-fruits of such things as every God bestows upon us; by which he nourishes and supports our existence, and which are subservient to the purposes of sacrifice. As the husbandman, therefore, performs sacred rites, by presenting handfuls of pulse and fruits, so ought we to sacrifice our purest thoughts, and other goods of the soul, thanking the divinities for the sublime contemplations they afford us, and for truly seeding our intellectual part with the speculation of their essences; for, conversing with us, and appearing to our mental sight; for shining upon us with divine splendours, and by this means procuring for us true salvation.

"But an exercise of this kind is performed in an indolent manner, by many who apply themselves to philosophy, and who, more sedulously cultivating fame than honouring the divinity, are wholly employed about statues, taking no care to learn after what manner, or whether or not these intellectual beings are to be adored; nor by properly consulting divine concerns, are they anxious to know in how great a degree we ought to strive after an union with these exalted natures. With such as these we by no means contend; since our only endeavour is to obtain a knowledge of divinity, and to imitate pious and ancient men, by frequently sacrificing of that contemplation which the Gods have bestowed upon us, and by the use of which we are partakers of real salvation.

"The Pythagoreans indeed who were very studious of numbers and lines, for the most part sacrificed of these to the Gods; denominating this number Minerva,[19] another Apollo; and again, this Justice, and another Temperance. They proceeded also in a similar manner in geometrical figures. Hence they pleased the divinities by sacrifices of this kind, calling each of them by their

[19] In the latter part of this Dissertation, we shall shew the wonderful agreement of the following Hymns, with the names given by Pythagoras to numbers.

proper names, for the purpose of obtaining their particular requests. They often besides made such invocations subservient to the purposes of divination; and if they required the investigation of any thing particular, they used the visible celestial Gods, also the wandering and fixed stars, of all which the sun ought to be placed as a leader, next to this the moon; and, as a theologian observes, we should make fire allied to these by a proximate conjunction. But the same person asserts that the Pythagoreans sacrificed no animal, but offered the first fruits of flour and honey, and of the diversified productions of the earth; nor kindled fire on the bloody altar, says he, with other things of a similar nature: but why should I transcribe such relations? For he who is truly studious of piety, knows why he ought not to sacrifice any thing animated to Gods; but alone to genii, and other powers superior to man, whether good or bad: he likewise knows to what kind of men it belongs to sacrifice these, and every circumstance respecting those beings, who require such sacrifices to be performed. With regard to other particulars I shall be silent. But what some Platonists have divulged will perspicuously illustrate the subject before us, which I shall relate as follows.

"The first God, since he is incorporeal, immoveable, and indivisible, neither existing in any being, place, or time, nor even circumscribed by, and as it were invested with himself, is in no respect indigent of any thing external to his nature, as we have already observed. But this last property of a divine essence is likewise true of the soul of the world, possessing a triple divisibility, and being naturally self-motive, yet so constituted that it chuses to move in an orderly and beautiful manner, and to agitate the corporeal fabric of the world according to the most excellent and harmonious reasons. But it associates to itself and is circularly invested with body, although incorporeal and entirely destitute of passion. But to the other Gods, to the world, and to the erratic and fixed stars, composed from body and soul, and to the visible divinities, testimonials of gratitude are to be offered by sacrificing with inanimate substances. After these there remains that multitude of invisible beings, which Plato indiscriminately calls daemons. Some of these are allotted a peculiar name by mankind, from whom they obtain divine honours and other kinds of religious worship: but others of these are for the most part called by no peculiar name, but are obscurely worshipped by some men, and are denominated according to certain streets of cities. But the remaining multitude are called by the common name of daemons. Concerning all these, a general persuasion obtains, that their influence is noxious and malignant if they are once angered because their accustomed worship is neglected; and that they are again beneficent if appeased by prayers and supplications, by sacrifices and convenient rites.

"But the confused opinion which subsists concerning these beings, and which has proceeded to great infamy, requires that we should distinguish their nature according to the decisions of reason. After this manner then they are distributed. As many souls as, proceeding from the universal soul, administer considerable parts of those places contained under the lunar orb, who are indeed connected with an aerial part, but subject it to the dominion of reason, are to be esteemed good daemons. We ought to believe that all their operations tend to the utility of the concerns subject to their dominion, whether they preside over certain animals, or over fruits assigned to their charge, or over things subservient to these particulars; such as prolific showers, moderate winds, serene weather, and whatever is calculated to promote these, as a good temperament of the seasons of the year, &c. They likewise administer to us the use of music, and of every discipline, together with the medicinal and gymnastic arts, and whatever else is allied to these. For it is impossible that such daemons can supply what is convenient and proper; and at the same time be the authors of things destructive and improper. In this class the messengers, as Plato calls them, between Gods and men must be numbered, who convey our prayers and pious offerings to the Gods as judges of our conduct, and bring back to us in return divine warnings, exhortations, and oracles. But as many souls as do not properly govern the aerial part with which they are connected, but are for the most part subdued by its influence, and are agitated and hurried away by its brutal power in a rash and disorderly manner, whenever the wrathful irritations and desires of the pneumatic part grow strong; souls of this kind are properly denominated daemons, but ought at the same time to be called malevolent and base.

"All these, together with those who obtain a contrary power, are invisible, and entirely imperceptible to human sensation; for they are not invested like terrene animals with a solid body; nor are they all endued with one shape; but they possess a diversity of forms. However, the forms impressed on their aerial part, are sometimes apparent, and at other times obscured. Sometimes too evil daemons change their shapes. But this pneumatic part, so far as corporeal, is subject to passion and change; and although it is so confined by the coercive power of these demoniacal souls, that its form continues for a long time, yet it is not by this means eternal. For it is reasonable to believe, that something continually flows from this aerial part; and that it receives a nutriment accommodated to its nature. Indeed the πνευμα, or aerial part of the good daemons, consists in a certain commensurate proportion, in the same manner as those bodies which are the objects of our present perception. But the bodies of the malevolent daemons are of a discordant temperament, on which account they inhabit that aerial space proximate to the earth, with a passive affection; and for the most part govern things subject to their dominion with a turbulent malignity. Hence there is no evil which they do not endeavour to perpetrate. For their manners are entirely violent and fraudulent, and destitute of the guardian perservation of better daemons; so that they machinate vehement and sudden snares with which they rush on the unwary; sometimes endeavouring to conceal their incursions, and sometimes acting with open violence against the subjects of their oppression." Thus far Porphyry: the length of which quotation needs no apology; both on account of its excellence, and because the unlearned reader will not find it elsewhere in English. I would also add that I wish (with a proper sense of the greatness of the undertaking) to offer this, together with the preceding and subsequent paraphrases, as specimens of that method mentioned in the Preface to this Work; and which I cannot but consider as the best means of exhibiting the Greek philosophy in modern languages.

Having then discoursed so largely from Porphyry concerning sacrifice, and as he particularly recommends the sacrifice performed by contemplation and divine hymns; let us hear his sentiments concerning the nature of prayer, as they are preserved to us by Proclus in his excellent Commentary on the Timaeus, p. 64. "It is requisite (says Proclus) before all things, that we understand something perspicuously concerning the nature of prayer: I mean in what its essence consists, what its perfection is, and from whence it becomes natural to our souls." He then proceeds to relate the opinion of Porphyry as follows. "For Porphyry, discoursing concerning such of the ancients as either approved of or exploded prayer, leads us through various opinions, which I shall now summarily relate. Neither those who labour under the first kind of impiety, I mean denying the existence of the Gods, claim any advantage to themselves from prayer: nor yet those of the second class, who entirely subvert a providence; for though they acknowledge the existence of the Gods, yet they deny their provident concern for the affairs of the universe. Nor again those of a third order, who though they confess that there are Gods, and that their providence extends to the world, yet consider all things as produced by the divinities from necessity: for the utility of prayer is derived from such things as are contingent, and may have a different existence. But those who both acknowledge the being of the Gods, and their continual providence, and that some events are contingent, and may subsist in a different manner; these men indeed may be truly said to approve of prayer, and to confess that the Gods correct our life, and establish in it safety." Proclus then proceeds to relate the reasons by which Porphyry confirms its utility. "He adds that prayer in a particular manner pertains to worthy men, because it conjoins them with divinity; for similars love to be united together: but a worthy man is in an eminent degree similar to the divine natures. We may likewise add, that since good men are placed in custody, and confined by the dark bands of the body as in a prison, they ought to pray to the Gods, that it may be lawful for them to depart from hence. Besides, since we are as children torn from the bosom of our parent, we ought on this account to request by our prayers that we may return to the Gods our true intellectual parents. If this is the case, do not they who deny that prayers are to be offered to the Gods, and who prevent their souls from being united with the divinities, that is with beings more excellent than themselves, appear similar to those who are deprived of their parents? Lastly, all nations who have flourished in the exercise of wisdom, have applied themselves to divine prayers: as the Brahmans among the Indians, the Magi among the Persians, and amongst the Greeks also, those who have excelled in the science of theology: for on this account they instituted mysteries and initiatory rites (τελεται). Besides, this consideration is not to be omitted, that since we are a part of this universe, it is consonant to reason that we should be dependent on it for support. For a conversion to the universe procures safety to every thing which it contains. If therefore you possess virtue, it is requisite you should invoke that divinity which previously comprehended in himself every virtue: for universal good is the cause of that good which belongs to you by participation. And if you seek after some corporeal good, the world is endued with a power which contains universal body. From hence therefore it is necessary that perfection should also extend to the parts." Thus far that most excellent philosopher Porphyry; in which quotation, as well as the preceding, the reader must doubtless confess, that Proclus did not without reason admire him, for what he calls his τὰ ἱεροπεπῆ νοήματα, or conceptions adapted to holy concerns; for surely no philosopher ever possessed them in a more eminent degree.

If it should be asked, in what the power of prayer consists, according to these philosophers? I answer, in a certain sympathy and similitude of natures to each other: just as in an extended chord, where when the lowest part is moved, the highest presently after gives a responsive motion. Or as in the strings of a musical instrument, attempered to the same harmony; one chord trembling from the pulsation of another, as if it were endued with sensation from symphony. So in the universe, there is one harmony though composed from contraries; since they are at the same time similar and allied to each other. For from the soul of the world, like an immortal self-motive lyre, life every where resounds, but in some things more inferior and remote from perfection than in others. And with respect to the super-mundane Gods, sympathy and similitude subsists in these as in their most perfect exemplars; from whence they are participated by sensible natures, their obscure and imperfect images. Hence (say they) we must not conceive, that our prayers cause any animadversion in the Gods, or, properly speaking, draw down their beneficence; but that they are rather the means of elevating the soul to these divinities, and disposing it for the reception of their supernal illumination. For the divine irradiation, which takes place in prayer, shines and energizes spontaneously, restoring unity to the soul, and causing our energy to become one with divine energy. For such, according to these philosophers, is the efficacy of prayer, that it unites all inferior with all superior beings. Since, as the great Theodorus says, all things pray except the first.

Indeed so great is the power of similitude, that through its unifying nature all things coalesce, and impart their particular properties to others. Whilst primary natures distribute their gifts to such as are secondary, by an abundant illumination, and effects are established in the causes from which they proceed. But the connection and indissoluble society of active universals, and of passive particulars, is every where beheld. For the generative causes of things are contained by similitude in their effects; and in causes themselves their progeny subsist, comprehended in perfect union and consent. Hence the celestial orbs impart a copious defluxion of good to this terrestrial region; while sublunary parts, assimilated in a certain respect to the heavens, participate a perfection convenient to their nature.

Hence too, from the progressions of similitude, there are various leaders in the universe. And many orders of angels dancing harmoniously round their ruling deities; together with a multitude of daemons, heroes, and particular souls. There are besides multiform kinds of mortal animals, and various powers of plants. So that all things tend to their respective leaders, and are as it were stamped with one sign of domestic unity; which is in some more evident, and others more obscure. For indeed similitude in first productions subsists more apparently; but in those of the middle and extreme orders is obscured in consequence of the gradations of progression. Hence images and exemplars derive their hypostasis from conciliating similitude; and every thing through this is familiar to itself, and to its kindred natures.

But it is time to return from this digression to the business of sacrifice and prayer. That we may therefore have a clearer view of the nature and efficacy of each, let us hear the elegant and subtle Proclus,[20] upon sacrifice and magic, of which the following is a paraphrase.

"In the same manner as lovers gradually advance from that beauty which is apparent in sensible forms, to that which is divine; so the ancient priests, when they considered that there was a certain alliance and sympathy in natural things to each other, and of things manifest to occult powers, and by this means discovered that all things subsist in all, they fabricated a sacred science from this mutual sympathy and similarity. Thus they recognized things supreme, in such as are subordinate, and the subordinate in the supreme: in the celestial regions terrene properties subsisting in a causal and celestial manner; and in earth celestial properties, but according to a terrene condition. For how shall we account for those plants called heliotropes, that is attendants on the sun, moving in correspondence with the revolution of its orb; but selenitropes, or attendants on the moon, turning in exact conformity with her motion? it is because all things pray, and compose hymns to the leaders of their respective orders; but some intellectually, and others rationally; some in a

[20] As a Latin version only of this valuable work is published, the reader will please to make allowances for the Paraphrase, where it may be requisite.

natural, and others after a sensible manner. Hence the sunflower, as far as it is able, moves in a circular dance towards the sun; so that if any one could hear the pulsation made by its circuit in the air, he would perceive something composed by a sound of this kind, in honour of its king, such as a plant is capable of framing. Hence we may behold the sun and moon in the earth, but according to a terrene quality. But in the celestial regions, all plants, and stones, and animals, possess an intellectual life according to a celestial nature. Now the ancients having contemplated this mutual sympathy of things, applied for occult purposes both celestial and terrene natures, by means of which through a certain similitude they deduced divine virtues into this inferior abode. For indeed similitude itself is a sufficient cause of binding things together in union and consent. Thus if a piece of paper is heated, and afterwards placed near a lamp, though it does not touch the fire, the paper will be suddenly inflamed, and the flame will descend from the superior to the inferior parts. This heated paper we may compare to a certain relation of inferiors to superiors; and its approximation to the lamp, to the opportune use of things according to time, place, and matter. But the procession of fire in the paper aptly represents the presence of divine light, to that nature which is capable of its reception. Lastly, the inflammation of the paper may be compared to the deification of mortals, and to the illumination of material natures, which are afterwards carried upwards like the fire of the paper, from a certain participation of divine seed. Again, the lotus before the rising of the sun, folds its leaves into itself, but gradually expands them on its rising: unfolding them in proportion to the sun's ascent to the zenith; but as gradually contracting them as that luminary descends to the west. Hence this plant by the expansion and contraction of its leaves appears no less to honour the sun than men by the gesture of their eye-lids, and the motion of their lips. But this imitation and certain participation of supernal light is not only visible in plants, which possess but a vestige of life, but likewise in particular stones. Thus the sun-stone, by its golden rays, imitates those of the sun;

but the stone called the eye of heaven, or of the sun, has a figure similar to the pupil of an eye, and a ray shines from the middle of the pupil. Thus too the lunar stone, which has a figure similar to the moon when horned, by a certain change of itself, follows the lunar motion. Lastly, the stone called Helioselenus, i.e. of the sun and moon, imitates after a manner the congress of those luminaries, which it images by its colour. So that all things are full of divine natures; terrestrial natures receiving the plenitude of such as are celestial, but celestial of supercelestial essences; while every order of things proceeds gradually in a beautiful descent, from the highest to the lowest. For whatever is collected into one above the order of things is afterwards dilated in descending, various souls being distributed under their various ruling divinities. In fine, some things turn round correspondent to the revolutions of the sun, and others after a manner imitate the solar rays, as the palm and the date: some the fiery nature of the sun, as the laurel, and others a different property. For indeed we may perceive the properties which are collected in the sun every where distributed to subsequent natures constituted in a solar order; that is, to angels, daemons, souls, animals, plants, and stones. Hence the authors of the ancient priesthood, discovered from things apparent, the worship of superior powers, while they mingled some things, and purified with others. They mingled many things indeed together, because they saw that some simple substances possessed a divine property (though not taken singly) sufficient to call down that particular power, of which they were participants. Hence by the mingling of many things together, they attracted upon us a supernal influx; and by the composition of one thing from many, they symbolised with that one, which is above many; and composed statues from the mixtures of various substances, conspiring in sympathy and consent. Besides this, they collected composite odours, by a divine art, into one, comprehending a multitude of powers, and symbolising with the unity of a divine essence. Considering besides, that division debilitates each of these, but that mingling them together restores them to the idea of their exemplar; hence the ancient priests, by the mutual relation and sympathy of things to one another, collected their virtues into one, but expelled them by repugnancy and antipathy; purifying, when it was requisite, with sulphur and bitumen, and the sprinkling of marine water. For sulphur purifies from the sharpness of its odour; but marine water on account of its fiery portion. Besides this, in the worship of the Gods, they offered animals, and other substances congruous to their nature; and received in the first place the powers of daemons as proximate to natural substances and operations, by whose assistance they evocated these natural bodies to which they approached into their presence. Afterwards they proceeded from daemons to the powers and energies of the Gods, partly indeed from daemoniacal instruction, but partly by their own industry, aptly interpreting symbols, and ascending to a proper intelligence of the Gods. And lastly laying aside natural substances and their operations, they received themselves into the communion and fellowship of the Gods." Thus far Proclus, and thus much for the theological doctrine of Orpheus, as contained in the works of the latter Platonists. I persuade myself enough has been said in this Dissertation to convince every thinking and liberal mind, that the Greek theology as professed and understood by the Greek philosophers is not that absurd and nonsensical system represented by modern prejudice and ignorance as the creed of the ancients. In consequence of a blind and mistaken zeal it is common to ridicule the opinions of the ancient philosophers, in order to establish the certainty of the Christian religion. But surely revelation does not require so unwarrantable and feeble a support, which in reality only betrays the cause it endeavours to defend, by giving infidels occasion to suspect, either weakness in its evidence, or obscurity in its fundamental doctrines. Besides, the generality of these uncandid opponents know nothing of the Platonical writers, from whom alone genuine information can be derived on this sublime and intricate subject; and from whose works the preceding Dissertation has been so abundantly enriched. Were these invaluable books more generally known and understood, if they did not refine our taste, at present so depraved, they would at least teach us to admire the strength which human reason is capable of exerting, and to be more modest in our pretensions to wisdom; they would silence ignorant declaimers, and stop the immense increase of books on modern philosophy, which are so rapidly hastening to the abyss of forgetfulness, like streams into the ocean from which they originally flowed.

SECTION III

But it is now time to speak of the following Hymns, of which, as we have before observed, Onomacritus is the reputed author. And first, with regard to the dialect of these Hymns, Gesner well observes it ought to be no objection to their antiquity. For though, according to Iamblichus,[21] the Thracian Orpheus, who is more ancient than those noble poets Homer and Hesiod, used the Doric dialect; yet the Athenian Onomacritus, who, agreeable to the general opinion of antiquity, is the author of all the works now extant, ascribed to Orpheus,[22] might either, preserving the sentences and a great part of the words, only change the dialect, and teach the ancient Orpheus to speak Homerically, or as I may say Solonically: or might arbitrarily add or take away what he thought proper, which Herodotus relates was his practice, with respect to the oracles. Gesner adds, that it does not appear probable to him that Onomacritus would dare to invent all he writ, since Orpheus must necessarily, at that time, have been in great repute, and a variety of his verses in circulation: and he concludes with observing that the objection of the Doric dialect ought to be of no more weight against the antiquity of the present works, than the Pelasgic letters, which Orpheus used according to Diodorus Siculus.

The hymns of Orpheus are not only mentioned by Plato in

[21] De Vita Pythag. c. 34. p. 169. Kuft.

[22] Philoponus observes, in his Commentary on Aristotle's books of the Soul, that Aristotle calls the Orphic verses reputed, because they appear not to have been written by Orpheus himself, as Aristotle affirms in his book concerning philosophy. For the Dogmata contained in them were indeed his, but Onomacritus is reported to have put them into verse.

his Eighth Book of Laws, but also by Pausanias,[23] whose words
are translated as follows by the author of the Letters on Mythology.[24] "The Thracian Orpheus (says Pausanias) was represented
on mount Helicon, with ΤΕΛΕΤΗ (initiation or religion) by his
side, and the wild beasts of the woods, some in marble, some in
bronze, standing round him. His hymns are known by those
who have studied the poets to be both short and few in number.
The Lycomedes, an Athenian family dedicated to sacred music,
have them all by heart, and sing them at their solemn mysteries.
They are but of the second class for elegance, being far excelled
by Homer's in that respect. But our religion has adopted the
hymns of Orpheus, and has not done the same honour to the
hymns of Homer." To the testimony of Pausanias may be added
that of Suidas, who, among the writings of the Libethrian Orpheus mentions τελεται, or initiations, which he says are by
some ascribed to Onomacritus.[25] And Scaliger well observes, in
his notes to these hymns, that they ought rather to be called
initiations, because they contain only invocations of the Gods,
such as the initiated in mysteries are accustomed to use; but they
do not celebrate the nativities, actions, &c. of the divinities, as it
is usual in hymns. It is on this account we have entitled them
mystical initiations, which is doubtless their proper appellations.
The author too of the Allegories in the Theogony of Hesiod,[26]
relating the powers of the planets on things inferior, expressly
mentions these hymns, or rather initiations, and many of the
compound epithets with which they abound.[27] From all which
it is evident that the following Hymns were written by the
Athenian Onomacritus, and are the same with those so much
celebrated by antiquity. Indeed it is not probable they should be
the invention of any writer more modern than the above period,
as it must have been so easy to detect the forgery, from the orig-

[23] In Boeoticis p. 770.
[24] Page 167.
[25] It is remarkable that Sextus Empiricus more than once mentions
Onomacritus in the Orphics. Ονομάκριτος ἐν τοῖς Ορφικοῖς.
[26] Page 267.
[27] Vide Fabric. Bib. p. 124.

inal initiations which were even extant at the time in which Suidas lived.

In the former part of this Dissertation, we asserted that we should derive all our information concerning the Orphic theology from the writings of the Platonists; not indeed without reason. For this sublime theology descended from Orpheus to Pythagoras, and from Pythagoras to Plato; as the following testimonies evince. "Timaeus (says Proclus)[28] being a Pythagorean, follows the Pythagoric principles, and these are the Orphic traditions; for what Orpheus delivered mystically in secret discourses, these Pythagoras learned when he was initiated by Aglaophemus in the Orphic mysteries." Syrianus too makes the Orphic and Pythagoric principles to be one and the same; and, according to Suidas, the same Syrianus composed a book, entitled the Harmony of Orpheus, Pythagoras and Plato. And again Proclus:[29] "it is Pythagorical to follow the Orphic genealogies; for from the Orphic tradition downward by Pythagoras, the science concerning the Gods was derived to the Greeks." And elsewhere,[30] "All the theology of the Greeks is the progeny of the sacred initiations ($\mu\nu\sigma\tau\alpha\gamma\omega\gamma\acute{\iota}\alpha\iota$) of Orpheus. For Pythagoras first learned the orgies of the Gods from Aglaophemus; but Plato was the second who received a perfect science of these, both from the Pythagoric, and Orphic writings." Now in consequence of these testimonies, our hymns ought to agree with the doctrine of Pythagoras; especially since Onomacritus, their author, was of that school. And that they do so, the following discovery abundantly evinces.

Photius, in his Bibliotheca, has preserved to us part of a valuble work, written by Nicomachus the Pythagorean, entitled Theological Arithmetic; in which he ascribes particular epithets, and the names of various divinities to numbers, as far as to ten. There is likewise a curious work of the same title, by an anonymous writer, which is extant only in manuscript. From these two, and from occasional passages respecting numbers according to Pythagoras, found in the Platonic writers, Meursius has composed a

[28] In Timaeum. p. 291.   [29] In Tim. p. 289.
[30] In Theol. Plat. p. 13.

book, which he calls Denarius Pythagoricus; and which is an invaluable treasure to such as are studious of the ancient philosophy. On perusing this learned book, it seemed to me necessary, that as the divinities, ascribed to each number, had a particular relation to one another, they should also have a mutual agreement in the following hymns. And on the comparison I found the most perfect similitude: a few instances of which I shall select, leaving a more accurate investigation of this matter to the learned and philosophical reader.

In the first place then, among the various names ascribed to the monad or unity, are those of the following Gods; viz. the Sun, Jupiter, Love, Proteus, Vesta. Now in the hymn to the Sun we find the epithet ἀθάνατε Ζεῦ, O immortal Jove. In that to Love πυρίδρομος, or wandering fire, which is likewise found in the hymn to the Sun. In the hymn to Love, that deity is celebrated as having the keys of all things; viz. of aether, heaven, the deep, the earth, &c. And Proteus is invoked as possessing the keys of the deep. Again, Vesta, in the Orphic hymns, is the same with the mother of the Gods; and the mother of the Gods is celebrated as "always governing rivers, and every sea"; which perfectly agrees with the appellations given both to Love and Proteus. Again, among the various epithets ascribed to the duad, or number two, are, Phanes, Nature, Justice, Rhea, Diana, Cupid, Venus, Fate, Death, &c. Now Phanes, in the Orphic hymns, is the same with Protogonus; and Nature is called πρωτογενία, or first-born, and δίκη, or Justice, as also πεπρωμενή, or Fate. Likewise Rhea is denominated θύγατερ πολυμορφου Πωτογονόιο, or daughter, of much formed Protogonus; and in the same hymn the reader will find other epithets, which agree with the appellation given to Nature. Again, both Nature and Diana are called ὠκυλοχεία, or swiftly bringing forth; and Love as well as Nature is called διφυῆ, or two-fold. In like manner Rhea and Venus agree, for he says of Venus πάντα γὰρ ἐκ σέθεν ἐστὶν, for all things are from thee; and of Rhea, Μήτηρ μέν τε θεῶν ἠδε θνητῶν ἀνθρώτων, or mother of Gods and mortal men. After which he expressly says that earth and heaven, the sea and the air, proceed from her divinity. Besides this, he celebrates Venus as governing the three Fates; καὶ κρατέεις τρισσῶν μοιρῶν. And lastly he says of Love, after representing that Deity as invested with the keys of all things; thou alone rulest the governments of all these; which he likewise affirms of Death in the same words. And thus much for the duad. The triad, or number three, they denominated Juno, Latona, Thetis, Hecate or Diana, Pluto, Tritogenia or Minerva, &c. Now Latona and Thetis, are each of them called in these initiations, κυανόπεπλος, or dark-veiled; and Minerva and the Moon, who is the same with Diana, θῆλυς καὶ ἄρσην, female and male. The tetrad or number four, they denominated Hercules, Vulcan, Mercury, Bacchus, two-mothered, Bassarius, key-keeper of nature, Masculine, Feminine, the World, (which in these initiations is the same with Pan) Harmony, Justice. Now Onomacritus calls Hercules and Vulcan, Καρτεροχειρ, or strong-handed; and he celebrates Hercules and Mercury as "having an almighty heart." παγκρατὲς ἦτορ ἔχων. And so of the rest. The pentad or number five they called Nature, Pallas, Immortal, Providence, Nemesis, Venus, Justice, &c. Now Nature is called in these hymns, or rather initiations πολυμήχανε μῆτερ, or much-mechanic Mother, and παντοτεχνής, or universal Artist; and Minerva is denominated μητερ τεχνῶν, or Mother of Arts. Like-wise Nature is expressly called ἀθανάτη τε πρόνοια, or Immortal, and Providence. The hexad or number six, they denominated, Venus, Health, the World, Ἑκατηβελέτις, or far-darting, (be-cause compounded of the triad, which is called Hecate), Persaea, triform, Amphitrite, &c. Now Venus, as we have already ob-served in the names of the duad, is said to be the source of all things; and Health is expressly called μῆτερ ἀπαντων, or Mother of all things. Again the heptad, or number seven they called Fortune, Minerva, Mars, &c. And Fortune, in these initiations, is the same with Diana or the Moon, who is called male and female as well as Minerva; and Minerva and Mars are each of them denominated ὁπλοχαρής or armipotent, and Minerva πολεμοκλόνε, or full of warlike tumult. The ogdoad, or number eight, they called Rhea, Love, Neptune, Law. And the Mother of the Gods, who is the same with Rhea, is represented as we have observed on the monad, as governing rivers and every sea;

and Love is said to have the keys of all things; of heaven, the deep, &c. The ennead, or number nine, they denominate Ocean, Prometheus, Vulcan, Poean (i.e. Apollo or the Sun), Juno, Proserpine, &c. Now Saturn (who is called in these initiations Prometheus) and Ocean, are each of them celebrated as the source of Gods and men: and Vulcan is expressly called ἥλιος or the Sun. And lastly they denominated the decad, Heaven, the Sun, Unwearied, Fate, Phanes, Necessity, &c. Hence Heaven is called in these initiations φύλαξ πάντων, or Guardian of all things; and the Sun πιστοφύλαξ, or faithful Guardian; and ἀκάμα or Unwearied, is an appellation of the Sun, in the hymn to that Deity. The reader too will find many epithets in the hymn to Protogonus or Phanes, corresponding with those of the Sun. And thus much for the agreement of these hymns, with the Pythagoric names of numbers. The limits of the present work will not permit me to be more explicit on this particular; but he who wishes to understand the meaning of many of the preceding appellations, may consult the valuable book of Meursius, already cited, where he will meet with abundant matter for deep speculation. But before I conclude this Dissertation, I must beg leave to acquaint the reader with another discovery which I have made respecting these hymns, equally curious with the former.

Ficinus, on Plato's Theology,[31] has the following remarkable passage, translated, most likely from some manuscript work of Proclus, as I conjecture from its conclusion; for, unfortunately, he does not acquaint us with the author. "Those who profess, says he, the Orphic theology consider a two-fold power in souls and in the celestial orbs: the one consisting in knowledge, the other in vivifying and governing the orb with which that power is connected. Thus in the orb of the earth, they call the nostic power Pluto, the other Proserpine.[32] In water, the former power Ocean, and the latter Thetis. In air, that thundering Jove, and this Juno. In fire, that Phanes, and this Aurora. In the soul of the lunar sphere, they call the nostic power Licnitan Bacchus, the other

[31] Lib. iv. p. 128.

[32] The reader may observe that this two-fold power is divided into male and female; the reason of which distribution we have already assigned from Proclus.

Thalia. In the sphere of Mercury, that Bacchus Silenus, this Euterpe. In the orb of Venus, that Lysius Bacchus, this Erato. In the sphere of the sun, that Trietericus Bacchus, this Melpomene. In the orb of Mars, that Bassareus Bacchus, this Clio. In the sphere of Jove, that Sebazius, this Terpsichore. In the orb of Saturn, that Amphietus, this Polymnia. In the eighth sphere, that Pericionius, this Urania. But in the soul of the world, the nostic power, Bacchus Eribromus, but the animating power Calliope. From all which the Orphic theologers infer, that the particular epithets of Bacchus are compared with those of the Muses on this account, that we may understand the powers of the Muses, as intoxicated with the nectar of divine knowledge; and may consider the nine Muses, and nine Bacchuses, as revolving round one Apollo, that is about the splendor of one invisible Sun." The greater part of this fine passage is preserved by Gyraldus, in his Syntagma de Musis, and by Natales Comes, in his Mythology, but without mentioning the original author. Now if the Hymn to the Earth, is compared with the Hymns to Pluto and Proserpine; the one to Ocean, with that to Thetis; and so of the other elements agreeable to the preceding account, we shall discover a wonderful similitude. And with respect to the celestial spheres, Silenus Bacchus, who, according to the preceding account, should agree with Mercury, is called in these initiations τροφὴ, or Nourishment, and Mercury, τροφιουχε, or Nourisher. Venus, who should agree with Lysius Bacchus, is called κρυφία or Occult, and ἐρατοπλόκαμος, or lovely-haired, and σεμνὴ Βάκχοιο παρεδρε, or venerable attendant of Bacchus; and Lysius is denominated κρυψίγονος, or an occult offspring and καλλιέθειρα, or fair-haired. In like manner Trietericus Bacchus is called παιάν χρυσεγχὴς, or Apollo pouring golden light, which evidently agrees with the sun. Again, Bassarius Bacchus is celebrated as rejoicing in swords and blood, ὃς ξιφεσιν χαιρεις, ἠδ᾽ αἵμασι, κ. λ. which plainly corresponds with Mars, as the hymn to that Deity evinces in a particular manner. Sebazius and Jupiter evidently agree, for Sebazius is expressly called υἱος Κρονου, son of Saturn. And Amphietus is celebrated as moving in concert with the circling hours, Εὐάζων κινῶν τε χοροῦς ἐνι κυκλάσιν ὥραις, which corresponds with Saturn, who is called in these Hymns Τιταν, or the Sun.[33] And lastly, Dionysius who is called in these Initiations Eribromus, is denominated δικέρωτα, or two-horned, which is also an epithet of Pan, or the soul of the world. And thus much for the doctrine of these Hymns, so far as is requisite to an introductory Dissertation. What farther light we have been able to throw on these mysterious remains of antiquity, will appear in our following Notes. If the valuable Commentary of Proclus on the Cratylus of Plato was once published, I am persuaded we should find them full of the most recondite antiquity:[34] but as this is not to be expected in the present age, the lovers of ancient wisdom will, I doubt not, gratefully accept the preceding and subsequent elucidations. For on a subject so full of obscurity as the present, a glimmering light is as conspicuous, and as agreeable to the eye of the mind, as a small spark in profound darkness is to the corporeal sight.

[33] I have omitted a comparison between the eighth sphere and Pericionius from necessity, because there is no hymn among the following to that orb. And I have not contrasted Licnitan Bacchus with the lunar Sphere, because the resemblance is not apparent; though doubtless there is a concealed similitude.

[34] This is evident from the following epistle of Lucas Holstenius to P. Lambecius, preserved by Fabricius in that excellent work, his Bibliotheca Graeca. tom. i. p. 117:

"Habeo et Orphei exemplar non contemnendum, ex quo Argonautica plurimis locis emendavi. Auctor ille huc usque a Criticorum et Correctorum vulgo derelictus tuam exposcere videtur operam. Hymni autem reconditae antiquitatis plenissimi justum commentarium merentur, quem vel unius Procli scripta ἀνέκδοτα tibi instruent, ut ex notis meis ad Sallustium Philosophum prospicies: ne quid de caeteris, quos apud me habeo, Platonicis nunc dicam, in quibus τῆς μυθικης θεολογίας thesaurus latet."

[Tr.: I have also a copy of Orpheus which is not to be despised and from which I have emended the Argonautica in several passages. This author, who has so far been neglected by the body of Critics and Emendators, seems to demand your attention. Moreover, the hymns are steeped in remote antiquity, and deserve an adequate commentary which even the unedited writings of Proclus alone will provide for you, as you will see from my notes on Sallust the Philosopher—to say nothing at the moment of the other writers on Plato I have with me, in whom there is a great wealth of mystical theology.]

THE INITIATIONS OF
ORPHEUS

TO MUSAEUS[1]

Attend Musaeus to my sacred song,
And learn what rites to sacrifice belong.
Jove I invoke, the earth, and solar light,
The moon's pure splendor, and the stars of night;
Thee Neptune, ruler of the sea profound,
Dark-hair'd, whose waves begirt the solid ground;

[1] As these Hymns, though full of the most recondite antiquity, have never yet been commented on by any one, the design of the following notes is to elucidate, as much as possible, their concealed meaning, and evince their agreement with the Platonic philosophy. Hence they will be wholly of the philosophic kind: for they who desire critical and philological information will meet with ample satisfaction in the notes of the learned Gesner, to his excellent edition of the Orphic Remains.

The present Introduction to Musaeus, the son of Orpheus, is, as Gesner observes, a summary of the work, without being servilely confined to the exact number of divinities: and the reader will please to observe through the whole of these Hymns, that the Orphic method of instruction consists in signifying divine concerns by symbols alone. And here it will be necessary to speak of philosophical mythology; as an accurate conception of its nature will throw a general light on the Hymns, and, I hope, contribute to the dispersion of that gloom in which this sublime subject has been hitherto involved, through the barbarous systems of modern mythologists. Proclus then, on Plato's Republic, p. 170, observes, that there are two kinds of fables: one, accommodated to puerile institution, but the other full of divine fury, which regards universal nature more than the ingenuity of the auditors. He then observes that the hearers of fables are likewise to be distinguished: for some are of a puerile and simple ingenuity; but others are capable of rising higher, and of estimating intellectually the genera of the Gods, their progressions through all nature, and their various orders, which are extended to the utmost bounds of the universe. Hence, says he, having distributed both fables and the hearers of fables into two parts, we cannot allow that the fables of Homer and Hesiod are accommodated to puerile institution; since they follow the nature and order of the universe, and unite with true beings such minds as are capable of being elevated to divine considerations.

Indeed nature herself, fabricating the images of intelligible essences, and of ideas totally destitute of matter, pursues this design by many and various ways. For by parts she imitates things destitute of all parts, eternal natures by such as are temporal, intelligibles by sensibles, simple essences by such as are mixt, things void of quantity by dimensions, and things stable by unceasing mutations: all which she endeavours to express as

209

Ceres abundant, and of lovely mien,
And Proserpine infernal Pluto's queen;
The huntress Dian, and bright Phoebus rays,
Far-darting God, the theme of Delphic praise;
And Bacchus, honour'd by the heav'nly choir,
And raging Mars, and Vulcan god of fire;
The mighty pow'r who rose from foam to light,
And Pluto potent in the realms of night;
With Hebe young, and Hercules the strong,
And you to whom the cares of births belong:

---

much as she is able, and as much as the aptitude of appearances will permit. Now the authors of fables, having perceived this proceeding of nature, by inventing resemblances and images of divine concerns in their verses, imitated the exalted power of exemplars by contrary and most remote adumbrations: that is, by shadowing forth the excellency of the nature of the Gods by preternatural concerns: a power more divine than all reason, by such as are irrational: a beauty superior to all that is corporeal by things apparently base, and by this means placed before our eyes the excellence of divinity, which far exceeds all that can possibly be invented or said. After this, in another place of the same excellent work, he gives us some instances of the occult significations of fables: previously observing that those names which among us denote a worse condition of being, and have a worse signification, when applied to divine concerns, denote in the figments of the poets, a more excellent nature and power. Thus a bond among men is the impediment and retention of action: but in divine concerns it insinuates a conjunction and ineffable union with causes; and hence the Saturnian bonds signify the union of the demiurgus of the universe with the intelligible and paternal excellence of Saturn. A falling and precipitation signifies with us a violent motion; but in divine concerns, it indicates a prolific progression, and a presence every where loosened and free, which does not desert its proper principle, but depending from it pervades through every order. After this manner, the precipitation of Vulcan intimates the progression of divinity from the highest principle to the extreme artificers of sensible things; which process is moved, perfected, and deduced from the first demiurgus and parent. Thus too castration in bodies which are composed from parts and matter brings on a diminution of power: but in primary causes it shadows forth the progression of such as are secondary into a subject order: since primary causes revolve and produce the powers placed in their essences, yet are neither moved through the egression of secondaries, nor diminished by their separation, nor divided by the laceration of inferiors.

The Hymns of Orpheus

Justice and Piety august I call,
And much-fam'd nymphs, and Pan the god of all.
To Juno sacred, and to Mem'ry fair,
And the chaste Muses I address my pray'r;
The various year, the Graces, and the Hours,
Fair-hair'd Latona, and Dione's pow'rs;
Armed Curetes, household Gods I call,
With those who spring from Jove the king of all:
Th' Idaean Gods, the angel of the skies,
And righteous Themis, with sagacious eyes;
With ancient night, and day-light I implore,
And Faith, and Justice dealing right adore;
Saturn and Rhea, and great Thetis too,
Hid in a veil of bright celestial blue:
I call great Ocean, and the beauteous train
Of nymphs, who dwell in chambers of the main;
Atlas the strong, and ever in its prime,
Vig'rous Eternity, and endless Time;
The Stygian pool, and placid Gods beside,
And various Genii, that o'er men preside;
Illustrious Providence, the noble train
Of daemon forms, who fill th' aetherial plain;
Or live in air, in water, earth, or fire,
Or deep beneath the solid ground retire.
Bacchus and Semele the friends of all,
And white Leucothea of the sea I call;
Palaemon bounteous, and Adrastria great,
And sweet-tongu'd Victory, with success elate;
Great Esculapius, skill'd to cure disease,
And dread Minerva, whom fierce battles please;
Thunders and winds in mighty columns pent,
With dreadful roaring struggling hard for vent;
Attis, the mother of the pow'rs on high,
And fair Adonis, never doom'd to die,
End and beginning he is all to all,

211

These with propitious aid I gently call;
And to my holy sacrifice invite,
The pow'r who reigns in deepest hell and night;
I call Einodian Hecate, lovely dame,[2]
Of earthly, wat'ry, and celestial frame,
Sepulchral, in a saffron veil array'd,
Pleas'd with dark ghosts that wander thro' the shade;
Persian, unconquerable huntress hail![3]
The world's key-bearer never doom'd to fail;
On the rough rock to wander thee delights,
Leader and nurse be present to our rites;
Propitious grant our just desires success,
Accept our homage, and the incense bless.

[I]

TO THE GODDESS PROTHYRAEA[4]

THE FUMIGATION FROM STORAX

O venerable goddess, hear my pray'r,
For labour pains are thy peculiar care;
In thee, when stretch'd upon the bed of grief,
The sex as in a mirror view relief.
Guard of the race, endued with gentle mind,
To helpless youth, benevolent and kind;

---

[2] Jo. Diac. Allegor. ad Hesiodi Theog. p. 268. cites this line, upon which, and Hymn LXXI. 3. he observes, Εὑρίσκω, τὸν Ὀρφέα καὶ τὴν ΤΥΧΗΝ 'ΑΡΤΕΜΙΝ προσαγορεύοντα, ἀλλὰ καὶ την ΣΕΛΗΝΗΝ ΕΚΑΤΗΝ, i.e. "I find that Orpheus calls Fortune Artemis, or Diana, and also the Moon, Hecate."

[3] Diodorus informs us that Diana, who is to be understood by this epithet, was very much worshipped by the Persians, and that this goddess was called Persaea in his Time. See more concerning this epithet in Gyrald. Syntag. ii. p. 361.

[4] An epithet of Diana's, alluding to her presiding over gates, and being as it were the gate-keeper of life. It is remarkable that the first of these Hymns should be addressed to the goddess who ushers in our existence, and the last to Death. This certainly proves the collection is complete.

Benignant nourisher; great Nature's key
Belongs to no divinity but thee.
Thou dwell'st with all immanifest to sight,
And solemn festivals are thy delight.
Thine is the task to loose the virgin's zone,
And thou in ev'ry work art seen and known.
With births you sympathize, tho' pleas'd to see
The numerous offspring of fertility;
When rack'd with nature's pangs and sore disstress'd,
The sex invoke thee, as the soul's sure rest;
For thou alone can'st give relief to pain,
Which art attempts to ease, but tries in vain;
Assisting goddess, venerable pow'r,
Who bring'st relief in labour's dreadful hour;
Hear, blessed Dian, and accept my pray'r,
And make the infant race thy constant care.

[II]

TO NIGHT

THE FUMIGATION WITH TORCHES

Night, parent goddess, source of sweet repose,
From whom at first both Gods and men arose,
Hear, blessed Venus, deck'd with starry light[5]
In sleep's deep silence dwelling Ebon night!
Dreams and soft ease attend thy dusky train,
Pleas'd with the length'ned gloom and feastful strain.
Dissolving anxious care, the friend of Mirth,
With darkling coursers riding round the earth.
Goddess of phantoms and of shadowy play,
Whose drowsy pow'r divides the nat'ral day:
By Fate's decree you constant send the light
To deepest hell, remote from mortal sight;

[5] See the reason why Night is called Venus, in the notes to Hymn V
to Protogonus.

For dire Necessity which nought withstands,
Invests the world with adamantine bands.
Be present, Goddess, to thy suppliant's pray'r,
Desir'd by all, whom all alike revere,
Blessed, benevolent, with friendly aid
Dispell the fears of Twilight's dreadful shade.

[III]

TO HEAVEN

THE FUMIGATION FROM FRANKINCENSE

Great Heav'n, whose mighty frame no respite knows,
Father of all, from whom the world arose:
Hear, bounteous parent, source and end of all,
Forever whirling round this earthly ball;
Abode of Gods, whose guardian pow'r surrounds[6]
Th' eternal World with ever during bounds;
Whose ample bosom and encircling folds
The dire necessity of nature holds.
Aetherial, earthly, whose all-various frame[7]
Azure and full of forms, no power can tame.
All-seeing Heav'n, progenitor of Time,
Forever blessed, deity sublime,
Propitious on a novel mystic shine,
And crown his wishes with a life divine.

[6] *Whose guardian power surrounds,* &c. and line 11, *All-seeing Heaven,*
ὁ τοῦ Ὀρφέος οὐρανὸς οὖρος καὶ πάντων φυλὰξ εἶναι βούλεται. Damascius
περὶ ἀρχῶν, i.e. "according to Orpheus, Heaven is the inspector and guardian
of all things."

[7] We have already observed in our Dissertation, that according to the
Platonists, subordinate natures are contained in the supreme, and such as
are supreme in the subordinate: and this doctrine which is originally
Egyptian, is mentioned by Proclus in Tim. p. 292. as Orphical. ἔστι γὰρ
καὶ ἐν γῇ οὐρανὸς καὶ ἐν οὐρανῷ γῆ, καὶ ἐνταῦθα μὲν ὁ οὐρανὸς χθονίως, ἐκεῖ
δὲ οὐρανίως ἡ γῆ, i.e. "heaven is in earth, and earth in heaven; but here
heaven subsists in an earthly manner, and there earth in a celestial manner."

[IV]

TO FIRE

THE FUMIGATION FROM SAFFRON[8]

O ever untam'd Fire, who reign'st on high
In Jove's dominions ruler of the sky;
The glorious sun with dazzling lustre bright,
And moon and stars from thee derive their light;
All taming pow'r, aetherial shining fire,
Whose vivid blasts the heat of life inspire:
The world's best element, light-bearing pow'r,
With starry radiance shining, splendid flow'r,
O hear my suppliant pray'r, and may thy frame
Be ever innocent, serene, and tame.

[V]

TO PROTOGONUS
Or the FIRST-BORN[9]

THE FUMIGATION FROM MYRRH

O mighty first-begotten, hear my pray'r,
Two-fold, egg-born, and wand'ring thro' the air,

---

[8] Saturn.

[9] According to Orpheus, as related by Syrianus in Metaph. Aristot. p. 114, the first principle of all things is Unity or the Good itself, and after this the Duad, or Aether and Chaos, subsists, according to Pythagoras. The first of these, or Aether, approaches to a similitude of the one itself, and is the representative of bound; the other, Chaos, comprehends in its essence multitude and infinity. Afterwards (says Syrianus) the first and secret genera of the Gods subsists, among which the first apparent is the king and father of the universe, whom on this account they call Phanes. Now this first and secret genera of the Gods is no other than all the demiurgical and intellectual ideas, considered as proceeding to the production of the sensible World, from their occult subsistence in Aether and Chaos, whose mutual connection Orpheus represents under the symbol of an egg: upon the exclusion of which egg, by night considered as a principle, the God Phanes came forth, who is hence denominated Protogonus. Διὸ καὶ παρ᾽

Thomas Taylor the Platonist

Bull-roarer,[10] *glorying in thy golden wings,*
From whom the race of Gods and mortals springs.
Ericapaeus, celebrated pow'r,
Ineffable, occult, all shining flow'r.
From eyes obscure thou wip'st the gloom of night,
All-spreading splendour, pure and holy light;
Hence Phanes call'd, the glory of the sky,
On waving pinions thro' the world you fly.
Priapus, dark-ey'd splendour, thee I sing,
Genial, all-prudent, ever-blessed king,
With joyful aspect on our rights divine
And holy sacrifice propitious shine.

Ορφεῖ ὁ Φάνης περικαλλέος αἰθέρος υἱὸς ονομάζεται, καὶ ἁβρὸς Ἔρως, says Proclus, in Tim. ii. p. 132, I.e. "on this account Phanes is called by Orpheus, the son of beautiful Aether, and tender Love." There is likewise another valuable passage on this subject from Proclus, in Tim. p. 291. as follows. "Orpheus delivers the kings of the Gods, who preside over the universe according to a perfect number; Phanes, Night, Heaven, Saturn, Jupiter, Bacchus. For Phanes is first adorned with a sceptre, is the first king, and the celebrated Ericapaeus. But the second king is Night, who receives the sceptre from the father Phanes. The third is Heaven, invested with government from Night. The fourth Saturn, the oppressor as they say of his father. The fifth is Jupiter, the ruler of his father. And the sixth of these is Bacchus. But all these kings having a supernal origin from the intelligible and intellectual Gods, are received into the middle orders, and in the world, both which they adorn. For Phanes is not only among the intelligible Gods, but also among the intellectual ones; in the demiurgic order, and among the super-mundane and mundane Gods. And Night and Heaven in a similar manner: for the peculiarities of these are received through all the middle orders. But with respect to the great Saturn himself, has he not an order prior to that of Jupiter, and likewise posterior to the jovial king, distributing the Dionysiacal administration (δημιουργία) together with the other Titans? and this indeed in a different manner in the heavens and in things above the moon. And differently in the inerratic stars and in the planets; and in a similar manner Jupiter and Bacchus." Now on comparing the present hymn, and the hymns to Night, Heaven, Saturn and Jupiter together, we shall find them celebrated as the sources of all things; and Bacchus is expressly called Protogonus.

[10] Phanes, who, according to the preceding account, is the author of the sensible world, is represented by Orpheus (for the purpose of shadowing forth the causal, not the temporal production of the universe) as

[VI]

TO THE STARS

THE FUMIGATION FROM AROMATICS

With holy voice I call the stars on high,
Pure sacred lights and genii of the sky.
Celestial stars, the progeny of Night,
In whirling circles beaming far your light,
Refulgent rays around the heav'ns ye throw,
Eternal fires, the source of all below.
With flames significant of Fate ye shine,
And aptly rule for men a path divine.
In seven bright zones ye run with wand'ring flames,
And heaven and earth compose your lucid frames:[11]

---

adorned with the heads of a ram, a bull, a serpent, and a lion. Now Mithras, according to the Persian theology as related by Porphyry, de antro Nymph., is the father and creator of all things. And he informs us that the ancient priests of Ceres called the Moon who is the queen of generation ταῦρος or a Bull (p. 262.) and p. 265 ὡς καὶ ὁ ταῦρος δημιουργός ὤν ὁ Μίθρας, καὶ γενεσέως δεσπότης. I.e. "Mithras as well as the Bull is the demiurgus of the universe, and the lord of generation." The reason therefore is obvious why Phanes is called Bull-roarer. Hence too from the account of Phanes given by Proclus, it follows that what that divinity is in the intelligible, that Thetis must be in the sensible world. For Thetis according to Proclus, lib. v. in Timaeum, is Πρεσβυττατη Θεῶν, καὶ Πρόγονος, or the most ancient and progenitor of the Gods: and Thetis the mother of Venus, and Protogonus the father of Night. Venus therefore in the sensible world is the same as Night in the intelligible; and the reason is evident why Night in these Hymns is called Venus. I cannot conclude this note without observing how much it is to be lamented that the Platonical writers are so little known and understood in the present age: for surely if these valuable works had been consulted, it would have appeared that Protogonus and Noah resembled each other as much as the ancient and modern philosophy; or as much as an ancient commentator on Plato, and *a modern Mythologist.*

[11] It is an Orphic and Pythagoric opinion that the stars are inhabited; on which account they are called in this hymn, earthly. But the greatest geniuses of antiquity were of the same opinion; such as Anaxagoras, Aristarchus, Heraclitus, Plato, &c. and among the Platonists not a few, as Alcinous, Plotinus, and Plutarch. Thales too is said to have called the stars earthly, by which it is probable he was of the same opinion.

With course unwearied, pure and fiery bright
Forever shining thro' the veil of Night.
Hail twinkling, joyful, ever wakeful fires!
Propitious shine on all my just desires;
These sacred rites regard with conscious rays,
And end our works devoted to your praise.

[VII]

TO THE SUN

THE FUMIGATION FROM FRANKINCENSE AND MANNA

Hear golden Titan, whose eternal eye
With broad survey, illumines all the sky:
Self-born, unwearied in diffusing light,
And to all eyes the mirrour of delight:
Lord of the seasons, with thy fiery car
And leaping coursers, beaming light from far:
With thy right hand the source of morning light,[12]
And with thy left the father of the night.
Agile and vig'rous, venerable Sun,
Fiery and bright around the heav'ns you run.
Foe to the wicked, but the good man's guide,
O'er all his steps propitious you preside:
With various-sounding, golden lyre, 'tis thine
To fill the world with harmony divine.
Father of ages, guide of prosp'rous deeds,
The world's commander, borne by lucid steeds,
Immortal Jove,[13] *all-searching, bearing light,*

[12] Proclus, in lib. vi. Theol. Plat. p. 380, says that those who are skilled in divine concerns, attribute two hands to the Sun; denominating one the right hand, the other the left.

[13] According to the Orphic and Platonic philosophers, the Sun is the same in the sensible, as Apollo in the intellectual, and Good in the intelligible World. Hence Proclus, in Theol. Plat. p. 289, from the occult union subsisting between Good, Apollo, and the Sun, calls the Sun βασιλεὺς τοῦ παντός, or king of the universe: and it is well known that Jupiter is the demiurgus of the world. So that the Sun in perfect conformity to this Theology is called immortal Jove.

Source of existence, pure and fiery bright:
Bearer of fruit, almighty lord of years,
Agil and warm, whom ev'ry pow'r reveres.
Great eye of Nature and the starry skies,
Doom'd with immortal flames to set and rise:
Dispensing justice, lover of the stream,
The world's great despot, and o'er all supreme.
Faithful defender,[14] and the eye of right,
Of steeds the ruler, and of life the light:
With founding whip four fiery steeds you guide,
When in the car of day you glorious ride.
Propitious on these mystic labours shine,
And bless thy suppliants with a life divine.

[VIII]

TO THE MOON[15]

THE FUMIGATION FROM AROMATICS

Hear, Goddess queen, diffusing silver light,

[14] Proclus, lib. v. in Timaeum, informs us in the words of Orpheus
ὅτι ἥλιον μὲν ἐπέστησε τοῖς ὅλοις, ὁ δημιουργος, καὶ φύλακα αὐτὸν ἔτευξε,
κέλευσε τε πασιν ἀναάσσειν. "That the demiurgus placed the Sun in the
universe, and fabricated him as its guardian, commanding him to govern
all things."

[15] The Moon is called in this Hymn both σελήνη and μηνη: the former
of which words signifies the Moon in the language of the Gods; and the
latter is the appellation given to her by Men, as the following Orphic
fragment evinces.

> Μήσατο δ᾽ ἄλλην Γαιαη ἀπείριτον, ἤντε Σελήνην
> Ἀθάνατοι κλήζουσιν, ἐπιχθόνιοι δὲ τε Μηνην.
> Ἡ πολλ᾽ οὔρε ἔχει, πολλ᾽ ἄστεα, πολλα μέλαθρα.

That is, "But he (Jupiter) fabricated another boundless earth, which
the immorals call Selene, but Men, Mene. Which has many mountains,
many cities, many houses." Now this difference of names arises, according
to the Platonic philosophers, from the difference subsisting between divine
and human knowledge. For (say they) as the knowledge of the Gods is
different from that of particular souls: so with respect to names some
are divine, exhibiting the whole essence of that which is named; but
others are human, which only partially unfolds their signification. But

Bull-horn'd[16] *and wand'ring thro' the gloom of Night.*
With stars surrounded, and with circuit wide
Night's torch extending, thro' the heav'ns you ride:
Female and Male[17] *with borrow'd rays you shine,*
And now full-orb'd, now tending to decline.
Mother of ages, fruit-producing Moon,
Whose amber orb makes Night's reflected noon:
Lover of horses, splendid, queen of Night,
All-seeing pow'r bedeck'd with starry light.
Lover of vigilance, the foe of strife,
In peace rejoicing, and a prudent life:

---

a larger account of this curious particular is given by Proclus, in Theol. Plat. p. 69, as follows. There are three kinds of names: the first and most proper, and which are truly divine, subsist in the Gods themselves. But the second which are the resemblances of the first, having an intellectual subsistence, must be esteemed of divine condition. And the third kind which emanate from Truth itself, but are formed into words for the purpose of discourse, receiving the last signification of divine concerns, are enunciated by skillful men; at one time by a divine afflatus, at another time by energising intellectually, and generating the images of internal spectacles moving in a discursive procession. For as the demiurgic intellect represents about matter the significations of primary forms comprehended in its essence; temporal signatures of things eternal; divisible representatives of things indivisible, and produces as it were shadowy resemblances of true beings: after the same manner I think the science we possess, framing an intellectual action, fabricates by discourse both the resemblances of other things, and of the Gods themselves. So that it fashions by composition, that which in the Gods is void of composition: that which is simple by variety; and that which is united by multitude. And by this formation of names it demonstrates in the last place the images of divine concerns. And as the theurgic art provokes by certain signs, supernal illumination into artificial statues, and allures the unenvying goodness of the Gods; in the same manner the intellectual science of divine concerns, signifies the occult essence of the God by the compositions and divisions of sounds.

[16] For the mystical reason of this appellation, see note to the third line, of the Hymn to Protogonus.

[17] This is not wonderful, since according to the fragment of Ficinus in this Dissertation, all souls and the celestial spheres are endued with a two-fold power, nostic and animating; one of which is male and the other female. And these epithets are perpetually occurring in the Orphic Initiations.

Fair lamp of Night, its ornament and friend,
Who giv'st to Nature's works their destin'd end.[18]
Queen of the stars, all-wise Diana hail!
Deck'd with a graceful robe and shining veil;
Come, blessed Goddess, prudent, starry, bright,
Come moony-lamp with chaste and splendid light,
Shine on these sacred rites with prosp'rous rays,
And pleas'd accept thy suppliant's mystic praise.

[IX]

TO NATURE[19]

THE FUMIGATION FROM AROMATICS

Nature, all parent, ancient, and divine,
O much-mechanic mother, art is thine;
Heav'nly, abundant, venerable queen,
In ev'ry part of thy dominions seen.
Untam'd, all-taming, ever splendid light,

[18] In the original it is τελεσφορος, i.e. bringing to an end. And Proclus in Theol. Plat. p. 483. informs us that Diana (who is the same with the Moon) is so called, because she finishes or perfects the essential perfection of matter.

[19] Nature, according to the theologists, as related by Proclus, in Tim. p. iv, is the last of the dimiurgic causes of this sensible world, and the boundary of the latitude of incorporeal essences: and is full of reasons and powers, by which she governs the universe, every where connecting parts with their wholes. Hence Nature is represented in this Hymn as turning the still traces of her feet with a swift whirling. For since she is the last of the demiurgic causes, her operations aptly symbolize with the traces of feet. Now the reason why the epithets of much-mechanic, all-artist, connecting, all-wise, providence, &c. are given to nature, which evince her agreement with Minerva, is because that Goddess, according to the Orphic theology, fabricated the variegated veil of nature, from that wisdom and virtue of which she is the presiding divinity. And Proclus informs us, that she connects all the parts of the universe together: containing in herself intellectual life, by which she illuminates the whole, and unifying powers by which she superintends all the opposing natures of the world. Nature, therefore, from her connecting, and unifying power, and from her plenitude of seminal reasons, has an evident agreement with Minerva; whose divine arts according to the Orphic theology, reduce

All-ruling, honor'd, and supremely bright.
Immortal, first-born, ever still the same,
Nocturnal, starry, shining, glorious dame.
Thy feet's still traces in a circling course,
By thee are turn'd, with unremitting force.
Pure ornament of all the pow'rs divine,
Finite and infinite alike you shine;[20]
To all things common and in all things known,
Yet incommunicable and alone.
Without a father of thy wond'rous frame,
Thyself the father whence thy essence came.
All-flourishing, connecting, mingling soul,
Leader and ruler of this mighty whole.
Life-bearer, all-sustaining, various nam'd,
And for commanding grace and beauty fam'd.
Justice, supreme in might, whose general sway
The waters of the restless deep obey.
Aetherial, earthly, for the pious glad,
Sweet to the good, but bitter to the bad.

---

whatever in the universe is discordant and different, into union and consent.

Again, agreeable to this theology, primary natures impart their gifts to such as are secondary by an abundant illumination, and effects are established in the causes from which they proceed: so that in the obscure language of Heraclitus, all things are one, and one all things. Hence Nature though the last of the demiurgic causes, is with perfect conformity to this symbolical Theology, said to be both communicable and incommunicable; without a father and at the same time the father of her own being. For considered as full of operative reasons, she is communicable to every sensible nature: but considered as the representative of divine unity, she is incommunicable. And in like manner as symbolising with the first cause, she is both without any origin, and at the same time the source of her own essence.

[20] Philolaus according to Demetrius (in Laert.) published a discourse concerning Nature, of which this is the beginning: φύσις δὲ ἐν τῷ κόσμῳ ἁρμόχθη ἐξ ἀπείρον τε καὶ περαινότων, καὶ ὅλος κόσμος καὶ τὰ ἐν αυτῳ παντα. i.e. "Nature, and the whole world, and whatever it contains, are aptly connected together from infinites and finites."

All-wise, all-bounteous, provident, divine,
A rich increase of nutriment is thine;
Father of all, great nurse, and mother kind,
Abundant, blessed, all-spermatic mind:
Mature, impetuous, from whose fertile seeds
And plastic hand, this changing scene proceeds.
All-parent pow'r, to mortal eyes unseen,
Eternal, moving, all-sagacious queen.
By thee the world, whose parts in rapid flow,[21]
Like swift descending streams, no respite know,
On an eternal hinge, with steady course
Is whirl'd, with matchless, unremitting force.
Thron'd on a circling car, thy mighty hand
Holds and directs the reins of wide command.
Various thy essence, honor'd, and the best,
Of judgement too, the general end and test.
Intrepid, fatal, all-subduing dame,
Life-everlasting, Parca, breathing flame.
Immortal, Providence, the world is thine,
And thou art all things, architect divine.
O blessed Goddess, hear thy suppliant's pray'r,
And make my future life, thy constant care;
Give plenteous seasons, and sufficient wealth,
And crown my days with lasting peace and health.

[21] Since the world has an extended and composite essence, and is on this account continually separated from itself, it can alone be connected by a certain indivisible virtue infused from the divine unity. Again, since from a natural appetite, it is ever orderly moved towards good, the nature of such an appetite and motion must originate from a divine intellect and goodness. But since, from its material imperfection, it cannot receive the whole of divine infinity at once, but in a manner accommodated to its temporal nature: it can only derive it gradually and partially, as it were by drops, in a momentary succession. So that the corporeal world is in a continual state of flowing and formation, but never possesses real being; and is like the image of a lofty tree seen in a rapid torrent, which has the appearance of a tree without the reality; and which seems to endure perpetually the same, yet is continually renewed by the continual renovation of the stream.

[X]

TO PAN[22]

THE FUMIGATION FROM VARIOUS ODOURS

I call strong Pan, the substance of the whole,
Etherial, marine, earthly, general soul,
Immortal fire; for all the world is thine,
And all are parts of thee, O pow'r divine.
Come, blessed Pan, whom rural haunts delight,
Come, leaping, agile, wand'ring, starry light;
The Hours and Seasons, wait thy high command,
And round thy throne in graceful order stand.
Goat-footed, horned, Bacchanalian Pan,
Fanatic pow'r, from whom the world began,
Whose various parts by thee inspir'd, combine
In endless dance and melody divine.
In thee a refuge from our fears we find,
Those fears peculiar to the human kind.
Thee shepherds, streams of water, goats rejoice,
Thou lov'st the chace, and Echo's secret voice:[23]
The sportive nymphs,[24] *thy ev'ry step attend,*
And all thy works fulfill their destin'd end.

[22] Pan, it is well known, is the same with the Universe, and is called by Orpheus προτογονος (Protogonus), as we are informed by Damascius περὶ ἀρχῶν. Now Jupiter in the Orphic theology, is the demiurgus of the universe, or first intellect; and Apollo, in the intellectual world, is the same with Jupiter, as we have shewn in our notes to the Sun. Hence the reason is obvious why Pan is called in this Hymn, all-fertile Paean. And if we compare the Orphic fragment, given in the Dissertation, with the present Hymn, we shall find a striking resemblance; as the king and father of the universe, Protogonus or Jupiter is there celebrated as being all things; and is represented under the symbol of a divine body, whose members are the various parts of the world.

[23] Phurnutus informs us, that Pan is reported to dwell in solitary places, for the purpose of evincing his unity. For the World is one, and only-begotten. Opusc. Mythol. p. 203.

[24] This is because Pan rejoices in the exhalations produced from humid substances; without which the world cannot subsist.

O all-producing pow'r, much-fam'd, divine,
The world's great ruler, rich increase is thine.
All-fertile Paean, heav'nly splendor pure,
In fruits rejoicing, and in caves obscure.[25]
True serpent-horned Jove,[26] *whose dreadful rage*
When rous'd, 'tis hard for mortals to asswage.
By thee the earth wide-bosom'd deep and long,
Stands on a basis permanent and strong.
Th' unwearied waters of the rolling sea,
Profoundly spreading, yield to thy decree.
Old Ocean too reveres thy high command,
Whose liquid arms begirt the solid land.
The spacious air, whose nutrimental fire,
And vivid blasts, the heat of life inspire;
The lighter frame of fire, whose sparkling eye
Shines on the summit of the azure sky,
Submit alike to thee, whose general sway
All parts of matter, various form'd, obey.
All nature's change thro' thy protecting care,
And all mankind thy lib'ral bounties share:
For these where'er dispers'd thro' boundless space,
Still find thy providence support their race.
Come, Bacchanalian, blessed power draw near,

[25] A cave, as we learn from Porphyry, de Antro Nympharum, is an apt symbol of the material world; since it is agreeable at its first entrance on account of its participation of form, but is involved in the deepest obscurity to the intellectual eye, which endeavours to discern its dark foundation. So that, like a cave, its exterior and superficial parts are pleasant; but its interiour parts are obscure, and its very bottom, darkness itself.

[26] The reason why Pan is horned is because Jove is the mingler of all things, according to Orpheus, as we learn from Jo. Diac. Allegor. in Hesiod, p. 305; and the word κεραστής is as Gesner observes, derived from the verb κεράννυμι to mingle: so that horns are an occult symbol of the mingling and tempering power of the demiurgus of the world. But the literal meaning of the word κεραστής is horned serpent; and one of the heads of Protogonus is that of a serpent. We may add that Pan considered as the soul of the world is with great propriety called Jove; since that appellation is given by Orpheus to the mundane soul.

Fanatic Pan, thy humble suppliant hear,
Propitious to these holy rites attend,
And grant my life may meet a prosp'rous end;
Drive panic Fury too, wherever found,
From human kind, to earth's remotest bound.

[XI]

TO HERCULES

THE FUMIGATION FROM FRANKINCENSE

Hear, pow'rful, Hercules untam'd and strong,
To whom vast hands, and mighty works belong,
Almighty Titan, prudent and benign,
Of various forms, eternal and divine,
Father of Time, the theme of gen'ral praise,
Ineffable, ador'd in various ways.
Magnanimous, in divination skill'd,
And in the athletic labours of the field.
'Tis thine strong archer, all things to devour,
Supreme, all-helping, all-producing pow'r;
To thee mankind as their deliv'rer pray,
Whose arm can chase the savage tribes away:
Unweary'd, earth's best blossom,[27] *offspring fair,*

---

[27] Since, according to the Orphic theology, there are two worlds, the intelligible and the sensible, the former of which is the source of the latter; so, according to the same theology, the first contains in a primary, causal, and intellectual manner, what the second comprehends secondarily and sensibly. Hence it contains an intellectual heaven and earth, not like the material, existing in place, and affected with the circulations of Time; but subsisting immaterially in the stable essence of eternity. In this divine world, another sun, and moon, and stars shine with intellectual light; for every thing there is perfectly lucid, light continually mingling with light. There, as Plotinus divinely observes, every star is a sun: and though all things are beheld in every thing, yet some things are more excellent than others. Now from this intellectual heaven and earth, resident in Phanes, the king and father of the universe, Orpheus, according to Proclus, derives the orders of the Gods, subordinate to this sensible heaven and earth: and among these he relates the following progeny of the intellectual

The Hymns of Orpheus

To whom calm peace, and peaceful works are dear.
Self-born, with primogenial fires you shine,[28]
And various names and strength of heart are thine.
Thy mighty head supports the morning light,
And bears untam'd, the silent gloomy night;
From east to west endu'd with strength divine,
Twelve glorious labours to absolve is thine;

---

earth, as preserved by Proclus in his excellent Commentary on the Timaeus, p. 295, and by Athenagoras in Apol. "She produced seven beautiful pure virgins with voluble eyes, and seven sons, all of them kings, and covered with downy hair; the daughters are Themis and prudent Tethys, and fair-haired Mnemosyne, and blessed Thea; together with Dione, having an illustrious form, and Phoebe and Rhea the mother of king Jupiter. But this illustrious earth generated celestial sons, which are also sirnamed Titans, because they took revenge on the great starry heaven; and these are Caeus and great Craeus, and robust Phorcys, and Saturn, and Ocean, and Hyperion, and Iapetus." Now Hercules is celebrated in this Hymn as the Sun, as the nineteenth and twentieth lines particularly evince; and the Sun is the same with Hyperion; hence the reason is obvious why Hercules is called "earth's best blossom." And we shall find that Saturn in the following hymn is called "blossom of the earth"; and Themis, in Hymn 78, "young blossom of the earth"; and the Titans, in Hymn 36, "the illustrious progeny of heaven and earth."

[28] Since the intelligible world, which, as we have already observed, was produced from Aether and Chaos, is nothing else than the comprehension of all the demiurgic ideas in the divine mind, which is, according to Orpheus, the God Phanes; it remains that the sensible world, which is but the image τον Νοητον Παραδείγματος of an intelligible paradigm, should be produced according to its similitude, and filled with its proper divinities. Now Phanes, the author of the sensible world, is represented by Orpheus (for the purpose of symbolically representing the causal production of the universe) as adorned with the heads of various animals. According to Athenagoras, with the head of a dragon, of a lion, and the countenance of the God himself; but according to Proclus and others, in the words of Orpheus, with the countenance of a ram, a bull, a serpent, and a lion. And this Phanes, Athenagoras informs us, is denominated by Orpheus, Hercules and Time. Hence we see the reason why Hercules is said to shine with primogenial fires; since he is no other than Protogonus in the intelligible, and the Sun in the sensible, world. Hence too the reason is apparent why Saturn who is the same with Time, is called in the following hymn, τιτὰν i.e. Titan, or the Sun.

227

Supremely skill'd, thou reign'st in heav'n's abodes,
Thyself a God amid'st th' immortal Gods.
With arms unshaken, infinite, divine,
Come, blessed pow'r, and to our rites incline;
The mitigations of disease convey,
And drive disastrous maladies away.
Come, shake the branch with thy almighty arm,
Dismiss thy darts and noxious fate disarm.

[XII]

TO SATURN

THE FUMIGATION FROM STORAX

Etherial father, mighty Titan,[29] hear,
Great sire of Gods and men, whom all revere:
Endu'd with various council, pure and strong,
To whom perfection and decrease belong.
Consum'd by thee all forms that hourly die,
By thee restor'd, their former place supply;
The world immense in everlasting chains,
Strong and ineffable thy pow'r contains;
Father of vast eternity, divine,
O mighty Saturn, various speech is thine:
Blossom of earth and of the starry skies,
Husband of Rhea, and Prometheus wife.
Obstetric Nature, venerable root,
From which the various forms of being shoot;
No parts peculiar can thy pow'r enclose,
Diffus'd thro' all, from which the world arose.
O, best of beings, of a subtle mind,
Propitious hear to holy pray'rs inclin'd;
The sacred rites benevolent attend,
And grant a blameless life, a blessed end.

[29] See the notes to the preceding hymn.

[XIII]

TO RHEA[30]

THE FUMIGATION FROM AROMATICS

Daughter of great Protogonus,[31] *divine,*
Illustrious Rhea, to my pray'r incline,
Who driv'st thy holy car with speed along,
Drawn by fierce lions, terrible and strong.[32]
Mother of Jove, whose mighty arm can wield
Th' avenging bolt, and shake the dreadful shield.

[30] Rhea, according to the Orphic and Platonic theology, is one of the
zoogonic or vivific principles of the universe; have a maternal rank
among the universal paternal orders, i.e. between Saturn and Jupiter. Hence
she calls forth the causes latent in Saturn to the procreation of the universe;
and definitely unfolds all the genera of the Gods. So that she is filled from
Saturn, with an intelligible and prolific power, which she imparts to
Jupiter the demiurgus of the universe; filling his essence with a vivific
abundance. Since this Goddess then is a medium between the two intellectual parents of the universe, Saturn and Jupiter, the former of which
collects intellectual multitude into one, but the other scatters and divides it.
Hence says Proclus, in Theol. Plat. p. 266, this Goddess produces in herself the demiurgic causes of the universe; but imparts her diffusive power
abundantly to secondary natures. On this account Plato assimilates her
prolific abundance to the flowing of waters; signifying nothing more by
the word *flowing*, than that fontal power, by which she singularly contains the divisible rivers of life. And, p. 267, Proclus informs us, that this
Goddess, according to Orpheus, when considered as united to Saturn by
the most exalted part of her essence, is called Rhea: but considered as
producing Jupiter, and, together with Jove, unfolding the universal and
particular orders of the Gods, she is called Ceres.

[31] In the note to Hercules it appears that Rhea is one of the progeny of
the intellectual earth, resident in Phanes; and from the note to Hymn 5,
to Protogonus, we learn from Proclus, that Phanes is to be considered in
the intelligible as well as in the intellectual orders. Hence Rhea is, with
perfect agreement to the Orphic theology, the daughter of Protogonus,
considered as subsisting among the intelligible Gods.

[32] I have here followed the correction of Pierson, who reads ταυροφονων
for ταυροφορον: for Rhea is the same with the mother of the Gods, who
is celebrated in the Hymn to her, as seated in a car drawn by lions.

Drum-beating,[33] *frantic, of a splendid mien,*
Brass-sounding, honor'd, Saturn's blessed queen.
Thou joy'st in mountains and tumultuous fight,
And mankind's horrid howlings, thee delight.
War's parent, mighty, of majestic frame,
Deceitful saviour,[34] *liberating dame.*
Mother of Gods and men, from whom the earth
And lofty heav'ns derive their glorious birth;
Th' aetherial gales, the deeply spreading sea
Goddess aerial-form'd, proceed from thee.
Come, pleas'd with wand'rings, blessed and divine,
With peace attended on our labours shine;
Bring rich abundance, and wherever found
Drive dire disease, to earth's remotest bound.

[XIV]

TO JUPITER

THE FUMIGATION FROM STORAX

O Jove much-honor'd, Jove supremely great,
To thee our holy rites we consecrate,
Our pray'rs and expiations, king divine,

[33] Rhea, in the Orphic theology, is among the mundane divinities, the earth. Hence, according to Varro, she is represented with a drum; because that instrument is a symbol of the earth. August. de Civitat. lib. vii.

[34] When Jupiter was born (says the fable) his mother Rhea in order to deceive Saturn, gave him a stone wrapped in swaddling bands, in the place of Jove; informing him that was her offspring. Saturn immediately devoured the stone; and Jupiter who was privately educated, at length obtained the government of the world. With great propriety, therefore, is she called by the poet a deceitful saviour. This fable, according to Phurnutus, signifies the creation of the world. For at that time Nature (which among elementary essences is the same with Jupiter) was then nourished in the world, and at length prevailed. The stone devoured by Saturn is the earth, alluding to its firmly occupying the middle place: for, says Phurnutus, beings could not abide without such a foundation for their support. From this all things are produced, and derive their proper aliment. Opusc. Mythol. p. 147.

For all things round thy head exalted shine.
The earth is thine, and mountains swelling high,
The sea profound, and all within the sky.
Saturnian king, descending from above,
Magnanimous, commanding, sceptred Jove;
All-parent, principle and end of all,
Whose pow'r almighty, shakes this earthly ball;
Ev'n Nature trembles at thy mighty nod,
Loud-sounding, arm'd with light'ning, thund'ring God.
Source of abundance, purifying king,
O various-form'd from whom all natures spring;
Propitious hear my pray'r, give blameless health,
With peace divine, and necessary wealth.

[XV]

TO JUNO[35]

THE FUMIGATION FROM AROMATICS

O royal Juno of majestic mien,
Aerial-form'd, divine, Jove's blessed queen,
Thron'd in the bosom of caerulean air,
The race of mortals is thy constant care.
The cooling gales thy pow'r alone inspires,
Which nourish life, which ev'ry life desires.
Mother of clouds and winds, from thee alone
Producing all things, mortal life is known:
All natures share thy temp'rament divine,
And universal sway alone is thine.
With founding blasts of wind, the swelling sea
And rolling rivers roar, when shook by thee.
Come, blessed Goddess, fam'd almighty queen,
With aspect kind, rejoicing and serene.

[35] Juno is called by the Orphic theologers, according to Proclus Ζωογόνος Θεά, or the vivific Goddess: an epithet perfectly agreeing with the attributes ascribed to her in this Hymn. And in Theol. Plat. p. 483, he says that Juno is the source of the soul's procreation.

[XVI]

TO NEPTUNE

THE FUMIGATION FROM MYRRH

Hear, Neptune, ruler of the sea profound,
Whose liquid grasp begirts the solid ground;
Who, at the bottom of the stormy main,
Dark and deep-bosom'd, hold'st thy wat'ry reign;
Thy awful hand the brazen trident bears,
And ocean's utmost bound, thy will reveres:
Thee I invoke, whose steeds the foam divide,
From whose dark locks the briny waters glide;
Whose voice loud sounding thro' the roaring deep,
Drives all its billows, in a raging heap;
When fiercely riding thro' the boiling sea,
Thy hoarse command the trembling waves obey.
Earth shaking, dark-hair'd God, the liquid plains
(The third division) Fate to thee ordains,
'Tis thine, caerulian daemon, to survey
Well pleas'd the monsters of the ocean play,
Confirm earth's basis, and with prosp'rous gales
Waft ships along, and swell the spacious sails;
Add gentle Peace, and fair-hair'd Health beside,
And pour abundance in a blameless tide.

[XVII]

TO PLUTO

Pluto, magnanimous, whose realms profound
Are fix'd beneath the firm and solid ground,
In the Tartarian plains remote from sight,
And wrapt forever in the depths of night;
Terrestrial Jove,[36] *thy sacred ear incline,*

[36] Pluto, says Proclus in Theol. Plat. p. 368, is called terrestrial Jupiter, because he governs by his providence the earth, and all she contains.

And, pleas'd, accept thy mystic's hymn divine.
Earth's keys[37] *to thee, illustrious king belong,*
Its secret gates unlocking, deep and strong.
'Tis thine, abundant annual fruits to bear,
For needy mortals are thy constant care.
To thee, great king, Avernus is assign'd,
The seat of Gods, and basis of mankind.
Thy throne is fix'd in Hades' dismal plains,
Distant, unknown to rest, where darkness reigns;
Where, destitute of breath, pale spectres dwell,
In endless, dire, inexorable hell;
And in dread Acheron, whose depths obscure,
Earth's stable roots eternally secure.
O mighty daemon, whose decision dread,
The future fate determines of the dead,
With captive Proserpine, thro' grassy plains,
Drawn in a four-yok'd car with loosen'd reins,
Rapt o'er the deep, impell'd by love, you flew
'Till Eleusina's city rose to view:
There, in a wond'rous cave obscure and deep,
The sacred maid secure from search you keep,
The cave of Atthis, whose wide gates display
An entrance to the kingdoms void of day.
Of unapparent works, thou art alone
The dispensator, visible and known.
O pow'r all-ruling, holy, honor'd light,
Thee sacred poets and their hymns delight:
Propitious to thy mystic's works incline,
Rejoicing come, for holy rites are thine.

[37] Pausanias informs us, that Pluto is reported to have keys, as an illustrious distinction; in the same manner as a sceptre is attributed to Jupiter, and a trident to Neptune.

[XVIII]

TO THUNDRING JOVE

THE FUMIGATION FROM STORAX

O Father Jove, who shak'st with fiery light
The world deep-sounding from thy lofty height:
From thee, proceeds th' aetherial lightning's blaze,
Flashing around intolerable rays.
Thy sacred thunders shake the blest abodes,
The shining regions of th' immortal Gods:
Thy pow'r divine, the flaming lightning shrouds,
With dark investiture, in fluid clouds.
'Tis thine to brandish thunders strong and dire,
To scatter storms, and dreadful darts of fire;
With roaring flames involving all around,
And bolts of thunder of tremendous sound.
Thy rapid dart can raise the hair upright,
And shake the heart of man with wild afright.
Sudden, unconquer'd, holy, thund'ring God,
With noise unbounded, flying all abroad;
With all-devouring force, entire and strong,
Horrid, untam'd, thou roll'st the flames along.
Rapid, aetherial bolt, descending fire,
The earth all-parent, trembles at thy ire;
The sea all-shining; and each beast that hears
The sound terrific, with dread horror fears:
When Nature's face is bright with flashing fire,
And in the heavens resound thy thunders dire.
Thy thunders white, the azure garments tear,
And burst the veil of all surrounding air.
O Jove, all-blessed, may thy wrath severe,
Hurl'd in the bosom of the deep appear,
And on the tops of mountains be reveal'd,
For thy strong arm is not from us conceal'd.
Propitious to these sacred rites incline,

And crown my wishes with a life divine:
Add royal health, and gentle peace beside,
With equal reason, for my constant guide.

[XIX]

TO JOVE, AS THE AUTHOR OF LIGHTNING

THE FUMIGATION FROM FRANKINCENSE AND MANNA

I call the mighty, holy, splendid light,
Aerial, dreadful-sounding, fiery-bright;
Flaming, aerial-light, with angry voice,
Lightning thro' lucid clouds with horrid noise.
Untam'd, to whom resentments dire belong,
Pure, holy pow'r, all-parent, great and strong:
Come, and benevolent these rites attend,
And grant my days a peaceful, blessed end.

[XX]

TO THE CLOUDS

THE FUMIGATION FROM MYRRH

Aerial clouds, thro' heav'n's resplendent plains
Who wander, parents of prolific rains;
Who nourish fruits, whose wat'ry frames are hurl'd,
By winds impetuous, round the mighty world;
All-thund'ring, lion-roaring, flashing fire,
In Air's wide bosom, bearing thunders dire:
Impell'd by ev'ry stormy, sounding gale,
With rapid course, along the skies ye sail.
With blowing winds your wat'ry frames I call,
On mother Earth with fruitful show'rs to fall.

[XXI]

TO THE SEA, OR TETHYS[38]

THE FUMIGATION FROM FRANKINCENSE AND MANNA

Tethys I call, with eyes caerulean bright,
Hid in a veil obscure from human sight;
Great Ocean's empress, wand'ring thro' the deep,
And pleas'd with gentle gales, the earth to sweep;
Whose blessed waves in swift succession go,
And lash the rocky shore with endless flow:
Delighting in the Sea serene to play,
In ships exulting and the wat'ry way.
Mother of Venus, and of clouds obscure,
Great nurse of beasts, and source of fountains pure.
O venerable Goddess, hear my pray'r,
And make benevolent my life thy care;
Send, blessed queen, to ships a prosp'rous breeze,
And waft them safely o'er the stormy seas.

[XXII]

TO NEREUS

THE FUMIGATION FROM MYRRH

O Thou, who dost the roots of Ocean keep
In seats caerulean, daemon of the deep,
With fifty nymphs (attending in thy train,
Fair virgin artists) glorying thro' the main:
The dark foundation of the rolling sea
And Earth's wide bounds, belong much-fam'd to thee:
Great daemon, source of all, whose pow'r can make
The Earth's unmeasur'd, holy basis shake,
When blust'ring winds in secret caverns pent,
By thee excited, struggle hard for vent:

[38] See the last note to Hymn V for an explanation of the Goddess Tethys. [I.e., note 10; but the reference there is to Thetis.]

Come, blessed Nereus, listen to my pray'r,
And cease to shake the earth with wrath severe;
Send on our sacred rites abundant health,
With peace divine and necessary wealth.

[XXIII]

TO THE NEREIDS[39]

& see p. 260!

THE FUMIGATION FROM AROMATICS

Daughters of Nereus, resident in caves
Merg'd deep in Ocean, sporting thro' the waves;
Fanatic fifty nymphs, who thro' the main
Delight to follow in the Triton's train,
Rejoicing close behind their cars to keep;
Whose forms half wild, are nourish'd by the deep,
With other nymphs of different degree
Leaping and wand'ring thro' the liquid sea:
Bright, wat'ry dolphins, sonorous and gay,
Well pleas'd to sport with bachanalian play;
Nymphs beauteous-ey'd, whom sacrifice delights,
Send rich abundance on our mystic rites;
For you at first disclos'd the rites divine,
Of holy Bacchus and of Proserpine,
Of fair Calliope from whom I spring,
And of Apollo bright, the Muse's king.

[XXIV]

TO PROTEUS[39a]

THE FUMIGATION FROM STORAX

Proteus I call, whom Fate decrees, to keep
The keys which lock the chambers of the deep;

[39] [See Plate 14.]

[39a] According to Proclus, in Plat. Repub. p. 97, Proteus, though inferior to the primary Gods, is immortal: and though not a deity, is a certain angelic mind of the order of Neptune, comprehending in himself all the forms of things generated in the universe.

First-born, by whose illustrious pow'r alone
All Nature's principles are clearly shewn:
Matter to change with various forms is thine,
Matter unform'd, capacious, and divine.
All-honor'd, prudent, whose sagacious mind
Knows all that was, and is, of ev'ry kind,
With all that shall be in succeeding time;
So vast thy wisdom, wond'rous, and sublime:
For all things Nature first to thee consign'd,
And in thy essence omniform confin'd.
Come, blessed father, to our rites attend,
And grant our happy lives a prosp'rous end.

[XXV]

TO THE EARTH⁴⁰

THE FUMIGATION FROM EVERY KIND OF SEED,
EXCEPT BEANS AND AROMATICS

O Goddess, Earth, of Gods and men the source,
Endu'd with fertile, all destroying force;
All-parent, bounding, whose prolific pow'rs,
Produce a store of beauteous fruits and flow'rs,
All-various maid, th' eternal world's strong base
Immortal, blessed, crown'd with ev'ry grace;
From whose wide womb, as from an endless root,
Fruits, many-form'd, mature and grateful shoot.
Deep bosom'd, blessed, pleas'd with grassy plains,
Sweet to the smell, and with prolific rains.
All flow'ry daemon, centre of the world,
Around thy orb, the beauteous stars are hurl'd
With rapid whirl, eternal and divine,

⁴⁰ According to Orpheus, as related by Proclus, in Tim. p. 292, Earth
is the mother of every thing, of which Heaven is the father. And the
reader will please to observe, that, in the Orphic theology, Rhea, the
mother of the Gods, the Earth, and Vesta are all one and the same divinity,
considered according to her essential peculiarities.

Whose frames with matchless skill and wisdom shine.
Come, blessed Goddess, listen to my pray'r,
And make increase of fruits thy constant care;
With fertile Seasons in thy train, draw near,
And with propitious mind thy suppliant hear.

[XXVI]

TO THE MOTHER OF THE GODS

THE FUMIGATION FROM A VARIETY OF ODORIFEROUS SUBSTANCES

Mother of Gods, great nurse of all, draw near,
Divinely honor'd, and regard my pray'r:
Thron'd on a car, by lions drawn along,
By bull-destroying lions, swift and strong,
Thou sway'st the sceptre of the pole divine,[41]
And the world's middle seat, much-fam'd, is thine.
Hence earth is thine, and needy mortals share
Their constant food, from thy protecting care:
From thee at first both Gods and men arose;
From thee, the sea and ev'ry river flows.
Vesta, and source of good, thy name we find
To mortal men rejoicing to be kind;
For ev'ry good to give, thy soul delights;
Come, mighty pow'r, propitious to our rites,
All-taming, blessed, Phrygian saviour, come,
Saturn's great queen, rejoicing in the drum.
Celestial, ancient, life-supporting maid,
Fanatic Goddess, give thy suppliant aid;
With joyful aspect on our incense shine,
And, pleas'd, accept the sacrifice divine.

[41] We have already observed, that the mother of the Gods is the same with Rhea; and Proclus, in the second book of his Commentary on Euclid, informs us, that the pole of the world is called by the Pythagoreans the seal of Rhea.

[XXVII]

TO MERCURY

THE FUMIGATION FROM FRANKINCENSE

Hermes, draw near, and to my pray'r incline,
Angel of Jove, and Maia's son divine;
Studious of contests, ruler of mankind,
With heart almighty, and a prudent mind.
Celestial messenger, of various skill,
Whose pow'rful arts could watchful Argus kill:
With winged feet, 'tis thine thro' air to course,
O friend of man, and prophet of discourse:
Great life-supporter, to rejoice is thine,
In arts gymnastic, and in fraud divine:
With pow'r endu'd all language to explain,
Of care the loos'ner, and the source of gain.
Whose hand contains of blameless peace the rod,
Corucian, blessed, profitable God:
Of various speech, whose aid in works we find,
And in necessities to mortals kind:
Dire weapon of the tongue, which men revere,
Be present, Hermes, and thy suppliant hear;
Assist my works, conclude my life with peace,
Give graceful speech, and memory's increase.

[XXVIII]

TO PROSERPINE

A HYMN

Daughter of Jove, almighty and divine,
Come, blessed queen, and to these rites incline:
Only-begotten,[42] *Pluto's honor'd wife,*

---

[42] Καὶ γὰρ ὁ Θεολογός τὴν κόρην ΜΟΥΝΟΓΕΝΕΙΑΝ ἔιαθε προσαγορεύειν.
Proc. Tim. 2 extra. p. 139. 9, i.e. "I see that the theologist (meaning Orpheus) calls Proserpine, Only-begotten."

The Hymns of Orpheus

O venerable Goddess, source of life:
'Tis thine in earth's profundities to dwell,
Fast by the wide and dismal gates of hell:
Jove's holy offspring, of a beauteous mien,
Fatal, with lovely locks, infernal queen:
Source of the furies, whose blest frame proceeds
From Jove's ineffable and secret seeds:
Mother of Bacchus, sonorous, divine,
And many-form'd, the parent of the vine:
The dancing Hours attend thee, essence bright,
All-ruling virgin, bearing heav'nly light:
Illustrious, horned, of a bounteous mind,
Alone desir'd by those of mortal kind.
O, vernal queen, whom grassy plains delight,
Sweet to the smell, and pleasing to the sight:
Whose holy form in budding fruits we view,
Earth's vig'rous offspring of a various hue:
Espous'd in Autumn:[43] *life and death alone*
To wretched mortals from thy power is known:
For thine the task according to thy will,[44]

[43] We have already observed in the Dissertation, that the Orphic theologers considered a difference of sex in the divinities; attributing the male to some, and the female to others. Now the mutual commerce and energy subsisting between these Gods and Goddesses, they denominated ἱεροὶ Γαμοι, i.e. "holy marriages": or according to Proclus, on the Parmenides of Plato, as cited by Eschenbach, in Epig. p. 59, they mystically called the simple kindred conjunction, and communion of divine causes, a marriage. And Proserpine, or the animating part of the earth's soul, may be considered as resting in Autumn, from all farther productions; her powers at that time having attained their full perfection.

Hence at this period may we not say, that she is wholly abstracted from the animal life, and secretly united with Pluto, or the intellectual part of the earth's soul; from whom she receives the divine light of mind, and copious streams of the nectar of divine knowledge.

[44] Proclus, in Theol. Plat. p. 371, informs us, that, according to the Eleusinian mysteries, Proserpine, together with Pluto, governs terrestrial concerns, and the recesses of the earth: that she supplies life to the extreme parts of the universe, and imparts soul to those who, by her power, are rendered inanimate and dead. This is perfectly agreeable to the 23d and following line.

Life to produce, and all that lives to kill.
Hear, blessed Goddess, send a rich increase
Of various fruits from earth, with lovely Peace;
Send Health with gentle hand, and crown my life
With blest abundance, free from noisy strife;
Last in extreme old age the prey of Death,
Dismiss we willing to the realms beneath,
To thy fair palace, and the blissful plains
Where happy spirits dwell, and Pluto reigns.

[XXIX]

TO BACCHUS

THE FUMIGATION FROM STORAX

Bacchus I call, loud-sounding and divine,
Fanatic God, a two-fold shape is thine:
Thy various names and attributes I sing,
O, first-born,[45] thrice begotten, Bacchic king:
Rural, ineffable, two-form'd, obscure,
Two-horn'd, with ivy crown'd, Euion, pure:
Bull-fac'd, and martial, bearer of the vine,
Endu'd with counsel prudent and divine:
Triennial, whom the leaves of vines adorn,
Of Jove and Proserpine, occultly born.
Immortal daemon, hear my suppliant voice,
Give me in blameless plenty to rejoice;
And listen gracious to my mystic pray'r,
Surrounded with thy choir of nurses fair.

[XXX]

TO THE CURETES

A HYMN

Leaping Curetes, who with dancing feet
And circling measures, armed footsteps beat:

[45] See the notes to Hymn V to Protogonus. [I.e., n. 9.]

Whose bosom's mad, fanatic transports fire,
Who move in rythm to the sounding lyre:
Who traces deaf when lightly leaping tread,
Arm bearers, strong defenders, rulers dread:
Propitious omens, guards of Proserpine,[46]
Preserving rites, mysterious and divine:
Come, and benevolent my words attend,
(In herds rejoicing), and my life defend.

[XXXI]

TO PALLAS

A HYMN

Only-begotten, noble race of Jove,
Blessed and fierce, who joy'st in caves to rove:[47]
O, warlike Pallas, whose illustrious kind,
Ineffable and effable we find:
Magnanimous and fam'd, the rocky height,
And groves, and shady mountains thee delight:
In arms rejoicing, who with Furies dire
And wild, the souls of mortals dost inspire.
Gymnastic virgin of terrific mind,
Dire Gorgons bane, unmarried, blessed, kind:
Mother of arts, impetuous; understood,
Rage to the wicked, wisdom to the good:
Female and male, the arts of war are thine,

---

[46] Proclus calls the Curetes, guards of Proserpine, lib. vi. Theol. Plat. p. 383.

[47] Proclus, in Plat. Theol. p. 372, informs us, that there are three zoogonic or vivific monads, Diana, Proserpine, and Minerva; and that these three divinities exist together. Hence the reason is obvious why this Goddess is celebrated as living in caves, and delighting in rocks and mountains, from her agreement with Diana: and hence it appears, that Runkenius was mistaken in imagining these epithets were misplaced. We may likewise see the reason from hence, why Minerva is called, in line 14, Female and Male, as well as the Moon; and why the Moon is called in the Hymn to her πάνσοφε κούρη, i.e. "all-wise virgin."

Thomas Taylor the Platonist

Fanatic, much-form'd dragoness,[48] *divine:*
O'er the Phlegrean giants, rous'd to ire,[49]
Thy coursers driving, with destruction dire.
Sprung from the head of Jove, of splendid mien,

[48] It is easy to perceive the agreement between Minerva, who is the same with divine Wisdom and Providence, and a Dragon; since according to Phurnutus, a dragon is of a vigilant and guardian nature.

[49] The fable of the giants is common; but its philosophical explanation is, I fear, but little known and less understood. For the sake of the liberal, therefore, the following account of the battles of the Gods, from the excellent Commentary of Proclus, on Plato's Republic, p. 373, is inserted. "The divisible progressions of all beings, and the diversities of substances, receive a supernal origin, from a division of unknown primitive causes, which are mutually at strife with principles, subject to the universe. For some determine their essence about unity, on which they depend; and others receive in themselves a never-failing power of infinity, by which they generate universals, and a cause of multitude and progression, according to which they possess their peculiar essences. Hence, after the same manner as the first principles of beings, are mutually separated from each other; so all divine genera and true beings have among themselves a progression distinguished by order. In consequence of this, some insert in things posterior the principal cause of unity; but others afford the power of separation. Some are the causes of conversion to inferiors, and of collecting the multitude of progressive natures to their proper principles: while others promote their progression and procreation, emanating from principles, as their source. Some supply the power of generating to inferiors; and others exhibit a constant and undefiled purity. There are some, again, containing the cause of separable goods; and others, of such goods as subsist together with their recipients. Indeed, after this manner, the various contrariety of such kinds appears in all the administrations of true being. Thus the station or quiet of things constantly establishing being in themselves, resists efficacious and vital powers of motion. So the communication of identity, on every side similar to itself (if the expression may be allowed) is specially opposed to the discretions of diversity. Thus, too, similitude fights with dissimilitude, and equality with inequality. Since this is the case, can it be wonderful, that mythologists, perceiving a contrariety of this kind among the Gods, and the first principles of things, should represent it to their pupils by contentions and wars? For though the divine genera are always united with each other, yet they preside as well over those who administer to union, as over those who machinate confusion. And this is the first reason of the wars of the Gods. But it is lawful to produce another reason, and to affirm that the Gods are indeed indivisibly conjoined, and subsist together in mutual uniformity: but that their progressions into the universe, and participations by recipient natures,

Purger of evils, all-victorious queen.
Hear me, O Goddess, when to thee I pray,
With supplicating voice both night and day,
And in my latest hour, give peace and health,
Propitious times, and necessary wealth,
And, ever present, be thy vot'ries aid,
O, much implor'd, art's parent, blue-eyed maid.

[XXXII]

TO VICTORY

THE FUMIGATION FROM MANNA

O powerful victory, by men desir'd,
With adverse breasts to dreadful fury fir'd,

---

become disjoined and divisible, and by this means filled with contrariety. For things subject to the power of the Gods cannot receive their diffused powers, and multiform illustrations, without mixture and confusion. Hence, the last orders dependent on the Gods, since they are produced by a long interval from the first causes, but are contiguous to the concerns they administer, and adhere to matter, contract contrariety, and an all-various division; partially presiding over material affairs, and diminishing and dispersing those separate powers, which before subsisted in a superior manner, uniformly and indivisibly, in their primitive causes. Since, then, such and so many are the ways, by which, according to the mysteries of theologists, war is usually referred to the Gods; other poets who, seized with fury, have interpreted divine concerns, introduced the battles and wars of the Gods, according to the first reasons, i.e. so far as the divine genera admit of diversity, according to the first principles of all things. For fables, concealing truth under a veil, shew that such things as recall to principles, oppose and fight with the authors of generation: collecting with separating natures, things unifying with such as multiply by the progression of beings; and universal genera, with such as operate in a partial and particular manner. Hence they relate, that the Titans (or daemons subservient to Nature) fight with Bacchus (or Nature) and the giants with Jove. For union, and an indivisible work, is proper to Bacchus and Jupiter, as the demiurgic causes of the world; but Titans and Giants produce the demiurgic powers into multitude; partially administering the concerns of the universe, and existing as the proximate parents of material natures." Thus far Proclus. For a farther account of Minerva, see the note to Hymn IX to Nature. [I.e., n. 19 above.]

Thee I invoke, whose might alone can quell
Contending rage, and molestation fell:
'Tis thine in battle to confer the crown,
The victor's prize, the mark of sweet renown;
For thou rul'st all things, Victory divine!
And glorious strife, and joyful shouts are thine.
Come, mighty Goddess, and thy suppliant bless,
With sparkling eye, elated with success;
May deeds illustrious thy protection claim,
And find, led on by thee immortal Fame.

[XXXIII]

TO APOLLO

THE FUMIGATION FROM MANNA

Blest Paean, come, propitious to my pray'r,
Illustrious pow'r, whom Memphian tribes revere,
Slayer of Tityus, and the God of health,
Lycorian Phoebus, fruitful source of wealth:
Spermatic, golden-lyr'd, the field from thee
Receives its constant, rich fertility.
Titanic, Grunian,[50] *Smynthian, thee I sing,*
Python-destroying, hallow'd, Delphian king:
Rural, light-bearer, and the Muse's head,
Noble and lovely, arm'd with arrows dread:
Far-darting,[51] *Bacchian, two-fold, and divine,*
Pow'r far diffused, and course oblique is thine.
O, Delian king, whose light-producing eye
Views all within, and all beneath the sky:

[50] According to Strabo, lib. xiii., Grynaeus is a town of Myrinaeus: likewise, a temple of Apollo, and a most ancient oracle and temple, sumptuously built of white stone. Gyrald. Syntag. p. 237.

[51] *Far-darting.* ἑκατηβελετης. Proclus, on Plato's Cratylus, informs us he is so called, ὅτι χορηγὸς ὥς, καὶ ἐξερομενος ἐπι παντας ποιεῖ τας ενεργείας. i.e. "because since he is the choragus or leader of the choir of the Muses, he produces energies in all things."

Whose locks are gold, whose oracles are sure,
Who, omens good reveal'st, and precepts pure:
Hear me entreating for the human kind,
Hear, and be present with benignant mind;
For thou survey'st this boundless aether all,
And ev'ry part of this terrestrial ball
Abundant, blessed; and thy piercing sight,
Extends beneath the gloomy, silent night;
Beyond the darkness, starry-ey'd, profound,
The stable roots, deep fix'd by thee are found.
The world's wide bounds, all-flourishing are thine,
Thyself of all the source and end divine:
'Tis thine all Nature's music to inspire,
With various-sounding, harmonising lyre;
Now the last string thou tun'st to sweet accord,[52]

[52] Gesner well observes, in his notes to this Hymn, that the comparison and conjunction of the musical and astronomical elements are most ancient; being derived from Orpheus and Pythagoras, to Plato. Now, according to the Orphic and Pythagoric doctrine, the lyre of Apollo is an image of the celestial harmony, or the melody caused by the orderly revolutions of the celestial spheres. But I cannot believe that Orpheus and Pythagoras considered this harmony as attended with sensible sounds, according to the vulgar acceptation of the word: for it is surely more rational to suppose, that they meant nothing more by the music of the spheres, than their harmonical proportions to each other. Indeed these wise men, to whom metaphors were familiar, may be easily conceived by vulgar sound and vulgar harmony to insinuate internal sound, and harmony subsisting in its origin and cause. Hence we may consider the souls of the celestial spheres, together with the soul of the world, as composing the choir of the nine Muses (who are called by the Platonists nine Syrens), and dancing in numerical order round Apollo the sun of the intellectual world. But these nine Muses are far different from the marine Syrens of the poets who, resident as it were in the sea of material delights, draw us aside by their alluring melody, from the paths of rectitude. For these are divine Syrens inviting us to the proper end of our nature; and forming from the eight tones of the eight spheres, one perfect and everlasting harmony.

The following quotation from the Platonic Nichomachus, Harm. i. p. 6, illustrates the meaning of the Hypate and Nete, or the highest and lowest string. From the motion of Saturn, (says he) "The most remote of the planets, the appellation of the gravest sound, Hypate, is derived:

Divinely warbling now the highest chord;
Th' immortal golden lyre, now touch'd by thee,
Responsive yields a Dorian melody.
All Nature's tribes to thee their diff'rence owe,
And changing seasons from thy music flow:
Hence, mix'd by thee in equal parts, advance
Summer and Winter in alternate dance;
This claims the highest, that the lowest string,
The Dorian measure tunes the lovely spring:
Hence by mankind, Pan-royal,[53] *two-horn'd nam'd,*
Emitting whistling winds[54] *thro' Syrinx fam'd;*
Since to thy care, the figur'd seal's[55] *consign'd,*

---

but from the lunar motion, which is the lowest of all, the most acute sound is called νεάτη, Nete, or the lowest." But Gesner observes, that a more ancient, and as it were archetypal appellation, is derived from the ancient triangular lyre, a copy of which was found among the pictures lately dug out of the ruins of Herculaneum; where the highest chord next to the chin of the musician is the longest, and consequently (says he) the sound is the most grave. Gesner proceeds in observing, that the three seasons of the year are so compared together in a musical ratio, that Hypate signifies the Winter, Nete the Summer, and the Dorian measure represents the intermediate seasons, Spring and Autumn. Now the reason why the Dorian melody is assigned to the Spring, is because that measure wholly consists in temperament and moderation, as we learn from Plut. de Mus. p. 1136. E, and consequently is with great propriety attributed to the Spring, considered as placed between Summer and Winter; and gratefully tempering the fervent heat of the one, and the intense cold of the other.

[53] See the notes to the Hymn to Pan, to Hercules, and the Sun.

[54] Johannes Diaconus, in Allegorcis Theogoniae Hesiodi, quotes the following lines from Orpheus.

Ζεὺς δέ τε πάντων ἐστὶ θεός, πάντων τε κεραστὴς,

Πνένμασι συριζων, Φωναῖσι τε ἀερομικτοις.

That is, "But Jupiter is the God of all, and the mingler of all things; whistling with the breathing winds and aerial voices." And this perfectly agrees with Apollo, considered as Jupiter, or the sun of the intelligible world.

[55] Since Apollo in the intelligible world is the demiurgus of the universe, and consequently comprehends in his essence the archetypal ideas of all sensible forms, he may with great propriety be said to possess the figured seal, of which every visible species is nothing more than an impression.

Which stamps the world with forms of ev'ry kind.
Hear me, blest pow'r, and in these rites rejoice,
And save thy mystics with a suppliant voice.

[XXXIV]

TO LATONA

THE FUMIGATION FROM MYRRH

Dark veil'd Latona, much invoked queen,
Twin-bearing Goddess, of a noble mien;
Caeantis great, a mighty mind is thine,
Offspring prolific, blest of Jove divine:
Phoebus proceeds from thee, the God of light,
And Dian fair, whom winged darts delight;
She in Ortygia's honor'd regions born,
In Delos he, which mountains high adorn.
Hear me, O Goddess, with propitious mind,
And end these holy rites, with aspect kind.

[XXXV]

TO DIANA

THE FUMIGATION FROM MANNA

Hear me, Jove's daughter, celebrated queen,
Bacchian and Titan, of a noble mien:
In darts rejoicing and on all to shine,
Torch-bearing Goddess, Dictynna divine;
O'er births presiding,[56] and thyself a maid,
To labour-pangs imparting ready aid:

It is however necessary to observe, that in the great seal of ideas, all forms subsist in indivisible union and immaterial perfection: but in their imitative impressions in bodies, they are found full of boundless multitude, and material imperfection.

[56] In the original, λοχεία: and Proclus, in Plat. Theol. p. 403, observes that this epithet is given to Diana by theologians because she is the inspector of natural progression and generation.

Dissolver of the zone and wrinkl'd care,
Fierce huntress, glorying in the Sylvan war:
Swift in the course, in dreadful arrows skill'd,
Wandering by night, rejoicing in the field:
Of manly form, erect, of bounteous mind,
Illustrious daemon, nurse of human kind:
Immortal, earthly, bane of monsters fell,
'Tis thine, blest maid, on woody hills to dwell:
Foe of the stag, whom woods and dogs delight,
In endless youth who flourish fair and bright.
O, universal queen, august, divine,
A various form, Cydonian pow'r, is thine:
Dread guardian Goddess, with benignant mind
Auspicious, come to mystic rites inclin'd;
Give earth a store of beauteous fruits to bear,
Send gentle Peace, and Health with lovely hair,
And to the mountains drive Disease and Care.

[XXXVI]

TO THE TITANS[57]

THE FUMIGATION FROM FRANKINCENSE

O mighty Titans, who from heav'n and earth
Derive your noble and illustrious birth,
Our fathers sires, in Tartarus profound
Who dwell, deep merg'd beneath the solid ground:
Fountains and principles, from whom began
Th' afflicted, miserable, race of man:
Who not alone in earth's retreats abide,
But in the ocean and the air reside;
Since ev'ry species from your nature flows,
Which all prolific, nothing barren knows:
Avert your rage, if from th' infernal seats
One of your tribe should visit our retreats.

[57] See note to Hymn XXXI to Pallas. [I.e., n. 47.]

[XXXVII]

TO THE CURETES[58]

THE FUMIGATION FROM FRANKINCENSE

Brass-beating Salians, ministers of Mars,
Who guard his arms the instruments of wars;
Whose blessed frames, heav'n, earth and sea compose,
And from whose breath all animals arose:
Who dwell in Samothracia's sacred ground,
Defending mortals thro' the sea profound.
Deathless Curetes, by your pow'r alone,
Initial rites to men at first were shewn:
Who shake old Ocean thund'ring to the sky,
And stubborn oaks with branches waving high.
'Tis yours in glittering arms the earth to beat,
With lightly-leaping, rapid, sounding feet;
Then every beast the noise terrific flies,
And the loud tumult wanders thro' the skies:
The dust your feet excites with matchless force,
Flies to the clouds amidst their whirling course;
And ev'ry flower of variegated hue,
Grows in the dancing motion form'd by you.
Immortal daemons, to your pow'rs consign'd
The task to nourish, and destroy mankind.
When rushing furious with loud tumult dire,
O'erwhelm'd, they perish in your dreadful ire;
And live replenish'd with the balmy air,

[58] The Curetes are plainly celebrated in this Hymn as the winds; the reason of which is as follows. Saturn, who, according to the Orphic theology as related by Proclus, is allotted a supercelestial and intellectual essence produced Jupiter from Rhea. And Jupiter, or the demiurgus of the universe, silently emerged into light from the three principles, Aether, Chaos, and Night conflicting together, and mutually concurring with, and separating from each other. Now these three principles are interpreted by Julian, Orat. v, as the Corybantes: and hence with perfect agreement to the Orphic symbolical theology, the mutual conflict of these principles is represented by the impetuous Fury of the winds.

The food of life, committed to your care.
When shook by you, the seas, with wild uproar,
Wide-spreading, and profoundly whirling, roar:
The concave heav'ns, with Echo's voice resound,
When leaves with rustling noise bestrew the ground.
Curetes, Corybantes, ruling kings,
Whose praise the land of Samothracia sings:
From Jove descended; whose immortal breath
Sustains the soul, and wafts her back from death:
Aerial-form'd, much-fam'd, in heav'n ye shine
Two-fold, in heav'n all-lucid and divine:
Blowing, serene, from whom abundance springs,
Nurses of seasons, fruit-producing kings.

[XXXVIII]

TO CORYBAS[59]

THE FUMIGATION FROM FRANKINCENSE

The mighty ruler of this earthly ball,
For ever flowing, to these rites I call;
Martial and blest, unseen by mortal sight,
Preventing fears, and pleas'd with gloomy night:

[59] The following curious passage is preserved to us by Athenagoras, in Legat. i. pro Christianis; in which Orpheus describes the generation of the celestial or intellectual earth. "But Phanes or Protogonus produced another dire offspring from his holy womb; the dreadful form of a dragon. It has hairs on its head, and a beautiful countenance, but the rest of its body is that of a dragon, tremendous to the view." Now from this passage I conclude that Corybas, in the present Hymn, is the same with Protogonus: for he is celebrated, vv. 9, 10, as changing by his arts the holy body of Ceres (or the earth) into the form of a savage and obscure dragon. And as in the above lines the intellectual earth is represented under the form of a dragon with a beautiful countenance; the sensible earth, which is but the image of the intellectual, may with perfect agreement to this fragment be called an obscure dragon, since obscurity is an apt symbol of a material nature.

Corybas is likewise said, v. 7, to kill his two brothers. Now since Corybas is Protogonus, his two brothers may be considered as Aether and Chaos,

Hence, fancy's terrors are by thee allay'd,
All-various king, who lov'st the desart shade:
Each of thy brothers killing, blood is thine,
Two-fold Curete, many-form'd, divine.
By thee transmuted Ceres' body pure,
Became a dragon's savage and obscure:
Avert thy anger, hear me when I pray,
And by fix'd fate, drive fancy's fears away.

[XXXIX]

TO CERES

THE FUMIGATION FROM STORAX

O universal mother, Ceres fam'd
August, the source of wealth,[60] *and various nam'd:*
Great nurse, all-bounteous, blessed and divine,
Who joy'st in peace, to nourish corn is thine:
Goddess of seed, of fruits abundant, fair,
Harvest and threshing are thy constant care;
Who dwell'st in Eleusina's seats retir'd,
Lovely, delightful queen, by all desir'd.
Nurse of all mortals, whose benignant mind,
First ploughing oxen to the yoke confin'd;
And gave to men, what nature's wants require,
With plenteous means of bliss which all desire.
In verdure flourishing, in honor bright,
Assessor of great Bacchus, bearing light:

---

whose occult union formed the archetypal egg of the universe: and Protogonus bursting forth from this egg, and by this means dispersing Aether and Chaos, may be aptly represented under the symbol of Corybas destroying his two brothers. For, according to Proclus, it is customary with divine poets to imitate the exalted powers of exemplars, by contrary and most remote adumbrations.

[60] The following Orphic verse is preserved to us by Diodorus Siculus, i. 12, which perfectly agrees with the present Hymn.

Γῆ μήτηρ πάντων, Δημήτηρ, πλουτοδότειρα.

That is, "Earth, mother of all things, Ceres, source of wealth."

Rejoicing in the reaper's sickles, kind,
Whose nature lucid, earthly, pure, we find.
Prolific, venerable, Nurse divine,
Thy daughter loving, holy Proserpine:
A car with dragons yok'd,[61] *'tis thine to guide,*
And orgies singing round thy throne to ride:
Only-begotten, much-producing queen,
All flowers are thine and fruits of lovely green.
Bright Goddess, come, with Summer's rich increase
Swelling and pregnant, leading smiling Peace;
Come, with fair Concord and imperial Health,
And join with these a needful store of wealth.

[XL]

TO THE CERALIAN MOTHER

THE FUMIGATION FROM AROMATICS

Ceralian queen, of celebrated name,
From whom both men, and Gods immortal came;
Who widely wand'ring once, oppress'd with grief,
In Eleusina's valley found'st relief,
Discovering Proserpine thy daughter pure
In dread Avernus, dismal and obscure;
A sacred youth while thro' the world you stray
Bacchus, attending leader of the way;
The holy marriage of terrestrial Jove
Relating, while oppress'd with grief you rove;
Come, much invok'd, and to these rites inclin'd,
Thy mystic suppliant bless, with fav'ring mind.

[61] Since, according to our notes on the preceding Hymn to Corybas, Ceres, or the Earth, is represented by Orpheus under the form of an obscure dragon, it is not wonderful that she should be drawn by dragons.

[XLI]

TO MISES

THE FUMIGATION FROM STORAX

I call Thesmophorus,[62] spermatic God,
Of various names, who bears the leafy rod:
Mises, ineffable, pure, sacred queen,
Two-fold Iacchus, male and female seen:
Illustr'ous, whether to rejoice is thine
In incense offer'd, in the fane divine;[63]
Or if in Phrygia most thy soul delights,
Performing with thy mother sacred rites;
Or if the land of Cyprus is thy care,
Well pleas'd to dwell with Cytherea fair;
Or if exulting in the fertile plains
With thy dark mother Isis,[64] where she reigns,

[62] Or the legislator.
[63] Of Eleusina.
[64] According to Plutarch, in his Treatise of Isis and Osiris, Isis is the mother of Orus, who is called by the Greeks Apollo; and Iacchus it is well known is a mystic sirname of Bacchus. Now Apollo is frequently called in the Orphic writings Bacchus; as in the Hymn to that deity, Bacchian and Two-fold. And Apollo, as we have frequently observed, is in the intelligible world, the king and father of the universe, Protogonus, or Ericapaeus, and in the sensible world the Sun. So that Mises or Bacchus is celebrated in this Hymn by the same appellations as are given to Protogonus and Apollo: for he is called spermatic, ineffable, male and female, &c. which last appellation is given to Protogonus in the Orphic verse preserved by Proclus, lib. ii. in Timaeum.

Θῆλυς καὶ γενέτωρ κρατερὸς θεὸς ἠρικεπαῖος.

That is, "Female and father (or male), strong God Ericapaeus."
Indeed it is common with the Orphic theologers, to celebrate causes as the same with their effects, and effects with their causes; the supreme as the subordinate, and the subordinate as the supreme. And this in consequence of the mysterious union, subsisting between all the divine orders, and through every part of the universe; every thing, except the first cause, being stamped as it were with the same great seals of ideas, and existing on this account in sympathy and similitude with natures, both superior and subordinate to its essence. And here I cannot but take notice of the mistake of Macrobius, who imagines that all the Gods, according to Orpheus, may be reduced to the Sun; the other divinities being but so

Thomas Taylor the Platonist

With nurses pure attended, near the flood
Of sacred Egypt, thy divine abode:
Wherever resident, blest pow'r attend,
And with benignant mind these labours end.

---

many different appellations of that deity: for it is sufficiently evident to those who are skilled in the Orphic theology, that Orpheus was a Polytheist as well as a monarchist. But this mistake of Macrobius is not wonderful; as we may say of him what Plotinus said, on reading the book of Longinus *concerning principles,* φιλόλογος μὲν ὁ Λογγῖνος, φιλόσοφος δὲ οὐδαμῶς, i.e. "Longinus is a philologist, but by no means a philosopher." Similar to this is the mistake of modern Mythologists who, in conformity with the fashionable philosophy, call the material parts of nature the Gods of the ancients: the folly and impiety of which system cannot be better represented than in the words of Plutarch in his above mentioned curious Treatise of Isis and Osiris, which I shall give the reader in the elegant Translation of Dr. Squire, p. 90. "We ought to take the greatest care (says Plutarch) that we do not explain away the very nature of the Gods, by resolving it as it were into mere blasts of wind, or streams of rivers, into the sowing and earing of corn, or into the changes of the earth and seasons, as those persons have actually done, who make Bacchus to be Wine, and Vulcan Fire. Just as Cleanthes somewhere tells us, that by Proserpine nothing else is meant, but that air which, pervading the fruits of the earth, is thereby destroyed as it were, being deprived of its nutritive spirit: and as a certain poet, speaking of reaping corn, says,

Then, when the vigorous youth shall Ceres cut.

For those who indulge themselves in this manner of expression, act just as wisely as they would do, who should call the sails, the cables, and the anchors of the ship, the pilot; or the yarn and web, the weaver; or the emulsion, the easing draught, and the ptisan, the physician. "And, p. 91, he observes, that as the sun and the moon, and the heavens, and the earth, and the sea, though common to all mankind, have different names given them by different people; so may the same be affirmed, likewise, of that one supreme reason, who framed this world, and of that one providence which governs and watches over the whole, and of those *subordinate ministring powers that are set over the universe,* that they are the very same every where, though the honors which are paid them, as well as the appellations which are given them, are different in different places, according to the laws of each country, as are likewise those symbols, under which the mystics endeavour to lead their votaries to the knowledge of divine truths: and though some of these are more clear and explicit than others, yet are they not any of them without hazard; for whilst some persons, by wholly mistaking their meaning and appellation, have thereby plunged themselves into *superstition,* others, that they might avoid so fatal a quagmire, have unawares, dashed themselves upon the rock of *atheisim.*"

[XLII]

TO THE SEASONS

THE FUMIGATION FROM AROMATICS

Daughters of Jove and Themis, seasons bright,
Justice, and blessed peace, and lawful right,
Vernal and grassy, vivid, holy pow'rs,
Whose balmy breath exhales in lovely flow'rs:
All-colour'd seasons, rich increase your care,
Circling, for ever flourishing and fair:
Invested with a veil of shining dew,
A flow'ry veil delightful to the view:
Attending Proserpine, when back from night,
The Fates and Graces lead her up to light;
When in a band harmonious they advance,
And joyful round her, form the solemn dance:
With Ceres triumphing, and Jove divine;
Propitious come, and on our incense shine;
Give earth a blameless store of fruits to bear,
And make a novel mystic's life your care.

[XLIII]

TO SEMELE

THE FUMIGATION FROM STORAX

Cadmean Goddess, universal queen,
Thee, Semele I call, of beauteous mien;
Deep-bosom'd, lovely flowing locks are thine,
Mother of Bacchus, joyful and divine,
The mighty offspring, whom Jove's thunder bright,
Forc'd immature, and fright'ned into light:
Born from the deathless counsels, secret, high,
Of Jove Saturnian, regent of the sky;
Whom Proserpine permits to view the light,
And visit mortals from the realms of night:

257

Constant attending on the sacred rites,
And feast triennial, which thy soul delights;
When thy son's wond'rous birth mankind relate,
And secrets deep, and holy celebrate.
Now I invoke thee, great Cadmean queen,
To bless these rites with countenance serene.

[XLIV]

TO DIONYSIUS BASSAREUS TRIENNALIS[65]

A HYMN

Come, blessed Dionysius, various-nam'd,
Bull-fac'd, begot from Thunder, Bacchus fam'd:
Bassarian God, of universal might,
Whom swords, and blood, and sacred rage delight:
In heav'n rejoicing, mad, loud-sounding God,
Furious inspirer, bearer of the rod:
By Gods rever'd, who dwell'st with human kind,
Propitious come, with much-rejoicing mind.

[XLV]

TO LIKNITUS[66] BACCHUS

THE FUMIGATION FROM MANNA

Liknitan Bacchus, bearer of the vine,
Thee I invoke to bless these rites divine:
Florid and gay, of nymphs the blossom bright,
And of fair Venus, Goddess of delight,
'Tis thine mad footsteps with mad nymphs to beat,
Dancing thro' groves with lightly leaping feet:
From Jove's high counsels nurst by Proserpine,
And born the dread of all the pow'rs divine:
Come, blessed pow'r, regard thy suppliant's voice,
Propitious come, and in these rites rejoice.

[65] So called because his rites were performed every third year.
[66] Or the Fan-bearer. Concerning Liknitus and the following Bacchuses, see the last section of the Dissertation.

[XLVI]

TO BACCHUS PERICIONIUS[67]

THE FUMIGATION FROM AROMATICS

Bacchus Pericionius, hear my pray'r,
Who mad'st the house of Cadmus once thy care,
With matchless force, his pillars twining round,
(When burning thunders shook the solid ground,
In flaming, sounding torrents borne along),
Propt by thy grasp indissolubly strong.
Come mighty Bacchus to these rites inclin'd,
And bless thy suppliants with rejoicing mind.

[XLVII]

TO SABASIUS

THE FUMIGATION FROM AROMATICS

Hear me, illustrious father, daemon fam'd,
Great Saturn's offspring, and Sabasius nam'd;
Inserting Bacchus, bearer of the vine,
And founding God, within thy thigh divine,
That when mature, the Dionysian God
Might burst the bands of his conceal'd abode,
And come to sacred Tmolus, his delight,
Where Ippa dwells, all beautiful and bright.
Come blessed Phrygian God, the king of all,
And aid thy mystics, when on thee they call.

[XLVIII]

TO IPPA[68]

THE FUMIGATION FROM STORAX

Great nurse of Bacchus, to my pray'r incline,
For holy Sabus' secret rites are thine,

[67] So called from περι and κιονις, a little pillar.
[68] Ippa according to Proclus is the same with Juno.

The mystic rites of Bacchus' nightly choirs,
Compos'd of sacred, loud-resounding fires:
Hear me, terrestrial mother, mighty queen,
Whether on Phrygia's holy mountain[69] seen,
Or if to dwell in Tmolus thee delights,
With holy aspect come, and bless these rites.

[XLIX]

TO LYSIUS LENAEUS

A HYMN

Hear me, Jove's son, blest Bacchus, God of wine,
Born of two mothers, honor'd and divine;
Lysian, Euion[70] Bacchus, various-nam'd,
Of Gods the offspring-secret, holy, fam'd:
Fertile and nourishing, whose liberal care
Earth's fruits increases, flourishing and fair;
Sounding, magnanimous, Lenaean pow'r
O various form'd, medic'nal, holy flow'r:
Mortals in thee, repose from labour find,
Delightful charm, desir'd by all mankind:
Fair-hair'd Euion, Bromian, joyful God,
Lysian, invested with the leafy rod.
To these our rites, benignant pow'r incline,
When fav'ring men, or when on Gods you shine;
Be present to thy mystic's suppliant pray'r,
Rejoicing come, and fruits abundant bear.

[L] #50

TO THE NYMPHS

THE FUMIGATION FROM AROMATICS

Nymphs, who from Ocean's stream derive your birth,
Who dwell in liquid caverns of the earth;

[69] Ida.
[70] Euion ingeminat, reparabilis assonat Echo. *Persius.*

260

Nurses of Bacchus secret-coursing pow'r,
Who fruits sustain, and nourish ev'ry flow'r:
Earthly, rejoicing, who in meadows dwell,
And caves and dens, whose depths extend to hell:
Holy, oblique, who swiftly soar thro' air,
Fountains and dews, and mazy streams your care:
Seen and unseen, who joy with wand'rings wide
And gentle course, thro' flow'ry vales to glide;
With Pan exulting on the mountains height,
Loud-sounding, mad, whom rocks and woods delight:
Nymphs od'rous, rob'd in white, whose streams exhale
The breeze refreshing, and the balmy gale;
With goats and pastures pleas'd, and beasts of prey,
Nurses of fruits, unconscious of decay:
In cold rejoicing, and to cattle kind,
Sportive thro' ocean wand'ring unconfin'd:
Nysian, fanatic Nymphs, whom oaks delight,
Lovers of Spring, Paeonian virgins bright.
With Bacchus, and with Ceres, hear my pray'r,
And to mankind abundant favour bear;
Propitious listen to your suppliant's voice,
Come, and benignant in these rites rejoice;
Give plenteous Seasons, and sufficient wealth,
And pour, in lasting streams, continued Health.

[LI]

TO TRIETERICUS

THE FUMIGATION FROM AROMATICS

Bacchus fanatic, much-nam'd, blest, divine,
Bull-fac'd, Lenaean, bearer of the vine;
From fire descended, raging, Nysian king,
From whom initial ceremonies spring:
Liknitan Bacchus, pure and fiery bright,
Prudent, crown-bearer, wandering in the night;

Pupil of Proserpine, mysterious pow'r,
Triple, ineffable, Jove's secret flow'r:
Ericapaeus, first-begotten nam'd,
Of Gods the father, and the offspring fam'd:[71]
Bearing a sceptre, leader of the choir,
Whose dancing feet, fanatic Furies fire,
When the triennial band thou dost inspire.
Loud-sounding, Tages, of a fiery light,
Born of two mothers, Amphietus bright:
Wand'ring on mountains, cloth'd with skins of deer,
Apollo golden-ray'd, whom all revere.
God of the grape with leaves of ivy crown'd,
Bassarian, lovely, virgin-like, renown'd:
Come blessed pow'r, regard thy mystics voice,
Propitious come, and in these rites rejoice.

[LII]

TO AMPHIETUS BACCHUS

THE FUMIGATION FROM EVERY AROMATIC
EXCEPT FRANKINCENSE

Terrestrial Dionysius, hear my pray'r,
Awak'ned rise with nymphs of lovely hair:
Great Amphietus Bacchus, annual God,
Who laid asleep in Proserpine's abode,
Did'st lull to drowsy and oblivious rest,
The rites triennial, and the sacred feast;
Which rous'd again by thee, in graceful ring,

[71] According to the fragment preserved by Ficinus, and translated in our Dissertation, Trietericus is the nostic power, or intellect of the Sun; and the Sun is in the sensible world, what Protogonus or Phanes is in the intelligible world: or, in other words, the Sun is the Phanes of the material world, for Trietericus is expressly called in this Hymn Protogonus. With perfect agreement, therefore, to the Orphic theology, Protogonus, considered as the first of the secret genera of the Gods, is the father of the Gods; but considered as the Sun of the material world, he is the offspring of the Gods.

Thy nurses round thee mystic anthems sing;
When briskly dancing with rejoicing pow'rs,
Thou mov'st in concert with the circling hours.
Come, blessed, fruitful, horned, and divine,
And on these rites with joyful aspect shine;
Accept the general incense and the pray'r,
And make prolific holy fruits thy care.

[LIII]

TO SILENUS, SATYRUS, AND THE
PRIESTESSES OF BACCHUS

THE FUMIGATION FROM MANNA

Great nurse of Bacchus, to my pray'r incline,
Silenus, honor'd by the pow'rs divine;
And by mankind at the triennial feast
Illustrious daemon, reverenc'd as the best:
Holy, august, the source of lawful rites,
Rejoicing pow'r, whom vigilance delights;
With Sylvans dancing ever young and fair,
Head of the Bacchic Nymphs, who ivy bear.
With all thy Satyrs on our incense shine,
Daemons wild form'd, and bless the rites divine;
Come, rouse to sacred joy thy pupil king,[72]
And Brumal Nymphs with rites Lenaean bring;
Our orgies shining thro' the night inspire,
And bless triumphant pow'r the sacred choir.

[LIV]

TO VENUS

A HYMN

Heav'nly, illustrious, laughter-loving queen,
Sea-born, night-loving, of an awful mien;

[72] Because he was the nurse of Bacchus.

Crafty, from whom necessity first came,
Producing, nightly, all-connecting dame:
'Tis thine the world with harmony to join,[73]
For all things spring from thee, O pow'r divine.
The triple Fates are rul'd by thy decree,
And all productions yield alike to thee:
Whate'er the heav'ns, encircling all contain,
Earth fruit-producing, and the stormy main,
Thy sway confesses, and obeys thy nod,
Awful attendant of the brumal God:
Goddess of marriage, charming to the sight,
Mother of Loves, whom banquetings delight;
Source of persuasion, secret, sav'ring queen,
Illustrious born, apparent and unseen:
Spousal, lupercal, and to men inclin'd,
Prolific, most-desir'd, life-giving, kind:
Great sceptre-bearer of the Gods, 'tis thine,
Mortals in necessary bands to join;
And ev'ry tribe of savage monsters dire
In magic chains to bind, thro' mad desire.
Come, Cyprus-born, and to my pray'r incline,
Whether exalted in the heav'ns you shine,
Or pleas'd in Syria's temple to preside,
Or o'er th' Egyptian plains thy car to guide,
Fashion'd of gold; and near its sacred flood,
Fertile and fam'd to fix thy blest abode;
Or if rejoicing in the azure shores,
Near where the sea with foaming billows roars,
The circling choirs of mortals, thy delight,
Or beauteous nymphs, with eyes cerulean bright,

[73] According to the Orphic theology as related by Proclus, and from him by Eschenbach, in Epig. p. 52, Venus is the cause of all the harmony and analogy in the universe, and of the union of form with matter; connecting and comprehending the powers of all the mundane elements. And although this Goddess ranks among the supermundane divinities, yet her principal employment consists in beautifully illuminating the order, harmony, and communion of all mundane concerns.

Pleas'd by the dusty banks renown'd of old,
To drive thy rapid, two-yok'd car of gold;
Or if in Cyprus with thy mother fair,
Where married females praise thee ev'ry year,
And beauteous virgins in the chorus join,
Adonis pure to sing and thee divine;
Come, all-attractive to my pray'r inclin'd,
For thee, I call, with holy, reverent mind.

[LV]

TO ADONIS

THE FUMIGATION FROM AROMATICS

Much-nam'd, and best of daemons, hear my pray'r,
The desart-loving, deck'd with tender hair;
Joy to diffuse, by all desir'd is thine,
Much form'd, Eubulus, aliment divine:
Female and Male, all charming to the sight,
Adonis ever flourishing and bright;
At stated periods doom'd to set and rise,
With splendid lamp, the glory of the skies.[74]
Two-horn'd and lovely, reverenc'd with tears,
Of beauteous form, adorn'd with copious hairs.
Rejoicing in the chace, all-graceful pow'r,
Sweet plant of Venus, Love's delightful flow'r:
Descended from the secret bed divine,
Of lovely-hair'd, infernal Proserpine.
'Tis thine to sink in Tartarus profound,
And shine again thro' heav'ns illustrious round,
With beauteous temp'ral orb restor'd to sight;
Come, with earth's fruits, and in these flames delight.

[74] Proclus, in his elegant Hymn to the Sun, celebrates him as frequently called Adonis; and this perfectly agrees with the present epithet, and with many others in the Hymn.

[LVI]

TO THE TERRESTRIAL HERMES

THE FUMIGATION FROM STORAX

Hermes I call, whom Fate decrees to dwell
In the dire path which leads to deepest hell:
O Bacchic Hermes, progeny divine
Of Dionysius, parent of the vine,
And of celestial Venus Paphian queen,
Dark eye-lash'd Goddess of a lovely mien:
Who constant wand'rest thro' the sacred seats
Where hell's dread empress, Proserpine, retreats;
To wretched souls the leader of the way
When Fate decrees, to regions void of day:
Thine is the wand which causes sleep to fly,
Or lulls to slumb'rous rest the weary eye;
For Proserpine thro' Tart'rus dark and wide
Gave thee forever flowing souls to guide.
Come, blessed pow'r the sacrifice attend,
And grant our mystic works a happy end.

[LVII]

TO CUPID, OR LOVE

THE FUMIGATION FROM AROMATICS

I call great Cupid, source of sweet delight,
Holy and pure, and lovely to the sight;
Darting, and wing'd impetuous fierce desire,
With Gods and mortals playing, wand'ring fire:
Cautious, and two-fold, keeper of the keys
Of heav'n and earth, the air, and spreading seas;
Of all that Ceres' fertile realms contains,
By which th' all-parent Goddess life sustains,
Or dismal Tartarus is doom'd to keep,

266

Widely extended, or the sounding deep;
For thee, all Nature's various realms obey,
Who rul'st alone, with universal sway.
Come, blessed pow'r, regard these mystic fires,
And far avert, unlawful mad desires.

[LVIII]

TO THE FATES

THE FUMIGATION FROM AROMATICS

Daughters of darkling night, much-nam'd, draw near
Infinite Fates, and listen to my pray'r;
Who in the heav'nly lake[75] (where waters white
Burst from a fountain hid in depths of night,
And thro' a dark and stony cavern glide,
A cave profound, invisible) abide;
From whence, wide coursing round the boundless earth,
Your pow'r extends to those of mortal birth;
To men with hope elated, trifling, gay,
A race presumptuous, born but to decay;
Whose life 'tis yours in darkness to conceal
To sense impervious, in a purple veil,
When thro' the fatal plain they joyful ride
In one great car, Opinion for their guide;
'Till each completes his heav'n-appointed round
At Justice, Hope, and Care's concluding bound,

[75] Gesner confesses he is ignorant what the poet means by the λίμνη 'Ουρανία, or heavenly lake; as likewise of the dark cavern in which he places the Fates. At first sight indeed the whole seems impenetrably obscure, but on comparing this Hymn with the 68th, to the Furies, we shall find that the poet expressly calls them the Fates; and places them in an obscure cavern by the holy water of Styx. And from hence it appears, that the Heavenly Lake is the same with the Stygian Pool, which is called heavenly perhaps, because the Gods swear by it. But it is not wonderful that the water is called white, since Hesiod, in Theog. v. 791, speaks of the Stygian waters as falling into the sea with silvery whirls. And what strengthens the illustration still more, Fulgentius places the Fates with Pluto.

The terms absolv'd, prescrib'd by ancient law
Of pow'r immense, and just without a flaw;
For Fate alone with vision unconfin'd,
Surveys the conduct of the mortal kind.
Fate is Jove's perfect and eternal eye,
For Jove and Fate our ev'ry deed descry.
Come, gentle pow'rs, well-born, benignant, fam'd,
Atropos, Lachesis, and Clotho nam'd:
Unchang'd, aerial, wand'ring in the night,
Restless, invisible to mortal sight;
Fates all-producing, all-destroying hear,
Regard the incense and the holy pray'r;
Propitious listen to these rites inclin'd,
And far avert distress with placid mind.

[LIX]

TO THE GRACES

THE FUMIGATION FROM STORAX

Hear me, illustrious Graces, mighty nam'd,
From Jove descended and Eunomia fam'd;
Thalia, and Aglaia fair and bright,
And blest Euphrosyne whom joys delight:
Mothers of mirth, all lovely to the view,
Pleasure abundant pure belongs to you:
Various, forever flourishing and fair,
Desir'd by mortals, much invok'd in pray'r:
Circling, dark-ey'd, delightful to mankind,
Come, and your mystics bless with bounteous mind.

[LX]

TO NEMESIS

A HYMN

Thee, Nemesis I call, almighty queen,
By whom the deeds of mortal life are seen:

Eternal, much rever'd, of boundless sight,
Alone rejoicing in the just and right:
Changing the counsels of the human breast
For ever various, rolling without rest.
To every mortal is thy influence known,
And men beneath thy righteous bondage groan;
For ev'ry thought within the mind conceal'd
Is to thy sight perspicuously reveal'd.
The soul unwilling reason to obey
By lawless passion rul'd, thy eyes survey.
All to see, hear, and rule, O pow'r divine
Whose nature Equity contains, is thine.
Come, blessed, holy Goddess, hear my pray'r,
And make thy mystic's life, thy constant care:
Give aid benignant in the needful hour,
And strength abundant to the reas'ning pow'r;
And far avert the dire, unfriendly race
Of counsels impious, arrogant, and base.

[LXI]

TO JUSTICE

THE FUMIGATION FROM FRANKINCENSE

The piercing eye of Justice bright, I sing,[76]
Plac'd by the throne of heav'n's almighty king,
Perceiving thence, with vision unconfin'd,
The life and conduct of the human kind:
To thee, revenge and punishment belong,
Chastising ev'ry deed, unjust and wrong;

[76] This Hymn is cited by Demosthenes in his first speech against Aristogiton, as follows: "Let us, says the orator overlooking all custom, judge righteous judgment; let us reverence Eunomia that loves equity, and preserves states; and inexorable Δικη (right or justice) whom Orpheus, our instructor, in the most holy initiations, τελεταὶ, places by the throne of Jove, inspecting the affairs of men. Let each of us imagine her piercing eye is now upon us, and think and vote so as not to dishonour *her* from whom every judge has his name."

Whose pow'r alone, dissimilars can join,
And from th' equality of truth combine:
For all the ill, persuasion can inspire,
When urging bad designs, with counsel dire,
'Tis thine alone to punish; with the race
Of lawless passions, and incentives base;
For thou art ever to the good inclin'd,
And hostile to the men of evil mind.
Come, all-propitious, and thy suppliant hear,
When Fate's predestin'd, final hour draws near.

[LXII]

TO EQUITY

THE FUMIGATION FROM FRANKINCENSE

O Blessed Equity, mankind's delight,
Th' eternal friend of conduct just and right:
Abundant, venerable, honor'd maid,
To judgments pure, dispensing constant aid,
A stable conscience, and an upright mind;
For men unjust, by thee are undermin'd,
Whose souls perverse thy bondage ne'er desire,
But more untam'd decline thy scourges dire:
Harmonious, friendly power, averse to strife,
In peace rejoicing, and a stable life;
Lovely, loquacious, of a gentle mind,
Hating excess, to equal deeds inclin'd:
Wisdom, and virtue of whate'er degree,
Receive their proper bound alone in thee.
Hear, Goddess Equity, the deeds destroy
Of evil men, which human life annoy;
That all may yield to thee of mortal birth,
Whether supported by the fruits of earth,
Or in her kindly fertile bosom found,
Or in the depths of Marine Jove profound.

[LXIII]

TO LAW

A HYMN

The holy king of Gods and men I call,
Celestial Law, the righteous seal of all;
The seal which stamps whate'er the earth contains,
Nature's firm basis, and the liquid plains:
Stable, and starry, of harmonious frame,
Preserving laws eternally the same:
Thy all-composing pow'r in heav'n appears,
Connects its frame, and props the starry spheres;
And shakes weak Envy with tremendous sound,
Toss'd by thy arm in giddy whirls around.
'Tis thine, the life of mortals to defend,
And crown existence with a blessed end;
For thy command alone, of all that lives
Order and rule to ev'ry dwelling gives:
Ever observant of the upright mind,
And of just actions the companion kind;
Foe to the lawless, with avenging ire,
Their steps involving in destruction dire.
Come, blest, abundant pow'r, whom all revere,
By all desir'd, with fav'ring mind draw near;
Give me thro' life, on thee to fix my sight,
And ne'er forsake the equal paths of right.

[LXIV]

TO MARS[77]

THE FUMIGATION FROM FRANKINCENSE

Magnanimous, unconquer'd, boistrous Mars,
In darts rejoicing, and in bloody wars:

[77] This deity, according to Proclus, in Repub. p. 388, perpetually discerns and nourishes, and constantly excites the contrarieties of the universe, that

Fierce and untam'd, whose mighty pow'r can make
The strongest walls from their foundations shake:
Mortal destroying king, defil'd with gore,
Pleas'd with war's dreadful and tumultuous roar:
Thee, human blood, and swords, and spears delight,
And the dire ruin of mad savage fight.
Stay, furious contests, and avenging strife,
Whose works with woe, embitter human life;
To lovely Venus, and to Bacchus yield,
To Ceres give the weapons of the field;
Encourage peace, to gentle works inclin'd,
And give abundance, with benignant mind.

[LXV]

TO VULCAN[78]

THE FUMIGATION FROM FRANKINCENSE AND MANNA

Strong, mighty Vulcan, bearing splendid light,
Unweary'd fire, with flaming torrents bright:
Strong-handed, deathless, and of art divine,
Pure element, a portion of the world is thine:
All-taming artist, all-diffusive pow'r,
'Tis thine supreme, all substance to devour:
Aether, Sun, Moon, and Stars, light pure and clear,
For these thy lucid parts to men appear.
To thee, all dwellings, cities, tribes belong,
Diffus'd thro' mortal bodies bright and strong.
Hear, blessed power, to holy rites incline,
And all propitious on the incense shine:

---

the world may exist perfect and entire from all its parts. But he requires the assistance of Venus, that he may insert order and harmony into things contrary and discordant.

[78] This deity, according to Proclus, in Repub. p. 388, adorns by his artifice the sensible machine of the universe, which he fills with certain reasons, proportions, and powers of Nature. But he requires the assistance of Venus, that he may invest sensible effects with beauty, and by this means cause the pulchritude of the world.

Suppress the rage of fires unweary'd frame,
And still preserve our nature's vital flame.

[LXVI]

TO ESCULAPIUS

THE FUMIGATION FROM MANNA

Great Esculapius, skill'd to heal mankind,
All-ruling Paean, and physician kind;
Whose arts medic'nal, can alone assuage
Diseases dire, and stop their dreadful rage:
Strong lenient God, regard my suppliant pray'r,
Bring gentle Health, adorn'd with lovely hair;
Convey the means of mitigating pain,
And raging, deadly pestilence restrain.
O pow'r all-flourishing, abundant, bright,
Apollo's honor'd offspring, God of light;
Husband of blameless Health, the constant foe
Of dread Disease the minister of woe:
Come, blessed saviour, and my health defend,
And to my life afford a prosp'rous end.

[LXVII]

TO HEALTH

THE FUMIGATION FROM MANNA

O much-desir'd, prolific, gen'ral queen,
Hear me, life-bearing Health, of beauteous mien,
Mother of all; by thee diseases dire,
Of bliss destructive, from our life retire;
And ev'ry house is flourishing and fair,
If with rejoicing aspect thou art there:
Each daedal art, thy vig'rous force inspires,
And all the world thy helping hand desires;
Pluto life's bane alone resists thy will,

273

And ever hates thy all-preserving skill.
O fertile queen, from thee forever flows
To mortal life from agony repose;
And men without thy all-sustaining ease,
Find nothing useful, nothing form'd to please;
Without thy aid, not Plutus' self can thrive,
Nor man to much afflicted age arrive;
For thou alone of countenance serene,
Dost govern all things, universal queen.
Assist thy mystics with propitious mind,
And far avert disease of ev'ry kind.

[LXVIII]

TO THE FURIES[79]

THE FUMIGATION FROM AROMATICS

Vociferous, Bacchanalian Furies, hear!
Ye, I invoke, dread pow'rs, whom all revere;
Nightly, profound, in secret who retire,
Tisiphone, Alecto, and Megara dire:
Deep in a cavern merg'd, involv'd in night,
Near where Styx flows impervious to the sight;
Ever attendant on mysterious rites,
Furious and fierce, whom Fate's dread law delights;
Revenge and sorrows dire to you belong,
Hid in a savage veil, severe and strong.
Terrific virgins, who forever dwell
Endu'd with various forms, in deepest hell;
Aerial, and unseen by human kind,
And swiftly coursing, rapid as the mind.
In vain the Sun with wing'd refulgence bright,
In vain the Moon, far darting milder light,
Wisdom and Virtue may attempt in vain,
And pleasing Art, our transport to obtain;

[79] See the note to Hymn LVIII to the Fates. [I.e., note 75.]

Unless with these you readily conspire,
And far avert your all-destructive ire.
The boundless tribes of mortals you descry,
And justly rule with Right's impartial eye.
Come, snaky-hair'd, Fates many-form'd, divine,
Suppress your rage, and to our rites incline.

[LXIX]

TO THE FURIES

THE FUMIGATION FROM AROMATICS

Hear me, illustrious Furies, mighty nam'd,
Terrific pow'rs, for prudent counsel fam'd;
Holy and pure, from Jove terrestrial born
And Proserpine, whom lovely locks adorn:
Whose piercing sight, with vision unconfin'd,
Surveys the deeds of all the impious kind:
On Fate attendant, punishing the race
(With wrath severe) of deeds unjust and base.
Dark-colour'd queens, whose glittering eyes, are bright
With dreadful, radiant, life-destroying light:
Eternal rulers, terrible and strong,
To whom revenge, and tortures dire belong;
Fatal and horrid to the human sight,
With snaky tresses wand'ring in the night;
Hither approach, and in these rites rejoice,
For ye, I call, with holy, suppliant voice.

[LXX]

TO MELINOE

THE FUMIGATION FROM AROMATICS

I call Melinoe, saffron-veil'd, terrene,
Who from infernal Pluto's sacred queen,
Mixt with Saturnian Jupiter, arose,

275

Near where Cocytus' mournful river flows;
When under Pluto's semblance, Jove divine
Deceiv'd with guileful arts dark Proserpine.
Hence, partly black thy limbs and partly white,
From Pluto dark, from Jove etherial, bright.
Thy colour'd members, men by night inspire
When seen in specter'd forms with terrors dire;
Now darkly visible, involv'd in night,
Perspicuous now they meet the fearful sight.
Terrestrial queen expel wherever found
The soul's mad fears to earth's remotest bound;
With holy aspect on our incense shine,
And bless thy mystics, and the rites divine.

[LXXI]

TO FORTUNE

THE FUMIGATION FROM FRANKINCENSE

Approach strong Fortune, with propitious mind
And rich abundance, to my pray'r inclin'd:
Placid and gentle Trivia,[80] *mighty nam'd,*
Imperial Dian, born of Pluto fam'd;
Mankind's unconquer'd, endless praise is thine,
Sepulchral, widely-wand'ring pow'r divine!
In thee, our various mortal life is found,
And some from thee in copious wealth abound;
While others mourn thy hand averse to bless,
In all the bitterness of deep distress.
Be present, Goddess, to thy vot'ry kind,
And give abundance with benignant mind.

[80] See the note to the Introduction to Musaeus. [I.e., note 1.]

[LXXII]

TO THE DAEMON, OR GENIUS

THE FUMIGATION FROM FRANKINCENSE

Thee, mighty ruling, Daemon dread, I call,
Mild Jove, life-giving, and the source of all:
Great Jove, much-wand'ring, terrible and strong,
To whom revenge and tortures dire belong.
Mankind from thee, in plenteous wealth abound,
When in their dwellings joyful thou art found;
Or pass thro' life afflicted and distress'd,
The needful means of bliss by thee supprest.
'Tis thine alone endu'd with boundless might,
To keep the keys of sorrow and delight.
O holy, blessed father, hear my pray'r,
Disperse the seeds of life-consuming care;
With fav'ring mind the sacred rites attend,
And grant my days a glorious, blessed end.

[LXXIII]

TO LEUCOTHEA[81]

THE FUMIGATION FROM AROMATICS

I call Leucothea, of great Cadmus born,
And Bacchus' nurse, whom ivy leaves adorn.
Hear, pow'rful Goddess, in the mighty deep
Wide and profound, thy station doom'd to keep:
In waves rejoicing, guardian of mankind;
For ships from thee alone deliv'rance find
Amidst the fury of th' unstable main,
When art no more avail, and strength is vain;
When rushing billows with tempestuous ire
O'erwhelm the mariner in ruin dire,
Thou hear'st, with pity touch'd, his suppliant pray'r,
Resolv'd his life to succour and to spare.

[81] [See Plate 16.]

Be ever present, Goddess! in distress,
Waft ships along with prosperous success:
Thy mystics thro' the stormy sea defend,
And safe conduct them to their destin'd end.

[LXXIV]

TO PALAEMON

THE FUMIGATION FROM MANNA

O nurs'd with Dionysius, doom'd to keep
Thy dwelling in the widely-spreading deep:
With joyful aspect to my pray'r incline,
Propitious come, and bless the rites divine:
Thro' earth and sea thy ministers attend,
And from old Ocean's stormy waves defend:
For ships their safety ever owe to thee,
Who wand'rest with them thro' the raging sea.
Come, guardian pow'r, whom mortal tribes desire,
And far avert the deep's destructive ire.

[LXXV]

TO THE MUSES

THE FUMIGATION FROM FRANKINCENSE

Daughters of Jove,[81a] *dire-sounding and divine,*

[81a] Proclus, in some manuscript commentary, cited by Gyraldus, in Syntag. de Musis. p. 534, says that the Muses are called the daughters of Jove and Mnemosyne because to those who desire to possess disciplines and sciences, intellect and the power of memory are necessary as the first requisites: the latter of which the Greeks call μνημονικὸς, the former νοητικὸς. But as the best explanation of the nature of the Muses is given by Proclus, in his Commentary on Plato's Republic, p. 399, accompanied with all that philosophical elegance and subtilty, which he possessed in so remarkable a degree, I persuade myself the following Paraphrase on his discourse concerning the different kinds of poets will be highly acceptable to the liberal reader; and that its great excellence will amply compensate for its length. "In the first place then, there are three poetic forms corresponding to

The Hymns of Orpheus

Renown'd, Pierian, sweetly speaking Nine;
To those whose breasts your sacred furies fire
Much-form'd, the objects of supreme desire:
Sources of blameless virtue to mankind,

---

the three different powers of the soul, Intellect, Reason, and Opinion. These we shall explain according to the opinion of Plato; and produce from Homer examples of each. The first kind of poetry then, is similar to intellect. But intellect is the best, most perfect, and most divine power of the soul: it is the most similar to a divine life, in the contemplation of which it is wholly employed, and is swallowed up as it were in the essence of divinity; so that it enkindles its own light from the splendor of the Gods, and conjoins its own most simple essence with supernatural unity. In like manner the most excellent kind of poetry gives beatitude to the soul, from divinity, and places it among the Gods; participating by an ineffable union with the participated deities, and conjoining that which is filled with good, with its replenishing source. Hence it abstracts the soul from all material connections, illuminates it with celestial light, inflames it with a divine fire; and compels the whole inferior constitution of the soul to be obedient to intellect alone. Indeed, a Fury of this kind is more excellent than any temperance, since it furnishes the soul with such a symmetry and proportion of divinity, that the very words bursting forth as its last effects appear to be adorned with the beautiful bands of measure and number. For as prophetic Fury arises from truth, and the amatorial from beauty; so the poetic proceeds from divine symmetry, by means of which it most intimately unites the poets with the Gods. Plato, in the Phaedrus, speaking of this Fury, says that it is an occupation of the Muses; and a Fury sent from above on tender and untouched souls. That its employment is to suscitate and inspire the poet, according to odes and the other kinds of poetry: but its end, the instruction of posterity by celebrating the infinite deeds of antiquity. From these words it is plain, that Plato, in the first place, ascribes divinity to this kind of poetry, as being derived from the Muses; who fill as well intelligible as sensible works with paternal harmony, and elegant motion. But he calls it an occupation, because the whole illustrated soul, resigns itself to the present effect of illuminating divinity: and a Fury, because it relinquishes its own proper ingenuity, and is carried according to the vigorous impulse of a superior power. Again, in the second place he describes the habit of the soul thus occupied: for, he says, it ought to be tender and untouched; not rigid, hard, and filled with many and various opinions, foreign from inspiring divinity: but it should be soft and tender, that it may easily admit divine inspiration; and untouched, that it may be sincere and empty of all other concerns. In the third place, he adds its common employment; that it is perfected by the afflatus of the Muses, and by the soul properly disposed for its reception. Indeed suscitation is an elevation of the soul,

Thomas Taylor the Platonist

Who form to excellence the youthful mind;
Who nurse the soul, and give her to descry
The paths of right with Reason's steady eye.
Commanding queens who lead to sacred light

an operation but little depraved, and a vigorous conversion to the deity, from a lapse into the whirls of generation. But an afflatus is a divine motion, and an unwearied musical dance towards the inspiring deity. Lastly, he testifies that human concerns spoken from a divine mouth become more perfect, illustrious, and more convenient for the delivery of true doctrine to the hearers. Not that this kind of poetry is accommodated to juvenile tuition, but is the most convenient of all for the instruction of those who are perfect in politic discipline, and who earnestly desire the mystical tradition of divine concerns. On this account, Plato deservedly prefers it to all human arts. But he who (as he writes in the same place) approaches to the poetic gates, without the Fury of the Muses, trusting that he may become a good poet by a certain art, will be himself empty, as well as his poetry, in respect of that which proceeds from Fury; before whose presence, the poetry vanishes which is dictated by prudence alone." Thus far from the Phaedrus.

Again, not dissimilar to these, are the words of Socrates in the Iö. For when the rhapsodist affirms, that he abounds with a copiousness of discourse on Homer, but not upon the other poets, Socrates ascribes the cause of this to his being moved by divine force, and not by art. For unless he was peculiarly inclined to Homer by a divine instinct, he would be equally as copious on all other poets as upon Homer. But the first mover says he is a God or a Muse, that is a divine cause; from thence the poet is excited, and from him again the rhapsodist. Hence poetic Fury is a medium between a divine principle and the rhapsodists, moving, and at the same time moved, and distributing supernal gifts to inferiors, by a certain latent consent; by means of which, these degrees cohere among themselves in the same manner as many iron rings depending from a magnet, each of which communicates in gradation, its alluring and attractive power to the other. So in the poetic chain, it is requisite there should be something divine, which, through proper mediums, may connect the last to the first monad. This Fury Homer, as well as Plato, calls at one time in the plural number Muses, and at another time in the singular number a Muse: in the first case having respect to the multitude of the chain of the Muses; but in the second to the coherent union of all things, which is inserted from the first cause in inferior natures. For indeed poetry subsists in a secret and uniform manner in the first mover, and afterwards in poets excited by that unity, like the revolution of a thread from its bottom clew ἀνειλεγμένως, but in the rhapsodist's, according to the lowest and ministrant degree. And thus much it is sufficient for the present to have alleged from Plato's Iö. He who desires more, must

The Hymns of Orpheus

The intellect refin'd from Error's night;
And to mankind each holy rite disclose,
For mystic knowledge from your nature flows.
Clio, and Erato, who charms the sight,

---

consult that dialogue, where he will find many things commending this first and divine kind of poets.

We shall farther add the testimony of the Athenian guest and of Timaeus. For he exhorts us to follow poets seized with the Fury of Apollo, such being the sons of the Gods, and knowing in the best manner the concerns of their progenitors, although they deliver them without the assistance of arguments and demonstrations. And Plato, in the third book of his Laws, thus writes: "This genus of poets is divine, it is agitated by the Gods, composes sacred hymns, and every where embraces Truth attended with the Graces and Muses." To which may be added, that in the first Alcibiades, he says, the nature of poetry is aenigmatical, and is not manifest to every understanding.

Indeed, you will find in Homer all kinds of poetry; but he has less of imagination and imitation, and excels in the first, concerning which we are now discoursing. For, inspired by the Muses and full of fury, he proposes mystical senses of divinity; such as concerning demiurgical unity, the triple division of the universe, the chains of Vulcan, and the connection of Jupiter with Juno. But Homer speaking of Demodocus (under whose person he wishes to signify himself, and on this account reports he was blind) says that he was a divine bard, loved by the Muses and their leader Apollo.

And thus much for the first kind of poets and poetry, according to Proclus; among which it is evident these Hymns must be ranked; as all sacred poetical composition belongs to this highest order. He then proceeds to the second kind of poetry, which the Greeks call διανοια, or rational, as follows. Reason then is inferior to intellect in dignity and power, yet it follows intellect as the leader of its energies, between which, and opinion, it is the connecting medium. And as soul by intellect is conjoined with the divinities; so by the assistance of reason it is converted into itself. Hence it revolves the multitude of arguments, considers the various differences of forms, collects intellect and the intelligent into one; and imitates in its operations an intelligible essence. But since prudence is the employment of reason, we attribute to it the second kind of poetry, which is a medium between the preceding, and the third which we shall next explain. This rational poetry understands the essences of things, and is freely conversant about what is honest and good, as well in words as in actions, which are likewise the object of its contemplation. It produces every particular invested with elegant numbers and rythms; proposes moral sentences, the best counsels, intelligible moderation, and every virtue. Besides this, it teaches the circuits of the soul, its immortality and

With thee Euterpe minist'ring delight:
Thalia flourishing, Polymnia fam'd,
Melpomene from skill in music nam'd:
Terpsichore, Urania heav'nly bright,

various powers; explains to mortals many names of an incorporeal nature, and produces many probable Dogmata respecting corporeal substance. The Athenian guest (in Plato, lib. i. De Legibus) testifies, that the poetry of Theognis is of this kind, which, because it teaches and commends every virtue, is justly to be preferred to the poetry of Tyrtaeus, which exhorts to fortitude alone. But Homer represents this species of poetry, when he describes the life of the soul, the different essences of her parts, the difference between the image and the usurping soul, the variety subsisting in nature, the order of the elements of the universe, civil offices, and the like. But Homer himself appears to have made Phemius the lyrist skilled in this kind of poetry, where Penelope says to him, lib. i.

> *Alluring arts thou know'st, and what of old*
> *Of Gods and heroes, sacred bards have told.*

After the two superior kinds of poetry, that inspired by Fury, and the rational, it remains to speak of the imitative. This last kind of poetry, then, is far distant from the excellence of the others, since it employs imaginations, opinions, and the irrational senses; from whence it contracts many vices, especially in that part of it which is called phantastic. For it greatly raises moderate affections, disturbs the hearers, and, together with words, various harmonies, and numbers, changes the affections of the soul. It shadows over the nature of things not such as they are, but such as they appear to vulgar inspection; and explains them not according to an exact knowledge, but from a delusive imagination. Besides this, it proposes as its end the delight of its auditors; and particularly regards that part of the soul which is obnoxious to the passions of joy and grief. But it is subdivided into two other kinds, one of which is conjectural or assimilatory, and the other phantastic. The latter of these represents only the apparent imitation and similitude, not that which is true; and considers its end accomplished, if it produces in the hearers pleasure and delight, belonging to the phantasy alone. But the other does not so much study the gratification of the popular ear, as a proper imitation, that it may express the things themselves, and exhibit to the eyes an exquisite image of that, concerning which it treats, and may, as near as possible, express the exemplars which it imitates. But Plato himself, under the person of the Eleatean guest (in Sophista) describes the differences of each of these as follows. "I now appear to discern two species of imitation, one conjectural, or the art of assimilating, whose business is to fabricate an image emulous of its exemplar, as far as pertains to length, breadth, depth, and convenient colours. Theaet. Do not those who imitate some-

The Hymns of Orpheus

With thee[82] who gav'st me to behold the light.
Come, venerable, various, pow'rs divine,
With fav'ring aspect on your mystics shine;
Bring glorious, ardent, lovely, fam'd desire,
And warm my bosom with your sacred fire.

thing, perform this to the utmost of their ability? Guest. Not those who fashion or paint any great work. For if they bestowed on the resemblances the true commensuration of beautiful things, the superior members would appear less than is proper, and the inferior larger: because the one is beheld by us at a distance, the other near at hand. Theaet. Entirely so. Guest. Hence artists neglecting truth, do not accommodate to resemblances such commensurations as are really beautiful, but only such as appear so." From these words it is plain that Plato distinguishes each kind of imitation, not only in painting and statuary, but also in poetry; which he compares with those imitative arts. Again, the Athenian guest speaks separately of the conjectural kind, where he treats of that music which does not propose to itself pleasure, but a true and most similar imitation of its exemplar, as in the second book of Laws. Indeed, Socrates speaks of the phantastic kind in the tenth book of the Republic, comparing it to a picture which does not represent the works of nature, but of artists; and these not such as they are, but such as they appear, not imitating their reality, but only their phantastic representation. He likewise demonstrates that this kind of poetry is phantastic, and is in the third degree from truth. But each kind of imitation is found in Homer. For he is then to be esteemed phantastic when he affirms any thing according to vulgar opinion; such as when describing the rising and setting of the sun, not from true situations, but from such as appear so to the senses, which are deceived by distance of place. But where he preserves types of imitation convenient to persons and things, as when he imitates heroes fighting, consulting, and speaking, framing deeds and discourses adapted to the life and pursuits of each, he ought to be called a conjectural poet. And of this kind perhaps is the lyrist of Clytemnestra, who so learnedly imitated examples of temperance by right opinion, that Clytemnestra was free from fault, while he resided with her. But it is lawful to call the musician Thamyris, phantastic, who, instead of the ancient and simple music, endeavoured to introduce one more pleasant, diversified in many ways, and calculated to please the senses and the vulgar. Hence he is feigned to have contended with the Muses themselves, by whom, having raised their anger, he was blinded; not that in reality the Muses are affected with anger, but because he was incapable of the true, simple, and ancient music; and laboured only to move the affections and imagination, not following right opinion, or the science of imitation.

[82] Calliope.

[LXXVI]

TO MNEMOSYNE, OR THE GODDESS OF MEMORY[83]

THE FUMIGATION FROM FRANKINCENSE

The consort I invoke of Jove divine,
Source of the holy, sweetly-speaking Nine;
Free from th' oblivion of the fallen mind,
By whom the soul with intellect is join'd:

[83] Memory, according to the Platonic philosophy, is that power by which the soul is enabled to prosper in some future period, some former energy: and the energy of this power is reminiscence. Now the very essence of intellect is energy, and all its perceptions are nothing more than visions of itself: but all the energies of soul are derived from intellectual illumination. Hence we may compare intellect to light, the soul to an eye, and Memory to that power by which the soul is converted to the light, and actually perceives. But the visions of the soul participate of greater or less reality, in proportion as she is more or less intimately converted to the divine light of intellect. In the multitude of mankind, indeed, the eye of the soul perceives with but a glimmering light, being accustomed to look constantly abroad into the dark and fluctuating regions of sense, and to contemplate solely the shadowy forms of imagination; in consequence of which, their memory is solely employed on objects obscure, external, and low. But in the few who have purified that organ of the soul, by which truth can alone be perceived, and which, as Plato says, is better worth saving than ten thousand eyes of sense; who have disengaged this eye from that barbaric clay with which it was buried, and have by this means turned it as from some benighted day, to bright and real vision: in these, Souls, Memory, and Reminiscence are entirely conversant with those divine ideal forms, so familiar to the soul before her immersion in body. Hence, since we were formerly intellectual natures, we ought, as Porphyry observes, not only to think earnestly of the way, however long and laborious, by which we may return to things truly our own; but that we may meet with a more favourable reception from our proper kindred, we should meditate in what manner we may divest ourselves of every thing foreign from our true country, and recall to our memory those dispositions and habits, without which we cannot be admitted by our own, and which, from long disuse, have departed from our souls. For this purpose (says he) we must lay aside whatever we have associated to ourselves from a mortal nature; and hasten our return to the contemplation of the simple and immutable light of good. We must divest ourselves of the various garments

284

Reason's increase, and thought to thee belong,
All-powerful, pleasant, vigilant, and strong:
'Tis thine, to waken from lethargic rest
All thoughts deposited within the breast;
And nought neglecting, vigorous to excite
The mental eye from dark oblivion's night.
Come, blessed power, thy mystic's mem'ry wake
To holy rites, and Lethe's fetters break.

[LXXVII]

TO AURORA

THE FUMIGATION FROM MANNA

Hear me, O Goddess! whose emerging ray
Leads on the broad refulgence of the day;
Blushing Aurora, whose celestial light
Beams on the world with red'ning splendours bright:
Angel of Titan, whom with constant round,
Thy orient beams recall from night profound:
Labour of ev'ry kind to lead is thine,
Of mortal life the minister divine.
Mankind in thee eternally delight,
And none presumes to shun thy beauteous sight.
Soon as thy splendours break the bands of rest,
And eyes unclose with pleasing sleep oppress'd;
Men, reptiles, birds, and beasts, with gen'ral voice,
And all the nations of the deep, rejoice;
For all the culture of our life is thine.
Come, blessed pow'r! and to these rites incline:
Thy holy light increase, and unconfin'd
Diffuse its radiance on thy mystic's mind.

---

of mortality, by which our true beauty is concealed; and enter the place
of contest naked, and without the incumbrance of dress, striving for the
most glorious of all prizes, the Olympiad of the soul. Thus far Porphyry:
and thus it appears, that the poet, with great philosophical propriety,
celebrates Memory as uniting the soul with intellect.

[LXXVIII]

TO THEMIS

THE FUMIGATION FROM FRANKINCENSE

Illustrious Themis, of celestial birth,
Thee I invoke, young blossom of the earth:[84]
Beauteous-eyed virgin; first from thee alone,
Prophetic oracles to men were known,
Giv'n from the deep recesses of the fane
In sacred Pytho, where renown'd you reign;
From thee, Apollo's oracles arose,
And from thy pow'r his inspiration flows.
Honour'd by all, of form divinely bright,
Majestic virgin, wand'ring in the night:
Mankind from thee first learnt initial rites,
And Bacchus' nightly choirs thy soul delights;
For holy honours to disclose is thine,
With all the culture of the pow'rs divine.
Be present, Goddess, to my pray'r inclin'd,
And bless the mystic rites with fav'ring mind.

[LXXIX]

TO THE NORTH WIND[85]

THE FUMIGATION FROM FRANKINCENSE

Boreas, whose wint'ry blasts, terrific, tear
The bosom of the deep surrounding air;
Cold icy pow'r, approach, and fav'ring blow,
And Thrace a while desert expos'd to snow:
The misty station of the air dissolve,
With pregnant clouds, whose frames in show'rs resolve:
Serenely temper all within the sky,
And wipe from moisture, Aether's beauteous eye.

[84] See the note to Hymn XI to Hercules. [I.e. n. 27.]
[85] [See Plate 7.]

[LXXX]

TO THE WEST WIND

THE FUMIGATION FROM FRANKINCENSE

Sea-born, aerial, blowing from the west,
Sweet gales, who give to weary'd labour rest:
Vernal and grassy, and of gentle sound,
To ships delightful, thro' the sea profound;
For these, impell'd by you with gentle force,
Pursue with prosp'rous Fate their destin'd course.
With blameless gales regard my suppliant pray'r,
Zephyrs unseen, light-wing'd, and form'd from air.

[LXXXI]   8¹

TO THE SOUTH WIND

THE FUMIGATION FROM FRANKINCENSE

Wide coursing gales, whose lightly leaping feet
With rapid wings the air's wet bosom beat,
Approach benevolent, swift-whirling pow'rs,
With humid clouds the principles of show'rs:
For show'ry clouds are portion'd to your care,
To send on earth from all surrounding air.
Hear, blessed pow'rs, these holy rites attend,
And fruitful rains on earth all-parent send.

[LXXXII]

TO OCEAN

THE FUMIGATION FROM AROMATICS

Ocean I call, whose nature ever flows,
From whom at first both Gods and men arose;
Sire incorruptible, whose waves surround,[85a]

[85a] Gesner well observes, that this opinion of the ocean surrounding the earth, is exceeding ancient. See his Prael. i. de Navigationibus vet. § 1.

And earth's concluding mighty circle bound:
Hence every river, hence the spreading sea,
And earth's pure bubbling fountains spring from thee:
Hear, mighty sire, for boundless bliss is thine,
Whose waters purify the pow'rs divine:
Earth's friendly limit, fountain of the pole,
Whose waves wide spreading, and circumfluent roll.
Approach benevolent, with placid mind,
And be for ever to thy mystics kind.

[LXXXIII]

TO VESTA

THE FUMIGATION FROM AROMATICS

Daughter of Saturn, venerable dame,
The seat containing of unweary'd flame;[86]

[86] Vesta is celebrated in this Hymn as the earth, and is the same with the mother of the Gods; as is evident from the Hymn to that divinity, in which she is expressly called Vesta. Now this perfectly agrees with the fragment of Philolaus the Pythagorean, preserved by Stobaeus, in Eclog. Phys. p. 51. "Philolaus (says he) places fire in the middle at the centre, which he calls the Vesta of the universe, the house of Jupiter, the mother of the Gods, and the basis, coherence, and measure of nature." From whence it appears, that they are greatly mistaken who suppose the Pythagoreans meant the sun, by the fire at the centre: and this is still more evident, from the following words of Simplicius de Caelo, lib. ii. οἱ δὲ γενησιεστερον αυτων μετασχόντες, τὸ μὲν πῦρ ἐν τῷ μέσῳ φασὶ τὴν δημιουργικην δύναμιν, εκ τοῦ μέσου ὅλην τὴν γῆν τρέφουσαν, καὶ τὸ ψυχόμενον αὐτῆς ἀνεγειρουσαν. δι' ὅ οἱ μέν, ΖΗΝΟΣ ΠΥΡΓΟΝ αὐτὸ καλουσιν. ὡς αὐτὸς ἐν τοῖς Πυθαγορείοις διηγήσατο. οἱ δὲ ΔΙΟΣ ΦΥΛΑΚΗΝ ὡς ἐν τουτοις. οἱ δὲ, ΔΙΟΣ ΘΡΟΝΟΝ ὡς ἄλλοι φασίν. κεντρον (sic lege et non ἄντρον) δὲ τὴν γῆν ἔλεγον, ὡς ὄργανον καὶ αὐτην τοῦ χρονοῦ· ἡμερων γαρ ἔστιν αὕτη, καὶ νυκτων, αἰτία. That is, "But those who more clearly perceive these affairs, call the fire in the middle a demiurgic power, nourishing the whole earth from the midst, and exciting and enlivening whatever it contains of a frigid nature: on which account some call it the tower of Jupiter, as he (i.e. Aristotle) relates in his Pythagorics. But others, the keeper or guardian of Jove; as he relates in these (i.e. his books de Caelo). But according to others, it is the throne of Jupiter. But they called the earth a centre, as being itself an organ or instrument of time: for it is the cause of day and night."

In sacred rites these ministers are thine,
Mystics much-blessed, holy, and divine.
In thee, the Gods have fix'd their dwelling place,
Strong, stable basis of the mortal race:
Eternal, much-form'd, ever florid queen,
Laughing and blessed,[87] *and of lovely mien;*
Accept these rites, accord each just desire,
And gentle health, and needful good inspire.

[LXXXIV]

TO SLEEP

THE FUMIGATION FROM A POPPY

Sleep, king of Gods, and men of mortal birth,
Sov'reign of all sustain'd by mother Earth;

[87] Proclus, in Plat. Repub. p. 384, observes, that we ought to interpret the laughter of the Gods as an exuberant operation in the universe; and the gladness of mundane concerns, under the providence of a divine cause. But since such a providence, says he, is incomprehensible, and is a never failing communication of all divine goods; we must allow that Homer justly calls the laughter of the Gods ασβεστος or inextinguishable. He adds, that fables do not represent the Gods as always weeping, but affirm that they laugh without ceasing; because tears are symbols of their providence in mortal concerns, which are continually subject to existence and decay: but laughter is a sign of their effects in the universe, and of its principal parts, which are ever moved in one and the same orderly manner. Hence, since we divide demiurgical powers between Gods and men, we assign laughter to the generation of the Gods, but tears to the formation of men or animals. Hence, the poet sings in his Hymn to the Sun, *O Apollo, the mortal race of men is the subject of thy tears; but the celestial race of Gods springs from laughter.* But since we divide the works of divinity into things celestial, and those subject to the moon; after the same manner, we attribute laughter to the first, and grief to the second. Lastly, when we reason concerning the generations and corruptions of things below the moon, we refer the one to the weeping, and the other to the laughter of the Gods. And hence in our mysteries, the ministers of sacred rites, at a certain time order each of these to be celebrated. He then concludes with *an excellent observation,* that men of simple understandings are unable to comprehend intellectually mystical ceremonies and fables of this kind; since *such men* destitute of science, produce nothing but absurd confusion about the religion of the Gods.

For thy dominion is supreme alone,
O'er all extended, and by all things known.
'Tis thine all bodies with benignant mind
In other bands than those of brass to bind:
Tamer of cares, to weary toil repose,
From whom sweet solace in affliction flows.
Thy pleasing, gentle chains preserve the soul,
And e'en the dreadful cares of death controul;
For death and Lethe with oblivious stream,
Mankind thy genuine brothers justly deem.
With fav'ring aspect to my pray'r incline,
And save thy mystics in their works divine.

[LXXXV]
TO THE DIVINITY OF DREAMS

THE FUMIGATION FROM AROMATICS

Thee I invoke, blest pow'r of dreams divine,
Angel of future fates, swift wings are thine:
Great source of oracles to human kind,
When stealing soft, and whisp'ring to the mind,
Thro' sleep's sweet silence and the gloom of night,
Thy pow'r awake th' intellectual sight;
To silent souls the will of heav'n relates,
And silently reveals their future fates.
For ever friendly to the upright mind
Sacred and pure, to holy rites inclin'd;
For these with pleasing hope thy dreams inspire,
Bliss to anticipate, which all desire.
Thy visions manifest of fate disclose,
What methods best may mitigate our woes;
Reveal what rites the Gods immortal please,
And what the means their anger to appease:
For ever tranquil is the good man's end,
Whose life, thy dreams admonish and defend.
But from the wicked turn'd averse to bless,

290

Thy form unseen, the angel of distress;
No means to check approaching ill they find,
Pensive with fears, and to the future blind.
Come, blessed pow'r, the signatures reveal
Which heav'n's decrees mysteriously conceal,
Signs only present to the worthy mind,
Nor omens ill disclose of monstrous kind.

[LXXXVI]

TO DEATH

THE FUMIGATION FROM MANNA

Hear me, O Death, whose empire unconfin'd,
Extends to mortal tribes of ev'ry kind.
On thee, the portion of our time depends,
Whose absence lengthens life, whose presence ends.
Thy sleep perpetual bursts the vivid folds,
By which the soul, attracting body holds:[88]

[88] This is best explained by Porphyry in his excellent work entitled 'Αφορμαὶ πρὸς τὰ Νοητά. 8, as follows: "Whatever nature binds, nature again dissolves; and that which the soul conciliates into union, the soul disperses and dissolves. Nature, indeed, bound the body to the soul; but the soul ties herself to the body. Hence, nature frees the body from the soul, but the soul by the excercise of philosophy, separates herself from the deadly bands of the body." And again, in the next sentence, "Death is of two kinds, the one equally known to all men, when the body is separated from the soul; but the other peculiar to philosophers, when the soul is separated from the body: nor does the one always attend the other." Now this two-fold death we must understand in the following manner: that though some particular body may be loosened from the soul, yet while material passions and affections reside in the soul, the soul will continually verge to another body, and as long as this inclination continues, remain connected with the body. But when, from the dominion of an intellectual nature, the soul is separated from material affections, it is truly liberated from the body; though the body at the same time verges and clings to the soul, as to the immediate cause of its support. And thus much for a Commentary on the Hymns or Initiations of Orpheus. But before I conclude the present work, I beg leave to address a few words to the liberal and philosophical part of my readers. You then, as the votaries of truth,

Thomas Taylor the Platonist

Common to all of ev'ry sex and age,
For nought escapes thy all-destructive rage;
Not youth itself thy clemency can gain,
Vig'rous and strong, by thee untimely slain.
In thee, the end of nature's works is known,
In thee, all judgment is absolv'd alone:

---

will, I doubt not, unite with me in most earnest wishes, that every valuable work on the Platonic philosophy was well translated into our native tongue; that we might no longer be subject to the toil of learning the ancient languages. The mischief, indeed, resulting from the study of words is almost too apparent to need any illustration: as the understanding is generally contracted, its vigour exhausted; and the genius fettered to verbal criticism, and grammatical trifles. Hence an opinion is gradually formed, that the Greek philosophy can alone be understood in the Greek tongue: and thus the books containing the wisdom of antiquity are for the most part deposited in the hands of men incapable of comprehending their contents. While an opinion so sordid prevails, amidst all our refinements in arts, and increasing mass of experiments, we must remain with respect to philosophy in a state of barbarous ignorance. We may flourish, indeed, as a commercial people; and stretch the rod of empire over nations as yet unknown. The waters of Thames, heavy laden with the wealth of merchandize, and sonorous with the din of trade, may devolve abundance in a golden tide; but we must remember that the Daemon of commerce is at the same time advancing with giant strides, to trample on the most liberal pursuits, and is preparing with his extended savage arm to crush the votaries of truth, and depopulate the divine retreats of philosophy. Rise then ye liberal few, and vindicate the dignity of ancient wisdom. Bring truth from her silent and sacred concealments, and vigorously repel the growing empire of barbaric taste; which bids fair to extinguish the celestial fire of philosophy in the frigid embraces of philology, and to bury the divine light of mind, in the sordid gloom of sense. But if your labours should prove abortive; if the period is yet at a distance, when truth shall once more establish her kingdom; when another stream like that of Ilissus shall become tuneful with the music of philosophy; and other cities like those of Athens and Alexandria be filled with the sacred haunts of philosophers: there yet remains an inheritance for the lovers of wisdom in the regions of intellect, those fortunate islands of truth, where all is tranquil and serene, beyond the power of chance, and the reach of change. Let us then fly from hence my friends, to those delightful realms: for there, while connected with body, we may find a retreat from the storms and tempests of a corporeal life. Let us build for ourselves the raft of virtue, and departing from this region of sense, like Ulysses from the charms of Calypso, direct our course by the light of ideas, those bright

The Hymns of Orpheus

No suppliant arts thy dreadful rage controul,
No vows revoke the purpose of thy soul;
O blessed pow'r regard my ardent pray'r,
And human life to age abundant spare.

---

intellectual stars, through the dark ocean of a material nature, until we arrive at our father's land. For there having divested ourselves of the torn garments of mortality, as much as our union with body will permit, we may resume our natural appearance: and may each of us at length recover the ruined empire of his soul.

CONCERNING THE CAVE
OF THE NYMPHS

A Translation of Porphyry's *De Antro Nympharum*
from *The Commentaries of Proclus*

Taylor's paraphrase translation of Porphyry's *De Antro Nympharum* is a part of his long essay on the *History of the Restoration of the Platonic Theology, by the Latter Platonists*, which is in effect a plea for the revival of "Grecian theology." This essay is included in the second volume of the *Commentaries of Proclus* (1789), but it had already been published separately. The date of this first publication is not known, but it was presumably after *The Mystical Initiations* (1787). A second edition of the *Commentaries* appeared in 1792.

The *History* includes a life of Plotinus, paraphrased from Porphyry, followed by two specimens of his writings: *That Intelligibles Are Not External to Intellect, and Concerning the Good* (Ennead V, Book V) and *Concerning Intelligible Beauty* (Ennead V, Book VIII). The second section is devoted to Porphyry and an account of his works, including, as specimens, a passage *On the Regress and Reascent of the Soul* and the whole of the *Cave of the Nymphs*, given below. Section III gives an account of Iamblichus and the other late Platonists, concluding with a comparison of the Platonic and the Christian theology, which Taylor scorned. *On the Cave of the Nymphs* was republished in 1823 in *Select Works of Porphyry*, with revisions, the addition of paragraph numbers, and the omission of the note on "the people of dreams."

Taylor included the whole of Porphyry's "admirable work" because it "contains some deep arcana of the natural and symbolical theology of the ancients, together with some beautiful observations respecting the allegory of Ulysses." At least two of Taylor's contemporaries agreed: Coleridge owned and annotated the *Commentaries*, and Blake transformed the allegory of *The Cave of the Nymphs* into pictorial art. (See the reproduction of his Arlington Court tempera in Plate 18; see also p. 41.) It was also a favorite book of William Butler Yeats, who quoted Taylor at length to prove Shelley's indebtedness; and Taylor's long footnote on the "wanderings of Ulysses" may have been one of the stimulants for James Joyce's own version of the wanderings. Although Yeats might have known Taylor's *Select Works of Porphyry* (1823), which includes "His Treatise on the Homeric Cave of the Nymphs" and "an Appendix, Explaining the Allegory of the Wanderings of Ulysses," a more likely source is the 1895 reprint in Theosophical Siftings entitled *Porphyry, On the Cave of the Nymphs in the Thirteenth Book of Odyssey*, which was reprinted in 1917 by J. M. Watkins.

CONCERNING THE CAVE OF
THE NYMPHS

IN THE LAST PLACE, we may deservedly rank among the theological writings of Porphyry his treatise *Concerning the Cave
of the Nymphs*, in the 13th book of the Odyssey. This admirable
work is fortunately preserved: and as it contains some deep
arcana of the natural and symbolical theology of the ancients, together with some beautiful observations respecting the allegory
of Ulysses, I persuade myself the following paraphrased translation of this work will be acceptable to the lovers of ancient learning and philosophy.

What are we to understand by the Cave, in the island of Ithaca,
which Homer describes in the following verses?

> *High at the head a branching olive grows,*
> *And crowns the pointed cliffs with shady boughs.*
> *A cavern pleasant, though involv'd in night,*
> *Beneath it lies, the Naiades delight.*
> *Where bowls and urns, of workmanship divine,*
> *And massy beams in native marble shine;*
> *On which the Nymphs amazing webs display,*
> *Of purple hue, and exquisite array.*
> *The busy bees, within the urns secure*
> *Honey delicious, and like nectar pure.*
> *Perpetual waters thro' the grotto glide,*
> *A lofty gate unfolds on either side;*
> *That to the north is pervious by mankind:*
> *The sacred south t' immortals is consign'd.*[1]

I. e. "an olive with spreading branches stands at the head of the
Ithacensian port; and near it is a cave both pleasant and obscure,
which is sacred to the nymphs who are called Naiads. Within
the cavern, bowls and capacious amphora are formed from stone,
in which the bees deposit their delicious honey. There are like-

[1] There are three editions of this excellent work. The first Greek and
Latin are by Holstenius, Cantab. 1655; the second by Barnes, prefixed to
his Homer; and the third by some German editor, which I have not seen.

wise within the cave long stony beams, on which the nymphs weave purple webs wonderful to the sight. Perpetual waters flow within the grotto. But there are two gates: one towards the north gives entrance to mortals descending: but the other towards the south which is more divine, is impervious to mankind; and alone affords a passage to ascending immortals."

That the poet does not describe this cave according to truth is evident from hence, says Cronius, that none of those who have handed down to us the situation of that island make any mention of such a cave. This likewise, says he, is manifest, that it would be very absurd for a mortal man, such as Homer, to expect, that in describing a cave fabricated merely by poetical licence, and thus arbitrarily opening by a new art a path to gods and men in the region of Ithaca, he should gain the belief of mankind. It is equally as absurd to suppose, that nature herself should point out in this place, one path for the descent of all mankind, and again another path for all the gods. For indeed the whole world is full of gods and men: but it is impossible to be persuaded that in the Ithacensian cave men descend, and gods ascend. Cronius, having promised thus much, affirms that it was evident not only to the wise, but also to the vulgar and unlearned, that the poet under the veil of allegory, concealed some mysterious signification. But the investigation of the particular meaning of these gates, and of the cave of the nymphs, he leaves to others more disposed to such curious enquiries, as likewise why it is both pleasant and obscure, since darkness is by no means delightful, but is rather productive of aversion and horror. Also why it is not simply sacred to nymphs, but it is accurately added, which are called Naiads. Why likewise the cave is represented as containing bowls and urns, when no mention is made of their receiving any liquor, but the bees are said to deposit their honey in these vessels, as in hives? Then again, why are oblong beams placed here for the nymphs; and these not formed out of wood, or any other ductile matter, but from stone, as well as the bowls and urns? Which last circumstance is indeed less obscure; but that on these stony beams, the nymphs should weave purple garments is wonderful not only to the sight, but to the auditory sense. For who would believe that goddesses weave garments in a cave involved in darkness, and on stony beams; especially while he hears the poet affirming that the purple webs of the goddesses were exposed to human inspection. Besides this too is wonderful, that the cave should have a double entrance; one prepared for the descent of men, the other for the ascent of gods. And again, that the gate pervious by men should look to the north, but the portal of the gods to the south. Since the reason of this distribution affords just matter for surprize and enquiry: and why an eastern and western situation was not preferred. For almost all temples have their entrance and statues towards the east: but those who enter them look towards the west, when standing with their faces turned to the statues they honour and worship the gods. Hence since this narration abounds with obscurities, it follows that it is neither a fable, rashly devised for the purpose of procuring delight, nor contains a true and certain description of a place: but that something is signified by the poet, under its obscure disguise; who likewise places, with a mystic intent, an olive at the entrance of the cave. All which particulars the ancients thought very laborious to investigate and explain, and we who succeed them are of the same opinion, while endeavouring from our own inventions to unfold the concealed meaning of the allegory. Hence those men appear to have written very negligently concerning the situation of the place, who believe both the cave and its contents to be a mere poetical figment. But the best and most accurate writers of geography, and among these Artemidorus the Ephesian, in the fifth book of his work, which consists of eleven books, thus writes: "The island of Ithaca, containing an extent of 85 stadii,[2] is distant from Panormus, a port of Cephalenia, about 12 stadii.[3] It has a port named Phorcys; in which there is a shore, and on that shore a cave sacred to the nymphs, in which the Phaeacians are reported to have placed Ulysses."

By no means therefore is this cave a mere Homerical figment.

[2] I.e. about ten Italian miles.
[3] Viz. a mile and a half.

But whether the poet describes it according to its real nature, or adds something of his own invention, yet the same questions remain to be solved; whether you are disposed to investigate the intention of the poet, or of those who consecrated the cave. Since neither did the ancients consecrate temples without fabulous symbols; nor is it usual with Homer to relate any thing rashly concerning their peculiarities. For indeed, by how much the more any one endeavours to shew, that this description of the cave is not an Homeric fiction, but was consecrated to the gods, before Homer's time; by so much the more he evinces, that this sacred cave is filled with ancient wisdom. On which account it is highly worthy our investigation, and necessary that its symbolical consecration and obscure mysteries should be rendered evident by the light of philosophical enquiry.

Antiquity then with great propriety consecrated caves and dens to the world, whether taken collectively as the universe, or separately according to its parts. Hence they considered earth as the symbol of that matter from which the world is composed; so that, according to the opinion of some, matter and earth are the same; by the symbol of a cave, signifying the formation of the world from matter. For indeed caves are most commonly spontaneous productions, congenial with the earth herself, and comprehended by one uniform stone; whose interior part is concave, and whose exterior parts are extended over an immense space of earth. But the world being self-born (i. e. produced by no external cause but from a principle within), and in perfect symphony with itself, is allied to matter which they call, according to a secret signification, a stone and a rock. For like these hard bodies it is sluggish and inert, and receives the impression of ornamenting form: at the same time they considered it as infinite on account of its formless nature. But since it is continually flowing, and of itself destitute of the supervening investments of species by which it is formed and becomes visible, the flowing waters, darkness, or, as the poet says, obscurity of the cavern exhibit apt symbols of what the world contains on account of that matter with which it is connected. Hence through the dark union of matter, the world is obscure and dark, but from the presence and supervening ornaments of form (from which it derives its name) it is beautiful and pleasant. The world therefore may with great propriety be called a cave; agreeable indeed, at its first entrance, on account of its participation of form, but involved in the deepest obscurity to the intellectual eye which endeavours to discern its dark foundation. So that its exterior and superficial parts are pleasant, but its interior and profound parts obscure: and its very bottom is darkness itself. After the same manner the Persians, mystically signifying the descent of the soul into an inferior nature and its ascent into the intelligible world, initiate the priest or mystic in a place which they denominate a cave. For according to Eubulus, Zoroaster first of all among the neighbouring mountains of Persia, consecrated a natural cave, florid and watered with fountains, in honour of Mithras the father of all things: a cave in the opinion of Zoroaster bearing a resemblance of the world fabricated by Mithras. But the things contained in the cavern, being disposed by certain intervals, according to symmetry and order, were symbols of the elements and climates of the world. We find too that after Zoroaster it was usual with others to perform initiatory rites in caves and dens, whether natural or artificial. For as they consecrated temples, groves, and altars to the celestial gods; but to the terrestrial gods and to heroes altars alone, and to the subterranean divinities vaults and cells; so to the world they dedicated caves and dens; as likewise to nymphs, on account of the waters trickling, and dispersed through caverns, in which the nymphs called Naiads, as we shall shortly observe, preside. But the ancients not only considered a cave as the symbol of this generated and sensible world, but as the representative of every invisible power: because as a cave is obscure and dark, so the essence of these powers is unknown. Hence Saturn fabricated a cave in the ocean itself, and concealed his children in its dark retreats. Thus Ceres educated Proserpine with her nymphs in a cave; and many other particulars of this kind may be found by any one who peruses the writings of Theologists. But that caves are attributed to nymphs, and especially to Naiads, who dwell near fountains, and are called Naiads from the waters over whose flowing streams they preside, the hymn to Apollo indicates in these words:

"The nymphs residing in caves shall deduce fountains of intellectual waters to thee, (according to the divine voice of the Muses,) which are the progeny of a terrene spirit. Hence waters bursting through every river, shall exhibit to mankind perpetual effusions of sweet streams."[4] From hence as it appears to me the Pythagoreans, and after them Plato took occasion to call the world a cave and a den. For the powers which are the leaders and guides of souls thus speak in a verse of Empedocles.

We will enter into this cave covered with rocks.

And Plato in the seventh book of his Republic, speaking of the condition of mankind in this sensible world, says, "Behold men as if dwelling in a subterranean cavern, whose entrance opens through the whole cave to the admission of the light." But when the other person in the dialogue says, you relate an absurd similitude, he subjoins: "It is requisite, friend Glaucus, to apply this similitude to all that has been previously said: assimilating this terrene habitation which is the object of corporeal sight, to the dark residence of a prison: but accommodating the fire shining in the recesses of the cavern to the solar light." And thus it is sufficiently evident, that theologists have considered a cave as a symbol of the world, and of the powers it contains. But we observed that they likewise considered a cave as the symbol of an intelligible essence; led to this opinion by reasons very different from the former. For they placed it as a symbol of the sensible world, because caverns are dark, stony and humid; resembling in all these respects the world on account of the obscure nature of that matter from which it is composed, the continual impression of forms to which it is obnoxious, and the constant flowing of all its parts. But a cave resembles intelligible essence, both because in-

---

[4] These verses are not to be found in any of the hymns now extant, ascribed to Homer.

visible to the eyes and sense, and because its substance is solid, firm, and durable. And in the same manner particular virtues or powers are inconspicuous, especially such as are united with matter. For they did not consider a cave as the symbol of a material and immaterial nature on account of its figure as some have suspected: (since every cave is not circular as appears from this Homeric cavern with a double entrance) but from surveying the natural condition of caves, involved in the depths of obscurity and night, and formed from the union of a hard and stony substance. Again, since a cave has a twofold similitude, it must agree in some particulars with sensible substance, but in others with an intelligible essence. Thus the present cave since it contains perpetual waters, in this respect resembles a substance united with matter, and not that which is immaterial and intelligible. On this account the cave is not sacred to mountain divinities, to those who dwell on hills, or to other deities of this kind, but to Naiads so called by the Greeks from νάματα, fountains; because they preside over waters: and this term is commonly applied to all souls passing into the humid and flowing condition of a generative nature. These souls they considered as incumbent on the water, which is nourished by a divine spirit as Numenius affirms: and hence a prophet said, *that the spirit of God moved on the waters.* The Egyptians likewise on this account place all daemons, not connected with any thing solid or stable, but raised on a sailing vessel; and it is known that humor invades the sun itself, and all animals descending into generation. Hence Heraclitus observes "that it appears delightful, and not mortal to souls, when they are born connected with humidity." And he says in another place, speaking of unembodied souls, "we live their death, and we die their life." Hence the poet calls men existing in generation διερούς, i. e. humid, because their souls are drenched in moisture. On this account too, such souls delight in blood and humid seed: but water administers nutriment to the souls of plants. Besides, according to the opinions of some men aerial and celestial bodies, are nourished by the vapours of fountains and rivers and other exhalations. Thus the Stoics assert that the sun is nourished by the exhalation of the sea; the moon from the effluvia of fountains and rivers; but the stars from the exhalation of the earth. Hence according to them the sun is a certain intellectual composition formed from the sea; the moon from river waters; and the stars from terrene exhalations. It is necessary therefore that souls, whether they are corporeal or incorporeal, while they attract bodies, must verge to humidity, and be incorporated with humid natures; especially such souls, as from their material inclinations ought to be united with blood, and confined in humid bodies as in a watery tegument. Hence the souls of the dead are evocated by the effusion of bile and blood: and souls insnared by corporeal love, and attracting to their nature a humid spirit, condense this watery vehicle like a cloud; for a cloud is nothing more than humour condensed in the air. But the pneumatic part thus condensed, through too great an abundance of humour becomes the object of corporeal sight. And among the number of these we must reckon those apparitions of images, which from a spirit coloured by the influence of imagination, present themselves to mankind. But pure souls are averse from generation; on which account the same Heraclitus observes "a dry soul is the wisest." But souls thus desiring to be mingled with body, and attracting a humid vapour, by their propensity to generation render their pneumatic part moist and wet, and by thus verging to the ever-flowing waters of generation, are deservedly called Naiads. Hence it is customary with the Greeks to call nymphs γαμουμεναs, or married, as those who are copulated to generation; and to wash in a bath whose waters are derived from fountains or perpetual rills. This world then is sacred and pleasant to nymphs, i. e. to souls proceeding into a material nature, and to genii participating of generation, although it is naturally dark and opake; on which account some are of opinion that souls are composed from a certain aerial opacity. Hence a cave is a habitation peculiarly adapted to such souls; since it is both pleasant and obscure, like this material region, in which souls reside. A cave likewise through which perpetual waters flow is well adapted to nymphs, the divinities of waters. The present cave therefore must be allowed sacred to souls, and to those more particular powers denominated nymphs, who from their being praefects of rivers and fountains are called πηγαιαὶ and ναιδὲς, i. e. fountain and river divinities. What then are the different symbols, some of which correspond to souls, and others to the divinities of waters, by which it may be manifest that this cave is at the same time dedicated and consecrated to both? We reply that the stony bowls and urns are symbols of the aquatic nymphs. For vessels of the same form are symbols of Bacchus; but their composition is testaceous, that is, from baked earth. And indeed such as these are correspondent to the gift of this god; since the fruit of the vine is brought to a proper maturity by the celestial fire of the sun. But the stony bowls and urns are most admirably accommodated to nymphs residing over waters which flow from rocks. And what symbol is more proper to souls descending into generation, and the tenacious vestment of body, than as the poet says, "Nymphs weaving on stony beams purple garments wonderful to behold?" For the flesh is generated in and about the bones, which in the bodies of animals may be compared to stones. On which account these textorial instruments are fabricated from stones alone. But the purple garments plainly appear to be the flesh with which we are invested; and which is woven as it were and grows by the connecting and vivifying power of the blood, diffused through every part. Besides, purple garments are tinged with the blood of animals; and flesh is produced and subsists from blood. Add too that the body is a garment with which the soul is invested; a circumstance indeed wonderful to the sight, whether we regard its composition, or consider the connecting band by which it is knit to the soul. Thus according to Orpheus, Proserpine, who presides over every thing generated from seed, is represented weaving a web; and the ancients called heaven by the name of πεπλος, which is as it were the veil or tegument of the celestial gods. But why are the amphora represented filled with honey-combs, and not with water? For in these as he says the bees deposit their honey. But the word τιθαιβωσσειν, signi-

305

fies nothing more than τιθεναι την βοσιν, i. e. to deposit aliment. And honey is the nutriment of bees.

Indeed, theologists have made honey subservient to many and various symbols, because it is indued with a variety of powers: for it possesses a purging and preserving quality. Hence bodies are kept from putrefaction by its use, and ulcers of long standing are purified: besides it is sweet to the taste, and bees produced from putrid oxen collect it by a wonderful art from flowers. On this account when in the sacred rites called λεοντικα, those who are initiated pour honey instead of water on their hands, it is signified by this practice, that their hands should be pure from every sorrowful, noxious, and abominable concern. Thus, others purify the initiated by a purgatorial rite from fire, but are averse from water as the enemy of fire. Besides they purify the tongue from all the defilement of evil with honey. But when the Persians offer honey to the guardian of fruits, they regard its preserving power as a symbol of its similitude to a divine nature. In like manner when the poet pours nectar and ambrosia into the nostrils of the slain, for the purpose of preserving the body from putrefaction, some have interpreted honey as the aliment of the gods. For Homer in a certain place calls nectar yellow; which is also the colour of honey. But whether or not honey is to be taken for nectar, we shall hereafter more accurately examine. Again, we find in Orpheus that Jupiter employs stratagems against Saturn from honey. For Saturn full of honey is intoxicated, his senses are darkened as if from the effects of wine, and he sleeps: just as Porus, according to Plato, is distended with nectar; for wine (says he) was not yet known. But night admonishes Jupiter to employ the stratagem of honey, according to Orpheus, in these words, "As soon as you behold him spread under the lofty oaks, intoxicated with the sweet honey, produced by the bees, bind him in chains."

Saturn, therefore, intoxicated with honey is bound by Jupiter; and castrated in the same manner as Caelum. But the theological poet intimates by this fable that the divine essences are, as it were, bound, and drawn down by delight into the fluctuating empire of generation; and that when resolved in pleasure, they produce certain powers by their seminal virtue. Thus Saturn castrates Caelum, who, by his desire of coition descends to earth. But the intoxication of honey signifies among theologists nothing more than the desire of coition; by the ensnaring power of which Saturn is castrated. For Saturn and his orb is the first of the celestial spheres, which moves contrary to the course of Caelum or the heavens. But certain virtues descend as well from the heavens as from the wandering stars, and the influences of the heavens are received by Saturn, and those of Saturn by Jupiter. Hence, since honey is assumed in purgations, and as an antidote to putrefaction, and aptly represents the pleasure and delight of descending into the fascinating realms of generation, it is accounted a symbol well adapted to nymphs the divinities of waters; signifying the nature of the waters over which they preside free from putrefaction: intimating likewise the purgative quality of the waters and their co-operating in the business of generation. For water promotes generation. The poet, therefore, very properly represents the bees as depositing their honey in bowls and urns: since bowls signify fountains; and on this account a bowl or cup is placed next to Mithras instead of a fountain. But we draw the waters of fountains in Amphora; and fountains and rivers are proper to aquatic nymphs, and especially to the nymphs called by the ancients souls, which antiquity likewise peculiarly denominated μελισσας, i.e. artificers of sweetness or bees: for souls are, indeed, the authors of all the pleasure peculiar to our nature.

Hence Sophocles does not speak improperly, when he says, "The swarm of the dead utters a buzzing noise." But the priestesses of Ceres, as ministers to the terrene goddess, were formerly called bees; and her daughter Proserpine μελιτώδη, or delicious, alluding to the sweetness of honey. Besides' the moon who is the queen of generation was denominated by the ancients a bee, and likewise a bull: for the exaltation of the Moon is Taurus, and bees are generated from oxen; on which account they are called βουγενεις, which name is likewise attributed to souls proceeding into generation. Also the god Mercury is esteemed a stealer of oxen, who is secretly conscious of generation. Besides honey is considered as a symbol of death, in the same manner as gall is of life; whether they indicated by such similitudes that the life of the soul dies by the noxious embraces of pleasure, but enjoys life from bitterness, which by its disgustful sensation prevents the soul from sinking into that drowsy oblivion produced by corporeal delight (on which account they sacrificed gall to the gods); or whether the symbol originated from considering that death is the end of evils, but that the present life is laborious and bitter. But it is here necessary to observe that they did not promiscuously call all souls descending into the whirl of generation bees; but only those who, while residing in this fluctuating region, acted justly; and who, after being in a manner acceptable to the divinities returned to their pristine felicity. For the bee is an animal, accustomed to return to its former place; and is studious of justice and sobriety, on which account libations with honey are called νηφαλιοι, or sober. The ancients likewise refrained from sitting on beans, which they considered as a symbol of generation proceeding in a regular series without being intercepted; because this leguminous vegetable is almost the only one, amongst other fruits, whose stalk is perforated throughout without any intervening knots. We must, therefore, admit that honeycombs and bees are symbols, as well peculiar as common to nymphs the divinities of waters; and at the same time to souls wedded to the humid and fluctuating nature of generation.

But let us now return to the cave and consider its double entrance. The most ancient of mankind then, before temples were raised to divinity, consecrated caves and dens to the gods. Hence the Curetes in Crete dedicated a cave to Jupiter; in Arcadia a cave was sacred to the Moon, in Lyceum to Pan, and in the island Naxus to Bacchus. The worship of Mithras too, wherever this god was known was performed in caves. But with respect to this cave of the nymphs in Ithaca, Homer was not alone content with saying that it had two gates, but he adds that the one looks to the north, and the other, more divine, to the south; concerning which he does not mention whether it is pervious to the descent of either immortals or mankind, as is the case with the northern entrance, but he only says, "The other of these tends to the south, which is not pervious to men, but is alone open to immortals."

It remains, therefore, to investigate either the secret meaning of those who first instituted this cave, according to the poets' description; or what occult signification Homer himself intended to convey, if it is nothing more than a fiction of his own inventing. Since then, the present cave in an eminent degree is a symbol and image of the world, as Numenius and his familiar Cronius affirm, it is necessary, in order to elucidate the reason of the position of the gates, to observe that there are two extremities in the heavens; viz. the winter-solstice, than which no part of heaven is nearer to the south; and the summer-solstice which is situated next to the north. But the summer tropic, that is, the solstitial circle is in Cancer, and the winter tropic in Capricorn. And since Cancer is the nearest to the earth, it is deservedly attributed to the moon, which is itself proximate to the earth. But since the southern pole by its great distance is inconspicuous to us, Capricorn is ascribed to Saturn, who is the highest and most remote of all the planets. Again, the signs from Cancer to Capricorn are situated in the following order; the first is Leo called by astrologers the house of the sun; afterwards Virgo, or the house of Mercury; Libra of Venus; Scorpius of Mars; Sagittarius of Jupiter; and Capricornus or the house of Saturn. But from Capricorn in an inverse order, Sagittarius is attributed to Saturn; Pisces to Jupiter; Aries to Mars; Taurus to Venus; Gemini to Mercury; and last of all Cancer to the Moon. From among the number of these theologists consider Cancer and Capricorn as two ports; Plato calls them two gates. Of these, they affirm that Cancer is the gate through which souls descend, but Capricorn that through which they ascend, and exchange a material for a divine condition of being.[5] Cancer is, indeed, northern and adapted to descend: but

[5] Macrobius in the 12th chapter of his comment on Scipio's dream has derived some of the ancient arcana which it contains from the present part of this admirable work. What he has farther added, I shall translate

Capricorn, is southern, and accommodated to ascent. And, indeed, the gates of the cave which look to the north are with great propriety said to be pervious to the descent of men: but the southern gates are not the avenues of the gods, but of souls

on account of its excellence, and connection with the above passage of Porphyry. "Pythagoras (says he) thought that the empire of Pluto, began downwards from the milky way, because souls falling from thence, appear already to have receded from the gods. Hence he asserts, that the nutriment of milk is first offered to infants, because their first motion commences from the galaxy, when they begin to fall into terrene bodies. On this account, since those who are about to descend are yet in *Cancer*, and have not left the milky way, they rank in the order of the gods. But when by falling they arrive at the *Lion*, in this constellation, they enter on the exordium of their future condition. And, because in the *Lion*, the rudiments of birth, and certain primary exercises of human nature commence; but *Aquarius* is opposite to the lion, and presently sets, after the lion rises; hence, when the sun is in Aquarius, funeral rites are performed to departed souls; because he is then carried in a sign, which is contrary, or adverse to human life. From the confine, therefore, in which the zodiac and galaxy touch each other, the soul descending from a round figure, which is the only divine form, is produced into a cone by its defluxion. And as a line is generated from a point, and proceeds into length, from an indivisible, so the soul from its own point, which is a monad, passes into the duad, which is the first protraction. And this is the essence which Plato in the Timaeus calls indivisible, and at the same time divisible, when he speaks of the fabric of the mundane soul. For as the soul of the world, so likewise that of man will be found in one respect ignorant of division, if the simplicity of a divine nature is considered; and in another respect capacious of division, if we regard the diffusion of the former through the world, and of the latter through the members of the body.

"As soon, therefore, as the soul gravitates towards body, in this first production of herself, she begins to experience a material tumult, that is, matter flowing into her essence. And this is what Plato remarks in the Phaedo, that the soul is drawn into body, staggering with recent intoxication; signifying by this the new drink of matter's impetuous flood, through which the soul becoming defiled and heavy, is drawn into a terrene situation. But the starry *cup*, placed between Cancer and Lion, is a symbol of this mystic truth, signifying that descending souls first experience intoxication in that part of the heavens, through the influx of matter. Hence, oblivion, the companion of intoxication, there begins silently to creep into the recesses of the soul. For if souls retained in their descent to bodies the memory of divine concerns of which they were conscious in the heavens, there would be no dissension among men, concerning divinity. But all, indeed, in descending drink of oblivion; though some more, and others ascending to the gods. On this account the poet does not say it is the passage of the gods, but of immortals; which appellation is also common to our souls, whether in their whole essence or from some particular and most excellent part only they are denominated

---

less. On this account, though truth is not apparent to all men on the earth, yet all exercise their opinions about it: because *a defect of memory, is the origin of opinion.* But those discover most, who have drank least of oblivion: because they easily remember what they had known before in the heavens. Hence, that which is called *lectio* by the Latins, is called by the Greeks ἀναγνώσεις or repeated *knowledge*; because when we learn any truths, we recognize what we naturally knew, before material influxion, rushing into the body, had intoxicated the soul. But it is this *hyle* or matter which composes all that body of the world, which we every where perceive adorned with the impressions of forms. Its highest and purest part, however, by which divine natures are either sustained or composed is called *nectar*, and is believed to be the drink of the gods: but its more inferior and turbid part is the drink of souls. And this is what the ancients have denominated the river of Lethe. But according to the Orphic writers the νοῦς ὑλικὸς or *material intellect*, is Bacchus, who, proceeding from that indivisible part, is divided into particulars. Hence, in the Orphic mysteries, he is reported to have been torn in pieces, by Titanic fury, and the fragments being buried, are said to have risen entire, and collected into one; because intellect by passing into a divisible from an indivisible nature, and again returning from divisible to indivisible, both accomplishes the duties of the world, and does not desert the arcana of its own nature.

"The soul, therefore, falling with this first weight, from the zodiac, and milky-way into each of the subject spheres, is not only clothed with the accession of a luminous body, but produces the particular motions which it is to exercise in the respective orbs. Thus in Saturn, it energises according to a ratiocinative and intellective power, which they call λογιστικὸν and θεωρητικὸν: in the sphere of Jove, according to the power of acting, which is called πρακτικὸν: in that of Mars, according to the ardour of courage, which is denominated θυμικὸν: in the orb of the sun, according to a sensitive and phantastic nature, which they call αἰσθητικὸν and φανταστικὸν: but according to the motion of desire, which is denominated ἐπιθυμητικὸν, in the planet Venus: of pronouncing and interpreting what is perceives, which is called ἑρμηνευτικὸν, in the orb of Mercury; and according to a plantal nature, and a power of acting on body, which is denominated φυτικὸν, when it enters the lunar globe. And this sphere, as it is the last among the divine orders, so it is the first in our terrene situation. For this body, as it is the dregs of divine concerns, so it is the first substance of an animal. And this is the difference between terrene and supernal bodies (under which last, I comprehend the heavens, the

immortal. It is reported that Parmenides mentions these two ports in his book, concerning the nature of things: as likewise that they were not unknown to the Egyptians and Romans. For the Romans celebrate their Saturnalia when the sun is in Capricorn, and during this festivity the servants wear the shoes of those who are free, and all things are distributed among them in common; the legislator intimating by this ceremony, that those who are servants at present, by the condition of their birth, will be hereafter liberated by the Saturnalian feast, and by the house attributed to Saturn, i.e. Capricorn; when reviving in that sign, and being divested of the material garments of generation, they return to their pristine felicity, and to the fountain of life. But since the path beginning from Capricorn is retrograde, and pertains to descent; hence the origin of the word Januarius or January from Janua, a gate, which is the space of time measured by the sun while, returning from Capricorn towards the east, he directs his course to the northern parts. But with the Egyptians the beginning of the year is not Aquarius, as among the Romans, but Cancer. For the star Sothis (Sirius) borders on Cancer, which star the Greeks denominate Κυνος, or the Dog. When this star rises they celebrate the calends of the month, which begins their year; because this is the place of the heavens where generation commences, by which the world subsists. On this account the doors of the Homeric cavern are not dedicated to the east and west, nor to the equinoctial signs, Aries and Libra, but to the north and south, and particularly to those ports or celestial signs which are the

---

stars, and the other elements) that the latter are called upwards to be the seat of the soul, and merit immortality from the very nature of the region, and an imitation of sublimity; but the soul is drawn down to these terrene bodies, and is on this account reported to die, when it is inclosed in this fallen region, and the seat of mortality. Nor ought it to cause any disturbance, that we have so often named the death of the soul, which we have pronounced to be immortal. For the soul is not extinguished by its own proper death, but is only overwhelmed for a time. Nor does it lose the benefit of perpetuity, by its temporal demersion: since when it deserves to be purified from the contagion of vice, through its entire refinement from body; it will be restored to the light of perennial life, and will return to its pristine integrity and perfection."

nearest of all to these quarters of the world: and this because the present cave is sacred to souls, and to nymphs the divinities of waters. But these places are particularly adapted either to souls descending into generation, or to such as are separating from it. On this account they assigned a place congruous to Mithras, near the equinoctial; and hence he bears the sword of Aries, because this animal is martial, and is the sign of Mars: he is likewise carried in the Bull, the sign of Venus; because the Bull as well as Venus is the ruler of generation. But Mithras is placed near the equinoctial circle, comprehending the northern parts on his right, and the southern on his left hand. Likewise to the southern hemisphere they added the south, because it is hot, and to the northern hemisphere, the north, on account of the coldness of the wind in that quarter. Again, it was not without reason that they connected winds with souls sinking to generation, and again separating themselves from its stormy whirl: because, according to the opinion of some, souls attract a spirit, and obtain a pneumatic substance. Indeed, Boreas is proper to souls passing into generation: for the northern blasts recreate those who are on the verge of death; and refresh the soul reluctantly detained in the body. On the contrary, the southern gales dissolve life. For the north, from its superior coldness, collects into one, detains and strengthens the soul in the most moist and frigid embraces of terrene generation: but the south dissolves the humid bands, and by its superior heat, having freed the soul from the dark and cold tenement of the body, draws it upward to the incorporeal light and heat of divinity. But since our habitable orb verges mostly to the north, it is proper that souls born in this turbulent region should be conversant with the north wind; and those who depart from hence with the south. It is, indeed, on this account that wind blowing from the north is immediately on its commencement vehement; but the south, on the contrary, is more vehement towards the end. For the former hangs directly over the inhabitants of the north pole, but the latter is more distant, and the blast from places very remote is more tardy than from such as are near; but when it is gradually collected it blows abundantly and with vigour. Hence, because souls enter into generation, through the northern gate, they have feigned this wind to be amatorial; and hence the poet: "Boreas changed into the form of a horse mingled himself with the mares of Erichthonius; and they big with young produced twice six foal."[6] And they report that he committed a rape on Orithyia, from whom he begot Zetis and Calais. But attributing the south to the gods, when the sun is at his meridian, they draw the curtains before the statues of the Gods in temples; and conceal them from the view, observing the Homeric precept, that it is not lawful for men to enter temples when the sun is inclined to the south: "for this path is open to immortals alone."

Hence when the god is at his meridian they place a symbol of mid-day and of the south in the gate of the temple.[7] Besides, in other gates it was esteemed unlawful to speak at all times; because they considered gates as sacred. On this account too the Pythagoreans, and wise men among the Egyptians, forbade any person to speak while passing through gates or portals; for at that time the divinity who is the principle of the universe is to be worshipped in silence. But Homer was not ignorant that gates are sacred, because he represents Oeneus in the place of supplication knocking at the gate.

Before his gates the aged Oeneus came,
And suppliant shook their well-compacted frame.[8]

Besides he knew that the gates of heaven were committed to the care of the hours, commencing in cloudy places; and which are opened and shut by the clouds: for he says,

Whether they unfold, or close a dense cloud.[9]

Hence likewise they are said to resound because thunders roar through the clouds.

[6] Iliad. lib. xx. l. 223, &c.

[7] In the original: ἱστᾶσιν οὖν καὶ σύμβολον τῆς μεσημβρίας καὶ τοῦ νότου, ἐπὶ τῇ θύρᾳ μεσημβριαζοντος τοῦ θεοῦ. Which Holstenius translates most erroneously as follows: "Austrum igitur meridei symbolum flatuunt: cum Deus meridiano tempore ostio immineat."

[8] Iliad. lib. ix. l. 579.   [9] Iliad. lib. viii. l. 395.

Concerning the Cave of the Nymphs

Heaven's gates spontaneous open to the powers,
Heavens sounding gates kept by the winged hours.[10]

Besides Homer elsewhere makes mention of the gates of the sun, signifying by these Cancer and Capricorn: for the sun proceeds as far as these signs, when he descends from the north to the south; and from thence ascends again to the northern parts. But Capricorn and Cancer are situated about the milky circle, Cancer occupying the northern extremity of this circle, and Capricorn the southern. Again, according to Pythagoras *the people of dreams*[11] are souls, which are reported to be collected in the milky way;

[10] Iliad. lib. viii. l. 393.

[11] This assertion of Pythagoras that the people of dreams, δῆμος ὀνείρων, are souls situated in the milky way, admirably contributes to elucidate the following passage in the 24th book of the Odyssey, respecting the descent of the suitors' souls to the region of spirits:

Πὰρ δ' ἴσαν Ὠκεανοῦ τε ῥοὰς καὶ Λευκάδα πέτρην,
Ἠδὲ παρ' ἠελίοιο πύλας καὶ δῆμον ὀνείρων
Ἤισαν, αἶψα δ' ἵκοντο κατ' ἀσφοδελὸν λειμῶνα,
Ἔνθά τε ναίουσι ψυχαὶ εἴδωλα καμόντων.

I.e. "But they passed beyond the flowing waters of the ocean, and the rock Leucas, and the gates of the sun, and the people of dreams: and they immediately came into meadows of asphodel, where souls the images of the dead reside." For it is evident from hence that the souls of the suitors passed through the galaxy, or the seats of the blessed, according to the most ancient theology: and I doubt not but Homer describes in these lines the complicated progression of an impure soul until it regains its original habitation in the stars, and again begins to gravitate to this terrene abode. This, I presume, will be manifest from the following elucidation of these admirable lines.

In the first place these souls are said to pass over *the flowing waters of the ocean*, and *the Leucadian*, or *white rock*. Now by this nothing more is meant than the flight of the suitors' souls to the extremity of the earth, in order to a subterranean descent: for, according to the most ancient opinion, the earth is bounded by the ocean; and the Leucadian rock may, as Eustathius observes, be some rock on the earth's extremity, which receives the last rays of the sun. Afterwards they are said to pass through *the gates of the sun*, by which, as Porphyry informs us above, we must understand the tropics of Cancer and Capricorn: and as Capricorn is subterranean, and affords a passage to ascending immortals, we must conceive that they enter through this prior to the tropic of Cancer. But in order to comprehend the perfect propriety of this transition, we must observe that the

the appellation of which is derived from souls nourished with milk after their lapse into the whirls of generation. Hence those who desire to evocate departed souls sacrifice to them with milk sweetned with honey: convinced that by the allurements of pleasure, these souls would desire to pass into generation, with the very beginning of which milk is generally produced.

Besides the southern regions produce small bodies because being attenuated by the heat they are diminished and dried up: and by a contrary reason all bodies generated in the north are

---

souls of the suitors on account of their impurity, are punished in the recesses of the earth, before they enter the celestial tropics, and pass into the meadows of Pluto. This the poet evidently evinces by the *screaking noise* which they utter, and the squalid paths through which they descend: a noise of this kind as Proclus well observes, (in Plat. Repub.) "representing a species of life solely given to appetite and imagination." After they have been purified therefore by subterranean punishment, they are fit to ascend to *the people of dreams*, or the souls of the blessed situated in the milky way. However as the soul, on account of her middle nature, is incapable of a perpetual sameness of situation, but is formed for infinite circulations (as will be demonstrated in the following elements); hence Homer, without mentioning her duration among the gods, though it is doubtless very extended, agreeable to the mystic brevity of his Muse, makes her immediately pass into *the meadows of Asphodel, where souls the images of the dead reside.* Now these *meadows of Asphodel,* form the supreme part of Plato's dominions: for, according to Pythagoras, as we are informed by Macrobius, in the preceding note 5, above, the empire of Pluto commences downwards from the milky way; so that these meadows are most probably situated in *the Lion,* the constellation into which souls first fall, after they leave the tropic of Cancer. But the description of the Asphodel perfectly corresponds with, and confirms the preceding exposition. For the Asphodel is a plant, bearing a naked *starry flower,* which comprehends an ovarium, or *orbicular figure,* after the manner of a cup. And what can more aptly symbolize with the stars, than such a flower? It was usual too with the ancients to scatter this plant in the tombs of the deceased; occultly intimating most probably, the similitude of this flower to the pristine and proper habitations of the soul. And hence it derived its appellation from σποδός, ashes, διὰ τὴν τῶν καιομένων νεκρῶν σποδόν, i.e. *from the ashes of burnt dead bodies.*

In these meadows, then, *the images of the dead* are said to reside. Now these εἴδωλα, or *images,* are no other than those vehicles of the soul, which have been so copiously, and admirably discussed by Synesius, in the preceding quotation from his book on dreams, and which, from their residence in the starry regions, must be luciform, etherial, and pure. It is this

large, as is evident in the Celtae or Gauls, Thracians, and Scythians; and these regions are humid and abound with much pasture. For the word Boreas is derived from the Greek βορα, which signifies aliment. Hence also the wind which blows from a land abounding in nutriments is called βορρας or nutritive. From these causes therefore the northern parts are properly adapted to

---

phantastic spirit, or primary vehicle of the soul, which Virgil alludes to, in these beautiful lines:

> ... *exinde per amplum*
> *Mittimur Elysium, et pauci laeta arva tenemus:*
> *Donec longa dies perfecto temporis orbe*
> *Concretum exemit labem, purumque reliquit*
> *Aetherium sensum, atque auraï simplicis ignem.*

I.e. "We are afterwards sent through ample Elysium, and a few of us possess the joyful plains: till a long period, when the revolving orb of time has perfected its circulation, frees the soul from its concrete stains, and leaves the etherial sense pure, together with *the fire (or splendour) of simple ether.*" For here he evidently conjoins the rational soul, or *the etherial sense*, with its splendid vehicle, or *the fire of simple ether*; since it is well known that this vehicle, according to Plato, is rendered by proper purgation αὐγοειδές, or *luciform*, and divine. It must here however be observed that souls in these *meadows of asphodel*, or *summit of Pluto's empire*, are in a falling state; or in other words through the secret influx of matter begin to desire a terrene situation. And this explains the reason why Hercules in the infernal regions is represented by Homer boasting of his terrene exploits and glorying in his pristine valour; why Achilles laments his situation in these abodes; and souls in general are engaged in pursuits similar to their employment on the earth: for all this is the natural consequence of a propensity to a mortal nature, and a desertion of the regions every way lucid and divine. Let the reader too observe, that, according to the arcana of the Platonic doctrine, the first and truest seat of the soul is in the intelligible world, where she lives entirely divested of body, and enjoys the ultimate felicity of her nature. And this is what Homer divinely insinuates when he says:

> Τὸν δὲ μετ᾽, εἰσενόησα βίην Ἡρακληείην,
> Εἴδωλον· αὐτὸς δὲ μετ᾽ ἀθανάτοισι θεοῖσι
> Τέρπεται ἐν θαλίης, καὶ ἔχει καλλίσφυρον Ἥβην.—κ.τ.λ.

I.e. "after this I saw the Herculean power, or *image*: but Hercules himself is with the immortal gods, delighting in celestial banquets, and enjoying the beautiful-footed Hebe." Since for the soul to dwell with the gods, entirely separated from its vehicle, is to abide in the intelligible world, and to exercise, as Plotinus expresses it, the more sacred contests of wisdom.

Should it be enquired why departed souls, though in a state of felicity

the class of souls obnoxious to mortality and generation; but the southern quarter to immortals, exempt from the mutability inseparable from the flowing realms of generation: in the same manner as the east is attributed to the gods, and the west to daemons. Hence since diversity is the origin of nature, the ancients considered every thing with a double entrance, as the symbol of nature. For the progression of things is either through an intelligible or a sensible nature. And if through a sensible nature, either through the sphere of the fixed stars, or through the orbs of the planets; and again either with an immortal or a mortal motion. Likewise one centre or hinge of the world is above the earth, but the other is subterranean; and one part of the heavens is eastern, and another western. In like manner some parts of the world have a dexter, and others a sinister position. Thus too night is opposed to day; and the harmony of the universe consists from the amicable junction of contrary and not similar

---

are compared by Homer to *dreams* and shadows, I answer with Porphyry (apud Stob. p. 132) that they are shadows with respect to human concerns, both because they are destitute of body, and are void of memory: for after they have passed the Stygian river, they are entirely ignorant of their pristine life on the earth, though they recognize and converse with each other, as is evident from the discourses between Patroclus, Ajax, and Antilochus. Indeed together with memory, they lose all knowledge of corporeal resemblances, which are rendered apparent through the ministry of the phantasy. For since the phantasy consists from memory, as Plato asserts in the Philebus, whatever we imagine perishes with the memory; and when this is taken away all the perturbations of the soul are removed, as she then becomes wholly intellectual, and passes into a state divinely prudent and wise. However, by means of the blood, which, as we have before observed, is, according to Homer, the instrument of the phantastic soul, departed spirits recognize material forms, and recollect their pristine condition on the earth. And to the phantasy reasoning pertains; since it is nothing more than an aggregation of memory, collected through imaginations, into the judgment of universals. But this is very different from the *intellective energy*, acquired by the soul beyond Acheron, which Cocytus and Pyriphlegethon fill, from the whirling streams of the dreadful Styx. Let the reader, however, remember that the phantasy is twofold, communicating in its supreme part with the rational soul, and in its inferior part with sense; and that it is this inferior part which the soul deserts, when it acquires an intellectual condition of being.

natures. Plato also makes mention of two gates, one of which affords a passage to those ascending into the heavens, the other to those descending on the earth: and theologists place the sun and moon as the gates of souls, which ascend through the sun and descend through the moon. So, according to Homer,

Two urns by Jove's high throne have ever stood,
The source of evil one, and one of good.[12]

But Plato, in his Gorgias, by vases understands souls, some of which are beneficent and others malignant, and again some are rational and others irrational. But souls are denominated vases because they are capacious of certain energies and habits, after the manner of vessels. In Hesiod too we find one vase shut, but the other opened by pleasure, who diffuses its contents, and leaves nothing but hope behind. For in whatever concerns a depraved soul, diffused about the dark and turbulent nature of matter, deserts the proper order of its essence; in all these, it is accustomed to nourish itself with the pleasing though delusive prospects of hope.

Since then every twofold division is a symbol of nature, this Homeric cavern has with great propriety two gates, numerically different; the one peculiar to gods and pure souls; but the other to such as are mortal and depraved. Hence Plato took occasion to speak of bowls, and to substitute vases for Amphora, and two gates, as we have already observed, in the place of two ports. Also Pherecydes Syrus mentions recesses, and dens, caves, gates, and ports, by which he insinuates the generation of souls, and their separation from a material nature. And thus much for an interpretation of Homer's cave, which we appear to have sufficiently explained, without adducing any farther testimonies from ancient philosophers and theologists, which would give an unreasonable extent to our discourse.

One particular however remains to be explained, and that is the symbol of the olive at the top of the cavern; since Homer appears to insinuate something egregious by giving such a position:

[12] Iliad. xxiv. l. 527.

for he does not merely say that an olive grows in this place, but that it flourishes at the head or vertex of the cave.

> *High at the head a branching olive grows,*
> *Beneath a gloomy grotto's cool recess, &c.*

But the growth of the olive in such a situation is not fortuitous as some may suspect, since it finishes and contains the aenigma of the cave. For as the world was not produced by the blind concurrence of chance, but is the work of divine wisdom and an intellectual nature, hence an olive, the symbol of divine wisdom, flourishes near the present cavern, which is an emblem of the material world. For the olive is the plant of Minerva, and Minerva is wisdom. And since this goddess was produced from the head of Jupiter, the theological poet gives a proper position to the olive, consecrated at the head of the port: signifying by this symbol that the universe is the offspring of an intelligible nature, separated indeed by a diversity of essence, though not by distance of place from his work; and by unremitting and ever present energies, not remote from any part of the universe, but situated as it were on its very summit, that is governing the whole with perfect wisdom from the dignity and excellence of his nature. But since an olive always flourishes, it bears a similitude peculiar and convenient to the revolutions of souls in this material region. For in summer the white part of the leaves is upwards, but in winter it is bent downwards. On this account also in prayers and supplications they extend the branches of an olive, presaging from this omen that they shall exchange the sorrowful darkness of danger for the fair light of security and peace. But the olive is not only of an ever-flourishing nature, it likewise bears fruit, which is the reward of labour, is sacred to Minerva, supplies the victors in athletic labours with crowns, and affords a friendly branch to the suppliant petitioner. Thus too the world is governed by an intellectual nature, and a wisdom ever flourishing and vigilant, who also bestows on the conquerors in the athletic race of life, the crown of victory, as the reward of severe toil, and patient perseverance: and the mighty builder who supports the universe by his divine energies invigorates miserable and suppliant souls, contending for the most glorious of all prizes, the olympiad of the soul.

In this cave therefore, says Homer, all external possessions must be deposited; here, naked and assuming a suppliant habit, afflicted in body, and casting aside every thing superfluous, sense too being averse from needless possessions, it is requisite to sit at the foot of the olive, and consult with Minerva, by what means we may most effectually amputate and destroy that hostile rout of passions, which lurk in the secret recesses of the soul. Indeed as it appears to me it was not without foundation that Numenius thought the person of Ulysses in the Odyssey represented to us a man who passes in a regular manner over the dark and stormy sea of generation;[13] and thus at length arrives at that region, where tempests and seas are unknown, and finds a nation

Who ne'er knew salt, or heard the billows roar.

Again, according to Plato, the deep, the sea, and a tempest are so many symbols of the constitution of matter: and on this account, I think, the poet called that port by the name of the marine god Phorcys.

But it is the port of the ancient marine Phorcys.[14]

Likewise his daughter Thoosa is mentioned in the beginning of the Odyssey. But from Thoosa the Cyclops was born, whom Ulysses deprived of sight that he might by this means while sailing over the stormy ocean be reminded of his sins, till he was safely landed in his native country. On this account too, a seat under the olive is proper to Ulysses, as to one who supplicates divinity, and would please his natal daemon with a suppliant branch. For indeed it will not be lawful for any one to depart from this sensible life in a regular way and in the shortest time, who blinds and irritates his material daemon; but he who dares to do this will be pursued by the anger of the marine and material

---

[13] [For the text of n. 13, see pp. 322 ff.]

[14] Φόρκυνος δέ τις ἐστὶ λιμὼν ἁλίοιο γέροντος.

gods, whom it is first requisite to appease, by sacrifices, labours, and patient endurance; at one time by contending with perturbations, at another time by employing stratagems of various kinds, by all which he transmutes himself into different forms; so that at length being stripped of the torn garments by which his true person was concealed, he may recover the ruined empire of his soul. Nor will he even then be freed from molestation, till he has entirely passed over the raging sea, and taken a long farewell of its storms; till though connected with a mortal nature, through deep attention to intelligible concerns, he becomes so ignorant of marine and material operations, as to mistake an oar for a corn-van.

Nor it is proper to believe that interpretations of this kind are forced, and are nothing more than the conjectures of ingenious men: but when we consider the great wisdom of antiquity, and how much Homer excelled in prudence and in every kind of virtue, we ought not to doubt but that he has secretly represented the images of divine things under the concealments of fable. For it is not possible that this whole exposition could be devised, unless from certain established truths, an occasion of fiction had been given. But rejecting the discussion of this to another work, we shall here finish our proposed explication of the cave of the nymphs.

[The text of n. 13 follows.]

This was no doubt fully proved by Porphyry, in some of his unfortunately lost writings; such as his book *on the philosophy of Homer*; or that, *on the Allegories of the Grecian and Egyptian Theology*, of which we have already made mention. However, it does not seem impossible, from the hints afforded us in this excellent treatise, for a person conversant in the Platonic philosophy to evince the truth of this assertion. Presuming, therefore, that an attempt of this kind will be acceptable to the liberal reader, though my abilities are far inferior to those of Porphyry, I shall request his attention to the contents, and his pardon for the length of the ensuing discourse. I only premise, that I shall make use of a small treatise in Greek, on the wanderings of Ulysses, by an anonymous author, where he appears to have penetrated the sense of the allegory; and freely reject his interpretation, when foreign from the leading character of Ulysses, above mentioned, according to Numenius and Porphyry.

The first apparently fabulous adventure then of Ulysses, is that of the

Concerning the Cave of the Nymphs

Lotophagi; a coast upon which he was driven by the violence of the winds; and which produced a fruit called Lotos, whose enchanting taste caused oblivion, and a vehement desire of perpetually abiding with the Lotophagi. Or as it is beautifully described by Homer, in the elegant version of Mr. Pope:

> *The trees around them all their fruit produce,*
> *Lotos the name, divine, nectarious juice!*
> *(Thence call'd Lotophagi) which whoso tastes,*
> *Insatiate riots in the sweet repasts,*
> *Nor other home, nor other care intends,*
> *But quits his house, his country, and his friends:*
> *The three we sent from off th' enchanting ground*
> *We dragg'd reluctant, and by force we bound:*
> *The rest in haste forsook the pleasing shore,*
> *Or, the charm tasted, had return'd no more.*
>
> Lib. ix. l. 94, &c.

Here we view Ulysses subject to different desires, and blown about by contrary blasts of fortune, inconsiderately permitting the various affections of his soul to be engaged in improper employments; who, after they have tasted of sensual pleasures, and fraudulent manners, refuse to return to ruling intellect, and the natural good habits of the soul. Hence, fascinated by delight, they consign their country and kindred to oblivion; and desire to live forever lost in the intoxication of pleasure. Reason, however, no longer sustaining that her dignity should be obscured by depraved enjoyment, immediately recalls the affections from fraudulent deeds; which is represented by Ulysses withdrawing his men from the coasts of Lotophagi. After this she binds and restrains them, by the most weighty arguments, so as to prevent them from afterwards returning to evil. And indeed, she treats the affected parts of the soul, in a manner accommodated to their disease; and strengthens and fortifies such as are not affected, and removes them from the possession of noxious delight.

The next adventure of Ulysses is that of the Cyclops, whom he deprived of sight, and irritated with reproaches. Now, according to Porphyry in the above excellent treatise, this is no other than a malignant natal daemon, who destroys by his stratagems the good affections of the soul; which is occultly signified by Ulysses losing his companions, through the brutal appetite of the destructive daemon. Ulysses, however, lamenting the dreadful effects of his voluntary confinement, meditates, and at length accomplishes his deliverance, together with that of the remaining good habits of his soul; and glories in resuming the liberty he has lost. But this fable indeed contains one of the greatest arcana of philosophy: for this is what Synesius occultly intimates, in the preceding quotation from his book on dreams, when he speaks of matter marking her votaries in her secret volume, and severely punishing such as desert from her service. Thus Ulysses after a voluntary submission to his natal daemon, by indulging the irrational appetites and desires of his soul, flies from his base servitude; and adds irritations to his flight. He is, however, pursued by the anger of the marine and material daemons, and punished for his escape. For he who blinds the eye of sense, and extinguishes its light, after his will has profoundly assented to its use, must expect punishment for the attempt; as necessary to his own private good, and the general order of the universe. Indeed, troubles and misfortunes resulting from such undertakings, not only contribute to appease the anger of their malevolent authors, but likewise purify and benefit the subjects of their revenge. He, therefore, who in the present life perceives himself, like Ulysses, attended by uncommon misfortunes while he is in the road of virtue and eagerly searching for wisdom, may safely conclude, that either here, or in a prior state of existence, he has voluntarily submitted to the power of his natal daemon, and has now deprived him of sight; and that he has been profoundly delighted with the nature of matter, and is now abrogating the confessions which he made. This too is insinuated in the beautiful story of Psyche, by Apuleius, when the terrestrial Venus, sends Mercury, with a book in which her name is inscribed, to apprehend Psyche as a fugitive from her mistress. For this whole story relates to the descent of the soul into this terrene body, and its wanderings and punishments till it returns to its true country and pristine felicity. And this I may probably demonstrate in some future period, by publishing a translation of this admirable fable, and a comment on the divine mysteries it contains. We must here, however, observe, that as the advancements of Ulysses in virtue are but moderate, till he leaves Calypso; so the greatest of his troubles commence after that period, as our discourse will shortly evince.

In the next fable, which is that of Aeolus, a being, as the name implies, various and versatile, though hospitable and benignant, we see Ulysses sorrowful and wandering, through the anger of his natal daemon, enquiring after a refuge from misfortune; though not as becomes one studious of piety, but commiting himself to enchanters and magicians, and relying on their incantations for his deliverance from danger. He cannot, however, accomplish his end, by such undertakings, but remains frustrated of his hope, and filled with shame for his disappointment. The Poet too, by attributing the ill success of Ulysses to his sleep, egregiously insinuates that the rational soul was in a dormant state, when he confided in practices so incapable of producing the desired end, and so inconsistent with the goods which intellect confers. Such methods, indeed, as they increase the desire of success, so they present strongly to our view, the distant object of our pursuit; but this is immediately succeeded by the sleep of reason, and the destruction of hope. And this is what Homer appears to signify, by the following verses:

> *Nine prosp'rous days, we ply'd the lab'ring oar;*
> *The tenth presents our welcome native shore:*
> *The hills display the beacon's friendly light,*

Concerning the Cave of the Nymphs

And rising mountains gain upon our sight.
Then first my eyes by watchful toils opprest,
Comply'd to take the balmy gifts of rest;
Then first my hands did from the rudder part,
(So much the love of home possess'd my heart.)

Lib. x. l. 28, &c.

And hence:

. . . the thongs unbound,
The gushing tempest sweeps the ocean round;
Snatch'd in the whirl, the hurried navy flew,
The ocean widen'd, and the shores withdrew.

After this succeeds the adventure of the Lestrigons which seems to indicate the yet imperfect condition of Ulysses' nature, unable to distinguish the coast of virtue, from the infamous regions of vice. Hence he becomes an involuntary prey to the depredations of depraved manners; and is for some time incapable of exerting the power of reason. However, at length perceiving the magnitude of the evils with which he is surrounded, he cuts the detaining cables of vice, and flies from his dangerous situation; deploring, indeed the ruined slate of his better manners, but rejoicing that his principal part has escaped, and that he is not totally destroyed. And this the poet appears to me to insinuate by the following verses:

Whilst thus their fury rages at the bay,
My sword our cables cut, I call'd to weigh;
And charg'd my men, as they from fate would fly
Each nerve to strain, each bending oar to ply.
The sailors catch the word, their oars they seize,
And sweep with equal strokes the smoky seas;
Clear of the rocks th' impatient vessel flies;
Whilst in the port each wretch encumber'd dies.
With earnest haste my frighted sailors press,
While kindling transports glow'd at our success;
But the sad fate that did our friends destroy
Cool'd every breast, and damp'd the rising joy.

Lib. x. l. 125, &c.

In the next fable, which is the beautiful allegory of Circe, we shall find some deep arcana of philosophy contained, exclusive of its connection with Ulysses. By the Aegean island then, in which the palace of Circe was situated, we must conceive the region of sorrow and lamentation; for this word is evidently derived from the interjection αἰ, *alas!* and the adjective αἰηνὲς, *lamentable.* And by Circe we must understand the goddess of sense: for thus Porphyry in Stobaeus, p. 141. Ὅμηρος δὲ τον ἐν κύκλῳ περίοδον καὶ περιφορὰν παλιγγενεσίας, Κίρκην προσηγορευκεν, ἡλίου παῖδα, του πᾶσαν φθορὰν γενεσι, καὶ γενεσιν αὖ παλιν φθορᾷ συναπτοντος ἀει καὶ συνειροντος.

325

Thomas Taylor the Platonist

I.e. "Homer calls Circe, the daughter of the sun, the period and revolution of regeneration in a circle, who ever connects and combines all corruption with generation, and generation again with corruption." Hence, we may observe that the Aeean isle, or this region of sense, is with great propriety called the abode of trouble and lamentation. In this region then, the companions of Ulysses, that is, the thoughts and natural powers of his soul, are changed by the incantations of the goddess; and his opinions and natural motions, rashly wandering from the authority of ruling intellect, are converted through the allurements of delight, into an unworthy and irrational habit. Ulysses, however, or the rational soul, is by the assistance of Mercury, or reason, prevented from destruction. Hence, intellect, roused by its impassive power, and recollecting the ills which its natural faculties endure; at the same time, being armed with prudent anger, and the plant moly, or virtue, which is able to repel the allurements of pleasure, wars on the goddess of sense, and prevents the effects of her fascinating charms. Nor is reason alone free from the dire incantations of delight, but it likewise restores to their proper form the powers of nature, which had been previously corrupted; and thus departs a gainer by its loss. For he who returns to himself from the dominion of vice, derives at least this advantage in his return, that he becomes afterwards more prudent in resisting its incursions, and employs his first defeat as an incitement to the acquisition of virtue. It must here, however, be observed that Ulysses is an involuntary offender, in all his adventures posterior to that of the Cyclops. His passions, indeed, hurry him into various vices and misfortunes, but his will by no means concurs with their endurance. But his connection with his natal daemon was voluntary; and after his departure from hence, he must be considered as in a gradual course of purification, though his progress in virtue is but small, till the latter part of his abode with Calypso.

But Homer's account of Circe, exclusive of its relation to Ulysses, contains, according to Porphyry (in Stob. p. 141), an admirable explanation of the soul. For thus, (says he) Homer speaks:

> *No more was seen the human form divine;*
> *Head, face, and members, bristle into swine:*
> *Still curst with sense, their minds remain alone,*
> *And their own voice, affrights them when they groan.*
> Lib. x. l. 239, &c.

This fable, therefore, is the enigma of the opinions of Pythagoras and Plato respecting the soul; signifying that it is of an incorruptible and eternal nature, but not void of passion and mutability; since by dissolution and death, it is capable of being transmuted and changed, into other corporeal forms; and by its desire of pleasure it pursues a form adapted and allied to the condition of its life. And in this the assistance of learning and philosophy is perceived, if the soul, mindful of what is honest, and disdaining base and unlawful pleasures, can govern and defend herself

326

from being changed into a beast; and from embracing a brutal and impure body, which increases and nourishes a nature dull and irrational, together with desire and anger, rather than reason. Indeed, the order and nature of this transmutation is predicated by the daemon of Empedocles, when he says:

$$\Sigma\alpha\rho\kappa\omega\nu\ \dot{\alpha}\lambda\lambda\acute{o}\gamma\nu\omega\tau\iota\ \pi\epsilon\rho\iota\sigma\tau\acute{\epsilon}\lambda\lambda o\upsilon\sigma\alpha\ \chi\iota\tau\omega\nu\iota.$$
$$\text{K}\alpha\grave{\iota}\ \mu\epsilon\tau'\ \dot{\alpha}\mu\pi\epsilon\chi o\upsilon\sigma\alpha\ \tau\alpha\varsigma\ \psi\upsilon\chi\alpha\varsigma.$$

I.e. folding round the external garment of flesh, and afterwards investing souls with its covering. But the Aegean isle which receives the dead body is that part of the continent, into which souls first descending wander and lament, and are ignorant

. . . what coast before them lies
Or where the sun shall set, or where shall rise.

Indeed, since through the love of pleasure, they desire an association, and nourishment in the flesh, and in conjunction with its nature, they again fall into the confused mixture of generation, truly mingling things eternal and mortal, prudence and passion, celestials, and terrestrials; ensnared and fascinated by pleasures, again leading to the fluctuating realms of generation. And in this case, souls particularly require the greatest felicity and prudence; lest pursuing the most base concerns, and becoming bound to their parts and passions, they obtain an unhappy and brutal life. For that which is called the τριοδος, or triple path of Hades, is perceived in the *rational, irascible,* and *desiderative* parts of the soul; each of which contains the principle of a life convenient to its nature. And these assertions are not to be reckoned the figments of fables and the inventions of poets, but are to be esteemed as true and natural discourses. For those whose *desires,* in their mutation and generation, obtain the principality, will be changed into asinine bodies, and an impure life, through the dominion of gluttony and lust. But when the soul, raging with weighty contentions and odious cruelties, seeks a second generation, it betakes itself full of recent severity, into the nature of a wolf, or lion; acquiring a body of this kind as a defensive organ, adapted to its ruling affection. Hence, it is requisite that every one should be pure with respect to death, as in the sacred mysteries of initiation, by banishing every depraved affection, mitigating every desire, and expelling envy and anger from all connection with the body. And this is the true Mercury with his rod of gold, the clear indicator of honest conduct, who entirely prohibits and restrains the soul from the mixture of generation; or if she should drink the envenomed potion, preserves her in a human life, as long as can possibly be effected."

After this follows the allegory, respecting the descent of Ulysses into the infernal regions, which, exclusive of its connection with Ulysses, contains likewise some of the greatest arcana of the Grecian theology. As it respects Ulysses, it appears to me to insinuate his flying to the assistance of necromancy, in order to know the result of the ills with which he is surrounded, through the anger of his natal daemon. Hence Tiresias is nothing more than a departed spirit evocated by magical art, for the purpose of disclosing the secrets of futurity, and informing Ulysses how he may return to the true empire of his mind. The success, however, was not answerable to the certainty of the information: and perhaps Homer meant to intimate by his allegory, that the end of such illicit practices is never correspondent to the desires by which they are undertaken. Hence he plainly indicates the madness of such a conduct, by the consequences which may possibly attend its execution; and by the horror which forced Ulysses to hasten its conclusion: for thus Ulysses speaks:

> *Curious to view the kings of ancient days,*
> *The mighty dead that live in endless praise,*
> *Resolv'd I stand; and haply had survey'd*
> *The god-like Theseus, and Perithous' shade;*
> *But swarms of spectres rose from deepest hell,*
> *With bloodless visage, and with hideous yell,*
> *They scream, they shriek; sad groans and dismal sounds*
> *Stun my scar'd ears, and pierce hell's utmost bounds.*
> *No more my heart the dismal din sustains,*
> *And my cold blood hangs shiv'ring in my veins;*
> *Lest Gorgon rising from th' infernal lakes,*
> *With horrors arm'd, and curls of hissing snakes,*
> *Should fix me stiffen'd at the monstrous sight,*
> *A stony image, in eternal night!*
>
> Lib. ii. l. 627, &c.

Indeed by such a conduct, he becomes impious, profane, and execrable; till he returns to that condition of mind, in which the judgement of reason, and the light of intellect emerges through the gloom of impiety and folly, and prudent cogitations dance round the liberated soul. For in this case it may be truly said:

> *Here the gay morn resides in radiant bow'rs,*
> *Here keeps her revels with the dancing hours.*
>
> Lib. xii. ll. 3 & 4

With respect to the recondite wisdom contained in the description of the infernal regions, I shall only observe from Porphyry (ap. Stob. p. 131) that the reason why departed spirits are represented as possessing no knowledge of human concerns, till they inhale the vapour of blood, is because according to Homer and many of his successors, human intelligence or prudence consists in blood. And this says Porphyry is confirmed by the testimony of most writers posterior to Homer, who inform us that when the blood is inflamed by a fever or the bile, imprudence and foolishness is produced. But Empedocles considered the blood as an instrument of prudence, when he says:

Concerning the Cave of the Nymphs

Αἵματος ἐν πελάγεσι τετραμμένου ἀντιθρῶντος,
Τῇ τε νόημα μάλιστα κικλήσκεται ἀνθρωποισιν.
Αἷμα γὰρ ἀνθρώποις περικάρδιόν ἐστι νόημα.

The sense of which is, "that the blood surrounding the heart is the seat of intelligence in men."

But we must now view Ulysses passing from sense to imagination; in the course of which voyage, he is assailed by various temptations, of surprising power, and destructive effect. We shall perceive him victorious in some of these, and sinking under others; but struggling against the incursions of all. Among the first of these is the enchanting melody of the Sirens,

Whose song is death, and makes destruction please.

By which the poet evidently signifies alluring and fraudulent pleasures, which charm the soul in its passage from a sensible life, with flattering and mellifluous incantations. These delights however will be vanquished by him, who, imitating the example of Ulysses, closes, with divine reasons and energies as with wax, the powers of the soul, and the organs of sense; so that every passage being barred from access, they may in vain warble the song of extacy, and expect to ruin the soul by the enchanting strain. It will however be requisite that besides this, the corporeal assaults should be restrained by the bands of philosophy, and rendered irresistible by external machines; for thus like Ulysses, we shall employ the senses, without yielding to their impetuous invasions; and experience delight without resigning the empire of reason to its fascinating controul.

Ulysses having escaped the danger of the Syrens, passes on to the rocks of Scylla [see Plate 17] and Charybdis, of terrific appearance, and irresistible force. By these two rocks, the poet seems to signify the affections compressing human life on both sides; and which every one must experience, who proceeds like Ulysses in a regular manner to an intellectual state of existence. Some of these, which are conversant with the soul, are like Scylla, of a lofty malignity; fraudulent yet latent, and obscure, as concealed in the penetralia of the mind. And such is pride, and other depraved affections of the soul. In these recesses, a daemon, the prince of such affections, resides, a dire and enraged dog, who partly exposes his own malice, and partly hides it in impenetrable obscurity. Hence he is capable of producing mischief in a twofold respect: for he privately hurts by malignant stratagems, openly ravishes the soul, on the lofty rock of haughtiness, and rends it with the triple evil of deadly teeth, I mean revolt, hatred of humanity, and haughty arrogance. Indeed a daemon of this kind will be perpetually vigilant, in endeavouring to destroy, at one time the whole, and at another time a part of the soul, struggling like Ulysses against passion, and yielding reluctantly to its invasions.

But the other affections which belong to the body, are indeed lofty, and evidently destructive, but far inferior to the others; since their baseness is conspicuous, and not concealed by ostentation. A wild fig-tree, that is the will, is produced on the top of this rock, wild indeed, on account of its free nature, but sweet in fruition; and under which, often through the day, the impetuosities of the boiling body are accustomed to absorb and disturb the man, agitating upwards and downwards inflamed desire, so that mighty destruction, both to soul and body, is produced by their mutual consent. But it is highly proper that a rock of this last kind, should be anxiously avoided by one, who like Ulysses is labouring to return to his true country and friends. Hence if necessity requires he will rather expose himself to the other: for there the energy of cogitation, and of the soul's simple motion is alone necessary to be exerted; and it is easy to recover the pristine habit of the soul. In short the poet, seems to represent by this allegory of the two rocks, as well the dangers spontaneously arising from the soul, as those which happen from the external mass of matter; both of which must be sustained or one at least by a necessary consequence. For it is impossible that neither of them should be experienced by any one who is passing over the stormy ocean of a sensible life.

After this succeeds the allegory of the Trinacrean isle, containing the herds sacred to the god of day, which were violated by the companions of Ulysses; but not without destruction to the authors of this impiety, and the most dreadful danger to Ulysses. By the result of this fable, the poet evidently shews that punishment attends the sacrilegious, and the perjured; and teaches us that we should perpetually reverence divinity with the greatest sanctity of mind, and be cautious how we commit any thing in divine concerns contrary to piety of manners, and purity of thought. But Homer by attributing sense to the flesh and hides of the slain herds, manifestly evinces, that every base deed universally proclaims the iniquity of its author: but that perjury and sacrilege are attended with the most glaring indications of guilt, and the most horrid signatures of approaching vengeance, and inevitable ruin. We may here too observe that the will of Ulysses was far from consenting to this impious deed; and that though his passions prevailed at length over his reason, it was not till after frequent admonitions had been employed, and great diligence exerted to prevent its execution. This indeed is so eminently true, that his guilt was the consequence of surprize, and not of premeditated design; which Homer appears to insinuate, by relating that Ulysses was asleep, when his associates committed the offence.

In the next fable, we find Ulysses impelled, by the southern wind, towards the rocks of Scylla and Charybdis; in the latter of which he found safety, by clinging on the fig-tree which grew on its summit, till she refunded the mast, on which he rode after the tempest. But the secret meaning of the allegory appears to me as follows: Ulysses who has not yet taken his leave of a sensible life, is driven by the warmth of passion, represented by the southern gales, into the dire charybdis of insane desires, which frequently boiling over, and tossing on high the storms of depraved affections, plunges into ruin the soul obnoxious to its waves. However he is far from shameful idleness, and careless security; but perceiving the danger to which he is exposed, when the base storms begin to swell, and the whirlpools of depravity roar, he seizes the helm of temperance, and binds himself fast to the solid texture of his remaining virtue. The waves of desire are indeed tempestuous in the extreme; but before he is forcibly merged by the rage of the affections, into the depths of depravity, he tenaciously adheres to his unconsenting will, seated as it were on the lofty summit of terrene desire. For this like the wild fig-tree affords the best refuge to the soul struggling with the billows of base perturbations. Hence he by this means recovers the integrity which he had lost, and afterwards swims without danger over the waves of temptation; ever watchful and assiduous while he sails through this impetuous river of the flesh, and is exposed to the stormy blasts of heated passion and destructive vice. Hence too while he is thus affected, and anxious lest the loss from unworthy affections should return upon himself, he will escape being lacerated by the teeth of arrogance, though she should terribly and fiercely bark in the neighbourhood of desire, and endeavour like Scylla, to snatch him on her lofty rock. For those who are involuntarily disturbed like Ulysses by the billows of desire, suffer no inconvenience from the depraved rock of pride: but considering the danger of their present situation, they relinquish confident conceit, for modest diffidence, and anxious hope.

Hitherto we have followed Ulysses in his voyage over the turbulent and dangerous ocean of sense; in which we have seen him struggling against the storms of temptation, and in danger of perishing through the tempestuous billows of vice. We must now attend him in the region of imagination, and mark his progress from the enchanted island, till he regains the long lost empire of his soul. That the poet then by Calypso occultly signifies the phantasy, is I think evident from his description of her abode, (for the anonymous Greek author affords us no farther assistance). For she is represented as dwelling in a cavern, illuminated by a great fire; and this cave is surrounded with a thick wood, is watered by four fountains, and is situated in an island, far remote from any habitable parts, and invironed by the mighty ocean. All which particulars correspond with the phantasy, as I presume the following observations will evince. In the first place then, as the phantasy is situated between sense and cogitation, it communicates with each in such a manner that its beginning is the end of the cogitative power, and its end is the commencement of the senses. Hence on account of its twofold nature it partakes of a twofold light; receiving in its supreme part the splendor of cogitation, and in its inferior part, a light corresponding to that of sense. Now it is this inferior part or the common phantasy, which is represented by the cave of Calypso, for its light is artificial and external like that of fire: and this correspondence is evident from the etymology of the phantasy, which is derived from φαὸς, or *light*. In the next place the island is said to be surrounded with a thick wood, which evidently corresponds to a material nature, or this humid body, with which the phantasy is invested: for ὕλη, or *a wood*, implies matter according to its primary signification. But the four fountains by which the cave is watered occultly intimate those four gnostic powers of the soul discovered by the Pythagoreans, and embraced by Plato; *intelligence, cogitation, opinion*, and *imagination*. And these fountains are said, with great propriety and correspondence, to communicate with each other. In the last place the island is said to be invironed with the ocean, which admirably agrees with a corporeal nature, forever flowing without admitting any periods of repose. And thus much for the secret agreement of the cavern and island with the regions of imagination.

But the poet by denominating the goddess, Calypso, and the island, Ogygia, appears to me, very evidently to confirm the preceding exposition: for Calypso is derived from καλύπτω, which means *to cover as with a veil*; and Ogygia, is from ὠγύγιος, *ancient*. Now, as we have been previously informed by Synesius, the phantastic spirit is the primary vehicle of the rational soul, which it derived from the planetary spheres, and in which it descended to the corporeal world. It may therefore with great propriety be said to *cover* the soul, as with a fine garment, or veil; and it is no less properly denominated *ancient*, when considered as the first vehicle of the soul.

In this region of the phantasy then, Ulysses is represented as an involuntary captive; continually employed in bewailing his absence from his true country, and ardently longing to depart from the fascinating embraces of the goddess. For thus his situation is beautifully described by the poet:

> But sad Ulysses by himself apart,
> Pour'd the big sorrows of his swelling heart;
> All on the lonely shore he sat to weep,
> And roll'd his eyes around the restless deep;
> Tow'rd his lov'd coast, he roll'd his eyes in vain,
> 'Till dim'd with rising grief they stream'd again.
> Lib. v. l. 82, &c.

His return however is at length effected by means of Mercury, or reason, who prevails on the goddess to yield to his dismission. Hence after her consent, Ulysses is said with great propriety to have placed himself on the throne, where Mercury had sate: for reason now resumes her proper seat, and begins to exercise her authority with undisturbed controul. But Homer appears to me to insinuate something egregious, when he represents Ulysses on his departure from Calypso, sailing by night, and contemplating the order and light of the stars, in the following beautiful lines:

> And now rejoycing in the prosp'rous gales,
> With beating heart Ulysses spread his sails;
> Plac'd at the helm he sate, and mark'd the skies,
> Nor clos'd in sleep his ever watchful eyes.
> There view'd the Pleiads, and the northern team,
> And great Orion's more refulgent beam,
> To which around the axle of the sky
> The bear revolving, points his golden eye;
> Who shines exalted on th' aetherial plain,
> Nor bathes his blazing forehead in the main.

Concerning the Cave of the Nymphs

Far on the left those radiant fires to keep
The nymph directed, as he sail'd the deep.
Full seventeen nights he cut the foamy way;
The distant land appear'd the following day:
Then swell'd to sight Phaeacia's dusky coast,
And woody mountains half in vapour lost;
That lay before him, indistinct and vast,
Like a broad shield amid the wat'ry waste.

Lib. v. l. 269, &c.

Indeed as Ulysses is the image of a man passing in a regular manner from a sensible life, and advancing from darkness to light, he is very properly represented as sailing by the splendor of the stars, and directing his course by the most conspicuous of these illustrious orbs. For star-light corresponds to the light of the mathematical sciences, which are the proper employment of one who is departing from the sensible phantasy, and her detaining charms. And the stars themselves correspond to ideas, from which the light of science is derived. Ulysses therefore, who is hastening to an intellectual life, contemplates these lucid objects with vigilant eyes, rejoicing in the illuminations and assistance they afford him, while sailing over the dark ocean of a material nature.

But as he is now earnestly engaged in departing from sense, he must unavoidably be pursued by the anger of Neptune, whose service he has forsaken; and whose offspring he has blinded by stratagem, and irritated by reproach. Hence in the midst of these delightful contemplations, he is almost overwhelmed by the waves of misfortune, roused by the wrath of his implacable foe. He is however through divine assistance or Leucothea enabled to sustain the dreadful storm: for receiving from divinity, the immortal fillet of true fortitude, and binding it under his breast, (the proper seat of courage) he encounters the billows of adversity, and bravely shoots along the boisterous ocean of life. [See Plate 16.]

Ulysses therefore having with much difficulty escaped the dangers arising from the wrath of Neptune, lands at length on the island of Phaeacia, where he is hospitably received, and honourably dismissed. Now as it is proper that he who like Ulysses departs from the delusions of imagination, should immediately betake himself to the more intellectual light of thought, the land of Phaeacia, ought to correspond to the realms of cogitation: and that this is the case the following discourse will I persuade myself abundantly evince. In the first place then this island is represented by the poet as enjoying a perpetual spring; which plainly indicates, that it is not any terrene situation. Indeed the critical commentators have been so fully convinced of this, that they acknowledge Homer describes Phaeacia, as one of the Fortunate Islands; but they have not attempted to penetrate his design, by such a description. Now if we consider the perfect liberty, unfading variety, and endless delight, which the regions of cogitation afford, we shall find that it is truly the fortunate island of the soul. In the next place the poet by the description of the palace of Alcinous, the king of this island, egregiously insinuates the pure and splendid light of cogitation; for thus he speaks:

> *The front appear'd with radiant splendors gay,*
> *Bright as the lamp of night, or orb of day.*
> *The walls were massy brass: the cornice high*
> *Blue metals crown'd, in colours of the sky:*
> *Rich plates of gold the folding doors incase;*
> *The pillars silver, on a brazen base;*
> *Silver the lintels deep projecting o'er,*
> *And gold the ringlets that command the door.*
> *Two rows of stately dogs, on either hand,*
> *In sculptur'd gold, and labour'd silver stand.*
> *These Vulcan form'd intelligent to wait*
> *Immortal guardians at Alcinous' gate.*
>
> Lib. vii. l. 84, &c.

And he represents it, as no less luminous internally, by night.

> *Refulgent pedestals the walls surround,*
> *Which boys of gold with flaming torches crown'd;*
> *The polish'd ore reflecting ev'ry ray;*
> *Blaz'd on the banquets with a double day.*

For this palace is not like the cavern of Calypso naturally obscure, but remarkably bright and refulgent. Indeed Homer by his description of the outside of this palace, sufficiently indicates its agreement with the planet Mercury, who is the god of speech; and cogitation, as Plato beautifully observes in the Theaetetus, is nothing more than inward discourse. For, according to astronomers, the planet Mercury is resplendent with the colours of all the other planets. Thus Baptista Porta in Coelest. Physiog. p. 88: Videbis in eo Saturni luridum, Martis ignem, Jovis candidum, Veneris flavum, nec-non utriusque nitor, hilaritasque, et ob id non peculiaris formae, sed eorum formam capit, cum quibus associatur, ob id in describendo ejus colore astrologi differunt. That is, "you may perceive in this planet the pale colour of Saturn, the fire of Mars, the whiteness of Jupiter, and the yellow of Venus: likewise the brilliancy and hilarity of each; and on this account it is not of a peculiar form, but receives the form of its associates, and by this means causes astrologers to differ in describing its colour."

But that the island of Phaeacia is the region of cogitation is indisputably confirmed by Homer's account of the ships fabricated by its inhabitants: for thus he beautifully describes them:

> Ὄφρα σε τῇ πέμπωσι τιτυσκόμεναι φρεσὶ νῆες.
> Οὐ γὰρ Φαιήκεσσι κυβερνητῆρες ἔασιν,
> Οὐδέ τι πηδάλι' ἐστὶ, τὰ τ' ἄλλαι νῆες ἔχουσιν.
> Ἀλλ' αὐταὶ ἴσασι νοήματα καὶ φρένας ἀνδρῶν,
> Καὶ πάντων ἴσασι πόλιας καὶ πίονας ἀγροὺς
> Ἀνθρώπων, καὶ λαῖτμα τάχισθ' ἁλὸς ἐκπερόωσι,

334

Concerning the Cave of the Nymphs

Ἠέρι καὶ νεφέλη κεκαλυμμέναι· οὐδέ ποτέ σφιν
Οὔτε τι πημανθῆναι ἔπι δέος οὐδ᾽ ἀπολέσθαι.

Lib. viii. l. 556, &c.

I.e. "That ships intently directed by intellect may send you to your country. For the Phaeacians have no pilots, nor have the ships helms like others: but they know the thoughts and minds of men. They likewise know the cities and fertile fields of all men; and swiftly swim over the waters of the sea, covered with darkness and clouds: for they never are afraid of sustaining any damage, or of being utterly lost." Or in verse:

> So shalt thou instant reach the realm assign'd,
> In wond'rous ships self-mov'd, instinct with mind;
> No helm secures their course, no pilot guides,
> Like man intelligent they plow the tides,
> Conscious of ev'ry coast, and ev'ry bay,
> That lies beneath the sun's all seeing ray;
> And veil'd in clouds impervious to the eye,
> Fearless and rapid thro' the deep they fly.

Now it is absurd to suppose that Homer would ever employ such an hyperbole, in merely describing the excellency of the Phaeacian ships: for it so eminently surpasses the bounds of probability, and is so contrary to the admirable prudence, which Homer continually displays, that it can only be admitted as an allegory, pregnant with latent meaning, and the recondite wisdom of antiquity.

It must here however be observed, that as the energies of cogitation are twofold, according to the objects on which they are employed (for they are either sensible or intellectual); so the manners of Alcinous and his nobles are perfectly opposite to those of the other inhabitants. For these latter are thus described by the poet:

> A race of rugged mariners are these;
> Unpolish'd men, and boistrous as their seas;
> The native islanders alone their care,
> And hateful he that breathes a foreign air.
> These did the ruler of the deep ordain
> To build proud navies, and command the main;
> On canvas wings to cut the wat'ry way;
> No bird more light, no thought more swift than they.

Lib. vii. l. 33, &c.

The last of which lines, so remarkably agrees with the preceding account, that I presume no stronger confirmation can de desired. Nor is the original less satisfactory:

Τῶν νέες ὠκεῖαι ὡσεί πτερὸν ἠὲ νόημα.

I.e. "The ships of these are swift as a wing, or as *a conception of the mind*." But the inhabitants of the palace are represented as spending their days

335

in continual festivity, and unceasing mirth: in listening to the harmony
of the lyre; or in forming the tuneful mazes of the joyful dance. And this
distinction of manners admirably agrees with the difference between vulgar,
and intellectual cogitations: for the former of these are boisterous and
rough, selfish and proud; skilled indeed in rapidity, but groveling and
unpolished. But the latter are constantly employed in intellectual festivity
and mirth; in tuning the melodious lyre of divine recollection, or forming the responsive dance of refined imaginations. It was with the greatest
reason therefore, that Ulysses exclaimed on this occasion:

> *How sweet the products of a peaceful reign?*
> *The heav'n taught poet, and enchanting strain:*
> *The well fill'd palace, the perpetual feast,*
> *A land rejoycing, and a people blest.*
> *How goodly seems it ever to employ*
> *Man's social days in union, and in joy?*
> *The plenteous board high-heap'd with cates divine,*
> *And o'er the foaming bowl the laughing wine.*
>
> Lib. ix. l. 3, &c.

And here we may observe how much the behaviour of Ulysses at the
palace of Alcinous confirms the preceding exposition, and agrees with his
character as a man passing in a regular manner from the delusions of
sense, to the realities of intellectual enjoyment. For as he is now seated
in the palace of cogitation, it is highly proper that he should call to mind
his past conduct, and be afflicted with the survey; and that he should be
wakened to sorrow by the lyre of reminiscence, and weep over the follies
of his active life. Hence when the divine bard Demodocus, inspired by
the fury of the muses, sings the wrath of Ulysses and Achilles, on his
golden lyre, Ulysses is vehemently affected with the relation. For:

> *Touch'd at the song, Ulysses strait resign'd*
>
> *To soft affliction all his manly mind:*
> *Before his eyes the purple vest he drew,*
> *Industrious to conceal the falling dew:*
> *But when the music paus'd, he ceas'd to shed*
> *The flowing tear, and rais'd his drooping head.*
>
> Lib. viii. l. 83, &c.

And when the inhabitants of the palace, or refined cogitations, transported
with the song, demanded its repetition:

> *Again Ulysses veil'd his pensive head,*
> *Again unmann'd a shower of sorrow shed.*

For reminiscence is delightful to the former, because purified from
guilt: but afflictive to the latter, because he has not yet arrived at the summit of virtue, and acquired the perfection of contemplative good.

But while Ulysses is at the palace of Alcinous, Homer takes occasion of introducing some admirable mythological arcana, in the story of Mars and Venus; the explication of which from Proclus, on Plato's Republic, page 388, will I persuade myself be acceptable to the Platonic reader, and vindicate Homer from acting improperly by introducing this excellent fable. Both Vulcan and Mars then (says Proclus) operate about the universal world. And Mars indeed separates, perpetually nourishes, and constantly excites the contrarieties of the universe, that the world may exist perfect and entire from all its parts. But Vulcan adorns the whole sensible machine by his artifice, and fills it with certain reasons, proportions, and powers of nature. Hence he is feigned by Homer to construct twenty tripods about the heavens, that he may adorn them with the most perfect of many-sided figures: and he is likewise said to fashion a multitude of sublunary forms, variously figured, and artificially adorned; as when he says:

Chains, bracelets, pendants, all their toys I wrought.
Iliad. xviii.

But each of these deities requires the assistance of Venus; Mars that he may insert order and harmony in contrary natures; but Vulcan that he may induce beauty, in sensible operations, and thus render the world beautiful and divine. However since Venus is every where, Vulcan indeed always enjoys her, according to the superior orders of beings. As for instance, if Vulcan is super-mundane, Mars is mundane; and if the former is in the heavens, the latter enjoys Venus, in the regions subject to the moon. Hence Vulcan is said to have taken Venus for his wife according to the will of Jove; but Mars is reported to have committed adultery with Venus. For the cause of beauty, and conciliation, is naturally conjoined with the artificer of sensible concerns: but is after a manner foreign from the presiding deity of division and contrariety: for the collective are opposed to the separating genera of gods. And hence fables have given the appellation of adultery, to this consent of dissimilar causes. But a consent of this kind was necessary to the world, that contraries might join in mutual conciliation, and the war of the universe terminate in peace. Indeed as in the celestial regions, beauty, elegance of form, and the fabrications of Vulcan are particularly conspicuous: but in the realms of generation, elementary war, opposition, contrariety of natural powers, and the gifts of Mars reside: on this account I say, the sun, beholding from the heavens the congress of Mars and Venus, betrays it to Vulcan, with all whose actions he unites in amicable co-operation.

After this, Vulcan entangles them with all-various bonds, invisible to other gods, that he may connect the mundane genera, with artificial reasons; and may produce one constitution from the contrarieties of Mars, and the conciliating benefits of Venus. For both are required in generation. But according to Timaeus, there are some bonds of celestial, and others of sublunary concerns: and the latter are dissoluble, but the former of a perpetual nature. Hence Vulcan at last dissolves the bonds with which he had confined Venus and Mars; and this he effects through the persuasion of Neptune.

Who sues importunate to loose the god.

For Neptune desirous that the perpetual continuity of generation may be preserved, and that the circle of mutation may revolve into itself, causes begotten natures to be corrupted, and such as are corrupted to be renewed. Is there any reason then, why we should wonder at Homer's feigning Mars and Venus to be fettered with the bonds of Vulcan, since Timaeus also gives the appellation of bonds, to the demiurgic reasons, by which the celestial gods constitute generated natures? Is it not likewise congruous to the nature of things, that these bonds should be again dissolved, since they are the bonds of generation? Indeed the first, and most perfect artificer of things seems to have composed the world from contrary elements, and to have given them friendship in a certain proportion, by uniting the effects of Vulcan, Venus, and Mars, in association with each other. For producing the contrarieties of the elements, he operates within himself, according to Mars: but when he fabricates friendship, he energizes according to the power of Venus; and by connecting the natures of Venus and Mars, he appears to contain in himself the primitive exemplar of Vulcan's art. *Hence he is all, and operates with all the gods.* Besides the junior artificers, imitating their father, produce mortal animals, and again receive them when they perish, fabricating at the same time with Vulcan, mundane bonds, and primarily containing in themselves the causes of their dissolution. For every where, he who possesses a bond knows also the necessity of its solution."

We may here too observe that Ulysses, with the greatest propriety relates his past adventures in the palace of Alcinous: for as he now betakes himself to the intellectual light of thought, it is highly necessary that he should review his past conduct, faithfully enumerate the errors of his life, and anxiously solicit a return to true manners, and perfect rectitude of mind. But the description of his departure from Phaeacia is no less pregnant with philosophical mystery, than poetical beauty. For as he is now passing by the pure energy of thought, to his true country, the rational soul, he is represented as departing by night, and falling into so profound a sleep in his voyage, as to be insensible for some time of its happy consummation. For thus according to the poet:

> He climb'd the lofty stern; then gently prest
> The swelling couch, and lay compos'd to rest.
>
> Lib. xiii. l. 75.

And the vehemence of his thoughts is finely represented by the rapidity of the vessel:

> Now plac'd in order the Phaeacian train
> Their cables loose, and launch into the main:

Concerning the Cave of the Nymphs

At once they bend, and strike their equal oars,
And leave the sinking hills, and less'ning shores.
While on the deck the chief in silence lies,
And pleasing slumbers steal upon his eyes.
As fiery coursers in the rapid race
Urg'd by fierce drivers thro' the dusty space,
Toss their high heads, and scour along the plain;
So mounts the bounding vessel o'er the main.
Back to the stern the parted billows flow,
And the black ocean foams and roars below.
Thus with spread sails the winged galley flies;
Less swift an eagle cuts the liquid skies;
Divine Ulysses was her sacred load,
A man in wisdom equal to a god!
Much danger long and mighty toils he bore,
In storms by sea, and combats on the shore;
All which soft sleep now banish'd from his breast,
Wrapt in a pleasing, deep, and death-like rest.

By the night, therefore, Homer intimates the stillness and tranquillity which attends intellectual contemplation: and by the sweet and death-like sleep of Ulysses, his being abstracted from all sensible concerns, while merged in the profound and delightful energies of thought. For he has now bid adieu to the storms of passion, and the conflicts of desire; and is hastening to expel these dangerous foes, from the secret recesses of his soul.

Nor is it without reason that the poet represents Ithaca as presenting itself to the mariner's view, when the bright morning star emerges from the darkness of night. For thus he speaks:

But when the morning star, with early ray,
Flam'd in the front of heav'n, and promis'd day;
Like distant clouds the mariner descries
Fair Ithaca's emerging hills arise.

Lib. xiii. l. 93, &c.

Since it is only by the dawning beams of intellect, that cogitation can gain a glimpse of the native country, and proper empire of the soul.

But when Ulysses awakes from the delightful sleep of his corporeal energies, and, through the assistance of Minerva, recognizes his native land, he immediately enters into a consultation with the goddess, how he may effectually banish the various perturbations and inordinate desires which yet lurk in the penetralia of his soul. For this purpose it is necessary that he should relinquish all external possessions, mortify every sense, and employ every stratagem, which may finally destroy these malevolent foes. On this occasion the garb of poverty, the wrinkles of age, and the wants of life are symbols of mortified habits, desertion of sensible pursuits, and an intimate conversion to intellectual good. For the sensitive eye must now give place to the purer sight of the rational soul; and the strength and energies of a corporeal nature must yield to the superior vigour of intellectual exertion, and the severe labour of moral investigation. And this Homer appears most evidently to insinuate by the following beautiful lines:

> *Now seated in the olive's sacred shade,*
> *Confer the hero and the martial maid,*
> *The goddess of the azure eyes began:*
> *Son of Laertes! much-experienc'd man!*
> *The suitor train thy earliest care demand,*
> *Of that luxurious race to rid the land:*
> *Three years thy house their lawless rule has seen,*
> *And proud addresses to the matchless queen.*
> *But she thy absence mourns from day to day,*
> *And inly bleeds, and silent wastes away:*
> *Elusive of the bridal hour she gives*
> *Fond hopes to all, and all with hopes deceives.*
>
> Lib. xiii. l. 372.

Hence:

> *It fits thee now to wear a dark disguise,*
> *And secret walk unknown to mortal eyes,*
> *For this my hand shall wither ev'ry grace,*
> *And ev'ry elegance of form and face,*
> *O'er thy smooth skin a bark of wrinkles spread,*
> *Turn hoar the auburn honours of thy head,*
> *Disfigure every limb with coarse attire,*
> *And in thy eyes extinguish all the fire;*
> *Add all the wants and the decays of life,*
> *Estrange thee from thy own; thy son, thy wife;*
> *From the loath'd object ev'ry sight shall turn,*
> *And the blind suitors their destruction scorn.*
>
> Lib. xiii. l. 397, &c.

After this follows the discovery of Ulysses to Telemachus, which is no less philosophically sublime than poetically beautiful. For by Telemachus we must understand intellectual virtue, the true progeny of Ulysses, or the rational soul. Hence Ulysses, while employed in the great work of mortification, recognizes his legitimate offspring, and secretly plans with him the destruction of his insidious foes. The assistance however of Minerva, or wisdom, is requisite to this discovery, who beautifies and adorns the rational soul, and restores it on this occasion, to its pristine dignity and excellence of form. But it is necessary that this should be nothing more than a temporary change, till the enemies of reason are destroyed, and the dominion of intellect regained. With great propriety, therefore, is Telemachus represented as exploring his absent father, and impatient for his return: for the rational soul then alone associates with true virtue, when it withdraws itself from sensible delights, and earnestly meditates a restoration of its fallen dignity, and original sway.

And now Ulysses presents himself to our view in the habits of mortification, hastening to his long deserted palace, or the occult recesses of his soul, that he may mark the conduct, and plan the destruction of the malevolent passions, who are secretly attempting to subvert the empire of his mind. Hence the poet very properly and pathetically exclaims:

> *And now his city strikes the monarch's eyes,*
> *Alas! how chang'd! a man of miseries;*
> *Propt on a staff, a beggar old and bare,*
> *In tatter'd garments, flutt'ring with the air!*
> Lib. xvii. l. 201, &c.

However as this disguise was solely assumed for the purpose of procuring ancient purity and lawful rule, he divests himself of the torn garments of mortification, as soon as he begins the destruction of occult desires; and resumes the proper dignity and strength of his genuine form. But it is not without reason that Penelope, who is the image of intellectual purity, furnishes the instrument by which the hostile rout of passions are destroyed; for what besides the arrows of purity can be sufficient to extirpate the leading bands of impurity and vice? Hence as soon as he is furnished with this irresistible weapon, he no longer defers the ruin of his insidious foes, but:

> *Then fierce the hero o'er the threshold strode;*
> *Stript of his rags, he blaz'd out like a god.*
> *Full in their face the lifted bow he bore,*
> *And quiver'd deaths a formidable store;*
> *Before his feet the rattling show'r he threw,*
> *And thus terrific to the suitor crew.*
> Lib. xxii. l. i., &c.

But Homer represents Penelope as remaining ignorant of Ulysses, even after the suitors are destroyed; and he is seated on the throne of majesty, anxious to be known, and impatient to return her chaste and affectionate embrace. For thus he describes her:

> *Then gliding through the marble valves in state,*
> *Oppos'd before the shining fire she sate.*
> *The monarch by a column high enthron'd,*
> *His eye withdrew, and fix'd it on the ground*
> *Anxious to hear his queen the silence break:*
> *Amaz'd she sate, and impotent to speak;*
> *O'er all the man her eyes she rolls in vain,*
> *Now hopes, now fears, now knows, then doubts again.*
> Lib. xxiii. l. 88, &c.

Nor ought this to appear strange, for purity has been so long absent from his soul, that it is difficult to obtain a recollection of their pristine union, and legitimate association with each other. However in order to facilitate this discovery, he renders all harmonious and pure, within the recesses of his soul; and by the assistance of Minerva, or wisdom, resumes the garb and dignity which he had formerly displayed.

> *Then instant to the bath, (the monarch cries)*
> *Bid the gay youth and sprightly virgins rise,*
> *Thence all descend in pomp, and proud array,*
> *And bid the dome resound the mirthful lay;*
> *While the sweet lyrist airs of raptures sings,*
> *And forms the dance responsive to the strings.*
>
> Lib. xxiii. l. 131, &c.

And afterwards Ulysses is described, as appearing through the interposition of Minerva, *like one of the immortals:*

> *So Pallas his heroic form improves*
> *With bloom divine, and like a god he moves.*
>
> Lib. xxiii. l. 163

For indeed he who, like Ulysses, has destroyed the power of his passions, and purified himself from their defiling nature, no longer ranks in the order of mortals, but assimilates with divinity itself. And now that he may become entirely known to intellectual purity, that chaste Penelope of the soul, he need only relate the secrets of their mystic union, and recognize the bower of celestial love. For then perfect recollection will ensue; and the anxiety of diffidence will be changed into transports of assurance, and tears of rapturous delight.

And thus we have attended Ulysses through his various wanderings and woes, till he recovers the ruined empire of his soul. We must however remember, according to the beautiful observation of Porphyry, in the above treatise, that he is not freed from molestation till he has passed over the raging sea of a material nature, has entirely appeased the anger of divinity, and is become so insensible to the concerns of a corporeal life, as to be ignorant of their nature and use. For:

> *Then heav'n decrees in peace to end his days,*
> *And steal himself from life by slow decays;*
> *Unknown to pain, in age resign his breath,*
> *When late stern Neptune points the shaft of death;*
> *To the dark grave retiring as to rest;*
> *His people blessing, by his people blest.*
>
> Lib. iii. l. 281, &c.

*A DISSERTATION
ON THE ELEUSINIAN AND
BACCHIC MYSTERIES*

Of all Taylor's essays this remains the one whose value is least impaired by time. It remains unsurpassed as an exposition of mythological themes in the context of the philosophy with which they are traditionally and integrally associated. There is no publication date on the title page, and the presumed date is 1790 or 1791; the imprint of Amsterdam is considered to be fictitious. The volume, published anonymously in 184 duodecimo pages, contains an "advertisement," the dissertation in two sections (the first, untitled, on the Eleusinian Mysteries; the second, *On the Mysteries of Bacchus*), and an appendix on a passage in Psellus. On the title page is a motto from Proclus.

Proclus's *Commentaries* had been prefaced by an extract, prominently displayed, from *Curiosities of Literature* (second edition): "Mr. T. Taylor, the Platonic Philosopher and *the modern Plethon*, consonant to that philosophy, professes Polytheism." Possibly it may have seemed necessary to the printer and publisher of his next work to conceal his identity.

The *Dissertation* was reprinted with some changes as the second edition in the *Pamphleteer*, VIII (1816), 33–66, 455–86. The third edition (1875) and the fourth (1891) were "Edited, with Introduction, Notes, Emendations, and Glossary" by Alexander Wilder, one of Taylor's American disciples, whose translation of Iamblichus's *Mysteries of the Egyptians, Chaldeans, and Assyrians* is heavily indebted to Taylor's translation (1821). The fourth edition includes 85 sketches "drawn from the antique by A. L. Rawson" to illustrate "the two or three theories of human life held by the ancient Greeks."

For passages of Latin verse, the following translations have been provided: for Virgil's *Aeneid*, that of Dryden, edited by James Kinsley (Oxford, 1958), reproduced here by permission of Clarendon Press; for Claudian's *Rape of Proserpine*, that of Jacob George Strutt (London, 1814).

ADVERTISEMENT

As THERE IS NOTHING more celebrated than the mysteries of the antients, so there is perhaps nothing which has hitherto been less solidly known. Of the truth of this observation, the liberal reader will, I persuade myself, be fully convinced, from an attentive perusal of the following sheets; in which the secret meaning of the Eleusinian and Bacchic Mysteries is unfolded, from authority the most respectable, and from a philosophy of all others the most venerable and august. The authority, indeed, is principally derived from manuscript writings, which are of course in the possession of but a few; but its respectability is no more lessened by its concealment, than the value of a diamond when secluded from the light. And as to the philosophy, by whose assistance these mysteries are developed, it is coeval with the universe itself; and however its continuity may be broken by opposing systems, it will make its appearance at different periods of time, as long as the sun himself shall continue to illuminate the world. It has, indeed, and may hereafter, be violently assaulted by delusive opinions; but the opposition will be just as imbecil as that of the waves of the sea against a temple built on a rock, which majestically pours them back,

Broken and vanquish'd foaming to the main.

SECTION I

[ON THE ELEUSINIAN MYSTERIES]

Dr. Warburton, in his Divine Legation of Moses, has ingeniously proved, that the sixth book of Virgil's Aeneid represents some of the shews of the Eleusinian Mysteries; but, at the same time, has miserably failed in attempting to unfold their latent meaning, and obscure, though important, end. By the assistance, however, of the Platonic philosophy, I have been enabled to correct his errors, and to vindicate the wisdom of antiquity from his malevolent and ignorant aspersions, by a genuine account of this sublime institution; of which the following observations are designed as a comprehensive view.

345

In the first place, then, I shall present the reader with two remarkable authorities, and these perfectly demonstrative, in support of the assertion, that a part of the shews consisted in a representation of the infernal regions; authorities which, though of the last consequence, were unknown to Dr. Warburton himself. The first of these is from no less a person than the immortal Pindar, in a fragment preserved by Clemens Alexandrinus in Stromat. lib. 3. "ἀλλα και Πινδαρος περι των εν Ελευσινι μυστηριων λεγων επιφερει. Ολβιος, οστις ιδων εκεινα κοινα εις υποχθονια, οιδεν μεν βιον τελευταν, οιδεν δε διος δοτον αρχαν." I.e. "But Pindar, speaking of the Eleusinian Mysteries, says, Blessed is he who, on seeing those *common concerns under the earth*, knows both the end of life and the given empire of Jupiter." The other of these is from Proclus in his Commentary on Plato's Politics, p. 372, who, speaking concerning the sacerdotal and symbolical mythology, observes, that from this mythology Plato himself establishes many of his own peculiar dogmata, "since in the Phaedo he venerates, with a becoming silence, the assertion delivered in the arcane discourses, that men are placed in body as in a certain prison, secured by a guard, *and testifies, according to the mystic ceremonies, the different allotments of pure and impure souls in Hades, their habits, and the triple path arising from their essences; and this according to paternal and sacred institutions; all which are full of a symbolical theory, and of the poetical descriptions concerning the ascent and descent of souls, of dyonisiacal signs, the punishments of the Titans, the trivia and wanderings in Hades, and every thing of a similar kind."*—"Δηλοι δε εν φαιδωνι τον τε εν απορρητοις λεγομενον, ως εν τινι φρουρα εσμεν οι ανθρωποι, σιγη τη πρεπουση σεβων, καὶ τας τελετας (lege καὶ κατα τας τελετας) μαρτυρομενος των διαφορων ληξεων της ψυχης κεκαθαρμενης τε καὶ ακαθαρτου εις αδου απιουσης, καὶ τας τε σχεσεις αυ, καὶ τας τριοδους απο των ουσιων καὶ των (lege καὶ κατα των) πατρικων θεσμων τεκμαιρομενος. α δη της συμβολικης απαντα θεωριας εστι μεστα, καὶ των παρα τοις ποιηταις θρυλλουμενων ανοδων τε καὶ καθοδων, των τε διονυσιακων συνθηματων, καὶ των τιτανικων αμαρτηματων λεγομενων, και των εν ᾳδου τριοδων, και της πλανης, και των τοιουτων απαντων."

Having premised thus much, I now proceed to prove that the shews of the lesser mysteries were designed by the antient theologists, their founders, to signify occultly the condition of the impure soul invested with a terrene body, and merged in a material nature: or, in other words, to signify that such a soul in the present life might be said to die, as far as it is possible for soul to die; and that on the dissolution of the present body, while in a state of impurity, it would experience a death still more durable and profound. That the soul, indeed, till purified by philosophy, suffers death through its union with body was obvious to the philologist Macrobius, who, not penetrating the secret depth of the antients, concluded from hence that they signified nothing more than the present body, by their descriptions of the infernal abodes. But this is manifestly absurd; since it is universally agreed, that all the antient theological poets and philosophers inculcated the doctrine of a future state of rewards and punishments in the most full and decisive terms; at the same time occultly intimating that the death of the soul was nothing more than a profound union with the ruinous bonds of the body. Indeed if these wise men believed in a future state of retribution, and at the same time considered a connection with body as the death of the soul, it necessarily follows, that the soul's punishment and subsistence hereafter is nothing more than a continuation of its state at present, and a transmigration, as it were, from sleep to sleep, and from dream to dream. But let us attend to the assertions of these divine men concerning the soul's conjunction with a material nature. And to begin with the obscure and profound Heraclitus, speaking of souls unembodied: "We live," says he, "their death, and we die their life."
Ζωμεν τον εκεινων θανατον, τεθνηκαμεν δε τον εκεινων βιον.

And Empedocles, blaming generation, beautifully says of her:

> *The species changing with destruction dread,*
> *She makes the living pass into the dead.*

Εκ μεν γαρ ζωων ετιθει νεκρα, ειδε αμειβων.

And again, lamenting his connection with this corporeal world, he pathetically exclaims:

For this I weep, for this indulge my woe,
That e'er my soul such novel realms should know.

Κλαυσα τε και κωκυσα, ιδων ασυνηθεα χωρον.

Plato, too, it is well known, considered the body as the sepulchre of the soul; and in the Cratylus consents with the doctrine of Orpheus, that the soul is punished through its union with body. This was likewise the opinion of the celebrated Pythagorean, Philolaus, as is evident from the following remarkable passage in the Doric dialect, preserved by Clemens Alexandrinus in Stromat. lib. 3. p. 413. "Μαρτυρεονται δε και οι παλαιοι θεολογοι τε και μαντεις, ως δια τινας τιμωριας, α ψυχα τω σωματι συνεζευκται, και καθαπερ εν σωματι τουτω τεθαπται." I.e. "The antient theologists and priests also testify, that the soul is united with body for the sake of suffering punishment; and that it is buried in body as in a sepulchre." And lastly, Pythagoras himself confirms the above sentiments, when he beautifully observes, according to Clemens in the same book, "that whatever we see when awake, is death; and when asleep, a dream." Θανατος εστιν, οκοσα εγερθεντες ορεομεν· οκοσα δε ευδοντες, υπνος.

But that the mysteries occultly signified this sublime truth, that the soul by being merged in matter resides among the dead both here and hereafter, though it follows by a necessary consequence from the preceding observations, yet it is indisputably confirmed, by the testimony of the great and truly divine Plotinus, in Ennead 1. lib. 8 p. 80. "When the soul," says he, "has descended into generation she participates of evil, and profoundly rushes into the region of dissimilitude, *to be entirely merged in which is nothing more than to fall into dark mire.*" And again, soon after: "The soul therefore *dies* through vice, as much as it is possible for the soul to die: *and the death of the soul is, while merged, or baptized, as it were, in the present body, to*

348

Eleusinian and Bacchic Mysteries

descend into matter, and be filled with its impurity, and after departing from this body, to lye absorbed in its filth till it returns to a superior condition, and elevates its eye from the overwhelming mire. For to be plunged in matter is to descend into Hades, and there fall asleep."[1] Γινομενω δε η μεταληψις αυτου. Γινεται γαρ πανταπασιν εν τω της ανομοιοτητος τοπω, ενθα δυς εις αυτην εις βορβορον σκοτεινον εσται πεσων.—αποθνησκει ουν, ως ψυχη αν θανοι· και ο θανατος αυτη, και ετι εν τω σωματι βεβαπτισμενη, εν υλη εστι καταδυναι, και πλησθηναι αυτης. και εξελθουσης εκει κεισθαι, εως αναδραμη και αφελη πως την οψιν εκ του βορβορου. και τουτο εστι το εν ᾳδου ελθοντα επικαταδαρθειν. Here the reader may observe that the obscure doctrine of the mysteries mentioned by Plato in the Phaedo, that the unpurified soul in a future state lies merged in mire, is beau-

[1] This passage doubtless alludes to the antient and beautiful story of Cupid and Psyche, in which Psyche is said to fall asleep in Hades; and this through rashly attempting to behold corporeal beauty: and the observation of Plotinus will enable the profound and contemplative reader to unfold the greater part of the mysteries contained in this elegant fable. But, prior to Plotinus, Plato, in the seventh book of his Republic, asserts, that such as are unable in the present life to perceive *the idea of the good*, will descend to Hades after death, and fall asleep in its dark abodes. Ος αν μη εχῃ διορισαθαι τω λογῳ, απο των αλλων παντων αφελων την του αγαθου ιδεαν, και ωσπερ εν μαχῃ δια παντων ελεγχων διεξιων, με κατα δοξαν αλλα κατ' ουσιαν προθυμουμενος ελεγχειν, εν πασι τουτοις απτωτι τω λογῳ διαπορευηται, ουτε αυτο το αγαθον ουδεν φησεις ειδεναι τον οντως εχοντα, ουτε αλλο αγαθον ουδεν; αλλ' ει πη ειδωλου τινος εφαπτεται, δοξῃ ουκ επιστημῃ εφαπτεσθαι; και τον νυν βιον ονειροπολουντα, και υπν ωττοντα, πριν ενθαδ' εξεργεσθαι, εις αδου προτερον αφικομενον τελεως επικαταδαρθανειν; *i.e.*, "He who is not able, by the exercise of his reason, *to define the idea of the good*, separating it from all other objects, and piercing, as in a battle, through every kind of argument; endeavouring to confute, not according to opinion, but according to essence, and proceeding through all these dialectical energies with an unshaken reason;—he who cannot accomplish this, would you not say, that he neither knows the good itself, nor any thing which is properly denominated good? And would you not assert, that such a one, when he apprehends any certain image of reality, apprehends it rather through the medium of opinion than of science; that in the present life he is sunk in sleep, and conversant with the delusions of dreams; and that before he is roused to a vigilant state, he will descend to Hades, and be overwhelmed with a sleep perfectly profound."

349

tifully explained; at the same time that our assertion concerning their secret meaning is no less solidly confirmed. In a similar manner the same divine philosopher, in his book on the beautiful, Ennead. 1. lib. 6, explains the fable of Narcissus as an emblem of one who rushes to the contemplation of sensible forms as if they were perfect realities, when at the same time they are nothing more than like beautiful images appearing in water, fallacious and vain. "Hence," says he, "as Narcissus, by catching at the shadow, merged himself in the stream and disappeared, so he who is captivated by beautiful bodies, and does not depart from their embrace, is precipitated, not with his body, but with his soul, into a darkness profound and horrid to intellect, through which, becoming blind both here and in Hades, he converses with nothing but shadows." Τον αυτον δη τροπον ο εχομενος των καλων σωματων, και μη αφιεις, ου τω σωματι, τη δε ψυχη καταδυσεται, εις σκοτεινα και ατερπη τω νω βαθη, ενθα τυφλος εν αδου μενων, και ενταυθα κακει σκιαις συνεστι. And what still farther confirms our exposition is, that matter was considered by the Egyptians as a certain mire or mud. "The Egyptians," says Simplicius, in Arist. Phys. p. 50, "called matter, (which they symbolically denominated water,) the dregs or sediment of the first life; matter being, as it were, a certain mire or mud." Διο και Αιγυπτιοι την της πρωτης ζωης, ην υδωρ συμβολικως εκαλουν, υποσταθμην την υλην ελεγον, οιον ιλυν τινα ουσαν. So that from all that has been said we may safely conclude with Ficinus, whose words are as express to our purpose as possible. "Lastly," says he, "that I may comprehend the opinion of the antient theologists, on the state of the soul after death, in a few words: they considered, as we have elsewhere asserted, things divine as the only realities, and that all others were only the images and shadows of truth. Hence they asserted that prudent men, who earnestly employed themselves in divine concerns, were above all others in a vigilant state. But that imprudent men, who pursued objects of a different nature, being laid asleep, as it were, were only engaged in the delusions of dreams: and that if they happened to die in this sleep, before they were roused, they would be afflicted with similar and still sharper visions in a future state. And that as he who in this life pursued realities, would, after death, enjoy the highest truth, so he who was conversant with fallacies, would hereafter be tormented with fallacies and delusions in the extreme: as the one would be delighted with true objects of enjoyment, so the other would be tormented with delusive semblances of reality."—Denique ut priscorum theologorum sententiam de statu animae post mortem paucis comprehendam: sola divina (ut alias diximus) arbitrantur res veras existere, reliqua esse rerum verarum imagines atque umbras. Ideo prudentes homines, qui divinis incumbunt, prae ceteris vigilare. Imprudentes autem qui sectantur alia, insomniis omnino quasi dormientes illudi, ac si in hoc somno priusquam expergefacti fuerint moriantur similibus post discessum et acrioribus visconibus angi. Et sicut eum qui in vita veris incubuit, post mortem summa veritate potiri, sic eum qui falsa fectatus est, fallacia extrema torqueri, ut ille rebus veris oblectetur, hic falsis vexetur simulachris." (Ficin. de immortal anim. lib. 18, p. 411.)

But notwithstanding this important truth was obscurely shewn by the lesser mysteries, we must not suppose that it was generally known even to the initiated themselves: for as people of almost all descriptions were admitted to these rites, it would have been a ridiculous prostitution to disclose to the multitude a theory so abstracted and sublime. It was sufficient to instruct these in the doctrine of a future state of rewards and punishments, and in the means of returning to the principles from which they originally fell: for this last piece of information was, according to Plato in the Phaedo, the ultimate design of the mysteries; and the former is necessarily inferred from the present discourse. Hence the reason why it was obvious to none but the Pythagoric and Platonic philosophers, who derived their theology from Orpheus himself, the original founder of these sacred institutions; and why we meet with no information in this particular in any writer prior to Plotinus; as he was the first who, having penetrated the profound wisdom of antiquity, delivered it to posterity without the concealments of mystic symbols and fabulous narrations.

Hence too, I think, we may infer, with the greatest probability, that this recondite meaning of the mysteries was not known even to Virgil himself, who has so elegantly described their external form; for notwithstanding the traces of Platonism which are to be found in the Aeneid, nothing of any great depth occurs throughout the whole, except what a superficial reading of Plato and the shews of the mysteries might easily afford. But this is not perceived by the moderns, who, entirely unskilled themselves in Platonism, and fascinated by the charms of his poetry, imagine him to be deeply knowing in a subject with which he was most likely but slightly acquainted. This opinion is still farther strengthened by considering that the doctrine delivered in his Eclogues is perfectly Epicurean, which was the fashionable philosophy of the Augustan age; and that there is no trace of Platonism in any other part of his works but the present book, which, in consequence of its containing a representation of the mysteries, was necessarily obliged to display some of the principal tenets of this philosophy, so far as they illustrated and made a part of these mystic exhibitions. However, on the supposition that this book presents us with a faithful view of some part of these sacred rites, and this accompanied with the utmost elegance, harmony, and purity of versification, it ought to be considered as an invaluable relic of antiquity, and a precious monument of venerable mysticism, recondite wisdom, and theological information. This will be sufficiently evident from what has been already delivered, by considering some of the beautiful descriptions of this book in their natural order; at the same time that the descriptions themselves will corroborate the present elucidations.

In the first place, then, when he says,

> . . . *facilis descensus Averno.*
> *Noctes atque dies patet atra janua Ditis:*
> *Sed revocare gradum, superasque evadere ad auras,*

Eleusinian and Bacchic Mysteries

*Hcc opus, hic labor est. Pauci quos aequus amavit
Jupiter, aut ardens evexit ad aethera virtus,
Dis geniti potuere. Tenent media omnia silvae,
Cocytusque sinu labens, circumvenit atro. . . ,*

[*The Gates of Hell are open Night and Day;
Smooth the Descent, and easie is the Way:
But, to return, and view the chearful S*kies;
*In this the Task, and mighty Labour lies.
To few great* Jupiter *imparts this Grace:
And those of shining Worth, and Heav'nly Race.
Betwixt those Regions, and our upper Light.
Deep Forrests, and impenetrable Night
Possess the middle space: Th' Infernal Bounds*
Cocytus, *with his sable Waves, surrounds.* . . ,

VI. 192–201]

is it not obvious, from the preceding explanation, that by Avernus,
in this place, and the dark gates of Pluto, we must understand a
corporeal nature, the descent into which is indeed at all times
obvious and easy, but to recall our steps, and ascend into the upper
regions, or, in other words, to separate the soul from body by the
cathartic virtues, is indeed a mighty work, and a laborious task?
For a few only, the favourites of heaven, that is, born with the
true philosophic genius, and whom ardent virtue has elevated to
divine contemplations, have been enabled to accomplish the
arduous design. But when he says that all the middle regions are
covered with woods, this too plainly intimates a material nature;
the word silva, as is well known, being used by antient writers to
signify matter, and implies nothing more than that the passage
leading to the barathrum of body, i.e. into profound darkness
and oblivion, is through the medium of a material nature: and
this medium is surrounded by the black bosom of Cocytus, that is,
by bitter weeping and lamentations, the necessary consequence
of the soul's union with a nature entirely foreign to her own. So
that the poet in this particular perfectly corresponds with Emped-

353

ocles in the line we have cited above, where he exclaims, alluding
to this union,

> *For this I* weep, *for this* indulge my woe,
> *That e'er my soul such novel realms should know.*

In the next place, when he thus describes the cave, through
which Aeneas descended to the infernal regions:

> *Spelunca alta fuit, vastoque immanis hiatu,*
> *Scrupea, tuta lacu nigro, nemorumque tenebris:*
> *Quam super haud ullae poterant impune volantes*
> *Tendere iter pennis: talis sese halitus atris*
> *Faucibus effundens supera ad convexa ferebat:*
> *Unde locum Graii dixerunt nomine Aornum.*

> [*Deep was the Cave; and downward as it went*
> *From the wide Mouth, a rocky rough Descent;*
> *And here th' access a gloomy Grove defends;*
> *And there th' unnavigable Lake extends.*
> *O're whose unhappy Waters, void of Light,*
> *No Bird presumes to steer his Airy Flight;*
> *Such deadly Stenches from the depth arise,*
> *And steaming Sulphur, that infects the Skies.*
> *From hence the* Grecian *Bards their Legends make,*
> *And give the name* Avernus *to the Lake.* VI. 338–47]

Does it not afford a beautiful representation of a corporeal nature,
of which a cave, defended with a black lake, and dark woods, is
an obvious emblem? For it occultly reminds us of the ever-flowing and obscure condition of such a nature, which may be said

> *To roll incessant with impetuous speed,*
> *Like some dark river, into Matter's sea.*

Nor is it with less propriety denominated Aornus, *i.e.* destitute
of birds, or a winged nature; for on account of its native sluggish-
ness and inactivity, and its merged condition, being situated in
the extremity of things, it is perfectly debile and languid, incapable of ascending into the regions of reality, and exchanging its

obscure and degraded station for one every way splendid and divine. The propriety too of sacrificing, previous to his entrance, to Night and Earth, is obvious, as both these are proper emblems of a corporeal nature.

In the verses which immediately follow,

Ecce autem, primi sub limina solis et ortus,
Sub pedibus mugire solum, et juga coepta movere
Silvarum, visaque canes ululare per umbram,
Adventante dea,

[*Late, the Nocturnal Sacrifice begun;*
Nor ended, 'till the next returning Sun.
Then Earth began to bellow, Trees to dance;
And howling Dogs in glimm'ring Light advance;
E're Hecate *came . . . ,*   VI. 364–68]

we may perceive an evident allusion to the earthquakes, &c. attending the descent of the soul into body, mentioned by Plato in the tenth book of his Republic; since the lapse of the soul, as we shall see more fully hereafter, was one of the important truths which these mysteries were intended to reveal. And the howling dogs are symbols of material daemons, who are thus denominated by the magic oracles of Zoroaster, on account of their ferocious and malevolent dispositions, ever baneful to the felicity of the human soul. And hence matter herself is represented by Synesius in his first hymn, with great propriety and beauty, as barking at the soul with devouring rage: for thus he sings, addressing himself to the Deity:

Μακαρ ος τις βορον υλας
Προφυγων υλαγμα, και γας
Αναδυς, αλματι κουφῳ
Ιχνος ες θεον τιταινει.

Which may be thus paraphrased:

Blessed! thrice blessed! who, with winged speed,
From Hyle's dread voracious barking flies,

355

And, leaving Earth's obscurity behind,
By a light leap, directs his steps to thee.

And that material daemons actually appeared to the initiated previous to the lucid visions of the gods themselves, is evident from the following passage of Proclus in his MS. Commentary on the first Alcibiades: εν ταις αγιοταταις των τελετων προ της θεου παρουσιας δαιμονων χθονιων εκβολαι προφαινονται, και απο των αχραντων αγαθων εις την υλην προκαλουμεναι. *I.e.* "In the most holy of the mysteries, before the presence of the god, the impulsive forms of certain terrestrial daemons appear, which call the attention from undefiled advantages to matter." And Pletho, on the Oracles, expressly asserts, that these spectres appeared in the shape of dogs.

After this Aeneas is described as proceeding to the infernal regions, through profound night and darkness:

Ibant obscuri sola sub nocte per umbram,
Perque domos Ditis vacuas, et inania regna.
Quale per incertam lunam sub luce maligna
Est iter in silvis: ubi caelum condidit umbra
Jupiter, et rebus nox abstulit atra colorem.

[*Obscure they went thro dreery Shades, that led*
Along the waste Dominions of the dead:
Thus wander Travellers in Woods by Night,
By the Moon's doubtful, and malignant Light:
When Jove *in dusky Clouds involves the Skies;*
And the faint Crescent shoots by fits before their Eyes.

VI. 378–83]

And this with the greatest propriety; for the mysteries, as is well known, were celebrated by night: and in the Republic of Plato, as cited above, souls are described as falling into generation at midnight; this period being peculiarly accommodated to the darkness and oblivion of a corporeal nature; and to this circumstance the nocturnal celebration of the mysteries doubtless alluded.

In the next place, the following beautiful description presents itself to our view:

Vestibulum ante ipsum, primisque in faucibus orci
Luctus, et ultrices posuere cubilia curae:
Pallentesque habitant morbi, tristisque senectus,
Et metus, et mala suada fames, ac turpis egestas;
Terribiles visu formae; Lethumque Laborque:
Tum consanguineus Lethi sopor, et mala mentis
Gaudia, mortiferumque adverso in limine bellum,
Ferreique Eumenidum thalami, et discordia demens,
Vipereum crinem vittis innexa cruentis.
In medio ramos annosaque brachia pandit
Ulmus opaca ingens: quam sedem somnia vulgo
Vana tenere ferunt, foliisque sub omnibus haerent.
Multaque praeterea variarum monstra ferarum:
Centauri in foribus stabulant, Scyllaeque biformes,
Et centumgeminus Briareus, ac bellua Lernae,
Horrendum stridens, flammisque armata Chimaera,
Gorgones, Harpyiaeque, et forma tricorporis umbrae.

[Just in the Gate, and in the Jaws of Hell,
Revengeful Cares, and sullen Sorrows dwell;
And pale Diseases, and repining Age;
Want, Fear, and Famine's unresisted rage.
Here Toils, and Death, and Death's half-brother, Sleep,
Forms terrible to view, their Centry keep:
With anxious Pleasures of a guilty Mind,
Deep Frauds before, and open Force behind:
The Furies' Iron Beds, and Strife that shakes
Her hissing Tresses, and unfolds her Snakes.
Full in the midst of this infernal Road,
An Elm displays her dusky Arms abroad;
The God of Sleep there hides his heavy Head:
And empty Dreams on ev'ry Leaf are spread.
Of various Forms unnumber'd Specters more;
Centaurs, *and double Shapes, besiege the Door:*
Before the Passage horrid Hydra *stands,*
And Briareus[2] *with all his hundred Hands:*

[2] [See Plate 15.]

Gorgons, Geryon *with his triple Frame;*
And vain Chimaera *vomits empty Flame.* VI. 384-403]

And surely it is impossible to draw a more lively picture of the
maladies with which a material nature is connected; of the soul's
dormant condition through its union with body; and of the various
mental diseases to which, through such a conjunction, it becomes
unavoidably subject: for this description contains a threefold division; representing, in the first place, the external evils with
which this material region is replete; in the second place, intimating that the life of the soul when merged in body is nothing
but a dream; and, in the third place, under the disguise of omniform and terrific monsters, exhibiting the various vices of our
irrational part. Hence Empedocles, in perfect conformity with
the first part of this description, calls this material abode, or the
realms of generation,—ατερπεα χωρον,[2a] a *"joyless region,"*

> *Where slaughter, rage, and countless ills reside;*
> Ενθα φονος τε κολος τε και αλλων εθνεα κηρων;

and into which those who fall,

> *Through Ate's meads and dreadful darkness stray.*
> Ατης
> ανα λειμωνα τε και σκοτος ηλασκουσιν.

And hence he justly says of such a soul, that

> *She flies from deity and heav'nly light,*
> *To serve* mad discord *in the realms of night.*
> . . . φυγας θεοθεν, και αλητης,
> Νεικεï μαινομενῳ πισυνος. . . .

Where too you may observe that the *discordia demens* of Virgil
is an exact translation of the νειχεï μαινομενῳ of Empedocles.

In the lines too which immediately succeed, the *sorrows* and
mournful miseries attending the soul's union with a material
nature, are beautifully described.

[2a] This and the other citations from Empedocles are to be found in
Hierocles in Aur. Carm. p. 186.

Hinc via, Tartarei quae fert Acherontis *ad undas;*
Turbidus hic caeno vastaque voragine gurges
Aestuat, atque omnem Cocyto *eructat arenam.*

[*Hence to deep* Acheron *they take their way;*
Whose troubled Eddies, thick with Ooze and Clay,
Are whirl'd aloft, and in Cocytus *lost. . . .*

VI. 410–12]

And when Charon calls out to Aeneas to desist from entering any farther, and tells him,

Here to reside delusive Shades delight;
For nought dwells here but Sleep and drowsy Night,

Umbrarum hic locus est, Somni Noctisque soporae,

nothing can more aptly express the condition of the dark regions of body, into which the soul, when descending, meets with nothing but shadows and drowsy night: and by persisting in her ruinous course, is at length lulled into profound sleep, and becomes a true inhabitant of the phantom abodes of the dead.

Aeneas, having now passed over the Stygian lake, meets with the three-headed monster Cerberus, the guardian of these infernal abodes:

Tandem trans fluvium incolumis vatemque virumque
Informi limo glaucaque exponit in ulva.
Cerberus haec ingens latratu regna trifauci
Personat, adverso recubans immanis in antro . . .

[*His Passengers at length are wafted o're;*
Expos'd in muddy Weeds, upon the miry Shore.
No sooner landed, in his Den they found
The triple Porter of the Stygian *Sound:*
Grim Cerberus. . . .   VI. 560–64]

Where by Cerberus we must understand the discriminative part of the soul, of which a dog, on account of its sagacity, is an emblem; and the three heads signify the triple distinction of this part, into the intellective, cogitative, and opinionative powers.—With respect to the three kinds of persons described as situated on the borders of the infernal realms, the poet doubtless intended by this enumeration to represent to us the three most remarkable characters, who, though not apparently deserving of punishment, are yet each of them similarly merged in matter, and consequently require a similar degree of purification. The persons described are, as is well known, first, the souls of infants snatched away by untimely ends; secondly, such as are condemned to death unjustly; and, thirdly, those who, weary of their lives, become guilty of suicide. And with respect to the first of these, or infants, their connection with a material nature is obvious. The second sort, too, who are condemned to death unjustly, must be supposed to represent the souls of men who, though innocent of one crime for which they were wrongfully punished, have, notwithstanding, been guilty of many crimes, for which they are receiving proper chastisement in Hades, *i.e.* through a profound union with a material nature. And the third sort, or suicides, though apparently separated from body, have only exchanged one place for another of a similar nature; since a conduct of this kind, according to the arcana of divine philosophy, instead of separating the soul from body, only restores it to a condition perfectly correspondent to its former inclinations and habits, lamentations and woes. But if we examine this affair more profoundly, we shall find that these three characters are justly placed in the same situation, because the reason of punishment is in each equally obscure. For is it not a just matter of doubt, why the souls of infants should be punished? And is it not equally dubious and wonderful why those who have been unjustly condemned to death in one period of existence should be punished in another? And as to suicides, Plato in his Phaedo says, that the prohibition of this crime in the ἀπορρητα is a profound doctrine, and not easy to be understood. Indeed the true cause why the two first of these characters are in Hades can only be obtained from regarding a prior state of existence, in surveying which, the latent justice of punishment will be manifestly revealed; the apparent inconsistencies in the administration of providence fully reconciled; and the doubts con-

cerning the wisdom of its proceedings entirely dissolved. And as
to the last of these, or suicides, since the reason of their punishment, and why an action of this kind is in general highly atrocious, is extremely mystical and obscure, the following solution
of this difficulty will, no doubt, be gratefully received by the
Platonic reader, as the whole of it is no where else to be found but
in manuscript. Olympiodorus, then, a most learned and excellent
commentator on Plato, in his commentary on that part of the
Phaedo where Plato speaks of the prohibition of suicide in the
απορρητα, observes as follows: "The argument," says he, "which
Plato employs in this place against suicide is derived from the
Orphic mythology, in which four kingdoms are celebrated: the
first of *Heaven,* whom Saturn assaulted, cutting off the genitals
of his father. But after Saturn, Jupiter succeeded to the government of the world, having hurled his father into Tartarus. And
after Jupiter, Bacchus rose to light, who, according to report,
was, through the stratagems of Juno, torn in pieces by the Titans,
by whom he was surrounded, and who afterwards tasted his
flesh: but Jupiter, enraged at the deed, hurled his thunder at
the guilty offenders and consumed them to ashes. Hence a certain matter being formed from the vapour of the smoke ascending
from their burning bodies, out of this mankind were produced.
It is unlawful therefore to destroy ourselves, not as the words of
Plato seem to import, because we are in body, as in a prison, secured by a guard; (for this is evident, and Plato would not have
called such an assertion arcane) but because our body is Dionysiacal, or the property of Bacchus: for we are a part of this god, since
we are composed from the vapours of the Titans who tasted his
flesh. Socrates, therefore, fearful of disclosing the arcane part of
this narration, adds nothing more of the fable but that we are
placed as in a certain prison secured by a guard: but the interpreters
relate the fable openly." Και εστι το μυθικον επιχειρημα τοιουτον.
Παρα τῳ Ορφει τεσσαρες βασιλειαι παραδιδονται. Πρωτη μεν, η
του Ουρανου, ην ο Κρονος διεδεξατο, εκτεμων τα αιδοια του
πατρος. Μετα δη τον Κρονον, ο Ζευς εβασιλευσεν καταταρτα-
ρωσας τον πατερα. Ειτα τον Δια διεδεξατο ο Διοννσος, ον φασι

κατ᾽ επιβουλην της Ηρας τους περι αυτου Τιτανας σπαραττειν, καὶ των σαρκων αυτου απογευεσθαι. Και τουτους οργισθεις ο Ζευς εκεραυνωσε, καὶ εκ της αιθαλης των ατμων των αναδοθεντων εξ αυτων, υλης γενομενης γενεσθαι τους ανθρωπους. Ου δει ουν εξαγαγειν ημας εαυτους, ουχ οτι ως δοκει λεγειν η λεξις, διοτι εν τινι δεσμῳ εσμεν τῳ σωματι · τουτο γαρ δηλον εστι, καὶ ουκ αν τουτο απορρητον ελεγε, αλλ᾽ οτι ου δει εξαγαγειν ημας εαυτους ως του σωματος ημων διονυσιακου οντος· μερος γαρ αυτου εσμεν, ειγε εκ της αιθαλης των τιτανων συγκειμεθα γευσαμενων των σαρκων τουτου. Ο μεν ουν Σωκρατης εργῳ το απορρητον δεικνυς, του μυθου ουδεν πλεον προστιθησι του ως εν τινι φρουρα εσμεν. Οι δε εξηγηται τον μυθον προστιθεασιν εξωθεν. After this he beautifully observes, "that these four governments obscurely signify the different gradations of virtues, according to which our soul contains the symbols of all the virtues, both theoretical and cathartical, political and ethical; for it either energizes according to the theoretic virtues, the paradigm of which is the government of *heaven,* that we may begin from on high; and on this account heaven receives its denomination παρα του τα ανω οραν, from beholding the things above:—or it lives cathartically, the exemplar of which is the Saturnian kingdom; and on this account Saturn is denominated, from being a pure intellect, through a survey of himself; and hence he is said to devour his own offspring, signifying the conversion of himself to himself:— or it energizes according to the politic virtues, the symbol of which is the government of Jupiter; and hence Jupiter is the Demiurgus, so called from operating about secondary natures:— or the soul energizes according to both the ethical and physical virtues, the symbol of which is the kingdom of Bacchus; and on this account he is fabled to be torn in pieces by the Titans, because the virtues do not follow but are separated from each other." Αινυττονται (lege αινιττονται) δε τους διαφερους βαθμους των αρετων καθ᾽ ας η ημετερα ψυχη συμβολα εχουσα πασων των αρετων, των τε θεωρητικων, καὶ καθαρτικων, καὶ πολιτικων, καὶ ηθικων. Η γαρ κατα τας θεωρητικας ενεργει ων παραδειγμα η του ουρανου βασιλεια, ινα ανωθεν αρξαμεθα, διο καὶ ουρανος

ειρηται παρα του τα ανω οραν. Η καθαρτικως ζη, ης παραδειγμα
η κρονεια βασιλεια, διο και κρονος ειρηται οιον ο κορονους τις
ων δια το εαυτον οραν. Διο και καταπινειν τα οικεια γεννηματα
λεγεται, ως αυτος προς εαυτον επιστρεφων. Η κατα τας πολιτικας
ων συμβολον η του διος βασιλεια, διο και δημιουργος ο Ζευς,
ως περι τα δευτερα ενεργων. Η κατα τας ηθικας και φυσικας
αρετας, ων συμβολον, η του Διονυσου βασιλεια, διο και σπαραττεται, διοτι ουκ αντακολουθουσιν αλληλαις αι αρεται. And thus
far Olympiodorus; in which passages it is necessary to observe,
that as the Titans are the ultimate artificers of things, and the most
proximate to their fabrications, men are said to be composed from
their fragments, because the human soul has a partial life capable
of proceeding to the most extreme division united with its proper
nature. And while the soul is in a state of servitude to the body,
she lives confined, as it were, in bonds, through the dominion of
this Titanical life. We may observe farther concerning these
shews of the lesser mysteries, that as they were intended to represent the condition of the soul while subservient to the body,
we shall find that a liberation from this servitude, through the
cathartic virtues, was what the wisdom of the antients intended
to signify by the descent of Hercules, Ulysses, &c., into Hades,
and their speedy return from its dark abodes. "Hence," says
Proclus in Plat. Polit. p. 382, "Hercules being purified by *sacred
initiations*, and enjoying undefiled fruits, obtained at length a
perfect establishment among the gods": that is, well knowing the
dreadful condition of his soul while in captivity to a corporeal
nature, and purifying himself according to the cathartic virtues, of
which certain purifications in the mystic ceremonies were symbolic, he at length fled from the bondage of matter, and ascended
beyond the reach of her hands. On this account, it is said of
him, that

He dragg'd the three-mouth'd dog to upper day;

intimating that by temperance, continence, and the other virtues,
he drew upwards the intellective, cogitative, and opinionative
part of the soul. And as to Theseus, who is represented as suffer-

ing eternal punishment in Hades, we must consider him too as an allegorical character, of which Proclus, in the above-cited admirable work, p. 384, gives the following beautiful explanation: "Theseus and Pirithous," says he, "are fabled to have ravished Helen, and descended to the infernal regions, *i.e.* were lovers both of intelligible and visible beauty; afterwards one of these (Theseus) on account of his magnanimity, was liberated by Hercules from Hades; but the other (Pirithous) remained there, because he could not sustain the arduous altitude of divine contemplation." This account, indeed, of Theseus can by no means be reconciled with Virgil's:

> . . . *sedet, aeternumque sedebit,*
> *Infelix Theseus.*

Nor do I see how Virgil can be reconciled with himself, who, a little before this, represents him as liberated from Hades. The conjecture therefore of Hyginus is most probable, that Virgil in this particular committed an oversight, which, had he lived, he would doubtless have detected, and amended. This is at least much more probable than the opinion of Dr. Warburton, that Theseus was a living character, who once entered into the Eleusinian mysteries by force, for which he was imprisoned upon earth, and afterwards damned in the infernal realms. For if this was the case, why is not Hercules also represented as in punishment? and this with much greater reason, since he actually dragged Cerberus from Hades; whereas the fabulous descent of Theseus was attended with no real, but only intentional, mischief—Not to mention that Virgil appears to be the only writer of antiquity who condemns this hero to an eternity of pain.

Nor is the secret meaning of the fables concerning the punishment of impure souls less beautiful and profound, as the following extract from the manuscript commentary of Olympiodorus on the Gorgias of Plato will abundantly affirm:—"Ulysses," says he, "descending into Hades, saw, among others, Sysiphus, and Titius, and Tantalus: and Titius he saw lying on the earth, and a vulture devouring his liver; the liver signifying that he lived solely according to the desiderative part of his nature, and through this was indeed internally prudent; but earth signifying the terrestrial condition of his prudence. But Sysiphus, living under the dominion of ambition and anger, was employed in continually rolling a stone up an eminence, because it perpetually descended again; its descent implying the vicious government of himself; and his rolling the stone, the hard, refractory, and, as it were, rebounding condition of his life. And, lastly, he saw Tantalus extended by the side of a lake, and that there was a tree before him, with abundance of fruit on its branches, which he desired to gather, but it vanished from his view; and this indeed indicates, that he lived under the dominion of the phantasy; but his hanging over the lake, and in vain attempting to drink, implies the elusive, humid, and rapidly-gliding condition of such a life."

Ο Οδυσσευς κατελθων εις αδου, ειδε τον Συσιφον, και τον Τιτυον, και τον Τανταλον. Και τον μεν Τιτυον, επι της γης ειδε κειμενον, και οτι το ηπαρ αυτου ησθιειν γυψ. Το μεν ουν ηπαρ σημαινει οτι κατα το επιθυμητικον μερος εζησε, και δια τουτο εσω φροντιζετο. Η δε γη σημαινει το χθονιον αυτου φρονημα. Ο δε Σισυφος, κατα το φιλοτιμον, και θυμοειδες ζησας εκυλιε τον λιθον, και παλιν κατεφερεν, επειδε περι αυτα καταρρει, ο κακως πολιτευομενος. Λιθον δε εκυλιε, δια το σκληρον, και αντιτυπον της αυτου ζωης. Τον δε Τανταλον ειδεν εν λιμν (lege λιμνη) και οτι εν δενδροις ησαν οπωραι, και ηθελε τρυγαν, και αφανεις εγινοντο αι οπωραι. Τουτο δε σημαινει την κατα φαντασιαν ζωην. Αυτη δε σημαινει το ολισθηρον, και διυγρον, και θαττον αποπανομενον. So that according to the wisdom of the antients, and the most sublime philosophy, the misery which a soul endures in the present life, when giving itself up to the dominion of the irrational part, is nothing more than the commencement, as it were, of that torment which it will experience hereafter: a torment the same in kind though different in degree, as it will be much more dreadful, vehement, and extended. And by the above specimen, the reader may perceive how infinitely superior the explanation which the Platonic philosophy affords of these fables is to the frigid and trifling interpretations of Bacon and other modern mythologists; who are able indeed to point out their correspondence to something in the natural or moral world, because such is the wonderful connection of things, that all things sympathize with all, but are at the same time ignorant that these fables were composed by men divinely wise, who framed them after the model of the highest originals, from the contemplation of real and permanent being, and not from regarding the delusive and fluctuating objects of sense. This, indeed, will be evident to every ingenuous mind, from reflecting that these wise men universally considered Hades as commencing in the present life, (as we have already abundantly proved,) and that, consequently, sense is nothing more than the energy of the dormant soul, and a perception, as it were, of the delusions of dreams. In consequence of this, it is absurd in the highest degree to imagine that such men would compose fables from the contemplation of shadows only, without regarding the splendid originals from which these dark phantoms were produced:—not to mention that their harmonizing so much more perfectly with intellectual explications is an indisputable proof that they were derived from an intellectual source.

And thus much for the shews of the lesser mysteries, or the first part of these sacred institutions, which was properly denominated τελετη and μνησις, as containing certain perfective rites and appearances, and the tradition of sacred doctrines, previously necessary to the inspection of the most splendid visions, or εποπτεια. For thus the gradation of the mysteries is disposed by Proclus in Theol. Plat. lib. 4. p. 220. "The *perfective part*," says he, "precedes *initiation*, and *initiation* precedes *inspection*." Προηγειται γαρ, η μεν τελετη της μνησεως, αυτη δε της εποπτειας. At the same time it is proper to observe, that the whole business of initiation was distributed into five parts, as we are informed by Theo of Smyrna, in Mathemat. p. 18, who thus elegantly compares philosophy to these mystic rites: "Again," says he, "philosophy may be called the initiation into true sacred ceremonies, and the tradition of genuine mysteries; for there are five parts of initiation: the first of which is previous purgation;

for neither are the mysteries communicated to all who are willing to receive them; but there are certain characters who are prevented by the voice of the cryer, such as those who possess impure hands and an inarticulate voice; since it is necessary that such as are not expelled from the mysteries should first be refined by certain purgations: but after purgation, the tradition of the sacred rites succeeds. The third part is denominated inspection. And the fourth, which is the end and design of inspection, is the binding of the head and fixing the crowns; so that the initiated may, by this means, be enabled to communicate to others the sacred rites in which he has been instructed; whether after this he becomes a torch bearer, or an interpreter of the mysteries, or sustains some other part of the sacerdotal office. But the fifth, which is produced from all these, is friendship with divinity, and the enjoyment of that felicity which arises from intimate converse with the gods. Similar to this is the tradition of political reasons; for, in the first place, a certain purgation precedes, or an exercise in convenient mathematical disciplines from early youth. For thus Empedocles asserts, that it is necessary to be purified from sordid concerns, by drawing from five fountains, with a vessel of indissoluble brass: but Plato, that purification is to be derived from the five mathematical disciplines, viz. from arithmetic, geometry, stereometry, music, and astronomy; but the philosophical tradition of theorems, logical, political, and physical, is similar to initiation. But he (that is, Plato,) denominates εποπτεια, or inspection, an occupation about intelligibles, true beings, and ideas. But he considers the binding of the head, and coronation, as analogous to the power which any one receives from his instructors, of leading others to the same contemplation. And the fifth gradation is the most perfect felicity arising from hence, and, according to Plato, an assimilation to divinity, as far as is possible to mankind." But though εποπτεια, or inspection, principally characterized the greater mysteries, yet this was likewise accompanied with μυησις, or initiation, as will be evident in the course of this inquiry.

But let us now proceed to the doctrine of the greater mysteries:

and here I shall endeavour to prove, that as the shews of the lesser mysteries occultly signified the miseries of the soul while in subjection to body, so those of the greater obscurely intimated, by mystic and splendid visions, the felicity of the soul both here and hereafter, when purified from the defilements of a material nature, and constantly elevated to the realities of intellectual vision. Hence, as the ultimate design of the mysteries, according to Plato, was to lead us back to the principles from which we descended, that is, to a perfect enjoyment of intellectual good, the tradition of these principles was doubtless one part of the doctrine contained in the *απορρητα*, or secret discourses; and the different purifications exhibited in these rites, in conjunction with initiation and inspection, were symbols of the gradation of virtues requisite to this reascent of the soul. And hence too, if this be the case, a representation of the descent of the soul must certainly form no inconsiderable part of these mystic shews; all which the following observations will, I doubt not, abundantly evince.

In the first place, then, that the shews of the greater mysteries occultly signified the felicity of the soul both here and hereafter, when separated from the contagion of body, is evident from what has been demonstrated in the former part of this discourse: for if he who in the present life is in subjection to his irrational part is truly in Hades, he who is superior to its dominion is likewise an inhabitant of a place totally different from Hades. If Hades therefore is the region of punishment and misery, the purified soul must reside in the regions of bliss; cathartically, indeed, and theoretically, in the present life, and *ενθεαστικως*, or according to a deific energy, in the next. This being admitted, let us proceed to consider the description which Virgil gives us of these fortunate abodes, and the latent signification which it contains. Aeneas and his guide, then, having passed through Hades, and seen Tartarus, or the utmost profundity of a material nature, at a distance, advance to the Elysian fields.

Devenere locos laetos, et amoena vireta
Fortunatorum nemorum, sedesque beatas.
Largior hic campos aether et lumine vestit
Purpureo; solemque suum, sua sidera norunt.

[... *they took their Way,*
Where long extended Plains of Pleasure lay.
The verdant Fields with those of Heav'n may vye;
With Aether *vested, and a Purple Sky:*
The blissful Seats of Happy Souls below:
Stars of their own, and their own Suns they know.
VI. 867–72]

Now the secret meaning of these joyful places is thus beautifully
unfolded by Olympiodorus in his MS. Commentary on the
Gorgias of Plato. "It is necessary to know," says he, "that the
fortunate islands are said to be raised above the sea; and hence
a condition of being transcending this corporeal life and generation is denominated the islands of the blessed; but these are
the same with the Elysian fields. And on this account Hercules
is reported to have accomplished his last labour in the Hesperian
regions; signifying by this, that having vanquished an obscure
and terrestrial life, he afterwards lived in open day, that is, in
truth and resplendent light." Δει δε ειδεναι οτι αι νησοι υπερ-
κυπτουσι της θαλασσης ανωτερω ουσαι. Την ουν πολιτειαν την
υπερκυψασαν του βιου και της γενησεως, μακαρων νησους
καλουσι. Ταυτον δε εστι και το Ηλυσιον πεδιον. Δια τοι τουτο
και ο Ηρακλης τελευταιον αθλον εν τοις Εσπεριοις μερεσιν
εποιησατο, αντι κατηγωνισατο τον σκοτεινον και χθονιον βιον,
και λοιπον εν ημερα, ο εστιν εν αληθεια και φωτι εζη. So that
he who in the present state vanquishes as much as possible a
corporeal life, through the exercise of the cathartic virtues, passes
in reality into the fortunate islands of the soul, and lives surrounded with the bright splendours of truth and wisdom proceeding from the sun of good.

But when the poet, in describing the employments of the blessed, says,

> *Pars in gramineis exercent membra palaestris;*
> *Contendunt ludo, et fulva luctantur arena:*
> *Pars pedibus plaudunt choreas, et carmina dicunt.*
> *Nec non Threicius longa cum veste sacerdos*
> *Obloquitur numeris septem discrimina vocum:*
> *Iamque eadem digitis, jam pectine pulsat eburno.*
> *Hic genus antiquum Teucri, pulcherrima proles,*
> *Magnanimi heroes, nati melioribus annis,*
> *Ilusque, Assaracusque, et Trojae Dardanus auctor.*
> *Arma procul, currusque virum miratur inanis.*
> *Stant terra defixae hastae, passimque soluti*
> *Per campum pascuntur equi. Quae gratia curruum*
> *Armorumque fuit vivis, quae cura nitentis*
> *Pascere equos, eadem sequitur tellure repostos.*
> *Conspicit, ecce alios, dextra laevaque per herbam*
> *Vescentis, laetumque choro Paeana canentis,*
> *Inter odoratum lauri nemus: unde superne*
> *Plurimus Eridani per silvam volvitur amnis.*

[Their Airy Limbs in Sports they exercise,
And, on the Green, contend the Wrestler's Prize.
Some, in Heroick Verse, divinely sing;
Others in artful Measures lead the ring.
The Thracian *Bard, surrounded by the rest,*
There stands conspicuous in his flowing Vest.
His flying Fingers, and harmonious Quill,
Strike sev'n distinguish'd Notes, and sev'n at once they fill.
Here found they Teucer's *old Heroick Race;*
Born better times and happier Years to grace.
Assaracus *and* Ilus *here enjoy*
Perpetual Fame, with him who founded Troy.
The Chief beheld their Chariots from afar;
Their shining Arms, and Coursers train'd to War:
Their Lances fix'd in Earth, their Steeds around,

Free from their Harness, graze the flow'ry Ground.
The love of Horses which they had, alive,
And care of Chariots, after Death survive.
Some chearful Souls, were feasting on the Plain;
Some did the Song, and some their Choir maintain:
Beneath a Laurel Shade, where mighty Po
Mounts up to Woods above, and hides his Head below.

VI. 873–94]

This must not be understood as if the soul in the regions of felicity retained any affection for material concerns, or was engaged in the trifling pursuits of a corporeal life; but that when separated from generation, she is constantly engaged in intellectual employments; either in exercising the divine contests of the most exalted wisdom; in forming the responsive dance of refined imaginations; in tuning the sacred lyre of mystic piety to strains of deific fury and ineffable delight; in giving free scope to the splendid and winged powers of the soul; or in nourishing the intellect with the substantial banquets of intelligible food. Nor is it without reason that the river Eridanus is represented as flowing through these delightful abodes; and is at the same time denominated *plurimus*, because a great part of it was absorbed in the earth without emerging from thence: for a river is the symbol of life, and consequently signifies in this place the nature of an intellectual life, proceeding from on high, that is, from divinity itself, and gliding with prolific energy through the occult and profound recesses of the soul.

But when, in the following lines, he says,

Nulli certa domus. Lucis habitamus opacis,
Riparumque toros, et prata recentia rivis
Incolimus. . . ,

[*In no fix'd place the Happy Souls reside.*
In Groves we live; and lye on mossy Beds
By Crystal Streams, that murmur through the Meads. . . ,

VI. 913–15]

371

by the blessed being confined to no particular habitation, the liberal condition of their existence is plainly implied; since they are entirely free from all material restraint, and purified from all inclination to the dark and cold tenement of body. The shady groves are symbols of the soul's retiring to the depth of her essence, and there, by a divinely solitary energy, establishing herself in the ineffable principle of things. And the meadows are symbols of that prolific power of the gods through which all the variety of reasons, animals, and forms was produced, and which is here the refreshing pasture and retreat of the liberated soul.

But that the tradition of the principles from which the soul descended formed a part of the sacred mysteries is evident from Virgil; and that this was accompanied with a vision of these principles or gods, is no less certain, from the testimony of Plato, Apuleius, and Proclus. The first part of this assertion is evinced by the following beautiful lines:

Principio caelum ac terras, camposque liquentes
Lucentemque globum lunae, Titaniaque astra
Spiritus intus alit, totamque infusa per artus
Mens agitat molem, et magno se corpore miscet.
Inde hominum pecudumque genus, vitaeque volantum,
Et quae marmoreo fert monstra sub aequore pontus.
Igneus est ollis vigor, et caelestis origo
Seminibus, quantum non noxia corpora tardant,
Terrienique hebetant artus, moribundaque membra.
Hinc metuunt cupiuntque: dolent, gaudentque: neque auras
Despiciunt clausae tenebris et carcere caeco.

> [*Know first, that Heav'n, and Earth's compacted Frame,*
> *And flowing Waters, and the starry Flame,*
> *And both the Radiant Lights, one Common Soul*
> *Inspires, and feeds, and animates the whole.*
> *This Active Mind infus'd through all the Space,*
> *Unites and mingles with the mighty Mass.*
> *Hence Men and Beasts the Breath of Life obtain;*

And Birds of Air, and Monsters of the Main.
Th' Etherial Vigour is in all the same,
And every soul is fill'd with equal Flame:
As much as Earthy Limbs, and gross allay
Of Mortal Members, subject to decay,
Blunt not the Beams of Heav'n and edge of Day.
From this course Mixture of Terrestrial parts,
Desire, and Fear, by turns possess their Hearts:
And Grief, and Joy: Nor can the groveling Mind,
In the dark Dungeon of the Limbs confin'd,
Assert the Native Skies; or own its heav'nly Kind.

VI. 980–97]

For the sources of the soul's existence are also the principles from which it fell; and these, as we may learn from the Timaeus of Plato, are Jupiter, or the Demiurgus, the mundane soul, and the junior or mundane gods.—Now, of these, the mundane intellect, which, according to the antient theology, is Bacchus, is principally celebrated by the poet, and this because the soul is particularly distributed into generation Dionysiacally, as is evident from the preceding extracts from Olympiodorus; and is still more abundantly confirmed by the following curious passage from the same author, in his comment on the Phaedo of Plato. "The soul," says he, "descends Corically, or after the manner of Proserpine, into generation, but is distributed into generation Dionysiacally; and she is bound in body Prometheiacally and Titanically: she frees herself therefore from its bonds by exercising the strength of Hercules; but she is collected into one through the assistance of Apollo and the saviour Minerva, by philosophizing in a manner truly cathartic." Οτι κορικως μεν εις γενεσιν κατεισιν η ψυχη. Διονυσιακως δε μεριζεται υπο της γενεσεως. Προμηθειως δε, και τιτανικως, εγκαταδειται τω σωματι. Λυει μεν ουν εαυτην ηρακλειως ισχυσασα. Συναιρει δε δι Απολλωνος και της σωτηρας αθηνας, καθαρτικως τω οντι φιλοσοφουσα.

The poet, however, intimates the other causes of the soul's existence, when he says,

Igneus est ollis vigor, et caelestis origo
Seminibus . . . ,

which evidently alludes to the *sowing* of souls into generation, mention in the Timaeus. And from hence the reader will easily perceive the extreme ridiculousness of Dr. Warburton's system, that the grand secret of the mysteries consisted in exposing the errors of Polytheism, and in teaching the doctrine of the unity, or the existence of one deity alone. For he might as well have said, that the great secret consisted in teaching a man how, by writing notes on the works of a poet, he might become a *bishop!* But it is by no means wonderful that men who have not the smallest conception of the true nature of the gods; who have persuaded themselves that they were only dead men deified; and who measure the understandings of the antients by their own, should be led to fabricate a system so improbable and absurd. Indeed the sophistry throughout his whole treatise is perpetual, and every where exhibits to our view the leading features of a Christian priest in complete perfection; I mean consummate arrogance united with a profound ignorance of antient wisdom and blended with matchless hypocrisy and fraud. For, indeed, from the earliest of the fathers down to the most modern and vile plebeian teacher among the Methodists, the same character displays itself and is alike productive of the same deplorable mischief to the real welfare of mankind. But it is necessary that impiety should sometimes prevail on the earth; though at the same time, it is no less necessary that its consequent maladies should be lamented and strenuously resisted by every genuine lover of virtue and truth.

But that this tradition was accompanied with a vision of the causes from which the soul descended is evident from the express testimony, in the first place, of Apuleius, who thus describes his initiation into the mysteries. "Accessi confinium mortis; et calcato Proserpinae limine, per omnia vectus elementa remeavi. Nocte media vidi solem candido coruscantem lumine, *deos inferos, et deos superos.* Accessi coram, et adoravi de proximo."[3] That is,

---

[3] Apul. Metamorph. lib. 11. prope finem.

"I approached the confines of death; and treading on the threshold of Proserpine, and being carried through all the elements, I came back again to my pristine situation. In the depths of midnight I saw the sun glittering with a splendid light, *together with the infernal and supernal gods*: and to these divinities approaching near, I paid the tribute of devout adoration." And this is no less evidently implied by Plato in the Phaedrus, who thus describes the felicity of the virtuous soul prior to its descent, in a beautiful allusion to the arcane visions of the mysteries.
Καλλος δε τοτε ην ιδειν λαμπρον, οτε συν ευδαιμονι χορω μακαριαν οψιν τε και θεαν επομενοι μετα μεν Διος ημεις, αλλοι δε μετ'αλλου θεων, ειδον τε και ετελουντο τελετων ην θεμις λεγειν μακαριωτατην· ην οργιαζομεν ολοκληροι μεν αυτοι οντες, και απαθεις κακων οσα ημας εν υστερω χρονω υπεμενεν. Ολοκληρα δε και απλα και ατρεμη και ευδαιμονα φασματα μυουμενοι τε και εποπτευοντες εν αυγη καθαρα καθαροι οντες και ασημαντοι τουτου ο νυν δη σωμα περιφεροντες ονομαζομεν οστρεου τροπον δεδεσμευμενοι. That is, "But it was then lawful to survey the most splendid beauty, when we obtained, together with that blessed choir, this happy vision and contemplation. And we indeed enjoyed this blessed spectacle together with Jupiter; but others in conjunction with some other god; at the same time being *initiated* in those *mysteries*, which it is lawful to call the most blessed of all mysteries. And these divine *Orgies* were celebrated by us, while we possessed the proper integrity of our nature, and were freed from the molestations of evil which awaited us in a succeeding period of time. Likewise, in consequence of this divine *initiation*, we became *spectators* of entire, simple, immoveable, and *blessed visions*, resident in a pure light; and were ourselves pure and immaculate, and liberated from this surrounding vestment, which we denominate body, and to which we are now bound like an oyster to its shell." Upon this beautiful passage Proclus observes, in Theol. Plat. lib. 4. p. 193, that "*initiation* and *inspection* are symbols of ineffable silence, and of union with mystical natures, through intelligible visions."
Και γαρ η μυησις, και η εποπτεια, της αρρητου σιγης εστι συμβολον, και της προς τα μυστικα δια των νοητων φασματων

375

ενωσεως. Now, from all this, it may be inferred, that the most sublime part of εποπτεια or *inspection* consisted in beholding the gods themselves invested with a resplendent light; and that this was symbolical of those transporting visions, which the virtuous soul will constantly enjoy in a future state; and of which it is able to gain some ravishing glimpses, even while connected with the cumbrous vestment of body.

But that this was actually the case, is evident from the following unequivocal testimony of Proclus in Plat. Repub. p. 380. Εν απασι ταις τελεταις και τοις μυστηριοις, οι θεοι πολλας μεν εαυτων προτεινουσι μορφας, πολλα δε σχηματα εξαλλαττοντες φαινονται· και τοτε μεν ατυπωτον αυτων προβεβληται φως, τοτε δε εις ανθρωπειον μορφην εσχηματισμενον, τοτε δε εις αλλοιον τυπον προεληλυθως. *I.e.* "In all initiations and mysteries, the gods exhibit many forms of themselves, and appear in a variety of shapes: and sometimes, indeed, an unfigured light of themselves is held forth to the view; sometimes this light is figured according to a human form, and sometimes it proceeds into a different shape." This doctrine, too, of divine appearances in the mysteries, is clearly confirmed by Plotinus, Ennead. 1. lib. 6. p. 55, and Ennead. 9. lib. 9. p. 700. And, in short, that magical evocation formed a part of the sacerdotal office in the mysteries, and that this was universally believed by all antiquity, long before the aera of the latter Platonists, is plain from the testimony of Hippocrates, or at least Democritus, in his Treatise de Morbo Sacro. p. 86, fol. For speaking of those who attempt to cure this disease by magic, he observes: ει γαρ σεληνην τε καθαιρειν, και ηλιον αφανιζειν, χειμωνα τε και ευδιην ποιειν, και ομβρους και αυχμους, και θαλασσαν αφονον και γην, και τ'αλλα τα τοιουτο τροπα παντα επιδεχονται επιστασθαι, ειτε και εκ ΤΕΛΕΤΩΝ, ειτε και εξ αλλης τινος γνωμης η μελετης φασιν οιοι τε ειναι οι ταυτα επιτηδευοντες δυσεβεειν εμοι γε δοκεουσι. κ. λ. *I.e.* "For if they profess themselves able to draw down the moon, to obscure the sun, to produce stormy and pleasant weather, as likewise showers of rain, and heats, and to render the sea and the earth barren, and to accomplish every thing else of this kind;

whether they derive this knowledge from *the Mysteries*, or from some other institution or meditation, they appear to me to be impious, from the study of such concerns." From all which it is easy to see how egregiously Dr. Warburton was mistaken when, in p. 231 of his Divine Legation, he asserts that "the light beheld in the mysteries was nothing more than an illuminated image which the priests had thoroughly purified."

But he is likewise no less mistaken in transferring the injunction, given in one of the magic oracles of Zoroaster, to the business of the Eleusinian mysteries, and in perverting the meaning of the Oracle's admonition. For thus the Oracle speaks:

Μη φυσεως καλεσης αυτοπτον αγαλμα,

Ου γαρ χρη κεινους σε βλεπειν πριν σωμα τελεσθη.

That is, "Invoke not *the self-conspicuous image of Nature*, for you must not behold these things before your body has received the purification necessary to initiation."—Upon which he observes that *the self-conspicuous image was only a diffusive shining light, as the name partly declares.*[4] But this is a piece of gross ignorance, from which he might have been freed by an attentive perusal of Proclus on the Timaeus of Plato: for in these truly divine Commentaries we learn that "the moon is the cause of nature to mortals, *and the self-conspicuous image of fontal nature.*" Σεληνη μεν αιτια τοις θνητοις της φυσεως, το αυτοπτον αγαλμα ουσα της πηγαιας φυσεως (in Tim. p. 260). If the reader is desirous of knowing what we are to understand by the fontal nature of which the moon is the image, let him attend to the following information, derived from a long and deep study of the antient theology: for from hence I have learned, that there are many divine fountains contained in the essence of the Demiurgus of the world; and that among these there are three of a very distinguished rank, viz. the fountain of souls, or Juno, the fountain of virtues, or Minerva, and the fountain of nature, or Diana. This last fountain too immediately depends on the vivific goddess Rhea; and was assumed by the Demiurgus

[4] Divine Legation, p. 231.

among the rest, as necessary to the prolific production of himself. And this information will enable us besides to explain the meaning of the following passages in Apuleius, which, from not being understood, have induced the moderns to believe that Apuleius acknowledged but one deity alone. The first of these passages is in the beginning of the eleventh book of his Metamorphosis, in which the divinity of the moon is represented as addressing him in this sublime manner: En adsum tuis commota, Luci, precibus, rerum Natura parens, elementorum omnium domina, seculorum progenies initialis, summa numinum, regina Manium, prima caelitum, Deorum Dearumque facies uniformis: quae caeli luminosa culmina, maris salubria flamina, inferorum deplorata silentia nutibus meis dispenso: cujus numen unicum, multiformi specie, ritu vario, nomine multijugo totus veneratur orbis. Me primigenii Phryges Pessinunticam nominant Deûm matrem. Hinc Autochthones Attici Cecropiam Minervam; illinc fluctuantes Cyprii Paphiam Venerem: Cretes sagittiferi Dictynnam Dianam; Siculi trilingues Stygiam Proserpinam; Eleusinii vetustam Deam Cererem: Junonem alii, alii Bellonam, alii Hecaten, Rhamnusiam alii. Et qui nascentis dei Solis inchoantibus radiis illustrantur, Aethiopes, Arriique, priscaque doctrina pollentes Aegyptii caerimoniis me prorsus propriis percolentes appellant vero nomine reginam Isidem. That is, "Behold, Lucius, moved with thy supplications, I am present; I, who am *Nature*, the parent of things, queen of all the elements, initial progenitor of ages, the greatest of divinities, queen of departed spirits, the first of the celestials, and the uniform appearance of gods and goddesses: who rule by my nod the luminous heights of the heavens, the salubrious breezes of the sea, and the deplorable silences of the infernal regions; and whose divinity, in itself but one, is venerated by all the earth, according to a multiform shape, various rites, and different appellations.—Hence the primitive Phrygians call me Pessinuntica, the mother of the gods; the native Athenians, Cecropian Minerva; the floating Cyprians, Paphian Venus; the arrow-bearing Cretans, Dictynnian Diana; the three-tongued Sicilians, Stygian Proserpine; and the inhabitants of Eleusis, the antient goddess Ceres. Some again have invoked me as Juno, others as Bellona, others as Hecate, and others as Rhamnusia: and those who are enlightened by the emerging rays of the rising sun, the Aethiopians, Ariians, and Aegyptians, powerful in antient learning, who reverence my divinity with ceremonies perfectly proper, call me by a true appellation queen Isis." And, again, in another place of the same book, he says of the moon: "Te Superi colunt, observant Inferi: tu rotas orbem, luminas Solem, regis mundum, calcas Tartarum. Tibi respondent sidera, gaudent numina, redeunt tempora, serviunt elementa, &c." That is, "The supernal gods reverence thee, and those in the realms beneath attentively observe thy nod. Thou rollest the heavens round the steady poles, dost illuminate the sun, govern the world, and tread on the dark realms of Tartarus. The stars move responsive to thy command, the gods rejoice in thy divinity, the hours and seasons return by thy appointment, and the elements reverence thy decree." For all this easily follows, if we consider it as addressed to the fontal deity of nature, subsisting in the Demiurgus, and which is the exemplar of that nature which flourishes in the lunar orb, and throughout the material world, and from which the deity itself of the moon originally proceeds. Hence, as this fountain immediately depends on the vivific goddess Rhea, the reason is obvious why it was formerly worshipped as the mother of the gods: and as all the mundane are contained in the super-mundane gods, the other appellations are to be considered as names of the several mundane divinities produced by this fountain, and in whose essence they are likewise contained.

But to proceed with our inquiry, I shall, in the next place, prove that the different purifications exhibited in these rites, in conjunction with initiation and inspection, were symbols of the gradation of virtues requisite to the reascent of the soul. And the first part, indeed, of this proposition respecting the purifications immediately follows from the testimony of Plato in the passage already adduced, in which he asserts, that the ultimate design of the mysteries was to lead us back to the principles from which we originally fell. For if the mysteries were symbolical, as is universally acknowledged, this must likewise be true of the purifications as a part of the mysteries; and as inward purity, of which the external is symbolical, can only be obtained by the exercise of the virtues, it evidently follows, that the purifications were symbols of the purifying moral virtues. And the latter part of the proposition may be easily inferred from the passage already cited from the Phaedrus of Plato, in which he compares *initiation* and *inspection* to the blessed vision of intelligible natures; an employment which can alone belong to the energies of contemplative virtue. But the whole of this is rendered indisputable by the following remarkable testimony of Olympiodorus, in his excellent MS. Commentary on the Phaedo of Plato. "In the sacred rites," says he, "popular purifications are in the first place brought forth, and after these such as are more arcane. But in the third place, collections of various things into one are received; after which follows inspection. The ethical and political virtues therefore are analogous to the apparent (or popular) purifications. But such of the cathartic virtues as banish all external impressions correspond to the more occult purifications. The theoretical energies about intelligibles are analogous to the collections; but the contraction of these energies into an indivisible nature corresponds to initiation. And the simple self-inspection of simple forms is analogous to epoptic vision." Οτι εν τοις ιεροις ηγουντο μεν αι πανδημοι καθαρσεις. Ειτα επι ταυταις απορρητοτεραι· μετα δε ταυτας συστασεις παρελαμβανοντο, καὶ επι ταυταις μυησεις· εν τελει δε εποπτειαι. Αναλογουσι τοινυν αι μεν ηθικαι καὶ πολιτικαι αρεται, τοις εμφανεσι καθαρμοις. Αι δε καθαρτικαι οσαι αποσκευαζονται παντα τα εκτος τοις απορρητοτεροις. Αι δε περι τα νοητα θεωρητικαι τε ενεργειαι ταις συστασεσιν. Αι δε τουτων συναιρεσεις εις το αμεριστον ταις μυησεσιν. Αι δε απλαι των απλων ειδων αυτοψιαι ταις εποπτιαις. And here I cannot refrain from noticing, with indignation mingled with pity, the ignorance and arrogance of modern critics, who pretend that this distribution of the virtues is entirely the invention of the latter Platonists, and without any foundation in the writings of Plato. And among the supporters of such ignorance, I am sorry to find Fabricius, in his prolegomena to the life of Proclus. For nothing can be more obvious to every reader of Plato than that in his Laws he treats of the political virtues; in his Phaedo, and seventh book of the Republic, of the cathartic; and in his Thaetetus, of the contemplative and sublimer virtues. This observation is indeed so obvious, in the Phaedo, with respect to the cathartic virtues, that no one but a verbal critic could read this dialogue and be insensible to its truth: for Socrates in the very beginning expressly asserts, that it is the business of philosophers to study to die, and to be themselves dead,[5] and yet at the same time reprobates suicide. What then can such a death mean but philosophical death? And what is this but the true exercise of the cathartic virtues? But these poor men read only superficially, or for the sake of displaying some critical *acumen* in verbal emendations; and yet with such despicable preparations for philosophical discussion, they have the *impudence* to oppose their puerile conceptions to the decisions of men of elevated genius and profound investigation, who, happily freed from the danger and drudgery of learning any foreign language, directed all their attention without restraint to the acquisition of the most exalted truth.

It only now remains that we prove, in the last place, that a representation of the descent of the soul formed no inconsiderable part of these mystic shews. This indeed is doubtless occultly insinuated by Virgil, when speaking of the souls of the blessed in Elysium, he adds,

> *Has omnes, ubi mille rotam volvêre per annos,*
> *Lethaeum ad fluvium deus evocat agmine magno:*
> *Scilicet immemores supera ut convexa revisant,*
> *Rursus et incipiant in corpora velle reverti.*

> [*But, when a Thousand rowling years are past,*
> (*So long their Punishments and Penance last;*)[6]

---

[5] Κινδυνευουσι γαρ οσοι τυγχανουσιν ορθως απτομενοι φιλοσοφιας λεληθεναι τους αλλους, οτι ουδεν αλλο αυτος επιτηδευουσιν η αποθνησκειν τε και τεθναναι. Plat. in Phaed.

[6] [Here Dryden has taken liberties with the text, inserting line 2 in order to give a basis for his own interpretation of the drinking of Lethe—

Whole Droves of Minds are, by the driving God,
Compell'd to drink the deep Lethaean Flood:
In large forgetful draughts to steep the Cares
Of their past Labours, and their Irksom Years.
That, unrememb'ring of its former Pain,
The Soul may suffer mortal Flesh again.   VI. 1015–20][6a]

But openly by Apuleius, in the following prayer which Psyche addresses to Ceres: Per ego te frugiferam tuam dextram istam deprecor, per laetificas messium caerimonias, per tacita sacra cistarum, et per famulorum tuorum draconum pinnata curricula, et glebae Siculae sulcamina, et currum rapacem, et terram tenacem, et illuminarum Proserpinae nuptiarum demeacula, et caetera, quae silentio tegit Eleusis, Atticae sacrarium; miserandae Psyches animae, supplicis tuae, subsiste. That is, "I beseech thee, by thy fruit-bearing right hand, by the joyful ceremonies of thy harvests, by the occult sacred concerns of thy cistae, and by the winged car of thy attending dragons, and the furrows of the Sicilian soil, and the rapacious chariot, *and the dark descending ceremonies attending the marriage of Proserpine, and the ascending rites which accompanied the luminous invention of thy daughter, and by other arcana which Eleusis the Attic sanctuary conceals in profound silence,* relieve the sorrows of thy wretched supplicant Psyche." For the rape of Proserpine signifies the descent of the soul, as is evident from the passage previously adduced from Olympiodorus, in which he says the soul descends Corically; and this is confirmed by the authority of the philosopher Sallust, who, in his book de Diis et Mundo, p. 251, observes that "the rape of Proserpine is fabled to have taken place about the opposite equinoctial; and by this the descent of souls is implied." Περι γουν την εναντιαν ισημεριαν η της Κορης αρπαγη μυθολογειται γενεσθαι, ο δη καθοδος εστι των ψυχων.

---

i.e. that it is a kindly draught of forgetfulness intended to obliterate the memory of suffering. Plato's meaning is exactly the opposite: the soul descending from an eternal to a temporal world forgets its divine nature.]

[6a] [See Plate 10.]

And as the rape of Proserpine was exhibited in the shews of the mysteries, as is clear from Apuleius, it indisputably follows, that this represented the descent of the soul, and its union with the dark tenement of body. Indeed if the ascent and descent of the soul, and its condition while connected with a material nature, were represented in the shews of the mysteries, it is evident that this was implied by the rape of Proserpine. And the former part of this assertion is manifest from Apuleius when, describing his initiation, he says, in the passage already adduced, "I approached the confines of death, and treading on the threshold of Proserpine, *and being carried through all the elements, I came back again to my pristine situation.*" And as to the latter part, it has been amply proved, from the highest authority, in the first division of this discourse.

Nor must the reader be disturbed on finding that, according to Porphyry, as cited by Eusebius,[7] the fable of Proserpine alludes to seed placed in the ground; for this is likewise true of the fable, considered according to its material explanation. But it will be proper on this occasion to rise a little higher, and consider the various species of fables, according to their philosophical distribution; since by this means the present subject will receive an additional elucidation, and the wisdom of the antient authors of fables will be vindicated from the unjust aspersions of ignorant declaimers. I shall present the reader, therefore, with the following interesting division of fables, from the elegant book of the Platonic philosopher Sallust, on the gods and the universe. "Of fables," says he, "some are theological, others physical, others animastic, (or relating to soul) others material, and lastly, others mixed from these.—Fables are theological which employ nothing corporeal, but speculate the very essences of the gods; such as the fable which asserts that Saturn devoured his children: for it insinuates nothing more than the nature of an intellectual god; since every intellect returns into itself. But we speculate fables physically when we speak concerning the energies of the gods about the world; as when considering Saturn the same as time, and calling the parts

[7] Eveng. Praeper. lib. 3. cap. 2.

of time the children of the universe, we assert that the children are devoured by their parent. But we employ fables in an animastic mode when we contemplate the energies of soul; because the intellections of our souls, though by a discursive energy they run into other things, yet abide in their parents. Lastly, fables are material, such as the Egyptians ignorantly employ, considering and calling corporeal natures divinities: such as Isis, earth, Osiris, humidity, Typhon, heat: or, again, denominating Saturn, water, Adonis, fruits, and Bacchus, wine. And, indeed, to assert that these are dedicated to the gods, in the same manner as herbs, stones, and animals, is the part of wise men; but to call them gods is alone the province of fools and mad men; unless we speak in the same manner as when, from established custom, we call the orb of the sun and its rays the sun itself. But we may perceive the mixed kind of fables, as well in many other particulars, as when they relate, that Discord, at a banquet of the gods, threw a golden apple, and that a dispute about it arising among the goddesses, they were sent by Jupiter to take the judgement of Paris, who, charmed with the beauty of Venus, gave her the apple in preference to the rest. For in this fable the banquet denotes the supermundane powers of the gods; and on this account they subsist in conjunction with each other: but the golden apple denotes the world, which, on account of its composition from contrary natures, is not improperly said to be thrown by Discord, or strife. But again, since different gifts are imparted to the world by different gods, they appear to contest with each other for the apple. And a soul living according to sense, (for this is Paris) not perceiving other powers in the universe, asserts that the apple is alone the beauty of Venus. But of these species of fables, such as are theological belong to philosophers; the physical and animastic to poets; *but the mixt to initiatory rites (τελεταῖς); since the intention of all mystic ceremonies is to conjoin us with the world and the gods.*"

Thus far the excellent Sallust: from whence it is evident, that the fable of Proserpine, as belonging to the mysteries, is properly of a mixed nature, or composed from all the four species of fables, the theological, physical, animastic, and material. But in order to understand this divine fable, it is requisite to know, that according to the arcana of the antient theology, the Coric order (or the order belonging to Proserpine) is twofold, one part of which is super-mundane, subsisting with Jupiter, or the Demiurgus, and together with him establishing one artificer of divisible natures: but the other is mundane, in which Proserpine is said to be ravished by Pluto, and to animate the extremities of the universe. "Hence," says Proclus, "according to the rumor of theologists, who delivered to us the most holy Eleusinian initiations, Proserpine abides on high in those dwellings of her mother which she prepared for her in inaccessible places, exempt from the sensible world. But she likewise dwells beneath with Pluto, administering terrestrial concerns, governing the recesses of the earth, supplying life to the extremities of the universe, and imparting soul to beings which are rendered by her inanimate and dead," Και γαρ η των θεολογων φημη, των τας αγιωτατας ημιν εν Ελευσινι τελετας παραδεδωκοτων, ανω, μεν αυτην εν τοις μητρος οικοις μενειν φησιν, ους η μητηρ αυτη κατεσκευαζεν εν αβατοις εξηρημενος του παντος. Κατω δε μετα Πλουτωνος των χθονιων επαρχειν, καὶ τους της γης μυχους επιτροπευειν, καὶ ζωην επορεγειν τοις εσχατοις του παντος, καὶ ψυχης μεταδιδοναι τοις παρ' εαυτων αψυχοις, καὶ νεκροις (Procl. in Theol. Plat. p. 371). Hence we may easily perceive that this fable is truly of the mixed kind, one part of which relates to the super-mundane establishment of the secondary cause of life, and the other to the procession of life and soul to the extremity of things. Let us therefore more attentively consider the fable, in that part of it which is symbolical of the descent of souls; in order to which, it will be requisite to premise an abridgement of the arcane discourse, respecting the wanderings of Ceres, as preserved by Minutius Felix. "Proserpine," says he, "the daughter of Ceres by Jupiter, as she was gathering tender flowers, in the new spring, was ravished from her delightful abodes by Pluto; and being carried from thence through thick woods, and over a length of sea, was brought by Pluto into a cavern, the residence of departed spirits, over whom she afterwards ruled with absolute sway. But Ceres, upon discovering the loss of her daughter, with lighted torches, and begirt with a serpent, wandered over the whole earth for the purpose of finding her till she came to Eleusina; there she found her daughter, and discovered to the Eleusinians the plantation of corn." Now in this fable *Ceres* represents the evolution of that self-inspective part of our nature which we properly denominate *intellect* (or its being unfolded from its quiet and collected subsistence in the intelligible world); and *Proserpine* that vital, self-moving, and animating part which we call *soul*. But lest this analogy of unfolded intellect to Ceres should seem ridiculous to the reader, unacquainted with the Orphic theology, it is necessary to inform him that this goddess, from her intimate union with Rhea, in conjunction with whom she produced Jupiter, is evidently of a Saturnian and zoogonic, or intellectual and vivific rank; and hence, as we are informed by the philosopher Sallust, among the mundane divinities she is the deity of the planet Saturn.[8] So that in consequence of this, our intellect in a descending state must aptly symbolize with the divinity of Ceres; but Pluto signifies the whole of a material nature; since the empire of this god, according to Pythagoras, commences downwards from the Galaxy or milky way. And the cavern signifies the entrance, as it were, into the profundities of such a nature, which is accomplished by the soul's union with this terrestrial body. But in order to understand perfectly the secret meaning of the other parts of this fable, it will be necessary to give a more explicit detail of the particulars attending the rape, from the beautiful poem of Claudian on this subject. From this elegant performance, therefore, we learn that Ceres, who was afraid lest some violence should be offered to Proserpine, on account of her inimitable beauty, conveyed her privately to Sicily, and concealed her in a house built on purpose by the Cyclops, while she herself directs her course to the temple of Cybele, the mother of the Gods. Here, then, we see the first cause of the soul's

---

[8] Hence we may perceive the reason why Ceres as well as Saturn was denominated a legislative deity; and why illuminations were used in the celebration of the Saturnalia, as well as in the Eleusinian mysteries.

descent, viz. her desertion of a life wholly according to intellect, which is occultly signified by the separation of Proserpine from Ceres. Afterwards, we are told that Jupiter instructs Venus to go to this abode, and betray Proserpine from her retirement, that Pluto may be enabled to carry her away; and to prevent any suspicion in the virgin's mind, he commands Diana and Pallas to bear her company. The three goddesses arriving find Proserpine at work on a scarf for her mother; in which she had embroidered the primitive chaos, and the formation of the world. Now by Venus in this part of the narration we must understand *desire*, which, even in the celestial regions, (for such is the residence of Proserpine till she is ravished by Pluto) begins silently and fraudulently to creep into the recesses of the soul. By Minerva we must conceive *the rational power of the soul*, and by Diana, *nature*, or the merely natural and vegetable part of our composition; both which are now ensnared through the allurements of desire. And lastly, the web in which Proserpine had displayed all the fair variety of the material world beautifully represents the commencement of the phantastic energies through which the soul becomes ensnared with the beauty of imaginative forms.— But let us for a while attend to the poet's elegant description of her employment and abode:

> *Devenere locum, Cereris quo tecta nitebant*
> *Cyclopum firmata manu. Stant ardua ferro*
> *Maenia; ferrati postes: immensaque nectit*
> *Claustra chalybs. Nullum tanto sudore Pyracmon,*
> *Nec Steropes, construxit opus: nec talibus unquam*
> *Spiravere notis animae: nec flumine tanto*
> *Incoctum maduit lassa fornace metallum.*
> *Atria vestit ebur: trabibus solidatur aenis*
> *Culmen, et in celsas surgunt electra columnas.*
> *Ipsa domum tenero mulcens Proserpina cantu*
> *Irrita texebat rediturae munera matri.*
> *Hic elementorum seriem sedesque paternas*
> *Insignibat acu: veterem qua lege tumultum*

Thomas Taylor the Platonist

Discrevit natura parens, et femina justis
Discessere locis: quidquid leve fertur in altum:
In medium graviora cadunt: incanduit aether:
Egit flamma polum: fluxit mare: terra pependit.
Nec color unus inest. Stellas accendit in auro,
Ostro fundit aquos, attolit litora gemmis,
Filaque mentitos jam jam caelantia fluctus
Arte tument. Credas illidi cautibus algam,
Et raucum bibulis inserpere murmur arenis.
Addit quinque plagas: mediam subtemine rubro
Obsessam fervore notat: squalebat adustus
Limes, et assiduo sitiebant stamina sole.
Vitales utrimque duas; quas mitis oberrat
Temperies habitanda viris. Tum fine supremo
Torpentes traxit geminas, brumaque perenni
Foedat, et aeterno contristat frigore telas.
Nec non et patrui pingit sacraria Ditis,
Fatalesque sibi manes. Nec defuit omen.
Praescia nam subitis maduerunt fletibus ora.

[They reach the spot where shone the bright abode
Of Ceres, by Cyclopian hands uprear'd,
With towering walls of steel, and iron gates,
Secur'd by pond'rous bars: the toiling slaves
Of Vulcan never with more labor strove
Than when the structure rose; nor ever breathed
More lurid sighs; nor since that time have flow'd
Such fiery torrents from the blazing forge.
Ivory adorns each court, and ev'ry roof
With sculptur'd brass consolidated shines,
And sparkling ores in lofty columns rise.
In these fair halls sits lovely Proserpine,
And soothing with sweet song the tedious day,
Plies the swift loom, expectant of the hour
When Ceres should return. Her needle paints
The birth and order of the elements;

388

And shows by what true laws Nature appeased
Pristine confusion, when her parent hand
Assign'd each unfix'd principle a seat:
Up springs each subtle essence, while below
Matter more pond'rous sinks; transparent floats
The ether; ocean swells; earth's pictur'd orb
Hangs in the firmament. Rich colours grace
The various web; stars glitter bright in gold;
Dark purple flows the sea; the rocky shores
Sparkle in gems; so well the threads deceive,
That, whilst th' enchanted eye fancies the waves
To swell and ripple on the moving floods,
The ear, deluded, seems to catch the sound
Of murm'ring waters, breaking on the sand,
And sea-weed dashing on the marble rocks.
Five zones she forms; one the rich scarlet woof
Displays, as parch'd by fierce and burning suns
Barren and dry; two others, temperate
And habitable, glow with softer hues;
Joyless and cold the last, with sullen tract,
Cover each pole, wrapt in perpetual gloom.

I. 295-331]

After this, Proserpine, forgetful of her parent's commands, is represented venturing from her retreat, through the fraudulent persuasions of Venus:

Impulit Ionios praemisso lumine fluctus
Nondum pura dies: tremulis vibravit in undis
Ardor, et errantes ludunt per caerula flammae.
Jamque audax animi, fidaeque oblita parentis,
Fraude Dionaea riguos Proserpina saltus
(Sic Parcae voluere) petit. . . .

[The day yet scarcely ris'n, with warning light
Now touch'd th' Ionian deep, the gradual ray
Glanced on the trembling waves; and purpling beams
Irradiate, on the changeful waters play'd;

389

When all elate, and of her parent's will
Forgetful, Proserpine, by Venus led,
The dewy woods, and flow'ry pastures seeks.

II. 1–7]

And this with the greatest propriety: for oblivion necessarily follows a remission of intellectual energy, and is as necessarily attended with the allurements of desire. Nor is her dress less symbolical of the soul's acting in such a state, principally according to the energies of imagination and nature. For thus her garments are beautifully described by the poet:

Quas inter Cereris proles, nunc gloria matris,
Mox dolor, aequali tendit per gramina passu,
Nec membris nec honore minor; potuitque videri
Pallas, si clipeum, si ferret spicula, Phoebe.
Collectae tereti nodantur jaspide vestes.
Pectinis ingenio nunquam felicior arti
Contigit eventus. Nullae sic consona telae
Fila, nec in tantum veri duxere figuram.
Hic Hyperionis Solem de semine nasci
Fecerat, et pariter, sed forma dispare lunam,
Aurorae noctisque duces. Cunabula Tethys
Praebet, et infantes gremio solatur anhelos,
Caeruleusque sinus roseis radiatur alumnis.
Invalidum dextro portat Titana lacerto
Nondum luce gravem, nec pubescentibus alte
Cristatum radiis: primo clementior aevo
Fingitur, et tenerum vagitu despuit ignem.
Laeva parte soror vitrei libamina potat
Uberis, et parvo signatur tempora cornu.

[Among the goddesses, with equal gait,
The blooming daughter of fair Ceres walk'd,
Equal to them in majesty of face,
And form: graced with a shield she might appear
Minerva's self, or, quiver'd, rove the woods,

390

Like Dian. On her vest a jasper beam'd:
The skilful artist never from his loom
Produced a woof so rich as that she wore,
Nor with more pleasing subject interwove
The many-colour'd web. It show'd the birth
Of bright Hyperion's son, and Luna pale,
Supreme o'er day and night; how Tethys' nurse
Upon her bosom bore the breathing babes,
Whose rosy colour graced the azure breast.
The infant Phoebus on the right appear'd,
Not with those burning and resistless beams
Attired, that shine on his maturer brow;
But pictured in the earliest dawn of life,
And from his baby lips were seen to burst
Soft glowing flames, mingled with tender cries:
Upon the left his beauteous sister lay,
With mimic crescent; and, with coral lip,
Press'd the bland fluid from its crystal source.

II. 42–64]

In which description the sun represents the phantasy, and the moon nature, as is well known to every tyro in the Platonic philosophy. They are likewise, with great propriety, described in their infantine state: for these energies do not arrive to perfection previous to the soul's merging into the dark receptacle of matter. After this we behold her issuing on the plain with Minerva and Diana, and attended by a beauteous train of nymphs, who are evident symbols of generation, as is largely proved by Porphyry de Antr. Nymph.; and are, therefore, the proper companions of the soul about to fall into its fluctuating realms.

But the design of Proserpine, in venturing from her retreat, is beautifully significant of her approaching descent: for she rambles from home for the purpose of gathering flowers; and this in a lawn replete with the most enchanting variety, and exhaling the most delicious odours. A manifest image this of the soul's energizing principally according to the natural life, and of her becoming effeminated and ensnared through the delusive attrac-

tions of sensible form. Minerva, too, or the rational power in this
case, gives herself wholly to the dangerous employment, and
abandons the proper characteristics of her nature for the destructive revels of desire.

All which is thus described with the utmost elegance by the
poet:

Forma loci superat flores: curvata tumore
Parvo planities, et mollibus edita clivis
Creverat in collem. Vivo de pumice fontes
Roscida mobilibus lambebant gramina rivis.
Silvaque torrentes ramorum frigore soles
Temperat, et medio brumam sibi vindicat aestu.
Apta fretis abies, bellis accomoda cornus,
Quercus amica Jovi, tumulos tectura cupressus,
Ilex plena favis, venturi praescia laurus.
Fluctuat hic denso crispata cacumine buxus,
Hic ederae serpunt, hic pampinus induit ulmos.
Haud procul inde lacus (Pergum dixere Sicani)
Panditur, et nemorum frondoso margine cinctus
Vicinis pallescit aquis: admittit in altum
Cernentes oculos, et late pervius humor
Ducit inoffensus liquido sub gurgite visus,
Iamque perspicui prodit secreta profundi.

Huc elapsa cohors gaudent per florea rura
Hortatur Cytherea, legant. Nunc ite, sorores,
Dum matutinis praesudat solibus aer:
Dum meus humectat flaventes Lucifer agros,
Rotanti praevectus equo. Sic fata, doloris
Carpit signa sui. Varios tum caetera saltus
Invasere cohors. Credas examina fundi
Hyblaeum raptura thymum, cum cerea reges
Castra movent, fagique cava demissus ab alvo
Mellifer electis exercitus obstrepit herbis.
Pratorum spoliatur honos. Hac lilia fuscis
Intexit violis: hanc mollis amaracus ornat:

Eleusinian and Bacchic Mysteries

Haec graditur stellata rosis; haec alba ligustris.
Te quoque flebilibus maerens, Hyacinthe, figuris,
Narcissumque metunt, nunc inclita germina veris,
Praestantes olim pueros. Tu natus Amyclis:
Hunc Helicon genuit. Te disci perculit error:
Hunc fontis decepit amor. Te fronte retusa
Deluis, hunc fracta Cephissus arundine luget.
Aestuat ante alias avido fervore legendi
Frugiferae spes una Deae. Nunc vimine texto
Ridentes calathos spoliis agrestibus implet:
Nunc sociat flores, seseque ignara coronat.
Augurium fatale tori. Quin ipsa tubarum
Armorumque potens, dextram qua fortia turbat
Agmina; qua stabiles portas et moenia vellit,
Jam levibus laxat studiis, hastamque reponit,
Insolitisque docet galeam mitescere sertis.
Ferratus lascivit apex, horrorque recessit
Martius, et cristae pacato fulgure vernant.
Nec quae Parthenium canibus scrutatur odorem,
Aspernata choros, libertatemque comarum
Injecta tantum voluit frenare corona.

[The level lawns to gentle risings swell'd,
And tow'ring hills by soft ascent were form'd;
The crystal fountains gush'd from marble rocks,
And through the dewy herbage winding rills
Play'd with melodious murmur; lofty woods
Temper'd with grateful shade the noon-tide heat
To icy coolness, ev'ry various tree;
The fir for mariners, the cornel fit
For archers, and the statlier plant of Jove;
The mournful cypress, and the scarlet oak
Enrich'd by bees, and prescient laurels green.
Here rov'd the box, along the crisped paths;
Low ivies crept around, and flaunting vines
Bound their smooth tendrils to majestic elms.

393

Thomas Taylor the Platonist

Along the shady margin of the grove
A tranquil lake extends, whose clear profound
Invites the penetrating eye to trace
The secret wonders of its lucid caves.
Now in the flow'ring field the virgin train
Gaily disport. Venus persuades to cull
The scented blooms. "Come," she exclaims, "while
The morning sky glows with light's earliest ray,
And yonder star, shedding sweet influence,
Heralds th' approach of day's more fiery orb,
Come, sister-nymphs!" She spoke, and reach'd her hand,
And pluck'd her fav'rite grief-inwoven flow'r.
Meanwhile, dispersed around, the roving maids
Throng in each various path, as when a swarm
Of bees, led from their waxen citadel,
Built in some hollow oak, following their queen
O'er beds of thyme, cluster with pleasing hum,
And visit ev'ry flow'r in search of sweets.
They spoil the treasures of the field; some chuse
Pale lilies to entwine with violet buds;
Some seek the rich Amaracus; some walk
With roses crown'd; some deck'd with woodbine wreaths;
They spare not thee, sad Hyacinth, nor thee,
Pallid Narcissus, pride of all the plain;
Once graceful youths: the fatal disk to one
Brought timeless fate, and him Apollo mourns
With clouded beauty: Love the other doom'd
To end his being by a fountain side,
Pining for shadowy bliss, and him e'en now
Cephisus sad deplores with broken reed.
More ardent to collect the fragrant spoils,
The blooming maid, brown Ceres' only care,
Exceeds her train; now weaving pliant twigs,
She heaps her rural wealth in smiling stores,
Now joins in nuptial union many a bud,

And thoughtless crowns her temple with the wreath,
Too sure prognostic of her future fate!
She, too, who revels in the field, when arms
Resound, and trumpets bray, she, whose strong hand,
Invincible, resists embattled hosts,
And makes high walls and cities tremble,—now
In softer toil engages, drops the spear,
And with unusual garlands decks her helm:
Her iron crest shows gay with wanton pride,
Her martial terrors fly, and war no more
Sits on her rose-bound front. Neither did she,
Whose tuneful bounds Parthenian gales explore,
Disdain the sportive band: her tresses loose
A woven coronet of flow'rs confined.

II. 122–84]

But there is a circumstance relative to the narcissus which must not be passed over in silence, I mean its being, according to Ovid, the metamorphosis of a youth who fell a victim to the love of his own corporeal form; the secret meaning of which most admirably accords with the rape of Proserpine, which, according to Homer, in his hymn to Ceres, was the immediate consequence of her gathering this wonderful flower. For by Narcissus falling in love with his shadow appearing in the limpid stream we may behold a beautiful representation of a soul vehemently gazing on the flowing condition of a material body, and in consequence of this, becoming enamoured with a corporeal life, which is nothing more than the delusive image of the true man, or rational and immortal soul. Hence, by an immoderate attachment to this unsubstantial mockery and gliding semblance of the real soul, such an one becomes, at length, wholly changed, as far as is possible to his nature, into a plantal condition of being, into a beautiful but transient flower, that is, into a corporeal life, or a life totally consisting in the mere energies of nature. Proserpine, therefore, or the soul, at the very instant of her descent into matter, is, with the utmost propriety, represented as eagerly engaged in plucking this fatal flower; for her energies at this period are entirely conversant with a life divided about the fluctuating condition of body.

After this, Pluto, forcing his passage through the earth, seizes on Proserpine, and carries her away with him, notwithstanding the resistance of Minerva and Diana, who are forbid by Jupiter (who in this place signifies fate) to attempt her deliverance: where by the resistance of Minerva and Diana no more is signified than that the lapse of the soul into a material nature is contrary to the genuine wish and proper condition, as well of the corporeal life depending on her essence, as of her true and rational nature: well, therefore, may the soul, in such a situation, pathetically exclaim with Proserpine:

> *O male dilecti flores, despectaque matris*
> *Consilia: O Veneris deprensae serius artes!*

> [. . . *O sadly chosen flow'rs!*
> *Maternal counsel wantonly despised!*
> *O artful Venus!*   II. 329–31]

But, according to Minutius Felix, Proserpine was carried by Pluto through thick woods, and over a length of sea, and brought into a cavern, the residence of the dead: where by woods a material nature is plainly implied, as we have already observed in the first part of this discourse; and where the reader may likewise observe the agreement of the description in this particular with that of Virgil in the descent of his hero. For in the words,

> . . . *tenent media omnia* silvae
> *Cocytusque sinuque labens, circumvenit atro,*

> [. . . *Cocytus' fiery banks*
> *In shades of Erebus, and drink the wave*
> *Of stagnant Lethe, breathing then around*
> *Oblivious vapours,*   I. 351–54]

the woods are expressly mentioned; and the ocean has an evident agreement with Cocytus, signifying the flowing condition of a

material nature, and the sorrows attending its connection with
the soul.

Pluto, then, having hurried Proserpine into the infernal regions,
i.e. the soul having sunk into the profundities of a material nature, a description of her marriage next succeeds, or of her union
with the dark tenement of body:

> *Jam suus inferno processerat Hesperus orbi*
> *Ducitur in thalamum virgo. Stat pronuba juxta*
> *Stellantes Nox picta sinus, tangensque cubile*
> *Omnia perpetuo genitalia sidere sancit.*

> [. . . *Now Hesperus*
> *Descended to th' infernal shades, and led*
> *The virgin to the bridal bow'r. Night stood*
> *Attendant, in bright constellations robed,*
> *And glittering stars; while happiest omens shed*
> *Their kindly influence.* II. 441–46]

In which Night is with great beauty and propriety introduced
standing by the nuptial couch, and confirming the oblivious
league. For the soul through her union with a material body
becomes familiar with darkness, and subject to the empire of
night; in consequence of which she dwells wholly with delusive
phantoms, and till she breaks her fetters is deprived of the perception of that which is real and true.

In the next place, we are presented with the following beautiful and pathetic description of Proserpine appearing in a dream
to Ceres, and bewailing her captive and miserable condition:

> *Sed tunc ipsa, sui jam non ambagibus ullis*
> *Nuntia, materno facies ingesta sopori.*
> *Namque videbatur tenebroso obtecta recessu*
> *Carceris, et saevis Proserpina vincta catenis,*
> *Non qualem roseis nuper convallibus Aetnae*
> *Suspexere Deae. Squalebat pulchrior auro*
> *Caesaries, et nox oculorum infecerat ignes.*
> *Exhaustusque gelu pallet rubor. Ille superbi*

Flammeus oris honos, et non cessura pruinis
Membra colorantur picei caligine regni.
Ergo hanc ut dubio vix tandem agnoscere visu
Evaluit: cujus tot poenae criminis? inquit.
Unde haec informis macies? Cui tanta facultas
In me saevitiae est? Rigidi cur vincula ferri
Vix aptanda feris molles meruere lacerti?
Tu, mea tu proles? An vana fallimur umbra?

[At length, no more mysteriously veil'd,
In doubtful slumbers, the acknowledged shape
Of Proserpine appalls the mother's sleep;
For in a cave forlorn she saw her sit,
In bonds and hideous darkness; not that maid
Whom late, embosom'd in the isle, she left;
Nor with that beauty graced, which rivall'd well,
In Enna's flow'ry and enchanting vale,
Th' admiring goddesses: loaded with gold
Shone her encircled hair, and gloomy night
Added strange lustre to her sterner eyes;
Dead was the rose upon her cheek, illumed
With other fires, and all her air betray'd
Infectious gloom. Affrighted Ceres scarce
Dared trust the mournful vision, yet at length,
By dread anxiety compell'd, these words,
Mingled with frequent sighs, escaped her lips:
"What crime awakes this punishment! O whence
This spectre horrible? from whom proceeds
The hateful work of cruelty! O say,
Terrific form, art thou indeed my child?
Or does some idle phantom of the night
Thus, with unreal terrors, shake my soul?"
III. 110–32]

For such indeed is the wretched situation of the soul when profoundly merged in a corporeal nature: so that she not only becomes captive and fettered, but loses all her original splendour;

is defiled with the impurity of matter; and the piercing vigour of her rational sight is blunted and dim'd through the thick darkness of a material night. Where, too, the reader may observe how Proserpine, being represented as confined in the dark recess of a prison, and bound with fetters, confirms the explanation of the fable here given as symbolical of the descent of the soul; for such, as we have already largely proved, is the condition of the soul from its union with body, according to the uniform testimony of the most antient philosophers and priests.

After this, the wanderings of Ceres for the discovery of Proserpine commence; in which she is described, by Minutius Felix, begirt with a serpent, and bearing two lighted torches in her hands; but by Claudian, instead of being girt with a serpent, she commences her search by night in a car drawn by dragons. But the meaning of the allegory is the same in each; for both a serpent and a dragon are emblems of a divisible life, subject to transitions, with which, in this case, our intellectual part becomes connected: since as these animals put off their skins, and become young again, so the divisible life of the soul, falling into generation, is rejuvenized in its subsequent progression. But what emblem can more beautifully represent the evolutions and processions of an intellectual nature into the regions of sense than the wanderings of Ceres by the light of torches through the darkness of night, and her continuing the pursuit till she proceeds into the depths of Hades itself? For the intellectual part of the soul, when it verges towards body, enkindles, indeed, a light in its dark receptacle, but becomes itself situated in obscurity: and, as Proclus somewhere divinely observes, the mortal nature by this means participates of intellect, but the intellectual part becomes obnoxious to death. The tears and lamentations too, of Ceres, in her course, are symbolical both of the providential energies of intellect about a mortal nature, and the miseries with which such energies are (with respect to partial souls like ours) attended. Nor is it without reason that Jacchus, or Bacchus, is celebrated by Orpheus as the companion of her search: for Bacchus is the evident symbol of the partial energies of intellect, and its distribution into the obscure and lamentable dominions of sense.

But our explanation will receive additional strength from considering that these sacred rites occupied the space of nine days in their celebration; and this, doubtless, because, according to Homer in his hymn to Ceres, this goddess did not discover the residence of her daughter till the expiration of that period. For the soul, in falling from her original and divine abode in the heavens, passes through eight spheres, viz. the inerratic sphere, and the seven planets, assuming a different body, and employing different energies in each; and becomes connected with the sublunary world and a terrene body, as the ninth, and most abject gradation of her descent. Hence the first day of initiation into these mystic rites was called αγυρμον, *i.e.* according to Hesychius, εκκλησιαν, et παν το αγειρομενον, *an assembly, and every thing collecting together*: and this with the greatest propriety; for, according to Pythagoras, *the people of dreams are souls collected together in the Galaxy.* Δημος δε ονειρων κατα Πυθαγοραν αι ψυχαι, ας συναγεσθαι φησιν εις την γαλαξιαν.⁹ And from this part of the heavens souls first begin to descend. After this, the soul falls from the tropic of Cancer into the planet Saturn; and to this the second day of initiation was consecrated, which they called Αλαδε μυσται, because, says Meursius, on that day the cryer was accustomed to admonish the mystics to betake themselves to the sea. Now the meaning of this will be easily understood by considering that, according to the arcana of the antient theology, as may be learned from Proclus,¹⁰ the whole planetary system is under the dominion of Neptune; and this too is confirmed by Martianus Capella, who describes the several planets as so many streams. Hence when the soul falls into the planet Saturn, which Capella compares to a river voluminous, sluggish, and cold, she then first merges herself into fluctuating matter, though purer than that of a sublunary nature, and of which water is an antient and significant symbol. Besides the sea is an

⁹ Porphyr. de Antro. Nympharum. p. 267.
¹⁰ Theol. Plat. lib. 6.

emblem of purity, as is evident from the Orphic hymn to Ocean, in which that deity is called θεων αγνισμα μεγιστον, i.e. *greatest purifier of the gods*: and Saturn, as we have already observed, is *pure intellect*. And what still more confirms this observation is that Pythagoras, as we are informed by Porphyry, in his life of that philosopher, symbolically called the sea a tear of Saturn. But the eighth day of initiation, which is symbolical of the soul's falling into the lunar orb, was celebrated by the mystics with *repeated initiation and second sacred rites*; because the soul in this situation is about to bid adieu to every thing of a celestial nature; to sink into a perfect oblivion of her divine origin and pristine felicity; and to rush profoundly into the region of dissimilitude, ignorance, and error. And lastly, on the ninth day, when the soul falls into the sublunary world and becomes united with a terrestrial body, a libation was performed, such as is usual in sacred rites. Here the mystics, filling two earthen vessels of broad and spacious bottoms, which were called πλημοχοαι and κοτυλισκοι, the former of these words denoting vessels of a conical shape, and the latter small bowls or cups sacred to Bacchus, they placed one towards the east, and the other towards the west. And the first of these was doubtless, according to the interpretation of Proclus, sacred to the earth, and symbolical of the soul's proceeding from an orbicular figure, or divine form, into a conical defluxion and terrene situation: but the other was sacred to the soul, and symbolical of its celestial origin; since our intellect is the legitimate progeny of Bacchus. And this too was occultly signified by the position of the earthen vessels; for, according to a mundane distribution of the divinities, the eastern center of the universe, which is analogous to fire, belongs to Jupiter, who likewise governs the inerratic sphere; and the western to Pluto, who governs the earth, because the west is allied to earth on account of its dark and nocturnal nature.[11]

Again, according to Clemens Alexandrinus, the following confession was made by the new mystic in these sacred rites, in answer to the interrogations of the Hierophant: "I have fasted;

[11] Vide Procl. in Plat. Theol. lib. 6, cap. 10.

but I have drank a miscellaneous potion; and having done this, I have taken out of the Cista, and placed what I have taken out into the Calathus; and alternately I have taken out of the Calathus and put into the Cista." Κᾳστι το συνθημα Ελευσινιων μυστη-ριων· ενηστωσα· επιον τον κυκεωνα· ελαβον εκ κιστης, εργασα-μενος απεθεμην εις καλαθον, και εκ καλαθον εις κιστην. But as this pertains to a circumstance attending the wanderings of Ceres, which formed the most mystic part of the ceremonies, it is necessary to adduce the following arcane narration, summarily collected from the writings of Arnobius: "The goddess Ceres, when searching through the earth for her daughter, in the course of her wanderings arrived at the boundaries of Eleusis, in the Attic region, a place which was then inhabited by a people called Αυτοχθονες, or descended from the earth, whose names were as follows: Baubo and Triptolemus; Dysaules, a goat herd; Eubulus, a keeper of swine; and Eumolpus, a shepherd, from whom the race of the Eumolpidi descended, and the illustrious name of Cecropidae was derived; and who afterwards flourished as bearers of the caduceus, hierophants, and cryers belonging to the sacred rites. Baubo, therefore, who was of the female sex, received Ceres, wearied with complicated evils, as her guest, and endeavoured to soothe her sorrows by obsequious and flattering attendance. For this purpose she entreated her to pay attention to the refreshment of her body, and placed before her *a miscellaneous potion* to assuage the vehemence of her thirst. But the sorrowful goddess was averse from her solicitations, and rejected the friendly officiousness of the hospitable dame. The matron, however, who was not easily repulsed, still continued her entreaties, which were as obstinately resisted by Ceres, who persevered in her refusal with unshaken constancy and invincible rigour. But when Baubo had thus often exerted her endeavours to appease the sorrows of Ceres, but without any effect, she, at length, changed her arts, and determined to try if she could not exhilarate, by prodigies, a mind which she was not able to allure by serious attempts. For this purpose she freed from concealment that part of her body through which the female sex produces

children, and derives the appellation of woman. This she caused
to assume a purer appearance, and a smoothness such as is found
in the private parts of a stripling child. She then returns to the
afflicted goddess, and, in the midst of those attempts which are
usually employed to alleviate distress, she uncovers herself, and
exhibits her secret parts; upon which the goddess fixed her eyes,
and was delighted with the novel method of mitigating the
anguish of sorrow; and afterwards, becoming cheerful through
laughter, she assuages the ardour of her thirst with the miscellaneous potion which she had before despised." Thus far Arnobius; and the same narration is epitomised by Clemens Alexandrinus, who is very indignant at the indecency, as he conceives,
in the story, and in its composing the arcana of the Eleusinian
rites. Indeed as the simple father, with the usual ignorance of a
Christian priest, considered the fable literally, and as designed
to promote indecency and lust, we cannot wonder at his ill-timed
and malevolent abuse. But the fact is, this narration belonged
to the ἀπόρρητα, or arcane discourses, on account of its mystical
meaning, and to prevent it from becoming the object of ignorant
declamation, licentious perversion, and impious contempt: for
the purity and excellence of these institutions is perpetually
acknowledged even by Dr. Warburton himself, who, in this instance, has dispersed, for a moment, the mists of delusion necessarily produced by a religion full of barbarous impiety, wild fanaticism, and intolerant zeal. Besides, as Jamblichus beautifully
observes (de Mysteriis), "exhibitions of this kind in the mysteries
were designed to free us from licentious passions, by gratifying
the sight, and at the same time vanquishing desire, through the
awful sanctity with which these rites were accompanied: for,"
says he, "the proper way of freeing ourselves from the passions is,
first, to indulge them with moderation, by which means they
become satisfied; listen, as it were, to persuasion, and may thus
be entirely removed." This doctrine is indeed so rational, that
it can never be objected to by any but quacks in philosophy and
religion. For as he is nothing more than a quack in medicine
who endeavours to remove a latent bodily disease before he has

called it forth externally, and by this means diminished its fury; so he is nothing more than a pretender in philosophy who attempts to remove the passions by violence, instead of moderate compliance and gentle persuasion.

But, to return from this digression, the following appears to be the secret meaning of this mystic discourse:—The matron Baubo may be considered as a symbol of that passive, effeminate, and corporeal life through which the soul becomes united with this terrene body, and through which being at first ensnared, it descended, and, as it were, was born into the realms of generation, passing, by this means, from mature perfection, splendour, and reality, into infancy, darkness, and error. Ceres, therefore, or the intellectual part of the soul, in the course of her wanderings, that is, of her evolutions and processions into matter, is at length captivated with the arts of Baubo, or a corporeal life, and forgets her sorrows, that is, imbibes oblivion of her wretched state in the mingled potion which she prepares: the miscellaneous liquor being an obvious symbol of such a life, mixed and impure, and, on this account, obnoxious to corruption and death; since every thing pure and unmixed is incorruptible and divine. And here it is necessary to caution the reader from imagining that because, according to the fable, the wanderings of Ceres commence after the rape of Proserpine, hence intellect descends posterior to the soul, and in a separate manner: for nothing more is meant by this circumstance than that intellect, from the superior excellence of its nature, has a causal, though not a temporal, priority to soul; and that on this account a defection and revolt commences indeed from soul, and afterwards takes place in intellect, yet not so as that the former descends without the inseparable attendance of the latter.

From this explanation, then, of the fable, we may easily perceive the meaning of the mystic confession, *I have fasted, but I have drank a miscellaneous potion*, &c. for by the former part of the assertion, no more is meant than that intellect, previous to its imbibing oblivion, through the fraudulent arts of a corporeal life, abstains from all material concerns, and does not mingle itself (as far as its nature is capable of such abasement) with even the necessary delights of the body. And as to the latter part, it doubtless alludes to the descent of Proserpine to Hades, and her reascent to the abodes of her mother Ceres: that is, to the circulations of soul, and her alternately falling into generation, and ascending from thence into the intelligible world, and becoming perfectly converted to her divine and intellectual part. For *the Cista* contained the most arcane symbols of the mysteries, into which it was unlawful for the profane to look: and whatever were its contents, we learn from the hymn of Callimachus to Ceres, that they were formed from gold, which, from its incorruptibility, is an evident symbol of an immaterial nature. And as to the Calathus, this, as we are told by Claudian, was filled with *spoliis agrestibus, the spoils or fruits of the field*, which are manifest symbols of a life corporeal and terrene. So that the mystic, by confessing that he had taken from the Cista, and placed what he had taken into the Calathus, and the contrary, occultly acknowledged the descent of his soul from a condition of being wholly immaterial and immortal, into one material and mortal; and that, on the contrary, by living according to the purity which the mysteries inculcated, he should reascend to that perfection of his nature, from which he had unhappily fallen.

It only now remains that we consider the last part of this fabulous narration, or arcane discourse, in which it is said, that after the goddess Ceres, on arriving at Eleusina, had discovered her daughter, she instructed the Eleusinians in the plantation of corn: or, according to Claudian, the search of Ceres for her daughter, through the goddess discovering the art of tillage as she went, proved the occasion of a universal benefit to mankind. Now the secret meaning of this will be obvious, by considering that the descent of intellect into the realms of generation becomes, indeed, the greatest benefit and ornament which a material nature is capable of receiving: for without the participation of intellect in the lowest regions of matter, nothing but irrational soul and a brutal life would subsist in its dark and fluctuating abode. As the art of tillage, therefore, and particularly the plantation of corn, becomes the greatest possible benefit to our sensible life, no symbol can more aptly represent the unparalleled advantages arising from the evolution and procession of intellect into a corporeal life than the good resulting from agriculture and corn: for whatever of horrid and dismal can be conceived in night, supposing it to be perpetually destitute of the friendly illuminations of the moon and stars, such, and infinitely more dreadful, would be the condition of an earthly nature, if deprived of the beneficent irradiations and supervening ornaments of an intellectual life.

And thus much for an explanation of the Eleusinian mysteries, or the history of Ceres and Proserpine; in which it must be remembered, that as this fable, according to the excellent observation of Sallust already adduced, is of the mixed kind, though the descent of the soul was doubtless principally alluded to by these sacred rites, yet they likewise occultly signified, agreeable to the nature of the fable, the procession of divinity into the sublunary world. But when we view the fable in this part of its meaning, we must be careful not to confound the nature of a partial intellect like ours with one universal and divine; for as every thing subsisting about the gods is deified, intellect in the highest degree, and next to this soul, hence wanderings and ravishments, lamentations and tears, can here only signify the participations and providential energies of these about inferior natures; and this in such a manner as not to derogate from the dignity, or impair the perfection, of the divine participated essence. I only add, that the preceding exposition will enable us to perceive the meaning and beauty of the following representation of the rape of Proserpine, from the Heliacan tables of Hieronymus Aleander, as delivered by Kircher in his Obeliscus Pamphilius, p. 227. For here, first of all, we behold Ceres in a car drawn by two dragons, and afterwards, Diana and Minerva, with an inverted calathus at their feet, and pointing out to Ceres, Proserpine, who is hurried away by Pluto in his car, and is in the attitude of one struggling to be free. In the next place, Hercules is represented with his club, in the attitude of one opposing the violence of Pluto: and last of all, Jupiter is represented extending his hand, as if willing to assist Proserpine in escaping from the embraces of Pluto. I shall therefore conclude this section with the following remarkable passage from Plutarch, which will not only confirm, but be itself corroborated by the preceding exposition. Ο τι μεν ουν η παλαια φυσιολογια, και παρ Ελλησι και Βαρβαροις, λογος ην φυσικος εγκεκαλυμμενος μυθοις, τα πολλα δι' αινιγματων και υπονοιων επικρυφος, και μυστηριωδης θεολογια. Τα τε λαλουμενα των σιγωμενων σαφεστερα τοις πολλοις εχοντα. Και τα σιγωμενα των λαλουμενων υποπτοτερα. Δηλον εστι, pergit, εν τοις Ορφικοις επεσι, και τοις Αιγυπτιακοις και Φρυγιοις λογοις. Μαλιστα δε οι περι τας τελετας οργιασμοι, και τα δρωμενα συμβολικως εν ταις ιερουργιαις, την των παλαιων εμφαινει διανοιαν.[12] I.e. "That the antient physiology, therefore, as well of the Greeks as the Barbarians, was nothing else than a physical discourse involved in fables, concealing many things through aenigmas and conjectures, and among the rest a mystic theology, in which the things spoken were clearer to the multitude than those delivered in silence, and the things delivered in silence were more subject to conjecture than what was spoken, is manifest from the *Orphic verses*, and the Egyptian and Phrygian discourses. *But the orgies of initiations, and the symbolical operations of sacred rites especially, exhibit the conceptions of the antients.*"

[12] Vide Plutarch apud Euseb.

THE Dionysiacal sacred rites instituted by Orpheus depended on the following arcane narration, part of which has been already related in the preceding section, and the rest may be found in a variety of authors. "Dionysius, or Bacchus, while he was yet a boy, was engaged by the Titans, through the stratagems of Juno, in a variety of sports, with which that period of life is so vehemently allured; and among the rest, he was particularly captivated with beholding his image in a mirror; during his admiration of which, he was miserably torn in pieces by the Titans; who, not content with this cruelty, first boiled his members in water, and afterwards roasted them by the fire. But while they were tasting his flesh thus dressed, Jupiter, excited by the steam, and perceiving the cruelty of the deed, hurled his thunder at the Titans; but committed his members to Apollo, the brother of Bacchus, that they might be properly interred. And this being performed, Dionysius, (whose heart during his laceration was snatched away by Pallas and preserved,) by a new regeneration, again emerged, and being restored to his pristine life and integrity, he afterwards filled up the number of the gods. But in the mean time, from the exhalations formed from the ashes of the burning bodies of the Titans, mankind were produced." Now, in order to understand properly the secret meaning of this narration, it is necessary to repeat the observation already made in the preceding section, that "all fables belonging to mystic ceremonies are of the mixed kind": and consequently the present fable, as well as that of Proserpine, must in one part have reference to the gods, and in the other to the human soul, as the following exposition will abundantly evince.

In the first place, then, by Dionysius, or Bacchus, according to the highest establishment of this deity, we must understand the intellect of the mundane soul; for there are various processions of this god, or Bacchuses, derived from his essence. But by the Titans we must understand the mundane gods, of whom Bacchus is the summit: by Jupiter, the Demiurgus, or artificer of the universe: by Apollo, the deity of the Sun, who has both a mundane and super-mundane establishment, and by whom the universe is bound in symmetry and consent, through splendid reasons and harmonizing power: and, lastly, by Minerva we must understand that fontal, intellectual, imperatorial, and providential deity, who guards and preserves all middle lives in an immutable condition, through intelligence and a self-energizing life, and by this means sustains them from the depredations of matter. Again, by the puerile state of Bacchus at the period of his laceration, the flourishing condition of an intellectual nature is implied; since, according to the Orphic theology, souls, while under the government of Saturn, who is pure intellect, instead of proceeding, as now, from youth to age, advance in a retrograde progression from age to youth. The arts employed by the Titans, in order to ensnare Dionysius, are symbolical of those apparent and divisible energies of the mundane gods, through which the participated intellect of Bacchus becomes, as it were, torn in pieces: and by the mirror we must understand, in the language of Proclus, the inaptitude of the universe to receive the plenitude of intellectual perfection; but the symbolical meaning of his laceration, through the stratagems of Juno, and the consequent punishment of the Titans, is thus beautifully unfolded by Olympiodorus, in his MS. Commentary on the Phaedo of Plato: "The form," says he, "of that which is universal is pluckt off, torn in pieces, and scattered into generation; and Dionysius is the *monad* of the Titans. But his laceration is said to take place through the stratagems of Juno, because this goddess is the inspective guardian of motion and progression; and on this account, in the Iliad, she perpetually rouses and excites Jupiter to providential energies about secondary concerns: and, in another respect, Dionysius is the inspective guardian of generation, because he presides over life and death; for he is the guardian of life because of generation, but of death because wine produces an enthusiastic energy: and we become more enthusiastic at the period of dissolution, as Proclus evinces agreeable to Homer; for he became prophetic at the time of his death. They likewise assert, that tragedy and comedy are referred to Dionysius: comedy, indeed, because this is the *play* or *joke* of life; but tragedy on account of the *passions* and *death*, which it represents. Comedians, therefore, do not properly denominate tragedians, as if they were not Dionysiacal; asserting, at the same time, that nothing tragical belongs to Dionysius. But Jupiter hurled his thunder at the Titans; the thunder signifying a conversion on high: for fire naturally ascends; and hence Jupiter, by this means, converts the Titans to himself."—Σπαραττεται δε το καθολου ειδος εν τη γενεσει, μονας δε τιτανων ο Διονυσος. —κατ᾽ επιβουλην δε της ηρας διοτι κινησεως εφορος η θεος καὶ προοδου. Διο καὶ συνεχως εν τη Ιλιασι εξανιστησιν αυτη, καὶ διεγορει τον δια εις προνοιαν των δευτερων. Και γενεσεως αλλως εφορος εστιν ο Διονυσος, διοτι καὶ ζωης καὶ τελευτης. Ζωης μεν γαρ εφορος, επειδη καὶ της γενεσεως, τελευτης δε διοτι ενθουσιαν ο οινος ποιει. Και περι την τελευτην δε ενθουσιαστικωτεροι γινομεθα, ως δηλοι ο παρ᾽ Ομηρω Προκλος, μαντικος γεγονως περι την τελευτην· καὶ την τραγωδιαν, καὶ την κωμωδιαν ανεισθαι φασι τω Διονυσω. Την μεν κωμωδιαν παιγνιον ουσαν του βιου· την δε τραγωδιαν δια τα παθη, καὶ την τελευτην. ουκ αρα καλως οι κωμικοι τοις τραγικοις εγκαλουσιν, ως μη διοννυσιακοις ουσιν, λεγοντες οτι ουδεν ταυτα προς τον Διονυσον. Κεραυνοι δε τουτοις ο Ζευς, του κεραυνου δηλουντος την επιστροφην· πυρ γαρ επι τα ανω κινουμενα. Επιστρεφει ουν αυτους προς εαυτον. But by the members of Dionysius being first boiled in water by the Titans, and afterwards roasted by the fire, the procession or distribution of intellect into matter, and its subsequent conversion from thence, is evidently implied: for water was considered by the Egyptians, as we have already observed, as the symbol of matter; and fire is the natural symbol of ascent. The heart of Dionysius too, is, with the greatest propriety, said to be preserved by Minerva; for this goddess is the guardian of life, of which the heart is a symbol. So that this part of the fable plainly signifies, that while intellectual life is distributed into the universe, its principle is preserved entire by the guardian power and providence of unpolluted intelligence. And as Apollo is the source of all union and harmony, and as he is called by Proclus, in his elegant hymn to the Sun, "the key-keeper of the fountain of life," the reason is obvious why the members of Dionysius, which were buried by this deity, by a new generation again emerged, and were restored to their pristine integrity and life. But let it here be carefully observed, that renovation, when applied to the gods, is to be considered as secretly implying the rising of their proper light, and its consequent appearance to subordinate natures. And that punishment, when considered as taking place about beings more excellent than mankind, signifies nothing more than a secondary providence of such beings which is of a punishing characteristic, and which subsists about apostatizing souls. Hence, then, from what has been said, we may easily collect the ultimate design of the first part of this mystic fable; for it appears to be no other than to represent the manner in which the form of the mundane intellect is distributed into the universe;—that such an intellect (and every one which is total) remains entire during its participations, and that the participations themselves are continually converted to their source, with which they become finally united. So that intellectual illumination, while it proceeds into the dark and rebounding receptacle of matter, and invests its obscurity with the supervening ornaments of deific light, returns at the same time without intermission to the principle of its descent.

Let us now consider the latter part of the fable, in which it is said that our souls were formed from the vapours produced by the ashes of the burning bodies of the Titans; at the same time connecting it with the former part of the fable, which is also applicable in a certain degree to the condition of a partial intellect like ours. In the first place, then, we are composed from *fragments*, (says Olympiodorus,) because, through falling into generation, our life has proceeded into the most distant and extreme division; but from *Titannic fragments*, because the Titans are the ultimate artificers of things, and the most proximate to their fabrications. But farther, our irrational life is Titannic, under which the rational life is torn in pieces. And hence, when we disperse the Dionysius, or intellect contained in the secret recesses of our nature, breaking in pieces the kindred and divine form of our essence, and which communicates, as it were, both with things subordinate and supreme, then we become Titans; but when we establish ourselves in union with this Dionysiacal or kindred form, then we become Bacchuses, or perfect guardians of our irrational life: for Dionysius, whom in this respect we resemble, is himself a guardian deity, dissolving at his pleasure the bonds by which the soul is united to the body, since he is the cause of a partial life. But it is necessary that the passive nature of our irrational part, through which we are bound in body, and which is nothing more than the resounding echo, as it were, of soul, should suffer the punishment incurred by descent; for when the soul casts aside the peculiarity of her nature, she requires a certain proper, but at the same time multiform body, that she may again become indigent of a common form, which she has lost through Titannic dispersion into matter.

But in order to see the perfect and beautiful resemblance between the manner in which our souls descend and the participation of intellect by mundane natures, let the reader attend to the following admirable citation from the MS. Commentary of Olympiodorus on the Phaedo of Plato:—"In order," says he, "to the soul's descent, it is necessary that she should first establish an animating image of herself in the body; and in the second place, that she should sympathize with the image, according to a similitude of form: for every form passes into a sameness with itself, through naturally verging to itself. In the third place, being situated in a divisible nature, it is necessary that she should be lacerated and scattered together with such a nature, and that she should fall into an ultimate distribution, till, through the energies of a cathartic life, she raises herself from the extreme dispersion, and loosens the bond of sympathy through which she is united with body; and till, at the same time, energizing without the image, she becomes established according to her primary life. And we may behold a resemblance of all this in the fable respecting Bacchus, the exemplar of our intellect. For it is said that

Dionysius, establishing his image in a mirror, pursued it, and thus became distributed into the universe. But Apollo excited and elevated Bacchus; this god being a cathartic deity, and the true saviour of Dionysius; and on this account he is celebrated as Dionysites." Ὅτι δεῖ πρῶτον ὑποστῆσαι εἰκόνα τὴν ψυχὴν ἑαυτοῦ ἐν τῷ σώματι. Τοῦτο γάρ ἐστι ψυχῶσαι τὸ σῶμα. Δεύτερον δὲ συμπαθεῖν τῷ εἰδώλῳ, κατὰ τὴν ὁμοείδειαν. Πᾶν γὰρ εἶδος ἐπείγεται εἰς τὴν πρὸς ἑαυτὸ ταυτότητα διὰ τὴν πρὸς ἑαυτὸ συνεῦσιν ἔμφυτον. Τρίτον ἐν τῷ μερισμῷ γενομένην συνδιασπασθῆναι αὐτῷ, καὶ εἰς τὸν ἔσχατον ἐκπεσεῖν μερισμόν. Ἕως ἂν διὰ τῆς καθαρτικῆς ζωῆς συναγείρει μὲν ἑαυτὴν ἀπὸ τοῦ σκορπισμοῦ, λύσῃ δὲ τὸν δεσμὸν τῆς συμπαθείας, προβάλλεται δὲ τὴν ἄνευ τοῦ εἰδώλου, καθ' ἑαυτὴν ἑστῶσαν πρωτουργὸν ζωήν. Ὅτι τὰ ὅμοια μυθεύεται, καὶ ἐν τῷ παραδείγματι. Ὁ γὰρ Διόνυσος, ὅτι τὸ εἴδωλον ἐνέθηκε τῷ ἐσόπτρῳ τούτῳ ἐφέσπετο. Καὶ οὕτως εἰς τὸ πᾶν ἐμερίσθη. Ὁ δὲ Ἀπόλλων συναγείρει τε αὐτὸν καὶ ἀνάγει, καθαρτικὸς ὢν θεός, καὶ τοῦ Διονύσου σωτὴρ ὡς ἀληθῶς. Καὶ διὰ τοῦτο διονυσότης ἀνυμνεῖται. Hence, as the same author beautifully observes, the soul revolves according to a mystic and mundane circulation: for flying from an indivisible and Dionysiacal life, and energizing according to a Titannic and revolting energy, she becomes bound in body as in a prison. Hence, too, she abides in punishment and takes care of her partial concerns; and being purified from Titannic defilements, and collected into one, she becomes a Bacchus; that is, she passes into the proper integrity of her nature according to the Dionysius who abides on high. From all which it evidently follows, that he who lives Dionysiacally rests from labours and is freed from his bonds; that he leaves his prison, or rather his apostatizing life; and that he who does this is a cathartic philosopher. But farther from this account of Dionysius, we may perceive the truth of Plato's observation that "the design of the mysteries is to lead us back to the perfection from which, as a principle, we first made our descent." For in this perfection Dionysius himself subsists, establishing perfect souls in the throne of his proper father; that is, in the whole of a life according to

Jupiter. So that he who is perfect necessarily resides with the gods, according to the design of those deities, who are the sources of consummate perfection to the soul. And lastly, the Thyrsus itself, which was used in the Bacchic procession, as it was a reed full of knots, is an apt symbol of the distribution of an intellectual nature into the sensible world. And agreeable to this, Olympiodorus on the Phaedo observes that "the Thyrsus is a symbol of material and partial fabrication from its dissipated continuity; and that on this account it is a Titannic plant. This it was customary to extend before Bacchus instead of his paternal sceptre; and through this they called him down into a partial nature. And, indeed, the Titans are Thyrsus-bearers; and Prometheus concealed fire in a Thyrsus or reed; whether he is considered as deducing celestial light into generation; or producing soul into body; or calling forth divine illumination (the whole of which is without generation) into generation. Hence Socrates calls the multitude Orphically Thyrsus-bearers, because they live according to a Titannic life." Οτι ο ναρθηξ συμβολον εστι της ενυλου δημιουργιας, καὶ μεριστης, δια την μαλιστα διεσπαρμενην συνεχειαν, οθεν καὶ τιτανικον το φυτον. Και γαρ τῷ Διονυσῳ προτεινουσιν αυτῷ, αντι του πατρικου σκηπτρου. Και ταυτῃ προκαλουνται αυτον εις τον μερικον. Και μεντοι, καὶ ναρθηκοφορουσιν οι Τιτανες, καὶ ο Προμηθευς, εν ναρθηκϊ ἐκλεττε το πυρ, ειτε το ουρανιον φως εις την γενεσιν κατασπων, ειτε την ψυχην εις το σωμα προαγων, ειτε την θειαν ελλαμψιν ολην αγεννητον ουσαν, εις την γενεσιν προκαλουμενος. Δια δε τουτο, καὶ ο Σωκρατης τους πολλους καλει ναρθηκοφορους Ορφικως, ως ζωντας τιτανικως.

And thus much for the secret meaning of the fable, which formed a principal part of these mystic rites. Let us now proceed to consider the signification of the symbols, which, according to Clemens Alexandrinus, belonged to the Bacchic ceremonies; and which are comprehended in the following Orphic verses:

Κωνος, και ρομβος, και παιγνια καμπεσιγνια
Μηλα τε χρυσεα καλα παρ' εσπεριδων λιγυφώνων.

That is,

> *A wheel, a pine-nut, and the wanton plays,*
> *Which move and bend the limbs in various ways:*
> *With these th' Hesperian golden-fruit combine,*
> *Which beauteous nymphs defend of voice divine.*

To all which Clemens adds εσοπτρον, *a mirror*, ποκος, *a fleece of wool*, and αστραγαλος, *the ankle-bone.* In the first place, then, with respect to the wheel, since Dionysius, as we have already explained, is the mundane intellect, and intellect is of a reductorial, or convertive nature, nothing can be a more apt symbol of intellectual energy than a wheel or sphere: besides, as the laceration of Dionysius signifies the procession of intellectual illumination into matter, and its conversion at the same time to its source, this too will be aptly symbolized by a wheel. In the second place, a pine-nut, from its conical shape, is a perspicuous symbol of the manner in which intellectual illumination proceeds from its principle into a material nature. "For the soul," says Macrobius,[13] "proceeding from a round figure, which is the only divine form, is produced into a cone by its defluxion." And the same is true symbolically of intellect. And as to the wanton sports which bend the limbs, this evidently alludes to the Titannic arts, by which Dionysius was allured, and occultly signifies the energies of the mundane intellect, considered as subsisting according to an apparent and divisible condition. But the Hesperian golden-apples, signify the pure and incorruptible nature of that intellect, or Dionysius, which is participated by the world; for a golden apple, according to the philosopher Sallust, is a symbol of the world; and this doubtless, both on account of its external figure, and the incorruptible intellect which it contains, and with the illuminations of which it is externally adorned; since gold, on account of its never being subject to rust, aptly denotes an incorruptible and immaterial nature. The mirror, which is the next symbol, we have already explained. And as to the fleece of wool, this is a symbol of the laceration, or

[13] In som. Scip. cap. 12.

distribution of intellect, or Dionysius, into matter; for the verb σπαραττω, *dilanio*, which is used in the relation of the Bacchic discerption, signifies to tear in pieces like wool: and hence Isidorus derives the Latin word lana, *wool*, from laniando, as *vellus a vellendo*. Nor must it pass unobserved, that λῆνος, in Greek, signifies wool, and ληνὸς, a wine-press. And, indeed, the pressing of grapes is as evident a symbol of dispersion as the tearing of wool; and this circumstance was doubtless one principal reason why grapes were consecrated to Bacchus: for a grape, previous to its pressure, aptly represents that which is collected into one; and when it is pressed into juice, it no less aptly represents the diffusion of that which was before collected and entire. And lastly, the αστραγαλος, or *ankle-bone*, as it is principally subservient to the progressive motion of animals, so it belongs, with great propriety, to the mystic symbols of Bacchus; since it doubtless signifies the progressions of that deity into the regions of nature: for nature, or that divisible life which subsists about body, and which is productive of seeds, immediately depends on Bacchus. And hence we are informed by Proclus, in Tim. p. 184, that the genital parts of this god are denominated by theologists, *Diana*, who, says he, presides over the whole of the generation in nature, leads forth into light all natural reasons, and extends a prolific power from on high even to the subterranean realms. And hence we may perceive the reason why, in the Orphic hymn to Nature, that goddess is described as, *"turning round silent traces with the* ankle-bones *of her feet."*

Αψοφον αστραγαλοισι ποδων ιχνος ειλισσουσα.

And it is highly worthy our observation that in this verse of the hymn Nature is celebrated as Fortune, according to that description of the goddess in which she is represented as standing with her feet on a wheel, which she continually turns round with a progressive motion; as the following verse from the same hymn abundantly confirms:

Αεναῳ στροφαλιγγι θοον ρυμα δινενουσα.

The sense of which is, "moving with rapid motion on an eternal wheel." Nor ought it to seem wonderful that Nature should be celebrated as Fortune; for Fortune in the Orphic hymn to that deity is invoked as Diana: and the moon, as we have observed in the preceding section, is the αυτοπτον αγαλμα φυσεως, *the self-conspicuous image of Nature*; and indeed the apparent inconstancy of Fortune has an evident agreement with the fluctuating condition in which the dominions of nature are perpetually involved."

It only now remains that we explain the secret meaning of the sacred dress with which the initiated in the Dionysiacal mysteries were invested, in order to the θρονισμος taking place; or sitting in a solemn manner on a throne, about which it was customary for the other mystics to dance. But the particulars of this habit are thus described in the Orphic verses preserved by Macrobius in the first book of his Saturnalia, cap. 18.

> Ταυτα γε παντα τελειν ιερᾳ σκηνῃ πυκασαντα,
> Σωμα θεου πλαττειν εριαυγους ηελιοιο.
> Πρωτα μεν αργυφεαις εναλιγκιον ακτινεσσιν
> Πεπλον φοινικερον (lege φοινικεον) πυρῐκελον
>   αμφιβαλεσθαι.
> Αυταρ υπερθε νεβροιο παναιολου ευρυ καθαψαι
> Δερμα πολυστικτον θηρος κατα δεξιον ωμων,
> Αστρων δαιδαλεων μιμημ' ιερου τε πολοιο.
> Ειτα δ' υπερθε νεβρης χρυσεον ζωστηρα βαλεσθαι
> Παμφανοωντα περιξ στερνων φορεειν μεγα σημα
> Ευθυς οτ' εκ περατων γαιης φαεθων ανορουσων
> Χρυσειαις ακτισι βαλῃ ροον ωκεανοιο,
> Αυγη δ' ασπετος η, ανα δ' δροσῳ αμφιμιγεισα
> Μαρμαιρῃ δινῃσιν ελισσομενη κατα κυκλον,
> Προσθε θεου. ζωνη δ' αρ' υπο στερνων αμετρητων
> Φαινετ' αρ' ωκεανου κυκλος, μεγα θαυμ' εισιδεσθαι.

That is,

> *He who desires in pomp of sacred dress*
> *The sun's resplendant body to express,*

Should first a veil assume of purple bright,
Like fair white beams combin'd with fiery light:
On his right shoulder, next, a mule's broad hide,
Widely diversify'd with spotted pride
Should hang, an image of the pole divine,
And daedal stars, whose orbs eternal shine.
A golden splendid zone, then, o'er the vest
He next should throw, and bind it round his breast;
In mighty token, how with golden light,
The rising sun, from earth's last bounds and night
Sudden emerges, and, with matchless force,
Darts through old Ocean's billows in his course.
A boundless splendor hence, enshrin'd in dew,
Plays on his whirlpools, glorious to the view;
While his circumfluent waters spread abroad,
Full in the presence of the radiant god:
But Ocean's circle, like a zone of light,
The sun's wide bosom girds, and charms the wond'ring
    sight.

In the first place, then, let us consider why this mystic dress belonging to Bacchus is to represent the sun. Now the reason of this will be evident from the following observations: according to the Orphic theology, the intellect of every planet is denominated a Bacchus, who is characterized in each by a different appellation; so that the intellect of the solar deity is called Trietericus Bacchus. And in the second place, since the divinity of the sun, according to the arcana of the antient theology, has a supermundane as well as mundane establishment, and is wholly of a reductorial or intellectual nature; hence considered as supermundane, he must both produce and contain the mundane intellect, or Dionysius, in his essence; for all the mundane are contained in the super-mundane deities, by whom also they are produced. Hence Proclus, in his elegant hymn to the sun, says,

Σε κλυτον υμνειουσι Διωνυσσοιο τοκηα.

That is, "they celebrate thee in hymns as the illustrious parent of

Dionysius." And thirdly, it is through the subsistence of Dionysius in the sun that that luminary derives its circular progression, as is evident from the following Orphic verse, in which, speaking of the sun, it is said of him, that

. . . Διονυσος δ᾽ επεκληθη,
Ουνεκα δινειται κατ᾽ απειρονα μακρον ολυμπον. . . ,

"he is called Dionysius, because he is carried with a circular motion through the immensely-extended heavens." And this with the greatest propriety, since intellect, as we have already observed, is entirely of a convertive and reductorial nature: so that from all this, it is sufficiently evident why the dress of Dionysius is represented as belonging to the sun. In the second place, the veil, resembling a mixture of fiery light, is an obvious image of the solar fire. And as to the spotted mule-skin, which is to represent the starry heavens, this is nothing more than an image of the moon; this luminary, according to Proclus on Hesiod, resembling the mixed nature of a mule; "becoming dark through her participation of earth, and deriving her proper light from the sun." Γης μεν εχουσα το σκοτιζεσθαι, ηλιου δε το οικειον ειληχεναι φως. Ταυτη μεν ουν οικειωται προς αυτην η ημιονος. in Hes. p. 174. So that the spotted hyde of the mule signifies the moon attended with a multitude of stars: and hence, in the Orphic hymn to the moon, that deity is celebrated "as shining surrounded with beautiful stars":

. . . καλοις αστροισι βρυουσα

and is likewise called αστραρχη, or *queen of the stars*.

In the next place, the golden zone is the circle of the Ocean, as the last verses plainly evince. But, you will ask, what has the rising of the sun through the ocean, from the boundaries of earth and night, to do with the adventures of Bacchus? I answer, that it is impossible to devise a symbol more beautifully accommodated to the purpose: for, in the first place, is not the ocean a proper emblem of a material nature, whirling and stormy, and perpetually rolling without admitting any periods of repose?

419

And is not the sun emerging from its boisterous deeps a perspicuous symbol of an intellectual nature, apparently rising from the dark and fluctuating receptacle of matter, and conferring form and beauty on the sensible universe through its light? I say apparently rising, for though intellect always diffuses its splendor with invariable energy, yet it is not always perceived by the subjects of its illuminations; besides, as sensible natures can only receive partially and successively the benefits of divine irradiation, hence fables regarding this temporal participation transfer, for the purpose of concealment and in conformity to the phaenomena, the imperfection of subordinate natures to such as are supreme. This description, therefore, of the rising sun is a most beautiful symbol of the renovation of Bacchus, which, as we have already observed, implies nothing more than the rising of intellectual light, and its consequent appearance to subordinate forms.

And thus much for the mysteries of Bacchus, which, as well as those of Ceres, relate in one part to the descent of a partial intellect into matter, and its condition while united with the dark tenement of body: but there appears to be this difference between the two, that in the fable of Ceres and Proserpine, the descent of the whole rational soul is considered; and in that of Bacchus, the distribution and procession of that supreme part alone of our nature which we properly characterize by the appellation of intellect. In the composition of each we may discern the same traces of exalted wisdom and recondite theology; of a theology the most venerable of all others for its antiquity, and the most admirable for its excellence and reality: in each we may easily perceive the ignorance and malevolence of Christian priests, from the most early fathers to the most modern retailers of hypocrisy and cant; and in each every intelligent reader must be alternately excited to grief and indignation, to pity and contempt, at the barbarous mythological systems of the moderns: for in these we meet with nothing but folly and delusion; opinions founded either on fanaticism or atheism, inconceivably absurd and inextricably obscure, ridiculously vain and monstrously deformed, stupidly dull and contemptibly zealous, Apostolically delirious, or historically dry; and, in one word, such only as arrogance and ignorance could conceive, impiety propagate, and the vapid spirit of the moderns be induced to admit.

I shall therefore conclude this treatise by presenting the reader with a valuable and most elegant hymn of Proclus[14] to Minerva, which I have discovered in the British Museum; and the existence of which appears to have been hitherto utterly unknown. This hymn is to be found among the Harleian MSS., in a volume containing several of the Orphic hymns, with which, through the ignorance of the transcriber, it is indiscriminately ranked, as well as the other four hymns of Proclus, already printed in the Bibliotheca Graeca of Fabricius. Unfortunately too, it is transcribed in a character so obscure, and with such great inaccuracy, that, notwithstanding the pains I have taken to restore the text to its original purity, I have been obliged to omit two lines, and part of a third, as beyond my abilities to read or amend; however, the greatest, and doubtless the most important part, is fortunately intelligible, which I now present to the reader's inspection, accompanied with some corrections, and an English paraphrased translation. The original is highly elegant and pious, and contains one mythological particular which is no where else to be found. It has likewise an evident connection with the preceding fable of Bacchus, as will be obvious from the perusal; and on this account principally it was inserted in the present discourse.

TO MINERVA

DAUGHTER of aegis-bearing Jove, divine,
Propitious to thy vot'ries prayer incline;
From thy great father's fount supremely bright,
Like fire resounding, leaping into light.

[14] That the following hymn was composed by Proclus, cannot be doubted by any one who is conversant with those already extant of this incomparable man, since the spirit and manner in both is perfectly the same.

Thomas Taylor the Platonist

Shield-bearing goddess, hear, to whom belong
A manly mind, and power to tame the strong!
Oh, sprung from matchless might, with joyful mind
Accept this hymn; benevolent and kind!
The holy gates of wisdom, by thy hand
Are wide unfolded; and the daring band
Of earth-born giants, that in impious fight
Strove with thy sire, were vanquished by thy might.
Once by thy care, as sacred poets sing,
The heart of Bacchus, swiftly-slaughter'd king,
Was sav'd in aether, when, with fury fir'd,
The Titans fell against his life conspir'd;
And with relentless rage and thirst for gore,
Their hands his members into fragments tore:
But ever watchful of thy father's will,
Thy pow'r preserv'd him from succeeding ill,
Till from the secret counsels of his sire,
And born from Semele through heav'nly sire,
Great Dionysius to the world at length
Again appear'd with renovated strength.
Once, too, thy warlike axe, with matchless sway,
Lopp'd from their savage necks the heads away
Of furious beasts, and thus the pests destroy'd
Which long all-seeing Hecate annoy'd.
By thee benevolent great Juno's might
Was rous'd, to furnish mortals with delight.
And thro' life's wide and various range, 'tis thine
Each part to beautify with arts divine:
Invigorated hence by thee, we find
A demiurgic impulse in the mind.
Towers proudly rais'd, and for protection strong,
To thee dread guardian deity belong,
As proper symbols of th' exalted height
Thy series claims amidst the courts of light.
Lands are belov'd by thee, to learning prone,
And Athens, O Athena, is thy own!

Great goddess, hear! and on my dark'ned mind
Pour thy pure light in measure unconfin'd;—
That sacred light, O all-protecting queen,
Which beams eternal from thy face serene.
My soul, while wand'ring on the earth, inspire
With thy own blessed and impulsive fire:
And from thy fables, mystic and divine,
Give all her powers with holy light to shine.
Give love, give wisdom, and a power to love,
Incessant tending to the realms above;
Such as unconscious of base earth's controul
Gently attracts the vice subduing soul:
From night's dark region aids her to retire,
And once more gain the palace of her sire.
O all-propitious to my prayer incline!
Nor let those horrid punishments be mine
Which guilty souls in Tartarus confine,
With fetters fast'ned to its brazen floors,
And lock'd by hell's tremendous iron doors.
Hear me, and save (for power is all thine own)
A soul desirous to be thine alone.[15]

It is very remarkable in this hymn, that the exploits of Minerva relative to her cutting off the heads of wild beasts with an axe, &c., is mentioned by no writer whatever; nor can I find the least trace of a circumstance either in the history of Minerva or Hecate to which it alludes. And from hence, I think, we may reasonably conclude that it belonged to the arcane Orphic narrations concerning these goddesses, which were consequently but rarely mentioned, and this but by a few, whose works, which might afford us some clearer information, are unfortunately lost.

[15] If I should ever be able to publish a second edition of my translation of the hymns of Orpheus, I shall add to it a translation of all those hymns of Proclus, which are fortunately extant; but which are nothing more than the wreck of a great multitude which he composed. [Taylor published a second edition of *The Mystical Hymns of Orpheus* (see above, p. 162) in 1824, but he did not add the hymns of Proclus.]

APPENDIX

Since my writing the above Dissertation, I have met with a curious Greek MS. of Psellus, *on Daemons, according to the opinion of the Greeks*: του Ψελλου τινα περι δαιμονων δοξαζουσιν Ελληνες: in the course of which he describes the machinery of the Eleusinian mysteries as follows:—Α δε γε μυστηρια τουτων, οιον αυτικα τα ελευσινια, τον μυθικον υποκρινεται δια μιγνυμενον τη δηοι, ἢ τη Δημητερι, και τη θυγατερει ταυτης Φερσεφαττη τη και κορη. Επειδη δε εμελλον και αφροδισιοι επι τη μυησει γινεσθαι συμπλοκαι, αναδυεται πως η αφροδιτη απο τινων πεπλασμενων μηδεων πελαγιος. Ειτα δε γαμηλιος επι τη κορη υμεναιος. Και επαδουσιν οι τελουμενοι, εκ τυμπανου εφαγον, εκ κυμβαλων επιον, εκιρνοφορησα (lege εκερνοφορησα) υπο τον παστον εισεδυν. Υποκρινεται δε και τας δηους ωδινας. Ικετηριαι γουν αυτικα δηους. Και χολης ποσις, και καρδιαλγιαι. Εφ᾽ οις και τραγοσκελες μιμημα παθαινομενον περι τοις διδυμοις· οτι περ ο Ζευς δικας αποτιννυς της βιας τη Δημητερι τεραγου (lege τραγου) ορχεις αποτεμων, τω κολπω ταυτης κατεθετο, ωσπερ δη και εαυτου. Επι πασιν αι του Διονυσου τιμαι, και η κυστις, και τα πολυομφαλα ποπανα, και οι τω σαβαζιω τελουμενοι, κληδονες τε και μιμαλωνες, και τις ηχων λεβης θεσπρωτειος και δωδωναιον χαλκειον, και κορυβας αλλος και κουρης ετερος, δαιμονων μιμηματα. Εφ᾽ οις η βαβωτους (lege η βαυβω τους) μηρους ανασυρομενη, και ο γυναικος κτεις, ουτω γαρ ονομαζουσι την αιδω αισχυνομενοι. Και ουτως εν αισχρω την τελετην καταλυουσιν. *I.e.* "The mysteries of these daemons," (for Psellus being a Christian, considered the gods of the antients as nothing more than evil daemons,) "such as the Eleusinian mysteries, consisted in representing the fabulous narration of Jupiter mingling with Ceres and her daughter Proserpine. But as venereal connections take place along with the initiation,[16] a marine Venus is represented rising from certain fictitious genital parts: afterwards the celebrated marriage of Proserpine (*with Pluto*) takes place; and those who are initiated sing, I have eat out of the drum, I have drank out of the cymbal, I have

---

[16] I.e. a representation of them.

borne the mystic cup, I have entered into the bed. But the pregnant throes likewise of Ceres are represented: hence the supplications of Ceres are exhibited; her drinking of bile, and the pains
of her heart. After this, an image with the thighs of a goat makes
its appearance, and which at the same time suffers vehemently
about the testicles: because Jupiter, in order to expiate the crime
of the violence which he offered to Ceres, is represented as cutting off the testicles of a goat, and placing them on the bosom
of Ceres, as likewise on his own bosom. But after all this, the
honours of Bacchus succeed; the Cista, and the cakes with many
bosses, like those of a shield. Likewise the mysteries of Sabazius,
divinations, and the priestesses of Bacchus; a certain sound of
the Thesprotian kettle; the Dodonaean brass; another Corybas,
and another Proserpine, who are resemblances of Daemons. After
these succeed the uncovering the thighs of Baubo, and a woman's
comb; for thus, through shame, they denominate the privities of a
woman. And thus, in the indecent, they finish the initiation."

From this curious passage, it appears that the Eleusinian mysteries comprehended those of almost all the gods; and this account
will not only throw light on the relation of the mysteries given
by Clemens Alexandrinus, but likewise be elucidated by it in
several particulars. I would willingly unfold to the reader the
mystic meaning of the whole of this machinery, but this cannot
be accomplished by any one, without at least the possession of all
the Platonic manuscripts which are extant. This acquisition,
which I should infinitely prize above the wealth of the Indies,
will, I hope, speedily and fortunately be mine, and then I shall
be no less anxious to communicate this arcane information,
than the *liberal* reader will be to receive it. I shall only therefore
observe, that the mutual communication of energies among the
gods was called by antient theologists ιερος γαμος, *a sacred marriage*; concerning which Proclus, in the second book of his MS.
Commentary on the Parmenides, admirably remarks as follows:
ταυτην δε την κοινωνιαν, ποτε μεν εν τοις συστοιχοις ορωσι
θεοις (οι θεολογοι) και καλουσι γαμον Ηρας και Διος, ουρανου
και γης, Κρονου και Ρεας· ποτε δε των καταδεεστερων προς τα
κρειττω, και καλουσι γαμον Διος και Δημητρας· ποτε δε και

εμπαλιν των κρειττωνων προς τα υφειμενα, και λεγουσι Διος και Κορης γαμον. Επειδη των θεων αλλαι μεν εισιν αι προς τα συστοιχα κοινωνιαι, αλλαι δε αι προς τα προ αυτων· αλλαι δε αι προς τα μετα ταυτα. Και δει την εκαστης ιδιοτητα κατανοειν και μεταγειν απο των θεων επι τα ειδη την τοιαυτην διαπλοκην. *I.e.* "Theologists at one time considered this communion of the gods in divinities co-ordinate with each other; and then they called it the marriage of Jupiter and Juno, of Heaven and Earth, of Saturn and Rhea: but at another time, they considered it as subsisting between subordinate and superior divinities; and then they called it the marriage of Jupiter and Ceres: but at another time, on the contrary, they beheld it as subsisting between superior and subordinate divinities; and then they called it the marriage of Jupiter and Proserpine. For in the gods there is one kind of communion between such as are of a co-ordinate nature; another between the subordinate and supreme; and another again between the supreme and subordinate. And it is necessary to understand the idiom of each, and to transfer a conjunction of this kind from the gods to the communion of ideas with each other." And in lib. 1. in Tim. p. 16, he observes: και το την αυτην (supply θεαν) ετεροις ἠ τον αυτον θεον πλειοσι συζευγνυσθαι, λαβοις αν εκ των μυστικων λογων, και των εν απορρητοις λεγομενων ιερων γαμων. *I.e.* "And that the same goddess is conjoined with other gods, or the same god with many goddesses, may be collected from *the mystic discourses,* and those marriages which are called in *the mysteries Sacred Marriages.*"—Thus far the divine Proclus; from the first of which passages the reader may perceive how adultery and rapes, as represented in the machinery of the mysteries, are to be understood when applied to the gods; and that they mean nothing more than a communication of divine energies, either between a superior and subordinate, or subordinate and superior, divinity. I only add, that the apparent indecency of these exhibitions was, as I have already observed, exclusive of its mystic meaning, designed as a remedy for the passions of the soul: and hence mystic ceremonies were very properly called ακεα, *medicines,* by the obscure and noble Heraclitus.[17]

[17] Vid. Jamblich. de Mysteriis, p. 22.

INTRODUCTION TO

THE FABLE OF CUPID AND PSYCHE

As part of the explanatory matter on the title page of the original edition (London, 1795), Taylor pointed out that the object of this Introduction was to unfold "the meaning of the fable," and he included a condensed version in an extended footnote in *The Metamorphosis, or Golden Ass, and Philosophical Works, of Apuleius* (1822), pp. 87–91. The reissue of 1893 omits the footnote.

Taylor also hoped to convince his readers that Apuleius "held a distinguished place among the Platonic philosophers" of his time, and was indeed "the greatest of the ancient Latin Platonists," though clearly inferior to "that golden race . . . of which the great Plotinus stands at the head."

Hoping no doubt to attract attention to his struggle against "the forces of darkness," Taylor dedicated "To the President, Council, and Members of the Royal Academy, the Following Translation and Explanation of *The Fable of Cupid and Psyche*." It was reviewed in four prominent periodicals: *Critical Review*, XIV, 2d Series (1795), 269; *Monthly Review*, XVIII, 2d Series (1795), 51–55; *British Critic*, VII (1796), 571–72; and *Analytical Review*, XXVI (1797), 388–90.

For representations of the *Fable*, see Plates 11a, 12, and 13.

INTRODUCTION

THE FOLLOWING well-known fable is extracted from the Metamorphoses of Apuleius, a work replete with elegance and erudition,
in which the marvelous and mystic are happily combined with
historical precision, and the whole of which is composed in a
style inimitably glowing and diffuse.

Its author was by birth an African, and, by profession, a Platonic
philosopher. From the account which he gives of himself, it appears most probable that he lived in the times of Antoninus Pius,
and his illustrious brothers. He seems to have been very much
addicted to the study of magic, but has very ably cleared himself
from the accusation of practising it, which was brought against
him, in an Oration, the whole of which is still extant. However,
though he was a man of extraordinary abilities, and held a distinguished place among the Platonic philosophers of that period,
yet he was inferior to any one of that golden race of philosophers,
of which the great Plotinus stands at the head. Of the truth of this
observation few indeed of the present age are likely to be convinced, from that base prejudice which has taken such deep root
in the minds of men of every description, through the declamations
of those literary bullies, the verbal critics, on the one hand, and
the fraudulent harangues of sophistical priests on the other. Posterity, however, will warmly patronize my assertion, and vindicate
the honours of those venerable heroes, the latter Platonists, when
such critics and *such* priests are covered with the shades of eternal
oblivion.

The following beautiful fable, which was designed to represent
the lapse of the human soul from the intelligible world to the
earth, was certainly not invented by Apuleius; for, as will appear
in the course of the Introduction, it is evidently alluded to by
Synesius, in his book *On Dreams*, and obscurely by Plato and
Plotinus. It is clear, therefore, that Plato could not derive his
allusion from Apuleius; and as to Plotinus and Synesius, those
who are at all acquainted with the writings of the Greek philosophers, well know that they never borrowed from Latin authors,

from a just conviction that they had the sources of perfection among themselves.

I have said that this fable represented the lapse of the human soul; of the truth of this the philosophical reader will be convinced by the following observations: In the first place, the gods, as I have elsewhere shown, are super-essential natures, from their profound union with the first cause, who is super-essential without any addition. But though the gods, through their summits or unities, transcend essence, yet their unities are participated either by intellect alone, or by intellect and soul, or by intellect, soul, and body; from which participations the various orders of the gods are deduced. When, therefore, intellect, soul, and body are in conjunction suspended from this super-essential unity, which is the center flower or blossom of a divine nature, then the god from whom they are suspended is called a mundane god. In the next place, the common parents of the human soul are the intellect and soul of the world; but its proximate parents are the intellect and soul of the particular star about which it was originally distributed, and from which it first descends. In the third place, those powers of every mundane god, which are participated by the body suspended from his nature, are called mundane; but those which are participated by his intellect, are called super-mundane; and the soul, while subsisting in union with these super-mundane powers, is said to be in the intelligible world; but when she wholly directs her attention to the mundane powers of her god, she is said to descend from the intelligible world, even while subsisting in the Heavens.

Thus much being premised, let us proceed to the explanation of the fable: Psyche, then, or soul, is described as transcendantly beautiful; and this indeed is true of every human soul, before it profoundly merges itself in the defiling folds of dark matter. In the next place, when Psyche is represented as descending from the summit of a lofty mountain into a beautiful valley, this signifies the descent of the soul from the intelligible world into a mundane condition of being, but yet without abandoning its establishment in the Heavens. Hence the palace which Psyche beholds in the valley is, with great propriety, said to be "a royal house, which was not raised by human, but by divine, hands and art." The gems, too, on which Psyche is said to have trod in every part of this palace, are evidently symbolical of the stars. Of this mundane, yet celestial, condition of being, the incorporeal voices which attend upon Psyche are likewise symbolical: for outward discourse is the last image of intellectual energy, according to which the soul alone operates in the intelligible world. As voices, therefore, they signify an establishment subordinate to that which is intelligible, but so far as denudated of body, they also signify a condition of being superior to a terrene allotment.

Psyche, in this delightful situation, is married to an invisible being, whom she alone recognizes by her ears and hands. This invisible husband proves afterwards to be Love; that is to say, the soul, while established in the Heavens, is united with pure *desire* (for *Love* is the same with *desire*), or, in other words, is not fascinated with outward form. But in this beautiful palace she is attacked by the machinations of her two sisters, who endeavour to persuade her to explore the form of her unknown husband. The sisters, therefore, signify imagination and nature; just in the same manner as reason is signified by Psyche. Their stratagems at length take effect, and Psyche beholds and falls in love with Love; that is to say, the rational part, through the incentives of phantasy and the vegetable power, becomes united with impure or terrene desire; for vision is symbolical of union between the perceiver and thing perceived. In consequence of this illicit perception Cupid, or *pure desire*, flies away, and Psyche, or soul, is precipitated to earth. It is remarkable that Psyche, after falling to the ground, is represented as having "*a stumbling and often reeling gait*"; for Plato, in the Phaedo, says, that the soul is drawn into body with a *staggering* motion.

After this commence the wanderings of Psyche, or soul, in search of Love, or pure desire, from whose embraces she is unhappily torn away. In the course of her journey she arrives at the temples of Ceres and Juno, whose aid she suppliantly implores. Her conduct, indeed, in this respect is highly becoming; for Ceres comprehends in her essence Juno, who is the foundation of souls; and the safety of the soul arises from converting herself to the divine sources of her being.

In the next place Venus is represented desiring Mercury to proclaim Psyche through all lands, as one of her female slaves that has fled from her service. It is likewise said that she gave him a small volume, in which the name of Psyche was written, and every other particular respecting her. Now I think it cannot be doubted but that Synesius alludes to this part of the fable in the following passage from his admirable book *On Dreams*: "When the soul descends spontaneously to its former life, with mercenary views, it receives servitude as the reward of its mercenary labours. But this is the design of descent, that the soul may accomplish a certain servitude to the nature of the universe, prescribed by the laws of Adrastia, or inevitable fate. Hence when the soul is fascinated with material endowments, she is similarly affected to those who, though free born, are, for a certain time, hired by wages to employments, and in this condition captivated with the beauty of some female servant, determine to act in a menial capacity under the master of their beloved object. Thus, in a similar manner, when we are profoundly delighted with external and corporeal goods, we confess that the nature of matter is beautiful, who marks our assent in her secret book; *and if, considering ourselves as free, we at any time determine to depart, she proclaims us deserters, endeavours to bring us back, and openly presenting her mystic volume to the view, apprehends us as fugitives from our mistress.* Then, indeed, the soul particularly requires fortitude and divine assistance, as it is no trifling contest to abrogate the confession and compact which she made. Besides, in this case force will be employed; for the material inflicters of punishments will then be roused to revenge by the decrees of fate against the rebels to her laws."[1]

Venus, however, must not be considered here as the nature of

[1] See my History of the Restoration of the Platonic Theology, at the end of Vol. II of Proclus on Euclid, in which a translation of the greater part of this excellent piece is given.

matter; for though she is not the celestial Venus, but the offspring of Dione, yet she is that divine power which governs all the co-ordinations in the celestial world and the earth, binds them to each other, and perfects their generative progressions through a kindred conjunction. As the celestial Venus, therefore, separates the pure soul from generation, so she that proceeds from Dione binds the impure soul, as her legitimate slave, to a corporeal life.

After this follows an account of the difficult tasks which Psyche is obliged to execute by the commands of Venus; all which are images of the mighty toils and anxious cares which the soul must necessarily endure after her lapse, in order to atone for her guilt, and recover her ancient residence in the intelligible world. In accomplishing the last of these labours she is represented as forced to descend even to the dark regions of Hades; by which it is evident that Psyche is the image of a soul that descends to the very extremity of things, or that makes the most extended progression before it returns. But Psyche, in returning from Hades, is oppressed with a profound sleep, through indiscreetly opening the box given her by Proserpine, in which she expected to find a portion of divine beauty, but met with nothing but an infernal Stygian sleep. This obscurely signifies that the soul, by considering a corporeal life as truly beautiful, passes into a profoundly dormant state: and it appears to me that both Plato and Plotinus allude to this part of our fable in the following passages, for the originals of which I refer the reader to my Dissertation on the Eleusinian and Bacchic Mysteries, p. 10.[2] In the first place, then Plato, in the seventh book of his *Republic*, observes that "He who is not able, by the exercise of his reason, to define the idea of *the good* separating it from all other objects, and, piercing, as in a battle, through every kind of argument: endeavouring to confute, not according to opinion, but according to essence, and proceeding through all the dialectical energies with an unshaken reason, is in the present life sunk in sleep, and conversant with the delusions of dreams; and that before he is roused to a vigilant state, *he will descend to Hades, and be overwhelmed with a sleep*

[2] [See above, p. 349n.]

perfectly profound." And Plotinus, in Ennead 1. lib. 8, p. 80, says, "The death of the soul is, while merged, or baptized, as it were, in the present body, to descend into matter, and be filled with its impurity, and after departing from this body, to lie absorbed in its filth till it returns to a superior condition, and elevates its eye from the overwhelming mire. *For to be plunged into matter is to descend to Hades, and fall asleep."*

Cupid, however, or pure desire, at length recovering his pristine vigor, rouses Psyche, or soul, from her deadly lethargy. In consequence of this, having accomplished her destined toils, she ascends to her native heaven, becomes lawfully united with Cupid, (for while descending her union might be called illegitimate) lives the life of the immortals; and the natural result of this union with pure desire is pleasure or delight. And thus much for an explanation of the fable of Cupid and Psyche. For farther particulars respecting the lapse of the soul, see my Introduction to, and Translation of, Plotinus on the Descent of the Soul, and my Dissertation on the Eleusinian and Bacchic Mysteries.

I only add, that the Paraphrase on the Speech of Diotima, the Hymns, some of which are illustrative of the Speech, and the other pieces of poetry, are added at the request of a gentleman, whose thirst after knowledge, endeavours to promote it, elegant taste, and friendship for the author, demand a panegyric executed in a more masterly manner at least, though not with greater sincerity, than by the following lines:

> *While some, the vilest of a puffing age,*
> *With fulsome adulation stain the page,*
> *And time's irrevocable moments waste*
> *In base compliance with degenerate taste,*
> *Rise honest muse; and to thy lib'ral lyre*
> *Symphonious sing what friendship shall inspire.*
> *Say, shall the wretch, to gain devoted, claim*
> *A place conspicuous 'midst the sons of fame;*
> *For ill-got wealth with dying accents giv'n,*
> *To bribe the vengeance of impartial Heav'n?*

Introduction to Cupid and Psyche

And shall not he *who,'midst the din of trade,*
Has homage at the Muse's altars paid;
Astonish'd view'd the depth of Plato's thought,
And strove to spread the truths sublime he taught—
Attention gain, and gratitude inspire,
And with his worth excite the poet's fire?
Yes, PHRONIMUS, *my muse, in lib'ral lays,*
This friendly tribute to thy merit pays;
And ardent hopes that ages yet unborn
May see well pleas'd thy name her works adorn!

THE PLATONIC
PHILOSOPHER'S CREED

This essay was included by Taylor in his *Miscellanies in Prose and Verse* (1805), which also contained the *Triumph of the Wise Man over Fortune according to the Doctrine of the Stoics and Platonists* and other short works.

THE PLATONIC PHILOSOPHER'S CREED

1. I BELIEVE in one first cause of all things, whose nature is so immensely transcendent, that it is even super-essential; and that in consequence of this it cannot properly either be named, or spoken of, or conceived by opinion, or be known, or perceived by any being.

2. I believe, however, that if it be lawful to give a name to that which is truly ineffable, the appellations of *the one* and *the good* are of all others the most adapted to it; the former of these names indicating that it is the principle of all things, and the latter that it is the ultimate object of desire to all things.

3. I believe that this immense principle produced such things as are first and proximate to itself, most similar to itself; just as the heat *immediately* proceeding from fire is most similar to the heat in the fire; and the light *immediately* emanating from the sun, to that which the sun essentially contains. Hence, this principle produces many principles proximately from itself.

4. I likewise believe that since all things differ from each other, and are multiplied with their proper differences, each of these multitudes is suspended from its one proper principle. That, in consequence of this, all beautiful things, whether in souls or in bodies, are suspended from one fountain of beauty. That whatever possesses symmetry, and whatever is true, and all principles are in a certain respect connate with the first principle, so far as they are principles, with an appropriate subjection and analogy. That all other principles are comprehended in this first principle, not with interval and multitude, but as parts in the whole, and number in the monad. That it is not a certain principle like each of the rest; for of these, one is the principle of beauty, another of truth, and another of something else, but it is *simply principle*. Nor is it simply the *principle of beings*, but it is *the principle of principles*; it being necessary that the characteristic property of principle, after the same manner as other things, should not begin from multitude, but should be collected into one monad as a summit, and which is the principle of principles.

5. I believe, therefore, that such things as are produced by the first good in consequence of being connascent with it, do not recede from essential goodness, since they are immoveable and unchanged, and are eternally established in the same blessedness. All other natures, however, being produced by the one good, and many goodnesses, since they fall off from essential goodness, and are not immoveably established in the nature of divine goodness, possess on this account the good according to participation.

6. I believe that as all things considered as subsisting *causally* in this immense principle are transcendently more excellent than they are when considered as effects proceeding from him; this principle is very properly said to be all things, *prior* to all; *priority* denoting exempt transcendency. Just as number may be considered as subsisting occultly in the monad, and the circle in the centre; this *occult* being the same in each with *causal* subsistence.

7. I believe that the most proper mode of venerating this great principle of principles is to extend in silence the ineffable parturitions of the soul to its ineffable co-sensation; and that if it be at all lawful to celebrate it, it is to be celebrated as a thrice unknown darkness, as the god of all gods, and the unity of all unities, as more ineffable than all silence, and more occult than all essence, as holy among the holies, and concealed in its first progeny, the intelligible gods.

8. I believe that self-subsistent natures are the immediate offspring of this principle, if it be lawful thus to denominate things which ought rather to be called ineffable unfoldings into light from the ineffable.

9. I believe that incorporeal forms or ideas resident in a divine intellect are the paradigms or models of every thing which has a perpetual subsistence according to nature. That these ideas subsist primarily in the highest intellects, secondarily in souls, and ultimately in sensible natures; and that they subsist in each, characterized by the essential properties of the beings in which they are contained. That they possess a *paternal, producing, guardian, connecting, perfective,* and *uniting* power. That in *divine beings* they possess a power fabricative and gnostic, in

nature a power fabricative but not gnostic, and in *human souls* in their present condition through a degradation of intellect, a power gnostic, but not fabricative.

10. I believe that this world, depending on its divine artificer, who is himself an intelligible world, replete with the archetypal ideas of all things, is perpetually flowing, and perpetually advancing to being, and, compared with its paradigm, has no stability, or reality of being. That considered, however, as animated by a divine soul, and as being the receptacle of divinities from whom bodies are suspended, it is justly called by Plato, a blessed god.

11. I believe that the great body of this world, which subsists in a perpetual dispersion of temporal extension, may be properly called a *whole, with a total subsistence*, or a *whole of wholes*,[1] on account of the perpetuity of its duration, though this is nothing more than a flowing eternity. That the other wholes which it contains are the celestial spheres, the sphere of aether, the whole of air considered as one great orb; the whole earth, and the whole sea. That these spheres are *parts with a total subsistence*, and through this subsistence are perpetual.

12. I believe that all the parts of the universe are unable to participate of the providence of divinity in a similar manner, but some of its parts enjoy this eternally, and others temporally; some in a primary and others in a secondary degree; for the universe being a perfect whole, must have a first, a middle, and a last part. But its first parts, as having the most excellent subsistence, must always exist according to nature; and its last parts must sometimes exist according to, and sometimes contrary to, nature. Hence, the celestial bodies, which are the first parts of the universe, perpetually subsist according to nature, both the whole spheres, and the multitude co-ordinate to these wholes; and the only alteration which they experience is a mutation of figure, and

---

[1] As little as the eye of a fly at the bottom of the largest of the Egyptian pyramids sees of the whole of that pyramid, compared with what is seen of it by the eye of a man, so little does the greatest experimentalist see of the whole of things, compared with what Plato and Aristotle saw of it, through scientific reasoning founded on self-evident principles.

variation of light at different periods; but in the sublunary region, while the spheres of the elements remain on account of their subsistence, as wholes, always according to nature; the parts of the wholes have sometimes a natural, and sometimes an unnatural subsistence: for thus alone can the circle of generation unfold all the variety which it contains. I believe, therefore, that the different periods in which these mutations happen, are with great propriety called by Plato, periods of *fertility*[2] and *sterility*: for in these periods a fertility or sterility of men, animals, and plants takes place; so that in fertile periods mankind will be both more numerous, and upon the whole superior in mental and bodily endowments to the men of a barren period. And that a similar reasoning must be extended to irrational animals and plants. I also believe that the most dreadful consequence attending a barren period with respect to mankind is this, that in such a period they have no scientific theology, and deny the existence of the immediate progeny of the ineffable cause of all things.

13. I believe that as the world considered as one great comprehending whole is a divine animal, so likewise every whole which it contains is a world, possessing in the first place a self-perfect unity proceeding from the ineffable by which it becomes a god; in the second place, a divine intellect; in the third place, a divine soul; and in the last place a deified body. That each of these wholes is the producing cause of all the multitude which it contains, and on this account is said to be a whole prior to parts; because considered as possessing an eternal form which holds all its parts together, and gives to the whole perpetuity of subsistence, it is not indigent of such parts to the perfection of its being. And that it follows by a geometrical necessity, that these wholes which rank thus high in the universe must be animated.

14. Hence I believe that after the immense principle of principles in which all things causally subsist absorbed in super-essential light, and involved in unfathomable depths, a beautiful

---

[2] The so much celebrated *heroic age* was the result of one of these fertile periods, in which men, transcending the herd of mankind both in *practical* and *intellectual* virtue abounded on the earth.

series of principles proceeds, all largely partaking of the ineffable, all stamped with the occult characters of deity, all possessing an overflowing fulness of good. That from these dazzling summits, these ineffable blossoms, these divine propagations, being, life, intellect, soul, nature, and body depend; *monads*[3] suspended from *unities*, deified natures proceeding from deities. That each of these monads is the leader of a series which extends to the last of things, and which, while it proceeds from, at the same time abides in, and returns to its leader. Thus all beings proceed from and are comprehended in the first being; all intellects emanate from one first intellect; all souls from one first soul; all natures blossom from one first nature; and all bodies proceed from the vital and luminous body of the world. That all these great monads are comprehended in the first one, from which both they and all their depending series are unfolded into light. And that hence this first one is truly the unity of unities, the monad of monads, the principle of principles, the god of gods, one and all things, and yet one prior to all.

15. I also believe that man is a microcosm, comprehending in himself *partially* every thing which the world contains divinely and *totally*. That hence he is endued with an intellect subsisting in energy, and a rational soul proceeding from the same causes as those from which the intellect and soul of the universe proceed. And that he has likewise an ethereal vehicle analogous to the heavens, and a terrestrial body composed from the four elements, and with which also it is co-ordinate.

16. I believe that the rational part of man, in which his essence consists, is of a self-motive nature, and that it subsists between intellect, which is immoveable both in essence and energy, and nature, which both moves and is moved.

17. I believe that the human as well as every mundane soul uses periods and restitutions of its proper life. For in consequence

[3] *The monad* is that which contains things separated from each other unitedly; just as the inerratic sphere contains the fixed stars. But *the one* is *the summit* of multitude. And hence *the one* is more simple than *the monad*.

of being measured by time, it energizes transitively, and possesses a proper motion. But every thing which is moved perpetually, and participates of time, revolves periodically, and proceeds from the same to the same.

18. I also believe that as the human soul ranks among the number of those souls that *sometimes* follow the mundane divinities, in consequence of subsisting immediately after daemons and heroes the *perpetual* attendants of the gods, it possesses a power of descending infinitely into the sublunary region, and of ascending from thence to real being. That in consequence of this, the soul while an inhabitant of earth is in a fallen condition, an apostate from deity, an exile from the orb of light. That she can only be restored while on earth to the divine likeness, and be able after death to reascend to the intelligible world, by the exercise of the *cathartic* and *theoretic* virtues; the former purifying her from the defilements of a mortal nature, and the latter elevating her to the vision of true being. And that such a soul returns after death to her kindred star from which she fell, and enjoys a blessed life.

19. I believe that the human soul essentially contains all knowledge, and that whatever knowledge she acquires in the present life is nothing more than a recovery of what she once possessed; and which discipline evocates from its dormant retreats.

20. I also believe that the soul is punished in a future for the crimes she has committed in the present life; but that this punishment is proportioned to the crimes, and is not perpetual; divinity punishing, not from anger or revenge, but in order to purify the guilty soul, and restore her to the proper perfection of her nature.

21. I also believe that the human soul on its departure from the present life will, if not properly purified, pass into other terrene bodies; and that if it passes into a human body, it becomes the soul of that body; but if into the body of a brute, it does not become the soul of the brute, but is externally connected with the brutal soul in the same manner as presiding daemons are connected in their beneficent operations with mankind; for the rational part never becomes the soul of the irrational nature.

22. Lastly, I believe that souls that live according to virtue shall in other respects be happy; and when separated from the irrational nature, and purified from all body, shall be conjoined with the gods, and govern the whole world, together with the deities by whom it was produced.

AN APOLOGY
FOR THE FABLES OF HOMER

Translated from the Greek of Proclus
(Introduction to the Second and
Third Books of the *Republic*,
from *The Works of Plato*)

Taylor's translation of Proclus's essay on the fables of Homer is indebted to "the epitome made by Gesner of this apology." As an "Introduction to the Second and Third Books of the *Republic*," from Volume I of *The Works of Plato* (5 vols., London, 1804), the *Apology* seems over-long and hard to justify simply as a "defence of Homer and divine fables in general," but Taylor as usual had a further motive: not only to demonstrate that Homer's epics as well as Plato's *Republic* are complex cosmological allegories, but also to prove that "Homer and Plato are so admirably reconciled."

AN APOLOGY FOR THE
FABLES OF HOMER

AS A VERY considerable part both of the second and third books of The Republic consists in examining and reprobating the assertions of the poets and particularly the fables of Homer, concerning divine natures, it appeared to me that I could not more essentially benefit the reader than by presenting him with the following defence of Homer and divine fables in general, from the exposition of the more difficult questions in this dialogue, by that coryphaeus of all true philosophers Proclus. For in this apology Homer and Plato are so admirably reconciled, that the poetry of the one and the philosophy of the other are in the highest degree honoured by the expulsion of the former from the polity of the latter. In short, it will be found, however paradoxical it may appear, that the most divine of poets ought beyond all others to be banished from a republic planned by the prince of philosophers. Such readers, too, as may fortunately possess a genius adapted for these speculations will find that the fables of Homer are replete with a theory no less grand than scientific, no less accurate than sublime; that they are truly the progeny of divine fury; are worthy to be ascribed to the Muses as their origin; are capable of exciting in those that understand them the most exalted conceptions, and of raising the imagination in conjunction with intellect, and thus purifying and illuminating its figured eye.

Though I availed myself in this translation of the epitome made by Gesner of this apology, who seems to have consulted a more perfect manuscript than that from which the Basil edition was printed, yet I frequently found it necessary to correct the Greek text from my own conjecture, as the learned reader will readily perceive. Some of these emendations I have noted in the course of the translation; but as they are numerous many are omitted.

Thomas Taylor the Platonist

I. CONCERNING THE MODE OF THE
APPARATUS OF DIVINE FABLES
WITH THEOLOGISTS.—THE CAUSES
OF SUCH FABLES ASSIGNED; AND A
SOLUTION OF THE OBJECTIONS
AGAINST THEM

Since Socrates accuses the mode of fables according to which Homer and Hesiod have delivered doctrines concerning the Gods, and prior to these Orpheus, and any other poets, who with a divine mouth, ειθεω στοματι, have interpreted things which have a perpetual sameness of subsistence, it is necessary that we should in the first place show that the disposition of the Homeric fables is adapted to the things which it indicates. For it may be said, How can things which are remote from the good and the beautiful, and which deviate from order,—how can base and illegal names ever be adapted to those natures whose essence is characterized by the good, and is consubsistent with the beautiful, in whom there is the first order, and from whom all things are unfolded into light, in conjunction with beauty and undefiled power? How then can things which are full of tragical portents and phantasms which subsist with material natures, and are deprived of the whole of justice and the whole of divinity, be adapted to such natures as these? For is it not unlawful to ascribe to the nature of the Gods, who are exempt from all things through transcendent excellence, adulteries, and thefts, precipitations from heaven, injurious conduct towards parents, bonds, and castrations, and such other particulars as are celebrated by Homer and other antient poets? But, as the Gods are separated from other things, are united with *the good*, or the ineffable principle of things, and have nothing of the imperfection of inferior natures belonging to them, but are unmingled and undefiled with respect to all things, presubsisting uniformly according to one bound and order,—in like manner it is requisite to employ the most excellent language in speaking of them, and such appellations as are full of intellect, and which are able to assimilate us, according to their proper order, to their ineffable transcendency. It is also necessary to purify the notions of the soul from material phantasms, in the mystic intellectual conceptions of a divine nature; and, rejecting every thing foreign and all false opinions, to conceive every thing as small with respect to the undefiled transcendency of the Gods, and believe in right opinion alone, and the more excellent spectacles of intellect in the truth concerning the first of essences.

Let no one therefore say to us that such things harmonize with the Gods as are adapted to men, nor endeavour to introduce the passions of material irrationality to natures expanded above intellect, and an intellectual essence and life: for these symbols do not appear similar to the hyparxes[1] of the Gods. It is therefore requisite that fables, if they do not entirely wander from the truth inherent in things, should be in a certain respect assimilated to the particulars, the occult theory of which they endeavour to conceal by apparent veils. Indeed, as Plato himself often mystically teaches us divine concerns through certain images, and neither any thing base, nor any representation of disorder, nor material and turbulent phantasm is inserted in his fables,—but the intellectual conceptions concerning the Gods are concealed with purity, before which the fables are placed like conspicuous statues, and most similar representations of the inward arcane theory,— in like manner it is requisite that poets, and Homer himself, if they devise fables adapted to the Gods, should reject these multiform compositions, and which are at the same time replete with names most contrary to things, but employing such as regard the beautiful and the good, should, through these, exclude the multitude from a knowledge concerning the Gods, which does not pertain to them, and at the same time employ in a pious manner fabulous devices respecting divine natures.

These are the things which, as it appears to me, Socrates objects to the fables of Homer, and for which perhaps some one besides

---

[1] Hyparxis signifies the summit of essence; and, in all the divinities except the first God, is *the one* considered as participated by essence. See the Introduction to the Parmenides.

may accuse other poets, in consequence of not admitting the apparently monstrous signification of names. In answer then to these objections, we reply that fables fabricate all that apparatus pertaining to them, which first presents itself to our view, instead of the truth which is established in the arcana, and employ apparent veils of conceptions invisible and unknown to the multitude. This indeed is their distinguishing excellence, that they narrate nothing belonging to natures truly good to the profane, but only extend certain vestiges of the whole mystic discipline to such as are naturally adapted to be led from these to a theory inaccessible to the vulgar. For these, instead of investigating the truth which they contain, use only the pretext of fabulous devices; and, instead of the purification of intellect, follow phantastic and figured conceptions. Is it not therefore absurd in these men to accuse fables of their own illegitimate conduct, and not themselves for the erroneous manner in which they consider them?

In the next place, do we not see that the multitude are injured by such things as are remarkably venerable and honourable, from among all other things, and which are established in and produced by the Gods themselves? For who will not acknowledge that the mysteries and perfective rites lead souls upwards from a material and mortal life, and conjoin them with the Gods, and that they suppress all that tumult which insinuates itself from the irrational part into intellectual illuminations, and expel whatever is indefinite and dark from those that are initiated, through the light proceeding from the Gods? Yet at the same time nothing can restrain the multitude from sustaining from these all-various distortions, and, in consequence of using the good, and the powers proceeding from these, according to their perverted habit, departing from the Gods, and truly sacred ceremonies, and falling into a passive and irrational life. Those indeed that accuse the mysteries for producing these effects in the multitude may also accuse the fabrication of the universe, the order of wholes, and the providence of all things, because those that receive the gifts of these, use them badly; but neither is such an accusation holy, nor is it fit that fables should be calumniated on account of the perverted conceptions of the multitude. For the virtue and vice of things are not to be determined from those that use them perversely; but it is fit that every thing should be estimated from its own proper nature, and the rectitude which it contains. Hence the Athenian guest, in the Laws of Plato, is of opinion that even intoxication ought not to be expelled from a well-instituted city, on account of the views of the multitude and its corrupt use; for he says it greatly contributes to education, if it is properly and prudently employed. And yet it may be said that intoxication corrupts both the bodies and souls of those that are subject to it; but the legislator does not on this account detract from its proper worth, and the aid it affords to virtue.

But if any one accuses fables on account of their apparent depravity, and the base names which they employ,—since things of this kind are by no means similar to the divine exemplars of which fables are the images,—we reply in the first place, that there are two kinds of fables, those adapted to the education of youth, and those full of a divine fury, and which rather regard the universe itself than the habit of those that hear them. In the next place we must distinguish the lives of those that use fables; and we must consider that some are juvenile, and conversant with simple habits; but that others are able to be excited to intellect, to the whole genera of the Gods, to their progressions through all things, their series, and their terminations, which hasten to be extended as far as to the last of things. This being premised, we must say that the fables of Homer and Hesiod are not adapted to the education of youth, but that they follow the nature of wholes, and the order of things, and conjoin with true beings such as are capable of being led to the elevated survey of divine concerns. For the fathers of fables—perceiving that nature, fabricating images of immaterial and intelligible forms, and diversifying the sensible world with the imitations of these, adumbrated things impartible partibly, but expressed things eternal through such as proceed according to time, things intelligible through sensibles, that which is immaterial materially, that which is without interval with interval, and through mutation

453

that which is firmly established, conformably to the nature and the progression of the phaenomena,—they also, devising the resemblances and images of things divine in their verses, imitated the transcendent power of exemplars by contrary and most remote adumbrations. Hence they indicated that which is supernatural in things divine by things contrary to nature, that which is more divine than all reason, by that which is contrary to reason, and that which is expanded above all partial beauty, by things apparently base. And thus by an assimilative method they recalled to our memory the exempt supremacy of divine natures.

Besides this, according to every order of the Gods, which beginning from on high gradually proceeds as far as to the last of things, and penetrates through all the genera of beings, we may perceive the terminations of their series exhibiting such idioms as fables attributed to the Gods themselves, and that they give subsistence to, and are connective of, such things as those through which fables conceal the arcane theory of first essences. For the last of the daemoniacal genera, and which revolve about matter, preside over the perversion of natural powers, the baseness of material natures, the lapse into vice, and a disorderly and confused motion. For it is necessary that these things should take place in the universe, and should contribute to fill the variety of the whole order of things, and that the cause of their shadowy subsistence, and of their duration, should be comprehended in perpetual genera. The leaders of sacred rites, perceiving these things, ordered that laughter and lamentations should be consecrated to such-like genera in certain definite periods of time, and that they should be allotted a convenient portion of the whole of the sacred ceremonies pertaining to a divine nature. As therefore the art of sacred rites, distributing in a becoming manner the whole of piety to the Gods and the attendants of the Gods, that no part of worship might be omitted adapted to such attendants, conciliated the divinities by the most holy mysteries and mystic symbols, but called down the gifts of daemons by apparent passions, through a certain arcane sympathy,—in like manner the fathers of these fables, looking, as I may say, to all

454

the progressions of divine natures, and hastening to refer fables to the whole series proceeding from each, established the imagery in their fables, and which first presents itself to the view, analogous to the last genera, and to those that preside over ultimate and material passions; but to the contemplators of true being they delivered the concealed meaning, and which is unknown to the multitude, as declarative of the exempt and inaccessible essence of the Gods. Thus, every fable is daemoniacal according to that which is apparent in it, but is divine according to its recondite theory. If these things then are rightly asserted, neither is it proper to deprive the fables of Homer of an alliance to things which have a true subsistence, because they are not serviceable to the education of youth; for the end of such fables is not juvenile tuition, nor did the authors of fables devise them looking to this, nor are those written by Plato to be referred to the same idea with those of a more divinely inspired nature, but each is to be considered separately; and the latter are to be established as more philosophic, but the former as adapted to sacred ceremonies and institutions. The latter likewise are fit to be heard by youth, but the former by those who have been properly conducted through all the other parts of learning.

Socrates, indeed, sufficiently indicates this to those who are able to perceive his meaning, and also that he only blames the fables of Homer so far as they are neither adapted to education, nor accord with the restless and simple manners of youth. He likewise signifies that the recondite and occult good of fables requires a certain mystic and entheastic (i.e. divinely inspired) intelligence. But the multitude, not perceiving the meaning of the Socratic assertions, and widely deviating from the conceptions of the philosopher, accuse every such-like kind of fables. But it is worth while to hear the words of Socrates, and through what cause he rejects such a mythology: "The young person (says he) is not able to judge what is allegory, and what is not; but whatever opinions he receives at such an age are with difficulty washed away, and are generally immoveable. On these accounts, care should be taken, above all things, that what they are first to hear be composed in the most handsome manner for exciting them to virtue." With great propriety, therefore, do we say that the Homeric fables do not well imitate a divine nature; for they are not useful to legislators for the purposes of virtue and education, nor for the proper tuition of youth, but in this respect indeed they do not appear at all similar to things themselves, nor adapted to those that preside over the politic science; but, after another manner, they harmonize with the Gods, and lead those who possess a naturally good disposition to the contemplation of divine natures; and the good which they contain is not disciplinative, but mystic, nor does it regard a juvenile, but an aged habit of soul. This also Socrates himself testifies, when he says that "such fables should be heard in secrecy, by as few as possible, after they had sacrificed not a hog, but some great and wonderful sacrifice." Socrates therefore is very far from despising this kind of fables, according to the opinion of the multitude; for he evinces that the hearing of them is coordinated with the most holy initiations, and the most subtle mysteries.[2] For to assert that such fables ought to be used in secret with a sacrifice the *greatest* and *most perfect* manifests that the contemplation of them is mystic, and that they elevate the souls of the hearers to sublime speculations. Whoever therefore has divested himself of every puerile and juvenile habit of the soul, and of the indefinite impulses of the phantasy, and who has established intellect as the leader of his life, such a one will most opportunely participate of the spectacles concealed in such-like fables; but he who still requires instruction, and symmetry of manners, cannot with safety engage in their speculation.

It follows therefore, according to Socrates himself, that there is a two-fold species of fables, one of which is adapted to the instruction of youth, but the other is mystic; one is preparatory to

[2] The Eleusinian, which Proclus calls the most holy of the mysteries, are likewise always denominated by him τελεται: and Suidas informs us that τελετη signifies a mysterious sacrifice, the *greatest* and *most honourable*. So that Socrates in the above passage clearly indicates that such fables belong to the most sacred of the mysteries.

moral virtue, but the other imparts a conjunction with a divine nature; one is capable of benefiting the many, the other is adapted to the few; the one is common and known to most men, but the other is recondite and unadapted to those who do not hasten to become perfectly established in a divine nature; and the one is co-ordinate with juvenile habits, but the other scarcely unfolds itself with sacrifices and mystic tradition. If therefore Socrates teaches us these things, must we not say that he harmonizes with Homer respecting fables? But he only rejects and reprobates them so far as they appear unadapted to the hypothesis of his discourse, and the narration of the education of youth.

But if it be requisite that legislators should in one way be conversant with mythical fictions, and those who endeavour to cultivate more imperfect habits, but in another way those who indicate by the divinely-inspired intuitive perceptions of intellect the ineffable essence of the Gods to those who are able to follow the most elevated contemplations, we shall not hesitate to refer the precipitations of Vulcan to the irreprehensible science concerning the Gods, nor the Saturnian bonds, nor the castrations of Heaven, which Socrates says are unadapted to the ears of youth, and by no means harmonize with those habits which require juvenile tuition. For, in short, the mystic knowledge of divine natures can never subsist in foreign receptacles. To those therefore that are capable of such sublime speculations we must say, that the precipitation of Vulcan indicates the progression of a divine nature from on high, as far as to the last fabrication in sensibles, and this so as to be moved and perfected and directed by the demiurgus and father of all things. But the Saturnian bonds manifest the union of the whole fabrication of the universe,[3] with the intellectual and paternal supremacy of Saturn. The castrations of Heaven obscurely signify the separation of the Titanic[4] series from the connective[5] order. By thus speaking

---

[3] Hence, according to the fable, Saturn was bound by Jupiter, who is the demiurgus or artificer of the universe.

[4] The Titans are the ultimate artificers of things.

[5] See the notes to the Cratylus.

we shall perhaps assert things that are known, and refer that which is tragical and fictitious in fables to the intellectual theory of the divine genera. For whatever among us appears to be of a worse condition, and to belong to the inferior coordination of things, fables assume according to a better nature and power. Thus, for instance, a bond with us impedes and restrains energy, but there it is a contact and ineffable union with causes. A precipitation here is a violent motion from another; but with the Gods it indicates prolific progression, and an unrestrained and free presence to all things, without departing from its proper principle, but in an orderly manner proceeding from it through all things. And castrations in things partial and material cause a diminution of power, but in primary causes they obscurely signify the progression of secondary natures into a subject order, from their proper causes; things first at the same time remaining established in themselves undiminished, neither moved from themselves through the progression of these, nor mutilated by their separation, nor divided by their distribution in things subordinate. These things, which Socrates justly says are not fit to be heard by youth, are not on that account to be entirely rejected. For the same thing takes place with respect to these fables, which Plato somewhere says happens to divine and all-holy dogmas: For these are ridiculous to the multitude, but to the few who are excited to intellectual energy they unfold their sympathy with things, and through sacred operations themselves procure credibility of their possessing a power connate with all that is divine. For the Gods, hearing these symbols, rejoice, and readily obey those that invoke them, and proclaim the characteristic of their natures through these, as signs domestic and especially known to them. The mysteries likewise and the greatest and most perfect of sacrifices ($\tau\epsilon\lambda\epsilon\tau\alpha\iota$) possess their efficacy in these, and enable the mystics to perceive through these, entire, stable, and simple visions, which a youth by his age, and much more his manners, is incapable of receiving. We must not therefore say that such-like fables do not instruct in virtue, but those that object to them should show that they do not in the highest degree accord with

458

the laws pertaining to sacred rites. Nor must it be said that they dissimilarly imitate divine natures, through obscure symbols, but it must be shown that they do not prepare for us an ineffable sympathy towards the participation of the Gods. For fables which are composed with a view to juvenile discipline should possess much of the probable, and much of that which is decorous in the fabulous, in their apparent forms, but should be entirely pure from contrary appellations, and be conjoined with divine natures through a similitude of symbols. But those fables which regard a more divinely inspired habit, which co-harmonize things last with such as are first through analogy alone, and which are composed with a view to the sympathy in the universe between effects and their generative causes,—such fables, despising the multitude, employ names in an all-various manner, for the purpose of indicating divine concerns. Since also, with respect to harmony, we say that one kind is poetic, and which through melodies exciting to virtue cultivates the souls of youth; but another divine, which moves the hearers, and produces a divine mania, and which we denominate better than temperance: and we admit the former as completing the whole of education, but we reject the latter as not adapted to political administration. Or does not Socrates expel the Phrygian harmony from his Republic as producing ecstasy in the soul, and on this account separate it from other harmonies which are subservient to education?

As, therefore, harmony is twofold, and one kind is adapted to erudition, but the other is foreign from it; in a similar manner, likewise, is mythology divided; into that which contributes to the proper tuition of youth, and into that which is subservient to the sacred and symbolic invocation of a divine nature. And the one, viz. the method through images, is adapted to those that philosophize in a genuine manner; but the other, which indicates a divine essence through recondite signs, to the leaders of a more mystically-perfective operation; from which Plato himself also renders many of his peculiar dogmas more credible and clear. Thus, in the Phaedo, he venerates with a becoming silence that recondite assertion, that we are confined in body as in a prison secured by a guard, and testifies, according to the mysteries, the different allotments of the soul, when in a pure or impure condition, on its departure to Hades; and again, its habitudes, and the triple paths arising from its essence, and this according to paternal sacred institutions; all which are full of a symbolic theory, and of the ascent and descent of souls celebrated by poets, of Dionysiacal signs, and what are called Titanic errors, the triviae, and wandering in Hades, and every thing else of this kind. So that Plato does not entirely despise this mode of mythologizing, but considers it as foreign from juvenile tuition, and, on this account, delivers types of theology commensurate with the manners of those that are instructed.

It likewise appears to me, that whatever is tragical, monstrous, and unnatural, in poetical fictions, excites the hearers, in an all-various manner, to the investigation of the truth, attracts us to recondite knowledge, and does not suffer us through apparent probability to rest satisfied with superficial conceptions, but compels us to penetrate into the interior parts of fables, to explore the obscure intention of their authors, and survey what natures and powers they intended to signify to posterity by such mystical symbols.[6]

Since therefore fables of this kind excite those of a naturally more excellent disposition to a desire of the concealed theory which they contain, and to an investigation of the truth established in the adyta[7] through their apparent absurdity, but prevent the profane from busying themselves about things which it is not lawful for them to touch, are they not eminently adapted to the Gods themselves, of whose nature they are the interpreters? For many genera are hurled forth before the Gods,[8] some of a

---

[6] Such fables, also, call forth our unperverted conceptions of divine natures, in which they efficaciously establish us, by untaught sacred disciplines; and, in short, they give perfection to the vital powers of the soul.

[7] Αδυνατοις is erroneously printed in the original for αδυτοις.

[8] Proclus says this with reference to what took place in the mysteries, as is evident from the following extract from his MS. Commentary on the

daemoniacal, and others of an angelic order, who terrify those that are excited to a participation of divinity, who are exercised for the reception of divine light, and are sublimely elevated to the union of the Gods. But we may especially perceive the alliance of these fables with the tribe of daemons, whose energies manifest many things symbolically, as those know who have met with daemons when awake,[9] or have enjoyed their inspiration in dreams, unfolding many past or future events. For, in all such phantasies, after the manner of the authors of fables, some things are indicated by others. Nor, of the things which take place through this, are some images, but others paradigms; but some are symbols, and others sympathize with these from analogy. If, therefore, this mode of composing fables is daemoniacal, must we not say that it is exempt from every other variety of fables, as well that which regards nature, and interprets natural powers, as that which presides over the instruction of the forms of the soul?

First Alcibiades: Εν ταις ἁγιωτάταις των τελετων προ της του θεου παρουσιας δαιμονων χθονιων τινων συμβολοι προφαινονται, και οψεις εκταραττουσαι τους τελουμενους, και αποσπωσαι των αχραντων αγαθων, και εις την ὑλην εκπροκαλουμεναι· δια το και οἱ θεοι παρακελευονται μη προτερον εις εκεινους βλεπειν, πριν ταις απο των τελετων φραχθωμεν δυναμεσιν· ου χρη κεινους σε βλεπειν πριν σωμα τελεσθεις, και δια τουτο τα λογια προστιθησιν, ὁτι τας ψυχας θελγοντες αει των τεγετων ἀπαγουσιν. I.e. "In the most holy of the mysteries, before the God appears, certain terrestrial daemons present themselves, and fights which disturb those that are to be initiated, tear them away from undefiled goods, and call forth their attention to matter. Hence the Gods exhort us not to look at these, till we are fortified by the powers which the mysteries confer. For thus they speak: It is not proper for you to behold them till your body is initiated. And on this account the oracles (i.e. the Chaldaean) add, that such daemons, alluring souls, seduce them from the mysteries." Agreeably to this, Proclus, also, in Plat. Theol. p. 7 observes, Εν ταις των τελετων ἁγιωτάταις φασι τους μυστας, την μεν πρωτην πολυειδεσι και πολυμορφοις των θεων προβεβλημενοις γενεσιν ἀπανταν. I.e. "In the most holy of the mysteries they say that the mystics at first meet with the multiform and many-shaped genera which are hurled forth before the gods."

[9] For ὑπερ as in the original, read ὑπαρ.

II. WHAT THE DIFFERENT MODES
OF THEOMACHY, OR, THE BATTLES
OF THE GODS, ARE, AMONG
THEOLOGISTS, AND AN
INTERPRETATION OF THE OCCULT
TRUTH WHICH THEY CONTAIN

And thus much concerning those forms of fables according to which other poets and Homer have delivered mystic conceptions respecting the Gods, and which are unapparent to the vulgar. After this, it follows I think that we should distinctly consider the several fables in the order in which they are mentioned by Socrates, and contemplate according to what conceptions of the soul Homer represents the Gods fighting, or doing or suffering any thing else, in his poems. And in the first place let us consider this *theomachy* as it is called, or battles of the Gods, which Homer devises, but Socrates thinks worthy of animadversion, as by no means adapted to the education of youth. For, that there is neither sedition, nor dissension and division, as with mortals, among the Gods, but peace and an inoffensive life, the poet himself testifies when he somewhere says concerning Olympus, that it is a substratum to the Gods, who possess every possible joy, and spectacles of immense beauty:

The blessed Gods in joy unceasing live.

What discord and war then can find any entrance among those who are allotted eternal delight, who are perpetually propitious, and rejoicing in the goods which they possess? But if it be proper that discourses concerning the Gods should regard as well their providence as the nature of the beings for whom they provide, I think we may interpret as follows their opposition to each other:

In the first place, the divided progressions of all things, and their separations according to essence, supernally originate from that division of first operating causes[10] which is unknown to all

[10] Viz. *bound* and *infinity*, which are the highest principles after the ineffable cause of all. See the Philebus, and the Notes to my Translation of Aristotle's Metaphysics.

things; and subsisting according to those principles which are expanded above wholes, they dissent from each other; some being suspended from the unifying monad *bound*, and about this determining their subsistence, but others receiving in themselves a never-failing power from that *infinity* which is generative of wholes, and is a cause productive of multitude and progression, and about this establishing their proper hyparxis. After the same manner, therefore, in which the first principles of things are separated from each other, all the divine genera and true beings have a progression orderly divided from each other; and some of them are the leaders of *union* to secondary natures, but others impart the power of *separation*; some are the causes of *conversion*, convolving the multitude of progressions to their proper principles; but others *bound the progressions*, and the subordinate *generation* from the principles. Again, some supply a *generative abundance* to inferior natures, but others impart an *immutable* and *undefiled purity*; some bind to themselves the cause of *separate* goods, but others, of those goods that are *consubsistent* with the beings by whom they are received. And thus in all the orders of being is such a contrariety of genera diversified. Hence *permanency*, which establishes things in themselves, is opposed to *efficacious powers*, and which are full of *life* and *motion*. Hence the kindred communion of *sameness* receives a division according to species, opposite to the separations of *difference*; but the genus of *similitude* is allotted an order contrary to *dissimilitude*, and that of *equality* to *inequality*, according to the same analogy. And the divisions of all these are supernally defined from that duad which subsists as a principle, according to which all beings are distinguished by their proper boundaries, proceed with an opposite division to each other from their generative causes, and from their connection with each other generate all the variety of secondary natures. Is it therefore any longer wonderful, if the authors of fables, perceiving such contrariety in the Gods themselves and the first of beings, obscurely signified this to their pupils, through battles? the divine genera indeed being perpetually united to each other, but at the same time containing in themselves the causes of the union and separation of all things.

We may also, I think, adduce another mode of solution: that the Gods themselves are impartibly connascent with each other, and subsist uniformly in each other, but that their progressions into the universe and their communications are separated in their participants, become divisible, and are thus filled with contrariety; the objects of their providential exertions not being able to receive in an unmingled manner the powers proceeding from thence, and without confusion their multiform illuminations. We may likewise say, that the last orders which are suspended from divine natures, as being generated remote from first causes, and as being proximate to the subjects of their government, which are involved in matter, participate themselves of all-various contrariety and separation, and partibly preside over material natures, minutely dividing those powers which presubsist uniformly and impartibly in their first operating causes. Such then and so many being the modes according to which the mystic rumours of theologists are wont to refer war to the Gods themselves, other poets, and those who in explaining divine concerns have been agitated with divine fury, have ascribed wars and battles to the Gods, according to the first of those modes we related, in which the divine genera are divided conformably to the first principles of wholes. For those powers which *elevate to causes* are after a manner opposed to those that are the *sources of generation*, and the *connective* to the *separating*; those that *unite*, to those that *multiply* the progression of things; *total* genera, to such as fabricate *partibly*; and those which are *expanded above*, to those that *preside over* partial natures: and hence fables concealing the truth assert that such powers fight and war with each other. On this account, as it appears to me, they assert that the Titans were the antagonists of Bacchus, and the Giants of Jupiter; for union, indivisible operation, and a wholeness prior[11] to parts are adapted to those artificers that have a subsistence prior to the world; but the Titans and Giants

[11] The form of a thing considered according to its causal subsistence, or a subsistence in its cause, is said to be a whole prior to parts.

produce the demiurgic powers into multitude, divisibly administer the affairs of the universe, and are the proximate fathers of material concerns.

We may also conceive that the Homeric fables after another manner have devised the battles of the Gods. For, in the first place, Homer exempts the demiurgic monad from all the multitude of the Gods, and neither represents him proceeding to the contrariety of generation, nor in any respect opposing it; but, while this is firmly established in itself, the number of the Gods proceeds from it, which number both abides and proceeds into the universe, and on this account is said to be divided about the providence of the natures which it governs. In the next place, of these Gods which are distributed from their father, some abide in him, and have an unproceeding subsistence in their proper monad, which the poetry of Homer says are established in the abode of Jupiter, and together with their father providentially preside in an exempt manner over wholes. That these war against, or oppose each other, the fable does not even according to the apparent description admit. But it represents those Gods as warring against each other, who proceeding from the demiurgic monad, subside into multiform orders, become more partial, and more proximate to the objects of their government, and give completion to the angelic or daemoniacal armies, through their abundant sympathy with subordinate natures and partial allotment of providential energy. For to these I think the passions of the subjects of their providential care are more allied, such as wounds, blows, and repercussions; and, in short, the contrariety of generation is not very remote from the administration of these Gods. That which is partial likewise in the fabrication of things secondary, and a minute distribution of providence, are adapted to such like powers, but not to those which rank as principles, and are exempt from all the objects of their providential energy, and subsist as separate causes.

Moreover, since the angelic orders are suspended from the government of the more excellent genera of Gods, and preserve the characteristics of their leaders though in a partial and multiplied manner, they are called by their names; and as they subsist analogously to the first Gods, they appear in their progressions to be the same with their more total causes. And this not only the fables of the Greeks have occultly devised,—I mean that leading Gods and their attendants should be called by the same names,—but this is also delivered in the initiatory rites of the Barbarians. For they say that angels suspended from the Gods, when invoked, particularly rejoice to be called by the appellations, and to be invested with the vehicles, of the leaders of their series, and exhibit themselves to theurgists in the place of these leading deities. If therefore we refer Minerva, Juno, and Vulcan when engaged in war below about generation, and likewise Latona, Diana, and the river Xanthus, to other secondary orders, and which are proximate to divisible and material things, we ought not to wonder on account of the communion of names. For each series bears the appellation of its monad, and partial spirits love to receive the same denomination with wholes. Hence there are many and all-various Apollos, Neptunes, and Vulcans; and some of them are separate from the universe, others have an allotment about the heavens, others preside over the whole elements, and to others the government of individuals belongs. It is not therefore wonderful if a more partial Vulcan, and who is allotted a daemoniacal order, possesses a providential dominion over material fire, and which subsists about the earth, or that he should be the inspective guardian of a certain art which operates in brass. For, if the providence of the Gods has a subjection according to an ultimate division, being allotted a well-ordered progression supernally from total and united causes, this Vulcanian daemon also will rejoice in the safety of that which he is allotted, and will be hostile to those causes which are corruptive of its constitution. War therefore in such like genera, a division of all-various powers, mutual familiarity and discord, a divisible sympathy with the objects of their government, verbal contentions, revenge through mockery, and other things of this kind, are very properly conceived to take place about the terminations of the divine orders. Hence fables, in representing such like powers discordant with and opposing each other on account of the subjects over which they providentially preside, do not appear to be very remote from the truth. For the passions of the things governed are proximately referred to these.

In short, since we may perceive two conceptions of battles celebrated by poets inspired by Phoebus, one of these considers the well-ordered division of the divine genera about those two principles of wholes which *the one*, the exempt cause of all things, produced, and according to the opposition of these principles represents the Gods also as acting contrary to each other. For, whether it be proper to call those first natures bound and infinity, or monad and indefinite duad, they will entirely appear to be oppositely divided with respect to each other, according to which the orders of the Gods are also separated from each other. But the other conception arises from considering the contrariety and variety about the last of things, and referring a discord of this kind to the powers that proximately preside over it, and thus feigning that the Gods, proceeding into a material nature, and distributed about this, war with each other. Homer, to those who consider his poems with attention, will appear to speak about the former mode of divine contention when he says,

> *When Saturn was by Jove all-seeing thrust*
> *Beneath the earth:*

and in another place[12] respecting Typhon,

> *Earth groan'd beneath them; as when angry Jove*
> *Hurls down the forky lightning from above,*
> *On Arimè when he the thunder throws,*
> *And fires Typhaeus with redoubled blows,*
> *Where Typhon, prest beneath the burning load,*
> *Still feels the fury of th' avenging God.*

For in these verses he obscurely signifies a Titanic war against Jupiter, and what the Orphic writers call precipitations into Tartarus (κατατρταρωσεις). But he particularly introduces the

[12] Iliad. lib. 2. ver. 288, &c.

Gods warring with each other, and dissenting about human affairs, according to the second conception of divine battles, in which the divine and intellectual disposition of the figments adopted by the poet is worthy of the greatest admiration. For, in describing their battles (who though they are allotted a subsistence at the extremities of the divine progressions, yet are suspended from the Gods, and are proximate to the subjects of their government, and are allied to their leaders), he indicates their sympathy with inferior natures, referring a divided life, battle, and opposition from things in subjection to the powers by which they are governed; just as Orpheus conjoins with Bacchic images compositions, divisions and lamentations, referring all these to them from presiding causes. But Homer represents the alliance of these divisible spirits with the series from which they proceed, by the same names through which he celebrates the powers exempt from material natures, and employs numbers and figures adapted to their whole orders. For those who engage in battle are eleven in number, imitating the army of the Gods and daemons following Jupiter, and distributed into eleven[13] parts. Of these, those that preside over the better coordination are contained in the pentad; for the odd number, the spheric,[14] and the power of leading all secondary natures according to justice, and of extending from the middle to every number, are adapted to those who desire to govern more intellectual and perfect natures, and such as are more allied to *the one*. But those of an inferior destiny, and who are the guardians of material natures, proceed according to the hexad, possessing indeed a perfective power over the subjects of their providential care through a proper[15] number; but in consequence of this number being even, and coordinate with a worse nature, they are subordinate to the other powers. Nor is it wonderful if some one should call these genera Gods, through their alliance to their leaders, and should

[13] See the Phaedrus.

[14] For five is not only an odd, but also a spheric number; for all its multiplications into itself terminate in five; and therefore end where they began.

[15] For six is a perfect number, being equal to the sum of all its parts.

represent them as warring through their proximate care of material natures. The opposition therefore of Neptune and Apollo signifies that these powers preside over the apparent contrariety of all sublunary wholes: and hence these Gods do not fight with each other. For parts are preserved by their containing wholes, as long as they subsist. But the opposition of Juno and Diana represents the opposite division of souls in the universe, whether rational or irrational, separate or inseparable, supernatural or natural; the former of these powers presiding over the more excellent order of souls, but the latter bringing forth and producing into light those of an inferior condition. Again, the discord of Minerva and Mars represents the division of the whole of the war in generation into providence subsisting according to intellect, and that which is perfected through necessity; the former power intellectually presiding over contraries, and the latter corroborating their natural powers, and exciting their mutual opposition. But the battle between Hermes and Latona insinuates the all-various differences of souls according to their gnostic and vital motions; Hermes giving perfection to their knowledge, and Latona to their lives; which two often differ from and are contrary to each other. Lastly, the battle between Vulcan and the river Xanthus adorns in a becoming manner the contrary principles of the whole corporeal system; the former assisting the powers of heat and dryness, and the latter of cold and moisture, from which the whole of generation receives its completion. But since it is requisite that all contrarieties should end in mutual concord, Venus is present, producing friendship[16] in the adverse parties, but at the same time assisting those powers that belong to the worse coordination; because these are especially adorned, when they possess symmetry and familiarity with the better order of contrary natures. And thus much concerning the divine battles of Homer.

[16] That is to say, though Venus is not represented by Homer as actually producing friendship in the adverse Gods, yet this is occultly signified by her being present; for she is the source of all the harmony, friendship, and analogy in the universe, and of the union of form with matter.

III. IN WHAT MANNER AN APOLOGY
IS TO BE MADE FOR THOSE
DIVINE FABLES WHICH APPEAR TO
MAKE THE GODS THE CAUSES
OF EVIL

In the next place let us consider how, since the Gods in the summit of their essence are particularly characterized by goodness, poetry makes them to be the authors of both evil and good, though it is proper to refer to them the principal cause of what is good alone. For this, Socrates, demonstrating that divinity gives subsistence to good alone, but to nothing evil, thinks worthy of animadversion in the poems of Homer. And it seems that he reprobates the battles of the Gods, as subverting divine union, but condemns what we now propose to investigate, as diminishing the goodness of the Gods. For,

> *Two vessels on Jove's threshold ever stand,*
> *The source of evil one, and one of good.*[17]

To this objection, we answer that there are two coordinations of things in the world, which, as we have before observed, supernally proceed from the Gods themselves. For all things are divided by the biformed principles[18] of things, viz. the orders of the Gods, the natures of beings, the genera of souls, physical powers, the circulations of the heavens, and the diversities of material things; and lastly human affairs, and allotments according to justice, thence receive a twofold generation. For, of these, some are of a better, and others of an inferior condition. I mean, for instance, that the natural habits of bodies, viz. beauty, strength, health, and also such things as, independent of the corporeal constitution, pertain to souls, viz. power, and honour, and riches, belong to allotments of a better condition; but those habits and circumstances which are opposite to these belong to those of an inferior condition. These things then being necessarily divided

[17] Iliad. lib. 24. ver. 527.
[18] Viz. *bound* and *infinity*.

after the above-mentioned manner, those which belong to the
better portion it was usual with the antients immediately to denominate good, but those of the contrary portion they denominated evil; yet not in the same signification as when we call an
unjust and intemperate habit of the soul evil; but as impediments
of energies, as darkening our natural dispositions, and disturbing the providence of the soul in its tranquil management of
human affairs, they admitted them to be evil, and to be so denominated, but after a different manner from what are called
the evils of the soul. Thus also they were accustomed to call
disease, imbecility, and a privation of the necessaries of life, evils.
And why is it necessary to adduce all poetry as a witness of the
use of this name? For the Pythagoraeans also, in establishing
twofold coordinations[19] of things in all orders, did not refuse to
call one of these good, and the other evil. Though, how can any
one admit that the even, the oblong, and motion, are to be enu-
merated among those evils which we define as privations of
good? How can we say that the feminine, the genus of difference
and of dissimilitude, are contrary to nature? But I think this
entirely evident, that, according to every progression of things,
they called the subordinate series of things opposite, evil, as deserting the other series, and being neither primarily beneficent,
nor distant by the same interval from the one cause of every
thing beautiful and good. It is requisite therefore to suspend
these twofold coordinations of good and evil in the universe from
the demiurgic monad. For the divisions of the Gods, and of the
genera posterior to the Gods, depend on that first principle. The
cause likewise of the good and evil which happen from fate,
and which are allotted to souls about generation, according to
justice, must be referred to the dispensator of the universe, who
also sends souls into the region of mortality. For the effects of
fate are suspended from demiurgic providence, about which the

[19] These twofold coordinations of the Pythagoraeans are as follow: Bound,
infinity; the odd, the even; the one, multitude; right hand, left hand; the
masculine, the feminine; the quiescent, that which is in motion; the
straight, the curved; light, darkness; good, evil; the square, the oblong.
See my Translation of Aristotle's Metaphysics, book 1.

series of justice also subsists, and the boundaries of which it follows, being, as the Athenian guest in Plato observes, the avenger of the divine law. Lastly, the gifts of fortune, and the distribution of all things according to justice, are determined according to the will of the father. The demiurgus and father therefore of the universe has pre-established in himself the cause of every thing good and evil, of more excellent and subordinate gifts, of prosperous events, and of such as are impediments to the energies of the soul in externals; and he governs all things according to intellect, distributing to every being such things as are fit, and referring all things to his own paternal administration. For he distributes to souls, with a view to good, both things of the better and of the inferior coordination; looking in his distribution to the perfection of the recipients.

If these things then are rightly asserted, we must admit the Homeric arrangement, which places in the demiurgic intellect of Jupiter twofold primary causes of the goods and the ills which he imparts to souls. For, of all the intellectual kings, the duad especially belongs to the demiurgus of the universe: since, according to the Oracle, "the duad is seated with him; and, by his governing all things, and disposing every thing in its proper place, he shows virtue to be victorious, and vice to be vanquished in the universe." For what difference is there between asserting these things, and comparing the demiurgus to one playing at chess, and sending souls into lives adapted to their respective natures? These two fountains therefore of a better and worse condition of things, by which the demiurgus conducts souls according to justice, the poet mythologizing denominates *tubs*;[20] whether indicating that divinity assigns to every thing its proper boundary through intellectual *persuasion* (for intellect, says Timaeus, is the principle of necessity, persuading it to lead all things to that which is best), or the capaciousness of these principles, and their comprehending all-various effects. For the demiurgus and father of the universe contains unitedly in himself the dispersed multitude of all that he distributes to souls. So that,

---

[20] For πειθω signifies persuasion, and πιθος is a tub.

according to this reasoning, Plato and the Homeric poetry accord with each other. For the former says that it is not proper to make God the cause of any evil; but the other perpetually produces every thing good from thence: yet, since goods are twofold, and each kind benefits those by whom it is received, hence the Homeric poetry distributes them into twofold coordinations, and, indicating their difference with respect to each other, denominates the one as absolutely good, but places the other separate, as contrary to good. But that what is called evil by Homer is not such as that which Plato denies to be given by the Gods, the poet himself declares in the following verses,[21]

> *The Gods on Peleus from his birth bestow'd*
> *Illustrious gifts. . . .*
> *With these God also evil join'd. . . .*

What this evil is he immediately tells us:

> *No race succeeding to imperial sway;*
> *An only son, and he (alas!) ordain'd*
> *To fall untimely in a foreign land.*
> *See him in Troy the pious care decline*
> *Of his weak age, to live the curse of thine!*

In these verses, it appears that Homer does not make divinity the cause of real evils, since he calls the loss of a son, and the being deprived of his attendance in old age, evils. But in what manner these are evils, we have above explained, viz. so far as they cause difficulty in the present life, and sorrow in the soul. For, though it is not lawful for those who philosophize in a genuine manner to call these evils, yet they appear to be impediments of a life according to virtue, to those who make choice of a practical life. Hence the Athenian guest also contends that all such things are, in a certain respect, evil to good men, but good to such as are depraved; though he makes God to be the cause, both of these, and of every thing imparted from the universe. So that not only Homer, and Achilles in Homer assert these things, but Plato himself, and the legislator according to Plato.

[21] Iliad. lib. 24. ver. 534, &c.

IV. HOW THE POETRY OF HOMER
SEEMS TO REFER A VIOLATION
OF OATHS TO THE GODS:—THE
TRUTH RESPECTING THIS UNFOLDED

In the next place let us consider how leagues and oaths, according to the poetry of Homer, are violated with the will of the mighty Jupiter, and of Minerva acting in subserviency to the will of her father: for this also Socrates reprobates, as referring the principle of evils to the first of the Gods.

And here indeed it is worth while especially to doubt how he who makes divinity to be the cause of these things does not make him to be the cause of the greatest and real evils. For Homer cannot here be defended by saying, that he represents poverty, disease, and things of this kind, as proceeding from the Gods, but he ascribes to divinity the cause of those things which are acknowledged by all men to be evils. Timaeus, indeed, in Plato, represents the demiurgus as entirely prescribing laws to souls prior to their descent into generation, that he may not be accused as the cause of their consequent evils; but these verses of Homer admit that the principle of the greatest evils is imparted to them from divinity, when they have descended, and are conversant with generation. How then shall we reply to these animadversions, so as to harmonize the doctrine of Homer with the nature of things, and the narration of Plato? We may reply as follows: That fables of this kind are not adapted to the habit of youth, as has been asserted by us before, and we shall now, and in all that follows, repeat the assertion. For it is not possible for youth to distinguish the nature of things, nor to refer the apparent signs of truth to an unapparent theory, nor to see how every thing in the universe is accomplished according to the will of divinity, through other intervening causes. But we shall show that these things are agreeable to the philosophy of Plato.

The Athenian guest then, in the Laws, says that "God is the beginning, the middle, and end of all things, and that justice follows him, taking vengeance on those that desert the divine law: but these, as he informs us, are such as through youth and folly have their soul inflamed with insolence, and for a certain time appear to themselves to govern, but afterwards suffer the proper punishment of their conduct from justice, and entirely subvert themselves, their city, and their family." These things are asserted by the Athenian guest politically; but Homer,[22] relating them in a divinely inspired manner ($\epsilon\nu\theta\epsilon\alpha\sigma\tau\iota\kappa\omega\varsigma$), says that those who have often sinned, and committed the greatest crimes, are punished for their offences according to the single will of Jupiter, and are deprived of life together with their wives and children. He further informs us, that Jupiter first of all accomplishes this punishment, and in a manner exempt and unapparent to all; but Minerva in the second place, being subservient to and cooperating with the paternal providence of Jupiter: for, as Orpheus says, "she is the powerful queen of the intellect of Saturnian Jove."[23] The same poet likewise adds, that "his brain who violates leagues and oaths flows on the ground like wine." In consequence, therefore, of this violation, such men subject themselves to justice, and render themselves adapted to punishment. Hence the violation of leagues and oaths is especially perpetrated by those who, prior to this, have deserved the vengeance of the Gods, who justly govern mortal affairs, and thus punish former crimes. But such are said to be moved, and led forth into energy by the Gods themselves: not that the Gods render men who are to be punished impious and unjust, but as calling into energy those that are adapted to the perpetration of such-like actions, that by once energizing according to their inward habit, and producing into light the progeny of depraved actions with which they are pregnant, they may become worthy of punishment. For we should rather say, according to Plato, that vengeance, the attendant of justice, is perfected in such, than divine justice itself; since the just and justice are beautiful things. But both he on whom vengeance is inflicted, and he on whom it is not, are miserable. Men therefore, who have committed many

---

[22] For ὁ δε ὁμως, as in the original, read ὁ δε Ὁμηρος.

[23] Δεινη γαρ Κρονιδαο νοου κραντειρα τετυκται.

and the greatest crimes, and who have a depraved habit which is parturient with greater and more weighty evils, in the first place sustain vengeance, which appears indeed to crush those that suffer it, leading them to the violation of oaths, but in reality brings them to suffer the punishment of their crimes, effecting that which is similar to the opening of ulcers by the surgeon's instrument, which produces an increase of pain at the time, but, by discharging the putridity and the latent humour, becomes the cause of future health. But the poetry of Homer says that this punishment, beginning supernally from Jupiter (for justice, as we have before observed, follows him, taking vengeance on those that desert the divine law), is perfected through Minerva as the medium. For the Trojans, seeing into what an evil they had brought themselves, and that their life was obnoxious to deserved punishment, rendered this inevitable to themselves, by the violation of oaths and leagues.

Again then, it must be in the first place said that the Gods were not the causes of this confused and disorderly conduct to the Trojans, but that they through their own depravity rendered themselves worthy of an energy of this kind, and among these Pandarus in an eminent degree, as being a man ambitious, avaricious, and leading an atheistical life. Hence Minerva, proceeding according to the intellect of her father, does not excite any one causally to this action, but is said to seek Pandarus,[24] as particularly adapted to an avenging energy.

She ev'ry where the godlike Pandarus explor'd.[25]

For a man who is capable of doing and suffering any thing, and who also opposes himself to divinity, through a certain gigantic and audacious habit of soul, is rare, and truly difficult to be found. As therefore physicians are not the causes of cuttings and burnings, but the diseases of those that are cured, so neither are

---

[24] *Pandarus* seems to be derived απο του παντα δραν, that is, as we commonly say of a very depraved character, he was a man *capable of any thing*.

[25] Iliad. lib. 4. ver. 86.

the Gods the causes of the impiety respecting oaths and leagues, but the habits of those by whom it is committed.

In the second place, this also must be considered, that Minerva is not said to prepare Pandarus for the deed, but only to try if he gave himself up to this energy. For divinity does not destroy the freedom of the will, not even in such as are consummately wicked:

> *Lycaon's warlike son, what I suggest,*
> Wilt *thou obey?*

But Pandarus, incited by an immoderate desire of riches and power, leaps to unjust energies, the poet all but exclaiming in the very words of Socrates in the Republic,[26] that "many things are extended to souls from the universe, which astonish the stupid, and cause them to err respecting the elections of lives." As therefore the prophet extends a tyrannic life, and he who first chooses this is said to be stupid, although he by whom it was extended was entirely a divine nature; so here, when Minerva offers to the choice of Pandarus a more powerful and rich condition with impiety, or one entirely contrary to this, he makes choice of the worse. And in this case Minerva is not the cause of the election, but the improbity of him by whom the election is made. For neither is the prophet in Plato the cause of a tyrannic life, but the intemperance of him that chose it. Hence Pandarus, in obeying Minerva, is said to suffer this through his stupidity. For indeed (to speak accurately) he did not obey Minerva, but the avaricious and stupid habit of his soul. Though, is it not wonderful that Minerva, in this instance, is not the cause of wisdom, but of folly? But, says Plotinus, "Craft is produced from a defluxion of intellect; an illumination of temperance becomes intemperance; and audacity is the gift of fortitude." For such as are the forms of life, such also from necessity must be the participations from more excellent natures. Hence some participate of intelligibles intellectually, others according to opinion, and others phantastically. Others again participate of passions impas-

[26] See the 10th Book.

477

sively, others with mediocrity of passion, and others with perfect passivity. But all things are moved by the Gods, according to their respective aptitudes. So that the violation of oaths did not proceed from Jupiter and Minerva, but from Pandarus and the Trojans. This action however is suspended from the Gods, as being the forerunner of justice, and as preparing those by whom it was perpetrated for the perfect punishment of their guilt.

Nor is a divine nature the cause of true evils to souls, but the depraved habits of these are the sources to them of their depraved energies. But every energy, though it proceeds with depravity into the universe, is under the direction of presiding Gods, and of a more total or partial providence. For it becomes, says Plotinus, an unjust action to him who does it, so far as pertains to the doing it, but just to him who suffers for it, so far as he suffers. And so far as an action of this kind is atheistical, it originates from a partial cause, which gives perfection to an action full of passion; but so far as it is good, it obtains from presiding powers its proper end. For it is necessary that the authors of the greatest crimes should some time or other be called to punishment; but this would never take place, unless their depravity received its completion. Many habits therefore, remaining unenergetic, render those by whom they are possessed incapable of obtaining their proper cure. Hence, on the Gods consulting concerning bringing the war to an end, and saving the Trojans, the Goddess who presides over justice prevents any energy of this kind, that the Trojans may more swiftly suffer the punishment of their crimes; and Minerva, who cooperates with this divinity, excites to the violation of the oath, that, energizing according to the whole of their depravity, they may receive the punishment of the whole of it. For neither was it good for them to remain without a cure, nor that their latent depravity should be healed prior to their second offences. All their unjust life therefore being unfolded, punishment follows, correcting the whole of their impious conduct.

An Apology for the Fables of Homer

V. THE WHOLE THEORY OF THE
FABLE UNFOLDED, IN WHICH
JUPITER, THROUGH THEMIS,
EXCITES THE GODS TO CONTENTION

In the next place, since Socrates mentions the judgment of the
Gods in Homer, and the strife to which Jupiter excites the multitude of the Gods, through Themis elevating all of them to himself, let us also speak concerning these things. That Jupiter then
is a monad separated from the universe, and the multitude of
mundane Gods, and that he is able to produce all things from,
and again convert them to himself, has often been said. But since
his energy proceeding to the multitude of Gods is twofold, one
of which converts and the other moves the Gods to the providence of inferior natures, poetry also describes twofold speeches[27]
of Jupiter to the Gods. According to the first of these, the one
and whole demiurgus of the universe is represented as communicating an unmingled purity to the multitude of the Gods, and
imparting to them powers separate from all division about the
world. Hence he orders all the Gods to desist from the war and
the contrariety of mundane affairs. But, according to the second
of these speeches, he excites them to the providence of subordinate
natures, and permits their divided progressions into the universe,
that they may not only be contained in one demiurgic intellect,
which, as the poet says,

None can escape, or soaring run beyond—

but may energize in the subjects of their providential care, according to their own characteristics. Hence Jupiter says to them,

Each, as your minds incline, to either host
Your succour lend.[28]

But as the progressions of the Gods are not divulsed from the
demiurgic monad, Themis first converts them to this monad,

[27] For δημιουργίας read δημηγορίας.
[28] Iliad. lib. 20.

But Jove to Themis gives command, to call
The Gods to council—

that, acting providentially according to the will of their father, they may also energize according to the judgment of Themis. And the poet indeed delivers to us separate speeches of the one demiurgus of the universe to the junior Gods; but Timaeus represents him in one speech converting the multitude of these Gods to himself, and exciting them to the providence of mortal affairs, that they may govern all secondary natures according to justice. But these things in no respect differ from exciting them to war, and through Themis converting them to himself. For those who preside over generation govern the war in matter; and those who energize according to justice are suspended from the whole of Themis, of whom Justice is the daughter, and imitate the one demiurgic intellect, to whom it is not lawful to do any thing but what is most beautiful, as Timaeus himself asserts.

VI. WHAT THE JUDGMENT OF THE
GODS IS IN THE FABLES OF THE
POET, AND WHAT DIFFERENCES
OF LIVES IT OBSCURELY SIGNIFIES

Again, it is not proper to think that the celebrated judgment of the Gods, which fables say was accomplished by Paris, was in reality a strife of the Gods with each other, under the judgment of a barbarian; but we ought to consider the elections of lives, which Plato delivers in many places, as subsisting under the Gods who are the inspective guardians of souls. And this indeed Plato clearly teaches us in the Phaedrus, when he says that a royal life is the gift of Juno, a philosophic life of Jupiter, and an amatory life of Venus. Since therefore souls, from among a multitude of lives proposed to them from the universe, embrace some according to their own judgment and reject others, hence fables, transferring to the Gods themselves the peculiarities of lives, assert that not the diversities of living, but the Gods that preside over these diversities, are judged by those that choose them. According to this reasoning, Paris also is said to have been appointed a judge of Minerva, Juno and Venus; and that of three lives which were proposed to him, he chose the amatory life: and this not with prudence, but recurring to apparent beauty, and pursuing the image of that beauty which is intelligible. For he who is truly amatory, taking intellect and prudence for his guides, and with these contemplating both true and apparent beauty, is no less the votary of Minerva than of Venus. But he who alone pursues the amatory form of life by itself, and this accompanied with passion, deserts true beauty, but through folly and luxury leaps to the image of beauty, lies about it in a fallen condition, and does not attain to a perfection adapted to an amatory character. For he who is truly amatory and studious of Venus, is led to divine beauty, and despises all that is beautiful in the regions of sense. Since however there are certain daemons with the characteristics of Venus, who preside over apparent beauty, and which subsists in matter, hence he who embraces the image of beauty, is said to have Venus cooperating with him in all his undertakings.

VII. WHAT THE MUTATIONS OF THE
GODS ARE, WHICH ARE
INTRODUCED IN FABLES, AND
IN HOW MANY WAYS, AND
THROUGH WHAT CAUSES, THEY
ARE DEVISED

Since a divine nature is not only beneficent, but likewise immutable, without form, simple, and always subsisting according to the same, and after the same manner, Socrates very properly considers the following verses of Homer worthy of animadversion,

The Gods at times, resembling foreign guests,
Wander o'er cities in all-various forms.[29]

And again those respecting Proteus and Thetis, in which they are represented as changing their forms, and variously appearing. Indeed, that fables of this kind ought not to be heard by those

[29] Odyss. lib. 17. ver. 485.

who genuinely receive a political education, is perfectly evident;
since it is requisite that the paradigm of a polity which is to be
stable should be immutable, and not obnoxious to all-various
mutations. But here also it is requisite to collect by reasoning
the divine dianoëtic conceptions of Homer, though I am not
ignorant that the above verses are ascribed to one of the suitors,
and that on this account the poet is free from blame. For neither
should we think it right to take the opinion of Plato from what
is said by Callicles or Thrasymachus, or any other sophists that
are introduced in his writings; but when Parmenides or Socrates,
or Timaeus, or any other of such divine men speaks, then we
think that we hear the dogmas of Plato. In like manner we should
form a judgment of the conceptions of Homer, not from what is
said by the suitors, or any other depraved character in his poems,
but from what the poet himself, or Nestor, or Ulysses, appears
to say.

If any one however is willing to ascribe this dogma concerning
the mutation of the Gods to Homer himself, he will not be
destitute of arguments which accord with all sacred concerns,
with the greatest sacrifices and mysteries, and with those appearances of the Gods which both in dreams and true visions, the
rumour of mankind has supernally received. For in all these the
Gods extend many forms of themselves, and appear passing into
many figures. And sometimes an unfigured light of them presents itself to the view; at other times this light is fashioned in a
human form, and at others again assumes a different shape. These
things also the discipline of divine origin pertaining to sacred
concerns delivers. For thus the Oracles[30] speak: "A similar fire
extending itself by leaps through the waves of the air; or an unfigured fire whence a voice runs before; or a light beheld near,
every way splendid, resounding and convolved. But also to behold a horse full of refulgent light; or a boy carried on the swift
back of a horse,—a boy fiery, or clothed with gold, or, on the
contrary, naked; or shooting an arrow, and standing on the back

[30] Viz. the Chaldaean Oracles. See my Collection of these Oracles in the
third volume of the Monthly Magazine.

of the horse." And such things as the oracles add after these, not at any time attributing either internal change, or variety, or any mutation to a divine nature, but indicating its various participations. For that which is simple in the Gods appears various to those by whom it is seen, they neither being changed, nor wishing to deceive; but nature herself giving a determination to the characteristics of the Gods, according to the measures of the participants. For that which is participated, being one, is variously participated by intellect, the rational soul, the phantasy, and sense. For the first of these participates it impartibly, the second in an expanded manner, the third accompanied with figure, and the fourth with passivity. Hence that which is participated is uniform according to the summit of its subsistence, but multiform according to participation. It is also essentially immutable and firmly established, but at different times appearing various to its participants through the imbecility of their nature. And not only these things follow, but that which is without weight appears heavy to those that are filled with it: "The miserable heart by whom I am received cannot bear[31] me," says some one of the Gods. Whence Homer also perceiving the truth of these things through divine inspiration says concerning Minerva:

> *Loud crash'd the beechen axle with the weight,*
> *For strong and dreadful was the power it bore.*[32]

Though here it may be said, how can that which is without weight be the cause of weight? But such as is the participant, such necessarily must that which is participated appear.[33] Whether, therefore, some of the Gods have appeared similar to guests, or have been seen in some other form, it is not proper to attribute the apparent mutation to them, but we should say that the

---

[31] Hence also Homer, Iliad. lib. 20. ver. 131. says, χαλεποι δε θεοι φαινεσθαι εναργεις—i.e. O'erpowering are the Gods when clearly seen.

[32] Iliad. lib. 5.

[33] A divine nature must necessarily produce the sensation of weight in the body by which it is received, from its overpowering energy; for body lies like non-entity before such a nature, and fails, and dies away, as it were, under its influence.

phantasy is varied in the different recipients. And this is one way in which the poetry of Homer delivers multiform mutations of immutable natures.

But there is another way, when a divine nature itself, which is all-powerful and full of all-various forms, extends various spectacles to those that behold it. For then, according to the variety of powers which it possesses, it is said to be changed into many forms, at different times extending different powers; always indeed energizing according to all its powers, but perpetually appearing various to the transitive intellections of souls, through the multitude which it comprehends. According to this mode, Proteus also is said to change his proper form to those that behold it, perpetually exhibiting a different appearance. For though he is subordinate to the first Gods, and immortal indeed, but not a God; the minister of Neptune, but not allotted a leading dignity; yet he is a certain angelic intellect belonging to the series of Neptune, possessing and comprehending in himself all the forms of generated natures. Idothea has the first arrangement under him; she being a certain daemoniacal soul conjoined to Proteus as to her proper divine intellect, and connecting her intellections with his intelligible forms. Another number of rational and perpetual souls follows, which the fable denominates Phocae. Hence Proteus is represented as *numbering* these, poetry indicating by this the perpetuity of their nature. For the multitude of things which are generated and perish is *indefinite*. Partial souls therefore beholding Proteus, who is an intellect possessing many powers and full of forms, whilst at different times they convert themselves to the different forms which he contains, fancy that the transition of their own intellections is a mutation of the intelligible objects. Hence to those that retain him he appears to become all things—

> *Water, and fire divine, and all that creeps*
> *On earth.*

For such forms as he possesses and comprehends, or rather such as he perpetually is, such does he appear to become when these forms are considered separately, through the divisible conception of those that behold them.

In the third place, therefore, we say that the Gods appear to be changed, when the same divinity proceeds according to different orders, and subsides as far as to the last of things, multiplying himself according to number, and descending into subject distinctions; for then again fables say, that the divinity, which supernally proceeds into this form, is changed to that into which it makes its progression. Thus they say that Minerva was assimilated to Mentor, Mercury to the bird called the sea-gull, and Apollo to a hawk; indicating by this their more daemoniacal orders, into which they proceed from those of a superior rank. Hence, when they describe the *divine* advents of the Gods, they endeavour to preserve them formless and unfigured. Thus, when Minerva appears to Achilles,[34] and becomes visible to him alone, the whole camp being present, there Homer does not even fabulously ascribe any form and figure to the goddess, but only says that she was present, without expressing the manner in which she was present. But when they intend to signify *angelic* appearances, they introduce the Gods under various forms, but these such as are total; as for instance, a human form, or one common to man or woman indefinitely. For thus, again, Neptune and Minerva were present with Achilles:

> *Neptune and Pallas haste to his relief,*
> *And thus in* human form *address the chief.*[35]

Lastly, when they relate daemoniacal advents, then they do not think it improper to describe their mutations into individuals and partial natures; whether into particular men, or other animals. For the last of those genera that are the perpetual attendants of the Gods are manifested by these figures. And here you may see how particulars of this kind are devised according to the order of things. For that which is simple is adapted to a divine nature, that

[34] Iliad. lib. 1.
[35] Iliad. 21. ver. 285.

which is universal to an angelic, and the rational nature to both these; and that which is partial and irrational accords with a daemoniacal nature: for a life of this kind is connected with the daemoniacal order. And thus much concerning the modes according to which the Homeric fables devise mutations of things immutable, and introduce various forms to uniform natures.

VIII. CONCERNING THE DREAM SENT
TO AGAMEMNON, WHICH APPEARS
TO ACCUSE THE GODS OF FALSE-
HOOD, AND HOW IT MAY BE
SHOWN THAT A DIVINE NATURE
IS VOID OF FALSEHOOD

It now remains that we speak concerning the dream sent by Jupiter to Agamemnon; for Socrates, at the end of his theological types, reprobates this, because the whole of a divine and daemoniacal nature is without falsehood, as he collects by demonstrative arguments. But Homer says that Agamemnon was deceived through this dream. Though, is it not absurd, if this dream is from Jupiter, according to the assertion of the poet, that this alone nearly, of all the particulars which are mentioned as deriving their origin from Jupiter, should be attended with fraud?

In answer to this objection, we may say what is usually asserted by most of the interpreters, that the fallacy had its subsistence in the phantasy of Agamemnon. For Jupiter in his speech to the dream, and the dream again in its address to Agamemnon, evidently indicate that it would be requisite to call together *all* the army, and to attack the enemy with *all* his forces; for this is the meaning of the word πανουδιη, which is used in both the speeches. But Agamemnon, not understanding the mandate, neglected the greatest part of his army, and, engaging in battle without the aid of Achilles, was frustrated in his expectations through his unskilfulness in judging of divine visions. So that Jupiter is not the cause of the deception, but he who did not properly understand the mandates of Jupiter.

We shall also add the solution given by our preceptor Syrianus, which both accedes to the meaning of Homer and the truth of things. For, if Jupiter is represented as providing for the honour of the hero Achilles, and consulting how he may destroy the greatest number of the Greeks, is it not necessary that he must previously comprehend in himself the cause of the deception? For, if Achilles had been associated with the army, the Greeks would not have been destroyed, nor would they have been punished for their unjust conduct towards him. It is better therefore to say that the deception was from divinity for the good of the deceived. For good is better than truth. And among the Gods, indeed, they are conjoined with each other: for neither is intellect without divinity, nor divinity without an intellectual essence. But in their participants they are often separated; and good is produced through falsehood, and truth is frustrated of good. Whence also Socrates himself, when he is framing laws for the guardians of his republic, orders falsehood to be employed, through the opinion of the stupid, who are not otherwise able to obtain the good which is adapted to their condition. If therefore it be said that divinity benefits some through truth, and others through falsehood, and at the same time leads all of them to good, it is by no means wonderful. For, of generated natures, some subsist without matter, but others with matter, in which fallacy is inherent; or, rather, matter is true fallacy itself. So that, in the providence of souls, if they are, as we have said, variously benefited by divinity, some immaterially through truth, but others materially through falsehood, such providential energy will be adapted to the nature of the Gods.

But, if it be requisite, this also may be asserted, that deception and falsehood are generated in the participant, and that this takes place according to the will of divinity, that he who has acted erroneously may through the deception become more worthy: just as that which is material is generated in these lower regions, but subsists according to demiurgic providence, that there may be generation and corruption in order to the completion of the universe. Divinity therefore does not deceive, but he who is deceived is deceived by himself; and this takes place, according to the will of divinity for the good of him who sustains the deception. For, God making immaterially, that which is generated is generated materially; and he energizing impartibly, that which proceeds from this energy, receives its completion partibly; and he signifying intellectually, falsehood obtains a shadowy subsistence in the being that receives what is signified. But the divine poet himself manifests, that, truth dwelling with the Gods, deception is generated from the opinion of the recipients, when he makes Jupiter commanding the dream say—

All that I order tell with perfect truth.

How then is there falsehood in divinity, according to Homer? And how is divinity the cause of deception? Unless it should be said he is the cause in such a manner, as that neither is the shadowy subsistence of deception in these lower regions contrary to his will. But the habit of youth is incapable of distinguishing and contemplating how, wholes remaining void of evil, in the natures which receive them divisibly evil appears; how, natures more excellent than ours not deceiving, we are often deceived; and how, when deceived, we suffer this according to the will of providence. Hence Socrates is not willing that young men should hear things of this kind, as being incapable of forming properly distinct opinions of things.

IX. A COMMON APOLOGY BOTH FOR
THE HOMERIC AND PLATONIC
FABLES, IN WHICH THEY SPEAK
OF THE JUDGMENTS IN HADES, OF
SOULS, AND THE DIFFERENT
ALLOTMENTS WHICH THEY RECEIVE
ON DEPARTING FROM THEIR
BODIES, ACCORDING TO THE
IDIOMS OF THE LIFE IN THE BODY

Having then discussed these things, let us examine what is written in the third book of the Republic, and, prior to other things, what the poet either himself asserts, or introduces another asserting, mythologically concerning Hades; and let us consider whether they contain any thing of truth, and accord with the narrations of Plato. What then are we to understand, when the poet represents Achilles as preferring servitude in the present life to the possession of every thing in Hades? What is the meaning of those dreadful habitations, which are odious to the Gods, of the image and the soul, of shades wandering without intellect, of lives compared to shadows, of the lamentations of souls passing thither, of their being assimilated to bats, of smoke, a crashing noise, and such like particulars, which the poems of Homer contain? What likewise are the rivers in Hades, and those appellations which are the most tragical? For these Socrates reprobates, but at the same time adds, what is common to all fables, "that they contribute to something else; but we (says he) are afraid for our guardians, lest from these terrible relations, they should think death to be dreadful."

However, that Socrates himself in many places uses names and aenigmas of this kind is obvious to every one. For, that I may omit the rivers mentioned in the Phaedo, the wanderings of souls, their anxieties, the three roads, the punishments, the being carried in rivers, the lamentations and exclamations there, and the supplications of injurers to the injured, of all which Plato says Hades is full;—though these things should be omitted, yet does not what we find written at the end of the Republic accord with the intention of the Homeric poetry, viz. the bellowing mouth, Tartarus, fiery daemons, the tearing off the flesh of the tyrant Aridaeus, and souls full of dust and filth? For, what is there in these which falls short of the tragical in the extreme? So that for the same reason these also are to be rejected, or the Homeric doctrine is not to be reprehended. In defence of both therefore, whether some Epicurean or any other endeavours to accuse such-like fables, we say, that the habits of souls liberated from the body are different, and the places of the universe are multiform, into which they are introduced. Of these also some are so separated from mortal instruments, as neither to have any habitude to things of a worse condition, nor to be filled with the tumult which they contain, and material inanity. The vehicles of such are necessarily pure and luciform, not disturbed by material vapours, nor thickened by a terrestrial nature. But others who are not yet perfectly purified by philosophy, but are drawn down to an affection towards the testaceous body, and pursue a life conjoined with this,—these exhibit such-like vehicles suspended from their essence to those who are capable of beholding them, viz. shadowy, material, drawing downwards by their weight, and attracting much of a mortal condition. Hence Socrates, in the Phaedo, says that such souls, rolling about sepulchres, exhibit shadowy phantasms; and the poet relates that they are impelled along similar to shadows.

Further still, of those souls which yet embrace a corporeal life there are many differences. For some live a more practic life, and, not yet deserting a life of this kind, embrace an organ adapted to practical energies, from which when they are separated they are indignant; as was the case with the soul of Patroclus,

Which leaving youth and manhood wail'd its fate.

And when in Hades, they still desire an association with this organ, as did the soul of Achilles,[36] because he preferred a life on earth to a separate life, according to which he was not able to energize, but very much excelled in an active life. Others again, through the infelicity of their condition, eagerly embrace the testaceous body, and think that the life conjoined with it differs in no respect from the proper life of the soul. Such as these the divine poetry of Homer assimilates to bats, as looking to that which is dark in the universe, and its very extremity, and which may be denominated a stupendous cavern; and as having the winged nature of the soul gross and terrestrial. Is it therefore wonderful that Achilles, who possessed practical virtue, should desire a life in conjunction with body, and which was capable of

[36] Heroes are divided into two kinds: those that energize according to practical, and those that energize according to intellectual virtue. Achilles was a hero of the former class, and Hercules of the latter. For an ample account of the characteristics of these two kinds, see my Pausanias, vol. iii. p. 229.

being subservient to his actions? For Hercules, being purified through the telestic science, and partaking of undefiled fruits, obtained a perfect restoration among the Gods; whence the poet says of him,

> *He with th' immortal Gods delighted lives,*
> *And beauteous Hebe crowns his joys. . . .*

But Achilles, since he embraces rectitude in practical affairs, and the present life, pursues also and desires an instrument adapted to this life. Plato himself, therefore, also says that souls according to the manners to which they have been accustomed make choice of secondary lives. Is not this likewise worthy of admiration in the divine tradition of Homer—I mean the separation of the soul from its image, and intellect from the soul? Also that the soul is said to use the image,[37] but that intellect is more divine than both these? And again, that the image and the soul may in a certain respect be known while yet detained in the body; and that the soul takes care of and providentially attends to the testaceous body, and, when this is not effected, desires its accomplishment; but that intellect is incomprehensible by our phantastic and figured motions? Hence Achilles, on beholding Patroclus speaking concerning the burial of his body, was led to believe that the soul and its image were in Hades, but that intellect was not there, nor prudence, by which these are used. For the energies of the irrational life hastened to adopt this position, but could not credit the reception of the intellectual soul in Hades from the visions of dreams.

Does it not also most perfectly accord with things themselves to say, that the multitude of souls depart from their bodies lamenting, and are divulsed from them with difficulty, through the alluring life and manifold pleasures which they enjoy in them? For every corporeal pleasure, as Socrates says in the Phaedo, as if armed with a nail, fastens the soul to the body. And such souls

---

[37] The irrational part of the soul is the *image* of the rational, in the same manner as the rational soul is the image of intellect. Body also is the image of the irrational soul, and matter, or the last of things, is the image of body.

after deserting their bodies use shadowy vehicles, which are disturbed by the ponderous and terrene vapours[38] of the Sirens, and utter an uncertain voice, and a material sound, which the Homeric poetry denominates a crashing noise. For, as the instruments of ascending souls emit a harmonious sound, and appear to possess an elegant and well-measured motion, so the sound of more irrational souls descending under the earth is similar to a crashing noise, bearing an image of an appetitive and phantastic life alone. Nor must we think that the places in Hades, and the tribunals under the earth, and the rivers which both Homer and Plato teach us are there, are merely fabulous prodigies: but, as many and all-various places are assigned to souls ascending to the heavens, according to the allotments which are there; in like manner it is proper to believe that places under the earth are prepared for those souls that still require punishment and purification. These places, as they contain the various defluxions of the elements on the earth, are called by poets rivers and streams. They likewise contain different orders of presiding daemons; some of whom are of an avenging, others of a punishing, others of a purifying, and, lastly, others of a judicial characteristic. But if the Homeric poetry calls these places

Horrid and dark, and odious to the Gods,

neither is it proper to condemn it for this. For souls are terrified through the variety and phantasy of the presiding daemons which are there. The infernal region likewise is extended according to all-various allotments, adapted to the different habits of those that descend thither.[39] It is also most remote from the Gods, as being the extremity of the universe, and as possessing much of material disorder, and never enjoying the splendor of the solar rays. And thus much concerning those verses which Socrates thinks should be obliterated, and should by no means be heard by

[38] For αγμων here read ατμων.

[39] Instead of reading the latter part of this sentence, and the beginning of the next, as it is erroneously printed in the original, viz. φερομενων πορρωτατω. Τα δε εστι &c. it is necessary to read, as in the translation, φερομενων. Πορρωτατω δε εστι &c.

those whom he educates: for through these, says he, the love of the soul for the body will be increased, and a separation from it will appear to be of all things most dreadful.

X. WHAT THE CAUSES ARE THROUGH
WHICH THE POETRY OF HOMER
ASCRIBES LAMENTATIONS BOTH
TO HEROES AND GODS; AND
LIKEWISE TO THE BEST OF
HEROES AND THE GREATEST OF
THE GODS

It now follows that we should consider how the poetry of Homer does not represent one of us weeping and lamenting, when he also ascribes these effects of sorrow to his heroes, but makes the Gods themselves to weep, for the death of mortals whom they loved; though, according to Plato, Socrates neither wept, nor suffered any perturbation of mind, when his familiars wept on account of his approaching death; but Apollodorus, who wept abundantly, and any other who was similarly affected, were reproved by their master. But the divine poet represents his heroes immoderately lamenting the loss of their familiars. And, though some one should say that such things as the following became Priam who was a barbarian, and more irrational in his conduct:

> *Roll'd in the dust he suppliant call'd on all,*
> *And nam'd them one by one . . .*[40]

yet is it not absurd that Achilles, the son of a goddess, should at one time lie supine, at another prone, and, at another on his side, and, defiling his head with dust, weep in a very puerile manner? And even if such passions were proper in men who are allotted a mortal nature, yet they ought not to be ascribed to the Gods themselves. Why then is it requisite that Thetis should say weeping:

> *Ah wretched me! unfortunately brave*
> *A son I bore.*[41]

[40] Iliad. 22.   [41] Iliad. 18.

493

For a divine nature is established very remote from pleasure and pain. But though some one should dare to introduce the Gods affected in this manner,[42] yet it is not fit that the greatest of the Gods should lament and mourn both for Hector when pursued by Achilles, and for his son Sarpedon, and exclaim respecting both, Ah me! For such an imitation does not appear to be in any respect adapted to its paradigms, since it ascribes tears to things without tears, pain to things void of pain, and in short passion to things free from passion. These things Socrates reprobates in Homer, and expels from the education of youth, fearful lest some impediment should arise, through such-like assertions, to a right discipline according to virtue. For education is particularly conversant with pleasure and pain; which being increased, the legislator must necessarily be frustrated of his proper end.

To these objections we reply, that since the poet introduces heroes engaged in practical affairs, and living a life adapted to these, he very properly represents them as affected with particular events, and living conformably to such affections. For to philosophers, and those who energize cathartically, pleasures and pains, and the mixtures of these, are by no means adapted; since they are separated from these, lay aside all the trifling of mortality, and hasten to be divested of the forms of life with which they are surrounded from the elements, rapidly withdrawing themselves from material passions the offspring of generation. But pleasures, pains, sympathies, and a scene of all-various passions, are coordinated to those engaged in war, and who energize according to the passive part of the soul. And how could the vehement about actions take place, without the impulse of the appetites? Priam, therefore, and Achilles, neither being philosophers, nor willing to separate themselves from generation, nor living after the manner of the guardians of Plato's republic,—if they lament and com-

---

[42] I.e., Jupiter, who is called the *greatest* of the Gods, with reference to the mundane Gods, of whom he is the demiurgus and father. For, that he is not the first God, is evident from the Cratylus, Timaeus and Parmenides of Plato; which see.

miserate their familiars, it is by no means wonderful. For the loss of friends, the being destitute of children, and the subversions of cities appear to warriors to impart a great portion of misery. The accomplishment of mighty deeds, therefore, is adapted to these, as being allotted an heroic nature; and in conjunction with this the pathetic, from their being conversant with particulars.

With respect to the Gods, however, when they are said to weep for or lament those that are most dear to them, another mode of interpretation is to be adopted, and which was formerly admitted by the authors of fables, who indicated by tears the providence of the Gods about mortal, generated, and perishable natures. For this object of providential energy naturally calling for tears afforded a pretext to the inventors of fables; and through these they obscurely signified providence itself. Hence some one, in a hymn to the Sun, says,

> *Phoebus, the much-enduring race of men*
> *Thy tears excite. . . .*[43]

And on this account, in the mysteries also, we mystically assume sacred lamentations, as symbols of the providence pertaining to us from more excellent natures. Thetis therefore, and Jupiter, are said to lament those most dear to them, when in extreme danger—not that they are passively disposed after the manner of men, but because a certain separate providence proceeds from them, and gifts to particulars. And when the order of the universe concurs with this divisible providence, the preserving energy of that which provides is unimpeded; but when this order opposes, and that which is the object of a particular providence, as being a part of the universe, and allotted generation, sustains that corruption which is adapted to its nature, then fables, adducing the idiom or peculiarity of the providence which this object received according to its order, say that the powers who exert this providential energy lament, but not with exclamation: so that grief with them is a sign of the energy of a particular providence about individuals. After this manner, then, we attribute lamentations to the first

---

[43] Δακρυα μεν σεθεν εστι πολυπλημων (lege πολυτλημων) γενος ανδρων.

Gods; since the greatest and most perfect[44] of mystical sacrifices (τελεται) deliver in the arcana certain sacred lamentations of Proserpine and Ceres, and of the greatest[45] goddess herself.

But it is by no means wonderful if the last of the genera which are the perpetual attendants of the Gods, and which proximately attend to the affairs of mortals, in consequence of employing appetites and passions, and having their life in these, should rejoice in the safety of the objects of their providence, but be afflicted and indignant when they are corrupted, and should suffer a mutation according to passions:

> *The Nymphs lament when trees are leafless found;*
> *But when the trees through fertilizing rain*
> *In leaves abound, the Nymphs rejoice again—*

says a certain poet. For all things subsist divinely in the Gods, but divisibly and daemoniacally in the divided guardians of our nature. And thus much may suffice concerning the lamentations of the Gods.

XI. WHAT THE CAUSE IS OF THE LAUGHTER ASCRIBED TO THE GODS IN FABLES, AND WHY THE POETRY OF HOMER MAKES THE GODS TO LAUGH IMMODERATELY AT VULCAN

Let us in the next place consider whether fables properly attribute to the Gods a passion contrary to that which we have just now discussed, viz. immoderate laughter, and which is thought worthy of reprehension by Socrates.

> *Vulcan ministrant when the Gods beheld,*
> *Amidst them laughter unextinguish'd rose.*[46]

---

[44] Viz. the Eleusinian mysteries.
[45] Viz. Rhea, who is the mother of the Gods.
[46] Iliad. lib. i. circa finem.

An Apology for the Fables of Homer

What then is the laughter of the Gods? and why do they laugh in consequence of Vulcan moving and energizing? Theologists, therefore, say that Vulcan, as we have elsewhere observed, is the demiurgus and maker of every thing apparent.[47] Hence he is said to have constructed habitations for the Gods:

> *Then to their proper domes the Gods depart,*
> *Form'd by lame Vulcan with transcendent art.*

And this, in consequence of preparing for them mundane receptacles. He is also said to be lame in both his feet, because his fabrication is without legs. For that which is moved with a motion about intellect and prudence does not, says Timaeus, require feet. He is likewise said to preside over the brazier's art, and he himself energizes working in brass. Hence, in the poetry of Homer, heaven is often celebrated as brazen; and many other particulars confirm this opinion. But since every providential energy about a *sensible nature*, according to which the Gods assist the fabrication of Vulcan, is said to be the *sport* of divinity, hence Timaeus also appears to me to call the mundane Gods *junior*, as presiding over things which are perpetually in generation, or becoming to be, and which may be considered as ludicrous. The authors of fables are accustomed to call this peculiarity of the providence of the Gods energizing about the world, *laughter*. And when the poet says that the Gods, being delighted with the motion of Vulcan, laughed with inextinguishable laughter, nothing else is indicated than that they are cooperating artificers; that they jointly give perfection to the art of Vulcan, and supernally impart joy to the universe. For Vulcan suspends all their mundane receptacles, and extends to the providence of the Gods whole physical powers. But the Gods, energizing with a facility adapted to their nature, and

---

[47] Viz. He is the artificer of the whole of a corporeal nature. Proclus also, somewhere in his comment on the Timaeus, assigns another reason for the fiction of Vulcan's lameness, viz. because he is the fabricator of things last in the progressions of being (for such are bodies), and which are not able to proceed into another order. I prefer this explanation to the former.

not departing[48] from their proper hilarity, confer on these powers also their characteristic gifts, and move wholes by their perfective providence. In short, we must define the laughter of the Gods to be their exuberant energy in the universe, and the cause of the gladness of all mundane natures. But, as such a providence is incomprehensible, and the communication of all goods from the Gods is never-failing, we must allow that the poet very properly calls their laughter unextinguished. And here you may again see how what we have said is conformable to the nature of things. For fables do not assert that the Gods always weep, but that they laugh without ceasing. For tears are symbols of their providence in mortal and frail concerns, and which now rise into existence, and then perish; but laughter is a sign of their energy in wholes, and those perfect natures in the universe which are perpetually moved with undeviating sameness. On which account I think, when we divide demiurgic productions into Gods and men, we attribute laughter to the generation of the Gods, but tears to the formation of men and animals; whence the poet whom we have before mentioned, in his hymn to the Sun, says,

> Mankind's laborious race thy tears excite,
> But the Gods, laughing, blossom'd into light.

But when we make a division into things celestial and sublunary, again after the same manner we must assign laughter to the former, and tears to the latter; and when we reason concerning the generations and corruptions of sublunary natures themselves, we must refer the former to the laughter, and the latter to the tears, of the Gods. Hence, in the mysteries also, those who preside over sacred institutions order both these to be celebrated at stated times. And we have elsewhere observed, that the stupid are neither able to understand things employed by theurgists in secrecy, nor fictions of this kind. For the hearing of both these, when unac-

---

[48] Instead of και της οικειας ευπαθειας αφισταμενοι, read και της οικειας ευπαθειας ουχ αφισταμενοι.

companied with science, produces dire and absurd confusion in the lives of the multitude, with respect to the reverence pertaining to divinity.

XII. AN APOLOGY FOR THOSE PARTS IN THE POETRY OF HOMER, WHICH APPEAR IN ALL-VARIOUS WAYS TO EXCITE THE HEARERS TO A CONTEMPT OF TEMPERANCE

It now follows that we should consider whether the poems of Homer are inimical to the acquisition of temperance. The greatest species therefore of temperance, says Socrates, is reverence towards governors; the next to this is a command over the pleasures and desires of the soul; and there is a third consequent to these, which we shall shortly after contemplate. Achilles appears to have erred according to the first of these, when he freely says to the commander of all the Grecian forces,

Drunkard, dog-eyed, with heart of deer![49]

But Ulysses according to the third of these, when, defining the most beautiful life, he says that he particularly approves that polity of men in which there are

The heav'n-taught poet, and enchanting strain;
The well-fill'd palace, the perpetual feast,
A land rejoicing, and a people blest!
The plenteous board high-heap'd with cates divine,
And o'er the foaming bowl the laughing wine![50]

For in these verses he places the end of life in nothing else than variety of pleasure, and the gratification of desire. Such then being the objections made by Socrates to the verses of Homer, in answer to the first we say, that those guardians which he places over his

[49] Iliad. lib. 1.
[50] Odyss. lib. 10. at the beginning.

city, and who are allotted such a transcendency, on account of
their erudition and virtue, over those whom they govern, demand
the most abundant and the greatest honour, both from their associates and all others; as they are truly the saviours and benefactors
of the whole polity over which they preside: nor is it to be supposed that the governed will ever suffer any thing unholy or unjust from them, governing as they do according to intellect and
justice. But the poet neither admits that Agamemnon excels all
those that are subject to him, in virtue, nor in benefiting others;
but he ranks him among those that are benefited by others, and
particularly by the military science of Achilles. Very properly,
therefore, does he represent him as reviled by those more excellent
than himself, and consider the general good of the governed,
against which Agamemnon sinned, as of more consequence than
gratifying the passions of the chief. The poet therefore introduces
the best of the Greeks freely speaking to Agamemnon, without
regarding the multitude of soldiers that followed him, or his
naval power. For virtue is every where honourable, but not the
instruments of virtue. We must not therefore say, that he who
employs such disgraceful epithets sins against the rulers and
saviours of the whole army, when they are only superior by the
multitude of those that are subject to their command, but are far
inferior in virtue. For even the commander himself of so great an
army, and so difficult to be numbered, acknowledges, a little
after, how much Achilles excels him in virtue, laments his own
infelicity, and says,

> *For I have err'd, nor this will I deny.*

And,

> *That happy man whom Jove still honours most,*
> *Is more than armies, and himself an host.*

With respect to the words of Ulysses, we may say in their
defence, that every thing of this kind is interpreted more symbolically by those who transfer to other conceptions his wander-

ings, and who think it proper to rank both the Phaeacians and their felicity[51] higher than human nature. For with them the festival, the dainties, and the enchanting strain, have a different signification from that which is obvious to the multitude. It may also be said, that even those who do not depart from the apparent meaning of the poet, may nevertheless reply to such objections, and show, in the first place, that Ulysses, the wisest of the Greeks, does not think it fit that pleasure should have dominion in well-instituted polities, but worthy joy ($\epsilon\upsilon\phi\rho\sigma\sigma\upsilon\nu\eta$). And how much these differ from each other, we may learn from Plato himself. In the second place, Ulysses approves of the whole city becoming harmonized and unanimous with itself through music, being an auditor of such melodies as lead to virtue. For it is of great consequence to the whole polity, and to true erudition and virtue, that he who exercises music among the vulgar should not be any casual person, but one who derives his knowledge of it supernally through divine inspiration, from its presiding deity. In the third place, such harmony, to those that partake of it, adds an abundance of things necessary, which the multitude in cities very much require. For Ulysses does not remarkably praise a life filled with things of this kind, but that life which is in want of nothing necessary to mortal existence. The wisest of the Greeks, therefore, appears to speak conformably to our dogmas, and to unperverted preconceptions respecting divine felicity. But if Ulysses thought that he deserves approbation who takes away worthy delight, and the discipline subsisting through divine music, alone regarding feasting, and immoderate enjoyments, destitute of the Muse, and directs his attention to pleasure, Socrates with great propriety says that things of this kind are remote from his polity. For it is by no means fit that immoderate pleasure, and a life adapted to gluttony, should have dominion in a city consisting of the happy.

[51] See these explained in my History of the Platonic Theology, annexed to my Translation of Proclus on Euclid.

XIII. WHAT THE CONNEXION OF
JUPITER WITH JUNO OBSCURELY
SIGNIFIES; WHAT THE ORNAMENT
OF JUNO IS; AND WHAT THE
PLACE IN WHICH THEY WERE
CONNECTED. WHAT THE LOVE OF
JUPITER SIGNIFIES; WHAT THE
DIVINE SLEEP IS; AND, IN SHORT,
THE WHOLE INTERPRETATION OF
THAT FABLE

To such objections therefore of Socrates it is not difficult to reply; but a doubt yet remains to be solved by us, greater and more difficult, respecting the connexion of Jupiter with Juno; for this Socrates reprehends, as by no means fit to be heard by youth. For, does it not appear to be perfectly impious, to suspect of the greatest of the Gods, that through his love to Juno he should be forgetful of all his former decrees, should have connexion with the goddess on the ground, not waiting to enter into her bed-chamber, and should condescend to speak in the language of human lovers? For these in the first place prefer before all things a conjunction with the objects of their love; and in the next place say, that they experience the power of love more than in any former time. For Jupiter is made to speak in this manner in the following verses:

> *Ne'er did my soul so strong a passion prove,*
> *Or for an earthly, or a heavenly love.*[52]

And also that he loved her more

> *Than when, ascending to the nuptial couch,*
> *In love they mingled, from their parents hid.*

Our preceptor[53] in a most divinely inspired manner has unfolded the occult theory of this fable; from whose writings extracting as much as is sufficient to the present purpose, we shall

[52] Iliad. lib. 14.
[53] Viz. the great Syrianus.

briefly explain the several parts of the fable, and show that Homer is free from all blasphemy in the preceding verses.

All the divine orders, therefore, proceeding from the one principle of wholes, which Plato usually calls *the good*, and from those biformed causes proximately appearing after this principle, which Socrates in the Philebus denominates *bound* and *infinity*, but other wise men have venerated by other names; these orders likewise being divided and separated from each other, in a manner adapted to the Gods, through those second biformed principles,—the interpreters of the truth concerning the Gods usually oppose in their divisions the male to the female, the even to the odd, and the paternal to the maternal genera. But these divine orders again hastening to union and a connate communion, through the first cause, which is the leader of united goods to all beings, hence I think the authors of fables took occasion in their symbolical theory to ascribe marriage to the Gods, connexions, and a progeny from these, and also celebrated the connexions and conjunctions of their progeny, till they had perfectly contemplated the whole extent of a divine nature, diversified by such like progressions and conjunctions supernally, as far as to mundane natures. As therefore, among the Gods prior to the fabrication of the world, they celebrate the connexions of Saturn and Rhea, of Heaven and Earth, and their cogenerations, in the same manner also, among the fabricators of the universe, they inform us that the first conjunction is that of Jupiter and Juno; Jupiter being allotted a paternal dignity, but Juno being the mother of every thing of which Jupiter is the father. The former likewise produces all things in the rank of a monad, but the latter in conjunction with him gives subsistence to secondary natures, according to the prolific duad: and the former is assimilated to intelligible bound, but the latter to intelligible infinity. For, according to every order of Gods, it is requisite that there should be primary causes subsisting analogously to those two principles. But, to the union of these greatest divinities, it is necessary that there should previously subsist a oneness of transcendency of the monadic and demiurgic God, and a perfect conversion to him of the generative and dyadic cause. For the connate communion of more excellent natures is after this manner effected, more elevated causes being established in themselves, and in natures more divine than themselves, but such as are subordinate giving themselves up to those that are superior. Through these causes, as it appears to me, Juno hastening to a connexion with Jupiter, perfects her whole essence, and prepares it with all-various powers, the undefiled, the generative, the intellectual, and the unific; but Jupiter excites the divine love in himself, according to which he also fills his proximate participants with good, and extends to them a cause collective of multitude, and an energy convertive of secondary natures to himself. But the union and indissoluble conjunction of both these divinities is effected separate from the universe, and exempt from the mundane receptacles. For Jupiter elevates to this communion, Juno extending to him that which is subordinate and mundane; the Gods indeed being always united, but fables separating them from each other; and referring a connexion separate[54] from the universe to the will of Jupiter, but the common cooperation of these divinities proceeding into the world, to the providence of Juno. The reason of this is, that every where the paternal cause is the leader of exempt and more uniform good, but the maternal of that good which is proximate to its participants, and is multiplied according to all-various progressions. With great propriety, therefore, are sleep and wakefulness usurped separately in the symbols of fables; wakefulness manifesting the providence of the Gods about the world, but sleep a life separate from all subordinate natures; though the Gods at the same time both providentially energize about the universe, and are established in themselves. But as Timaeus represents the demiurgus of wholes, at one time energizing, and giving subsistence to the earth, the heavens, the planets, the fixed stars, the circles of the soul, and the mundane intellect, but at another time abiding in himself, after his accustomed manner, and exempt from all those powers that energize

[54] In the original μεριστην; but it is necessary to read χωριστην as in our translation.

in the universe; so, long before Timaeus, fables represent the father of all mundane natures, at one time awake, and at another asleep, for the purpose of indicating his twofold life and energy. "For he contains intelligibles in his intellect, but introduces sense to the worlds,"[55] says one of the Gods. According to the former energy, therefore, he may be said to be awake; for wakefulness with us is an energy of sense; but according to the latter to sleep, as separated from sensibles, and exhibiting a life defined according to a perfect intellect. It may also be said, that he consults about human affairs when awake; for according to this life he provides for all mundane concerns; but that when asleep, and led together with Juno to a separate union, he is not forgetful of the other energy, but, possessing and energizing according to it, at the same time contains both. For he does not, like nature, produce secondary things without intelligence, nor through intelligence is his providence in subordinate natures diminished, but at the same time he both governs the objects of his providence according to justice, and ascends to his intelligible watch-tower. The fable, therefore, indicates this exempt transcendency, when it says that his connexion with Juno was on mount Ida; for there Juno arriving gave herself to the embraces of the mighty Jupiter. What else, then, shall we say mount *Ida* obscurely signifies, but the region of *ideas* and an intelligible nature, to which Jupiter ascends, and elevates Juno through love;—not converting himself to the participant, but through excess of goodness imparting this second union with himself, and with that which is intelligible? For such are the loves of more excellent natures,—they are convertive of things subordinate to things first, give completion to the good which they contain, and are perfective of subject natures. The fable, therefore, does not diminish the dignity of the mighty Jupiter, by representing him as having connexion on the ground with Juno, and refusing to enter into her bed-chamber; for by this it insinuates that the connexion was supermundane, and not mundane. The chamber, therefore, constructed by Vulcan in-

[55] This is a part of one of the Chaldaean Oracles, to my collection of which I have already referred the reader.

dicates the orderly composition of the universe, and the sensible region; for Vulcan, as we have said before, is the artificer of the universe.

If you are also willing to consider the dress of Juno, through which she conjoined herself to the greatest of the Gods, and called forth the paternal providence of Jupiter to a communion with her own prolific powers, you will, I think, in a still greater degree behold the excess of the separate union of the Gods, celebrated in this fable. For she assimilates herself all-variously to the mother of the Gods, from whom she also proceeds, and is adorned with the more partial powers of those natures which presubsist in her totally, and, becoming all but another Rhea, proceeds to the demiurgus of the universe, who had then ascended to his proper intelligible. For she who is about to be conjoined with him who imitates his father, through a life separate from mundane natures, assimilates also her own perfection to the mother of all the divine orders, and thus enters into a connate communion with him. The hairs therefore of the Goddess, and her ringlets widely spreading, which she again binds, are evidently analogous to the hairs of the mother of the Gods: "for her hairs appear similar to rays of light ending in a sharp point," says some one of the Gods. And the poet calls the hairs of Juno *shining*. But her zone, with the fringes depending on and not cut off from it, resembles the whole and all-perfect girdle of Rhea. For Juno also is a vivific Goddess, and is generative of all the multitude of souls, which the number of the depending fringes symbolically indicates. Her ear-rings and her sandals represent the first and the last of the partial[56] powers which flow from thence, some of which subsist about the highest powers of the Goddess, and thence depend, but others are situated about her lowest progressions. The ambrosia and the oil are signs of the undefiled powers of the Goddess; for the inflexible[57] order of Gods subsists about her. What therefore that untamed genus of Gods and cause of purity is to Juno, that is here signified through these

[56] Viz. Daemoniacal powers. The dress therefore of Juno signifies her being invested with powers of this kind.
[57] Viz. The Curetes.

symbols. For ambrosia represents a power superior to all impurity and all defilement, and oil, as it produces strength, and is adapted to gymnastic exercises, properly belongs to Curetic deity. For the first Curetes are in other respects ascribed to the order of Minerva, and are said by Orpheus to be crowned with a branch of olive.

The Goddess, therefore, being perfectly furnished with such like symbols, and becoming as it were a partial Rhea, proceeds to the demiurgus of the universe, that she may be conjoined with him according to that life by which he particularly imitates Saturn; not proceeding into the universe, but being separate from mundane natures; nor consulting about things which are here, according to the sleepless providence of wholes, but exempt from sensibles, according to divine sleep; and in this respect emulating his father, who is represented as sleeping, the first of the Gods.

When Saturn tasted the deceitful food,
Loud snoring lay the God.

Since therefore Jupiter thus imitates his father Saturn, with great propriety does the dress of Juno regard the whole of Rhea; and hence Jupiter, through his similitude to Saturn, prefers a connexion on mount Ida to that which proceeds into the universe.

The girdle also, and the assistance of Venus, assimilate Juno still more to Rhea. For there also was the presubsisting monad of this Goddess, proceeding supernally from the connective divinity of Heaven, through Saturn as a medium, and illuminating the whole of an intellectual life with the light of beauty. Venus is said to carry this girdle in her bosom, as possessing its powers conspicuously extended; but Juno after a manner conceals it in her bosom, as being allotted a different idiom of hyparxis, but as possessing the girdle also, so far as she likewise is filled with the whole of Venus. For she does not externally derive the power which conjoins her with the demiurgus, but comprehends it also in herself. But the general opinion of mankind evinces the communion of these Goddesses: for they honour Juno as Nuptial and Pronuba, as beginning such like energies from herself. For she conjoins herself with the demiurgus through the girdle in herself; and hence she likewise imparts to all others a legitimate communion with each other.

But how are Jupiter and Juno said to have been at first connected with each other, concealed from their parents, but that now they are connected in a greater degree, through the excess of love with which Jupiter then loved Juno? Shall we say that the peculiarities of other goods are also twofold; and that, of union, one kind is connate to those that are united, but that the other supernally proceeds to them from more perfect causes? According to the former of these, therefore, they are said to be concealed from their parents, in consequence of being allotted this union as peculiar to themselves; but according to the other they are elevated to their causes, and hence this is said to be a greater and more perfect union than the former. But both these unions eternally subsisting together, with the Gods, fables separate them, in the same manner as sleep and wakefulness, progression and conversion, a communication of proper goods to things secondary, and a participation of primary causes: for these the authors of fables, concealing the truth, separate, though they are consubsistent with each other. Every thing, therefore, is asserted by Homer respecting the connexion of the great Jupiter and Juno after a theological manner; which is also testified by Socrates in the Cratylus, who derives the etymology of Juno from nothing else than *love*, as being, says he, lovely to Jupiter. According to an occult theory, therefore, we must not accuse Homer for writing such things concerning these mighty divinities. But if it should be objected that things of this kind are not fit to be heard by youth, according to their apparent signification, poets the authors of such fables will say, Our fables are not for youth, nor did we write such things with a view to juvenile discipline, but with an insane mouth; for these are the productions of the mania of the Muses, of which whoever being deprived arrives at the poetic gates, will be both as to himself and his poetry imperfect. And thus much may suffice for these particulars.

An Apology for the Fables of Homer

XIV. WHAT THE MYTHOLOGY OF
HOMER OBSCURELY SIGNIFIES
CONCERNING VENUS AND MARS,
AND THE BONDS OF VULCAN,
WITH WHICH BOTH ARE SAID
TO BE BOUND

Let us now consider the connexion between Mars and Venus, and the bonds of Vulcan. For Socrates says that neither must these be admitted, nor must such fables be delivered to youth. Let us, therefore, concisely relate what the poetry of Homer obscurely signifies by these things. Both these divinities then, I mean Vulcan and Mars, energize about the whole world, the latter separating the contrarieties of the universe, which he also perpetually excites, and immutably preserves, that the world may be perfect, and filled with forms of every kind; but the former artificially fabricating the whole sensible order, and filling it with physical reasons and powers. He also fashions twenty tripods about the heavens, that he may adorn them with the most perfect of many-sided[58] figures, and fabricates various and many-formed sublunary species,

Clasps, winding bracelets, necklaces, and chains.[59]

Both these divinities require the assistance of Venus to their energies; the one, that he may insert order and harmony in contraries; and the other, that he may introduce beauty and splendour as much as possible, into sensible fabrications, and render this world the most beautiful of things visible. But, as Venus is every where, Vulcan always enjoys her according to the superior, but Mars according to the inferior, orders of things. Thus, for instance, if Vulcan is supermundane, Mars is mundane; and if the

[58] Viz. The dodecaedron, which is bounded by twelve equal and equilateral pentagons, and consists of twenty solid angles, of which the tripods of Vulcan are images; for every angle of the dodecaedron is formed from the junction of three lines.

[59] Iliad. lib. 18. ver. 402.

former is coelestial, the latter is sublunary. Hence the one is said to have married Venus according to the will of Jupiter, but the other is fabled to have committed adultery with her. For a communion with the cause of beauty and conciliation is *natural* to the demiurgus of sensibles; but is in a certain respect foreign to the power which presides over division, and imparts the contrariety of mundane natures; for the separating are opposed to the collective genera of Gods. Fables therefore denominate this conspiring union of dissimilar causes adultery. But a communion of this kind is necessary to the universe, that contraries may be co-harmonized, and the mundane war terminate in peace. Since, however, on high among celestial natures, beauty shines forth, together with forms, elegance, and the fabrications of Vulcan, but beneath, in the realms of generation, the opposition and war of the elements, contrariety of powers, and in short the gifts of Mars, are conspicuous, on this account the sun from on high beholds the connexion of Mars and Venus, and discloses it to Vulcan, in consequence of cooperating with the whole productions of this divinity. But Vulcan is said to throw over them all-various bonds, unapparent to the other Gods, as adorning the mundane genera with artificial reasons, and producing one system from martial contrarieties, and the co-harmonizing goods of Venus. For both are necessary to generation. Since too, of bonds, some are coelestial, but others sublunary (for some are indissoluble, as Timaeus says, but others dissoluble); on this account, Vulcan again dissolves the bonds with which he had bound Mars and Venus, and this he particularly accomplishes in compliance with the request of Neptune; who being willing that the perpetuity of generation should be preserved, and the circle of mutation revolve into itself, thinks it proper that generated natures should be corrupted, and things corrupted be sent back again to generation. What wonder is it, then, if Homer says that Mars and Venus were bound by the bonds of Vulcan, since Timaeus also denominates those demiurgic reasons bonds, by which the coelestial Gods give subsistence to generated natures? And does not Homer speak conformably to the nature of things when he says the bonds were dissolved, since these are the bonds of generation? Indeed the demiurgus of wholes, by composing the world from contrary elements, and causing it through analogy to be in friendship with itself, appears to have collected into union the energies of Vulcan, Mars and Venus. In producing the contrarieties of the elements, too, he may be said to have generated them according to the Mars which he contains in himself; but, in devising friendship, to have energized according to the power of Venus. And in binding together the productions of Venus with those of Mars, he appears to have previously comprehended in himself, paradigmatically, the art of Vulcan. He is therefore all things, and energizes in conjunction with all the Gods. The junior artificers also, imitating their father, fabricate mortal animals, and again receive them when they are corrupted, generating, in conjunction with Vulcan, sublunary bonds, and previously containing in themselves the causes of their solution. For every where, he who comprehends in himself a bond, knows also the necessity of its solution.

XV. WHAT MUST BE SAID TO THE
ANIMADVERSIONS OF SOCRATES,
RESPECTING THE AVARICE
ASCRIBED BY HOMER TO HIS
HEROES

Let us now consider those places in the poems of Homer, which, according to Socrates, increase the love of riches in our souls. For why does Phoenix advise Achilles to receive gifts when he lays aside his anger, but otherwise not to lay it aside? Why also does Achilles receive gifts from Agamemnon for his insolence, and refuse to restore the dead body of Hector, unless it was redeemed with money? For he who becomes an auditor of things of this kind is in danger of falling into a dire and insatiable avarice. To these objections we shall briefly say, that Phoenix advises Achilles to lay aside his anger on receiving the gifts, and

Achilles, on receiving them, did lay it aside, both of them considering the gifts as an argument of the repentance of the giver; but not that they might satisfy the avaricious disposition of their soul, nor considering an increase of riches as the boundary of felicity. For they did not from the first demand these presents, but received them when they were spontaneously offered. But if Achilles restored the dead body of Hector to Priam, on its being redeemed by money, perhaps we may say that it was at that time customary to receive a ransom for the bodies of enemies. This also must be considered, that it belongs to the art of commanding an army, to cut off the riches of the enemy, but to increase the property of those who are compelled to oppose the enemy in a foreign country. But all these and such-like particulars may be defended as the transactions of those heroes who energized according to circumstances, and whose actions are to be estimated according to other manners than those of common men: they are, however, entirely unfit to be heard by those educated under the legislator of Socrates, whose geniuses are philosophic, whose erudition regards a philosophic life, and who are entirely deprived of possessions and property.

If you are willing, we may also add to what has been said respecting Achilles, that he himself accuses Agamemnon of avarice, and reprobates this passion as disgraceful.

> *Atrides, who in glory art the first,*
> *And no less avaricious than renown'd!*[60]

Besides, he indicates to us his contempt of wealth, when he says to Agamemnon,

> *Thine in each contest is the wealthy prey,*
> *Though mine the sweat and danger of the day.*
> *Some trivial present to my ships I bear,*
> *Or barren praises pay the wounds of war.*[61]

Further still, neither would he accept the gifts at first, when they

[60] Iliad. lib. 1.   [61] Iliad. lib. 1.

were offered by Agamemnon, because he did not think it was then fit to be reconciled to him. So that it was not the promise of riches which made him more mild to Agamemnon, by whom he had been treated with insolence; but, when he thought it was proper to lay aside his anger, he prepared himself for battle that he might revenge his friend. And when Agamemnon sent him the gifts, he neither looked at them, nor thought that any accession would thence be made to his own goods. Besides, his contempt of these things is evident from the multitude of rewards proposed by him in the funeral games: for he honoured the several champions with proper gifts; and magnificently bestowed upon Nestor, who through his age was unable to engage in the games, a golden bowl. How therefore, according to Homer, could he be avaricious, who used riches in a proper manner, who when they were present despised them, when absent did not anxiously desire them, and could endure to receive less of them than others? To which we may add, that he reprobated, in the midst of the Greeks, that passion of the soul as a disease, which aspires after immoderate wealth. How likewise can it be said that Phoenix was the teacher of avarice, who exhorts Achilles to imitate the antient custom of the Greeks? For he says,

> *Thus antient heroes, when with rage inflam'd,*
> *By words were soften'd, and by gifts appeas'd.*[62]

But these things, which are adapted to heroic times, and to the customs which then subsisted among heroes, were considered by Homer as deserving the highest imitation; though they are by no means adapted to the youth educated by Socrates, who are assigned no other employment by the legislator, than discipline and the study of virtue. But an attention to riches, and such things as are necessary to the preservation of the life of mortals, is assigned to others who are necessary to the perfection of an inferior republic.

[62] Iliad. lib. 9.

XVI. IN WHAT MANNER IT IS
REQUISITE TO APOLOGIZE FOR
THE NEGLIGENCE OF HEROES
RESPECTING A DIVINE NATURE,
WHICH APPEARS TO TAKE PLACE
IN THE POETRY OF HOMER

It now follows that we should consider how we are to answer Socrates, when he accuses Achilles of negligence respecting a divine nature. For how can he be pious and a worshipper of the Gods, who dares to say to Apollo,

Me thou hast injur'd most pernicious God?[63]

who also opposes the river Xanthus though a God, and presents his locks to the dead body of Patroclus, though he had promised them to the river Sperchius? That Achilles therefore, according to Homer, was remarkably cautious respecting a divine nature, is evident from his advising the Greeks to reverence Apollo, to send a sacrifice to him, and to appease Chryses the priest of Apollo. This also follows from his readily obeying the commands of Minerva, when she appeared to him, though contrary to the impulse of his wrath. He likewise asserts that a subserviency to the Gods, and a compliance with the will of more excellent natures, is of all things the most useful; and offers a libation and prays to Jupiter, with science adapted to the Gods. For his first purifying the bowl, and in an especial manner consecrating it to Jupiter alone, and standing in the middle of the enclosure, invoking the power that pervades every where from the middle of the universe, afford a sufficiently conspicuous argument of his piety to a divine nature, and of his knowledge of the signs adapted to the objects of worship.

But if he appears to have spoken to Apollo more boldly than is fit, it is requisite to know that the Apolloniacal orders pervade from on high, as far as to the last of things; and some of them are divine, others angelic, and others daemoniacal, and these

[63] Iliad. lib. 22.

multiformly divided. It must be considered, therefore, that these words were not addressed to a God, but to a daemoniacal Apollo, and this not the first in rank, and coordinated with those that have a total dominion, but one who proximately presides over individuals; and, in short, (for why should I not speak clearly?) the guardian of Hector himself. For the poet perspicuously says,

> *Apollo now before Achilles stood,*
> *In all things like Agenor....*

This Apollo, therefore, Achilles calls most pernicious, so far as he was a hindrance to his actions, by preserving his enemy uninjured. Nor does he by thus speaking sin against a God, but against a power who ranks amongst the most partial of the Apolloniacal series. For it is not proper to refer either all the speeches or energies to that first Apollo, but we should also attend to his second and third progressions. Thus, for instance, we should consider who the Apollo is that sits with Jupiter and the Olympian Gods; who, that convolves the solar sphere; who the aërial Apollo is; who the terrestrial; who, that presides over Troy; and who, that is the peculiar guardian of Hector, concerning whom the poet also says,

> *He fled to Hades by Apollo left.*

For, by looking to all these orders, we shall be able to refer the speeches of Achilles to some such partial power, who was willing to preserve the object of his care, and impede Achilles in his strenuous exertions. For the words "thou hast injured me" are very properly addressed to a daemon of this kind, who deprives him of the end of his present labours; and the epithet "most pernicious" clearly evinces that this power is more adverse to him than any other God or daemon. For he who preserves uninjured a principal enemy, becomes more than any one noxious to the person injured, by impeding his avenging the injury. But, as such language even to such an inferior power is not unattended with punishment, it is said that Achilles shortly after was slain by a certain power of the Apolloniacal order, which Hector when he was dying thus predicts to him:

515

Paris and Phoebus shall avenge my fate,
And stretch thee here before this Scaean gate.

Does not therefore the poetry of Homer by these things make us more modest respecting a divine nature, since we learn from it that even the most subordinate powers cannot be offended with impunity? Though I am not ignorant that those who are skilled in mystic sacrifices dare many things of this kind respecting dae-mons; but perhaps they are defended by more divine natures from sustaining any such injury from subordinate powers. In the meantime justice follows other men, correcting the improbity of their speech.

It is also not difficult to reply to what is said in objection to the contest of Achilles with the river Xanthus. For he was not dis-obedient to the God himself, but he either contended with the apparent water which hindered his impulse against the enemy, or with some one of the indigenous powers, the associate of the Gods in battle: for Minerva and Neptune were present with him, and afforded him assistance. And it appears to me, indeed, that the poetry of Homer devises contests according to all possible diversities; sometimes relating the battles of men with men, and sometimes of the more excellent genera with each other, as in what is called *theomachy*, or the battles of the Gods; and some-times, as in the instance before us, the oppositions of heroes to certain daemoniacal natures; indicating to those that are able to understand things of this kind, that the first of last natures are after a manner equal to the last of such as are first, and particu-larly when they are guarded and moved by the Gods. Hence, not only Achilles is said to have contended with Xanthus, but Hercules also with the river Achelous, of whose life Achilles being emulous, he did not avoid similar contests.

Lastly, we may solve the third of the proposed inquiries by saying that the first and principal design of Achilles was, on returning to his country, to offer to the river Sperchius his locks, as he had promised; but when he despaired of his return, in con-sequence of hearing from his mother,

Soon after Hector shall thy death succeed,

was it not then necessary that he should cut off his hair in honour of his friend? For Socrates in Plato received the crowns which Alcibiades was to have offered to a God, and was crowned with them; nor did he think that he sinned by so doing, or injured the young man. I omit to say that the hairs of Achilles were not yet sacred to the river: for he who had promised to consecrate them on his return, when deprived of this, was also deprived of the consecration of his hairs.

XVII. AN APOLOGY FOR THE
UNWORTHY TREATMENT OF THE
DEAD BODY OF HECTOR, AND FOR
THE TWELVE TROJANS SLAIN AND
BURNT ON THE FUNERAL PILE
OF PATROCLUS, SINCE THESE
THINGS EVIDENTLY APPEAR TO
BE CRUEL, ABSURD, AND
UNBECOMING THE CHARACTER
OF HEROES

It now remains that we consider the conduct of Achilles to Hector, his dragging him round the tomb of Patroclus, and his sacrificing twelve Trojan youths on his pile; for these things, says Socrates, cannot be truly ascribed to Achilles, who was the son of a Goddess, and of the most temperate Peleus descended from Jupiter, and who was educated by the wise Chiron. In the first place, then, it is said by the antients that this was the custom of the Thessalians, as the Cyrenaean poet also testifies, when he informs us, "that it is an antient Thessalian custom, to drag round the tomb of the slain the body of the slaughterer."

Achilles therefore thus acted conformably to the custom of his country, that all due honours might be paid to the funeral of Patroclus. But if Hector dragged Patroclus when a dead body, threatened to cut off his head, and cast his corpse to the Trojan dogs, which is also told to Achilles by Iris—

A prey to dogs he dooms the corse to lie,
And marks the place to fix his head on high.[64]
Rise and prevent (if yet you think of fame)
Thy friend's disgrace, thy own eternal shame!

does not Achilles, therefore, inflict a proper punishment on Hector, in dragging him round the tomb of Patroclus? For thus he both revenges the cruelty of Hector, and openly testifies his benevolence to his friend. He does not, however, accomplish what he intended; for he restores the dead body of Hector to his friends, and suffers him to be buried. He therefore who introduces such measures to his actions energizes according to the whole of justice, and the providence of the Gods. Hence the poet also says, that, by complying with the will of more excellent natures, he was rendered so mild with respect to Hector, that with his own hands he placed him on the bier.

Two splendid mantles, and a carpet spread,
They leave, to cover and inwrap the dead;
Then call the handmaids with assistant toil
To wash the body, and anoint with oil.
This done, the garments o'er the corse they spread;
Achilles lifts it to the funeral bed.[65]

Achilles, therefore, performed every thing pertaining to the dead in a manner adapted to his character. For he illustriously honoured his friend by the vengeance which he inflicted on his enemy, and, afterwards becoming more mild, behaved with great philanthropy to Priam, and paid him the utmost attention and respect.

With respect to the Trojan youths that were slaughtered at the funeral pile of Patroclus, it may be said, that by this action, according to appearance, Achilles perfectly honoured his friend, and that he did nothing more to these Trojans than he was accustomed to do to other enemies, viz. slaying those whom he happened to meet. For what difference is there between dying at

[64] Iliad. lib. 18.   [65] Iliad. lib. 24.

a funeral pyre, or in a river? Does he not indeed act better by these, whose bodies were totally destroyed by fire, than by those whose bodies were torn in pieces by savage beasts, and who suffer the same things with Lycaon? to whom Achilles says,

> *Lie there, Lycaon! let the fish surround*
> *Thy bloated corse, and suck thy gory wound.*[66]

But if it be requisite to recall to our memory the more occult speculations of our preceptor respecting these particulars, we must say that the whole transaction of Achilles concerning the pyre imitates the immortalizing of the soul (της ψυχης; αποθανατισμος) by theurgists, and pertains to the separate soul of Patroclus. Hence, before the pyre was enkindled, he is said to have invoked the winds, the north and the west, that the apparent vehicle of Patroclus, through their visible motion, might obtain a convenient culture, and that the vehicle, which is more divine than this, might be invisibly purified, and restored to its proper allotment, "being drawn upwards by aerial, lunar and solar splendors," as one of the Gods somewhere asserts. It is also related of him, that he made a libation all night on the pyre:

> *All night Achilles hails Patroclus' soul*
> *With large libations from the golden bowl.*[67]

The poet all but proclaiming to us, in these verses, that Achilles was busily employed about the soul of his friend, and not about his visible body only, and that all things are symbolically usurped by him. For the libation from a golden bowl signifies the defluxion of souls from their fountain; which defluxion imparts a more excellent life to a partial soul, and is able through undefiled purity to lead it from bodies to an invisible and divine condition of being. And, in short, many arguments in confirmation of this opinion may be derived from the writings of our preceptor.

Since then it appears that Achilles celebrated the funeral of Patroclus mystically, it may be not improperly said, that these twelve Trojans that were slaughtered at the pyre were coordinated

[66] Iliad. lib. 21.   [67] Iliad. lib. 23.

as attendants with the soul of Patroclus, the ruling nature of which was both known and reverenced by Achilles. Hence, he chose this number as most adapted to attendants, and as sacred to the all-perfect progressions of the Gods.[68] By no means, therefore, did Achilles slay these Trojans from a certain dire and savage cruelty of soul, but performed the whole of this transaction in conformity with certain sacred laws pertaining to the souls of those that die in battle. Nor ought he to be accused of a proud contempt of Gods and men; nor ought we to deny that he was the son of a Goddess and Peleus, and the disciple of Chiron, for acting in this manner. For some of his actions he performed as regarding universal justice, others as a warrior, and others as employing sacred methods. But in all these the poet has perfectly preserved the measures of imitation. And such is the answer to all that Socrates objects to in Homer, as deserving reprehension.

But if any one should say that the fable is not to be admitted, which says that Theseus and Pirithous ravished Helen, and descended into Hades, perhaps these things also, which are asserted more mythologically, may be properly solved by saying that these heroes, being lovers both of unapparent and visible beauty, are fabled to have ravished Helen, and to have descended into the invisible regions; and that, when there, one of them (Pirithous), through the elevation of his intellect, was led back by Hercules, but that the other in a certain respect remained in Hades, from not being able to raise himself to the arduous altitude of contemplation. And though some one should contend that this is not the true meaning of the fable, it does not affect the poetry of Homer, which every where attributes, according to imitation, that which is adapted to the Gods, to the genera more excellent than human nature, and to heroic lives; indicating some things more occultly, teaching us other particulars about these things, with intellect and science, and leaving no genus of beings uninvestigated, but delivering each as energizing with respect to itself and other things, according to its own order.

[68] For τον θεον in the original, read των θεων.

BIBLIOGRAPHY

INDEX

1. THOMAS TAYLOR THE PLATONIST

Including original works, translations, and later editions.
Place of publication is always London unless otherwise
given.

1780   The Elements of a New Method of Reasoning in Geometry: Applied to the Rectification of the Circle.

1782   "On the Nature of the Universe," *European Magazine*, II (Sept. 1782), 180–182; 262–263; 350–351; 429–430. Reprinted in *Collectanea*, 1806. Note: Preceded by a "Note to the editors of the European magazine," signed: T.T.

1787   [Tr.] Concerning the Beautiful; or, a Paraphrase Translation from the Greek of Plotinus. Ennead I. Book VI.

        [Tr.] The Mystical Initiations; or, Hymns of Orpheus. Translated from the Original Greek, with a Preliminary Dissertation on the Life and Theology of Orpheus.

1788– [Tr.] The Philosophical and Mathematical Commentaries of
1789   Proclus; Surnamed Plato's Successor, on the First Book of Euclid's Elements and His Life by Marinus. Translated from the Greek with a Preliminary Dissertation on the Platonic Doctrine of Ideas, etc. Vol. I, 1788.

        [Tr.] The Philosophical and Mathematical Commentaries of Proclus on the First Book of Euclid's Elements. To Which Are Added, a History of the Restoration of the Platonic Theology, by the Latter Platonists: and a Translation from the Greek of Proclus's Theological Elements. Vol. II, 1789.

1790   Tr. A Dissertation on the Eleusinian and Bacchic Mysteries. Amsterdam. Note: Fictitious imprint, printed in London.

1791   A New System of Religion.
        Note: Fictitious imprint, printed in London. J. M. Rigg, in *DNB*, XIX (1921–1922), 469, attributes this book to Taylor, but few other critics do. Taylor himself never claimed it.

1792   [Tr.] The Phaedrus of Plato. A Dialogue Concerning Beauty and Love. Translated from the Greek.
        A Vindication of the Rights of Brutes.
        Note: Said to be a satire on Paine's *Rights of Man* and also no doubt on Mary Wollstonecraft's *Vindication of the Rights of Women*.

Bibliography

[Tr.] An Essay on the Beautiful from the Greek of Plotinus. Second edition.

[Tr.] The Hymns of Orpheus. Translated from the Original Greek: with a Dissertation on the Life and Theology of Orpheus. Second edition.

[Tr.] The Philosophical and Mathematical Commentaries of Proclus, on the First Book of Euclid's Elements. . . . Second edition.

1793   [Tr.] Two Orations of the Emperor Julian. One to the Sovereign Sun, and the Other to the Mother of the Gods. Translated from the Greek. With Notes, and a Copious Introduction, in Which Some of the Greatest Arcana of the Grecian Theology Are Unfolded.

[Tr.] The Cratylus, Phaedo, Parmenides and Timaeus of Plato. Translated from the Greek. With Notes on the Cratylus, and an Explanatory Introduction to Each Dialogue.

[Tr.] Sallust on the Gods and the World; and the Pythagoric Sentences of Demophilus, Translated from the Greek; and Five Hymns by Proclus, in the Original Greek, with a Poetical Version. To Which Are Added, Five Hymns by the Translator.

1794   [Tr.] The Description of Greece, by Pausanias. Translated from the Greek. With Notes, in Which Much of the Mythology of the Greeks Is Unfolded from a Theory Which Has Been for Many Ages Unknown. And Illustrated with Maps and Views Elegantly Engraved. 3 vols.
Note: For this Taylor received £60, the only one of his works for which he was paid by the booksellers.

[Tr.] Five Books of Plotinus, viz. On Felicity; On the Nature and Origin of Evil; On Providence, On Nature, Contemplation and the One; and On the Descent of the Soul. Translated from the Greek, with an Introduction, Containing Additional Information on These Important Subjects.

An Abridgement to Mr. [Bryan] Edwards's Civil and Commercial History of the British West Indies. 3 vols.
Note: ". . . attributed to Taylor, and was probably but one among other pieces of anonymous hackwork by which he eked out his slender means." J. M. Rigg, *DNB*, XIX (1921–1922), 469.

1795   [Tr.] The Fable of Cupid and Psyche, Translated from the Latin of Apuleius: To Which Are Added, A Poetical Paraphrase of the Speech of Diotima, in the Banquet of Plato; Four Hymns, etc. With an Introduction in Which the Meaning of the Fable Is Unfolded.

Bibliography

1797 "Chaldean Oracles," *Monthly Magazine*, Supplementary Number XIX, Vol. 3 (June 1797).

Biographical Anecdotes of the Founders of the French Revolution (London-printed and Dublin-reprinted, 1797. Wrongly attributed to John Adolphus, and attributed by Mrs. Louise Schutz Boas in *The Journal of the Royal Society of Arts* (Sept. 1967) to Richard (later Sir Richard) Phillips. The article on Godefroi Izarn, Marquis de Valady is almost certainly by Taylor.

1801 [Tr.] The Metaphysics of Aristotle, Translated from the Greek; with Copious Notes, in Which the Pythagoric and Platonic Dogmas Respecting Numbers and Ideas Are Unfolded from Antient Sources. To Which Is Added, a Dissertation on Nullities and Diverging Series; in Which the Conclusions of the Greatest Modern Mathematicians on This Subject Are Shown to be Erroneous, the Nature of Infinitely Small Quantities Is Explained, and the TO 'EN or THE ONE of the Pythagoreans and Platonists, so often Alluded to by Aristotle in This Work, Is Elucidated.
Note: This work was sold at one guinea to subscribers, two guineas after publication.

1803 An Edition of Hederic's Greek Lexicon.

1804 [Tr.] The Dissertations of Maximus Tyrius. Translated from the Greek. 2 vols.
An Answer to Dr. Gillies's Supplement to His New Analysis of Aristotle's Works; in Which the Unfaithfulness of His Translation of Aristotle's Ethics Is Unfolded.

❋ [Tr.] The Works of Plato, viz. His Fifty-five Dialogues, and Twelve Epistles, Translated from the Greek; Nine of the Dialogues by the Late Floyer Sydenham, and the Remainder by Thomas Taylor: with Occasional Annotations on the Nine Dialogues Translated by Sydenham, and Copious Notes, by the Latter Translator; in Which Is Given the Substance of Nearly All the Existing Greek MS Commentaries on the Philosophy of Plato, and a Considerable Portion of Such as Are Already Published. 5 vols.
Note: Published at 10 guineas.

Bridgman, William F.L.S. and Taylor, Thomas. Translations from the Greek, viz. Aristotle's Synopsis of the Virtues and Vices. The Similitudes of Demophilus. The Golden Sentences of Democrates. And the Pythagoric Symbols, with the Explanations of Jamblichus. To Which Are Added, the Pythagoric Sentences of Demophilus by Mr. Taylor.

1805 Miscellanies in Prose and Verse: Containing the Triumph of the Wise Man over Fortune, According to the Doctrine of the Stoics and

Platonists; the Creed of the Platonic Philosopher; a Panegyric on Sydenham, etc. etc.

1806   Collectanea; or, Collections, Consisting of Miscellanies Inserted by Thomas Taylor in the European and Monthly Magazines, with an Appendix Containing Some Hymns by the Same Author Never Before Printed.
Note: Only 50 copies printed, at the expense of Mr. William Meredith.

1806– [Tr.] The Works of Aristotle. Translated from the Greek. With
1812 Copious Elucidations from the Best of his Greek Commentators, viz. Alexander Aphrodisiensis, Syrianus, Ammonius Hermaeus, Priscianus, Olympiodorus, Simplicius, etc. 10 vols.
Note: Binder's title: Aristotle's Works. Taylor. Note: No general title page. Each volume has special title page.
Note: *Metaphysics*, second edition, as Vol. 9 of the *Works*.

1807   [Tr.] The Treatises of Aristotle on the Heavens; on Generation and Corruption; and on Meteors. Translated from the Greek, with Copious Elucidations from the Commentaries of Simplicius and Olympiodorus.

1809   [Tr.] The Elements of the True Arithmetic of Infinities. In Which All the Propositions in the Arithmetic of Infinities Invented by Dr. Wallis, Relative to the Summation of Infinite Series, and, also the Principles of the Doctrine of Fluxions Are Demonstrated To Be False; and the Nature of Infinitesimals Is Unfolded.
Note: Also in *Works of Aristotle*, Vol. 6.

[Tr.] The Arguments of the Emperor Julian against the Christians. Translated from the Greek Fragments Preserved by Cyril, Bishop of Alexandria. To Which Are Added Extracts from the Other Works of Julian Relative to the Christians. Printed for the Translator.
Note: Privately printed edition of 25 copies.
Note: The title in Lowndes' Bibliographer's Manual makes this change: ". . . preserved by Cyril of Jerusalem. . . ."

[Tr.] The History of Animals of Aristotle and His Treatise on Physiognomy.

1810   [Tr.] Commentaries of Proclus on the Timaeus of Plato, in Five Books; Containing a Treasury of Pythagoric and Platonic Physiology. 2 vols.

1811   [Tr.] The Great and Eudemian Ethics, the Politics, and Economics of Aristotle.

1812   [Tr.] A Dissertation on the Philosophy of Aristotle, in Four Books.

Bibliography

In Which his Principal Physical and Metaphysical Dogmas Are Unfolded; and It Is Shown, from Indubitable Evidence, that His Philosophy Has Not Been Accurately Known since the Destruction of the Greeks. The Insufficiency also of the Philosophy That Has Been Substituted by the Moderns for That of Aristotle, Is Demonstrated.
Note: Also in *Works of Aristotle*, Vol. 10.

1816 Theoretic Arithmetic in Three Books; Containing the Substance of All That Has Been Written on This Subject by Theo of Smyrna, Nicomachus, Iamblichus, and Boetius.—Together with Some Remarkable Particulars Respecting Perfect, Amicable, and Other Numbers, Which Are Not To Be Found in the Writings of Any Ancient or Modern Mathematicians. Likewise, a Specimen of the Manner in Which the Pythagoreans Philosophized about Numbers; and a Development of Their Mystical and Theological Arithmetic.

[Tr.] The Six Books of Proclus, the Platonic Successor: On the Theology of Plato, Translated from the Greek; to Which a Seventh Book [by the translator] Is Added, in order to Supply the Deficiency of Another Book on This Subject, Which Was Written by Proclus, but Since Lost. Also a Translation from the Greek of Proclus's Elements of Theology. To Which Are Added a Translation of the Treatise of Proclus on Providence and Fate; a Translation of Extracts from His Treatise, Entitled: Ten Doubts Concerning Providence; and a Translation of Extracts from His Treatise on the Subsistence of Evil; as Preserved in the Bibliotheca Graeca of Fabricius.
Note: 2 vols. in one.

"A Dissertation on the Eleusinian and Bacchic Mysteries," *Pamphleteer*, VIII (1816), 33–66, 455–486.
Note: Taylor always called this the second edition.

1817 [Tr.] Select Works of Plotinus, the Great Restorer of the Philosophy of Plato; and Extracts from the Treatise of Synesius on Providence. Translated from the Greek. With an Introduction Containing the Substance of Porphyry's Life of Plotinus.

"Remarks on the Daemon of Socrates," *Classical Journal*, XVI (Sept. 1817), 160–164.

"Use of Arches Known among the Ancients," *Classical Journal*, XVI (Sept. 1817), 184–185.

1817– "Collection of the Chaldean Oracles," *Classical Journal* XVI (Sept.
1818 and Dec. 1817), 333–344; XVII (Mar. and June 1818), 128–133, 243–264.

1818 [Tr.] Iamblichus' Life of Pythagoras, or Pythagoric Life. Accompanied by Fragments of the Ethical Writings of Certain Pythago-

527

reans in the Doric Dialect; and a Collection of Pythagoric Sentences from Stobaeus and Others, Which Are Omitted by Gale in His Opuscula Mythologica, and Have Not Been Noticed by Any Editor. Note: "A list of translations and original works by T. Taylor." Pp. [355]-360.

[Tr.] The Rhetoric, Poetic, and Nicomachean Ethics of Aristotle, Translated from the Greek. 2 vols.

"Orphic Fragments, Hitherto Unedited," *Classical Journal*, XVII (Mar. and June 1818), 158-163.

"Remarks on a Passage in Stobaeus," *Classical Journal*, XVII (Mar. and June 1818), 455-456.

"On a Peculiar Signification of the Words *Demos* and *Soma*," *Classical Journal*, XVIII (Sept. and Dec. 1818), 202-203.

1819   "On the Philosophical Meaning of the Words *Bios, Kinema, Energema*, and *Aisthema*," *Classical Journal*, XIX (Mar. and June 1819), 363-364.

"On the Antiquity of Alchemy," *Classical Journal*, XX (Sept. and Dec. 1819), 75-78.

"On the Coincidence between the Belts of the Planet Jupiter and the Fabulous Bonds of Jupiter the Demiurgus," *Classical Journal*, XX (Sept. and Dec. 1819), 324-326.

1820   A Poetical Paraphrase on the Speech of Diotima in the Banquet of Plato. Included in ΕΚ ΤΩΝ, ΠΡΟΚΛΟΥ ΣΧΟΛΙΩΝ, ΕΙΣ ΠΛΑΤΩΝΟΣ ΚΑΡΤΥΛΟΝ ΕΚΛΟΓΑΙ, Ex Procli Scholiis in Cratylum Platonis Excerpta. Lipsiae.
Note: The copy in the University of Florida Library has many manuscript notes by Taylor.

Miscellanies in Prose and Verse, . . . Second edition, with Additions.

[Tr.] Commentaries of Proclus on the Timaeus of Plato, in Five Books, . . . Second edition.

"Important Additions to the First Alcibiades, and Timaeus of Plato," *Classical Journal*, XXI (Mar. and June 1820), 141-142.

"Discovery of a Verse of Homer, and Error of Kiessling," *Classical Journal*, XXI (Mar. and June 1820), 361-362.

"Important Discovery of the Original of Many of the Sentences of Sextus Pythagoricus, Which Have Been Hitherto Supposed to Be Alone Extant in the Fraudulent Version of the Presbyter Ruffinus," *Classical Journal*, XXI (Mar. and June 1820), 266-270.

Bibliography

"On the Theology of the Greeks," *Classical Journal*, XXII (Sept. and Dec. 1820), 89–104; 301–314.

"Platonic Demonstration of the Immortality of the Soul," *Classical Journal*, XXI (Mar. and June 1820), 201–230 [pages 205–224 skipped in numbering], XXII (Sept. and Dec. 1820), 40–51.

1821 [Tr.] Iamblichus on the Mysteries of the Egyptians, Chaldeans, ✓ and Assyrians. Translated from the Greek. Chiswick.

[Tr.] The Rhetoric, Poetic and Nicomachean Ethics of Aristotle. Translated from the Greek. Second edition.
Note: The Ethics are omitted in this edition.

"On the Mythology of the Greeks," *Classical Journal*, XXIII (Mar. and June 1821), 33–41; XXIV (Sept. and Dec. 1821), 54–67.

"Notice of Professor Cousin's Edition of the Two First Books of Proclus on the Parmenides of Plato," *Classical Journal*, XXIV (Sept. and Dec. 1821), 336–347.

1822 [Tr.] The Metamorphoses, or Golden Ass, and Philosophical Works of Apuleius. Translated from the Original Latin.
Note: Some copies contain four unpaged leaves of suppressed passages, printed on one side of the paper only, and one other leaf printed on both sides.

[Tr.] Political Fragments of Archytas, Charondas, Zaleucus, and Other Ancient Pythagoreans, Preserved by Stobaeus; and also, Ethical Fragments of Hierocles, the Celebrated Commentator on the Golden Pythagoric Verses, Preserved by the Same Author. Translated from the Greek. Chiswick.
Note: Binder's title reads: Taylor's Political Fragments.

"Observations on Professor Cousin's Edition of the Commentaries of Proclus on the First Alcibiades of Plato . . . and also on Creuzer's Edition of the Same Commentaries, together with Those of Olympiodorus on That Dialogue . . . ," *Classical Journal*, XXV (Mar. and June 1822), 134–142, 300–305.

"Observations on That Part of a Work Entitled, Empedoclis et Parmenidis Fragmenta ex Codice Taurinensis Bibliothecae Restituta et Illustrata, ab Amedeo Peyron, Lipsiae, 1810, in Which the Author Treats of the Genuine Greek Text of the Commentary of Simplicius in Aristotelem de Coelo et Mundo," *Classical Journal*, XXVI (Sept. and Dec. 1822), 250–259.

1823 The Elements of a New Arithmetical Notation, and of a New Arithmetic of Infinities; in Two Books: in Which the Series Discovered by Modern Mathematicians, for the Quadrature of the Circle and Hyperbola, Are Demonstrated to Be Aggregately Incommensurable Quantities, and a Criterion Is Given, by Which the Commeasurability or Incommeasurability of Infinite Series May Be Accurately Ascertained. With an Appendix, Concerning Some Properties of Perfect, Amicable, and Other Numbers, no Less Remarkable than Novel.

[Tr.] Select Works of Porphyry. Containing His Four Books on Abstinence from Animal Food; His Treatise on the Homeric Cave of the Nymphs, and His Auxiliaries to the Perception of Intelligible Natures. Translated from the Greek. With an Appendix, Explaining the Allegory of the Wanderings of Ulysses. By the Translator.

"Observations on Creuzer's Edition of the Commentary of Olympiodorus on the First Alcibiades of Plato," *Classical Journal*, XXVII (Jan. and Mar. 1823), 39–47.

"Observations on the Scholia of Hermes on the Phaedrus of Plato, Published by Fredericus Astius," *Classical Journal*, XXVIII (Sept. and Dec. 1823), 79–83, 268–273.

1824   [Tr.] The Mystical Hymns of Orpheus, Translated from the Greek and Demonstrated to Be the Invocations Which Were Used in the Eleusinian Mysteries. The Second Edition, with Considerable Emendations, Alterations, and Additions. Chiswick.

[Tr.] The Description of Greece, by Pausanias, Translated from the Greek. . . . A New Edition, with Considerable Augmentations. 3 vols.

"Introduction to the Second Edition of the Translation of the Mystical Hymns of Orpheus," *Classical Journal*, XXXIX (Mar. and June 1824), 322–331; XXX (Sept. and Dec. 1824), 81–92.

"Emendations of the Text of Plato," *Classical Journal*, XXX (Sept. and Dec. 1824), 304–306.

"Observations on the Excerpta from the Scholia of Proclus on the Cratylus of Plato, Published by Professor Boissonade," *Classical Journal*, XXX (Sept. and Dec. 1824), 3–9, 247–253.

1825   [Tr.] The Fragments That Remain of the Last Writings of Proclus, Surnamed the Platonic Successor. Translated from the Greek.

"Classical Allusion," *Classical Journal*, XXXI (Mar. and June 1825), 195.

"Notice of Professor Cousin's Edition of the Third, Fourth, and

Bibliography

Fifth Books of Proclus on the Parmenides of Plato," *Classical Journal*, XXXI (Mar. and June 1825), 16–21, 271–279.

"Biblical Criticism," *Classical Journal*, XXXII (Sept. and Dec. 1825), 31.

1829 "Corruption of Demiurgus," *Classical Journal*, XXXIX (Mar. and June 1829), 101–103.

"Extracts from Some of the Last Works of Aristotle, Xenocrates, and Theophrastus," *Classical Journal*, XL (Sept. and Dec. 1829), 332–335.

1830 [Ed. and Tr.] Arguments of Celsus, Porphyry, and the Emperor Julian, Against the Christians; Also Extracts from Diodorus Siculus, Josephus, and Tacitus, Relating to the Jews. Together with an Appendix; Containing the Oration of Libanius in Defence of the Temples of the Heathens, Translated by Dr. Lardner; and Extracts from Bingham's Antiquities of the Christian Church.
Note: Cover-title reads: Fragments of Porphyry, Julian, &c. against the Christians.

1831 [Tr.] Ocellus Lucanus. On the Nature of the Universe. Tauras, the Platonic Philosopher, on the Eternity of the World. Julius Firmicus Maternus of the Thema Mundi; in Which the Positions of the Stars at the Commencement of the Several Mundane Periods Is Given. Select Theorems on the Perpetuity of Time, by Proclus. Translated from the Originals.

1833 [Tr.] Two Treatises of Proclus, the Platonic Successor; the Former Consisting of Ten Doubts Concerning Providence, and a Solution of Those Doubts; and the Latter Containing a Development of the Nature of Evil. Translated from the Edition of These Works by Victor Cousin, Professor of Philosophy in the University of Paris.

1834 [Tr.] Translations from the Greek of the Following Treatises of Plotinus; viz. On Suicide, to Which Is Added an Extract from the Harleian MS. of the Scholia of Olympiodorus on the Phaedo of Plato Respecting Suicide, Accompanied by the Greek Text; Two Books on Truly Existing Being; and Extracts from his Treatise on the Manner in Which the Multitude of Ideas Subsists, and Concerning the Good; with Additional Notes from Porphyry and Proclus.

n.d. "Medicina Mentis: or, A Specimen of Theological Arithmetic." Unpublished manuscript, 21 pages. Now in the Houghton Library, Harvard University.

History of the Restoration of Platonic Theology.
Note: First published in Volume II of The Philosophical and Mathematical Commentaries of Proclus. . . , 1789.

Bibliography

1841   [Tr.] Two Treatises of Proclus, the Platonic Successor. . . . Second edition.

1862   "The Pythagoric Sentences of Demophilus, Translated from the Greek," *Philobiblion*, II (June 1862), 152–154. New York.

1873   [Tr.] The Arguments of the Emperor Julian against the Christians. . . . Reprinted and edited by W. Nevins.

1875   A Dissertation on the Eleusinian and Bacchic Mysteries. Third edition. Edited, with Introduction, Notes, Emendations, and Glossary, by Alexander Wilder. New York.

1880   Our Birth is But a Sleep and a Forgetting. Three treatises of Plotinus (two on the Essence of the Soul [the second translated by T. Taylor] and one on the Descent of [the] Soul). Translated from the Original Greek by Thomas M. Johnson. Osceola, Missouri.

1891   The Eleusinian and Bacchic Mysteries. A Dissertation. Fourth edition. Edited, with Introduction, Notes, Emendations, and Glossary, by Alexander Wilder. With 85 illustrations by A. L. Rawson. New York.

1893   [Tr.] The Metamorphoses; or, Golden Ass, and Philosophical Works of Apuleius. Translated from the Original Latin. Reprinted, Birmingham.
Note: "Of this re-issue only 600 copies have been printed." "Passages suppressed," 4 pp. (inserted) in Library of Congress copy.

1894   [Tr.] The Republic [of Plato]. The Scott Library.

1895   [Tr.] Select Works of Plotinus, Translated . . . with an Introduction Containing the Substance of Porphyry's Life of Plotinus. A New Edition with Preface and Bibliography, by G.R.S. Mead. Bohn Philological Series.

[Tr.] Plotinus, An Essay on the Beautiful. Reprint, Theosophical Siftings.

√   [Tr.] Porphyry, On the Cave of the Nymphs in the Thirteenth —
Book of the Odyssey. Reprint, Theosophical Siftings.

1896   [Tr.] Orpheus (The Theosophy of the Greeks). Reprint of Hymns of Orpheus, edited by George Robert Stow, Theosophical Publishing Society.

→   [Tr.] The Mystical Hymns of Orpheus. Translated from the Greek, and Demonstrated to Be the Invocations Which Were Used in the Eleusinian Mysteries, . . . New edition. (Bertram Dobell)

1906   Thomas Taylor and Floyer Sydenham (trans.). The Republic of

Bibliography

Plato. Revised by W.H.D. Rouse. With Introduction by Ernest Baker. Methuen's Standard Library.

1909   [Tr.] Select Works of Plotinus. . . . Reprint of 1895 edition.

1912   [Tr.] Select Works of Plotinus. . . . Reprint of 1895 edition, W. Rider and Son.

1917   [Tr.] Plotinus, An Essay on the Beautiful. . . . Reprint, J. M. Watkins.

       [Tr.] On the Cave of the Nymphs in the Thirteenth Book of the Odyssey. From the Greek of Porphyry. Translated by T. Taylor. Reprint, J. M. Watkins.

1926   [Tr.] Iamblichus' Life of Pythagoras. Translated by Thomas Taylor. Reprint, J. M. Watkins.

1929   [Tr.] Select Works of Plotinus. . . . Reprint of 1895 edition.

1932   [Tr.] Plotinus on the Beautiful. Ennead I. 6. Translated by the Editors of the Shrine of Wisdom and On Intelligible Beauty. Ennead V. 8. Translated by T. Taylor. Shrine of Wisdom Manual, No. 13.

1934   The Theoretic Arithmetic of the Pythagoreans. Introductory Essay by Manly Hall. Phoenix Press, Los Angeles.

1944   [Tr.] Plato. The Timaeus and the Critias or Atlanticus. The Thomas Taylor Translation. Foreword by R. Catesby Taliaferro. Bollingen Series III, New York.

1952   [Tr.] Plato. The Timaeus and The Critias. . . . Reprint of 1944 edition.

1959   A Vindication of the Rights of Brutes, 1792. Reproduced by the University of Florida from Microfilm Supplied by the University of California from the British Museum. Gainesville.

1965   [Tr.] Iamblichus's Life of Pythagoras. Translated by Thomas Taylor. Reprint, J. M. Watkins.

1966   A Vindication of the Rights of Brutes, 1792. With an Introduction by Louise Schutz Boas. Scholars' Facsimiles & Reprints, Gainesville.

1968   Iamblichus on the Mysteries of the Egyptians, Chaldeans, and Assyrians. Translated from the Greek. Third edition.

       [Tr.] Plato. The Timaeus and the Critias. . . . Reprint of 1944 edition. Bollingen Series III, Princeton.

533

2. REFERENCES TO TAYLOR

This list of references to and about Taylor, of necessity selective, is in two parts: one essentially primary, of contemporaries and acquaintances; the other secondary, of scholars and critics who have written about Taylor. The occasional notes will suggest the special significance of several items.

I. PRIMARY

Barker, E. H. "A Brief Notice of Mr. Thomas Taylor, the Celebrated Platonist, with a Complete List of His Published Works." *Literary Anecdotes.* London, 1852, I, 261–274.

——. *Literary Anecdotes and Contemporary Reminiscences, of Professor Porson and Others.* London, 1852, I, xvi, 3, 62, 88; II, 60.

Barthelémy–Saint Hilaire, Jules. *Victor Cousin, sa vie, et sa correspondance.* Paris, 1895, III, 238–245.

Bridgman, William. *Translations from the Greek.* London, 1804. See especially pp. xi-xii.

Coleridge, Samuel Taylor. *Collected Letters of Samuel Taylor Coleridge,* ed. Earl Leslie Griggs. Oxford and New York, 1956, I, 260; II, 608, 987; III, 279 and n. Also, of course, many references to Plato and the Neoplatonists are frequently indirect references to Taylor through his translations.

——. *The Complete Works of Samuel Taylor Coleridge . . . ,* ed. W.G.T. Shedd. New York, 1871, IV, 30.

——. *The Notebooks of Samuel Taylor Coleridge,* ed. Kathleen Coburn. Vol. 1. New York (Bollingen Series L) and London, 1957. Entries 1626, 1727, 1728, 1740, and Appendix B (pp. 455–458).

——. *The Philosophical Lectures of Samuel Taylor Coleridge,* ed. Kathleen Coburn. New York and London, 1949. See especially pp. 400, 429, 430, 443.

Collier, John Payne. *An Old Man's Diary, Forty Years Ago.* London, 1871, Part II, pp. 90, 91.

Cory, Isaac Preston. *Ancient Fragments . . . ,* 2d edn. London, 1832. This book is much indebted to Taylor and cites him in the introduction and several notes. Cory was a close friend and intended to write a biography of Taylor.

de Quincey, Thomas. *Works.* Edinburgh, 1860, XIII, 60.

Disraeli, Isaac. *Curiosities of Literature,* 12th edn. London, 1841. See p. 77.

——. *Vaurien.* London, 1797. The character of "The Platonist" is modeled on Thomas Taylor.

Dyce, Alexander, ed. *Recollections of the Table Talk of Samuel Rogers: To Which Is Added Porsoniana.* New York, 1856. See pp. 323–325.

Bibliography

Godwin, William. *Memoirs and Posthumous Works of Mary Wollstone-craft Godwin*. Dublin, 1798, pp. 12–20.

Mathias, Thomas James. *The Pursuits of Literature*, 7th edn. London, 1798, p. 181.

Shelley, Percy Bysshe. *The Complete Works of Percy Bysshe Shelley*, ed. Roger Ingpen and Walter E. Peck. New York, 1907, VII, 151.

——. *The Letters of Percy Bysshe Shelley*, ed. Roger Ingpen. London, 1909, II, 548.

——. *Shelley's Prose in the Bodleian Manuscripts*, ed. A. H. Koszul. London, 1910. See especially Appendix, pp. 124–125.

Southey, Robert. *Selections from the Letters of Robert Southey*, ed. J. W. Warter. London, 1856, I, 192.

Walpole, Horace. *Letters of Horace Walpole*, ed. Mrs. Paget Toynbee. Oxford, 1903–1905, XIV, 238.

Wordsworth, William. *Transactions of the Wordsworth Society*, VI (1884), 188, 213, 234. These references are to items in the Sale Catalogue of the library at Rydal Mount.

II. SECONDARY

A. F. "Mr. Emerson in the Lecture Room," *Atlantic Monthly*, LI (1883), 818–832.

Alcott, A. Bronson. *The Journals of Bronson Alcott*, ed. Odell Shepard. Boston, 1938. Alcott read widely in the Neoplatonists, almost entirely through Taylor's translations.

Anderson, Paul R. *Platonism in the Midwest*. New York and London, 1963.

Anonymous. *Analytical Review*, XVII (1793), 176.

——. *The Dial*, III (1843), 545–548. A notice about the Alcott library at Fruitlands, this list includes sixteen titles by Taylor.

——. *Edinburgh Review*, XIV (1809), 187–211. This long untitled review of Taylor's *Works of Plato* is usually attributed to James Mill.

——. *Gentleman's Magazine*, XCIII, Part 1 (1823), 571. This is an obituary notice for Taylor's second wife.

——. Review of R. M. Milnes. *Life, Letters, and Literary Remains of John Keats*. *North British Review*, X (1848), 38–52. Probably written by Coventry Patmore, who collected Taylor's books, this review praises Taylor as a poet.

——. *Monthly Review*, LXIV (1781), 72. This is a scornful notice of Taylor's *Elements of a New Method of Reasoning in Geometry*.

——. "Note-Book of a Literary Idler, No. 1," *Blackwoods Magazine*, XVII (1825), 736–744.

——. *Nouvelle Biographie Générale*. Paris, 1865, XLIV, 942–943. According to Axon, "par Hoefer."

——. "On the Mysteries of Eleusis," *Classical Journal*, XXXIX–XL (1829), 332–337, 56–70.

——. "The Survival of Paganism," *Fraser's Magazine*, XII, New Series (1875), 640–651. Pages 643–648 discuss Taylor in detail.

Bibliography

Anonymous. "Mr. Taylor, the Platonist," *Public Characters of 1798*. Dublin, 1798–1799, pp. 100–124. Unsigned, but written by Taylor himself, this article is the basis for all subsequent biographical studies.

——. "Thomas Taylor," *Encyclopedia Americana*, ed. Francis Lieber. XII (1832).

——. "Mr. Thomas Taylor." Obituary Notice. *Athenaeum*, VIII (Nov. 21, 1835), 874–875. Reprinted in *The Gentleman's Magazine*, CLIX (Jan. 1836), 91–92. [Vol. V, New Series.] Edward Peacock says Mr. John Inglis is the author.

Axon, W.E.A. "Thomas Taylor the Platonist," *The Library*, II (1890), 245–250, 292–300.

Beer, John. *Coleridge the Visionary*. London, 1959, *passim*.

Bentley, Gerald E., Jr. "Thomas Taylor's Biography," *Studies in Bibliography*, XIV (1961), 234–236.

Blackstone, Bernard. *The Consecrated Urn*. London, 1959, *passim*.

Blakey, Robert. *History of the Philosophy of Mind*. London, 1848. See especially IV, 66.

Boas, Louise Schutz. "Thomas Taylor, Platonist, at the Society of Arts," *Journal of the Royal Society of Arts* (London, Aug., Sept., and Oct. 1967).

Burnett, Alexander. "Shelley and His Pythagorean Friends," *Book-Lore*, III (1885–1886), 121–130. Reprinted from *The Medical Examiner* for 1824.

Carpenter, Frederic I. *Emerson and Asia*. Cambridge, Mass. 1930. See especially pp. 15, 40, 52, 54, 55, 220, 222.

Damon, S. Foster. *A Blake Dictionary*. Providence, Rhode Island, 1965. See especially pp. 396–397.

——. *William Blake: His Philosophy and Symbols*. London, 1924, *passim*.

Emerson, Ralph Waldo. *The Complete Works of Ralph Waldo Emerson*, ed. Edward Waldo Emerson. Boston and New York, 1903–1904. See especially III, 296; V, 224, 295, 374; VII, 202–203, 408–409; VIII, 50, 370. In addition to these references to Taylor himself there are many to his translations of Plato, Aristotle, and the Neoplatonists.

——. *Journals of Ralph Waldo Emerson*, ed. E. W. Emerson and W. E. Forbes. Boston and New York, 1909–1914. See especially VI, 470–471, 509–510; VII, 36; VIII, 361; X, 185. Here also there are many references to the translations as well as to Taylor himself.

Evans, Frank B. "The Background of the Romantic Revival of Platonism." Unpublished dissertation, Princeton University, 1938. This is a valuable collection of references to Taylor and a sound analysis of his importance to the Romantic Movement.

——. "Thomas Taylor, Platonist of the Romantic Period," *PMLA*, LV (1940), 1060–1079.

Fisher, Peter F. *The Valley of Vision: Blake as Prophet and Revolutionary*, ed. Northrop Frye. Toronto, 1961.

Bibliography

Haller, W. *The Early Life of Robert Southey*. New York, 1917, p. 336.

Harper, George M. "Mary Wollstonecraft's Residence with Thomas Taylor the Platonist," *Notes and Queries*, IX (1962), 461–463.

——. *The Neoplatonism of William Blake*. Chapel Hill and Oxford, 1961.

——. "A Source of Wordsworth's Ages of Man," *Texas Studies in Literature and Language*, I (1959), 277–280.

——. " 'Toward the Holy Land': A Chapter in the Platonism of the Middle West," *South Atlantic Bulletin* (1967), pp. 1–6.

Harrison, John S. *The Teachers of Emerson*. New York, 1910. The many citations from the Neoplatonists are almost all from Taylor.

Hirst, Desirée. *Hidden Riches: Traditional Symbolism from the Renaissance to Blake*. London, 1964. See especially pp. 4, 5, 6, 67, 153, 266, 294–297, 310, 335.

Holcroft, Thomas. *The Life of Thomas Holcroft*, ed. Elbridge Colby. London, 1925, II, 194–195.

Johnson, Franklin P. "Neo-Platonic Hymns by Thomas Taylor," *Philological Quarterly*, VIII (1929), 145–156.

Johnson, Thomas M. "The Life and Works of Thomas Taylor the Platonist," *The Platonist*, I (1881), 61–64, 102–109, 147–154, 179–187. *The Platonist* could hardly have existed without Taylor. His works are the justification for numerous articles and new translations, and he is referred to or quoted with approval in almost every issue of the four volumes (1881 to 1888).

Levinson, Ronald B. "Thomas Taylor, the Platonist." Unpublished dissertation, University of Chicago, 1924.

Lowes, J. L. *The Road to Xanadu*. Boston, 1927, pp. 231–232, 236, 393–394.

Mead, George Robert Stow. *Orpheus (The Theosophy of the Greeks)*. Theosophical Publishing Society: London, 1896. This book is based largely upon Taylor's Introduction to the *Mystical Hymns of Orpheus*, second edition.

Nichols, John. *Literary Anecdotes of the Eighteenth Century*. London, 1814, VIII, 484.

Niebuhr, B. G. *Life and Letters*. London, 1852, I, 142–143.

Notopoulos, James A. "Shelley and Thomas Taylor," *PMLA*, LI (1936), 502–517.

——. *The Platonism of Shelley*. Durham, N.C., 1949. Numerous references cite Taylor's influence on Peacock and others as well as Shelley.

Peacock, Edward. "Taylor the Platonist," *Notes and Queries*, 3d Series, X (1866), 302–303. Peacock was an early admirer who hoped to write a biography of Taylor.

——. "Thomas Taylor, the Platonist," *The Antiquary*, XVIII (1888), 1–5.

Peacock, Thomas Love. *Melincourt*. London, 1891, I, 66; II, 96–108, 151. Mr. Mystic is a thinly disguised fictional portrait of Taylor.

Percival, Milton O. *William Blake's Circle of Destiny*. New York, 1938. This book contains many references to and quotations from Taylor.

Bibliography

Pierce, Frederick E. "Blake and Thomas Taylor," *PMLA*, XLIII (1928), 1121–1141.

——. "Taylor, Aristotle, and Blake," *Philological Quarterly*, IX (1930), 363–370.

——. "Wordsworth and Thomas Taylor," *Philological Quarterly*, VII (1928), 60–64.

Politella, Joseph. " 'Plato Taylor,' a Greek Born out of His Time," *The Serif*, III (1966), 13–23.

Raine, Kathleen. *Blake and Tradition*. (The A. W. Mellon Lectures in the Fine Arts, 1962.) Princeton (Bollingen Series XXXV:11) and London, 1969.

——. "Blake's Debt to Antiquity," *Sewanee Review*, LXXI:3 (Summer 1963), 352–450. An abridged version of the A. W. Mellon Lecture above.

——. "The Sea of Time and Space," *Journal of the Warburg and Courtauld Institute*, XX (1957), 318–337. This article deals at length with the Neoplatonic symbolism of Blake's Arlington Court picture. See Fig. 10.

Rigg, James McMullen. "Thomas Taylor," *DNB*, XIX (1921–1922), 468–470.

Rollins, Hyder Edward, ed. *The Keats Circle*. Cambridge, Mass., 1948, I, 10, 21, 36.

Sandford, Orlin Mead. *An Annotated Catalogue . . . of the Works of Thomas Taylor*. New York, 1885. Reprinted in *Book-Lore* (1885–1886), II, 169; III, 11.

Sears, Clara Endicott. *Bronson Alcott's Fruitlands*. Boston and New York, 1915. A list of the books in the library at Fruitlands, which includes sixteen titles by Taylor, appears on pp. 177–185.

Van Doren, Carl. *Thomas Love Peacock*. London, 1911, p. 129.

Watson, John Selby. *The Life of Richard Porson*. London, 1861, p. 204.

Welsh, James Jacob. "A Brief Notice of Mr. Thomas Taylor, the Celebrated Platonist, with a Complete List of his Published Works," *Philobiblion*, II (1863), 151–158. Originally published in 1831.

Wilson, F.A.C. *W. B. Yeats and Tradition*. London, 1958. Wilson makes numerous references to the influence of Taylor on Yeats.

Yeats, William Butler. *Essays and Introductions*. London, 1961. See especially "The Philosophy of Shelley's Poetry," pp. 65–95. Yeats's early knowledge of the Neoplatonists, Plotinus in particular, came through Taylor's translations.

INDEX

This index includes only names and titles of literary and historical interest.

Index

Index

Index

543

Index